# The Book History Reader

Since the invention of the printing press in the fifteenth century, books and print culture have been central to the shaping of culture and society. *The Book History Reader* is the first comprehensive volume to bring together a variety of work – much of which is now out of print or impossible to access – examining key aspects of book history. International in scope and interdisciplinary in nature, book history studies is a rapidly growing subject which analyses books and print as cultural artefacts.

*The Book History Reader* is an essential collection of writings examining different aspects of the history of books and print culture: the development of the book, the move from spoken word to written texts, the commodification of books and authors, the power and profile of readers, and the future of the book in the electronic age. Arranged in thematic sections and featuring a general introduction to the Reader as well as an introduction to each section, the editors illustrate how book history studies have developed a broad approach which incorporates social and cultural considerations governing the production, dissemination and reception of print and texts.

This pioneering book will be a vital resource for all those involved in book publishing studies, library studies, book history and also those studying English literature, cultural studies, sociology and history.

**Essays by**: Richard Altick, Roland Barthes, C.A. Bayly, Pierre Bourdieu, John Brewer, Roger Chartier, Robert Darnton, Elisabeth Eisenstein, N.N. Feltes, Kate Flint, Stanley Fish, Michel Foucault, Wolfgang Iser, Adrian Johns, Jerome McGann, D.F. McKenzie, E. Jennifer Monaghan, Jan Dirk Müller, Walter Ong, Janice Radway, Jonathan Rose, Mark Rose, John Sutherland, Jane Tompkins, James L. W. West III.

**David Finkelstein** is Head of the Media and Communication department at Queen Margaret University College, Edinburgh. His recent publications include co-editing *Negotiating India in the Nineteenth-century Media*, and *Nineteenth-century Media and the Construction of Identities*. He is also author of *The House of Blackwood: Author–Publisher Relations in the Victorian Era*.

**Alistair McCleery** is Professor of Literature and Communications at Napier University, Edinburgh, and Director of the Scottish Centre for the Book. He is co-editor of *The Bibliotheck* and author of *The Porpoise Press 1922–1939*.

# The Book History Reader

Edited by David Finkelstein and
Alistair McCleery

London and New York

First published 2002
by Routledge
11 New Fetter Lane, London EC4P 4EE

Simultaneously published in the USA and Canada
by Routledge
29 West 35th Street, New York, NY 10001

Reprinted 2003

*Routledge is an imprint of the Taylor & Francis Group*

Typeset in Perpetua and Bell Gothic by Keystroke, Jacaranda Lodge, Wolverhampton
Printed and bound in Great Britain by TJ International Ltd, Padstow, Cornwall

*British Library Cataloguing in Publication Data*
A catalogue record for this book is available from the British Library

*Library of Congress Cataloging in Publication Data*
has been applied for

ISBN 0–415–22657–0 (hbk)
ISBN 0–415–22658–9 (pbk)

# CONTENTS

**PART THREE**
**Commodifying print: Books and authors**

## PART FOUR
## Books and readers

# ACKNOWLEDGEMENTS

The editors and publisher gratefully acknowledge permission to reproduce copyright material from the following:

Richard Altick, Chicago University Press, and Ohio State University Press for permission to reprint from Richard Altick, *The English Common Reader*, Chicago: Chicago University Press, 1957; revised edition, Ohio State University Press, 1998.

Éditions du Seuil for permission to reprint Roland Barthes, 'The death of the author' from *Oevres complètes, Tome 2. 1966–1973*, Éditions du Seuil, 1994.

Cambridge University Press for permission to reprint C. A. Bayly, 'The Indian ecumene: An indigenous public sphere', from *Empire and Information: Intelligence Gathering and Social Communication in India 1780–1870*, Cambridge University Press, 1996.

Blackwell/Polity Press for permission to reprint extract from Pierre Bourdieu, *The Field of Cultural Production*, ed. Randal Johnson, Cambridge: Polity Press, 1993, pp. 27–73.

HarperCollins for permission to reprint John Brewer, 'Authors, publishers and the making of a literary culture', from *The Pleasures of the Imagination: English Culture in the Eighteenth Century*, Glasgow: HarperCollins, 1997, pp. 125–66.

Roger Chartier and Johns Hopkins University Press for permission to reprint Roger Chartier, 'Labourers and voyagers: From the text to the reader', *Diacritics* 22.2 (1992): 49–61. © Johns Hopkins University Press. Reprinted with the permission of The Johns Hopkins University Press.

Roger Chartier and Harvard University Press for permission to reprint Roger Chartier, 'The practical impact of writing', from *A History of Private Life, volume 3*, Harvard University Press, 1989, pp. 111–59. Reprinted by permission of the publisher from *A History of Private Life, volume 3: Passions of the Renaissance*, Roger Chartier, vol. Ed., translated by Arthur Goldhammer, Cambridge, Mass.: The Belknap Press of Harvard University Press. © 1989 by the President and Fellows of Harvard College.

W. W. Norton & Company, Inc. for permission to reprint Robert Darnton, 'What is the history of books?', from *The Kiss of Lamourette: Reflections in Cultural History*, revised edition 1990, pp. 107–36.

Cambridge University Press for permission to reprint Elisabeth Eisenstein, 'Defining the initial shift: Some features of print culture', from *The Printing Press as an Agent of Change*, Cambridge University Press, 1979, pp. 43–71.

University of Chicago for permission to reprint N. N. Feltes, 'Anyone of everybody: Net books and *Howards End*', from *Modes of Production of Victorian Novels*, University of Chicago Press, 1986, pp. 76–98.

Stanley Fish and Chicago University Press for permission to reprint Stanley Fish, 'Interpreting the *Variorum*', from 'Is there a text in this class?', *Critical Enquiry*, 2.3 (Winter 1976): 465–86.

Oxford University Press for permission to reprint Kate Flint, 'Reading practices', from *The Woman Reader, 1837–1914*, Oxford University Press, 1993, pp. 187–249. © Kate Flint 1993.

Cornell University Press for permission to reprint Michel Foucault, 'What is an author?'

Princeton University Press for permission to reprint Wolfgang Iser, 'Interaction between text and reader', from Susan K. Suleiman and Inge Crosman, eds, *The Reader in the Text: Essays on Audience and Interpretation*, New Jersey: Princeton University Press, 1980, pp. 106–19. © 1980 by Princeton University Press.

Adrian Johns and the University of Chicago Press for permission to reprint from Adrian Johns, *The Book of Nature and the Nature of the Book*, 1998, pp. 1–36, The University of Chicago Press, 1998.

Princeton University Press for permission to reprint Jerome McGann, 'The socialization of texts', from *The Textual Condition*, Princeton University Press, 1991, pp. 69–83. © 1991 by Princeton University Press.

The Estate of the late D. F. McKenzie for permission to reprint D. F. McKenzie, 'The book as an expressive form', from D. F. McKenzie, *The Panizzi Lectures, 1985: Bibliography and the Sociology of Texts*, London: British Library, 1986, pp. 1–20; and D. F. McKenzie, 'The sociology of a text: Orality, literacy and print in early New Zealand', *The Library*, Sixth Series, 6.4 (December 1984): 333–65.

The Johns Hopkins University Press and E. Jennifer Monaghan for permission to reprint E. Jennifer Monaghan, 'Literacy instruction and gender in Colonial New England', from Cathy N. Davidson, ed., *Reading in America: Literature and Social History*, Johns Hopkins University Press, 1989, pp. 53–80. © 1989 Johns Hopkins University Press.

Stanford University Press for permission to reprint Jan-Dirk Müller, 'The body of the book: The media transition from manuscript to print', reprinted from *Materialities of Communication*, edited by Hans Ulrich Gumbrecht and K. Ludwig Pfeiffer, translated by William Whobrey, with the permission of the publisher, Stanford University Press. © 1994 by the Board of Trustees of the Leland Stanford Junior University.

Taylor and Francis Books Ltd for permission to reprint Walter Ong, 'Writing restructures consciousness', *Orality and Literacy: The Technologizing of the Word*, Routledge, rev. edn 1997, pp. 78–138.

University of North Carolina Press for permission to reprint Janice Radway, 'A feeling for books: The Book-of-the-Month Club, literary taste and middle-class desire', from *A Feeling for Books: The Book of the Month Club, Literary Taste, and Middle Class Desire* by Janice A. Radway, Chapel Hill: University of North Carolina Press, 1997, pp. 263–79. © 1997 by the University of North Carolina Press.

Jonathan Rose and Johns Hopkins University Press for permission to reprint Jonathan Rose, 'Rereading the English common reader: A preface to a history of audiences', *Journal of the History of Ideas* 53 (1992): 47–70. © The Journal of the History of Ideas, Inc. Reprinted by permission of The Johns Hopkins University Press.

Mark Rose and Harvard University Press for permission to reprint Mark Rose, 'Literary property determined', from *Authors and Owners: the invention of copyright*, Cambridge, Mass.: Harvard University Press, 1993, pp. 92–112. © 1993 by the President and Fellows of Harvard College.

Macmillan Press Ltd for permission to reprint John Sutherland, 'The Victorian novelists: Who were they?' from *Victorian Fiction: Writers, Publishers, Readers*, Basingstoke: Macmillan Press, 1995, pp. 151–64. © Macmillan Press Ltd.

Oxford University Press, Inc. for permission to reprint Jane Tompkins, 'Masterpiece theatre: The politics of Hawthorne's literary reputation', from *Sensational Designs: The Cultural Work of American Fiction 1790–1860*, Oxford: Oxford University Press, 1985, pp. 20–34. © 1985 by Oxford University Press, Inc.

James L. W. West III for permission to reprint 'The magazine market' from *American Authors and the Literary Marketplace since 1900*, University of Pennsylvania Press, 1990, pp. 103–13.

Every attempt has been made to obtain permission to reproduce copyright material. If any proper acknowledgement has not been made, we would invite copyright holders to inform us of the oversight.

# Chapter 1

# David Finkelstein and Alistair McCleery

## INTRODUCTION

In Ray Bradbury's novel *Fahrenheit 451* (1953) a society is described in which books are prohibited objects to be burnt when discovered (the title refers to the ignition point of paper). Books are regarded as carriers of social dissent; but the story ends on a generally comforting note with its description of living books, men and women who have committed classic texts to memory and preserve in themselves that cultural heritage. In pursuing his theme, Bradbury makes a common distinction between texts, composed of words, and books, composed of paper and ink, which act only as vehicles for texts. Books can be replaced by memory and oral recitation, or in contemporary terms by digitized and downloadable text. Books, from this latter viewpoint, are a passing phase, albeit one which has lasted five hundred years. The setting of Umberto Eco's novel *The Name of the Rose* (1983), a monastery before the coming of print, provides a view of the reproduction and conservation of texts in manuscript in which the authority of the author is sacrosanct. Indeed, the murders in the monastery which the Sherlock Holmes-like Baskerville (itself an allusion to the eighteenth-century English typographer) investigates originate in a concern to preserve the reputation of Aristotle. The author's authority and the accuracy of his texts represent central tenets of the textual scholars. Both these novels address issues which form part of the substance of this Reader. These are issues, on the one hand, of the significance of the book as a physical object, and, on the other, of authorial status, which in their historical development fall within the field of book history.

Book history has emerged as a field of study in relatively recent times. Although its ancestors can be traced through prior disciplines such as bibliography and social history, it achieves its relative distinctiveness from both its emphasis upon print culture and the role of the book as material object within that culture. The use of the term 'culture' also underpins a recurrent emphasis within the field upon broad social movements drawing on detailed statistical evidence, a methodology heavily influenced by the French *annales* school of historians. This aspect of book history stands in contrast to both the technical analysis of individual books or editions characteristic of bibliography in the Anglo-American tradition and the narrow remit of most publishing 'house histories', themselves also typified by an often adulatory attitude towards their subjects.

Bibliography traditionally dealt with the recension of manuscripts in order to produce the most complete and least corrupted version of a text possible. The intervention of agents other than the author in the transmission of the text was seen as part of that corrupting process. This approach was applied by scholars such as McKerrow (1927), Greg (1966) and Bowers (1949) to the printed book. The operation of agents in the printing process, including editors and proof-readers, was painstakingly retraced in order to distinguish their interference and establish the text which most accurately reflected the author's final intention. How the author's final intention was itself to be deciphered was the subject at times of a much less rigorous analysis and the doubt remains whether the author's intention existed only as an editorial concept disguising the editor's own predilections and decisions (see Tanselle 1979). However, two key elements were inherited from bibliography by book history: the very recognition that a book is a result of a collaborative, albeit for bibliographers a corrupting, process; and a detailed system for describing books on the basis of their production attributes, which provided a universal standard drawing attention to the material object rather than its contents.

The vogue for producing publishing 'house histories', on the other hand, characterized a self-satisfied industry desirous of ensuring its own immortality through promotion of its role in literature. If there is anything of value to be salvaged from these self-congratulatory tomes, it is not so much the recognition of the publisher's role in the gestation of great works but the emphasis upon the entrepreneurial and dynamic individuals responsible for the establishment of our oldest publishing houses and the slow trajectory from family to corporate ownership through succeeding generations. If book history were to be represented by these histories alone, then it would be fairly criticized as a field lacking in objectivity and rigour. That it can not may be due to the purgative value of social history.

The application of *annales* methodology, of quantitative social history drawing on detail to produce the overall pattern, was found in Robert Escarpit's *Sociologie de la Littérature* (1958) and also in the same year in Febvre and Martin's *L'Apparition du Livre* (1958). Escarpit's work is notable for his attempt to isolate models of book production, dissemination and reception from the accumulation of data in a manner taken up by Darnton (Chapter 2 in this Reader) and Adams and Barker (1993). The *annales* approach differs, moreover, from attempts such as Elizabeth Eisenstein's to relate the development of the printed book to broader social and political movements in what has more recently been criticized as an over-determinist and simplistic approach, itself indicated in the title of her major work, *The Printing Press as an Agent of Change* (1979) (see A. Johns, Chapter 6 in this Reader). Febvre and Martin are perhaps more accurate in their chapter headed 'The Book as a Force for Change'. For them, the printing press is only one of a number of actors in a social and political drama; Lucien Febvre offers the alternative title for their study, *The Book in the Service of History*. Where the book was primarily active in the promotion of change was in the language of texts; 'the unified Latin culture of Europe was finally dissolved by the rise of the vernacular languages which was consolidated by the printing press' (Febvre and Martin, English translation 1976, 332).

## Book history

That book history as a field of study has come to prominence in the past few decades partly derives from both a recognition of the key role print has played in our culture for the past five hundred years and a realization that the role has now been usurped by other media. The book will continue as a cultural component (it will not die), but its dominance has disappeared and this in some way has licensed the study of its past. Perhaps the very ubiquity of printed texts in our history prevented previous scholars from appreciating and evaluating the fuller complexities of textual functions, procedures and nature.

Since Darnton's formulation of the 'communication circuit' as a means of examining the role of texts in society, and the subsequent modifications suggested by critics such as Adams and Barker, book history has begun increasingly to focus on what McGann has described as the 'socialization of texts', that is, the impact of books as artefacts travelling from private to public spaces (see Chapter 4 in this Reader). In this formulation, production becomes very much part of a process of, as Duguid notes, 'producing a public artifact and inserting it in a particular social circuit' (Duguid 1996: 81). But at the same time, the picture has become more complex and more interesting. Textual production is no longer to be viewed simply as a straightforward linear paradigm of production, progressing from composition to publication and reception. Rather, in the words of Jordan and Patten, what are now becoming increasingly important are conceptions of 'the activity of producing and consuming books that decenter the principal elements and make them interactive and inter-dependent: publishing history, in other words, as hypertext' (Jordan and Patten 1995: 11).

While past traditions in bibliographic and textual studies have sought to establish stable texts and precise textual intentions, the field of book history now operates within a context of unstable texts. With new media practices and the World Wide Web challenging the fixity of print and creating new links between visual, oral and textual communication forms, print culture studies is shifting to acknowledge the need to view texts, past and present, in wider contexts. In order to do this, book history is drawing on and borrowing from a combination of analytical tools and insights derived from various disciplines, ranging from literary studies to history, media and communication studies. Book history is no longer simply the province of bibliographers or literary critics, but rather can be seen as an integral part of the history of human communication.

## The future of the book

Book history as a field of study marks both an end and a beginning. It is clear that as we move into an era marked by discussions of the 'new' electronic revolution, the 'old' print revolution, begun in the fifteenth century, assumes a clearer focus and a natural closure. Just as manuscript traditions merged with new print technologies, so too we are now seeing similar mergings and complementarities between new and old media. The embedding of visual culture in cultural formations from the twentieth century onwards (the advance of film, television, the World Wide Web) has meant also a reshaping of print culture to accommodate such media of communication. We can see this in the manner in which books now form a part of contemporary Western cultural industries, where creativity, capitalism and consumption are linked through production of mass media products based on texts (books to films and subsequent film 'novelizations'). It is also evident in the manner in which texts (newspapers, journals) are now only one among many media communication systems competing for the attention of mass audiences. One has only to survey the multiple media through which humanity now communicates to see that print culture is slowly being displaced from the centre of social communication to the periphery, still necessary but no longer the sole form of information in an electronic age.

The history of human communication can be interpreted as comprising three major revolutions: in the movements from orality to literacy, from the written text to the printed text, and from print to computer-generated content. The development of alphabets, and of writing systems generally, provided an enabling technology which empowered minorities within societies. The coming of the printing press took that technology of writing and provided materials for mass consumption within society. The third revolution, through which we are still living, has used computing, not so much desktop publishing as Internet-based applications such as e-mail and the World Wide Web, to move from mass consumption to mass creation. Unlike the book, the technologies and economies of which mean that authorship can only ever be a minority pursuit, the computer has the potential to turn us all into creators as well as consumers (see Duguid 1996; Landow 1997; and Nunberg 1993).

## Conclusion

But if the book in the future will no longer be the main form of human communication, this does not signify, as some critics would have us believe, the death of the book. Nor does it lessen the impact of print on social formations. Book history is important for what it says about human development. For well over five hundred years, print has been central to the shaping of Western society, and to the transmission of its values outwards (whether imposed or voluntarily) into colonized and connected societies and territories (as extracts in this Reader by Bayly and McKenzie suggest). Without the portability and reach of print and texts, social, cultural, legal, humanistic and religious formations would not have developed, been transmitted and shaped beliefs and systems around the world.

In 1984, Robert Darnton surveyed the field of book history and declared that it was so scattered in approach that it resembled 'interdisciplinarity run riot'. At the same time, he predicted it was an area that 'seems likely to win a place alongside fields like the history of science and the history of art in the canon of scholarly discipline' (Chapter 2 in this Reader). The explosion in studies in book history since Darnton's pronouncement bears him out, as the selections in this Reader demonstrate.

The Reader is divided into four major parts covering definitions of book history, the move from oral to print culture, the development of authorship as a profession, and books and their readers. Each part has its own introduction drawing out specific themes and issues touched on briefly in this preliminary general introduction. There is also a concluding bibliography of further readings, both general and section-specific.

On reviewing the variety of texts represented in this Reader, we feel it is fair to conclude that interdisciplinarity is a key strength of book history. This may well be one of its attractions for students, as the various undergraduate and graduate studies courses in book history that are now developing attest to. At the same time, book history has emerged as a field in which common structures, methodologies and frameworks for investigating texts are now being embedded, offering a combination of empirically grounded and theoretically informed approaches to the subject. There is much here for future scholars to take advantage of.

PART ONE

# What is book history?

# EDITORS' INTRODUCTION

Throughout the first half of the twentieth century, the study of the nature of books in Anglo-American circles was dominated by a preoccupation with the physical materiality of books. The works of Ronald McKerrow (1927), W. W. Greg (1966), and Fredson Bowers (1949) are classic exemplars of this tradition of scholarly endeavour, still utilized today to a certain extent in courses on bibliographic methods. Book history studies has since evolved over the last half of the twentieth century to incorporate work on the social and cultural conditions governing the production, dissemination and reception of print and texts. Much of this shift is a result of critical authorities represented in this part's extracts.

Crucial to any student's understanding of book history is Robert Darnton's piece which, borrowing from French sociological models, was one of the first to suggest a practical model of study for the 'newly' constituted book history field, one which emphasized locating cultural and social investigations of texts within an overarching cycle of print production, dissemination and reception. His 'communication circuit', a processive and circular model of the 'life cycle' of books, running between and returning to author, reader and publisher, has been a point of departure for much work undertaken on print culture history. Similarly, Don McKenzie's Panizzi Lectures of 1985, of which we have extracted the first section, offered the resonating clarion call to view book history in sociological contexts, to delve into 'the sociology of texts'. This too has become central to the formation of new directions in book history studies.

An influential reassessment and redevelopment of these models (unfortunately not available for inclusion in this Reader) has since been provided by Adams and Barker (1993), who refer to McKenzie while at the same time expanding on Darnton's work to suggest stronger linkages of social investigations of print culture to textual conditions and bio-bibliographical evidence. Jerome McGann is among those whose fusion of literary history and bibliographical methods has also been influential in moving textual editing and bibliographic activity towards integrating social and cultural considerations in the shaping of the production of texts. McGann's 'socialization of the text' echoes Darnton's 'communication circuit' and Don McKenzie's 'sociology of the text' as memorable phrases used to encapsulate what book history is now about.

One of the most influential and prolific exponents of book history as a physical and social phenomenon over the past twenty years has been the French analyst Roger Chartier. Chartier's work on reading and the reception of texts in particular follows the traditions of the *annales* school of literary historiography, and has been tremendously influential in focusing attention on the importance of integrating readership studies into book history studies. The extract included here is one of his best-known pieces. Taking his inspiration from the historian and ethnologist Michel de Certeau, Chartier offers an examination of the possibilities for a history of reading. His proposal for a definition of print culture intertwined with studies of readership expresses and explores some of the tensions to be found between the material and cultural analyses of textual production which demarcate bibliographic and sociological views of book history.

More recently, Adrian Johns's prize-winning work challenges whether there can be such a thing as print culture studies. Johns argues in particular against Elisabeth Eisenstein's groundbreaking 1978 assessment of the revolutionary impact of the printing press on Western Renaissance culture (extracted in Part Two), suggesting that the effect was less overwhelming than we believe. The result is a radical reworking of previously uncontested views of Western print culture history.

Finally, an extract is included of Pierre Bourdieu's sociological theorization of the 'literary field'. Bourdieu's theory of the field has gained much currency recently among book historians, stressing as it does the juncture between culture, society and material production. In this case, the literary field is seen as representing self-contained literary, artistic and social microcosms with their own structures and codes, operating within and affected indirectly by changing social, economic, political and technological conditions. Like Darnton, Bourdieu is interested in the material production and distribution of textual culture; unlike him, however, Bourdieu uses these as a starting point for investigating how 'cultural status' is acquired and retained for aesthetic products and by literary elites.

There is no doubt that current approaches to the study of book history will continue to evolve as further work is done in the areas demarcated in these extracts. What is also true is that book history studies no longer relies solely on the simple paradigm of linear production from author to publishers to reader. In an era dominated by new technology, the study of texts acquires new significance, as a recent survey effectively suggests: book historians now have theoretical models to choose from that offer 'conceptions of the activity of producing and consuming books that decenter the principal elements and make them interactive and interdependent: publishing history, in other words, as hypertext' (Jordan and Patten 1995: 11).

# Chapter 2

# Robert Darnton

## WHAT IS THE HISTORY OF BOOKS?

'*Histoire du livre*' in France, '*Geschichte des Buchwesens*' in Germany, 'history of books' or 'of the book' in English-speaking countries — its name varies from place to place, but everywhere it is being recognized as an important new discipline. It might even be called the social and cultural history of communication by print, if that were not such a mouthful, because its purpose is to understand how ideas were transmitted through print and how exposure to the printed word affected the thought and behavior of mankind during the last five hundred years. Some book historians pursue their subject deep into the period before the invention of movable type. Some students of printing concentrate on newspapers, broadsides, and other forms besides the book. The field can be extended and expanded in many ways; but for the most part, it concerns books since the time of Gutenberg, an area of research that has developed so rapidly during the last few years that it seems likely to win a place alongside fields like the history of science and the history of art in the canon of scholarly disciplines.

Whatever the history of books may become in the future, its past shows how a field of knowledge can take on a distinct scholarly identity. It arose from the convergence of several disciplines on a common set of problems, all of them having to do with the process of communication. Initially, the problems took the form of concrete questions in unrelated branches of scholarship: What were Shakespeare's original texts? What caused the French Revolution? What is the connection between culture and social stratification? In pursuing those questions, scholars found themselves crossing paths in a no-man's land located at the intersection of a half-dozen fields of study. They decided to constitute a field of their own and to invite in historians, literary scholars, sociologists, librarians, and anyone else who wanted to understand the book as a force in history. The history of books began to acquire its own journals, research centers, conferences, and lecture circuits. It accumulated tribal elders as well as Young Turks. And although it has not yet developed passwords or secret handshakes or its own population of Ph.D.s, its adherents can recognize one another by the glint in their eyes. They belong to a common cause, one of the few sectors in the human sciences where there is a mood of expansion and a flurry of fresh ideas.

To be sure, the history of the history of books did not begin yesterday. It stretches back to the scholarship of the Renaissance, if not beyond; and it began in earnest during the nineteenth century when the study of books as material objects led to the rise of analytical bibliography in England. But the current work represents a departure from the established strains of scholarship, which may be traced to their nineteenth-century origins through back issues of *The Library* and *Börsenblatt für den Deutschen Buchhandel* or theses in the Ecole des Chartes. The new strain developed during the 1960s in France, where it took root in institutions like the Ecole Pratique des Hautes Etudes and spread through publications like *L'Apparition du livre* (1958), by Lucien Febvre and Henri-Jean Martin, and *Livre et société dans la France du XVIIIᵉ siècle* (two volumes 1965 and 1970) by a group connected with the VIᵉ section of the Ecole Pratique des Hautes Etudes.

The new book historians brought the subject within the range of themes studied by the 'Annales school' of socioeconomic history. Instead of dwelling on fine points of bibliography, they tried to uncover the general pattern of book production and consumption over long stretches of time. They compiled statistics from requests for *privilèges* (a kind of copyright), analyzed the contents of private libraries, and traced ideological currents through neglected genres like the *bibliothèque bleue* (primitive paperbacks). Rare books and fine editions had no interest for them; they concentrated instead on the most ordinary sort of books because they wanted to discover the literary experience of ordinary readers. They put familiar phenomena like the Counter Reformation and the Enlightenment in an unfamiliar light by showing how much traditional culture outweighed the avant-garde in the literary fare of the entire society. Although they did not come up with a firm set of conclusions, they demonstrated the importance of asking new questions, using new methods, and tapping new sources.[1]

Their example spread throughout Europe and the United States, reinforcing indigenous traditions, such as reception studies in Germany and printing history in Britain. Drawn together by their commitment to a common enterprise, and animated by enthusiasm for new ideas, book historians began to meet, first in cafés, then in conferences. They created new journals – *Publishing History*, *Bibliography Newsletter*, *Nouvelles du livre ancien*, *Revue française d'histoire du livre* (new series), *Buchhandelsgeschichte*, and *Wolfenbütteler Notizen zur Buchgeschichte*. They founded new centers – the Institut d'Etude du Livre in Paris, the Arbeitskreis für Geschichte des Buchwesens in Wolfenbüttel, the Center for the Book in the Library of Congress. Special colloquia – in Geneva, Paris, Boston, Worcester, Wolfenbüttel, and Athens, to name only a few that took place in the late 1970s – disseminated their research on an international scale. In the brief span of two decades, the history of books had become a rich and varied field of study.

So rich did it prove, in fact, that it now looks less like a field than a tropical rain forest. The explorer can hardly make his way across it. At every step he becomes entangled in a luxuriant undergrowth of journal articles and disoriented by the crisscrossing of disciplines – analytical bibliography pointing in this direction, the sociology of knowledge in that, while history, English, and comparative literature stake out overlapping territories. He is beset by claims to newness – '*la nouvelle bibliographie matérielle*', 'the new literary history' – and bewildered by competing methodologies, which would have him collating editions, compiling statistics, decoding copyright law, wading through reams of manuscript, heaving at the bar of a reconstructed common press, and psychoanalyzing the mental processes of readers. The history of books has become so crowded with ancillary disciplines that one can no longer see its general contours. How can the book historian neglect the history of libraries, of publishing, of paper, type, and reading? But how can he master their technologies, especially when they appear in imposing foreign formulations, like *Geschichte der Appellstruktur* and *Bibliométrie bibliologique*? It is enough to make one want to retire to a rare book room and count watermarks.

To get some distance from interdisciplinarity run riot, and to see the subject as a whole, it might be useful to propose a general model for analyzing the way books come into being and spread through society. To be sure, conditions have varied so much from place to place and from time to time since the invention of movable type that it would be vain to expect the biography of every book to conform to the same pattern. But printed books generally pass through roughly the same life cycle. It could be described as a communications circuit that runs from the author to the publisher (if the bookseller does not assume that role), the printer, the shipper, the bookseller, and the reader. The reader completes the circuit because he influences the author both before and after the act of composition. Authors are readers themselves. By reading and associating with other readers and writers, they form notions of genre and style and a general sense of the literary enterprise, which affects their texts, whether they are composing Shakespearean sonnets or directions for assembling radio kits. A writer may respond in his writing to criticisms of his previous work or anticipate reactions that his text will elicit. He addresses implicit readers and hears from explicit reviewers. So the circuit runs full cycle. It transmits messages, transforming them en route, as they pass from thought to writing to printed characters and back to thought again. Book history concerns each phase of this process and the process as a whole, in all its variations over space and time and in all its relations with other systems, economic, social, political, and cultural, in the surrounding environment.

That is a large undertaking. To keep their task within manageable proportions, book historians generally cut into one segment of the communications circuit and analyze it according to the procedures of a single discipline – printing, for example, which they study by means of analytical bibliography. But the parts do not take on their full significance unless they are related to the whole, and some holistic view of the book as a means of communication seems necessary if book history is to avoid being fragmented into esoteric specializations cut off from each other by arcane techniques and mutual misunderstanding. The model shown in Figure 2.1 provides a way of envisaging the entire communication process. With minor adjustments, it should apply to all periods in the history of the printed book (manuscript books and book illustrations will have to be considered elsewhere), but I would like to discuss it in connection with the period I know best, the eighteenth century, and to take it up phase by phase, showing how each phase is related to (1) other activities that a given person has underway at a given point in the circuit, (2) other persons at the same point in other circuits, (3) other persons at other points in the same circuit, and (4) other elements in society. The first three considerations bear directly on the transmission of a text, while the last concerns outside influences, which could vary endlessly. For the sake of simplicity, I have reduced the latter to the three general categories in the center of the diagram.

Models have a way of freezing human beings out of history. To put some flesh and blood on this one, and to show how it can make sense of an actual case, I will apply it to the publishing history of Voltaire's *Questions sur l'Encyclopédie*, an important work of the Enlightenment, and one that touched the lives of a great many eighteenth-century bookmen. One could study the circuit of its transmission at any point – at the stage of its composition, for example, when Voltaire shaped its text and orchestrated its diffusion in order to promote his campaign against religious intolerance, as his biographers have shown; or at its printing, a stage in which bibliographical analysis helps to establish the multiplication of editions; or at the point of its assimilation in libraries, where, according to statistical studies by literary historians, Voltaire's works occupied an impressive share of shelf space.[2] But I would like to consider the least familiar link in the diffusion process, the role of the bookseller, taking Isaac-Pierre Rigaud of Montpellier as an example, and working through the four considerations mentioned above.[3]

**I**

On August 16, 1770, Rigaud ordered thirty copies of the nine-volume octavo edition of the *Questions*, which the Société typographique de Neuchâtel (STN) had recently begun to print in the Prussian principality of Neuchâtel on the Swiss side of the French–Swiss border. Rigaud

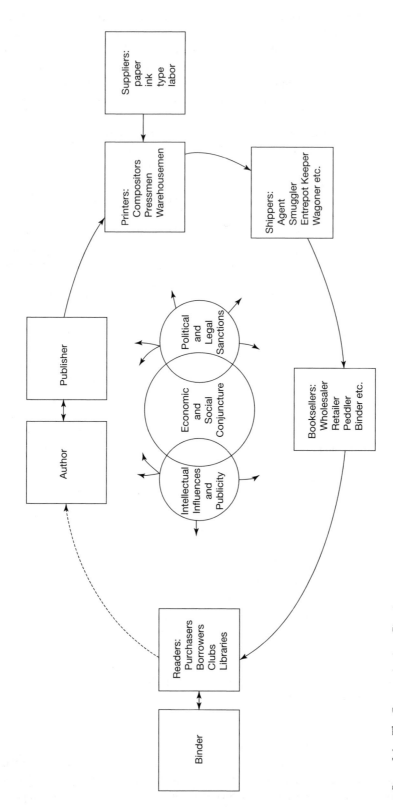

*Figure 2.1* The Communications Circuit

generally preferred to read at least a few pages of a new book before stocking it, but he considered the *Questions* such a good bet that he risked making a fairly large order for it, sight unseen. He did not have any personal sympathy for Voltaire. On the contrary, he deplored the philosophe's tendency to tinker with his books, adding and amending passages while cooperating with pirated editions behind the backs of the original publishers. Such practices produced complaints from customers, who objected to receiving inferior (or insufficiently audacious) texts. 'It is astonishing that at the end of his career M. de Voltaire cannot refrain from duping booksellers', Rigaud complained to the STN. 'It would not matter if all these little ruses, frauds, and deceits were blamed on the author. But unfortunately the printers and still more the retail booksellers are usually held responsible'.[4] Voltaire made life hard for booksellers, but he sold well.

There was nothing Voltairean about most of the other books in Rigaud's shop. His sales catalogues show that he specialized somewhat in medical books, which were always in demand in Montpellier, thanks to the university's famous faculty of medicine. Rigaud also kept a discreet line of Protestant works, because Montpellier lay in Huguenot territory. And when the authorities looked the other way, he brought in a few shipments of forbidden books.[5] But he generally supplied his customers with books of all kinds, which he drew from an inventory worth at least forty-five thousand livres, the largest in Montpellier and probably in all Languedoc, according to a report from the intendant's *subdélégué*.[6]

Rigaud's way of ordering from the STN illustrates the character of his business. Unlike other large provincial dealers, who speculated on a hundred or more copies of a book when they smelled a best seller, he rarely ordered more than a half dozen copies of a single work. He read widely, consulted his customers, took soundings by means of his commercial correspondence, and studied the catalogues that the STN and his other suppliers sent to him (by 1785 the STN's catalogue included seven hundred and fifty titles). Then he chose about ten titles and ordered just enough copies of them to make up a crate of fifty pounds, the minimum weight for shipment at the cheaper rate charged by the wagoners. If the books sold well, he reordered them; but he usually kept his orders rather small, and made four or five of them a year. In this way, he conserved capital, minimized risks, and built up such a large and varied stock that his shop became a clearinghouse for literary demand of every kind in the region.

The pattern of Rigaud's orders, which stands out clearly from the STN's account books, shows that he offered his customers a little of everything – travel books, histories, novels, religious works, and the occasional scientific or philosophical treatise. Instead of following his own preferences, he seemed to transmit demand fairly accurately and to live according to the accepted wisdom of the book trade, which one of the STN's other customers summarized as follows: 'The best book for a bookseller is a book that sells'.[7] Given his cautious style of business, Rigaud's decision to place an advance order for thirty nine-volume sets of the *Questions sur l'Encyclopédie* seems especially significant. He would not have put so much money on a single work if he had not felt certain of the demand – and his later orders show that he had calculated correctly. On June 19, 1772, soon after receiving the last shipment of the last volume, Rigaud ordered another dozen sets; and he ordered two more two years later, although by then the STN had exhausted its stock. It had printed a huge edition, twenty-five hundred copies, approximately twice its usual press run, and the booksellers had fallen all over themselves in the rush to purchase it. So Rigaud's purchase was no aberration. It expressed a current of Voltaireanism that had spread far and wide among the reading public of the Old Regime.

## II

How does the purchase of the *Questions* look when examined from the perspective of Rigaud's relations with the other booksellers of Montpellier? A book-trade almanac listed nine of them in 1777:[8]

| | |
|---|---|
| *Printer-Booksellers*: | Aug. Franç Rochard |
| | Jean Martel |
| *Booksellers*: | Isaac-Pierre Rigaud |
| | J. B. Faure |
| | Albert Pons |
| | Tournel |
| | Bascon |
| | Cézary |
| | Fontanel |

But according to a report from a traveling salesman of the STN, there were only seven.[9] Rigaud and Pons had merged and completely dominated the local trade; Cézary and Faure scraped along in the middle ranks; and the rest teetered on the brink of bankruptcy in precarious boutiques. The occasional binder and under-the-cloak peddler also provided a few books, most of them illegal, to the more adventuresome readers of the city. For example, the demoiselle Bringand, known as 'the students' mother', stocked some forbidden fruit 'under the bed on the room to the right on the second floor', according to the report of a raid that was engineered by the established booksellers.[10] The trade in most provincial cities fell into the same pattern, which can be envisaged as a series of concentric circles: at the center, one or two firms tried to monopolize the market; around the margin, a few small dealers survived by specializing in chapbooks and old volumes, by setting up reading clubs (*cabinets littéraires*) and binderies, or by peddling their wares in the back country; and beyond the fringe of legality, adventurers moved in and out of the market, selling forbidden literature.

When he ordered his shipment of the *Questions*, Rigaud was consolidating his position at the center of the local trade. His merger with Pons in 1770 provided him with enough capital and assets to ride out the mishaps – delayed shipments, defaulting debtors, liquidity crises – that often upset smaller businesses. Also, he played rough. When Cézary, one of the middling dealers, failed to meet some of his payments in 1781, Rigaud drove him out of business by organizing a cabal of his creditors. They refused to let him reschedule the payments, had him thrown in prison for debt, and forced him to sell off his stock at an auction, where they kept down the prices and gobbled up the books. By dispensing patronage, Rigaud controlled most of Montpellier's binderies; and by exerting pressure on the binders, he produced delays and snags in the affairs of the other booksellers. In 1789 only one of them remained, Abraham Fontanel, and he stayed solvent only by maintaining a *cabinet littéraire*, 'which provokes terrible fits of jealousy by the sieur Rigaud, who wants to be the only one left and who shows his hatred of me every day',[11] as Fontanel confided to the STN.

Rigaud did not eliminate his competitors simply by outdoing them in the dog-eat-dog style of commercial capitalism of early modern France. His letters, theirs, and the correspondence of many other booksellers show that the book trade contracted during the late 1770s and 1780s. In hard times, the big booksellers squeezed out the small, and the tough outlasted the tender. Rigaud had been a tough customer from the very beginning of his relations with the STN. He had ordered his copies of the *Questions* from Neuchâtel, where the STN was printing a pirated edition, rather than from Geneva, where Voltaire's regular printer, Gabriel Cramer, was producing the original, because he had extracted better terms. He also demanded better service, especially when the other booksellers in Montpellier, who had dealt with Cramer, received their copies first. The delay produced a volley of letters from Rigaud to the STN. Why couldn't the STN work faster? Didn't it know that it was making him lose customers to his competitors? He would have to order from Cramer in the future if it could not provide quicker shipments at a lower price. When volumes one through three finally arrived from Neuchâtel, volumes four through six from Geneva were already on sale in the other shops. Rigaud compared the texts, word for word, and found that the STN's edition contained none of the additional material that it had claimed to receive on the sly from Voltaire. So how could he push the theme of 'additions and corrections' in his sales talk? The recriminations flew thick and fast in the mail between Montpellier and Neuchâtel, and they showed that Rigaud meant to exploit every inch of every advantage that he could gain on his competitors. More important, they also revealed that the *Questions* were being sold all over Montpellier, even though in principle they could not circulate legally in France. Far from being confined to the under-the-cloak trade of marginal characters like 'the students' mother', Voltaire's work turned out to be a prize item in the scramble for profits at the very heart of the established book trade. When dealers like Rigaud scratched and clawed for their shipments of it, Voltaire could be sure that he was succeeding in his attempt to propel his ideas through the main lines of France's communications system.

## III

The role of Voltaire and Cramer in the diffusion process raises the problem of how Rigaud's operation fits into the other stages in the life cycle of the *Questions*. Rigaud knew that he was not getting a first edition; the STN had sent a circular letter to him and its other main customers explaining that it would reproduce Cramer's text, but with corrections and additions provided by the author himself, so that its version would be superior to the original. One of the STN's directors had visited Voltaire at Ferney in April 1770 and had returned with a promise that Voltaire would touch up the printed sheets he was to receive from Cramer and then would forward them to Neuchâtel for a pirated edition.[12] Voltaire often played such tricks. They provided a way to improve the quality and increase the quantity of his books, and therefore served his main purpose – which was not to make money, for he did not sell his prose to the printers, but to spread Enlightenment. The profit motive kept the rest of the system going, however. So when Cramer got wind of the STN's attempt to raid his market, he protested to Voltaire, Voltaire retracted his promise to the STN, and the STN had to settle for a delayed version of the text, which it received from Ferney, but with only minimal additions and corrections.[13] In fact, this setback did not hurt its sales, because the market had plenty of room to absorb editions, not only the STN's but also one that Marc Michel Rey produced in Amsterdam, and probably others as well. The booksellers had their choice of suppliers, and they chose according to whatever marginal advantage they could obtain on matters of price, quality, speed, and reliability in delivery. Rigaud dealt regularly with publishers in Paris, Lyon, Rouen, Avignon, and Geneva. He played them off against each other and sometimes ordered the same book from two or three of them so as to be certain of getting it before his competitors did. By working several circuits at the same time, he increased his room for maneuver. But in the case of the *Questions*, he was outmaneuvered and had to receive his goods from the circuitous Voltaire–Cramer–Voltaire–STN route.

That route merely took the copy from the author to the printer. For the printed sheets to reach Rigaud in Montpellier from the STN's shop in Neuchâtel, they had to wind their way through one of the most complex stages in the book's circuit. They could follow two main routes. One led from Neuchâtel to Geneva, Turin, Nice (which was not yet French), and Marseilles. It had the advantage of skirting French territory – and therefore the danger of confiscation – but it involved huge detours and expenses. The books had to be lugged over the Alps and pass through a whole army of middlemen – shipping agents, bargemen, wagoners, entrepôt keepers, ship captains, and dockers – before they arrived in Rigaud's storeroom. The best Swiss shippers claimed they could get a crate to Nice in a month for thirteen livres, eight sous per hundredweight; but their estimates proved to be far too low. The direct route from Neuchâtel to Lyon and down the Rhône was fast, cheap, and easy – but dangerous. The crates had to be sealed at their point of entry into France and inspected by the booksellers' guild and the royal book inspector in Lyon, then reshipped and inspected once more in Montpellier.[14]

Always cautious, Rigaud asked the STN to ship the first volumes of the *Questions* by the roundabout route, because he knew he could rely on his agent in Marseilles, Joseph Coulomb, to get the books into France without mishap. They left on December 9, 1771, but did not arrive until after March, when the first three volumes of Cramer's edition were already being sold by Rigaud's competitors. The second and third volumes arrived in July, but loaded down with shipping charges and damaged by rough handling. 'It seems that we are five or six thousand leagues apart', Rigaud complained, adding that he regretted he had not given his business to Cramer, whose shipments had already reached volume six.[15] By this time, the STN was worried enough about losing customers throughout southern France to set up a smuggling operation in Lyon. Their man, a marginal bookdealer named Joseph-Louis Berthoud, got volumes four and five past the guild inspectors, but then his business collapsed in bankruptcy; and to make matters worse, the French government imposed a tax of sixty livres per hundredweight on all book imports. The STN fell back on the Alpine route, offering to get its shipments as far as Nice for fifteen livres per hundredweight if Rigaud would pay the rest of the expenses, including the import duty. But Rigaud considered the duty such a heavy blow to the international trade that he suspended all his orders with foreign suppliers. The new tariff policy had made it prohibitively expensive to disguise illegal books as legal ones and to pass them through normal commercial channels.

In December, the STN's agent in Nice, Jacques Deandreis, somehow got a shipment of volume six of the *Questions* to Rigaud through the port of Sète, which was supposed to be closed to book imports. Then the French government, realizing that it had nearly destroyed the foreign book trade, lowered the tariff to twenty-six livres per hundredweight. Rigaud proposed sharing the cost with his suppliers: he would pay one third if they would pay two thirds. This proposal suited the STN, but in the spring of 1772 Rigaud decided that the Nice route was too expensive to be used under any conditions. Having heard enough complaints from its other customers to reach the same conclusion, the STN dispatched one of its directors to Lyon, and he persuaded a more dependable Lyonnais dealer, J.-M. Barret, to clear its shipments through the local guild and forward them to its provincial clients. Thanks to this arrangement, the last three volumes of Rigaud's *Questions* arrived safely in the summer.

It had required continuous effort and considerable expense to get the entire order to Montpellier, and Rigaud and the STN did not stop realigning their supply routes once they had completed this transaction. Because economic and political pressures kept shifting, they had constantly to readjust their arrangements within the complex world of middlemen, who linked printing houses with bookshops and often determined, in the last analysis, what literature reached French readers.

How the readers assimilated their books cannot be determined. Bibliographical analysis of all the copies that can be located would show what varieties of the text were available. A study of notarial archives in Montpellier might indicate how many copies turned up in inheritances, and statistics drawn from auction catalogues might make it possible to estimate the number in substantial private libraries. But given the present state of documentation, one cannot know who Voltaire's readers were or how they responded to his text. Reading remains the most difficult stage to study in the circuit that books follow.

## IV

All stages were affected by the social, economic, political, and intellectual conditions of the time; but for Rigaud, these general influences made themselves felt within a local context. He sold books in a city of thirty-one thousand inhabitants. Despite an important textile industry, Montpellier was essentially an old-fashioned administrative and religious center, richly endowed with cultural institutions, including a university, an academy of sciences, twelve Masonic lodges, and sixteen monastic communities. And because it was a seat of the provincial estates of Languedoc and an intendancy, and had as well an array of courts, the city had a large population of lawyers and royal officials. If they resembled their counterparts in other provincial centers,[16] they probably provided Rigaud with a good many of his customers and probably had a taste for Enlightenment literature. He did not discuss their social background in his correspondence, but he noted that they clamored for the works of Voltaire, Rousseau, and Raynal. They subscribed heavily to the *Encyclopédie*, and even asked for atheistic treatises like *Système de la nature* and *Philosophie de la nature*. Montpellier was no intellectual backwater, and it was good book territory. 'The book trade is quite extensive in this town', an observer remarked in 1768. 'The booksellers have kept their shops well stocked ever since the inhabitants developed a taste for having libraries.'[17]

These favorable conditions prevailed when Rigaud ordered his *Questions*. But hard times set in during the early 1770s; and in the 1780s Rigaud, like most booksellers, complained of a severe decline in his trade. The whole French economy contracted during those years, according to the standard account of C. E. Labrousse.[18] Certainly, the state's finances went into a tailspin: hence the disastrous book tariff of 1771, which belonged to Terray's unsuccessful attempt to reduce the deficit accumulated during the Seven Years' War. The government also tried to stamp out pirated and forbidden books, first by more severe police work in 1771–74, then by a general reform of the book trade in 1777. These measures eventually ruined Rigaud's commerce with the STN and with the other publishing houses that had grown up around France's borders during the prosperous mid-century years. Foreign publishers produced both original editions of books that could not pass the censorship in Paris and pirated editions of books put out by the Parisian publishers. Because the Parisians had acquired a virtual monopoly over the legal publishing industry, their rivals in the provinces formed alliances with the foreign houses and looked the other way when shipments from abroad arrived for inspection in the provincial guild halls (*chambres syndicales*). Under Louis XIV, the government had used the Parisian guild as an instrument to suppress the illegal trade: but under Louis XV it became increasingly lax, until a new era of severity began with the fall of Choiseul's ministry (December 1770). Thus Rigaud's relations with the STN fit perfectly into an economic and political pattern that had prevailed in the book trade since the early eighteenth century and that began to fall apart just as the first crates of the *Questions* were making their way between Neuchâtel and Montpellier.

Other patterns might show up in other research, for the model need not be applied in this manner, nor need it be applied at all. I am not arguing that book history should be written according to a standard formula but trying to show how its disparate segments can be brought together within a single conceptual scheme. Different book historians might prefer different schemata. They might concentrate on the book trade of all Languedoc, as Madeleine Ventre has done; or on the general bibliography of Voltaire, as Giles Barber, Jeroom Vercruysse, and others are doing; or on the overall pattern of book production in eighteenth-century France, in the manner of François Furet and Robert Estivals.[19] But however they define their subject, they will not draw out its full significance unless they relate it to all the elements that worked together as a circuit for transmitting texts. To make the point clearer, I will go over the model circuit once more, noting questions that have been investigated successfully or that seem ripe for further research.

## I  Authors

Despite the proliferation of biographies of great writers, the basic conditions of authorship remain obscure for most periods of history. At what point did writers free themselves from the patronage of wealthy noblemen and the state in order to live by their pens? What was the nature of a literary career, and how was it pursued? How did writers deal with publishers, printers, booksellers, reviewers, and one another? Until those questions are answered, we will not have a full understanding of the transmission of texts. Voltaire was able to manipulate secret alliances with pirate publishers because he did not depend on writing for a living. A century later, Zola proclaimed that a writer's independence came from selling his prose to the highest bidder.[20] How did this transformation take place? The work of John Lough begins to provide an answer, but more systematic research on the evolution of the republic of letters in France could be done from police records, literary almanacs, and bibliographies (*La France littéraire* gives the names and publications of 1,187 writers in 1757 and 3,089 in 1784). The situation in Germany is more obscure, owing to the fragmentation of the German states before 1871. But German scholars are beginning to tap sources like *Das gelehrte Teutschland*, which lists four thousand writers in 1779, and to trace the links between authors, publishers, and readers in regional and monographic studies.[21] Marino Berengo has shown how much can be discovered about author–publisher relations in Italy.[22] And the work of A. S. Collins still provides an excellent account of authorship in England, although it needs to be brought up to date and extended beyond the eighteenth century.[23]

## II  Publishers

The key role of publishers is now becoming clearer, thanks to articles appearing in the *Journal of Publishing History* and monographs like Martin Lowry's *The World of Aldus Manutius*, Robert Patten's *Charles Dickens and His Publishers*, and Gary Stark's *Entrepreneurs of Ideology: Neoconservative Publishers in Germany, 1890–1933*. But the evolution of the publisher as a distinct figure in contrast to the master bookseller and the printer still needs systematic study. Historians have barely begun to tap the papers of publishers, although they are the richest of all sources for the history of books. The archives of the Cotta Verlag in Marbach, for example, contain at least one hundred fifty thousand documents, yet they have only been skimmed for references to Goethe, Schiller, and other famous writers. Further investigation almost certainly would turn up a great deal of information about the book as a force in nineteenth-century Germany. How did publishers draw up contracts with authors, build alliances with booksellers, negotiate with political authorities, and handle finances, supplies, shipments, and publicity? The answers to those questions would carry the history of books deep into the territory of social, economic, and political history, to their mutual benefit.

    The Project for Historical Biobibliography at Newcastle upon Tyne and the Institut de Littérature et de Techniques Artistiques de Masse at Bordeaux illustrate the directions that such interdisciplinary work has already taken. The Bordeaux group has tried to trace books through different distribution systems in order to uncover the literary experience of different groups in contemporary France.[24] The researchers in Newcastle have studied the diffusion process through quantitative analysis of subscription lists, which were widely used in the sales campaigns of British publishers from the early seventeenth to the early nineteenth centuries.[25] Similar work could be done on publishers' catalogues and prospectuses, which have been collected in research centers like the Newberry Library. The whole subject of book advertising needs investigation. One could learn a great deal about attitudes toward books and the context of their use by studying the way they were presented – the strategy of the appeal, the values invoked by the phrasing – in all kinds of publicity, from journal notices to wall posters. American historians have used newspaper advertisements to map the spread of the printed word into the back reaches of colonial society.[26] By consulting the papers of publishers, they could make deeper inroads in the nineteenth and twentieth centuries.[27] Unfortunately, however, publishers usually treat their archives as garbage. Although they save the occasional letter from a famous author, they throw away account books and commercial correspondence, which usually are the most important sources of information for the book historian. The Center for the Book in the Library of Congress is now compiling a guide to publishers' archives. If they can be preserved and studied, they might provide a different perspective on the whole course of American history.

## III  Printers

The printing shop is far better known than the other stages in the production and diffusion of books because it has been a favorite subject of study in the field of analytical bibliography, whose purpose, as defined by R. B. McKerrow and Philip Gaskell, is 'to elucidate the transmission of texts by explaining the processes of book production.'[28] Bibliographers have made important contributions to textual criticism, especially in Shakespearean scholarship, by building inferences backward from the structure of a book to the process of its printing and hence to an original text, such as the missing Shakespeare manuscripts. That line of reasoning has been undercut recently by D. F. McKenzie.[29] But even if they can never reconstruct an Ur-Shakespeare, bibliographers can demonstrate the existence of different editions of a text and of different states of an edition, a necessary skill in diffusion studies. Their techniques also make it possible to decipher the records of printers and so have opened up a new, archival phase in the history of printing. Thanks to the work of McKenzie, Leon Voet, Raymond de Roover, and Jacques Rychner, we now have a clear picture of how printing shops operated throughout the handpress period (roughly 1500–1800).[30] More work needs to be done on later periods, and new questions could be asked: How did printers calculate costs and organize production, especially after the spread of job printing and journalism? How did book budgets change after the introduction of machine-made paper in the first decade of the nineteenth century and Linotype in the 1880s? How did the technological changes affect the management of labor? And what part did journeymen printers, an unusually articulate and militant sector of the working class, play in labor history? Analytical bibliography may seem arcane to the outsider, but it could make a great contribution to social as well as literary history, especially if it were seasoned with a reading of printers' manuals and autobiographies, beginning with those of Thomas Platter, Thomas Gent, N. E. Restif de la Bretonne, Benjamin Franklin, and Charles Manby Smith.

## IV  Shippers

Little is known about the way books reached bookstores from printing shops. The wagon, the canal barge, the merchant vessel, the post office, and the railroad may have influenced the history of literature more than one would suspect. Although transport facilities probably had little effect on the trade in great publishing centers like London and Paris, they sometimes determined the ebb and flow of business in remote areas. Before the nineteenth century, books were usually sent in sheets, so that the customer could have them bound according to his taste and his ability to pay. They traveled in large bales wrapped in heavy paper and were easily damaged by rain and the friction of ropes. Compared with commodities like textiles, their intrinsic value was slight, yet their shipping costs were high, owing to the size and weight of the sheets. So shipping often took up a large proportion of a book's total cost and a large place in the marketing strategy of publishers. In many parts of Europe, printers could not count on getting shipments to booksellers in August and September because wagoners abandoned their routes to work the harvest. The Baltic trade frequently ground to a halt after October, because ice closed the ports. Routes opened and shut everywhere in response to the pressures of war, politics, and even insurance rates. Unorthodox literature has traveled underground in huge quantities from the sixteenth century to the present, so its influence has varied according to the effectiveness of the smuggling industry. And other genres, like chapbooks and penny dreadfuls, circulated through special distribution systems, which need much more study, although book historians are now beginning to clear some of the ground.[31]

## V  Booksellers

Thanks to some classic studies – H. W. Bennett on early modern England, L. C. Wroth on colonial America, H.-J. Martin on seventeenth-century France, and Johann Goldfriedrich on Germany – it is possible to piece together a general picture of the evolution of the book trade.[32] But more work needs to be done on the bookseller as a cultural agent, the middleman who mediated between supply and demand at their key point of contact. We still do not know enough about the social and intellectual world of men like Rigaud, about their values and tastes and the way they fit into their communities. They also operated within commercial networks, which expanded and collapsed like alliances in the diplomatic world. What laws governed the rise and fall of trade empires in publishing? A comparison of national histories could reveal some general tendencies, such as the centripetal force of great centers like London, Paris, Frankfurt, and Leipzig, which drew provincial houses into their orbits, and the countervailing trend toward alignments between provincial dealers and suppliers in independent enclaves like Liège, Bouillon, Neuchâtel, Geneva, and Avignon. But comparisons are difficult because the trade operated through different institutions in different countries, which generated different kinds of archives. The records of the London Stationers' company, the Communauté des Libraires et Imprimeurs de Paris, and the Leipzig and Frankfurt book fairs have had a great deal to do with the different courses that book history has taken in England, France, and Germany.[33]

Nevertheless, books were sold as commodities everywhere. A more unabashedly economic study of them would provide a new perspective to the history of literature. James Barnes, John Tebbel, and Frédéric Barbier have demonstrated the importance of the economic element in the book trades of nineteenth-century England, America, and France.[34] But more work could be done – on credit mechanisms, for example, and the techniques of negotiating bills of exchange, of defense against suspensions of payment, and of exchanging printed sheets in lieu of payment in specie. The book trade, like other businesses during the Renaissance and early modern periods, was largely a confidence game, but we still do not know how it was played.

## VI  Readers

Despite a considerable literature on its psychology, phenomenology, textology, and sociology, reading remains mysterious. How do readers make sense of the signs on the printed page? What are the social effects of that experience? And how has it varied? Literary scholars like Wayne Booth, Stanley Fish, Wolfgang Iser, Walter Ong, and Jonathan Culler have made reading a central concern of textual criticism because they understand literature as an activity, the construal of meaning within a system of communication, rather than a canon of texts.[35] The book historian could make use of their notions of fictitious audiences, implicit readers, and interpretive communities. But he may find their observations somewhat time-bound. Although the critics know their way around literary history (they are especially strong on seventeenth-century England), they seem to assume that texts have always worked on the sensibilities of readers in the same way. But a seventeenth-century London burgher inhabited a different mental universe from that of a twentieth-century American professor. Reading itself has changed over time. It was often done aloud and in groups, or in secret and with an intensity we may not be able to imagine today. Carlo Ginsburg has shown how much meaning a sixteenth-century miller could infuse into a text, and Margaret Spufford has demonstrated that still humbler workmen fought their way to mastery over the printed word in the era of *Areopagitica*.[36] Everywhere in early modern Europe, from the ranks of Montaigne to those of Menocchio, readers wrung significance from books; they did not merely decipher them. Reading was a passion long before the '*Lesewut*' and the '*Wertherfieber*' of the romantic era; and there is *Sturm und Drang* in it yet, despite the vogue for speed-reading and the mechanistic view of literature as the encoding and decoding of messages.

But texts shape the response of readers, however active they may be. As Walter Ong has observed, the opening pages of *The Canterbury Tales* and *A Farewell to Arms* create a frame and cast the reader in a role, which he cannot avoid no matter what he thinks of pilgrimages and civil wars.[37] In fact, typography as well as style and syntax determine the ways in which texts convey meanings. McKenzie has shown that the bawdy, unruly Congreve of the early quarto editions settled down into the decorous neoclassicist of the *Works* of 1709 as a consequence of book design rather than bowdlerization.[38] The history of reading will have to take account of the ways that texts constrain readers as well as the ways that readers take liberties with texts. The tension between those tendencies has existed wherever men confronted books, and it has produced some extraordinary results, as in Luther's reading of the Psalms, Rousseau's reading of *Le Misanthrope*, and Kierkegaard's reading of the sacrifice of Isaac.

If it is not possible to recapture the great rereadings of the past, the inner experience of ordinary readers may always elude us. But we should at least be able to reconstruct a good deal of the social context of reading. The debate about silent reading during the Middle Ages has produced some impressive evidence about reading habits,[39] and studies of reading societies in Germany, where they proliferated to an extraordinary degree in the eighteenth and nineteenth centuries, have shown the importance of reading in the development of a distinct bourgeois cultural style.[40] German scholars have also done a great deal in the history of libraries and in reception studies of all kinds.[41] Following a notion of Rolf Engelsing, they often maintain that reading habits became transformed at the end of the eighteenth century. Before this '*Leserevolution*', readers tended to work laboriously through a small number of texts, especially the Bible, over and over again. After-wards, they raced through all kinds of material, seeking amusement rather than edification. The shift from intensive to extensive reading coincided with a desacralization of the printed word. The world began to be cluttered with reading matter, and texts began to be treated as commodities that could be discarded as casually as yesterday's newspaper. This interpretation has recently been disputed by Reinhart Siegert, Martin Welke, and other young scholars, who have discovered 'intensive' reading in the reception of fugitive works like almanacs and newspapers, notably the *Noth- und Hülfsbüchlein* of Rudolph Zacharias Becker, an extraordinary best seller of the *Goethezeit*.[42] But whether or not the concept of a reading revolution will hold up, it has helped to align research on reading with general questions of social and cultural history.[43] The same can be said of research on literacy,[44] which has made it possible for scholars to detect the vague outline of diverse reading publics two and three centuries ago and to trace books to readers at several levels of society. The lower the level, the more intense the study. Popular literature has been a favorite topic of research during the last decade,[45] despite a growing tendency to question the notion that cheap booklets like the *bibliothèque bleue* represented an autonomous culture of the common people or that one can distinguish clearly between strains of 'elite' and 'popular' culture. It now seems inadequate to view cultural change as a linear, or trickle-down, movement of influences. Currents flowed up as well as down, merging and blending as they went. Characters like Gargantua, Cinderella, and Buscon moved back and forth through oral traditions, chapbooks, and sophisticated literature, changing in nationality as well as genre.[46] One could even trace the metamorphoses of stock figures in almanacs. What does Poor Richard's reincarnation as *le Bonhomme Richard* reveal about literary culture in America and France? And what can be learned about German–French relations by following the Lame Messenger (*der hinkende Bote, le messager boiteux*) through the traffic of almanacs across the Rhine?

Questions about who reads what, in what conditions, at what time, and with what effect, link reading studies with sociology. The book historian could learn how to pursue such questions from the work of Douglas Waples, Bernard Berelson, Paul Lazarsfeld, and Pierre Bourdieu. He could draw on the reading research that flourished in the Graduate Library School of the University of Chicago from 1930 to 1950, and that still turns up in the occasional Gallup report.[47] And as an example of the sociological strain in historical writing, he could consult the studies of reading (and nonreading) in the English working class during the last two centuries by Richard Altick, Robert Webb, and Richard Hoggart.[48] All this work opens onto the larger problem of how exposure to the printed word affects the way men think. Did the invention of movable type transform man's mental universe? There may be no single satisfactory answer to that question because it bears on so many different aspects of life in early modern Europe, as Elizabeth Eisenstein has shown.[49] But it should be possible to arrive at a firmer understanding of what books meant to people. Their use in the taking of oaths, the exchanging of gifts, the awarding of prizes, and the bestowing of legacies would provide clues to their significance within different societies. The iconography of books could indicate the weight of their authority, even for illiterate laborers who sat in church before pictures of the tablets of Moses. The place of books in folklore, and of folk motifs in books, shows that influences ran both ways when oral traditions came into contact with printed texts, and that books need to be studied in relation to other media.[50] The lines of research could lead in many directions, but they all should issue ultimately in a larger understanding of how printing has shaped man's attempts to make sense of the human condition.

One can easily lose sight of the larger dimensions of the enterprise because book historians often stray into esoteric byways and unconnected specializations. Their work can be so fragmented, even within the limits of the literature on a single country, that it may seem hopeless to conceive of book history as a single subject, to be studied from a comparative perspective across the whole range of historical disciplines. But books themselves do not respect limits either linguistic or national. They have often been written by authors who belonged to an international republic of letters, composed by printers who did not work in their native tongue, sold by booksellers who operated across national boundaries, and read in one language by readers who spoke another. Books also refuse to be contained within the confines of a single discipline when treated as objects of study. Neither history nor literature nor economics nor sociology nor bibliography can do justice to all the aspects of the life of a book. By its very nature, therefore, the history of books must be international in scale and interdisciplinary in method. But it need not lack conceptual coherence, because books belong to circuits of communication that operate in consistent patterns, however complex they may be. By unearthing those circuits, historians can show that books do not merely recount history; they make it.

## Notes

This essay first appeared in *Daedalus* (Summer 1982): 65–83. Since then I have attempted to develop its themes further in an essay on the history of reading (Chapter 9 this volume) and in 'Histoire du livre–Geschichte des Buchwesens: An Agenda for Comparative History', *Publishing History*, no. 22 (1987): 33–41.

1    For examples of this work, see, in addition to the books named in the essay, Henri-Jean Martin, *Livre, pouvoirs et société à Paris au XVIIᵉ siècle (1598–1701)* (Geneva, 1969), 2 volumes; Jean Quéniart, *L'Imprimerie et la librairie à Rouen au XVIIIᵉ siècle* (Paris, 1969); René Moulinas, *L'Imprimerie, la librairie et la presse à Avignon au XVIIIᵉ siècle* (Grenoble, 1974); and Frédéric Barbier, *Trois cents ans de librairie et d'imprimerie: Berger-Levrault, 1676–1830* (Geneva, 1979), in the series 'Histoire et civilisation du livre', which includes several monographs written along similar lines. Much of the French work has appeared as articles in the *Revue française d'histoire du livre*. For a survey of the field by two of the most important contributors to it, see Roger Chartier and Daniel Roche, 'Le livre, un changement de perspective', *Faire de l'histoire* (Paris, 1974), III: 115–36, and Chartier and Roche, 'L'Histoire quantitative du livre', *Revue française d'histoire du livre* 16 (1977): 3–27. For sympathetic assessments by two American fellow travelers, see Robert Darnton, 'Reading, Writing, and Publishing in Eighteenth-Century France: A Case Study in the Sociology of Literature', *Daedalus* (Winter 1971): 214–56, and Raymond Birn, 'Livre et Société After Ten Years: Formation of a Discipline', *Studies on Voltaire and the Eighteenth Century* 151 (1976): 287–312.

2    As examples of these approaches, see Theodore Besterman, *Voltaire* (New York, 1969), pp. 433–34; Daniel Mornet, 'Les Enseignements des bibliothèques privées (1750–1780)', *Revue d'histoire littéraire de la France* 17 (1910): 449–92; and the bibliographical studies now being prepared under the direction of the Voltaire Foundation, which will replace the outdated bibliography by Georges Bengesco.

3    The following account is based on the ninety-nine letters in Rigaud's dossier in the papers of the Société typographique de Neuchâtel, Bibliothèque de la ville de Neuchâtel, Switzerland (henceforth referred to as STN), supplemented by other relevant material from the vast archives of the STN.

4    Rigaud to STN, July 27, 1771.

5    The pattern of Rigaud's orders is evident from his letters to the STN and STN's 'Livres de Commission', where it tabulated its orders. Rigaud included catalogues of his major holdings in his letters of June 29, 1774, and May 23, 1777.

6    Madeleine Ventre, *L'Imprimerie et la librairie en Languedoc au dernier siècle de l'Ancien Régime* (Paris and The Hague, 1958), p. 227.

7    B. André to STN, August 22, 1784.

8    *Manuel de l'auteur et du libraire* (Paris, 1777), p. 67.

9    Jean-François Favarger to STN, August 29, 1778.

10    The *procès-verbal* of the raids is in the Bibliothèque Nationale, Ms. français 22075, fo. 355.

11    Fontanel to STN, March 6, 1781.

12    STN to Gosse and Pinet, booksellers of The Hague, April 19, 1770.

13    STN to Voltaire, September 15, 1770.

14    This account is based on the STN's correspondence with intermediaries all along its routes, notably the shipping agents Nicole and Galliard of Nyon and Secrétan and De la Serve of Ouchy.

15    Rigaud to STN, August 28, 1771.

16    Robert Darnton, *The Business of Enlightenment: A Publishing History of the Encyclopédie 1775–1800* (Cambridge, Mass., 1979), pp. 273–99.

17    Anonymous, 'Etat et description de la ville de Montpellier, fait en 1768', in *Montpellier en 1768 et en 1836 d'après deux manuscrits inédits*, edited by J. Berthelé (Montpellier, 1909), p. 55. This rich contemporary description of Montpellier is the main source of the above account.

18   C. E. Labrousse, *La Crise de l'économie française à la fin de l'Ancien Régime et au début de la Révolution* (Paris, 1944).

19   Ventre, *L'Imprimerie et la librairie en Languedoc*; François Furet, 'La "librairie" du royaume de France au 18ᵉ siècle', *Livre et société*, 1, 3–32; and Robert Estivals, *La Statistique bibliographique de la France sous la monarchie au XVIIIᵉ siècle* (Paris and The Hague, 1965). The bibliographical work will be published under the auspices of the Voltaire Foundation.

20   John Lough, *Writer and Public in France from the Middle Ages to the Present Day* (Oxford, 1978), p. 303.

21   For surveys and selections of recent German research, see Helmuth Kiesel and Paul Münch, *Gesellschaft und Literatur im 18. Jahrhundert. Voraussetzung und Entstehung des literarischen Marktes in Deutschland* (Munich, 1977); *Aufklärung, Absolutismus und Bürgertum in Deutschland*, edited by Franklin Kopitzsch (Munich, 1976); and Herbert G. Göpfert, *Vom Autor zum Leser* (Munich: 1978).

22   Marino Berengo, *Intellettuali e librai nella Milano della Restaurazione* (Turin, 1980). On the whole, however, the French version of *histoire du livre* has received a less enthusiastic reception in Italy than in Germany: see Furio Diaz, 'Metodo quantitativo e storia delle idee', *Rivista storica italiana* 78 (1966): 932–47.

23   A. S. Collins, *Authorship in the Days of Johnson* (London, 1927) and *The Profession of Letters (1780–1832)* (London, 1928). For more recent work, see John Feather, 'John Nourse and His Authors', *Studies in Bibliography* 34 (1981): 205–26.

24   Robert Escarpit, *Le littéraire et le social. Eléments pour une sociologie de la littérature* (Paris, 1970).

25   Peter John Wallis, *The Social Index: A New Technique for Measuring Social Trends* (Newcastle upon Tyne, 1978).

26   William Gilmore is now completing an extensive research project on the diffusion of books in colonial New England. On the political and economic aspects of the colonial press, see Stephen Botein, ' "Meer Mechanics" and an Open Press: The Business and Political Strategies of Colonial American Printers', *Perspectives in American History* 9 (1975): 127–225; and *The Press and the American Revolution*, edited by Bernard Bailyn and John B. Hench (Worcester, Mass., 1980), which contain ample references to work on the early history of the book in America.

27   For a general survey of work on the later history of books in this country, see Hellmut Lehmann-Haupt, *The Book in America*, rev. ed. (New York, 1952).

28   Philip Gaskell, *A New Introduction to Bibliography* (New York and Oxford, 1972), preface. Gaskell's work provides an excellent general survey of the subject.

29   D. F. McKenzie, 'Printers of the Mind: Some Notes on Bibliographical Theories and Printing House Practices', *Studies in Bibliography* 22 (1969): 1–75.

30   D. F. McKenzie, *The Cambridge University Press 1696–1712* (Cambridge, 1966), 2 volumes; Leon Voet, *The Golden Compasses* (Amsterdam, 1969 and 1972), 2 volumes; Raymond de Roover, 'The Business Organization of the Plantin Press in the Setting of Sixteenth-Century Antwerp', *De gulden passer* 24 (1956): 104–20; and Jacques Rychner, 'A L'Ombre des Lumières: coup d'oeil sur la main-d'oeuvre de quelques imprimeries du XVIIIᵉ siècle', *Studies on Voltaire and the Eighteenth Century*, 155 (1976): 1925–55, and 'Running a Printing House in Eighteenth-Century Switzerland: the Workshop of the Société typographique de Neuchâtel', *The Library*, sixth series, 1 (1979): 1–24.

31   For example, see J.-P. Belin, *Le Commerce des livres prohibés à Paris de 1750 à 1789* (Paris, 1913); Jean-Jacques Darmon, *Le Colportage de librairie en France sous le second empire* (Paris, 1972); and Reinhart Siegert, *Aufklärung und Volkslektüre exemplarisch dargestellt an Rudolph Zacharias Becker und seinem 'Noth- und Hülfsbüchlein' mit einer Bibliographie zum Gesamtthema* (Frankfurt am Main, 1978).

32   H. S. Bennett, *English Books and Readers 1475 to 1557* (Cambridge, 1952) and *English Books and Readers 1558–1603* (Cambridge, 1965); L. C. Wroth, *The Colonial Printer* (Portland: 1938);

Martin, *Livre, pouvoirs et société*; and Johann Goldfriedrich and Friedrich Kapp, *Geschichte des Deutschen Buchhandels* (Leipzig, 1886–1913), 4 volumes.

33    Compare Cyprian Blagden, *The Stationers' Company, A History, 1403–1959* (Cambridge: 1960); Martin, *Livre, pouvoirs et société*; and Rudolf Jentzsch, *Der deutsch-lateinische Büchermarkt nach den Leipziger Ostermesskatalogen von 1740, 1770 und 1800 in seiner Gliederung und Wandlung* (Leipzig, 1912).

34    James Barnes, *Free Trade in Books: A Study of the London Book Trade Since 1800* (Oxford, 1964); John Tebbel, *A History of Book Publishing in the United States* (New York, 1972–78), 3 volumes; and Barbier, *Trois cents ans de librairie et d'imprimerie.*

35    See, for example, Wolfgang Iser, *The Implied Reader: Patterns of Communication in Prose Fiction from Bunyan to Beckett* (Baltimore, 1974); Stanley Fish, *Self-Consuming Artifacts: The Experience of Seventeenth-Century Literature* (Berkeley and Los Angeles, 1972) and *Is There a Text in This Class? The Authority of Interpretive Communities* (Cambridge, Mass., 1980); Walter Ong, 'The Writer's Audience Is Always a Fiction', *PMLA (Publication of the Modern Language Association of America)* 90 (1975): 9–21; and for a sampling of other variations on these themes, Susan R. Suleiman and Inge Crosman, *The Reader in the Text: Essays on Audience and Interpretation* (Princeton: Princeton University Press, 1980).

36    Carlo Ginzburg, *The Cheese and the Worms: The Cosmos of a Sixteenth-Century Miller* (Baltimore: Johns Hopkins University Press, 1980); Margaret Spufford, 'First Steps in Literacy: The Reading and Writing Experiences of the Humblest Seventeenth-Century Spiritual Autobiographers, *Social History* 4 (1979): 407–35.

37    Ong, 'The Writer's Audience Is Always a Fiction'.

38    D. F. McKenzie, 'Typography and Meaning: The Case of William Congreve', *Wolfenbütteler Schriften zur Geschichte des Buchwesens* (Hamburg: Dr. Ernst Hauswedell, 1981), IV: 81–125.

39    See Paul Saenger, 'Silent Reading: Its Impact on Late Medieval Script and Society', *Viator* 13 (1982): 367–414.

40    See *Lesegesellschaften und bürgerliche Emanzipation. Ein Europäischer Vergleich*, edited by Otto Dann (Munich: C. H. Beck, 1981), which has a thorough bibliography.

41    For examples of recent work, see *Öffentliche und Private Bibliotheken im 17. und 18. Jahrhundert: Raritätenkammern, Forschungsinstrumente oder Bildungsstätten?* edited by Paul Raabe (Bremen and Wolfenbüttel, 1977). Much of the stimulus for recent reception studies has come from the theoretical work of Hans Robert Jauss, notably *Literaturgeschichte als Provokation* (Frankfurt am Main, 1970).

42    Engelsing, *Analphabetentum und Lektüre. Zur Sozialgeschichte des Lesens in Deutschland zwischen feudaler und industrieller Gesellschaft* (Stuttgart, 1973), and *Der Bürger als Leser. Lesergeschichte in Deutschland 1500–1800* (Stuttgart, 1974); Siegert, *Aufklärung und Volkslektüre*; and Martin Welke, 'Gemeinsame Lektüre und frühe Formen von Gruppenbildungen im 17. and 18. Jahrhundert: Zeitungslesen in Deutschland', in *Lesegesellschaften und bürgerliche Emanzipation*, pp. 29–53.

43    As an example of this alignment, see Rudolf Schenda, *Volk ohne Buch* (Frankfurt am Main, 1970), and for examples of more recent work, *Leser und Lesen im Achtzehnten Jahrhundert*, edited by Rainer Gruenter (Heidelberg, 1977) and *Lesen und Leben*, edited by Herbert G. Göpfert (Frankfurt am Main, 1975).

44    See François Furet and Jacques Ozouf, *Lire et écrire: L'Alphabétisation des français de Calvin à Jules Ferry* (Paris, 1978); Lawrence Stone, 'Literacy and Education in England, 1640–1900', *Past and Present* 42 (1969): 69–139; David Cressy, *Literacy and the Social Order: Reading and Writing in Tudor and Stuart England* (Cambridge, 1980); Kenneth A. Lockridge, *Literacy in Colonial New England* (New York, 1974); and Carlo Cipolla, *Literacy and Development in the West* (Harmondsworth: 1969).

45    For a survey and a synthesis of this research, see Peter Burke, *Popular Culture in Early Modern Europe* (New York, 1978).

46  As an example of the older view, in which the *bibliothèque bleue* serves as a key to the understanding of popular culture, see Robert Mandrou, *De la culture populaire aux XVIIᵉ et XVIIIᵉ siècles: La Bibliothèque bleue de Troyes* (Paris, 1964). For a more nuanced and up-to-date view, see Roger Chartier, *Figures de la gueuserie* (Paris, 1982).

47  Douglas Waples, Bernard Berelson, and Franklyn Bradshaw, *What Reading Does to People* (Chicago, 1940); Bernard Berelson, *The Library's Public* (New York, 1949); Elihu Katz, 'Communication Research and the Image of Society: The Convergence of Two Traditions', *American Journal of Sociology* 65 (1960): 435–40; and John Y. Cole and Carol S. Gold, eds., *Reading in America 1978* (Washington, D.C., 1979). For the Gallup report, see the volume published by the American Library Association, *Book Reading and Library Usage: A Study of Habits and Perceptions* (Chicago, 1978). Much in this older variety of sociology still seems valid, and it can be studied in conjunction with the current work of Pierre Bourdieu; see especially his *La distinction: Critique sociale du jugement* (Paris, 1979).

48  Richard D. Altick, *The English Common Reader: A Social History of the Mass Reading Public 1800–1900* (Chicago, 1957); Robert K. Webb, *The British Working Class Reader* (London, 1955); and Richard Hoggart, *The Uses of Literacy* (Harmondsworth, 1960; 1st edition, 1957).

49  Elisabeth L. Eisenstein, *The Printing Press as an Agent of Change* (Cambridge, 1979), 2 volumes. For a discussion of Eisenstein's thesis, see Anthony T. Grafton, 'The Importance of Being Printed', *Journal of Interdisciplinary History* 11 (1980): 265–86; Michael Hunter, 'The Impact of Print', *The Book Collector* 28 (1979): 335–52; and Roger Chartier, 'L'Ancien Régime typographique: Réflexions sur quelques travaux récents', *Annales: Economies, sociétés, civilisations* 36 (1981): 191–209.

50  Some of these general themes are taken up in Eric Havelock, *Origins of Western Literacy* (Toronto, 1976); *Literacy in Traditional Societies*, edited by Jack Goody (Cambridge, 1968); Jack Goody, *The Domestication of the Savage Mind* (Cambridge, 1977); Walter Ong, *The Presence of the Word* (New York, 1970); and Natalie Z. Davis, *Society and Culture in Early Modern France* (Stanford, 1975).

# Chapter 3

# D. F. McKenzie

## THE BOOK AS AN EXPRESSIVE FORM

My purpose in these lectures – one I hope that might be thought fitting for an inaugural occasion – is simply to consider anew what bibliography is and how it relates to other disciplines. To begin that inquiry, I should like to recall a classic statement by the late Sir Walter Greg. It is this: 'what the bibliographer is concerned with is pieces of paper or parchment covered with certain written or printed signs. With these signs he is concerned merely as arbitrary marks; their meaning is no business of his'.[1] This definition of bibliography, or at least of 'pure' bibliography, is still widely accepted, and it remains in essence the basis of any claim that the procedures of bibliography are scientific.

A recent study by Mr Ross Atkinson supports that view by drawing on the work of the American semiotician, C. S. Peirce.[2] It can be argued, for example, that the signs in a book, as a bibliographer must read them, are simply iconic or indexical. Briefly, iconic signs are those which involve similarity; they represent an object, much as a portrait represents the sitter. In enumerative bibliography, and, even more so in descriptive, the entries are iconic. They represent the object they describe. Textual bibliography, too, may be said to be iconic because it seeks, as Mr Atkinson puts it, 'to reproduce the Object with maximum precision in every detail'. In that way, enumerative, descriptive, and textual bibliography may be said to constitute a class of three *referential* sign systems. Analytical bibliography, however, would form a distinct class of indexical signs. Their significance lies only in the physical differences between them as an index to the ways in which a particular document came physically to be what it is. It is their *causal* status that, in Peirce's terms, makes the signs *indexical*. In the words of Professor Bowers, writing of analytical bibliography, the physical features of a book are 'significant in the order and manner of their shapes but indifferent in symbolic meaning'.[3]

I must say at once that this account comes closer than any other I know to justifying Greg's definition of the discipline. I am also convinced, however, that the premise informing Greg's classic statement, and therefore this refinement of it, is no longer adequate as a definition of what bibliography is and does.

In an attempt to escape the embarrassment of such a strict definition, it is often said that bibliography is not a subject at all but only, as Mr G. Thomas Tanselle once put it, 'a related group of subjects that happen to be commonly referred to by the same term'.[4] Professor Bowers virtually concedes as much in dividing it into enumerative or systematic bibliography, and descriptive, analytical, textual, and historical bibliography.[5] The purity of the discipline which Greg aspired to is to that extent qualified by its particular applications and these in turn imply that the definition does not fully serve its uses.

The problem is, I think, that the moment we are required to explain signs in a book, as distinct from describing or copying them, they assume a symbolic status. If a medium in any sense affects a message, then bibliography cannot exclude from its own proper concerns the relation between form, function and symbolic meaning. If textual bibliography were merely iconic, it could produce only facsimiles of different versions. As for bibliographical analysis, that depends absolutely upon antecedent historical knowledge, for it can only function 'with the assistance of previously gathered information on the techniques of book production'.[6] But the most striking weakness of the definition is precisely its incapacity to accommodate history. Mr Atkinson is quite frank about this. Accepting the bibliographer's presumed lack of concern for the meaning of signs, he writes: 'we are left now only with the problem of historical bibliography'. He cites with approval the comment by Professor Bowers that the numerous fields concerned with the study of printing and its processes both as art and craft are merely 'ancillary to analytical bibliography'.[7] He is therefore obliged to argue that

> historical bibliography is not, properly speaking, bibliography at all. This is because it does not have as its Object material sign systems or documents. Its Object rather consists of certain mechanical techniques and as such it must be considered not part of bibliography but a constituent of such fields as the history of technology or, perhaps, information science.

Such comments, although recent, and indeed advanced in seeking to accommodate bibliography to semiotics as the science of signs, are oddly out of touch with such developments as, for example, the founding of The Center for the Book by the Library of Congress, the American Antiquarian Society's Programme for the History of the Book in American Culture, or proposals for publication of national histories of the book, of which the most notable so far is *L'Histoire de l'Édition Française*.

I am not bold enough to speak of paradigm shifts, but I think I am safe in saying that the vital interests of most of those known to me as bibliographers are no longer fully served by description, or even by editing, but by the historical study of the making and the use of books and other documents. But is it right that in order to accomplish such projects as, for example, a history of the book in Britain, we must cease to be bibliographers and shift to another discipline? It is here, if anywhere, that other disciplines such as history, and especially cultural history, are now making demands of bibliography. Far from accepting that 'historical bibliography is not, properly speaking, bibliography at all', it is tempting to claim, now, that all bibliography, properly speaking, is historical bibliography.

In such a world, Greg's definition of the theoretical basis of bibliography is too limited. As long as we continue to think of it as confined to the study of the non-symbolic functions of signs, the risk it runs is relegation. Rare book rooms will simply become rarer. The politics of survival, if nothing else, require a more comprehensive justification of the discipline's function in promoting new knowledge.

If, by contrast, we were to delineate the field in a merely pragmatic way, take a panoptic view and describe what we severally *do* as bibliographers, we should note, rather, that it is the only discipline which has consistently studied the composition, formal design and transmission of texts by writers, printers, and publishers; their distribution through different communities by wholesalers, retailers, and teachers; their collection and classification by librarians; their meaning for, and – I must add – their creative regeneration by, readers. However we define it, no part of that series of human and institutional interactions is alien to bibliography as we have, traditionally, practised it.

But, like Panizzi himself, faced with everything printed in a world in change, we reach a point where the accretion of subjects, like the collection of books, demands that we also seek a new principle by which to order them. Recent changes in critical theory, subsuming linguistics, semiotics, and the psychology of reading and writing, in information theory and communications studies, in the status of texts and the forms of their transmission, represent a formidable challenge to traditional practice, but they may also, I believe, give to bibliographical principle a quite new centrality.

The principle I wish to suggest as basic is simply this: bibliography is the discipline that studies texts as recorded forms, and the processes of their transmission, including their production and reception. So stated, it will not seem very surprising. What the word 'texts' also allows, however, is the extension of present practice to include all forms of texts, not merely books or Greg's signs on pieces of parchment or paper. It also frankly accepts that bibliographers should be concerned to show that forms affect meaning. Beyond that, it allows us to describe not only the technical but the social processes of their transmission. In those quite specific ways, it accounts for non-book texts, their physical forms, textual versions, technical transmission, institutional control, their perceived meanings, and social effects. It accounts for a history of the book and, indeed, of all printed forms including all textual ephemera as a record of cultural change, whether in mass civilization or minority culture. For any history of the book which excluded study of the social, economic and political motivations of publishing, the reasons why texts were written and read as they were, why they were rewritten and redesigned, or allowed to die, would degenerate into a feebly degressive book list and never rise to a readable history. But such a phrase also accommodates what in recent critical theory is often called text production, and it therefore opens up the application of the discipline to the service of that field too.

In terms of the range of demands now made of it and of the diverse interests of those who think of themselves as bibliographers, it seems to me that it would now be more useful to describe bibliography as the study of the sociology of texts. If the principle which makes it distinct is its concern with texts in some physical form and their transmission, then I can think of no other phrase which so aptly describes its range. Both the words 'texts' and 'sociology', however, demand further comment.

I define 'texts' to include verbal, visual, oral, and numeric data, in the form of maps, prints, and music, of archives of recorded sound, of films, videos, and any computer-stored information, everything in fact from epigraphy to the latest forms of discography. There is no evading the challenge which those new forms have created.

We can find in the origins of the word 'text' itself some support for extending its meaning from manuscripts and print to other forms. It derives, of course, from the Latin *texere*, 'to weave', and therefore refers, not to any specific material as such, but to its woven state, the web or texture of the materials. Indeed, it was not restricted to the weaving of textiles, but might be applied equally well to the interlacing or entwining of any kind of material. The Oxford Latin Dictionary suggests that it is probably cognate with the Vedic 'tāṣṭi', to 'fashion by carpentry', and consequently with the Greek τέκτων and τέχνη.

The shift from fashioning a material medium to a conceptual system, from the weaving of fabrics to the web of words, is also implicit in the Greek ὗφος 'a web or net', from ὑφαίνω 'to weave'. As with the Latin, it is only by virtue of a metaphoric shift that it applies to language, that the verb 'to weave' serves for the verb 'to write', that the web of words becomes a text. In each case, therefore, the primary sense is one which defines a process of material construction. It creates an object, but it is not peculiar to any one substance or any one form. The idea that texts are written records on parchment or paper derives only from the secondary and metaphoric sense that the writing of words is like the weaving of threads.

As much could now be said of many constructions which are not in written form, but for which the same metaphoric shift would be just as proper. Until our own times, the only textual records created in any quantity were manuscripts and books. A slight extension of the principle – it is, I believe, the same principle – to cope with the new kinds of material constructions we have in the form of the non-book texts which now surround, inform, and pleasure us, does not seem to me a radical departure from precedent.

In turning briefly now to comment on the word 'sociology', it is not perhaps impertinent to note that its early history parallels Panizzi's. A neologism coined by Auguste Comte in 1830, the year before Panizzi joined the staff of the British Museum, it made a fleeting appearance in Britain in 1843 in *Blackwood's Magazine*, which referred to 'a new Science, to be called Social Ethics, or Sociology'. Seven years later it was still struggling for admission. *Fraser's Magazine* in 1851 acknowledged its function but derided its name in a reference to 'the new science of sociology, as it is barbarously called'. Only in 1873 did it find a local habitation and a respected name. Herbert Spencer's *The Study of Sociology*, published in that year, provides a succinct description of its role: 'Sociology has to recognize truths of social development, structure and function'.

As I see it, that stress on structure and function is important, although I should resist its abstraction to the point where it lost sight of human agency. At one level, a sociology simply reminds us of the full range of social realities which the medium of print had to serve, from receipt blanks to bibles. But it also directs us to consider the human motives and interactions which texts involve at every stage of their production, transmission and consumption. It alerts us to the roles of institutions, and their own complex structures, in affecting the forms of social discourse, past and present. Those are the realities which bibliographers and textual critics as such have, until very recently, either neglected, or by defining them as strictly non-bibliographical, have felt unable to denominate, logically and coherently, as central to what we do. Historical bibliography, we were told, was not strictly bibliography at all.

A 'sociology of texts', then, contrasts with a bibliography confined to logical inference from printed signs as arbitrary marks on parchment or paper. As I indicated earlier, claims were made for the 'scientific' status of the latter precisely because it worked only from the physical evidence of books themselves. Restricted to the non-symbolic values of the signs, it tried to exclude the distracting complexities of linguistic interpretation and historical explanation.

That orthodox view of bibliography is less compelling, and less surprising, if we note its affinities with other modes of thinking at the time when Greg was writing. These include certain formalist theories of art and literature which were concerned to exclude from the discussion of a work of art any intended or referential meaning. They were current not only in the years when Greg was formulating his definitions but were still active in the theory of the New Criticism when Professor Fredson Bowers was developing his. The congruence of bibliography and criticism lay precisely in their shared view of the self-sufficient nature of the work of art or text, and in their agreement on the significance of its every verbal detail, however small. In neither case were precedent or subsequent processes thought to be essential to critical or bibliographical practice. The New Criticism showed great ingenuity in discerning patterns in the poem-on-the-page as a self-contained verbal structure. It is not I think altogether fanciful to find a scholarly analogy in analytical bibliography. Compositor studies, for example, have shown a comparable virtuosity in discerning patterns in evidence which is entirely internal, if not wholly fictional.

I shall return to that analogy with the New Criticism, but I am more concerned for the moment to emphasize the point that this confinement of bibliography to non-symbolic meaning, in an attempt to give it some kind of objective or 'scientific' status, has seriously impeded its development as a discipline. By electing to ignore its inevitable dependence upon interpretive structures, it has obscured the role of human agents, and virtually denied the relevance to bibliography of anything we might now understand as a history of the book. Physical bibliography – the study of the signs which constitute texts and the materials on which they are recorded – is of course the starting point. But it cannot define the discipline because it has no adequate means of accounting for the processes, the technical and social dynamics, of transmission and reception, whether by one reader or a whole market of them.

In speaking of bibliography as the sociology of texts, I am not concerned to invent new names but only to draw attention to its actual nature. Derrida's 'Grammatology', the currently fashionable word 'Textuality', the French 'Textologie', or even 'Hyphologie' (a suggestion made, not altogether seriously, by Roland Barthes) would exclude more than we would wish to lose. Nor is bibliography a sub-field of semiotics, precisely because its functions are not merely synchronically descriptive. Our own word, 'Bibliography', will do. It unites us as collectors, editors, librarians, historians, makers and readers of books. It even has a new felicity in its literal meaning of 'the writing out of books', of generating new copies and therefore in time new versions. Its traditional concern with texts as recorded forms, and with the processes of their transmission, should make it hospitably open to new forms. No new names, then; but to conceive of the discipline as a sociology of texts is, I think, both to describe what the bibliography is that we actually do and to allow for its natural evolution.

Nevertheless, I must now turn to consider the special case of printed texts. In doing so, the particular inquiry I wish to pursue is whether or not the material forms of books, the non-verbal elements of the typographic notations within them, the very disposition of space itself, have an expressive function in conveying meaning, and whether or not it is, properly, a bibliographical task to discuss it.

Again, I sense that theory limps behind practice. At one end of the spectrum, we must of course recognize that Erwin Panofsky on perspective as symbolic form has long since made the theme familiar; at the other end, we find that Marshall McLuhan's *Understanding Media* has made it basic to media studies. In our own field, Mr Nicolas Barker, on 'Typography and the Meaning of Words: The Revolution in the Layout of Books in the Eighteenth Century'; Mr David Foxon on Pope's typography; Mr Giles Barber on Voltaire and the typographic presentation of *Candide*; Mr Roger Laufer on 'scripturation' or 'the material emergence of sense' are all distinguished bibliographers demonstrating in one way or another, not the iconic or indexical, but the symbolic function of typographic signs as an interpretive system.[8] Words like the 'articulation' or 'enunciation' of the book in this sense make similar assumptions. Discussions of the morphology of the book in relation to genre or to special classes of readers and markets assume a complex relation of medium to meaning. Journals like *Visible Language* and *Word & Image* were founded specifically to explore these questions. The persistent example of fine printing and the revival of the calligraphic manuscript, and numerous recent studies of the sophisticated displays of text and illumination in medieval manuscript production, also share a basic assumption that forms affect sense.[9]

Perhaps on this occasion the simplest way of exploring some of these issues as they relate to the expressive function of typography in book forms, as they bear on editing, and as they relate to critical theory, is to offer an exemplary case. I have chosen the four lines which serve as epigraph to 'The Intentional Fallacy', the distinguished essay by W. K. Wimsatt Jr. and M. C. Beardsley which was first published in *The Sewanee Review* in 1946.[10] It would, I think, be hard to name another essay which has so influenced critical theory and the teaching of literature in the past forty years. Briefly, they argued that it was pointless to use the concept of an author's intentions in trying to decide what a work of literature might mean, or if it was any good. And of course exactly the same objection must apply, if it holds at all, to the interpretation of a writer's or printer's intentions in presenting a text in a particular form, or a publisher's intentions in issuing it at all.

Let me say at once that my purpose in using an example from this essay is to show that in some cases significantly informative readings may be recovered from typographic signs as well as verbal ones, that these are relevant to editorial decisions about the manner in which one might reproduce a text, and that a reading of such bibliographical signs may seriously shape our judgement of an author's work. I think it is also possible to suggest that their own preconceptions may have led Wimsatt and Beardsley to misread a text, that their misreading may itself have been partly a function of the manner in which it was printed, and that its typographic style was in turn influenced by the culture at large. My argument therefore runs full circle from a defence of authorial meaning, on the grounds that it is in some measure recoverable, to a recognition that, for better or worse, readers inevitably make their own meanings. In other words, each reading is peculiar to its occasion, each can be at least partially recovered from the physical forms of the text, and the differences in readings constitute an informative history. What writers thought they were doing in writing texts, or printers and booksellers in designing and publishing them, or readers in making sense of them are issues which no history of the book can evade.

'The Intentional Fallacy' opens with an epigraph taken from Congreve's prologue to *The Way of the World* (1700). In it, as Wimsatt and Beardsley quote him,

> He owns with toil he wrote the following scenes;
> But, if they're naught, ne'er spare him for his pains:
> Damn him the more; have no commiseration
> For dullness on mature deliberation.
>                     WILLIAM CONGREVE, Prologue to
>                     *The Way of the World*

Congreve's authorized version of 1710 reads:

> *He owns, with Toil, he wrought the following*
>      *Scenes,*
> *But if they're naught ne'er ſpare him for his Pains:*
> *Damn him the more; have no Commiſeration*
> *For Dulneſs on mature Deliberation.*

It has not, I think, been observed before that, if we include its epigraph, this famous essay on the interpretation of literature opens with a misquotation in its very first line. Wimsatt and Beardsley say that Congreve 'wrote' the following scenes, but Congreve was a deliberate craftsman. He said he '*wrought*' them. Since the words quoted are ascribed to Congreve, I think we are clearly meant to accept them as his, even if the essay later persuades us that we cannot presume to know what Congreve might have intended them to mean. By adopting that simple change from '*wrought*' to 'wrote', Wimsatt and Beardsley oblige us to make our meaning from their misreading. The epigraph thereby directs us to weaken the emphasis that Congreve placed on his labour of composition: he writes of the '*Pains*' it cost him to hammer out *his* meaning. The changed wording destroys the carefully created internal rhyme, the resonance between what, in the first line, Congreve said he '*wrought*' and, in the second line, its fate in being reduced to '*naught*' by those who misquote, misconstrue, and misjudge him. Congreve's prologue to *The Way of the World* put, in 1700/1710, a point of view exactly opposite to the one which the lines are cited to support.

Less noticeable perhaps are the implications of the way in which the epigraph is printed. For Congreve's precise notation of spelling, punctuation and initial capitals, the 1946 version offers a flat, even insidiously open form. Congreve wrote that '*He owns*' – comma – '*with Toil*' – comma – '*he wrought the following Scenes*'. In their performance of the line, Wimsatt and Beardsley drop the commas. By isolating and emphasizing the phrase, Congreve may be read as affirming his seriousness of purpose, the deliberation of his art. Wimsatt and Beardsley speed past it, their eyes perhaps on a phrase more proper to their purpose in the next line. What their reading emphasizes instead, surrounding it with commas where Congreve had none, is the phrase 'if they're naught'. By that slight change they highlight Congreve's ironic concession that an author's intentions have no power to save him if an audience or reader thinks he is dull. Congreve, without commas, had preferred to skip quickly past that thought. Wimsatt and Beardsley allow us to dwell on it, for in their reading it would seem to justify their rather different argument.

Those shifts of meaning which result from the variants noted are, I believe, serious, however slight the signs which make them. But there are more. In his second couplet, Congreve writes:

> *Damn him the more; have no Commiseration*
> *For Dulness on mature Deliberation.*

Again, it suits the purpose of the epigraph to remove Congreve's irony, but as irony is crucially dependent upon context, the loss is perhaps inevitable. Reading the words literally, Wimsatt and Beardsley must take them to mean: 'If you really think my scenes are dull, don't waste your pity on their author'. But you will note that Congreve gives upper case *D*'s for '*Dulness*' and '*Deliberation*'. Those personified forms allow two readings to emerge which tell us something of Congreve's experience. The first is that these abstractions have human shapes (they were sitting there in the theatre); the second alludes to the age-old combat between Dulness and Deliberation, or Stupidity and Sense. By reducing all his nouns to lower case and thereby destroying the early eighteenth-century convention, the epigraph kills off Congreve's personified forms, and by muting his irony, it reverses his meaning. Where Congreve's irony contrasts his own '*mature Deliberation*' with the '*Dulness*' of his critics, their meaning has him saying the reader knows best.

If we look again at the form and relation of the words '*Toil*', '*Scenes*' and its rhyme-word '*Pains*', we note that they, too, have initial capitals. The convention thereby gives us in print a visual, semantic and ultimately moral identity between Congreve's own description of his labours ('*Toil . . . Pains*') and their human products who people his plays. The text as printed in the epigraph breaks down those visual links by depriving the words of their capitals. One set of meanings, which stress a writer's presence in his work, is weakened in favour of a preconceived reading which would remove him from it.

Small as it is, this example is so instructive that I should like to explore it further. It bears on the most obvious concerns of textual criticism – getting the right words in the right order; on the semiotics of print and the role of typography in forming meaning; on the critical theories of authorial intention and reader response; on the relation between the past meanings and present uses of verbal texts. It offers an illustration of the transmission of texts as the creation of the new versions which form, in turn, the new books, the products of later printers, and the stuff of subsequent bibliographical control. These are the primary documents for any history of the book. By reading one form of Congreve's text (1700/1710), we may with some authority affirm certain readings as his. By reading other forms of it (1946), we can chart meanings that later readers made from it under different historical imperatives.

I may believe – as I do – that Wimsatt and Beardsley have mistaken Congreve's meaning; that they have misconceived his relation to his tradition; that they have misreported his attitude to his own audience and readers. At the same time, their misreading has become an historical document in its own right. By speaking to what they perceived in 1946 to be the needs of their own time, not Congreve's in 1700/1710, they have left a record of the taste, thought and values of a critical school which significantly shaped our own choice of books, the way we read them and, in my own case, the way I taught them. The history of material objects as symbolic forms functions, therefore, in two ways. It can falsify certain readings; and it can demonstrate new ones.

To extend that line of argument, I should like to comment briefly on the word 'Scenes'. We recall first that Congreve's 'Scenes' cost him 'Pains'. Next, we should note that his editors and critics have, almost without exception, replaced his meaning of the word with a commoner one of their own. They have defined them by geography and carpentry, as when a scene shifts from a forest to the palace. For Congreve, by contrast, they were neoclassical scenes: not impersonal places in motion, but distinct groups of human beings in conversation. These made up his scenes. For him, it was the intrusion of another human voice, another mind, or its loss, that most changed the scene. The substance of his scenes, therefore, what he 'wrought with Toil', were men and women. Once we recover that context and follow Congreve's quite literal meaning in that sense, his rhyme of 'Scenes' with 'Pains' glows with an even subtler force. What he hints at is a serious critical judgement about all his work: beneath the rippling surface of his comedy there flows a sombre undercurrent of human pain. In a more mundane way, that perception may direct an editor to adopt a typography which divides Congreve's plays into neoclassical scenes, as he himself did in his edition of 1710.

With that last example, it could be argued that we reach the border between bibliography and textual criticism on the one hand and literary criticism and literary history on the other. My own view is that no such border exists. In the pursuit of historical meanings, we move from the most minute feature of the material form of the book to questions of authorial, literary and social context. These all bear in turn on the ways in which texts are then re-read, re-edited, re-designed, re-printed, and re-published. If a history of readings is made possible only by a comparative history of books, it is equally true that a history of books will have no point if it fails to account for the meanings they later come to make.

Though at times they may pretend otherwise, I suspect that few authors, with the kind of investment in their work that Congreve claims, are indifferent to the ways in which their art is presented and received. There is certainly a cruel irony in the fact that Congreve's own text is reshaped and misread to support an argument against himself. Far from offering a licence for his audience and readers to discount the author's meaning, Congreve is putting, with an exasperated irony, the case for the right of authors, as he says in another line of the prologue, 'to assert their Sense' against the taste of the town. When Jeremy Collier wrenched to his own purposes the meaning of Congreve's words, Congreve replied with his Amendments of Mr Collier's False and Imperfect Citations. He too had a way with epigraphs and chose for that occasion one from Martial which, translated, reads: 'That book you recite, O Fidentinus, is mine. But your vile re-citation begins to make it your own'.

With that thought in mind, I should like to pursue one further dimension of the epigraph's meaning which is not in itself a matter of book form. It nevertheless puts Congreve in the tradition of authors who thought about the smallest details of their work as it might be printed, and who directed, collaborated with, or fumed against, their printers and publishers. One such author is Ben Jonson. As it happens, Wimsatt and Beardsley might with equal point have quoted him to epitomize their argument that an author's intentions are irrelevant. This, for example:

> Playes in themselues haue neither hopes, nor feares,
> Their fate is only in their hearers ears . . .[11]

It chimes in perfectly with the very end of Congreve's prologue although, here, his irony is too heavy to miss:

*In short, our Play shall (with your leave to show it),*
*Give you one instance of a Passive Poet.*
*Who to your Judgments yields all Resignation;*
*So Save or Damn, after your own Discretion.*

To link Congreve with Jonson is to place his prologue and what it says in a developing tradition of the author's presence in his printed works. In that context, Congreve's lines become a form of homage to his mentor, an acceptance of succession, and a reminder that the fight for the author's right not to be mis-read can ultimately break even the best of us. For not only had Jonson inveighed against the usurpation of *his* meanings by those of his asinine critics, but he was a dramatist who for a time virtually quit the public stage to be, as he put it, 'Safe from the wolues black iaw, and the dull asses hoofe'. Jonson's rejection of free interpretation is venomous:

> Let their fastidious, vaine
> Commission of the braine
> Run on, rage, sweat, censure and condemn:
> They were not meant for thee, lesse, thou for them.[12]

Congreve's ironies allow him a more tactful, more decorous, farewell. Less tough, more delicate, than Jonson, he did leave the stage, sensing himself expelled by the misappropriation of his works, convinced that *his* meanings would rarely survive their reception. The imminence of that decision informs his prologue to *The Way of the World*. It was to be his last play. On '*mature Deliberation*', he found he could no longer bear the deadly '*Dulness*' of his critics. By respecting not only the words Congreve uses – a simple courtesy – but also the meanings which their precise notation gives, we can, if we wish, as an act of bibliographical scholarship, recover his irony, and read his pain.

In that long series of Pyrrhic victories which records the triumphs of critics and the deaths of authors, 'The Intentional Fallacy' has earned a distinguished place for the argument which follows its feat of misprision. Its epigraph is no celebration of Congreve's perspicacity in foreseeing a new cause; it is, rather, an epitaph to his own dismembered text. A vast critical literature has been generated by this essay, but I am unaware of any mention of the textual ironies which preface it. With what seems an undue reverence for the tainted text printed by Wimsatt and Beardsley, the epigraph has been reproduced in reprint after reprint with exceptional fidelity, its errors resistant to any further reworking of a classic moment of mis-statement, resistant even to the force of the argument which follows it. It is now incorporate with Congreve's history and with that of our own time.

Yet if the fine detail of typography and layout, the material signs which constitute a text, do signify in the ways I have tried to suggest, it must follow that any history of the book – subject as books are to typographic and material change – must be a history of misreadings. This is not so strange as it might sound. Every society rewrites its past, every reader rewrites its texts, and, if they have any continuing life at all, at some point every printer redesigns them. The changes in the way Congreve's text was printed as an epigraph were themselves designed to correct a late Victorian printing style which had come to seem too fussily expressive. In 1946, 'good printing' had a clean, clear, impersonal surface. It left the text to speak for itself.

This newly preferred form of printing had conspired with shifts in critical opinion. Eliot's theory of the impersonality of the poet affected to dissociate the writer from his text. The words on the page became what Wimsatt called a 'verbal icon', a freestanding artefact with its own inner coherence, what Cleanth Brooks was to call (as it happens) a '*well-wrought Urn*', a structure complete in itself which had within it all the linguistic signs we needed for the contemplation of its meaning.

The unprecedented rise of English studies and the decline of classics made quite new demands of teachers of literature. At one level, the critical analysis of set texts was an efficient way to teach reading from what was irreducibly common to a class, the text itself laid out on the page in a kind of lapidary state. At another level, it brought into sharper focus than ever before the fact that different readers brought the text to life in different ways. If a poem *is* only what its individual readers make it in their activity of constructing meaning from it, then a good poem will be one which most compels its own destruction in the service of its readers' new construction. When the specification of meaning is one with its discovery in the critical practice of writing, the generative force of texts is most active. In that context, the misreading of Congreve in 1946 may be seen as almost a matter of historical necessity, an interesting document itself in the nature of reading and the history of the book.

And it *is* a physical document. We can date it; we can read it; we can locate it in the context of *The Sewanee Review* and the interests of its readers; we can interpret it reasonably according to the propositional intentions of the anti-intentionalist essay which lies beneath it. It is, I hope, unnecessary to multiply instances. This scrap of prologue, this fragment of text, raises most of the issues we need to address as we think about books as texts which have been given a particular physical form.

But as a dramatic text, it was originally written to be spoken, and so other questions arise. Can we hear the voice of Thomas Betterton conveying orally the ironies we now read visually? Congreve's autograph letters show no concern for the niceties I suggested in the form of the epigraph. Am I therefore reading an interpretation of Congreve's meaning by his printer, John Watts? Is Watts merely following a general set of conventions imposed at this time, with or without Congreve's assent, by Congreve's publisher, Jacob Tonson? Who, in short, 'authored' Congreve? Whose concept of the reader do these forms of the text imply: the author's, the actor's, the printer's, or the publisher's? And what of the reader? Is a knowledge of Jonson, Betterton, Congreve, Watts, and Tonson a necessary condition of a 'true' reading? Does my reading betray a personal need to prove that a technical interest in books *and* in the teaching of texts, is not radically disjunctive, that bibliographical scholarship and criticism are in fact one? Visited by such questions, an author disperses into his collaborators, those who produced his texts and their meanings.

If we turn to the 1946 epigraph, similar questions insist on an answer. Does its removal from context entirely free it from irony? Do the slight changes of form alter the substance? Are they no more than a case of careless printing in a new convention? But the crucial questions for a history of reading, and the re-writing of texts, are these: did the intentions of these two authors (something extrinsic to their text) lead them to create from Congreve's lines a pre-text for their own writing; and, if so, did they do it consciously, unconsciously, or accidentally?

To venture into distinctions between conscious and unconscious intentions would be to enter upon troubled waters indeed. The probable answer is, I fear, banal, but as an illustration of the vagaries of textual transmission it should be given. The anthology of plays edited by Nettleton and Case, from which Wimsatt would almost certainly have taught, includes *The Way of the World*, the prologue to which in that edition inexplicably reads 'wrote' for '*wrought*'. We must therefore, I think, relieve Wimsatt and Beardsley of immediate responsibility, and we should certainly free them from any suggestion of deliberate contamination. But I wonder if they would have ventured to choose the lines had they been more carefully edited.[13]

The case, however, is not altered. If we think of the physical construction of Congreve's text in the quarto of 1700 or the octavo edition of 1710, and its physical re-presentation in 1946, then at least we begin by seeing two simple facts. One gives us the historical perspective of an author directing one set of meanings in a transaction with his contemporaries. The other gives us an equally historical perspective of two readers creating a reverse set of meanings for an academic – indeed, a scholarly – readership whose interests in the text were different. Each perspective can be studied distinctively in the signs of the text as printed. Those signs range in significance from the trivial to the serious, but far from importing the author's irrelevance, they take us back to human motive and intention. In Congreve's case, they reveal a man of compassion whose scenes record the human struggle they spring from as the very condition of writing.

In one sense at least, little has changed in critical theory since 1946. New Critical formalism and structuralism on the one hand, post-structuralism and deconstruction on the other, all share the same scepticism about recovering the past. One of the most impressive objections to this critical self-absorption, to the point of excluding a concern for the complexities of human agency in the production of texts, is Edward Said's *The World, the Text, and the Critic*. I can only agree with his judgement that 'As it is practised in the American academy today, literary theory has for the most part isolated textuality from the circumstances, the events, the physical senses that made it possible and render it intelligible as the result of human work'.[14] Commenting upon Said in his most recent book, *Textual Power*, Robert Scholes pursues the point: 'At the present time there are two major positions that can be taken with respect to this problem, and . . . it is extremely difficult to combine them or find any middle ground between them'.[15] Scholes describes those two positions as the hermetic and the secular.

To return now to my larger theme: Greg's definition of what bibliography is would have it entirely hermetic. By admitting history, we make it secular. The two positions are not entirely opposed, for books themselves are the middle ground. It is one bibliographers have long since explored, mapped, and tilled. Their descriptive methods far surpass other applications of semiotics as a science of signs. In the ubiquity and variety of its evidence, bibliography as a sociology of texts has an unrivalled power to resurrect authors in their own time, and their readers at any time. It enables what Michel Foucault called 'an insurrection of subjugated knowledges'.[16] One of its greatest strengths is the access it gives to social motives: by dealing with the facts of transmission and the material evidence of reception, it can make discoveries as distinct from inventing meanings. In focusing on the primary object, the text as a recorded form, it defines our common point of departure for any historical or critical enterprise. By abandoning the notion of degressive bibliography and recording *all* subsequent versions, bibliography, simply by its own comprehensive logic, its indiscriminate inclusiveness, testifies to the fact that new readers of course make new texts, and that their new meanings are a function of their new forms. The claim then is no longer for their truth as one might seek to define that by an authorial intention, but for their testimony, as defined by their historical use. There was a year 1710 in which Tonson published Congreve's *Works*, and there was a year 1946 in which some lines from the prologue to *The Way of the World* were quoted in *The Sewanee Review*. Wimsatt and Beardsley might be wrong from Congreve's point of view, but, given their published text, they indubitably *are*, and it is a very simple bibliographical function to record and to show their reading – indeed, in the interests of a history of cultural change, to show it up.

Reviewing Scholes in *The Times Literary Supplement*, Tzvetan Todorov gave a blunt appraisal of the relation of the present American literary scene to the traditions of western humanism: 'If we wish to call a spade a spade, we must conclude that the dominant tendency of American criticism is anti-humanism'.[17] Bibliography has a massive authority with which to correct that tendency. It can, in short, show the human presence in any recorded text.[18]

## Notes

1   'Bibliography – an Apologia', in *Collected Papers*, ed. J. C. Maxwell (Oxford: Clarendon Press, 1966), p.247.

2   Ross Atkinson, 'An Application of Semiotics to the Definition of Bibliography', *Studies in Bibliography* 33 (1980), 54–73.

3   *Bibliography and Textual Criticism* (Oxford: Clarendon Press, 1964), p.41; cited by Atkinson, p.63.

4   'Bibliography and Science', *Studies in Bibliography* 27 (1974), 88.

5   Principally in 'Bibliography, Pure Bibliography, and Literary Studies', *Papers of the Bibliographical Society of America* 47 (1952), 186–208; also in 'Bibliography', *Encyclopaedia Britannica* (1970), III, 588–92.

6   Atkinson, p.64.

7   *Encyclopaedia Britannica*, III, 588.

8   Nicolas Barker, 'Typography and the Meaning of Words', *Buch und Buchhandel in Europa im achtzehnten Jahrhundert*, ed. G. Barber and B. Fabian, *Wolfenbütteler Schriften zur Geschichte des Buchwesens* 4 (Hamburg, 1981), pp.126–65; Giles Barber, 'Voltaire et la présentation typographique de *Candide*', *Transmissione dei Testi a Stampa nel Periodo Moderno* I (Seminario Internationale, Rome 1985), 151–69; Roger Laufer, 'L'Énonciation typographique au dix-huitième siècle', *ibid.*, 113–23; 'L'Espace visuel du livre ancien', *Revue Française d'Histoire du Livre* 16 (1977), 569–81; 'L'Ésprit de la lettre', *Le Débat* 22 (November 1982), 147–59; see also Barbara R. Woshinsky, 'La Bruyère's *Caractères*: A Typographical Reading', *TEXT, Transactions of the Society for Textual Scholarship* 2 (1985), 209–28. Those examples from the past, implying a consciousness of the non-verbal resources of book forms to enhance and convey meaning, may be paralleled with others from current research into text design. A useful recent summary is James Hartley, 'Current Research on Text Design', *Scholarly Publishing* 16 (1985), 355–68; see also James Hartley and Peter Burnhill, 'Explorations in Space: A Critique of the Typography of BPS Publications', *Bulletin of the British Psychological Society* 29 (1976), 97–107.

9   For an excellent example, see Michael Camille, 'The Book of Signs: Writing and visual difference in Gothic manuscript illumination', *Word & Image* I, no.2 (April–June 1985), 133–48.

10  *The Sewanee Review* liv (Summer, 1946), 468–88; subsequently collected in *The Verbal Icon* (Lexington: University of Kentucky Press, 1954).

11  Ben Jonson, *The New Inne*, epilogue, ll. 1–2.

12  'Ode to *himselfe*', ll. 7–10.

13  I am indebted to Professor Albert Braunmuller for suggesting the probable source of the error. In fairness to Wimsatt and Beardsley, whose matching essay, 'The Subjective Fallacy', warns against readings uncontrolled by the formal limits of the words on the page, it should be said that they might well have welcomed and accepted as constituting a more acceptable text the lines as originally printed.

14  *The World, the Text, and the Critic* (London: Faber and Faber, 1984), p.4.

15  *Textual Power* (New Haven and London: Yale University Press, 1985), p.75.

16  Michel Foucault, 'Two Lectures: Lecture One: 7 January 1976', in *Power/Knowledge: Selected Interviews and Other Writings 1972–77*, ed. Colin Gordon (Brighton: Harvester Press, 1980), p.81.

17  'Against all humanity', *Times Literary Supplement*, 4 October 1985, p.1094.

18  The photo-construction is by Nicholas Wade. It appeared in *Word & Image* I, no.3 (July–September 1985), 259.

# Chapter 4

# Jerome McGann

## THE SOCIALIZATION OF TEXTS

### I

[Several] years ago G. Thomas Tanselle published an influential essay for scholars, 'The Editing of Historical Documents'. This paper was written as a strong, if also a friendly, critique of postwar work in historical editing. Tanselle argued that historical editing had, in general, been based upon an inadequate understanding of the nature of text. In this regard, according to Tanselle, many distinguished historical editing projects lagged far behind analogous projects undertaken by literary scholars. The problem was that historical editors, in contrast to their literary counterparts, had been too 'apt to neglect the physical form in which the evidence on which they subsist has been preserved'.[1]

This judgment must have come as a surprise to most historical editors, since the nature of their principal material – its documentary character – forces them to encounter the physique of their texts in ways that many literary editors do not experience. But Tanselle showed that historical editors were making excessive interventions into the documents being edited, changing text in misguided and often contradictory efforts to deliver the material in more efficient or accessible ways.

Today few people – certainly not I – would disagree with Tanselle's plea that editors should give the greatest respect to the physical integrity of the documents. Most of what I wish to argue here will involve an extrapolation of Tanselle's plea. But to the extent that Tanselle's essay focussed on the editing of manuscript-based materials, his representation of the problems confronting literary editors can be misleading.

The heart of his theoretical argument rests in his insistence that no sharp distinction should be made in the editorial policy applied to historical and to literary texts: 'No clear line can be drawn between writing which is "literature" and writing which is not' (495), Tanselle says, and he adduces various examples, all very much – so far as they go – to the point. He then adds, however, that 'a distinction does need to be made, not between literary and historical materials [but between] works intended for publication and private papers' (496). Tanselle gives about one-third of a single page to a discussion of this important matter – his essay is fifty-six pages long – and then proceeds to say that 'this is not the place to explore' the distinction he has drawn. 'The point here', he remarks, 'is to contrast that situation [i.e., text involved in a publishing venue] with the very different one which exists for private documents' (497).

When Tanselle rejects the distinction between a historical and a literary document – between informational and aesthetic works – he sets a gulf between himself and a textual theorist like Hershel Parker. Parker is aware, I am sure, that a historical work can be pursued or considered within an aesthetic horizon. Gibbon's *Decline and Fall* is probably as much a work of art as it is a work of history. He must be equally aware that literary works always disseminate historical information. Nonetheless, Parker, like Aristotle, would not want to collapse the distinction between these two kinds of work because they epitomize the difference between a form of writing that is committed to facticity and information, and a form that is, by contrast, devoted to creation.

History and literature differ, that is to say, along the line of their intentionalities. This being the case, we find in Parker's work a passionate engagement with the issue of literary intention. Parker's insistence that editors of literary works should return to authorial manuscripts wherever possible represents his desire to position the text in as close a relation to its authoritative source as possible. For literary work, in this view, is the creative expression of an individual's quest for meaning and order. The scholarly editor's task is to clarify as much as one can the artistic process of creative activity, for it is that process which *is* the literary work, whether we look at the work as a carrier of meaning (informational) or as a creative event (aesthetic).

Furthermore, if Parker, in contrast to Tanselle, maintains a clear distinction between historical and literary work, he reverses Tanselle's text-theoretical distinction between private papers and public (normally, for our period, printed) texts. Tanselle takes the distinction as a sign that some texts (typically, 'creative works') seek wide dissemination and a kind of iconic perfection, whereas others (typically, private documents) do not. But for Parker, the question of dissemination through printing is secondary, if not irrelevant, to the primary issue of artistic creativity.

For this reason Parker argues that Bowers and Tanselle are confused on the issue of intentionality. Their confusion is most apparent in the value they set upon so-called eclectic editing. To proceed with an editorial process along those lines is, for Parker, at best to court and at worst to ensure an unhappy result. The eclectic edition is by definition *not* a single authorial construct but a polyglot formation imagined by the editor. Furthermore, if the eclectic edition is based on a printed version of the work rather than an authorial manuscript version, the result will be to move even further from that moment 'when the artist was most in control' of his own work.[2]

I detail these matters here in order to position my argument with respect to this seminal debate. In what follows, therefore, I shall be trying to explain why I stand with Parker (and against Tanselle) in maintaining the distinction between historical and literary work, and why I support Tanselle (as against Parker) in Tanselle's view of the distinction between private and public documents. My own view of literary work, and hence of how to go about editing it, rests on this pair of distinctions. Furthermore, the distinctions highlight the centrality of literary texts for understanding the textual condition.

## II

I have no disagreement with Parker, or Bowers, or Tanselle on a great many issues of editorial procedure. I take it we all agree that no scholarly editing can take place which does not enumerate all the relevant texts and establish their genetic or collateral relations. We also agree that all such information should be made available to readers who wish to judge both the nature and the executive adequacy of the edition. On other technical matters we differ. We do not agree, for instance, on the criteria for establishing copy-text; we also differ, in various ways, on the appropriateness of copy-text editing (which is to say, 'eclectic' editing) for different kinds of text.

But these are not the subjects I mean to discuss here. Rather, I want to explore a pair of topics that expose the kind of approach I take toward editing literary works. The first deals with the question of multiple artistic intentionalities. The second concerns the aesthetic dimension of documentary materials.

Contemporary text theory, in the arena of literary scholarship, founded itself on the idea of authorial intentions. No one, of course, repudiates either the reality or the importance of authorial intentionality for the problem of text theory or editorial method. What is at issue is how absolutely the concept of authorial intention is to be understood *so far as the editing of literary works is concerned*. For Parker, the sole criterion on which a literary-editorial project ought to be based is the criterion of authorial intention. Furthermore, Parker postulates for every literary work an ideal process of creation. This process may become diverted or corrupted in many ways, by the author or by any number of other agents. The editor's task is to cut through those diversions and corruptions in order to reveal, as purely as possible, the original artist's creative intention.

Bowers and Tanselle also base their editorial theories on the concept of authorial intention. But because they discern in the production of literary works the presence of multiple authorial intentions, they seek to make compromises between the options offered by the diversity of textual witnesses. These compromises appear as the eclectic edition, which is an editorial construction built up from a copy-text. That copy-text becomes 'eclectic' when the editor, after examining the relevant documents, introduces readings from other textual witnesses which are judged to exhibit greater authority than the authority of the copy-text.

Parker criticizes the eclectic approach because it violates his notion of artistic integrity. The creative process for him is the artist's rage for order, which cannot be well approximated when an editor seeks for rationally derived compromises. It succeeds least of all if an editor grants equal authority to printed as to manuscript materials. In this situation, Parker devalues printed texts because they cannot embody the integrity of the artist's vision – too many other agents are involved in the production of such work. The job of the editor is to rescue the work from the chaos of conflicting and secondary authorities and agents – including the author's own secondary thoughts.

Eclectic editors, for their part, observe the scene somewhat differently. Where Parker sees randomness obscuring a hidden wholeness, the eclectic editor observes a kind of textual solar system, with the famous 'copy-text' standing as the center of gravity around which many textual planets move and have their being. 'Copy-text' is the still point in the turning world of a diversity of secondary or dependent texts.

But suppose the textual condition does not correspond to either of these imaginings. Suppose, for example, that the textual condition were to appear in the likeness of D. G. Rossetti's poetic sequence *The House of Life*. This work, as we have seen, was produced in multiple versions. Some of these versions stand in a genetic line of relation with each other, and hence could be taken for the dependencies of a primary authority. But one of the versions does not stand in such a relation, and the work breaks up into other kinds of independent units within each of the larger versions. Besides, the standard version of this work is a posthumous editorial construction made up from a decision about how to treat the heterodox amalgam of textual deposits.

Multiple versions of many Shakespeare works also come down to us – most notoriously, *King Lear* – and this situation is not merely common in the case of theatrical work, it is the rule. Today, the very concept of the famous 'bad quartos', once firmly established in editorial treatment of Shakespeare, has been undermined. Furthermore, it is equally typical that alterations in the texts of plays are the consequence of the collective efforts of the theatrical company. Texts change under the pressure of immediate events.

Charles Lamb's highly artistic essay — they are really types of prose poem — appear as one thing when they are first published in *The London Magazine*, and as quite other things when he moves to have them produced in book form. The Cuala Press editions of Yeats's poems differ sharply from the texts brought out (almost at the same time) under the Macmillan imprint.

But there is no call to multiply examples. The problem is well known. Let me just conclude with the startling case of Ezra Pound's last published installment of his *Cantos* project, the section known as *Drafts and Fragments*. Here it is not merely that an extreme indeterminacy governs the state of the texts. More difficult is the fact, now well documented, that various agents besides Pound were involved in the production of this work.[3] I should also make it clear that this case is just an extreme instance of something one discovers repeatedly in literary studies. Traditional ballads and songs typically descend to us through wildly heterodox lines of textual transmission. In such cases, trying to edit on the basis of any concept of 'authorial intention' or 'authorial control' is simply impossible.

Of course, each of these versions may be usefully studied as a singular example of a creative process, as may the two texts of *King Lear*, or the multiple versions of Stoppard's plays. Literary editing should encourage that kind of study. Nevertheless, literary work by its very nature sets in motion many kinds of creative intentionalities. These orbit in the universe of the creative work — but not around some imaginary and absolute center. Rather, they turn through many different kinds of motion, at many structural scales, and in various formal relationships. The universe of poiesis no more has an absolute center than does the stellar universe we have revealed through our astronomy. What it has are many relative centers which are brought to our attention by our own acts of observation. The universe of literature is socially generated and does not exist in a steady state. Authors themselves do not have, *as authors*, singular identities; an author is a plural identity and more resembles what William James liked to call the human world at large, a multiverse.

Literary texts differ from informational texts by being polyvocal. Whereas 'noise' is always a form of corruption for a channel of information, it can be exploited in literary texts for positive results. The thicker the description, so far as an artist is concerned, the better. (Minimalist styles of art thicken their media by processes of subtraction and absence.) A thickened text is a scene where metaphor and metonymy thrive (Coleridge's 'opposite or discordant qualities', his 'sameness with difference'). For Parker, the thickness comes from the artists' imaginative resources, who can be counted on to put into their texts far more than even they are aware of. Parker's 'intention' includes, crucially, the vast resources of the unconscious and preconscious.

But thickness is also built through the textual presence and activities of many non-authorial agents. These agencies may be the artist's contemporaries — these are the examples most often adduced — or they may not; furthermore, the agencies may hardly be imagined as 'individuals' at all. The texts of Sappho, for example, gain much of their peculiar power from their fragmented condition, and the same is true for various ballads and songs, which exploit their textual fractures and absences for poetic results.

Most important of all, however, so far as the *aesthesis* of texts is concerned, are the scholars and institutions of transmission who hand our cultural deposits down to us. Texts emerge from these workshops in ever more rich and strange forms. Indeed, readers sometimes complain that cultural transmitters interfere with the original texts too much, that they make them appear too difficult, too alien — too thick and encumbered. And no doubt there are many helpless and hopeless interventions. But who is to say for certain which they are? Besides, 'literary' work, in its textual condition, is not meant for transparency, is not designed to carry messages. Messages may be taken from such work, but always and only by acts of simplification and diminishment. So readers, in those ghostly shapes we call critics and scholars, hear many voices in the texts they study. Like Tennyson's sea, what is literary 'moans round' with many such voices. In doing and being so, texts put the features of textuality on fullest display.

## iii

To this point I have been taking the word 'text' to signify the linguistic text, the verbal outcome at every level (from the most elementary forms of single letters and punctuation marks up to the most complex rhetorical structures that comprise the particular linguistic event). And even if we agree, for practical purposes, to restrict the term 'text' to this linguistic signification, we cannot fail to see that literary works typically secure their effects by other than purely linguistic means. Every literary work that descends to us operates through the deployment of a double helix of perceptual codes: the linguistic codes, on one hand, and the bibliographical codes on the other.

We recognize the latter simply by *looking* at a medieval literary manuscript – or at any of William Blake's equivalent illuminated texts produced in (the teeth of) the age of mechanical reproduction. Or at Emily Dickinson's manuscript books of poetry, or her letters. In each of these cases the physique of the 'document' has been forced to play an aesthetic function, has been made part of the 'literary work'. That is to say, in these kinds of literary works the distinction between physical medium and conceptual message breaks down completely.

I could adduce scores of similar examples of works generated out of the production mechanisms developed by printing institutions. The most obvious are the ornamental texts produced, for example, by writers like William Morris, but the books published by Whitman, Yeats, W. C. Williams, and Pound – to name only the most obvious examples – make the same point. Less apparent, but no less significant, are the novels of Dickens and Thackeray, or the serial fictions produced throughout the nineteenth century – topics I shall elaborate upon in a moment. If Tanselle cannot easily draw a distinction between a historical and a literary work, it is just as difficult to distinguish, in all these cases, between that which is documentary and that which is literary. The physical presentation of these printed texts has been made to serve aesthetic ends.

Textual and editorial theory has heretofore concerned itself almost exclusively with the linguistic codes. The time has come, however, when we have to take greater theoretical account of the other coding network which operates at the documentary and bibliographical level of literary works.

Not that scholars have been unaware of the existence of these bibliographical codes. We have simply neglected to incorporate our knowledge into our theories of text. Surely no editor of Coleridge's 'The Rime of the Ancient Mariner' – if the editor chose to print the 1816 rather than the 1798 text – would consider placing the famous set of glosses anywhere except in the margin of the work. The glosses have to be *there*, and not set as either footnotes or endnotes, because their bibliographical position is in itself highly meaningful. Placed as they are, the glosses make an important historical allusion that affects the work in the most profound way. A similar kind of historical allusion operates in the ink, type-face, and paper used by William Morris in the first edition of his *The Story of the Glittering Plain* (1891). Both involve literary allusions: the one to medieval conventions of textual glossing, the other to fifteenth-century styles of typography and book production.

As Tanselle has argued, every documentary or bibliographical aspect of a literary work is meaningful, and potentially significant. But Tanselle's clear, practical sense of this matter has not led him to imagine how such materials are to be incorporated into a theory of texts and editing. On the contrary, in fact. He has neglected doing so, I believe, not because of his adherence to an eclectic model of editing, but because of his unnecessarily restricted view of the processes of literary signification.

A few more examples will clarify what I have in mind. In the current controversy over the edition of *Ulysses*, attention has been focussed on a number of specialized, and largely executive, issues (for example, the *Ulysses'* editors failure to work directly from original documents rather than from photocopies).[4] The overriding editorial question, however, has always been this: Should Gabler have chosen the 1922 *Ulysses* as copy-text instead of trying to construct as his copy-text (if that is the right term in this peculiar case) the theoretical entity he called in his edition 'the continuous manuscript text'? Without going into the technical issues involved, let me simply observe that John Kidd – Gabler's chief critic – originally took his own preference for the 1922 edition because he detected in that book an elaborate symbolism keyed to the sequence of page numbers. If Joyce's page numbering has been symbolically deployed, that fact has to be registered in the editorial reconstruction. Specifically, the 1922 pagination of *Ulysses* would have to be editorially preserved.

The example of *Ulysses* ought to remind us that many of the key works of the modernist movement in literature, especially the work produced before 1930, heavily exploit the signifying power of documentary and bibliographical materials. The first thirty of Pound's *Cantos*, published in three book installments between 1925 and 1930, are only the most outstanding examples of this fact about modernist texts. A great many similar examples could be cited from modernist writers working all across the Euro-American literary scene.

Nor does the situation change if we move back in time. The case of Thackeray is well known and typical, and the particular example of *Vanity Fair* eloquent. In the first 1848 edition Thackeray himself designed the sixty-six decorated initials and eighty-three vignettes – as well, of course, as the thirty-eight principal illustrations. His surviving manuscript of the novel with his markups shows where he wanted various cuts to appear. Yet most editions of *Vanity Fair* omit these materials altogether, even though they are clearly involved in the structure of the book's meaning. Gordon Ray has pointed out, for example, that while the verbal text 'leaves unanswered the question of whether or not Becky Sharp brought about the death of Jos Sedley[,] his etching of Becky's second appearance in the character of Clytemnestra more than hints that she did'.[5] Thackeray's decorated cover for the nineteen separate parts of the serially published text (1847–48) is an equally unmistakable case of the book's graphic materials being coded for significance. Indeed, in chapter 8 of the novel the narrator refers to that symbolic design and explicates its meaning.[6]

From a scholarly point of view, it would be difficult to justify an edition of Thackeray that omits the illustrative matter handled at the documentary level of the work. For the novel is not merely 'one of the best illustrated books in the world', it is also an important 'experiment in composite form as much as Edward Lear's *Book of Nonsense*' (1846)[7] – as much, indeed, as the more famous 'composite art' of William Blake. Indeed, Thackeray explicitly calls attention to his own composite art in the subtitle of his novel: 'Pen (i.e., linguistic) and Pencil (i.e., graphic) Sketches of English Society'.

Yet the same must be said in the case of Dickens, even though Dickens did not, like Blake, Thackeray, and Lear, design his own illustrations. For the texts of Dickens's novels were equally produced as works of composite art, though in this case Dickens supplied only the pen, while others worked with the pencil. The relevance of the illustrative material has been acknowledged throughout the editorial history of Dickens's works, both their scholarly and their commercial history.

Or what would one say of a critical edition of the Alice books that omitted the designs of Sir John Tenniel? So important was Tenniel's work for the first of the Alice books (*Alice's Adventures in Wonderland*, 1865) that his protest at the poor printing of the first edition caused the book to be cancelled altogether.

In fact, we have two distinct versions of this famous book: the version on which Carroll and Tenniel collaborated, published in 1865, and the fair manuscript copy with Carroll's own illustrations made as a Christmas gift for Anne Liddell, and eventually published in 1886. In both cases the verbal text and the documentary materials operate together to a single literary result.

Nor do I mean to isolate for importance, in the case of this work, only the marriage of illustration and text. As Tenniel's protest over the poor printing of the first edition indicates, the entire documentary level of the work must be understood as carrying significance. The fact that one version was conceived as a publishing event, and the other as a manuscript gift book, sets the bibliographical coding for each version on an entirely different footing.

The two versions of *Alice's Adventures in Wonderland* may well remind us of the variant versions of so many nineteenth-century books, especially the novels. Serial publication of one kind or another was the rule, as were the related publication mechanisms we associate with institutions like the circulating library. Writers worked within those particular sets of circulatory conventions (though they vary with place and time, such conventions always exist) and the literary results – the books issued – are coded for meaning accordingly.

Furthermore, different types of serialization were available. A novel written for weekly serial publication, like Dickens's *Hard Times* (1854),[8] is not merely *written* differently from one that is written for monthly circulation (or for no serial publication at all); it is *produced* differently and comes into the reader's view via differently defined bibliographical structures of meaning. Or consider the exemplary case of *Oliver Twist*. First issued in serial parts in the monthly magazine *Bentley's Miscellany* (1837–39), it was printed again in three volumes (1838) even before the serial run had been concluded. Then in 1846 it was published again, this time in ten serial installments (the run in *Bentley's Miscellany* had been twenty-four installments). In each of these cases the text is organized very differently. The *Bentley's* and the three volume publications comprise fifty-one chapters, whereas the 1846 serial publication has fifty-three. *Bentley's* is divided into three 'Books', but these do not correspond exactly to the three 'volumes' of 1838. The *Bentley's* serial typically prints two, sometimes three chapters per unit, whereas the monthly numbered parts of 1846 typically contain six, some times five (and in one case, four) chapters.[9]

These kinds of production structures can be exploited for aesthetic effects in particular and always highly individuated ways. *Pickwick Papers* first appeared in serial parts (1836–37), as did *Little Dorrit* (1855–57), but in each case the bibliographical codes are manipulated to unique effect. The latter is one of the late novels, produced twenty years after the groundbreaking effort of *Pickwick Papers*. The early work is far more episodic than the later, so much so that many would be reluctant to call *Pickwick Papers* a novel at all. Whatever it is, the work emerged through the mutual efforts of Dickens, two illustrators (Robert Seymour and Hablot Knight Browne ['Phiz']), and the production mechanisms set in motion by the publishers Chapman and Hall, all working together in cooperative consultation'.[10]

Literary works are distinct from other linguistic forms in their pursuit of extreme concrete particularity. That special feature of 'literature' has two consequences we all recognize. First, literary works tend toward textual and bibliographical dispersion (signalled at the earliest phases of the work by authorial changes of direction and revision, which may continue for protracted periods). Second, they are committed to work via the dimension of *aesthesis* (i.e., via the materiality of experience that Blake called 'the doors of perception' and that Morris named 'resistance'). In each case, literary works tend to multiply themselves through their means and modes of production. These processes of generation are executed in the most concrete and particular ways. *Oliver Twist* is produced during Dickens's lifetime in several important creative forms. But then there are equally important versions of that work – equally significant from an aesthetic point of view – that are produced later. Kathleen Tillotson's is a splendid edition of a great literary work, but perhaps we should want to argue that her edition is not the work of Charles Dickens. And perhaps we should be right in doing so.

Tillotson's edition stands in relation to Dickens's novel in the same kind of relation that (say) the Tate Gallery stands to the paintings of Turner. Both gallery and edition force us to engage with artistic work under a special kind of horizon. It is far from the horizon under which Dickens and Turner originally worked. It is nonetheless, still, an aesthetic and literary horizon, and that fact cannot be forgotten. Of course we cannot recover the earlier frame of reference; all we can do is make imaginative attempts at reconstituting or approximating it for later persons living under other skies. The vaunted immortality sought after by the poetic impulse will be achieved, if it is achieved at all, in the continuous socialization of the texts.

## Notes

1    Tanselle here is quoting with approval the words of Nicolas Barker. See G. Thomas Tanselle 'The Editing of Historical Documents', reprinted from *Studies in Bibliography* (1978) in *Selected Studies in Bibliography* (Charlottesville: University Press of Virginia, 1979), 454.

2    Hershel Parker, *Flawed Texts and Verbal Icons: Literary Authority in American Fiction* (Evanston: Northwestern University Press, 1984), 49.

3    Peter Stoicheff detailed the complex history of the *Drafts and Fragments* text in a lecture at the Yale conference on editing Pound, sponsored by Yale and the Beinecke Library in October, 1989. The lecture forms part of a book which is now in press. [Peter Stoicheff, *The Hall of Mirrors: Drafts and Fragments and the End of Ezra Pound's Cantos* (Ann Arbor: University of Michigan Press, 1995).]

4    John Kidd's recently published 'An Inquiry into *Ulysses*: *The Corrected Text*' supplies, in great detail, the case against the edition in this respect. See *The Papers of the Bibliographical Society of America* 82 (December 1988): 412–584.

5    See Gordon N. Ray, *The Illustrator and the Book in England from 1790 to 1914* (New York and Oxford: The Pierpont Morgan Library and Oxford University Press, 1976), 75.

6    See *Vanity Fair by William Makepeace Thackeray*, edited with an introduction by Geoffrey and Kathleen Tillotson (Boston: Houghton Mifflin Co., 1963); see pp. xxii and 80.

7    Gordon Ray, op. cit., xxxix.

8    *Hard Times* was first published in weekly parts in *Household Words* over five months, beginning 1 April 1854. It was then published separately.

9    See *Charles Dickens: Oliver Twist*, ed. Kathleen Tillotson (Oxford: Oxford University Press, 1966), especially pp. 369–71.

10    For the story of these events see Robert L. Patten, *Charles Dickens and His Publishers* (Oxford: Oxford University Press, 1978), chapter 3, especially pp. 63–68.

# Chapter 5

# Roger Chartier

## LABOURERS AND VOYAGERS
## From the text to the reader

Far from being writers – founders of their own place, heirs to the peasants of earlier ages now working on the soil of language, diggers of wells and builders of houses – readers are voyagers: they move across lands belonging to someone else, like nomads poaching their way across fields they did not write, despoiling the wealth of Egypt to enjoy it themselves. Writing accumulates, stocks up, resists time by the establishment of a place and multiplies its production through the expansionism of reproduction. Reading takes no measures against the erosion of time (one forgets oneself and also forgets), reading does not keep what it acquires, or it does so poorly, and each of the places through which it passes is a repetition of the lost paradise.

(Michel de Certeau, *The Practice of Everyday Life*)

This magnificent text by Michel de Certeau, which contrasts writing (conservative, durable, and fixed) with readings (always on the order of the ephemeral) constitutes at the same time a necessary foundation and a disquieting challenge for any history that intends to inventory and account for a practice – reading – that rarely leaves traces, is scattered into an infinity of singular acts, and purposely frees itself from all the constraints seeking to subdue it. Such a project fundamentally rests on a double assumption: that reading is not already inscribed in the text, with no conceivable difference between the sense assigned to it (by the author, usage, criticism, and so forth) and the interpretation constructable by its readers; and that, correlatively, a text does not exist except for a reader who gives it signification:

Whether it is a newspaper or Proust, the text has a meaning only through its readers; it changes along with them; it is ordered in accordance with codes of perception that it does not control. It becomes a text only in its relation to the exteriority of the reader, by an interplay of implication and ruses between two sorts of 'expectation'

Roger Chartier, 'Labourers and Voyagers: from the text to the reader', *Diacritics* 22:2, 1992: 49–61 © Johns Hopkins University Press. Reprinted with the permission of The Johns Hopkins University Press.

in combination: the expectation that organizes a readable space (a literality), and one that organizes a procedure necessary for the *actualization* of the work (a reading).
(Certeau, *Practice*, pp. 170–1)[1]

The task of the historian is, then, to reconstruct the variations that differentiate the 'readable space' (the texts in their material and discursive forms) and those which govern the circumstances of their 'actualization' (the readings seen as concrete practices and interpretive procedures).

Based upon de Certeau's suggestions, I would like to indicate some of the stakes, problems, and conditions of possibility for such an historical project. Three poles, generally separated by academic tradition, define the space of this history: first, the analysis of texts, either canonical or ordinary, deciphered in their structures, themes, and aims; second, the history of books and, more generally, of all the objects and forms that carry out the circulation of writing; and finally, the study of practices which in various ways take hold of these objects or forms and produce usages and differentiated meanings. A fundamental question underlies this approach in associating textual criticism, bibliography, and cultural history. That is to understand how in the societies of the ancien régime between the sixteenth and eighteenth centuries the increasing circulation of printed writing transformed the modes of social interaction (*sociabilité*), permitted new ways of thinking, and modified power relations.

Hence the attention placed upon the manner in which (to use the terms of Paul Ricoeur) the encounter between 'the world of the text' and 'the world of the reader' functions (*Time and Narrative*, 3: 6). To reconstruct in its historical dimensions this process of the 'actualization' of texts above all requires us to realize that their meaning depends upon the forms through which they are received and appropriated by their readers (or listeners). Readers, in fact, never confront abstract, idealized texts detached from any materiality. They hold in their hands or perceive objects and forms whose structures and modalities govern their reading or hearing, and consequently the possible comprehension of the text read or heard. In contrast to a purely semantic definition of the text, which characterizes not only structuralist criticism in all its variants but also literary theories concerned with reconstructing the modes of reception of works, it is necessary to maintain that forms produce meaning, and that even a fixed text is invested with new meaning and being (*statut*) when the physical form through which it is presented for interpretation changes. We must also realize that reading is always a practice embodied in gestures, spaces, and habits. Far from the phenomenology of reading, which erases the concrete modality of the act of reading and characterizes it by its effects, postulated as universals, a history of modes of reading must identify the specific dispositions that distinguish communities of readers and traditions of reading. This approach supposes the recognition of a series of contrasts: to begin with, the distinctions between reading competencies. The fundamental but rough separation between the literate and the illiterate does not exhaust the possible differences in the relation to writing. Those who can read texts do not all read them in the same fashion. There is a wide gap between the most skillful and the least competent readers – those who are obliged to read what they read aloud in order to understand it and who are at ease only with certain textual or typographical forms. Another contrast distinguishes between the norms and conventions of reading, defining for each community of readers the legitimate uses of the book, the forms of reading, and the instruments and procedures of interpretation. Finally, we have the contrast between the expectations and diverse interests that different groups of readers invest in the practice of reading. Upon these determining factors, which govern practice, depend the ways in which texts can be read – and read differently by readers who are equipped with different intellectual tools and maintain quite different relations to writing.

Michel de Certeau illustrated such an approach in describing the specific characteristics of the mystical reader: 'By "mystical readers" I have in mind all the procedures of reading which were suggested or practised in the field of solitary or collective experience designated in the sixteenth and seventeenth centuries as "illuminated", "mystical", or "spiritual" ' (Certeau, 'La lecture', p. 67).[2] In the minor, marginal, and dispersed community that was mysticism's milieu, reading, determined by norms and habits, invested the book with novel functions: to replace the ecclesiastical institution considered to be inadequate; to make a certain kind of speech possible (that of the prayer, the communication with God, the *conversar*); and to indicate the practices through which spiritual experience is constructed. The mystical relation to the book can also be understood as a trajectory in which several 'moments' of reading succeed one another: the establishment of an otherness (*altérité*) which founds the subjective quest; the development of ecstasy (*jouissance*); the marking of bodies physically reacting to the digestion (*manducation*) of the text; and, at the extreme, the interruption of reading, the abandonment of the book, and detachment. Consequently to locate the network of practices and rules of reading specific to diverse communities of readers (spiritual, intellectual, professional, and so forth) is a primary task for any history concerned with understanding, in its differentiations, the pragmatic figure of the 'poaching' reader (*lecteur braconnier*) (see, for example, Jardine and Grafton).

But to read is always to read something. Certainly, to exist at all, the history of reading must be radically distinguished from the history of what is read: 'The reader emerges from the history of the book, in which he was for a long time undifferentiated or indistinct. . . . The reader was taken as the effect of the book. Today he has become detached from the books of which he had seemed no more than a shadow. Suddenly this shadow has been released, has taken on a physiognomy, has acquired an independence' (de Certeau, 'La lecture', pp. 66–7). But this founding independence is not an arbitrary license. It is confined by the codes and conventions that govern the practices of a community. It is also confined by the discursive and material forms of the texts read. 'New readers make new texts, and their new meanings are a function of their new forms' (McKenzie, *Bibliography and the Sociology of Texts*, p. 20). D. F. McKenzie thus points out with great acuity the double network of variations – variations of the dispositions of readers and variations of textual and formal devices – which must be taken into account in any history seeking to recover the shifting and plural meaning of texts. One can make use of this analysis in different ways: by locating the major contrasts distinguishing different modes of reading by characterizing the most popular reading practices; or by paying attention to the publishing changes that offered old texts to new consumers, changes that made them more numerous and of more modest condition. Such a perspective translates a double dissatisfaction with the history of the book in France over the last twenty or thirty years, which has consistently taken as its objective to measure the unequal distribution of books in the different groups composing the society of the ancien régime. This led to the indispensable construction of factors revealing cultural divisions: for example, for a given location and time, the percentage of property inventories taken after death indicating the possession of books, the classification of collections according to the number of works they contain, or the thematic characterization of private libraries according to the proportion of different bibliographic categories present in them. From this perspective, to conceptualize reading in France between the sixteenth and eighteenth centuries was, above all, to put together series of quantitative data, to establish quantitative thresholds, and to locate how social differences were culturally translated.

This approach, pursued collectively (including by the author of this essay), produced a body of knowledge without which other inquiries would have been impossible. However, it poses a problem of its own. To begin with, it rests on a strictly sociographic conception which implicitly postulates that cultural separations are necessarily organized according to a preexisting social division. I believe it is necessary to challenge the analytic model which links differences in cultural practices with social oppositions constructed *a priori* – either on the scale of macroscopic contrasts (between the dominant and the dominated, between the elite and the people) or on a scale of finer differentiations (for example, between social groups hierarchized by distinctions of status or profession and levels of wealth).

Cultural separations are not necessarily ordered only according to a single grid of social divisions, conceived as determining the unequal possession of objects and the difference between behaviors. The perspective must be reversed to outline, first of all, the social areas where each corpus of texts and each variety of printed materials circulates. To start out thus from objects, and not from classes or groups, brings us to the realization that French sociocultural history has for too long been based on an incomplete conception of the social. In privileging only socioprofessional classifications, it has forgotten that other principles of differentiation, also fully social, could explain cultural divisions with greater pertinence. Thus there are also considerations of gender or generation, religious belief, community membership, academic or group traditions, and so on.

In another register, the history of the book in its social and serial definition sought to characterize cultural configurations according to categories of texts considered specific to them. Such an operation proves to be doubly reductive. For one thing, it simply equates the identification of differences to inequalities of distribution; and for another, it ignores the process by which a text takes on meaning for those who read it. Against these claims it is necessary to propose several modifications. The first of these situates the recognition of the most deeply embedded social divisions in the contrasting uses of shared material. More than we have tended to acknowledge, in the societies of the ancien régime it is the same texts which are taken up by readers from the popular classes and by those who are not. Sometimes readers of humble conditions owned books that were not particularly aimed at them (this was the case of Menocchio, the Friulian miller; of Jamerey Duval, the shepherd from Lorraine; and of Ménétra, the Parisian glazier: see Ginzburg, Hébrard, and Ménétra). Or sometimes creative and shrewd booksellers put within the reach of a broader clientele texts that previously had not circulated except in the narrow world of the wealthy and well read (as was the case with Castilian and Catalan *pliegos sueltos*, English chapbooks, or the collection known in France under the generic term Bibliothèque Bleue). What is essential, then, is to understand how the same texts could be diversely apprehended, handled, and understood.

The second modification is to reconstruct the networks of practices that organize the historically and socially differentiated modes of access to texts. Reading is not only an abstract operation of the intellect: it puts the body into play and is inscribed within a particular space, in a relation to the self or to others. This is why attention should particularly be paid to ways of reading that have been obliterated in our contemporary world: for example reading out loud in its double function – communicating that which is written to those who do not know how to decipher it, and binding together the interconnected forms of sociability which are all figures of the private sphere (the intimacy of the family, the conviviality of social life, the cooperation of scholars: *connivence lettré*). A history of reading, then, cannot limit itself only to the genealogy of our contemporary manner of reading – in silence and by sight. It must equally, perhaps above all, take on the task of discovering forgotten gestures and habits that have now disappeared. The stakes are important because they reveal not only the remote peculiarity of traditionally shared practices, but also the specific structures of texts composed for uses that are no longer those of their readers today. Often in the sixteenth and seventeenth centuries, the implicit reading of a text, literary or not, was construed as a vocalization and its 'reader' as the auditor of read speech (*parole lectrice*). Thus addressed to the ear as much as the eye, the work played with forms and processes designed to submit the written word to the requirements of oral 'performance'. From the motifs of the *Quijote* to the structures of texts published in the Bibliothèque Bleue, there are numerous examples of this link maintained between the text and the voice (see Chartier, 'Leisure and Sociability').

'Whatever they may do, authors do not write books. Books are not written at all. They are manufactured by scribes and other artisans, by mechanics and other engineers, and by printing presses and other machines' (Stoddard, 'Morphology', p. 4). This remark introduces the third modification that I would like to propose. Against the representation developed by literature itself and repeated by the most quantitative histories of the book, according to which the text exists in itself, separated from all materiality, we must insist that there is no text outside the material structure in which it is given to be read or heard. Thus there is no comprehension of writing, whatever it may be, which does not depend in part upon the forms in which it comes to its reader. Hence the necessary distinction between two groups of apparatuses: those which reveal strategies of writing and the intentions of the author, and those which are a result of the publishers' decisions or the constraints of the printing house. Authors do not write books. Rather they write texts which become objects copied, handwritten, etched, printed, and today computerized. This gap, which is rightly the space in which meaning is constructed, has too often been forgotten not only by classical literary history, which thinks of the work in itself as an abstract text for which the typographic forms are unimportant, but even by *Rezeptionstheorie*. Despite its desire to historicize the experience that readers have with works, *Rezeptionstheorie* postulates a pure and immediate relation between the 'signals' emitted by the text (which plays with accepted literary conventions) and the 'horizon of expectation' of the public to which they are addressed. In such a perspective the 'effect produced' does not depend at all upon the material forms the text takes.[3] Yet these forms contribute fully to shaping the anticipations of the reader *vis-à-vis* the text and to the production of new publics or innovative uses for it.

We thus return to the triangle with which we began, defined by the intricate relation between text, book, and reader. The variations of this relation outline some elementary figures in the connection between 'readable space' and 'actualization' of the text. The first variation considers a linguistically stable text presented in printed forms which themselves change. In studying the innovations occurring in the publication of the plays of William Congreve at the turn of the seventeenth and eighteenth centuries, McKenzie was able to demonstrate how some apparently insignificant formal transformations – the change from quarto to octavo formats, the numbering of scenes, the presence of an ornament between each scene, the list of the dramatis personae at the beginning of them, the marginal notation of the name of the character speaking, the indication of entrances and exits – had a major effect on the status of the works. A new readability was created by a format easier to handle and by a layout that reproduced in the book something of the movement of the actual production, thus breaking with the ancient conventions of printing plays with no rendering of their theatricality. A new manner of reading the same text resulted, but also a new horizon of reception. The forms used in the octavo edition of 1710, borrowed from those used in France for the edition of plays, gave an unofficial legitimacy to Congreve's plays, which from then on were inscribed in a classic canon. This is what could induce an author to refine his style in order to make the works conform to their new 'typographic' dignity (see McKenzie, 'Typography and Meaning'). Variations of the most formal modes of textual presentation can modify the register of reference and the mode of interpretation.

The same is true on a larger scale concerning the principal alteration of the layout in which texts were presented between the sixteenth and eighteenth centuries – what Henri-Jean Martin has termed 'the definitive triumph of white over black' (see Martin and Delmas, pp. 295–9): in other words, the opening up of the page through the multiplication of paragraphs that broke the uninterrupted continuity of the text common in the Renaissance and the indentations which, through varying the left margin, make the order of discourse immediately visible. A new reading of the same works or of the same genres was consequently suggested by their new publishers – a reading that fragments texts into small and separate units, an approach that reinforces the argument, whether intellectual or discursive, by a visual articulation of the page.

This textual segmentation (*découpage*) had fundamental implications when it was applied to sacred texts. The story of Locke's anxiety regarding the practice of dividing the text of the Bible into chapter and verse is well known. For him such a division presented a considerable risk of obliterating the powerful coherence of the Word of God. Referring to the Epistle of Paul, he thus noted that 'not only Common People take the Verses usually for distinct Aphorisms but even Men of more advanc'd Knowledge in reading them, lose very much of the strength and force of the Coherence and the Light that depends on it'. The effects of such a division he thought disastrous, authorizing each sect or religious body to found its legitimacy on the fragments of the Scriptures that supported its views:

> If a Bible was printed as it should be, and as the several Parts of it were writ, in continued Discourse where the Argument is continued, I doubt not that the several Parties would complain of it, as an Innovation, and a dangerous Change in the publishing of those holy Books. . . . He [i.e., the member of a particular sect] need but be furnished with Verses of Sacred Scriptures, containing Words and Expressions that are but flexible . . . and his System that has appropriated them to the Orthodoxie of His Church, makes them immediately strong and irrefragable Arguments for his Opinion. This is the Benefit of loose Sentences and Scripture crumbled into Verses, which quickly turn into independent Aphorism.
>
> (Quoted in McKenzie, *Bibliography and the Sociology of Texts*, pp. 46–7)

The second figure in our triangle of relations is that in which the text passes from one published form to another order, transforming the text itself and constituting a new public. This is clearly the case with the body of texts that constitute the catalogue of the Bibliothèque Bleue. If this collection has occupied French historians for a long time, it is because it seems to furnish direct access to the 'popular culture' of the ancien régime, a culture supposedly expressed and nourished by texts distributed 'en masse' to the humblest readers.[4] But such is not the case for three essential reasons. To begin with, it is clear that the texts which formed the stock of French book peddlers were almost never written for this purpose. The Bibliothèque Bleue drew from the repertoire of already published texts those which appeared to be best suited to attract a large public. Hence two necessary precautions: first, not to take the texts put into the books included in the Bibliothèque Bleue as 'popular' in themselves, because in fact they belonged to a wide variety of genres drawn from learned literature; and second, to consider that these texts generally had already had a published existence, sometimes quite lengthy, before entering the repertoire of 'popular' books (*livres pour le plus grand nombre*). The study of titles in this 'popular' catalogue has moreover permitted registering how the most formal and material arrangements can inscribe in themselves the indices of cultural differentiation. Indeed the fundamental specificity of the Bibliothèque Bleue is in the editorial interventions it imposed upon texts in order to make them readable by the large clientele at which they were aimed. All this work of adaptation – which shortened texts, simplified them, cut them up, and illustrated them – was determined according to the manner in which booksellers conceived the competencies and expectations of their customers. Thus the very structures of the book were governed by what the publishers thought to be the mode of reading of the clientele they were targeting.

Such a reading always required visible references, and this is my third assertion. Thus the anticipatory titles or the recapitulative summaries or even the wood engravings functioned as protocols of reading or sites of memory (*lieux de memoire*). Such a reading was comfortable only with brief, self-contained sequences, separated from one another – a reading that appears to have been satisfied with only minimal coherence. This manner of reading is not at all that of the lettered elite of the time – even if certain notables did not disdain to buy books from the Bibliothèque Bleue. These texts assumed their readers' foreknowledge. By the recurrence of highly coded forms, by the repetition of similar motifs from one title to another, and by the reuse of the same images, the knowledge of texts already encountered (either read or heard) was mobilized to help in the comprehension of new readings. The catalogue of the Bibliothèque Bleue thus organized a form of reading that was more recognition or recapitulation than discovery. It is therefore in the formal particularity of the Bibliothèque Bleue publications and in the modifications they impose on texts that they possess their 'popular' character.

In proposing this reevaluation of the Bibliothèque Bleue, my intention has been not only to better understand what was the single most powerful instrument of the acculturation to writing in ancien régime France.[5] It is also to argue that the detection of sociocultural differentiations and the study of formal and material devices, far from excluding one another, are necessarily linked. This is true not only because the forms are modeled on the expectations and competencies attributed to the public at which they are aimed, but above all because the works and objects produce the space of their social reception much more than they are produced by already concretized divisions. Recently Lawrence W. Levine provided a persuasive demonstration of this fact (see his 'William Shakespeare and the American People' and *Highbrow/Lowbrow*). Analyzing the manner in which the plays of Shakespeare were produced in America in the nineteenth century (that is to say, combined with other genres: melodrama, farce, circus, dance), he showed how this type of representation created a diverse public – 'popular' in the sense that it did not reduce down to just the lettered elite but actively participated in the production through its emotions and reactions. At the end of the century the strict separation established between genres, styles, and cultural sites dispersed this universal public, reserving a 'legitimate' Shakespeare for the few and relegating the other versions to the status of 'popular' entertainment. In establishing this 'bifurcated culture', transformations in the forms of presentation of a Shakespeare play (but also of symphony music, opera, or works of art) had a decisive role. Following a time of cultural mixing and sharing came another, in which the process of cultural distinction produced social separation. The traditional devices of representation in the American Shakespearean repertoire are thus of the same order as the 'typographic' transformations imposed by the publishers of the Bibliothèque Bleue upon the texts of which they took possession: both aim, in effect, to inscribe the text in a cultural matrix that was not its original destination, thereby permitting readings, understandings, and uses possibly disqualified by other intellectual practices.

These two cases lead us to the consideration of cultural differentiations not as the translation of already concretized and static divisions, but as the effect of a dynamic process. On the one hand, the transformation of forms and devices by which a text is presented authorizes new appropriations and consequently creates new publics for and uses of it. On the other hand, the sharing of the same objects by the whole of society gives rise to the search for new differences, suited to marking the divisions that were preserved. The trajectory of printed works in the French ancien régime bears witness to this situation. We could say that the distinctions between the manners of reading were progressively reinforced to the degree that printed works became less rare, less threatened by seizure, and more ordinary. Whereas the simple possession of a book had for a long time signified a cultural division in itself, with the conquests of printing it is, rather, specific reading attitudes and typographical objects which progressively take on this function. Against refined readings and carefully made books were henceforth counterposed hastily printed material and unskilled interpreters. But both groups, let us recall, often read the same texts, for which plural and contradictory significations were produced according to their contrasting uses. The question consequently becomes one of selection: why do certain texts lend themselves better than others to these continuing and recurrent uses (see Harlan)? Or at least, why do the makers (*faiseurs*) of books consider them capable of reaching a very diverse public? The answer lies in subtle relations between the structures of the works themselves, unequally suited to reappropriations, and the multiple determinations, as much institutional as formal, that establish their possible 'application' (in the phenomenological sense) to very different historical situations.

In the relation between the text, its printed form, and reading there is a third figure produced as soon as a text, fixed in its form and linguistically stable, is taken up by new readers who read differently from their predecessors. 'A book changes by the fact that it remains changeless while the world changes' (Bourdieu and Chartier, p. 236) – or, to make the proposition compatible with the scale of our reflection here, let us say, 'when its mode of being read changes'. The remark serves to justify the project of a history of the practices of reading, which attempts to mark the major contrasts that can give diverse meaning to the same text. It is surely time to reexamine three fundamental oppositions that have long been considered incontestable: to begin with, between a reading in which comprehension presupposes a required oral articulation, whether aloud or barely vocalized (*à basse voix*), and another species of reading that is purely visual (see Saenger, 'Silent Reading' and 'Physiologie de la lecture'). Let us recall (even if its chronology is questionable) a fundamental assertion of Michel de Certeau that associates the freedom of the reader with silent reading:

> In the last three centuries reading has become a gesture of the eye. It is no longer accompanied, as it used to be, by the murmur of vocal articulation, nor by the movement of a muscular mastication (*manducation*). To read without speaking the words or at least muttering them is a modern experience, unknown for millennia. In earlier times, the reader interiorized the text: he made his voice the body of the other; he was its actor. Today the text no longer imposes its own rhythm on the subject, it no longer manifests itself through the reader's voice. This withdrawal of the body, which is the condition of its autonomy, puts the text at a distance. It is the reader's *habeas corpus*.
>
> (*Practice of Everyday Life*, pp. 175–6; translation modified)

The second of these oppositions contrasts 'intensive' reading applied only to a few texts and sustained by hearing and memory with 'extensive' reading – consuming many texts, passing without constraint from one to another, granting little consecration (*sacralité*) to the object read (see Engelsing and Schön). Finally, the third of these oppositions is between the reading of intimacy, enclosure, and solitude – considered to be one of the essential foundations of the private sphere – and collective readings, whether orderly or unruly, in communal spaces (see Ariès, 'Introduction'; and Chartier, 'The Practical Impact of Writing').

In outlining a preliminary chronological thread, which marks as major transformations the progressive advances of silent reading in the Middle Ages and the entry into the world of extensive reading at the end of the eighteenth century, these now classic contrasts suggest several reflections. Some of these tend to complicate the oppositional pairs presented: shifting attention to the model's inaccuracies, complicating criteria that too rigidly differentiate styles of reading, reversing the image of an automatic connection between the collective and the 'popular' or between the elite and the private (see Darnton). Others invite the articulation of three series of transformations whose effects have often been imperfectly sorted out: first, the 'revolutions' that have occurred in the techniques of textual reproduction (with, most importantly, the passage from 'scribal culture' to 'print culture'); second, the changes in the forms of books themselves (the replacement of the *volumen* by the *codex* in the first centuries of the Christian era is the most fundamental; but others, certainly more subtle, alter the visual layout of the printed page between the sixteenth and eighteenth centuries – see Laufer); and finally, major alterations in reading abilities and in reading modes. These different evolutions do not proceed at the same pace and are not at all organized around the same turning points. The most interesting question posed to and by the history of reading today is without doubt that of the conjunction between these three sets of changes: technological, formal, and cultural.

The response we give to this question depends upon a re-evaluation of the trajectories and cultural divisions that characterize the society of the ancien régime. More than has been recognized, these were themselves ordered according to the role played by printed works. For a long time their distribution was measured by two restricted series of criteria: one, based upon the proportion of signatures, which sought to establish percentages of literacy and hence to estimate variations in the ability to read according to period, place, gender, and social situation; and another which, by inventorying the catalogues of libraries established by notaries or booksellers, sought to establish the circulation of books and the traditions of reading. But neither in ancien régime societies nor in our own can access to printing be reduced simply to the possession of books: not all books read are privately owned, and not all privately owned printed matter is in the form of books. Moreover written material occupies the very heart of the culture of the illiterate – in rituals, in public spaces, and in workplaces (see Chartier, *The Culture of Print*). Thanks to speech which deciphers it and to images which accentuate it, it is made accessible even to those who are incapable of reading or who cannot by themselves have more than a rudimentary understanding of the text. Rates of literacy, then, do not give a fair indication of familiarity with the written – particularly because in more traditional communities, where instruction in reading and instruction in writing were dissociated and successive, there were many individuals (especially among women) who left school knowing how to read, at least a little, but not how to write (see Spufford). Similarly, the private possession of books cannot adequately indicate the frequency with which printed texts were utilized by those who were too poor to have their own 'library'.

Even if it is impossible to establish the number of the reading-literate (lisants) who did not know how to set their names on paper, or how many possessed not a single book (at least none worth mentioning by a notary establishing the inventory of a decedent's possessions) but could still read posters and broadsheets, pamphlets and chapbooks, it is necessary to postulate that there were many such readers in order to comprehend the impact of print on the traditional forms of a culture that was still largely oral, gestural, and iconographic. The overlaps between the two modes of expression and communication are multiple: to begin with overlaps between writing and gesture, not only was writing at the center of everyday celebrations such as religious ceremonies, but numerous texts attempt to efface themselves as discourse and to produce, in practice, behavior conforming to social or religious norms. Such is the case, for example, of conduct books (traités de civilité), whose aim was to help individuals internalize the rules of worldly politesse or Christian decency (see Patrizi and Chartier). There is equally an interweaving between speech and writing, in two ways. First, texts intended by their author and, more often, by their publisher to reach the most popular audience often contain formulas or motifs that are themselves drawn from the oral tradition of tales and recitations. The writing styles in certain occasional pieces that plagiarize the speaking style of storytellers or the variations introduced in the fairy tales in the Bibliothèque Bleue, themselves originally drawn from written compilations, are good examples of the emergence of orality in print (see Chartier, 'The Hanged Woman Miraculously Saved' and Velay-Vallantin). Second, as mentioned above, a number of 'readers' do not understand texts except through the mediation of a voice. To understand the specificity of this relation to writing thus presumes that all reading is not necessarily individual, silent, and solitary but, on the contrary, marks the importance and diversity of a practice now largely lost – reading aloud.

From this initial assertion, which registers the powerful penetration of printed culture into the societies of the ancien régime, several others follow. It allows us to understand the importance given to writing, and the objects in which it is found, by the authorities whose intentions were to regulate behavior and to shape minds. Whence the pedagogical, acculturating, and disciplinary role attributed to texts placed in circulation for broad readerships; and the surveillance exercised over printing, subjected to a censor who was supposed to eliminate all that might endanger order, religion, or morals. Concerning these constraints, Michel de Certeau urges us to recognize both their power – all the stronger because of the strength of the institution that decreed them ('The creativity of the reader grows as the institution that controls him declines': *Practice of Everyday Life*, p. 172) – and their modalities, ranging from brutal prohibition to authorized interpretation, from exterior disciplines (administrative, judicial, inquisitorial, academic, and so forth) to the mechanisms which, in the book itself, seek to restrain the freedom of the reader.

Out of practices of writing and diverse treatments of printing, traditional texts constructed representations in which we can recognize the divisions that were considered decisive by the producers of books. These perceptions are fundamental because they found the strategies of writing and printing, regulated by the competencies and expectations of the different target audiences. They thereby acquire an efficacy of which the trace can be found in the protocols of explicit reading, in the forms given to typographic objects, or in the transformations that modified a text as soon as it was offered to new readers in a new published format. It is thus from these diverse representations of reading and from the dichotomies constructed in the modern age (between the reading of a text and the reading of an image, between literate reading and unskilled reading, between intimate reading and communal reading) that an attempt must be made to understand the agency and the uses of those printed texts, more modest than the book, but also more pervasive – texts ranging from individual images and posters (always accompanied by words) to occasional pieces and pamphlets like those found in the Bibliothèque Bleue (often illustrated with images). The representations of traditional ways of reading and of their differences from each other – revealed on the practical level by the transformations of printed materials (*mises en imprimé*) or in their normative purposes (*finalité*) by their literary, pictorial, or autobiographical stagings (*mises en scène*) – constitute the essential data for an archeology of reading practices. Yet while they may articulate the contrasts most apparent to the minds of their contemporaries, they should not be allowed to mask other divisions which may have been less clearly perceived. For example, it is certain that there are many practices that reverse the very terms of the frequently described opposition between readings in bourgeois or aristocratic solitude on the one hand, and mass communal readings on the other. Indeed, reading aloud (for others to listen to) remained an enduring, unifying element in elite society, and, conversely, printing penetrated to the very heart of intimate popular culture, capturing in unpretentious objects (not all of which were books) the traces of an important moment of existence, the memory of an emotion, the sign of an identity. Contrary to classic imagery – in fact, a product of the modern age – 'the people' are not always plural, and it is necessary to rediscover in their secret solitude the modest practices of those who cut out images of occasional works, colored printed etchings, and read books from the Bibliothèque Bleue for their personal pleasure.

Attached to a particular country (France between the sixteenth and eighteenth centuries) and having chosen a specific problem (the effects of the penetration of printed works into popular culture – *la culture du plus grand nombre*), the approach suggested in this text (and at work in several others) attempts to make functional two propositions of Michel de Certeau. The first reminds us, against all the reductions that cancel out the creative and inventive force of practices, that reading is never totally constrained and that it cannot be recursively deduced from the texts to which it is applied. The second emphasizes that the tactics of readers, infiltrating the 'special space' (*lieu propre*) produced by the strategies of writing, obey certain rules, logics, and models. Thus is articulated the founding paradox of any history of reading, which must postulate the freedom of a practice of which, broadly, it can only grasp the determinations. To construct communities of readers as 'interpretive communities' (to use the expression of Stanley Fish), to detect how material forms affect meaning, to locate social difference more in real practices than in statistical distributions – such are the paths outlined in our attempt to understand historically this 'silent production' which is the activity of reading.

## Notes

The translator and editors gratefully acknowledge support for the translation of this essay provided by the Center for Cultural Studies, University of California, Santa Cruz.

1    On the reading–writing duo in this book see the article by Anne-Marie Chartier and Jean Hébrard, 'L'invention du quotidien, une lecture, des usages', *Le Débat*, **49** (March–April 1988): 97–108.

2    The suggestions in this essay are reconsidered in one of Michel de Certeau's major works, *La Fable mystique* (Paris: Gallimard, 1982), in particular the third part, 'La Scène de l'énonciation' (pp. 209–73). This work has recently been translated into English: *The Mystic Fable*, trans. Michael B. Smith (Chicago: University of Chicago Press, 1992).

3    For a programmatic definition of *Rezeptionstheorie*, see Hans Robert Jauss, *Literaturgeschichte als Provokation* (Frankfurt-am-Main: Suhrkamp, 1974).

4    The fundamental but contested study on this issue is by Robert Mandrou, *De la culture populaire aux XVIIe et XVIIIe siècles*. Among the criticisms addressed to this book is de Certeau, 'La beauté du mort'; reconsidered in de Certeau, *La Culture au pluriel* (pp. 49–80).

5    See Chartier, 'The Bibliothèque Bleue and Popular Reading' and 'The Literature of Roguery in the Bibliothèque Bleue' in *The Cultural Uses of Print in Early Modern France* (pp. 240–64 and pp. 265–342).

## References

Ariès, Philippe 'Introduction', *Passions of the Renaissance*. Vol. 3 of *A History of Private Life*. Ed. Roger Chartier. Cambridge: Harvard University Press, 1989, pp. 1–11.

Bourdieu, Pierre and Roger Chartier 'La Lecture: Une pratique culturelle', *Pratiques de la lecture*. Ed. Roger Chartier. Marseille: Rivages, 1985.

Certeau, Michel de *La Culture au pluriel*. 1974. 2nd edn Paris: Bourgois, 1980.

—— 'La Lecture absolue (Théorie et pratique des mystiques chrétiens: XVIe–XVIIe siècles)', *Problèmes actuels de la lecture*. Ed. Lucien Dällenbach and Jean Ricardou. Paris: Clancier-Guénaud, 1982.

—— *The Practice of Everyday Life*. Trans. Steven F. Rendall. Berkeley: University of California Press, 1984.

Certeau, Michel de, Dominique Julia and Jacques Revel 'La Beauté du mort: Le concept de "culture populaire"', *Politique aujourd'hui* (December 1970): 3–23.

Chartier, Roger (ed.) *The Culture of Print: Power and the Uses of Print in Early Modern Europe*. Cambridge: Polity; Ithaca: Cornell University Press, 1989.

—— *The Cultural Uses of Print in Early Modern France*. Princeton: Princeton University Press, 1987.

—— 'The Hanged Woman Miraculously Saved: An Occasional', *Culture of Print*, pp. 59–91.

—— 'Leisure and Sociability: Reading Aloud in Early Modern Europe', *Urban Life in the Renaissance*.

Ed. S. Zimmermann and R. F. E. Weissman. Newark: University of Delaware Press; London: Associated University Press, 1989.

—— 'The Practical Impact of Writing', *Passions of the Renaissance*. Vol. 3 of *A History of Private Life*. Ed. Roger Chartier. Cambridge: Harvard University Press, 1989.

Darnton, Robert 'First Steps toward a History of Reading', *Australian Journal of French Studies*, **23**, 1 (1986): 5–30.

Engelsing, Rolf 'Die Perioden der Lesergeschichte in die Neuzeit. Das statistische Ausmass und die soziokulturelle Debeutung der Lektüre', *Archiv für Geschichte des Buchwesen*, **10** (1970): 945–1002.

Ginzburg, Carlo *The Cheese and the Worms: the Cosmos of a Sixteenth-Century Miller*. Trans. John and Anne Tedeschi. Baltimore: Johns Hopkins University Press, 1980.

Harlan, David 'Intellectual History and the Return of Literature', *American Historical Review*, **94** (June 1989): 581–609.

Hébrard, Jean 'Comment Valentin Jamerey-Duval apprit-il à lire? L'autodidaxie exemplaire?' *Pratiques de la lecture*. Ed. Roger Chartier. Marseille: Rivages, 1985.

Jardine, Lisa and Anthony Grafton '"Studied for Actions": How Gabriel Harvey Read his Livy', *Past and Present*, **129** (November 1990): 30–78.

Laufer, Roger 'L'espace visuel du livre ancien', Martin and Chartier, **1**, pp. 478–97.

—— 'Les espaces du livre', Martin and Chartier, **2**: 128–39.

Levine, Lawrence W. *Highbrow/Lowbrow: The Emergence of Cultural Hierarchy in America*. Cambridge: Harvard University Press, 1988.

—— 'William Shakespeare and the American People: A Study in Cultural Transformation', *American Historical Review*, **89** (February 1984): 34–66.

Mandrou, Robert *De la culture populaire aux XVIIe et XVIIIe siècles: La bibliothèque bleue de Troyes*. 1964. Paris: Stock, 1974.

Martin, Henri-Jean and Bruno Delmas *Histoire et pouvoirs de l'écrit*. Paris: Perrin, 1988.

Martin, Henri-Jean and Roger Chartier (eds) *Histoire de l'Edition française*. 2 vols, Paris: Promodis, 1982–84.

McKenzie, D. F. *Bibliography and the Sociology of Texts*. Panizzi Lectures, 1985. London: British Library, 1986.

—— 'Typography and Meaning: The Case of William Congreve', *Buch und Buchandel in Europa im achtzehnten Jahrhundert*. Ed. Giles Barber and Bernhard Fabian. Hamburg: Ernest Hauswedell, 1981.

Ménétra, Jacques-Louis *Journal de ma vie: Jacques-Louis Ménétra, compagnon vitrier au 18e siècle*. Ed. Daniel Roche. Paris: Montalba, 1982.

Patrizi, Giorgio 'Il libro del Cortegiano e la trattatistica sul comportamento', *La prosa*. Part 2 of *Le Forme del testo*. Vol. 3 of *Letteratura italiana*. Torino: Einaudi, 1984: pp. 855–90.

Patrizi, Giorgio and Roger Chartier 'From Texts to Manners: a Concept and its Books: *Civilité* between Aristocratic Distinction and Popular Appropriation', Chartier, *Cultural Uses of Print*, pp. 71–109.

Ricoeur, Paul *Time and Narrative*. Trans. Kathleen McLaughlin and David Pellauer. 3 vols. Chicago: University of Chicago Press, 1984–88.

Saenger, Paul 'Physiologie de la lecture et séparation des mots', *Annales E.S.C.* (1989): 939–52.

—— 'Silent Reading: Its Impact on Late Medieval Script and Society', *Viator*, **13** (1982): 367–414.

Schön, Erich *Der Verlust der Sinnlichkeit oder Die Verwandlungen des Lesers: Mentalitätswandel um 1800*. Stuttgart: Klett-Cotta, 1987.

Spufford, Margaret 'First Steps in Literacy: The Reading and Writing Experiences of the Humblest Seventeenth-Century Autobiographers', *Social History*, **4**, 3 (1979): 407–35.

Stoddard, Roger E. 'Morphology and the Book from an American Perspective', *Printing History*, **9**, 1 (1987): 2–14.

Velay-Vallantin, Catherine 'Tales as a Mirror: Perrault in the Bibliothèque Bleue', Chartier, *Culture of Print*, pp. 92–135.

# Chapter 6

# Adrian Johns

## THE BOOK OF NATURE AND THE
## NATURE OF THE BOOK

Pick up a modern book. This one will do: the one you are looking at right now. What sort of object is this? There are certain features about it of which you can be reasonably confident. Its professed author does indeed exist and did indeed write it. It contains information believed to be accurate, and it professes to impart knowledge to readers like you. It is produced with its author's consent, and it is indeed the edition it claims to be. If the dust jacket announces that it is the product of a given organization – for example the University of Chicago Press – then this too may be believed. Perhaps you may even say to yourself that that fact vouches for the quality of its content. You may safely assume that the book you now hold will have been printed in many copies, and a copy of the same book bought in Australia, say, will be identical in all relevant respects to one bought in the United States or in Great Britain.

Begin to use this object. It should immediately become clear that there are things about its proper utilization of which a reader like you can be equally confident. This book has not been produced with a specific, individual reader in mind. To some extent, at least, it is a commercial product, designed to appeal to purchasers. Its cost may have limited its readership somewhat, but its distribution will still have been fairly widespread, and it may be available for consultation in a number of libraries. Readers will not have to endure any formal vetting or approval process before being permitted to read this book. You yourself are free to carry it around and to lend it to others. You are not free, however – beyond certain legal limits – to reproduce its contents in your own right for commercial gain. Nor may you now proceed to issue translations, epitomes, or abridgments of those contents. It is improbable (but not impossible) that you will choose to declaim the text of this book aloud in a public place, and it is even more unlikely that you will make it the focus of a collective act of commemoration, worship, or similar ritual. Some books are indeed used in these ways, incidentally, but this is probably not going to be one of them. In short, while in some respects this book's usage is up to you, in others it appears to be quite closely constrained.

That we can assume all these things of such an object – that such an object actually exists – derives from our living in what many people call 'print culture'. Such phenomena, we say, are due to printing. Or rather, we would say this, but so infallibly reliable are they that we rarely even have to articulate the relation. It is obvious, self-evident, even necessary. The practical consequence is that we do not have to agonize over the reliability of a published book before we can put it to use. We do not need to undertake investigatory work to confirm that its author does exist and that its text is authorized. No literary spy need be hired to ascertain that it was indeed made by its stated publisher and that its contents will be the same as those of another copy of the same book found in any other place. In our world, all these characteristics are inherent in virtually any published book (and the duties of a 'literary agent' are comparatively mundane). We take them for granted, every day of our lives. We depend on them, and our reliance is, by and large, justified.

It is this very self-evidence that encourages us to ascribe all these characteristics to a technological order of reality. If called upon, we may assert that printed texts are identical and reliable because that is simply what printing *is*. The identification is as momentous as it is straightforward. It has become the point of departure for all current interpretations of print and its cultural consequences, and is the root from which the very concept of 'print culture' has grown.[1] It is thereby also the foundation of a conviction that that culture has rendered possible the establishment of veracious knowledge in modern society. Yet this book [i.e. Johns's book] argues that it is substantially false. Not only that: *The Nature of the Book* maintains that it is probably the most powerful force resisting the acceptance of a truly historical understanding of print and any cultural consequences it may foster.

This book contends that what we often regard as essential elements and necessary concomitants of print are in fact rather more contingent than generally acknowledged. Veracity in particular is, it argues, extrinsic to the press itself, and has had to be grafted onto it. The same may be said of other cognate attributes associated with printing. In short, *The Nature of the Book* claims that the very identity of print itself has had to be *made*. It came to be as we now experience it only by virtue of hard work, exercised over generations and across nations. That labor has long been overlooked, and is not now evident. But its very obscurity is revealing. It was dedicated to effacing its own traces, and necessarily so: only if such efforts disappeared could printing gain the air of intrinsic reliability on which its cultural and commercial success could be built. Recovering it is therefore a difficult task, but one well worth attempting. This book tries accordingly to excavate the complex issues involved in the historical shaping of print – issues that our conventional notion of print culture obscures with all the authority of a categorical definition. *The Nature of the Book* is the first real attempt to portray print culture in the making.

Yet how could print conceivably be anything else? If it were really the result of a significant process of historical construction, then surely we could not now find it so obvious, universal, and undeniable. If it could have developed differently, then surely it would now differ noticeably from place to place, and in any one place it would still bear the traces of its development. We would see the wreckage of failed alternatives all about us. In practical terms, we would indeed have to worry about the specific status of a given printed book in order to use it. Questions of where it had come from, who had made it, and whether or not its putative author acknowledged its content would all need to be posed and answered before we could safely trust any printed book. That they do not constitutes a powerful reason to accept the obvious.

Even a little reflection suggests that there is greater complexity to the subject than this. Any printed book is, as a matter of fact, both the product of one complex set of social and technological processes and also the starting point for another. In the first place, a large number of people, machines, and materials must converge and act together for it to come into existence at all. How exactly they do so will inevitably affect its finished character in a number of ways. In that sense a book is the material embodiment of, if not a consensus, then at least a collective consent. Its identity can be understood accordingly, in terms of these intricate processes. But the story of a book evidently does not end with its creation. How it is then put to use, by whom, in what circumstances, and to what effect are all equally complex issues. Each is worthy of attention in its own right. So a printed book can be seen as a nexus conjoining a wide range of worlds of work. Look closely and you are likely to find simplicity and inevitability in neither the manufacture of an object like this nor its subsequent construal. The processes leading to the deployment of a book and those consequent upon its use both depend on too many contingencies. That in turn means that print cannot be as straightforward as it seems.

One way to appreciate the implications is to examine more closely places where printing exists, but where its cultural consequences seem very different from those familiar to us. There are two such places, separated from us by space and by time. The first may be found in certain regions of the world where, to international publishers' disgust, so-called 'piracy' has become a prevalent commercial practice. You could not be so sure of all those 'selfevident' facts about this book if you had bought your copy in such a place. It might indeed prove reliable. But it might also have been produced by an anonymous manufacturer, and have different contents. Its purported author might have no idea of the claims it contained. Some such companies produce not just unauthorized reprints of existing books, but wholly new texts claiming to be written by best-selling authors. Their products threaten to compromise both the economic production of authorized works and, by generating correspondingly divergent readings, their reception. The potential effects are suggested by the most notorious of all recent controversies to arise from publishing. The author Salman Rushdie was complaining of piracy of his works in Pakistan and India long before the appearance of his *Satanic Verses*. When it did appear, the book was properly published in neither country; the protests that occurred in Lahore and elsewhere, and that first set in train the events leading eventually to Khomeini's fatwa, centered on the public reading of unauthorized copies and photocopied extracts. A Penguin representative even noted that piracy would permit readers to circumvent the Indian government's subsequent ban on the book.[2]

Rushdie's is admittedly an extreme case. But for good or ill, countless authors and publishers have encountered to some degree the loss of control induced by piracy. It means that the experiences associated with print are indeed different from those familiar to most Western readers. And any suggestion that the intrinsic cultural consequences of technology have simply been inadequately realized in such settings would be difficult to endorse. The evidence of recent international trade disputes indicates that modern technology, far from eliminating such practices, may even be facilitating them. The arguments currently raging over such matters are intense and important. Few claim to know how they will end.[3]

The alternative is to look not to other places in our own time, but to other times in our own place. It is possible to argue not only that print may differ from place to place, but also that its nature has changed over time even in our own society. If this is so, the implications are again substantial, but in rather different ways. Such an argument compels us to reappraise where our own concept of print culture comes from, how it developed, when it took hold, and why its sway continues to seem secure.

If an early modern reader picked up a printed book – *De Natura Libri*, perhaps – then he or she could not be immediately certain that it was what it claimed to be, and its proper use might not be so self-evident. Piracy was again one reason: illicit uses of the press threatened the credibility of all printed products. More broadly, ideas about the correct ways to make and use books varied markedly from place to place and time to time. But whatever the cause, it is not easy for us to imagine such a realm, in which printed records were not necessarily authorized or faithful. What could one know in such a realm, and how could one know it? We ourselves routinely rely on stable communications in our making and maintenance of knowledge, whether of the people around us or of the world in which we live. That stability helps to underpin the confidence we feel in our impressions and beliefs. Even the brisk skepticism we may express about certain printed materials – tabloid newspapers, say – rests on it, inasmuch as we feel confident that we can readily and consistently identify what it is that we are scorning. Instability in records would equally rapidly translate into uncertainty of judgment. The most immediate implication, then, would be epistemic.

In a sense, the point is a well-entrenched one. It has been made at least since the sixteenth century, when printers and others took to lauding their craft for its power to preserve. The contrast they drew was with previous scribal forms of reproduction, which they delineated as intrinsically corruptive. It now seems almost indisputable. We should recognize, however, that the first identification of that contrast was partly a product of interest. Printers stood to gain from what was originally a contentious argument, not a straightforward observation. If, on the other hand, it is not printing *per se* that possesses preservative power, but printing put to use in particular ways, then we ourselves may usefully draw some rather different distinctions. We may look not just for differences between print and manuscript reproduction, but for different ways in which the press itself and its products have been (and continue to be) employed. The roots of textual stability may be sought as much in these practices as in the press itself. And knowledge, such as it is, has come to depend on that stability. Here, then, is one way in which a social history of print can prove not just interesting, but consequential. A reappraisal of print in the making can contribute to our historical understanding of the conditions of knowledge itself.

## Tycho Brahe, Galileo Galilei, and the problems of 'print culture'

In 1576 the king of Denmark granted Tycho feudal powers over a small island named Hven, lying in the sound just north of Copenhagen. Here Tycho erected a remarkable castle-observatory, in which he lived and worked for the next two decades. His work at this palatial observatory, which he called Uraniborg, resulted in an unequaled series of observations and interpretations of the heavens. They secured for him a reputation as the greatest of all astronomers. Almost immediately, Tycho himself became an icon of the very enterprise of astronomy. Mathematical practitioners in succeeding generations came to see in him an unimpugnable model of the harmony of nobility and 'mechanic' skill. In the hands of modern historians, moreover, Tycho has again proved a powerful emblem, in two important and revealingly paradoxical respects. First, Uraniborg has become the outstanding Renaissance exemplar of the importance of locale in the making of knowledge.[4] This is an important issue, to be addressed later in this chapter. At the same time, however, Tycho has come to personify the role of print in transcending place and rendering natural knowledge universal. He has thus become emblematic of the transformation of local craft into global science. This latter apotheosis has been due above all to Elizabeth Eisenstein's *The Printing Press as an Agent of Change*. Published in 1979, this is still probably the most influential anglophonic interpretation of the cultural effects of printing. Yet *The Nature of the Book* pursues for the most part a quite different approach from hers. A consideration of Tycho Brahe provides the ideal opportunity to specify how and why it does so.[5]

The unifying concept of Eisenstein's argument is that of 'print culture'. This 'culture' is characterized primarily in terms of certain traits that print is taken to endow on texts. Specifically, those produced in such an environment are subject to conditions of *standardization*, *dissemination*, and *fixity*. The last of these is perhaps the most important. According to Eisenstein, printing meant the mass reproduction of precisely the same text, repeatable on subsequent occasions and in different locations. No longer need any work suffer the increasing corruption that Eisenstein assumes to be endemic to any 'script culture'. She focuses on this attribute of fixity as the most important corollary of the press, seeing it as central to most of the effects of print culture.[6] For example, in conditions of fixity the simple practice of juxtaposing texts became immensely significant. Newly available printed representations of opposing astronomical, anatomical, or other knowledge could be placed side by side, and their viewer could now be confident that conclusions drawn from comparing such reliable texts would be worthwhile. Correspondents on the other side of Europe could do the same, with representations that could be supposed identical.[7] Such

scholars no longer needed to concern themselves primarily with the fidelity of their representations, and were freed from spending their lives eradicating scribal mistakes. It was fixity that
liberated them from such labor and thus made possible the progressive improvement of knowledge.
This is the basis on which Eisenstein's main claim that the Renaissance and Reformation were
rendered permanent by the very permanence of their canonical texts, that nationalism developed
thanks to the stabilization of laws and languages, and that science itself became possible on the
basis of phenomena and theories reliably recorded.[8] With this new foundation of certainty at
their disposal, 'scientists' (as Eisenstein insists on calling them) could begin to develop new doubts
about their previous authority, namely antiquity. The 'Scientific Revolution' was thus inconceivable
without a preceding printing revolution.[9] And for Eisenstein Tycho Brahe personifies both.

Eisenstein's Tycho was an autodidact. This in itself was remarkable: before the printing
revolution, not enough faithful editions could have been amassed in one place to enable him to
teach himself. But while he was doing this, Tycho was able to place authoritative printed
representations of the Copernican and Ptolemaic systems of the heavens side by side before his
eyes. By this simple process of juxtaposition, he could immediately see that there were serious
discrepancies. Later, working on Hven, he instigated a program to rectify the data and theories
on which astronomy was based. He and his assistants labored for years to produce a systematic
corpus of recorded observations of the heavenly bodies, using not only Tycho's own careful
observations but those sent to him by astronomers across central Europe. When ready, Tycho could
then supervise the correct printing of this vital material in his own printing house, using paper
made in his own paper mill. As a result, one nova – 'Tycho's star', as it came to be called – became
'fixed' to the extent that it continued to be shown on celestial globes long after it had disappeared
from the sky.[10]

In this guise has Eisenstein's Tycho entered a current debate over science itself. Bruno Latour
has built an account of the making and power of science on her representation of a print culture,
first in his concept of 'immutable mobiles'[11] and more recently in that of 'mediators'.[12] Latour
identifies the collection and deployment of durable paper entities as the foundation of science's
success. The creation and circulation of such objects, Latour maintains, enabled Tycho to master
natural and social entities that were otherwise beyond reach. He could use print both to capture
heavenly bodies, as Eisenstein claimed, and, furthermore, effectively to turn every observatory
in Europe into an extension of Uraniborg. This he achieved by distributing printed forms on
which astronomers could enter their observations before returning them to the central site of
Hven.[13] In doing so, he pioneered a practice central to the development of modern science. For
this, Latour thinks, is essentially how the modern laboratory sustains its authority too. The Latourian
laboratory is an inscription engine, dedicated to the construction, collation, dispersal, and
accommodation of such materials. It is a compelling and enormously influential argument. And
it is consonant not only with Eisenstein herself, but more extensively still with her inspiration
and bête noire, Marshall McLuhan.[14] Latour's vision of science in action depends on Eisenstein's
'print culture' – and thereby implicitly on McLuhan's 'Gutenberg Galaxy' – to underwrite the
stability of both knowledge and society.[15]

The Tycho of Eisenstein and Latour has become the incarnation of textual, social, and
epistemic order. But just how credible is this Tycho? There is something altogether too neat, too
immaculate, about the figure and his achievements. As Philip Marlowe put it in The Big Sleep, such
testimony displays 'the austere simplicity of fiction rather than the tangled woof of fact'.[16] Maybe
the Tycho so far portrayed will change somewhat if we investigate more closely how his 'mediators'
actually came into being and were put to use. For Tycho does indeed represent perhaps the purest
example of a particular kind of printing, and a particular way of using the products of the press.
Like Regiomontanus before him, and Hevelius after, he controlled his own printing operation.

His was a singular printing house, however. It was as geographically isolated on the island of Hven as it was socially isolated from the companies of the European book trade. It was even physically embedded in the five-meter high, five-meter thick wall that enclosed his entire estate. Such isolation meant, at least in principle, that Tycho could produce books when, for whom, and in whatever form he liked.[17] Works like his *Astronomiae Instauratae Mechanica*, which described Uraniborg in all its glory, were scarcely intended to be *published* at all, but were to be distributed as gifts to patrons at courts and universities. The more prestigious were not just printed books, but hybrids – hand-colored, individualized tributes, presented to their intended recipients on specific dates.[18] Tycho meant to bypass the structures of the international book trade altogether.

The recipient of a book like Tycho's *Astronomiae Instauratae Mechanica* was thus likely to be found in a distinctive place: a royal court or a university. Here a book took its place and gained its meaning only amid a vast arsenal of other objects directed to similar ends. It would be encountered alongside natural curiosities, thaumaturgical wonders, mathematical devices, paintings, musical compositions, alchemical medallions, magical machines, and other books. In such surroundings, every aspect of appearance and handling mattered for creating an impact. The reader of such a work, in such a place, would be consciously engaging in a distinctive system of practices and ideas – in Tycho's case, feudal ones. The giving and receiving of such gifts was an important part of court culture, enmeshed in conventions of status recognition, reciprocation, and reward. This could not fail to affect the way in which that reader regarded the book. It was invested with enhanced credit, being untainted by 'mechanick' influence, and it was accorded the privileged reception due to such a noble gesture.[19] The veracity of its contents warranted respect. They could not be dismissed without cost. Yet at the same time such a gesture all but commanded creative responses – including challenges – from suitably prestigious interlocutors. Tycho's book would now fall subject to the conventions surrounding philosophical and mathematical disputes in these settings. The variables that determined both whether a 'scientific' debate would even take place, and, once battle had been joined, how it would proceed, were local ones: to whom one presented the book, through which channels it was distributed, with which patron it was identified. Disputes like this were affairs of honor, conducted through appropriate intermediaries and champions. Printed books were their vehicles. That was what they were *for*.[20]

When, therefore, Tycho found himself attacked by Nicolai Reymers Baer (or Ursus), a recognized mathematician but a man of low birth whom he himself had accused of plagiarism, a scientific debate was not the principal outcome. Rather unusually, Tycho did in fact deign to reply himself. But he did so with a series of elaborately indignant letters to his fellows across Europe, which he had printed on his press at Uraniborg and circulated in 1596. In this correspondence he recited the tale of Ursus's alleged theft and argued that, whatever the date of Ursus's publication, Tycho had *printed* the cosmology first. Ever willing to recall his opponent's low birth, he even seems to have suggested that Ursus be executed for his presumption. But the more philosophical side of the dispute he delegated to a second, the relatively humble Kepler. The result was Kepler's 'Defense of Tycho against Ursus', a remarkably sophisticated historical argument for the status of astronomical hypotheses and their creators. It was never printed.[21]

Much even of this story could be taken as reinforcing Eisenstein's image. However, two elements make it less confirmatory. The first is that Tycho was extremely atypical in his successful use of print. Other writers regarded him not as representative of their own situation, but as a model that they sought, with widely varying degrees of success, to emulate. Like most icons, he stood for an ideal that was unrealizable. The second is that, as his argument against Ursus implies, even Tycho himself found the ideal impossible to achieve. That was why he built his own printing house and paper mill: he discovered that he could not otherwise obtain acceptable materials and workmanship.[22] Even with these in place, moreover, most of his work remained unprinted until after his death.[23] Latour's preprinted forms, for example, seem to be mythical; Tycho did correspond extensively, but left no trace of having used such objects.[24] And while he began producing the images and descriptions for the *Astronomiae Instauratae Mechanica* as early as 1585, soon after building his printing house, the volume was not completed until thirteen years later. By that time he was in exile in Hamburg – the only place he could find with printers capable of finishing the book, even though he had brought his own press with him from Hven. Taken by his son to the Holy Roman Emperor, the book now became an instrument in Tycho's attempt to secure imperial patronage.[25] This proved successful, and he removed to Prague. But he soon discovered that even here, in the center of the empire, no printer able to undertake his prized star catalogue could be found. He was reduced to circulating hand-copied versions, and the catalogue remained unprinted on his death.[26]

At that point his works began to fall out of court circles altogether. They descended into the hands of the book trade. Even the *Astronomiae Instauratae Mechanica* was reprinted commercially. Such books were likely to be produced to different standards. They stood at risk of piracy and imitation, despite Rudolf II's stern commands forbidding such 'printers' frauds'. They were also likely to be read in different ways, by different people, in different places and for different reasons. Their accreditation became far more insecure. So, for example, the English astronomer royal, John Flamsteed – who, as we shall see, identified himself profoundly with Tycho – dismissed the posthumous printing of his star tables as, quite simply, a 'fraud'.[27] Tycho's inscriptions appear to have become distinctly mutable once they fell out of his control and left the courtly matrix.

If even Tycho Brahe found it so difficult to maintain his printed materials as mobile and immutable, what hope is there of explaining the achievements of less powerful figures in Eisenstein's terms? Attempting to do so would mean attributing to printed books themselves attributes of credibility and persuasion that actually took much work to maintain. It would thereby draw our attention away from important problems that any individual, even Tycho, had to overcome.[28] Talk of 'print culture' is strangely ethereal when compared to Tycho's struggles. It stands oddly disconnected from the professed experiences of real historical figures. For example, who actually printed (and reprinted) Tycho's pages? It is a question worth asking, since Tycho himself spent many frustrating years seeking suitable printers – and the astronomer Christoph Rothmann, at least, believed that Ursus had been able to plagiarize his world system because he had been employed in Tycho's printing house.[29] And how were those pages employed by their recipients? Of what use were they *to them*? How did Tycho ensure that such distant readers took them as authoritative, especially when, as was often the case in early modern testimony about celestial observations, they conflicted with figures produced locally? Eisenstein and Latour begin by decreeing such issues peripheral. *The Nature of the Book* does the opposite. If we are to understand how and why printed texts became trustworthy, it argues, we need to appreciate all of them, in something approaching their full 'woof'.

The disconnected air exhibited by Eisenstein's account is not accidental. In her work, printing itself stands outside history. The press is something '*sui generis*', we are told, lying beyond the reach of conventional historical analysis. Its 'culture' is correspondingly placeless and timeless. It is deemed to exist inasmuch as printed texts *possess* some key characteristic, fixity being the best candidate, and carry it with them as they are transported from place to place. The origins of this property are not analyzed. In fact, the accusations of technological determinism sometimes leveled against Eisenstein may even be wide of the mark, since she consistently declines to specify *any* position on the question of how print culture might emerge from print.[30] But the example of Tycho does suggest that the focus of her approach is *in practice* highly selective. The portrait it generates identifies as significant only the clearest instances of fixity. It regards instances when fixity was not manifested as exceptional failures, and even in the successful cases it neglects the labors through which success was achieved. It identifies the results of those labors instead as powers intrinsic to texts. Readers consequently suffer the fate of obliteration: their intelligence and skill is reattributed to the printed page. Tycho's labors deserve better. To put it brutally, what those labors really tell us is that Eisenstein's print culture does not exist.

There is an alternative. We may consider fixity not as an *inherent* quality, but as a *transitive* one. That is, it may be more useful to reverse our commonsense assumption. We may adopt the principle that fixity exists only inasmuch as it is recognized and acted upon by people — and not otherwise. The consequence of this change in perspective is that print culture itself is immediately laid open to analysis. It becomes a *result* of manifold representations, practices and conflicts, rather than just the monolithic *cause* with which we are often presented.[31] In contrast to talk of a 'print logic' imposed on humanity,[32] this approach allows us to recover the construction of different print cultures in particular historical circumstances. It recognizes that texts, printed or not, cannot compel readers to react in specific ways, but that they must be interpreted in cultural spaces the character of which helps to decide what counts as a proper reading. In short, this recasting has the advantage of positioning the cultural and the social where they should be: at the center of our attention. . . .

## From fixity to credit

A new historical understanding of print is needed. What will it look like? One immediately evident feature will be its regard for the labors of those actually involved in printing, publishing, and reading. Another will be its respect for their own representations of printing, embracing both its prospects and its dangers. The dangers in particular will loom larger and more substantial than they have hitherto. Historians tend to disregard such perils as accidental; early modern readers and writers knew otherwise. . . . Increasingly they articulated responses by which the culture of the learned gentleman could be saved from this 'mechanick art'. Perhaps we should remind ourselves of the extent to which those responses appeared to fail — of the extent to which the print culture of the eighteenth century could be perceived by contemporaries, not as a realization of the rationalizing effects now so often ascribed to the press, but as destabilizing and threatening to civility. Such a stance, artificial though it would be, might help us to distance ourselves from the apparent stability of our own print culture, with its uniform editions, mass reproduction, and typographical fixity. Early modern fears would then begin to appear not as incidental lapses, defined a priori as marginal, but as credible statements of experience. They would finally be recognized as no less substantial than the phenomenon of fixity itself.

*The Nature of the Book* tries to treat all sides of the world of print with equal historiographical respect. In so doing, it inherits and attempts to develop initiatives central to the current state of cultural history. In particular, it reflects the important French field of *histoire du livre*. This field, at first associated with the *Annales* movement, has since the 1950s developed into an academic industry in its own right.[33] At the same time, its approaches have changed substantially. Its original practitioners dedicated themselves to accounting for the effects of printing in terms of quantitative measures of manufacture and distribution. They divided up the realm of print by subject matter and by the social character of purchasers, hoping to arrive at objective indices of cultural change. In fact, fewer useful figures emerged than had been hoped for. But the approach, so representative of *Annales* historiography, nonetheless had — and still has — substantial advantages. Above all, it suited commonsense perceptions of what it is that most properly characterizes print: the large-scale reproduction and distribution of precisely the same objects. Eisenstein's representation of print culture effectively embodies those same perceptions, albeit without the quantification. However, as illustrated by the examples of Galileo and Tycho, there were also costs to such a strategy. One was that it was effectively 'indifferent to the objects themselves'. It assumed that successive editions of a work were essentially the same, whatever their variations in text, format, or appearance. . . . Another, equally serious, disadvantage was that it remained silent about how the objects being counted were employed by readers such that they could have divergent cultural consequences. It could not have explained the different receptions accorded Galileo's *Dialogo*, because it ignored what Roger Chartier calls the 'intellectual "labor"' required to put a book or paper to use.[34]

Chartier himself has been central to efforts to address these costs. He has worked to recover the different modes of labor surrounding printed materials, revealing how readers in local settings could 'appropriate' in different ways the books they read. From this perspective, ways of reading are recognized as 'social and cultural practices'. Like other such practices, they have a history, and one that can be reconstructed. The practical implications prove substantial. Sensitivity to the historical character of these practices often shows that an apparently authoritative text, however 'fixed', could not compel uniformity in the cultures of its reception. In practice, rather the reverse seems to have happened. Local cultures created their own meanings with and for such objects. For example, during the Counter-Reformation, printed images issued in large numbers in an attempt to standardize religious practice instead frequently served as vehicles for continued differentiation. The elements of a printed book – its format, layout, and typography – acted as no more than elements in an instrument, the book itself, that was useful for constructing knowledge. They were the tools, among others, with which users forged readings. In general, we may conclude that print entailed not one but many cultures, and that these cultures of the book were themselves local in character.[35]

As the opening pages of this chapter implied, there was one concern in particular that possessed early modern readers, and that may be used as a key to the rest. Could a printed book be trusted to be what it claimed? Perhaps a reader would be prudent to reserve judgment. On the most obvious level, whether a *Sidereus Nuncius* printed in Frankfurt was really Galileo's text, or an *Astronomiae Instauratae Mechanica* produced in Nuremburg was really Tycho's, could justifiably be doubted. More broadly, the very apprehension that printed books might not be self-evidently creditable was enough to rule out any possibility of their bearing the power attributed to them by most modern historians. And that apprehension was widespread. Piracy and plagiarism occupied readers' minds just as prominently as fixity and enlightenment. Unauthorized translations, epitomes, imitations, and other varieties of 'impropriety' were, they believed, routine hazards. Very few noteworthy publications seemed to escape altogether from such practices, and none at all could safely be regarded as immune a priori. It was regarded as extremely unusual for a book professing knowledge – from lowly almanacs to costly folios – to be published in the relatively unproblematic manner we now assume. Contemporaries had good reason to be wary. Their editions of Shakespeare, Donne, and Sir Thomas Browne were liable to be dubious. So were those of Robert Boyle, not to mention the first 'scientific' journal, the *Philosophical Transactions*. Even Isaac Newton's *Principia* suffered from unauthorized reprinting. From Galileo and Tycho to Newton and John Flamsteed, no significant learned author seemed to escape the kinds of practices soon colloquially subsumed under the label of piracy. This meant that even when a book was not so treated, the possibility that it might be still permeated the negotiations, practices, and conventions by which it was made, distributed, exchanged, and used. If piracy was as widespread as commonly feared, then trusting any printed report without knowledge of those processes could be rash. Profound problems of credit thus attended printed materials of all kinds. Without solutions there could be few meaningful uses for books – and perhaps no durable reasoning from them.

It should not be surprising, then, that contemporaries did not always identify fixity as a central characteristic of print. Surveying the books available to aid ocean navigators, Edmond

Halley, for one, noted that 'the first Editions have generally been the best; frequent Copying most commonly vitiating the Originals'.[36] Even when people did refer to enhanced reliability, it was often in the face of direct evidence to the contrary. Textual corruption of even such closely monitored texts as the Bible actually increased with the advent of print, due to various combinations of piracy and careless printing.[37] The first book reputed to have been printed without any errors appeared only in 1760. Before then, variety was the rule, even within single editions. Martin Luther's German translation of Scripture was actually beaten into print by its first piracy, and in succeeding years the proportion of unauthorized to authorized texts was roughly ninety to one; these included Luther's own translation, newly ascribed to others (including Catholics), and others' work reattributed to him. A century later, the first folio of Shakespeare boasted some six hundred different typefaces, along with non-uniform spelling and punctuation, erratic divisions and arrangement, mispaging, and irregular proofing. No two copies were identical. It is impossible to decide even that any one is 'typical'.[38] In such a world, questions of credit took the place of assumptions of fixity. . . .

When early modern readers determined a book not to be worthy of credit, they could do so on a number of grounds. It was in the attribution of 'piracy', however, that the issues of credibility and print particularly converged. The term seems to have been coined by John Fell, bishop of Oxford, to describe the rapacious practices of London printers and booksellers. It had a technical meaning: a pirate was someone who indulged in the unauthorized reprinting of a title recognized to belong to someone else by the formal conventions of the printing and bookselling community. But it soon came to stand for a wide range of perceived transgressions of civility emanating from print's practitioners. As such, almost any book could, in principle, find itself accounted a piracy, whatever its actual circumstances of production and distribution. Historians of printing have therefore misconstrued instances of alleged piracy in at least two senses. First, they have seen piracy, like fixity, as inherent in the object, and not as a contestable attribution. Second, furthermore, they have assumed cases of piracy to be exceptions, accidental (in the philosophical sense of the word) to the essentially stabilizing character of print. Contemporaries were not so sure of this. Incidents that have been retrospectively dismissed as isolated and exceptional often seemed to them commonplace and representative. They might even be seen as attempts to undermine, and thereby to reform, the whole structure of the book trade. Even when conducted in more humdrum circumstances, moreover, and with less ambitious ends in sight, piracy still had powerful implications. Its apparent prevalence affected the economic and cultural conditions of all printed and written communication. It conditioned the accreditation of printed materials of all sorts, from the humblest ABC to the most elaborate encyclopedia.[39]

For the learned, and for natural philosophers in particular, this had peculiarly important consequences. In the agonistic field of early modern natural knowledge, allegations of piracy readily shaded into charges of plagiarism. Such allegations therefore extended to the reputation of authors. That is, unauthorized printing threatened to 'unauthorize' authors themselves. Even more important, it threatened the credibility to be attributed to their ideas. Like print itself, piracy therefore had *epistemic* as well as *economic* implications: it affected the structure and content of knowledge. For an enterprise like experimental philosophy, in particular, which depended implicitly on the trust accorded to the printed reports issued by its protagonists, the consequences threatened to be nothing short of devastating. . . .

Printers and booksellers were manufacturers of credit. They had to be. The skills of those producing and trading in books, and the perceptions of those using them in learned work, might not intersect harmoniously. Whether or not they did at the moment of publication, moreover, accounts of printers' and booksellers' actions might still be drawn upon later by critics and rivals to challenge the value of any particular book, for example by alleging piracy. When they did succeed in remaining in the background – a rarer achievement than we might suppose – it was likely to be the result of hard and continuing work carried out 'behind the scenes'. . . .

The indispensable agency of printers and booksellers might remain unnoticed, for example, since the credit of their products depended on its being so. They themselves developed sophisticated ways of ensuring that they stayed just sufficiently in the background to avoid suspicion of either subterfuge or authorship. But in disputes the character of a bookseller or printer mattered. For readers attuned to its significance, anonymity itself might then become a source of suspicion.[40] Historians can put the resulting allegations to use as evidence. They need no longer be complicit in the cabal by their own silence. . . .

The sources of print culture are therefore to be sought in civility as much as in technology, and in historical labors as much as in immediate cause and effect. The 'printing revolution', if there was one, consisted of changes in the conventions of handling and investing credit in textual materials, as much as in transformations in their manufacture. The point deserves to be stressed explicitly. I do not question that print enabled the stabilization of texts, to some extent; although fixity was far rarer and harder to discern in early modern Europe than most modern historians assume. I do, however, question the character of the link between the two. Printed texts were not intrinsically trustworthy. When they were in fact trusted, it was only as a result of hard work. Fixity was in the eye of the beholder, and its recognition could not be maintained without continuing effort. At no point could it be counted on to reside irremissibly in the object itself, and it was always liable to contradiction. Those faced with using the press to create and sustain knowledge thus found themselves confronting a culture characterized by nothing so much as indeterminacy. If printing held no necessary bond to truth, neither did it show a necessary bond to falsity or corruption. Each link remained vulnerable to dispute. It is this epistemic indeterminacy that lends the history of the book its powerful impact on cultural history. Understanding how it could be overcome to make knowledge and hence cultural change is what the history of the book is for.

## Notes

1   For this term, see below, pp. 10–11, and Eisenstein, *Printing Press*, I, 43–159. I am not sure of its genesis; Eisenstein, its prime recent exponent, seems to take it from McLuhan (e.g., *Gutenberg Galaxy*, 146–9).

2   *The Times*, 24 November 1984; Appignanesi and Maitland, *Rushdie File*, 42; Pipes, *Rushdie Affair*, 24, 85, 113, 201–2.

3   These disputes extend far beyond 'copyright' as conventionally understood, and include conventions now being forged to cover the 'inventions' and 'texts' produced in areas such as biotechnology and genome research. The economic, cultural, and moral implications at stake in these, as in the battles raging over computer and music software, are truly massive. For confrontations between the USA and China over the latter, see Faison, 'Copyright Pirates'.

4   Hannaway, 'Laboratory Design'. Shackelford has responded to Hannaway, with more heat than really necessary, in 'Tycho Brahe'.

5   Eisenstein, *Printing Press*, abridged as *Printing Revolution*. For examples of Eisenstein's influence in a range of fields, see Tribble, *Margins and Marginality*, 3–4; Neuschel, *Word of Honor*, chap. 6; Olson, *World on Paper*, 37 and passim; Rose, *Authors and Owners*, 3–4; Sommerville, *Secularization*, 48, 70, 79, 178, 180, 219 n. 1; Anderson, *Imagined Communities*, 30–49; Eamon, *Science and the Secrets of Nature*, 6–9, 94–6; Lowood and Rider, 'Literary Technology and Typographic Culture' (where 'typographic culture' and 'print culture' are indistinguisable). Many more could be cited. It is difficult to be sure, but I would estimate that Tycho Brahe is referred to at least as frequently in *Printing Press* as any other Renaissance figure.

6   Eisenstein, *Printing Press*, 71–88, 113–26.

7   Eisenstein, *Printing Press*, 74–5, 597; *Printing Revolution*, 42–88. It is worth pointing out that these phenomena are similar to those attributed by anthropologists to the invention of writing, e.g., in Goody, *Logic of Writing*, 134–8, 174.

8   Eisenstein, *Printing Press*, 80, 117, 180–2, 200–10, 212, 646. The argument about nationalism has since been developed more thoroughly by Anderson in *Imagined Communities*, esp. 41–9.

9   Eisenstein, *Printing Press*, 107, 186, 193–4, 197, 640; Hunter, 'Impact of Print'; Leed, 'Elizabeth Eisenstein's *The Printing Press as an Agent of Change*'.

10  Eisenstein, *Printing Press*, 577, 583–4, 593, 596–603, 623–5, 629–30, 640, 699.

11  Latour, *Science in Action*, 52, 132–44, 226; Latour, 'On the Powers of Association'; Latour, 'Visualization and Cognition'. Compare also Latour, 'Give Me a Laboratory'; Latour and Woolgar, *Laboratory Life*, 45–53, 69–88; and Callon, Law, and Rip, *Mapping the Dynamics of Science and Technology*, 7–14, 35–99.

12  Latour, *We Have Never Been Modern*, 77–82, 128–9, 138; Latour, 'Technology Is Society Made Durable', 104–6, 127; Latour, 'Where Are the Missing Masses'? 237.

13  Latour, *Science in Action*, 52, 132–44, 226–7; Latour, 'Drawing Things Together'; Latour, 'Visualization and Cognition', 11–14; Latour, 'Politics of Explanation', 159; Callon, Law, and Rip, 'Putting Texts in Their Place', 223, 228–9.

14  A plausible summary of McLuhan's views in relation to Latour's might run as follows. Like Latour, McLuhan urged the importance of what he called the 'network' as a category of analysis, important in deciding ways of perceiving the world. He too identified a railway system as the representative network par excellence (compare Latour, *We Have Never Been Modern*, 117; and Latour, *Aramis*). What McLuhan's networks achieve – what lends them their power – is their ability to produce changes in scale. They permit individuals and organizations to localize and universalize by allowing them to magnify and reduce traces of the things on which they wish to operate to roughly the same size without destroying them. The 'message' of his networks is that they permit such control; and what is perceived as reality is in fact the current state of competing networks in dynamic interaction. The boundary between natural and social must therefore be forgotten when considering them. In such a world of natural/social hybrids, power comes from 'translation'. This is the agency by which we 'enlarge the scope of [our] action' and affect sites distant from ourselves. See McLuhan, *Understanding Media*, 3–21, 56–61, 89–105, 338–45, 346–59; compare Latour, *Science in Action*, 108–21, 223–32, 247–57, and *We Have Never Been Modern*, 10–12, 49–142. A reassessment of McLuhan is, I think, overdue, though attention to his work is currently reviving. Eisenstein herself roundly denied following him, but with an insistence and a perseverance that almost amounted to protesting too much: e.g., *Printing Press*, ix–xi, xvii, 40–1, 88, 129, 171.

15  Compare Shapin, 'Following Scientists Around', 541, 545–6.

16  Chandler, *Chandler Collection*, I, 143.

17  Thoren, *Lord of Uraniborg*, 144.

18  Brahe, *Astronomiae Instauratae Mechanica* (1598); Brahe, *Opera Omnia*, V, 317–8. A list of known copies with their recipients is in Norlind, *Tycho Brahe*, 286–93.

19  Westman, 'Astronomer's Role'. See also Hannaway, 'Laboratory Design'; and compare Eamon, 'Court, Academy and Printing House', 41.

20  In addition to the works of Biagioli and Hannaway cited here, see Findlen, 'Economy of Exchange'; Findlen, 'Courting Nature', esp. 61; Moran, *Alchemical World*, esp. 9, 93–4, 97, 110–2; Smith, *Business of Alchemy*, 49–50; Daston, 'Factual Sensibility'; and Davis, 'Beyond the Market'. Compare also the difficulties experienced by Becher in translating commercial documents for courtly readers: Smith, *Business of Alchemy*, 139.

21  Brahe, *Epistolarum Astronomicarum Libri*, 33–4, 148–51; Brahe, *Opera Omnia*, VI, 61–2, 179; Jardine, *Birth of History and Philosophy of Science*, 9–28 and *passim* (15 for Ursus's peasant background); Dreyer, *Tycho Brahe*, 183; Rosen, *Three Imperial Mathematicians*. Tycho's decision

to strike at Ursus personally (which Kepler, for one, found surprising) may well be related to the fact that, as Hannaway points out, his status was feudal in origin; Tycho was not a courtier. See Hannaway, 'Laboratory Design', 589 n. II. For Tycho's conflicts see also Gingerich and Westman, *Wittich Connection* (which contrasts Tycho's treatment of Ursus to his response to the relatively well-born Wittich), and Thoren, *Lord of Uraniborg*. I am grateful to Robert Westman for conversations about this affair, which remains one of the  more controversial among scholars of early modern astronomy.

22   Brahe, *Opera*, VI, 224, 365 n; VII, 214, 274; IX, 175; X, 302. Even with the mill in working order, he remained reliant on the cooperation of nearby parishioners to provide raw materials, as they were exhorted to do in regular 'rag sermons'.

23   In particular, the star catalogue (circulated only in manuscript until years after Tycho's death, and then inaccurately printed) and the *Astronomiae Instauratae Progymnasmata* (begun at Uraniborg, but completed only under the aegis of his heirs in 1602).

24   I have found no trace of these preprinted forms in Tycho's *Opera Omnia*, nor in any relevant secondary authority. I am also unable to find Latour's source for this central claim; it may well derive from an imaginative reading of certain passages in Eisenstein's *Printing Press*, e.g., 626–7.

25   Brahe, *Opera*, V, 317–8; VIII, 166, 177, 388.

26   Thoren, *Lord of Uraniborg*, 150, 185–7, 367, 381–97, 414–5, 421, 478. Tycho had planned to present the catalogue to Rudolf II on New Year's Day, apparently a customary occasion for gift-giving: Kaufmann, *Mastery of Nature*, 106. For Rudolf II's undertaking to provide a 'new Uraniborg', see Brahe, *Opera*, VIII, 178, 188. It is also likely, of course, that Tycho's circulation of the catalogue in manuscript was intended to enhance its status as a collectible object.

27   Brahe, *Astronomiae Instauratae Mechanica* (1602); Curtius, *Historia Cœlestis*; Flamsteed, *Preface to John Flamsteed's 'Historia Cœlestis Britannica'*, 99–100. For Rudolf's condemnation of 'Typographorum fraudem', see Brahe, *Opera*, II, 9.

28   Compare Schaffer, 'Eighteenth Brumaire', 178–92, on the concept of the 'ideal reader'.

29   Dreyer, *Tycho Brahe*, 184 n. 1.

30   Eisenstein, *Printing Press*, e.g., 159, 166–8, 609 n, 89–90, 702–3. See also Grafton, 'Importance of Being Printed'. The fact that Eisenstein is simultaneously too provincial (thus missing the contingent elements of print culture by her lack of a comparative perspective) and not local enough (thus missing the work needed to make print culture at all) may be inferred from Cohen's discussion in *Scientific Revolution*, 357–67.

31   Compare the discussions of power in Latour, 'On the Powers of Association', and Latour, 'Technology Is Society Made Durable'. This suggestion has obvious resonances with certain works in critical theory, such as Fish, *Is There a Text in This Class?* Since my aim is primarily historical I shall not be making many explicit links with such material, though the parallel deserves to be noted. Compare also McKenzie, *Bibliography and the Sociology of Texts*.

32   E.g., Kernan, *Printing Technology, Letters and Samuel Johnson*, 48 ff.

33   Its origin is conventionally dated to the appearance in 1958 of Febvre and Martin's *L'Apparition du Livre* (which has appeared in English translation as *The Coming of the Book*). Perhaps its most ambitious recent product has been Martin, *History and Power of Writing*. I have surveyed the field and its implications at greater length in Johns, 'Science and the Book'.

34   Chartier, *Cultural History*, 33–4.

35   These and similar points have been made in many contexts: Chartier, *Order of Books*, 16–17; Chartier, 'Culture as Appropriation'; Chartier, 'Publishing Strategies', 155–60; Chartier, 'Practical Impact of Writing', 122–6; Chartier, *Culture of Print*, 1–5; Chartier, 'Du Livre au Lire'; Chartier, *Cultural Uses of Print*, 3–12, 70; Chartier, *Lectures et Lecteurs*; Chartier, 'Texts, Printings, Readings'; Chartier, *Passions of the Renaissance*, 1–11, 110–59, 326–61, 362–95; Bourdieu and Chartier, 'La Lecture'; Martin, 'Pour une Histoire de la Lecture'; de Certeau, 'Reading as Poaching'; Darnton, 'History of Reading'; McKenzie, 'Typography and Meaning';

McKenzie, *Bibliography and the Sociology of Texts*; Martin and Vezin, *Mise en Page*. On the specific theme of *mise en page* see also Laufer, 'L'Espace Visuel du Livre Ancien'; Laufer, 'Espaces du Livre'; Pastoureau, 'L'Illustration du Livre'. Compare also the fascinating discussion of 'kitsch' in Clark, 'Scientific Revolution in the German Nations', 97–8.

36   *Atlas Maritimus & Commercialis*, i–iii.

37   Black, 'Printed Bible'. Eisenstein dismisses Black's argument out of hand: *Printing Press*, 80.

38   Newman, 'Word Made Print', 106–7 and *passim*; de Grazia, *Shakespeare Verbatim*, 15–19, 42; Kernan, *Printing Technology*, 48.

39   An inspiration for this treatment, as for other aspects of this book, has come from medieval history. Medievalists have devoted much attention to activities of 'forgery' and 'plagiarism'. They have constructed a sophisticated historiography addressing the diversity of acts since subsumed under such labels, immersing the subject in a detailed and authoritative treatment of the cultural uses of writing and reading in general. Medieval 'forgery' is appropriately seen as a form of truth-creation, justified (and perhaps even determined) by contemporary ideas about the nature and purposes of writing. It was also extraordinarily common. Perhaps half the documents known from Merovingian times are by our lights fake, and two-thirds of the documents known to have been issued to ecclesiastics before 1100 would now be reckoned forgeries. See Grafton, *Forgers and Critics*, 24–5, 30–32; Clanchy, *From Memory to Written Record*, 118–20, 231–57; Stock, *Implications of Literacy*, 59–87; Constable, 'Forgery and Plagiarism'. For a robust contrasting view, see Brown, '*Falsitas pia sive Reprehensibilis*'. For these medievalists' perspectives on print – which deserve more attention than they have received – see Clanchy, 'Looking Back', and Rouse and Rouse, *Authentic Witnesses*, 449–66.

40   For example, in his attacks on Ursus, Tycho Brahe was given to remarking upon his antagonist's book's having been published without a printer's name, as was customary for 'notorious libels': Jardine, *Birth of History and Philosophy of Science*, 16.

## References

### Primary sources

*Atlas Maritimus & Commercialis; Or, a General View of the World, so far as relates to Trade and Navigation*. London: printed for J. and J. Knapton, W. and J. Innys, J. Darby, A. Bettesworth, J. Osborn, T. Longman, J. Senex, E. Symon, A. Johnston, and the executors of W. Taylor, 1728.

Brahe, Tycho. *Astronomiae Instauratae Mechanica*. Wandesbek: n.p., 1598.

Brahe, Tycho. *Astronomiae Instauratae Mechanica*. Nuremburg: Levinus Hulsius, 1602.

Brahe, Tycho. *Epistolarum Astronomicarum Libri*. Vol. 1. Uraniborg: from the author's printing house, 1596.

Brahe, Tycho. *Opera Omnia*, 15 vols. Edited by J. L. E. Dreyer. Copenhagen: Gyldendal.

Curtius, A. [Lucius Barettus, pseud.]. *Historia Cœlestis*. Augsburg: S. Utzschneider, 1666; reissue Ratisbon: J. C. Emmrich, 1672.

Flamsteed, J. *The Preface to John Flamsteed's 'Historia Cœlestis Britannica' (1725)*. Translated and edited by A. D. Johnson and A. Chapman. London: National Maritime Museum, 1982.

### Secondary sources

Anderson, B. *Imagined Communities: Reflections on the Origin and Spread of Nationalism*. Rev. ed. London: Verso, 1983.

Appignanesi, L. and S. Maitland, eds. *The Rushdie File*. London: Fourth Estate, 1989.

Barber, G., and B. Fabian, eds. *Buch und Buchhandel in Europa im Achtzehnten Jahrhundert*. Hamburg: Hauswedell, 1981.

Biagioli, M. *Galileo, Courtier: The Practice of Science in the Culture of Absolutism*. Chicago: University of Chicago Press, 1993.

Biagioli, M. 'Galileo the Emblem Maker'. *Isis* 81 (1990): 230–58.

Biagioli, M. 'Galileo's System of Patronage'. *History of Science* 28 (1990): 1–62.

Biagioli, M. 'Playing with the Evidence'. *Early Science and Medicine* 1 (1996): 70–105.

Bijker, W. E., and J. Law, eds. *Shaping Technology / Building Society: Studies in Sociotechnical Change*. Cambridge: MIT Press, 1992.

Black, M. H. 'The Printed Bible'. In Greenslade, *Cambridge History of the Bible*, 408–75.

Bourdieu, P., and R. Chartier. 'La Lecture: Une Pratique Culturelle'. In Chartier, *Pratiques de la Lecture*, 218–39.

Brown, E. A. R. '*Falsitas pia sive Reprehensibilis*: Medieval Forgers and their Intentions'. In *Fälschungen in Mittelalter: Internationaler Kongress der Monumenta Germaniae Historica München, 16–19 September 1986. Teil I: Kongressdaten und Festvorträge Literatur und Fälschung*, 101–19. Hanover: Hahnsche Buchhandlung, 1988.

Burke, P., ed. *New Perspectives on Historical Writing*. Cambridge: Polity, 1991.

Callon, M., J. Law, and A. Rip. 'Putting Texts in Their Place'. In Callow, Law, and Rip, *Mapping the Dynamics of Science and Technology*, 221–30.

Callon, M., J. Law, and A. Rip, eds. *Mapping the Dynamics of Science and Technology: Sociology of Science in the Real World*. Basingstoke: Macmillan, 1986.

Chandler, R. *The Chandler Collection*. 3 vols. London: Picador, 1983–4.

Chartier, R. *Cultural History: Between Practices and Representations*. Translated by L. G. Cochrane. Cambridge: Polity, 1988.

Chartier, R. *The Cultural Uses of Print in Early Modern France*. Translated by L. G. Cochrane. Princeton: Princeton University Press, 1987.

Chartier, R. 'Culture as Appropriation: Popular Cultural Uses in Early Modern France'. In Kaplan, *Understanding Popular Culture*, 229–53.

Chartier, R. 'Du Livre au Lire'. In Chartier, *Pratiques de la Lecture*, 62–88.

Chartier, R. *Lectures et Lecteurs dans la France d'Ancien Régime*. Paris: Editions du Seuil, 1987.

Chartier, R. *The Order of Books: Readers, Authors, and Libraries in Europe between the Fourteenth and Eighteenth Centuries*. Translated by L. G. Cochrane. Cambridge: Polity Press, 1994.

Chartier, R., ed. *Passions of the Renaissance*. Vol. III of *A History of Private Life*, edited by P. Ariès and G. Duby. Translated by A. Goldhammer. Cambridge, Mass.: Belknap, 1989.

Chartier, R. 'The Practical Impact of Writing'. In Chartier, *Passions of the Renaissance*, 111–59.

Chartier, R. 'Publishing Strategies and What the People Read, 1530–1660'. In Chartier, *Cultural Uses of Print in Early Modern France*, 145–82.

Chartier, R., 'Texts, Printings, Readings.' In Hunt, *The New Cultural History*, 154–75.

Chartier, R., ed. *The Culture of Print: Power and the Uses of Print in Early Modern Europe*. Translated by L. G. Cochrane. Cambridge: Polity Press, 1989.

Chartier, R., ed. *Pratiques de la Lecture*. Marseille: Editions Rivages, 1985.

Chartier, R., and H.-J. Martin, eds. *Histoire de l'Edition Française*. 2d ed. 4 vols. Paris: Fayard, 1989–91.

Clanchy, M. T. *From Memory to Written Record: England 1066–1307*. London: Edward Arnold, 1979.

Clanchy, M. T. 'Looking Back from the Invention of Printing'. In Resnick, *Literacy in Historical Perspective*, 7–22.

Clark, W. 'The Scientific Revolution in the German Nations'. In Porter and Teich, *Scientific Revolution in National Context*, 90–114.

Cohen, H. F. *The Scientific Revolution: A Historiographical Inquiry*. Chicago: University of Chicago Press, 1994.

Constable, G. 'Forgery and Plagiarism in the Middle Ages'. *Archiv für Diplomatik* 29 (1983): 1–41.

Darnton, R. *The Great Cat Massacre, and Other Episodes in French Cultural History*. London: Allen Lane, 1984.

Darnton, R. 'History of Reading'. In Burke, *New Perspectives*, 140–67.

Daston, L. 'The Factual Sensibility'. *Isis* 79 (1988): 452–70.

Davis, N. Z. 'Beyond the Market: Books as Gifts in Sixteenth-Century France'. *Transactions of the Royal Historical Society*, 5th ser., 33 (1983): 69–88.

De Certeau, M. *The Practice of Everyday Life*. Translated by S. Rendall. Berkeley and Los Angeles: University of California Press, 1984.

De Certeau, M. 'Reading as Poaching'. In de Certeau, *Practice of Everyday Life*, 165–76.

De Grazia, M. *Shakespeare Verbatim: The Reproduction of Authenticity and the 1790 Apparatus*. Oxford: Oxford University Press, 1991.

Dreyer, J. L. E. *Tycho Brahe: A Picture of Scientific Life and Work in the Sixteenth Century*. Edinburgh: A. and C. Black, 1890.

Eamon, W. 'Court, Academy and Printing House: Patronage and Scientific Careers in Late Renaissance Italy'. In Moran, *Patronage and Institutions*, 25–50.

Eamon, W. *Science and the Secrets of Nature: Books of Secrets in Medieval and Early Modern Culture*. Princeton: Princeton University Press, 1994.

Eisenstein, E. L. *The Printing Press as an Agent of Change: Communications and Cultural Transformations in Early-Modern Europe*. 2 vols. Cambridge: Cambridge University Press, 1979.

Eisenstein, E. L. *The Printing Revolution in Early Modern Europe*. Cambridge: Cambridge University Press, 1983.

Faison, S. 'Copyright Pirates Prosper in China Despite Promises'. *New York Times*, 20 February 1996, 1, 4.

Febvre, L., and H.-J. Martin. *The Coming of the Book: The Impact of Printing 1450–1800*. Translated by D. Gerard. London: Verso, 1984. Originally published as *L'Apparition du Livre* (Paris: Albin Michel, 1958).

Findlen, P. 'The Economy of Exchange in Early Modern Italy'. In Moran, *Patronage and Institutions*, 5–24.

Fish, S. *Is There a Text in This Class? The Authority of Interpretive Communities*. Cambridge: Harvard University Press, 1980.

Gingerich, O., and R. S. Westman. *The Wittich Connection: Conflict and Priority in late Sixteenth-Century Cosmology*. Philadelphia: American Philosophical Society, 1988. Vol. 78, no. 7 of *Transactions of the American Philosophical Society*.

Goody, J. *The Logic of Writing and the Organization of Society*. Cambridge: Cambridge University Press, 1986.

Grafton, A. *Forgers and Critics: Creativity and Duplicity in Western Scholarship*. London: Collins and Brown, 1990.

Grafton, A. 'The Importance of Being Printed'. *Journal of Interdisciplinary History* 11 (1980): 265–86.

Greenslade, S. L., ed. *The Cambridge History of the Bible*, vol. 3. Cambridge: Cambridge University Press, 1963.

Hannaway, O. 'Laboratory Design and the Aim of Science: Andreas Libavius versus Tycho Brahe'. *Isis* 77 (1986): 585–610.

Hunt, L., ed. *The New Cultural History*. Berkeley and Los Angeles: University of California Press, 1989.

Hunter, M. 'The Impact of Print'. *The Book Collector* 28 (1979): 335–52.

Jardine, N. *The Birth of History and Philosophy of Science: Kepler's 'A Defence of Tycho Against Ursus' with Essays on Its Provenance and Significance*. Cambridge: Cambridge University Press, 1984.

Johns, A. 'Science and the Book in Modern Cultural Historiography'. *Studies in History and Philosophy of Science* 35 (1997): 23–59.

Kaplan, S. L., ed. *Understanding Popular Culture: Europe from the Middle Ages to the Nineteenth Century*. Berlin: Mouton, 1984.

Kaufmann, T. D. *The Mastery of Nature: Aspects of Art, Science, and Humanism in the Renaissance*. Princeton: Princeton University Press, 1993.

Kernan, A. *Printing Technology, Letters and Samuel Johnson*, Princeton: Princeton University Press, 1987.

Knorr-Cetina, K. D., and M. Mulkay, eds. *Science Observed: Perspectives on the Social Study of Science*. London: Sage, 1983.

Latour, B. *Aramis, ou l'Amour des Techniques*. Paris: Découverte, 1992.

Latour, B. 'Drawing Things Together'. In Lynch and Woolgar, *Representation in Scientific Practice*, 19–68.

Latour, B. 'Give Me a Laboratory and I Will Raise the World'. In Knorr-Cetina and Mulkay, *Science Observed*, 141–70.

Latour, B. 'On the Powers of Association'. In Law, *Power, Action and Belief*, 264–80.

Latour, B. 'The Politics of Explanation: An Alternative'. In Woolgar, *Knowledge and Reflexivity*, 155–76.

Latour, B. *Science in Action: How to Follow Scientists and Engineers through Society*. Milton Keynes: Open University Press, 1987.

Latour, B. 'Technology Is Society Made Durable'. In Law, *Sociology of Monsters*, 103–31.

Latour, B. 'Visualization and Cognition: Thinking with Eyes and Hands'. *Knowledge and Society* 6 (1986): 1–40.

Latour, B. *We Have Never Been Modern*. Translated by C. Porter. New York: Harvester Wheatsheaf, 1993.

Latour, B. 'Where Are the Missing Masses? The Sociology of a Few Mundane Artifacts'. In Bijker and Law, *Shaping Technology / Building Society*, 225–58.

Latour, B., and S. Woolgar. *Laboratory Life: The Social Construction of Scientific Facts*. London: Sage, 1979.

Laufer, R. 'Les Espaces du Livre'. In Chartier and Martin, *Histoire de l'Edition Française*, II, 156–72.

Laufer, R. 'L'Espace Visuel du Livre Ancien'. In Chartier and Martin, *Histoire de l'Edition Française*, I, 579–601.

Law, J., ed. *Power, Action and Belief: A New Sociology of Knowledge?* London: Routledge and Kegan Paul, 1986.

Law, J., ed. *A Sociology of Monsters: Essays on Power, Technology and Domination*. London: Routledge, 1991.

Leed, E. J. 'Elizabeth Eisenstein's *The Printing Press as an Agent of Change* and the Structure of Communications Revolutions'. *American Journal of Sociology* 88 (1982): 413–29.

Lowood, H. E., and R. E. Rider. 'Literary Technology and Typographic Culture: The Instrument of Print in Early Modern Science'. *Perspectives on Science* 2 (1994): 1–37.

Lynch, M., and S. Woolgar, eds. *Representation in Scientific Practice*. Cambridge: MIT Press, 1990.

Martin, H.-J. *The History and Power of Writing*. Translated by L. G. Cochrane. Chicago: University of Chicago Press, 1994.

Martin, H.-J. *Le Livre Française sous l'Ancien Régime*. Paris: Promodis, 1987.

Martin, H.-J. 'Pour une Histoire de la Lecture'. In Martin, *Le Livre Française*, 227–46.

Martin, H.-J., and J. Vezin, eds. *Mise en Page et Mise en Texte du Livre Manuscrit*. Paris: Promodis, 1990.

McKenzie, D. F. *Bibliography and the Sociology of Texts*. London: British Library, 1985.

McKenzie, D. F. 'Typography and Meaning: The Case of William Congreve'. In Barber and Fabian, *Buch und Buchhandel*, 81–123.

McLuhan, M. *The Gutenberg Galaxy*. London: Routledge and Kegan Paul, 1962.

McLuhan, M. *Understanding Media: The Extension of Man*. 1964. Reprint, London: Ark, 1987.

Moran, B. T. *The Alchemical World of the German Court: Occult Philosophy and Chemical Medicine in the Circle of Moritz of Hessen (1572–1632)*. Stuttgart: F. Steiner, 1991.

Moran, B. T., ed. *Patronage and Institutions: Science, Technology and Medicine at the European Court 1500–1700*. Woodbridge: Boydell, 1991.

Neuschel, K. B. *Word of Honor: Interpreting Noble Culture in Sixteenth-Century France*. Ithaca: Cornell University Press, 1989.

Newman, J. O. 'The Word Made Print: Luther's 1522 *New Testament* in an Age of Mechanical Reproduction'. *Representations* 11 (1985): 95–133.

Norlind, W. *Tycho Brahe: En levnadsteckning med nya bidrag belysande hans liv och verk*. Lund, Sweden: C. W. K. Gleerup, 1970.

Olson, D. R. *The World on Paper: The Conceptual and Cognitive Implications of Writing and Reading*. Cambridge: Cambridge University Press, 1994.

Pastoureau, M. 'L'Illustration du Livre: Comprendre ou Rêver'? In Chartier and Martin, *Histoire de l'Edition Française*, 1, 602–28.

Pipes, D. *The Rushdie Affair: The Novel, the Ayatollah, and the West*. London: Carol Publishing, 1990.

Porter, R., and M. Teich, eds. *The Scientific Revolution in National Context*. Cambridge: Cambridge University Press, 1992.

Resnick, D. P., ed. *Literacy in Historical Perspective*. Washington: Library of Congress, 1983.

Rose, M. *Authors and Owners: The Invention of Copyright*. Cambridge: Harvard University Press, 1993.

Rosen, E. *Three Imperial Mathematicians: Kepler Trapped between Tycho Brahe and Ursus*. New York: Abaris, 1986.

Rouse, M. A., and R. H. Rouse. *Authentic Witnesses: Approaches to Medieval Texts and Manuscripts*. Notre Dame, Ind.: University of Notre Dame Press, 1991.

Schaffer, S. J. 'The Eighteenth Brumaire of Bruno Latour'. *Studies in History and Philosophy of Science* 22 (1991): 174–92.

Shapin, S. 'Following Scientists Around'. *Social Studies of Science* 18 (1988): 533–50.

Smith, P. H. *The Business of Alchemy: Science and Culture in the Holy Roman Empire*. Princeton: Princeton University Press, 1994.

Sommerville, C. J. *The Secularization of Early Modern England: From Religious Culture to Religious Faith*. New York: Oxford University Press, 1992.

Stock, B. *The Implications of Literacy: Written Language and Models of Interpretation in the Eleventh and Twelfth Centuries*. Princeton: Princeton University Press, 1983.

Thoren, V. E. *The Lord of Uraniborg: A Biography of Tycho Brahe*. Cambridge: Cambridge University Press, 1990.

Tribble, E. B. *Margins and Marginality: The Printed Page in Early Modern England*. Charlottesville: University Press of Virginia, 1993.

Westman, R. S. 'The Astronomer's Role in the Sixteenth Century: A Preliminary Study'. *History of Science* 18 (1980): 105–47.

Woolgar, S., ed. *Knowledge and Reflexivity: New Frontiers in the Sociology of Knowledge*. London: Sage, 1988.

# Chapter 7

# Pierre Bourdieu

# THE FIELD OF CULTURAL PRODUCTION

## The struggle for the dominant principle of hierarchization

The literary or artistic field is at all times the site of a struggle between the two principles of hierarchization: the heteronomous principle, favourable to those who dominate the field economically and politically (e.g. 'bourgeois art') and the autonomous principle (e.g. 'art for art's sake'), which those of its advocates who are least endowed with specific capital tend to identify with degree of independence from the economy, seeing temporal failure as a sign of election and success as a sign of compromise.[1] The state of the power relations in this struggle depends on the overall degree of autonomy possessed by the field, that is, the extent to which it manages to impose its own norms and sanctions on the whole set of producers, including those who are closest to the dominant pole of the field of power and therefore most responsive to external demands (i.e. the most heteronomous); this degree of autonomy varies considerably from one period and one national tradition to another, and affects the whole structure of the field. Everything seems to indicate that it depends on the value which the specific capital of writers and artists represents for the dominant fractions, on the one hand in the struggle to conserve the established order and, perhaps especially, in the struggle between the fractions aspiring to domination within the field of power (bourgeoisie and aristocracy, old bourgeoisie and new bourgeoisie, etc.), and on the other hand in the production and reproduction of economic capital (with the aid of experts and cadres).[2] All the evidence suggests that, at a given level of overall autonomy, intellectuals are, other things being equal, proportionately more responsive to the seduction of the powers that be, the less well endowed they are with specific capital.[3]

The struggle in the field of cultural production over the imposition of the legitimate mode of cultural production is inseparable from the struggle within the dominant class (with the opposition between 'artists' and 'bourgeois') to impose the dominant principle of domination (that is to say – ultimately – the definition of human accomplishment). In this struggle, the artists and writers who are richest in specific capital and most concerned for their autonomy are considerably weakened by the fact that some of their competitors identify their interests with the dominant principles of hierarchization and seek to impose them even within the field, with the support of the temporal powers. The most heteronomous cultural producers (i.e. those with least symbolic capital) can offer the least resistance to external demands, of whatever sort.

To defend their own position, they have to produce weapons, which the dominant agents (within the field of power) can immediately turn against the cultural producers most attached to their autonomy. In endeavouring to discredit every attempt to impose an autonomous principle of hierarchization, and thus serving their own interests, they serve the interests of the dominant fractions of the dominant class, who obviously have an interest in there being only one hierarchy. In the struggle to impose the legitimate definition of art and literature, the most autonomous producers naturally tend to exclude 'bourgeois' writers and artists, whom they see as 'enemy agents'. This means, incidentally, that sampling problems cannot be resolved by one of those arbitrary decisions of positivist ignorance which are dignified by the term 'operational definition': these amount to blindly arbitrating on debates which are inscribed in reality itself, such as the question as to whether such and such a group ('bourgeois' theatre, the 'popular' novel, etc.) or such and such an individual claiming the title of writer or artist (or philosopher, or intellectual, etc.) belongs to the population of writers or artists or, more precisely, as to who is legitimately entitled to designate legitimate writers or artists.

The preliminary reflections on the definitions of the object and the boundaries of the population, which studies of writers, artists and, especially, intellectuals, often indulge in so as to give themselves an air of scientificity, ignore the fact, which is more than scientifically attested, that the definition of the writer (or artist, etc.) is an issue at stake in struggles in every literary (or artistic, etc.) field.[4] In other words, the field of cultural production is the site of struggles in which what is at stake is the power to impose the dominant definition of the writer and therefore to delimit the population of those entitled to take part in the struggle to define the writer. The established definition of the writer may be radically transformed by an enlargement of the set of people who have a legitimate voice in literary matters. It follows from this that every survey aimed at establishing the hierarchy of writers predetermines the hierarchy by determining the population deemed worthy of helping to establish it. In short, the fundamental stake in literary struggles is the monopoly of literary legitimacy, i.e., *inter alia*, the monopoly of the power to say with authority who are authorized to call themselves writers; or, to put it another way, it is the monopoly of the power to consecrate producers or products (we are dealing with a world of belief and the consecrated writer is the one who has the power to consecrate and to win assent when he or she consecrates an author or a work – with a preface, a favourable review, a prize, etc.).

While it is true that every literary field is the site of a struggle over the definition of the writer (a universal proposition), the fact remains that scientific analysts, if they are not to make the mistake of universalizing the particular case, need to know that they will only ever encounter historical definitions of the writer, corresponding to a particular state of the struggle to impose the legitimate definition of the writer. There is no other criterion of membership of a field than the objective fact of producing effects within it. One of the difficulties of orthodox defence against heretical transformation of the field by a redefinition of the tacit or explicit terms of entry is the fact that polemics imply a form of recognition; adversaries whom one would prefer to destroy by ignoring them cannot be combated without consecrating them. The '*Théâtre libre*' effectively entered the sub-field of drama once it came under attack from the accredited advocates of bourgeois theatre, who thus helped to produce the recognition they sought to prevent. The '*nouveaux philosophes*' came into existence as active elements in the philosophical field – and no longer just that of journalism – as soon as consecrated philosophers felt called upon to take issue with them.

The *boundary* of the field is a stake of struggles, and the social scientist's task is not to draw a dividing line between the agents involved in it by imposing a so-called operational definition, which is most likely to be imposed on him by his own prejudices or presuppositions, but to describe a *state* (long-lasting or temporary) of these struggles and therefore of the frontier delimiting the territory held by the competing agents. One could thus examine the characteristics of this boundary, which may or may not be institutionalized, that is to say, protected by conditions of entry that are tacitly and practically required (such as a certain cultural capital) or explicitly codified and legally guaranteed (e.g. all the forms of entrance examination aimed at ensuring a *numerus clausus*). It would be found that one of the most significant properties of the field of cultural production, explaining its extreme dispersion and the conflicts between rival principles of legitimacy, is the extreme permeability of its frontiers and, consequently, the extreme diversity of the 'posts' it offers, which defy any unilinear hierarchization. It is clear from comparison that the field of cultural production demands neither as much inherited economic capital as the economic field nor as much educational capital as the university sub-field or even sectors of the field of power such as the top civil service – or even the field of the 'liberal professions'.[5] However, precisely because it represents one of the *indeterminate sites* in the social structure, which offer ill-defined posts, waiting to be made rather than ready made, and therefore extremely elastic and undemanding, and career paths which are themselves full of uncertainty and extremely dispersed (unlike bureaucratic careers, such as those offered by the university system), it attracts agents who differ greatly in their properties and dispositions but the most favoured of whom are sufficiently secure to be able to disdain a university career and to take on the risks of an occupation which is not a 'job' (since it is almost always combined with a private income or a 'bread-and-butter' occupation).

> The 'profession' of writer or artist is one of the least professionalized there is, despite all the efforts of 'writers' associations', 'Pen Clubs', etc. This is shown clearly by (*inter alia*) the problems which arise in classifying these agents, who are able to exercise what they regard as their main occupation only on condition that they have a secondary occupation which provides their main income (problems very similar to those encountered in classifying students).

The most disputed frontier of all is the one which separates the field of cultural production and the field of power. It may be more or less clearly marked in different periods, positions occupied in each field may be more or less totally incompatible, moves from one universe to the other more or less frequent and the overall distance between the corresponding populations more or less great (e.g. in terms of social origin, educational background, etc.). . . .

## The structure of the field

Heteronomy arises from *demand*, which may take the form of personal *commission* (formulated by a 'patron' in Haskell's sense of a protector or client) or of the sanction of an autonomous *market*, which may be *anticipated* or *ignored*. Within this logic, the *relationship to the audience* and, more exactly, economic or political interest in the sense of interest in success and in the related economic or political profit, constitute one of the bases for evaluating the producers and their products. Thus, strict application of the autonomous principle of hierarchization means that producers and products will be distinguished according to their degree of success with the audience, which, it tends to be assumed, is evidence of their interest in the economic and political profits secured by success.

The duality of the principles of hierarchization means that there are few fields (other than the field of power itself) in which the antagonism between the occupants of the polar positions is more total (within the limits of the interests linked to membership of the field of power). Perfectly illustrating the distinction between relations of interaction and the structural relations which constitute a field, the polar individuals may never meet, may even ignore each other systematically, to the extent of refusing each other membership of the same class, and yet their practice remains determined by the negative relation which unites them. It could be said that the agents involved in the literary or artistic field may, in extreme cases, have nothing in common except the fact of taking part in a struggle to impose the legitimate definition of literary or artistic production.[6]

The hierarchy by degree of real or supposed dependence on audience, success or the economy itself overlaps with another one, which reflects the degree of specific consecration of the audience, i.e. its 'cultural' quality and its supposed distance from the centre of the specific values. Thus, within the sub-field of production-for-producers, which recognizes only the specific principle of legitimacy, those who are assured of the recognition of a certain fraction of the other producers, a presumed index of posthumous recognition, are opposed to those who, again from the standpoint of the specific criteria, are relegated to an inferior position and who, in accordance with the model of heresy, contest the legitimation principle dominant within the autonomous sub-field, either in the name of a new legitimation principle or in the name of a return to an old one. Likewise, at the other pole of the field, that of the market and of economic profit, authors who manage to secure 'high-society' successes and bourgeois consecration are opposed to those who are condemned to so-called 'popular' success – the authors of rural novels, music-hall artists, *chansonniers*, etc.

## The duality of literary hierarchies and genres

In the second half of the nineteenth century, the period in which the literary field attained its maximum autonomy, these two hierarchies seem to correspond, in the first place, to the specifically cultural hierarchy of the genres – poetry, the novel and drama – and secondarily to the hierarchy of ways of using them which, as is seen clearly in the case of the theatre and especially the novel, varies with the position of the audiences reached in the specifically cultural hierarchy.

> The literary field is itself defined by its position in the hierarchy of the arts, which varies from one period and one country to another. Here one can only allude to the effect of the hierarchy of the arts and in particular to the dominance which poetry, an intellectual art, exerted until the sixteenth century over painting, a manual art,[7] so that, for example, the hierarchy of pictorial genres tended to depend on their distance – as regards the subject and the more or less erudite manner of treating it – from the most elaborate model of poetic discourse. It is well known that throughout the nineteenth century, and perhaps until Duchamp, the stereotype which relegated the painter to a purely manual genre ('stupid as a painter') persisted, despite the increasing exchange of symbolic services (partly, no doubt, because the painters were generally less rich in cultural capital than the writers; we know, for example, that Monet, the son of a Le Havre grocer, and Renoir, the son of a Limoges tailor, were much intimidated in the meetings at the Café Guerbois on account of their lack of education). In the case of the field of painting, autonomy had to be won from the literary field too, with the emergence of specific criticism and above all the will to break free from the writers and their discourse by producing an intrinsically polysemic work beyond all discourse, and a discourse about the work which declares the essential inadequacy of all discourse. The history of the relations between Odilon Redon and the writers – especially Huysmans – shows in an exemplary way how the painters had to fight for autonomy from the *littérateur* who enhances the illustrator by advancing himself, and to assert the irreducibility of the pictorial work (which the professional critic is more ready to recognize).[8] The same logic can be used to

analyse the relations between the composers and the poets: the concern to use without being used, to possess without being possessed, led some composers (Debussy, for example) to choose to set mediocre texts which would not eclipse them.

From the economic point of view, the hierarchy is simple and relatively stable, despite cyclical fluctuations related to the fact, for example, that the more economically profitable the various genres, the more strongly and directly they are affected by recession.[9] At the top of the hierarchy is drama, which, as all observers note, secures big profits – provided by an essentially bourgeois, Parisian, and therefore relatively restricted, audience – for a very few producers (because of the small number of theatres). At the bottom is poetry, which, with a few, very rare exceptions (such as a few successes in verse drama), secures virtually zero profit for a small number of producers. Between the two is the novel, which can secure big profits (in the case of some naturalist novels), and sometimes very big profits (some 'popular' novels), for a relatively large number of producers, from an audience which may extend far beyond the audience made up of the writers themselves, as in the case of poetry, and beyond the bourgeois audience, as in the case of theatre, into the *petite bourgeoisie* or even, especially through municipal libraries, into the 'labour aristocracy'.

From the point of view of the symbolic hierarchies, things are less simple since, as can be seen from Figure 7.1, the hierarchies according to distance from profits are intersected by hierarchies internal to each of the genres (i.e. according to the degree to which the authors and works conform to the specific demands of the genre), which correspond to the social hierarchy of the audiences. This is seen particularly clearly in the case of the novel, where the hierarchy of specialities corresponds to the hierarchy of the audiences reached and also, fairly strictly, to the hierarchy of the social universes represented.

The complex structure of this space can be explained by means of a simple model taking into account, on the one hand, the properties of the different arts and the different genres considered as economic enterprises (price of the product, size of the audience and length of the economic cycle) and, on the other hand, the negative relationship which, as the field increasingly imposes its own logic, is established between symbolic profit and economic profit, whereby *discredit* increases as the audience grows and its specific competence declines, together with the value of the recognition implied in the act of consumption. The different kinds of cultural enterprise vary, from an economic standpoint, in terms of the unit price of the product (a painting, a play, a concert, a book, etc.) and the cumulative number of purchasers; but they also vary according to the length of the production cycle, particularly as regards the speed with which profits are obtained (and, secondarily, the length of time during which they are secured). It can be seen that, although the opposition between the short cycle of products which sell rapidly and the long cycle of products which sell belatedly or slowly is found in each of the arts, they differ radically in terms of the mode of profit acquisition and therefore, because of the connection that is made between the size of the audience and its *social quality*, in terms of the objective and subjective relationship between the producer and the market.

There is every difference between painters who, even when they set themselves in the avant-garde, can expect to sell to a *small number of connoisseurs* (nowadays including museums) works whose value derives partly from the fact that they are produced in limited numbers, and the writer who has to sell to an audience that is as wide as possible but one which, as it grows, is no doubt less and less composed of connoisseurs. This explains why the writers are, much more than painters, condemned to have an ambivalent attitude towards sales and their audience. They tend to be torn between

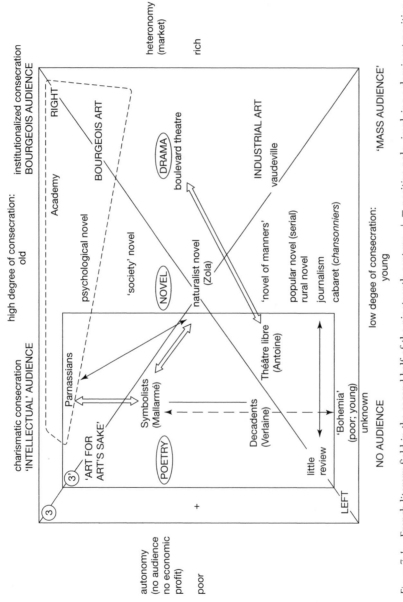

*Figure 7.1* French literary field in the second half of the nineteenth century; + = positive pole, implying a dominant position, − = negative pole, implying a dominated position

the internal demands of the field of production, which regard commercial successes as suspect and push them towards a heretical break with the established norms of production and consumption, and the expectations of their vast audience, which are to some degree transfigured into a populist mission (Zola, for example, endeavoured to invoke a popular legitimacy to sublimate commercial success by transforming it into popular success). As for the dramatists, they are situated between the two poles. Established playwrights can earn big profits through repeated performances of the same work; for the others, as for composers, the main difficulty is to get their work performed at all.

Thus, the relationship of mutual exclusion between material gratification and the sole legitimate profit (i.e recognition by one's peers) is increasingly asserted as the exclusive principle of evaluation as one moves down the hierarchy of economic gratifications. Successful authors will not fail to see this as the logic of resentment, which makes a virtue of necessity; and they are not necessarily wrong, since the absence of audience, and of profit, may be the effect of privation as much as a refusal, or a privation converted into refusal. The question is even harder to resolve, at least summarily, since the collective bad faith which is the basis of a universe sustained by denial of the economy helps to support the effort of individual bad faith which makes it possible to experience failure in this world as election hereafter, and the incomprehension of the audience as an effect of the prophetic refusal to compromise with the demands of an audience attached to old norms of production. It is no accident that ageing, which dissolves the ambiguities, converting the elective, provisional refusals of adolescent bohemian life into the unrelieved privation of the aged, embittered bohemian, so often takes the form of an emotional crisis, marked by reversals and abjurations which often lead to the meanest tasks of 'industrial art', such as vaudeville or cabaret, and of political pamphleteering. But, at the other end of the scale of economic profits, a homologous opposition is established, through the size of the audience, which is partly responsible for the volume of profit, and its recognized social quality, which determines the value of the consecration it can bestow, between bourgeois art, which has an honoured place in society, and industrial art, which is doubly suspect, being both mercantile and 'popular'.

Thus we find three competing principles of legitimacy. First, there is the specific principle of legitimacy, i.e., the recognition granted by the set of producers who produce for other producers, their competitors, i.e. by the autonomous self-sufficient world of 'art for art's sake', meaning art for artists. Secondly, there is the principle of legitimacy corresponding to 'bourgeois' taste and to the consecration bestowed by the dominant fractions of the dominant class and by private tribunals, such as *salons*, or public, state-guaranteed ones, such as academies, which sanction the inseparably ethical and aesthetic (and therefore political) taste of the dominant. Finally, there is the principle of legitimacy which its advocates call 'popular', i.e. the consecration bestowed by the choice of ordinary consumers, the 'mass audience'. It can be seen that poetry, by virtue of its restricted audience (often only a few hundred readers), the consequent low profits, which make it the disinterested activity *par excellence*, and also its prestige, linked to the historical tradition initiated by the Romantics, is destined to charismatic legitimation which is given to only a few individuals, sometimes only one per generation and, by the same token, to a continuous struggle for the monopoly of poetic legitimacy and a succession of successful or abortive revolutions: Parnassians against Romantics, Symbolists against Parnassians, neo-classicists against the early Symbolists, neo-Symbolists against neo-classicists.

Although the break between poetry and the mass readership has been virtually total since the late nineteenth century (it is one of the sectors in which there are still many books published at the author's expense), poetry continues to represent the ideal model of literature for the least cultured consumers. As is confirmed by analysis of a dictionary of writers (such as the *Annuaire national des lettres*), members of the working and lower middle classes who write have too elevated an idea of literature to write realist novels; and their production does indeed consist essentially of poetry – very conventional in its form – and history.

The theatre, which directly experiences the immediate sanction of the bourgeois public, with its values and conformisms, can earn the institutionalized consecration of academies and official honours, as well as money. The novel, occupying a central position in both dimensions of the literary space, is the most dispersed genre in terms of its forms of consecration. It was broadly perceived as typical of the new mercantile literature, linked to the newspaper and journalism by serialization and the impact they gave to it, and above all because, unlike the theatre, it reached a 'popular' audience; with Zola and Naturalism it achieved a wide audience which, although socially inferior, provided profits equivalent to those of the theatre, without renouncing the specific demands of the art and without making any of the concessions typical of 'industrial' literature; and, with the 'society' novel [*roman mondain*], it was even able to win bourgeois consecrations previously reserved for the theatre. . . .

## Structure and change

Changes which affect the structure of the field as a whole, such as major re-orderings of the hierarchy of genres, presuppose a concordance between internal changes, directly determined by modification of the chances of access to the literary field, and external changes which supply the new producers (the Romantics, the Naturalists, the Symbolists and the whole *fin-de-siècle* literary and artistic movement) and their new products with socially homologous consumers. This is not true to the same extent of changes which affect only the field of restricted production. These endless changes, which arise from the very structure of the field, i.e. the synchronic oppositions between the antagonistic positions (dominant/dominated, consecrated/novice, old/young, etc.), are largely independent of the external changes which may seem to determine them because they accompany them chronologically. This is true even when such internal changes owe their subsequent consecration mainly to a 'miraculous' encounter between (largely) independent causal series. This argument would have to be demonstrated, for example, in cases such as that of Mallarmé (or Debussy, or Fauré), in which the two opposing theses – the absolute independence of pure art, led solely by the autonomous logic of its own development, and the thesis of direct dependence on the historical situation – can both find arguments. Indeed, the *coincidence* between the properties of the social experience which privileged consumers may have had in a certain historical conjuncture and the properties of the work, in which are expressed the necessities inscribed in a *position* progressively instituted and containing a whole past and potential history, and in a *disposition*, itself progressively constituted through a whole social trajectory, is a sort of trap laid for those who, seeking to escape from internal reading of the work or the internal history of artistic life, condemn themselves to the *short circuit* of directly interrelating the period and the work. In such cases, both the period and the work are reduced to a few schematic properties, selected for the purposes of the argument, as in the Lukácsian or Goldmannian mythology of the writer as the unconscious spokesman of a group, which is simply an inversion of the Romantic myth of the poet *vates*. . . .

Without ever being a direct reflection of them, the internal struggles depend for their outcome on the correspondence they may have with the external struggles between the classes (or between the fractions of the dominant class) and on the reinforcement which one group or another may derive from them, through homology and the consequent synchronisms. When the newcomers are not disposed to enter the cycle of simple reproduction, based on recognition of the 'old' by the 'young' – homage, celebration, etc. – and recognition of the 'young' by the 'old' – prefaces, co-optation, consecration, etc. – but bring with them dispositions and position-takings which clash with the prevailing norms of production and the expectations of the field, they cannot succeed without the help of external changes. These may be political breaks, such as revolutionary crises, which change the power relations within the field (the 1848 revolution strengthened the dominated pole, causing writers to shift, very temporarily no doubt, to the left, i.e. towards 'social art'), or deep-seated changes in the audience of consumers who, because of their affinity with the new producers, ensure the success of their products.

> In fact, one never observes either total submission – and erudite reproduction presupposes a form of regulated innovation, even an obligatory, limited, break with predecessors – or an absolute break – and a break with the immediately preceding generation (fathers) is often supported by a return to the traditions of the next generation back (grandfathers), whose influence may have persisted in a shadowy way. For example, though there is no need to emphasize how much the Parnassians maintain of the Romantic tradition, it is less obvious that they tapped a current of Hellenism which had lived on despite the Romantic break with imitations of Antiquity. Events such as the publication in 1819 of the works of Chénier, impregnated with Hellenism, the discovery of the Venus de Milo in 1820, the Greek War of Independence and the death of Byron, turn attention to Grecian Antiquity; Greek myths are revitalized by the prose poems of Ballanche (*Antigone*, 1814; *Orphée*, 1827), and at the height of the Romantic period, there are the works of Paul-Louis Courier and Maurice de Guérin.

In the field of restricted production, each change at any one point in the space of positions objectively defined by their difference, their *écart*, induces a generalized change – which means that one should not look for a specific *site* of change. It is true that the initiative of change falls almost by definition on the newcomers, i.e. the youngest, who are also those least endowed with specific capital: in a universe in which to exist is to differ, i.e. to occupy a distinct, distinctive position, they must assert their difference, get it known and recognized, get themselves known and recognized ('make a name for themselves'), by. endeavouring to impose new modes of thought and expression, out of key with the prevailing modes of thought and with the doxa, and therefore bound to disconcert the orthodox by their 'obscurity' and 'pointlessness'. The fact remains that every new position, in asserting itself as such, determines a displacement of the whole structure and that, by the logic of action and reaction, it leads to all sorts of changes in the position-takings of the occupants of the other positions.

> As well as the countless labels too obviously intended to *produce* the differences they claim to express, one could point to 'manifestos', which often have no other content than the aim of distinguishing themselves from what already exists, even if they do not all go so far as the founders of the *Revue de métaphysique et de morale* and explicitly declare the aim of 'doing something different'.[10] As for the transformations induced by the effect of the structure, a characteristic example can be found in the changes which the Naturalist novelists made in their style and themes – Maupassant with *Une vie* and Zola with *Le rêve* – in response to the success of the psychological novel,[11]

and one may even suspect that the effect of the field explains some aspects of the sociology of Durkheim (classified by Bouglé among the representatives of the 'spiritualist initiative', alongside Bergson and Laberthonnière), in which Bouglé sees 'an effort to underpin and justify spiritualist tendencies in a new way'.[12]

Because position-takings arise quasi-mechanically – that is, almost independently of the agents' consciousness and wills – from the relationship between positions, they take relatively invariant forms, and being determined relationally, negatively, they may remain virtually empty, amounting to little more than a *parti pris* of refusal, difference, rupture. Structurally 'young' writers, i.e. those less advanced in the process of consecration (who may be biologically almost as old as the 'old' writers they seek to oust),[13] will refuse everything their 'elders' (in terms of legitimacy) are and do, and in particular all the indices of *social ageing*, starting with the signs of consecration, internal (academies, etc.) or external (success), whereas the 'old' writers will regard the social non-existence (in terms of success and consecration) and also the 'obscurity' of their young rivals as evidence of the voluntaristic, forced character of some endeavours to overtake them (as Zola puts it, 'a gigantic, empty pretension').

> The 'young' have an interest in describing every advance in the internal hierarchy of the sub-field of restricted production as an advance in the hierarchy of the field of cultural production as a whole, and therefore contest the independence of the internal hierarchy (cf. the contesting of the 'mandarins'). They may point to the fact that while 'bourgeois' consecration (academy places, prizes, etc.) is primarily awarded to writers who produce for the mass market, it also goes to the most acceptable members of the consecrated avant-garde (and the *Académie Française* has always made room, to a varying extent at different periods, for producers from the field of restricted production). It is also clear that the opposition, within the 'autonomous field, between professional writers, whose activity obliges them to lead an organized, regular, quasi-bourgeois life, and the 'bohemian' world of 'proletaroid intellectuals' who live on the odd jobs of journalism, publishing or teaching, may give rise to a political division, as was seen at the time of the Paris Commune.[14]

The history of the field arises from the struggle between the established figures and the young challengers. The ageing of authors, schools and works is far from being the product of a mechanical, chronological, slide into the past; it results from the struggle between those who have made their mark (*fait date* – 'made an epoch') and who are fighting to persist, and those who cannot make their own mark without pushing into the past those who have an interest in stopping the clock, eternalizing the present stage of things.[15] 'Making one's mark', initiating a new epoch, means winning recognition, in both senses, of one's difference from other producers, especially the most consecrated of them; it means, by the same token, creating a new position, ahead of the positions already occupied, in the vanguard. (Hence the importance, in this struggle for survival, of all distinctive marks, such as the names of schools or groups – words which make things, distinctive signs which produce existence.) The agents engaged in the struggle are both contemporaries – precisely by virtue of the struggle which synchronizes them – and separated by time and in respect of time: avant-garde writers have contemporaries who recognize them and whom they recognize – apart from other avant-garde writers – only in the future; consecrated writers recognize their contemporaries only in the past. The emergence of a group capable of 'making an epoch' by imposing a new, advanced position is accompanied by a displacement of the structure of temporally hierarchized positions opposed within a given field; each of them moves a step down the temporal hierarchy which is at the same time a social hierarchy; the avant-garde is separated by a generation from the consecrated avant-garde which is itself separated by another generation from the avant-garde that was already consecrated when it made its own entry into the field.[16] Each author, school or work which 'makes its mark' displaces the whole series of earlier authors, schools or works. As Shklovsky points out,[17] each period excludes certain hackneyed subjects: Tolstoy forbids mention of the 'romantic Caucasus' or moonlight, while Chekhov, in one of his juvenilia, lists the newly unacceptable commonplaces. Because the whole series of pertinent changes is present, practically, in the latest (just as the six figures already dialled on a telephone are present in the seventh), a work or an aesthetic movement is irreducible to any other situated elsewhere in the series; and *returns* to past styles (frequent in painting) are never 'the same thing', since they are separated from what they return to by negative reference to something which was itself the negation of it (or the negation of the negation, etc.).[18]

That is why, in an artistic field which has reached an advanced stage of this history, there is no place for *naïfs*; more precisely, the history is immanent to the functioning of the field, and to meet the objective demands it implies, as a producer but also as a consumer, one has to possess the whole history of the field. . . .

## Positions and dispositions

### The meeting of two histories

To understand the practices of writers and artists, and not least their products, entails understanding that they are the result of the meeting of two histories: the history of the positions they occupy and the history of their dispositions. Although position helps to shape dispositions, the latter, in so far as they are the product of independent conditions, have an existence and efficacy of their own and can help to shape positions. In no field is the confrontation between positions and dispositions more continuous or uncertain than in the literary and artistic field. Offering positions that are relatively uninstitutionalized, never legally guaranteed, therefore open to symbolic challenge, and non-hereditary (although there are specific forms of transmission), it is the arena *par excellence* of struggles over job definition. In fact, however great the effect of position – and we have seen many examples of it – it never operates mechanically, and the relationship between positions and *position-takings* is mediated by the dispositions of the agents.

> Likewise, morphological changes never produce their effects *mechanically*. For example, the influx, in the 1850s, of a large number of writers living with precarious means on the lower edges of the field is retranslated into a redefinition of the post, i.e. of the image of the writer, his sartorial symbolism, his political attitudes, his preferred haunts (café rather than *salon*), etc. More generally, a *numerus clausus* has the effect of protecting a definition of the function, and an increase in the number of legitimate performers of the function – whether architects, doctors or teachers – is sufficient to change the function more or less radically, through the objective devaluation which automatically ensues, the struggle by the guardians of the post to preserve the rarity which previously defined it, and the endeavours of the new occupants to adapt the position to their dispositions.

The 'post' of poet as it presents itself to the young aspirant in the 1880s is the crystallized product of the whole previous history. It is a position in the hierarchy of literary crafts, which, by a sort of effect of *caste*, gives its occupants, subjectively at least, the assurance of an essential superiority over all other writers; the lowest of the poets (Symbolist, at this time) sees himself as superior to the highest of the (Naturalist) novelists.[20] It is a set of 'exemplary figures' – Hugo, Gautier, etc. – who have composed the character and assigned roles, such as, for intellectuals (after Zola), that of the intellectual as the champion of great causes. It is a cluster of representations – that of the 'pure' artist, for example, indifferent to success and to the verdicts of the market – and mechanisms which, through their sanctions, support them and give them real efficacy. In short, one would need to work out the full social history of the *long, collective labour* which leads to the progressive invention of the crafts of writing, and in particular to *awareness* of the *fundamental law* of the field, i.e. the theory of art for art's sake, which is to the field of cultural production what the axiom 'business is business' (and 'in business there's no room for feelings') is to the economic field.[21] Nor, of course, must one forget the role of the mechanism which, here as elsewhere, leads people to make a virtue of necessity, in the constitution of the field of cultural production as a space radically independent of the economy and of politics and, as such, amenable to a sort of pure theory. The work of real emancipation, of which the 'post' of artist or poet is the culmination, can be performed and pursued only if the post encounters the appropriate dispositions, such as disinterestedness and daring, and the (external) conditions of these virtues, such as a private income. In this sense, the collective invention which results in the post of writer or artist has to be endlessly repeated, even if the objectification of past discoveries and the recognition ever more widely accorded to an activity of cultural production that is an end in itself, and the will to emancipation that it implies, tend constantly to reduce the cost of this permanent reinvention. The more the autonomizing process advances, the more possible it becomes to occupy the position of producer without having the properties – or not all of them, or not to the same degree – that had to be possessed to produce the position; the more, in other words, the newcomers who head for the most 'autonomous' positions can dispense with the more or less heroic sacrifices and breaks of the past.

The position of 'pure' writer or artist, like that of intellectual, is an institution of freedom, constructed against the 'bourgeoise' (in the artists' sense) and against institutions – in particular against the state bureaucracies, academies, salons, etc. – by a series of breaks, partly cumulative, but sometimes followed by regressions, which have often been made possible by diverting the resources of the market – and therefore the 'bourgeoisie' – and even the stage bureaucracies.[22] Owing to its objectively contradictory intention, it exists only at the lowest degree of institutionalization, in the form of words ('avant-garde', for example) or models (the avant-garde writer and his or her exemplary deeds) which constitute a tradition of freedom and criticism, and also, but above all, in the form of a field of competition, equipped with its own institutions (the paradigm of which might be the *Salon des refusés* or the little avant-garde review) and articulated by mechanisms of competition capable of providing incentives and gratification for emanicipatory endeavours. For example, the acts of prophetic denunciation of which *J'accuse* is the paradigm have become, since Zola, and perhaps especially since Sartre, so intrinsic to the personage of the intellectual that anyone who aspires to a position (especially a dominant one) in the intellectual field has to perform such exemplary acts.[23] This explains why it is that the producers most freed from external constraints – Mallarmé, Proust, Joyce or Virginia Woolf – are also those who have taken most advantage of a historical heritage accumulated through collective labour against external constraints.

Having established, in spite of the illusion of the constancy of the thing designated, which is encouraged by the constancy of the words artist, writer, bohemian, academy, etc., what each of the positions is at each moment, one still has to understand how those who occupy them have been formed and, more precisely, the shaping of the dispositions which help to lead them to these positions and to define their way of operating within them and staying in them. The field, as a field of possible forces, presents itself to each agent as a *space of possibles* which is defined in the relationship between the structure of average chances of access to the different positions (measured by the 'difficulty' of attaining them and, more precisely, by the relationship between the number of positions and the number of competitors) and the dispositions of each agent, the subjective basis of the perception and appreciation of the objective chances. In other words, the objective probabilities (of economic or symbolic profit, for example) inscribed in the field at a given moment only become operative and active through 'vocations', 'aspirations' and 'expectations', i.e. in so far as they are perceived and appreciated through the schemes of perception and appreciation which constitute a habitus. These schemes, which reproduce in their own logic the fundamental divisions of the field of positions – 'pure art' / 'commercial art', 'bohemian' / 'bourgeois', 'left bank' / 'right bank', etc. – are one of the mediations through which dispositions are adjusted to positions. Writers and artists, particularly newcomers, do not react to an 'objective reality' functioning as a sort of stimulus valid for every possible subject, but to a 'problem-raising situation', as Popper puts it; they help to create its intellectual and affective 'physiognomy' (horror, seduction, etc.) and therefore even the symbolic force it exerts on them. A position as it appears to the (more or less adequate) 'sense of investment' which each agent applies to it presents itself either as a sort of necessary locus which beckons those who are made for it ('vocation') or, by contrast, as an impossible destination, an unacceptable destiny or one that is acceptable only as temporary refuge or a secondary, accessory position. This sense of social direction which orients agents, according to their modesty or daring, their disinterestedness or thirst for profit, towards the risky, long-term investments of journalism, serials or the theatre, is the basis of the astonishingly close correspondence that is found between positions and dispositions, between the social characteristics of 'posts' and the social characteristics of the agents who fill them. The correspondence is such that in all cases of coincidence and concordance in which the position is in a sense materialized in the dispositions of its occupants, it would be equally wrong to impute everything solely to position or solely to dispositions.

> The mechanistic model that is, more or less consciously, put into operation when social origin, or any other variable, is made the principle of a linear series of determinations – e.g. father's occupation, more or less crudely defined, determining position, e.g. occupational position, which in turn determines opinions – totally ignores the effects of the field, in particular those which result from the way in which the influx of newcomers is quantitatively and qualitatively regulated.[24] Thus the absence of statistical relation between the agents' social origin and their *position-takings* may result from an unobserved transformation of the field and of the relationship between social origin and *position-taking*, such that, for two successive generations, the same dispositions will lead to different *position-takings*, or even opposing ones (which will tend to cancel each other out).

There is nothing mechanical about the relationship between the field and the habitus. The space of available positions does indeed help to determine the properties expected and even demanded of possible candidates, and therefore the categories of agents they can attract and above all *retain*; but the perception of the space of possible positions and trajectories and the appreciation of the value each of them derives from its location in the space depend on these dispositions. It follows as a point of method that one cannot give a full account of the relationship obtaining at a given moment between the space of positions and the space of dispositions, and, therefore, of the set of *social trajectories* (or constructed biographies),[25] unless one establishes the configuration, at the moment, and at the various critical turning-points in each career, of the space of available possibilities (in particular, the economic and symbolic hierarchy of the genres, schools, styles, manners, subjects, etc.), the social value attached to each of them, and also the meaning and value they received for the different agents or classes of agents in terms of the socially constituted categories of perception and appreciation they applied to them.

It would be quite unjust and futile to reject this demand for complete reconstitution on the ground (which is undeniable) that it is difficult to perform in practice and in some cases impossible (for example, a special study would be required in order to determine, for each relevant period, the *critical points* in the trajectories corresponding to each field, which are often unquestioningly assumed to be situated where they are today). Scientific progress may consist, in some cases, in identifying all the presuppositions and begged questions implicitly mobilized by the seemingly most impeccable research, and in proposing programmes for fundamental research which would really raise all the questions which ordinary research treats as resolved, simply because it has failed to raise them. In fact, if we are sufficiently attentive, we find numerous testimonies to this perception of the space of possibilities. We see it for example in the image of the great predecessors, who provide the terms for self-definition, such as the complementary figures of Taine and Renan, for one generation of novelists and intellectuals, or the opposing personalities of Mallarmé and Verlaine for a whole generation of poets; more simply, we see it in the exalted vision of the writer's or artist's craft which may shape the aspirations of a whole generation: 'The new literary generation grew up thoroughly impregnated with the spirit of 1830. The verses of Hugo and Musset, the plays of Alexandre Dumas and Alfred de Vigny circulated in the schools despite the hostility of the University; an infinite number of Mediaeval novels, lyrical confessions and despairing verses were composed under cover of classroom desks'.[26] One could quote whole pages in which Cassagne evokes the adolescent enthusiasms of Maxime Ducamp and Renan, Flaubert and Baudelaire or Fromentin. But one can also quote this very significant passage from *Manette Salomon*, in which Goncourt and Goncourt show that what attracts and fascinates in the occupation of artist is not so much the art itself as the artist's lifestyle, the artist's life (the same logic nowadays governs the diffusion of the model of the intellectual): 'At heart, Anatole was called by art much less than he was attracted by the artist's life. He dreamt of the studio. He aspired to it with a schoolboy's imaginings and the appetites of his nature. He saw in it those horizons of Bohemia which enchant from a distance: the novel of Poverty, the shedding of bonds and rules, a life of freedom, indiscipline and disorder, every day filled with accident, adventure and the unexpected, an escape from the tidy, orderly household, from the family and its tedious Sundays, the jeering of the bourgeois, the voluptuous mystery of the female model, work that entails no effort, the right to wear fancy dress all year, a sort of unending carnival; such were the images and temptations which arose for him from the austere pursuit of art'.[27]

Thus, writers and artists endowed with different, even opposing dispositions can coexist, for a time at least, in the same positions. The structural constraints inscribed in the field set limits to the free play of dispositions; but there are different ways of playing within these limits. Thus, whereas the occupants of the dominant positions, especially in economic terms, such as bourgeois theatre, are strongly homogeneous, the avant-garde positions, which are defined mainly negatively, by their opposition to the dominant positions, bring together for a certain time writers and artists from very different origins, whose interests will sooner or later diverge.[28] These dominated groups, whose unity is essentially oppositional, tend to fly apart when they achieve recognition, the symbolic profits of which often go to a small number, or even to only one of them, and when the external cohesive forces weaken. As is shown by the progressive separation between the Symbolists and the Decadents (analysed below), or the break-up of the Impressionist group, the factor of division does in this case lie in dispositions, the basis of aesthetic and political position-takings whose divergencies are felt the more strongly when associated with unequal degrees of consecration.[29]

Starting out from the same, barely marked, position in the field, and defined by the same opposition to Naturalism and the Parnasse group – from which Verlaine and Mallarmé, their leaders, were each excluded – the Decadents and the Symbolists diverged as they attained full social identity.[30] The latter, drawn from more comfortable social backgrounds (i.e. the middle or upper bourgeoisie or the aristocracy) and endowed with substantial educational capital, are opposed to the former, who are often the sons of craftsmen and virtually devoid of educational capital, as the *salon* (Mallarmé's 'Tuesdays') to the café, the right bank to the left bank and bohemia, audacity to prudence,[31] and, in aesthetic terms, as 'clarity' and 'simplicity' based on 'common sense' and 'naïveté' to a hermeticism based on an explicit theory which rejects all the old forms; politically, the Symbolists are indifferent and pessimistic, the Decadents committed and progressive.[32] It is clear that the field-effect which results from the opposition between the two schools, and which is intensified by the process of institutionalization that is needed to constitute a fully-fledged literary group, i.e. an instrument for accumulating and concentrating symbolic capital (with the adoption of a name, the drawing-up of manifestos and programmes and the setting-up of aggregation rites, such as regular meetings), tends to consecrate and underscore the critical differences. Verlaine, skilfully making a virtue of necessity, celebrated naïveté (just as Champfleury countered 'art for art's sake' with 'sincerity in art') whereas Mallarmé, who sets himself up as the theorist of 'the enigma in poetry', found himself pushed ever further into hermeticism by Verlaine's striving for sincerity and simplicity.[33] And as if to provide a crucial proof of the effect of dispositions, it was the richest Decadents who joined the Symbolists (Albert Aurier) or drew closer to them (Ernest Raynaud), whereas those Symbolists who were closest to the Decadents in terms of social origin, René Ghil and Ajalbert, were excluded from the Symbolist group, the former because of his faith in progress and the latter, who ended up as a realist novelist, because his works were not considered sufficiently obscure.

## The habitus and the possibles

The propensity to move towards the economically most risky positions, and above all the capacity to persist in them (a condition for all avant-garde undertakings which precede the demands of the market), even when they secure no short-term economic profit, seem to depend to a large extent on possession of substantial economic and social capital. This is, first, because economic capital provides the conditions for freedom from economic necessity, a private income [*la rente*] being one of the best substitutes for sales [*la vente*], as Théophile Gautier said to Feydeau: 'Flaubert was smarter than us . . . He had the wit to come into the world with money, something that is indispensable for anyone who wants to get anywhere in art'.[34]

> Those who do manage to stay in the risky positions long enough to receive the symbolic profit they can bring are indeed mainly drawn from the most privileged categories, who have also had the advantage of not having to devote time and energy to secondary, 'bread-and-butter' activities. Thus, as Ponton shows,[35] some of the Parnassians, all from the petite bourgeoisie, either had to abandon poetry at some stage and turn to better-paid literary activities, such as the 'novel of manners', or, from the outset, devoted part of their time to complementary activities such as plays or novels (e.g. François Coppée, Catulle Mendès, Jean Aicard), whereas the wealthier Parnassians could concentrate almost exclusively on their art (and when they did change to another genre, it was only after a long poetic career). We also find that the least well-off writers resign themselves more readily to 'industrial literature', in which writing becomes a job like any other.

It is also because economic capital provides the guarantees [*assurances*] which can be the basis of self-assurance, audacity and indifference to profit – dispositions which, together with the flair associated with possession of a large social capital and the corresponding familiarity with the field, i.e. the art of sensing the new hierarchies and the new structures of the chances of profit, point towards the outposts, the most exposed positions of the avant-garde, and towards the riskiest investments, which are also, however, very often the most profitable symbolically, and in the long run, at least for the earliest investors.

The sense of investment seems to be one of the dispositions most closely linked to social and geographical origin, and, consequently, through the associated social capital, one of the mediations through which the effects of the opposition between Parisian and provincial origin make themselves felt in the logic of the field.[36] Thus we find that as a rule those richest in economic, cultural and social capital are the first to move into the new positions (and this seems to be true in all fields: economic, scientific, etc.). This is the case with the writers around Paul Bourget, who abandoned Symbolist poetry for a new form of novel which broke with Naturalism and was better adjusted to the expectations of the cultivated audience. By contrast, a faulty sense of investment, linked to social distance (among writers from the working class or the petite bourgeoisie) or geographical distance (among provincials and foreigners) inclines beginners to aim for the dominant positions at a time when, precisely because of their attractiveness (due, for example, to the economic profits they secure, in the case of the Naturalist novel, or the symbolic profits they promise, in the case of Symbolist poetry) and the intensified competition for them, the profits are tending to decline. It may also make them persist in declining or threatened positions when the best-informed agents are abandoning them. Or again, it may lead them to be drawn by the attraction of the dominant sites towards positions incompatible with the dispositions they bring to them, and to discover their 'natural place' only when it is too late, i.e. after wasting much time, through the effect of the forces of the field and in the mode of relegation. An ideal-typical example of this is Léon Cladel (1835–92), the son of a Montauban saddler, who came to Paris in 1857, joined the Parnasse movement and, after seven years of fairly impoverished bohemian existence, returned to his native Quercy and devoted himself to the regionalist novel.[37] The whole oeuvre of this eternally displaced writer is marked by the antinomy between his dispositions, linked to his starting-point, to which he eventually returned, and the positions he aimed at and temporarily occupied: 'His ambition was to glorify his native Quercy, a Latin soil trodden by rustic Hercules, in a sort of ancient, barbarous '*geste*'. In distilling the arrogant poses of village champions from furious peasant scuffles, Cladel aspired to be numbered among the modest rivals of Hugo and Leconte de Lisle. Thus were born *Ompdrailles* and *La Fête votive de Bartholomé-Porte-Glaive*, bizarre epics, pastiching the *Iliad* and the *Odyssey* in inflated or Rabelaisian language'.[38] Tension and incoherence, oscillating between parody and utter seriousness, are manifest in this project of describing the peasants of Quercy in the style of Leconte de Lisle: 'Being instinctively led' he writes in the preface to his novel *Celui-de-la-croix-aux-boeufs* (1878), 'towards the study of plebeian types and milieux, it was almost inevitable that there would sooner or later be a conflict between the coarse and the refined'.[39] Always out of step, Cladel was a peasant among the Parnassians (who, objectively and subjectively, placed him with the 'populace', like his friend Courbet),[40] and a petit-bourgeois among the peasants of his native region. Not surprisingly, the very form and content of the rustic novel to which he resigned himself, in which rehabilitation gives way to self-indulgent depiction of peasant savagery, express the contradictions of a position entirely defined by the trajectory which led to it: 'A beggar's son, a beggar dreamer, he had an innate love of village life and country people. If, from the outset, without any shilly-shallying, he had sought to render them with that holy roughness of touch which distinguishes the early manner of the master painters, perhaps he would have made a place for himself among the most sparkling young writers of his generation'.[41]

But these forced returns to the 'people' are only particular cases of a more general model. And all the evidence suggests that the confrontation, within the artistic and literary field, with bourgeois, Parisian artists and writers, which impels them towards the 'people', induces writers and artists of working-class or petit-bourgeois origin to accept themselves for what they are and, like Courbet, to mark themselves positively with what is stigmatized – their provincial accent, dialect, 'proletarian' style, etc. – but the more strongly, the less successful their initial attempts at *assimilation* have been. Thus, Champfleury, a writer from very modest provincial petit-bourgeois origins, after having for some time been 'torn between two tendencies, a realism *à la* Monnier and German-style poetry, Romantic and sentimental',[42] found himself impelled towards militant realism by the failure of his first endeavours and perhaps especially by consciousness of his difference, provoked by contact or objective competition with the Parisian writers, which sent him towards 'the people', i.e. to realism in his manner and to objects excluded from the legitimate art of the day. And this negative return to the people is no less ambiguous, and suspect, than the regionalist writers' retreat to the peasantry. Hostility to the libertarian audacities and arbitrary populism of the bourgeois intellectuals can be the basis of an anti-intellectual populism, more or less conservative, in which 'the people are once again merely a projection in fantasy of relations internal to the intellectual field. A typical example of this field-effect can be seen in the trajectory of the same Champfleury, who, after having been the leader of the young realist writers of 1850 and the 'theorist' of the realist movement in literature and painting, was increasingly eclipsed by Flaubert and then by the Goncourts and Zola. He became a state official at the Sèvres porcelain factory and set himself up as the historian of popular imagery and literature, and, after a series of shifts and turns, the official theorist (awarded the Légion d'Honneur in 1867) of a conservatism based on exaltation of popular wisdom – in particular, of the resignation to hierarchies that is expressed in popular arts and traditions.[43]

Thus, it is within each state of the field that – as a function of the structure of the possibles which are manifested through the different positions and the properties of the occupants (particularly with respect to social origin and the corresponding dispositions), and also as a function of the positions actually and potentially occupied within the field (experienced as success or failure) – the dispositions associated with a certain social origin are specified by being enacted in structurally marked practices; and the same dispositions lead to opposite aesthetic or political positions, depending on the state of the field in relation to which they have to express themselves. One only has to consider the example of realism in literature or painting to see the futility of the attempts of some contemporary critics to relate the characteristics of this art directly to the characteristics of the social group – the peasantry – from which its inventors or advocates (Champfleury or Courbet) originate. It is only within a determinate state of an artistic field, and in the relationship with other artistic positions and their occupants, themselves socially characterized, that the dispositions of the realist painters and artists, which might have been expressed elsewhere in other forms of art, were fulfilled in a form of art which, within that structure, appeared as a form of aesthetic and political revolt against 'bourgeois' art and artists (or the spiritualist criticism which supported them) and, through them, against the 'bourgeois'.

To make this argument fully convincing, one would have to show how habitus, as systems of dispositions, are effectively realized only in relation to a determinate structure of positions socially marked by the social properties of their occupants, through which they manifest themselves. Thus, nothing would be more naïve than to endeavour to understand the differences between the *Théâtre de l'Oeuvre* and the *Théâtre libre* solely in terms of the differences of habitus between their respective founders, Lugné-Poe, the son of a Parisian bourgeois, and Antoine, a provincial petit-bourgeois.[44] Yet it seems quite impossible to understand them solely on the basis of the structural positions of the two institutions which, initially at least, seem to reproduce the opposition between the founders' dispositions. This is only to be expected, since the former are the realization of the latter in a certain state of the field, marked by the opposition between Symbolism, which is more bourgeois – not least in the characteristics of its advocates – and Naturalism, which is more petit-bourgeois. Antoine, who, like the Naturalists, and with their theoretical support, defined himself against bourgeois theatre, proposed a systematic transformation of *mise en scène*, a *specific* theatrical revolution based on a coherent thesis. Emphasizing milieu over characters, the determining context over the determined text, he made the stage 'a coherent, complete universe over which the director is sole master'.[45] By contrast, Lugné-Poe's 'scrappy but fertile' directing, which defined itself in relation to bourgeois theatre, but also in relation to Antoine's innovations, led to performances described as 'a mixture of refined invention and sloppiness'; inspired by a project that was 'sometimes demagogic, sometimes elitist', they brought together an audience in which anarchists rubbed shoulders with mystics.[46] In short, without exploring any further an opposition which appears everywhere, between the writers, newspapers or critics who support one or the other, between the authors performed and the content of the works, with, on one side, the 'slice of life', which in some ways resembles vaudeville, and, on the other, intellectual refinements inspired by the idea, enunciated by Mallarmé, of the multi-levelled work, it can be seen that the opposition between class dispositions receives its particular content in a particular space. There is every reason to think that, as this case suggests, the weight of dispositions – and the explanatory force of 'social origin' – is particularly strong when one is dealing with a position that is in the process of birth, still to be made (rather than already made, established and capable of imposing its own norms on its occupants); and, more generally, that the scope allowed to dispositions varies according to the state of the field (in particular, its autonomy), the position in the field and the degree of institutionalization of the position.

. Finally, we must ask explicitly a question which is bound to be asked: what is the degree of conscious strategy, cynical calculation, in the objective strategies which observation brings to light and which ensure the correspondence between positions and dispositions? One only has to read literary testimonies, correspondence, diaries and, especially perhaps, explicit position-takings on the literary world as such (like those collected by Huret) to see that there is no simple answer to these questions and that lucidity is always partial and is, once again, a matter of position and trajectory within the field, so that it varies from one agent and one moment to another. As for awareness of the logic of the game as such, and of the *illusio* on which it is based, I had been inclined to think that it was excluded by membership of the field, which presupposes (and induces) belief in everything which depends on the existence of the field, i.e. literature, the writer, etc., because such lucidity would make the literary or artistic undertaking itself a cynical mystification, a conscious trickery. So I thought, until I came across a text by Mallarmé which provides both the programme and the balance-sheet of a rigorous science of the literary field and the recognized fictions that are engendered within it: 'We know, captives of an absolute formula that, indeed, there is only that which is. Forthwith to dismiss the cheat, however, on a pretext, would indict our inconsequence, denying the pleasure we want to take: for that *beyond* is its agent, and the engine I might say were I not loath to perform, in public, the impious dismantling of the fiction and consequently of the literary mechanism, display the principal part or nothing. But I venerate how, by a trick, we project to a height forfended – and with thunder! – the conscious lack in us of what shines up there. What is it for? A game'.[47] This quasi-Feuerbachian theory reduces beauty, which is sometimes thought of as a Platonic Idea, endowed with an objective, transcendent existence, to no more than the projection into a metaphysical beyond of what is lacking in the here-and-now of literary life. But is that how it is to be taken? Hermeticism, in this case, perfectly fulfils its function: to utter 'in public' the true nature of the field, and of its mechanisms, is sacrilege *par excellence*, the unforgivable sin which all the censorships constituting the field seek to repress.

These are things that can only be said in such a way that they are not said. If Mallarmé can, without excluding himself from the field, utter the truth about a field which excludes the *publishing* of its own truth, this is because he says it in a language which is designed to be *recognized* within the field because everything, in its very *form*, that of euphemism and *Verneinung*, affirms that he *recognizes* its censorships. Marcel Duchamp was to do exactly the same thing when he made artistic acts out of his bluffs, demystificatory mystifications which denounce fiction as mere fiction, and with it the collective belief which is the basis of this 'legitimate' imposture (as Austin would have put it). But Mallarmé's hermeticism, which bespeaks his concern not to destroy the *illusio*, has another basis too: if the Platonic illusion is the 'agent' of a pleasure which we take only because 'we *want* to take it', if the pleasure of the love of art has its source in unawareness of producing the source of what produces it, then it is understandable that one might, by another willing suspension of disbelief, choose to 'venerate' the authorless trickery which places the fragile fetish beyond the reach of critical lucidity.

## Notes

1 The status of 'social art' is, in this respect, thoroughly ambiguous. Although it relates artistic or literary production to external functions (which is what the advocates of art for art's sake object to about it), it shares with art for art's sake a radical rejection of the dominant principle of hierarchy and of the 'bourgeois' art which recognizes it.

2 The specific, and therefore autonomous, power which writers and artists possess *qua* writers and artists must be distinguished from the alienated, heteronomous power they wield *qua* experts or cadres – a share in domination, but with the status of dominated mandatories, granted to them by the dominant.

3 Thus, writers and artists who are 'second-rank' in terms of the specific criteria may invoke populism and social art to impose their reign on the 'leading intellectuals' who, as has happened in China and elsewhere, will protest against the disparity between the revolutionary ideal and the reality, i.e. the reign of functionaries devoted to the Party. See M. Godman, *Literary Dissent in Communist China* (Cambridge, Mass.: Harvard University Press, 1967).

4 Throughout this passage, 'writer' can be replaced by 'artist', 'philosopher', 'intellectual', etc. The intensity of the struggle, and the degree to which it takes visible, and therefore conscious, forms, no doubt vary according to the genre and according to the rarity of the specific competence each genre requires in different periods, i.e. according to the probability of 'unfair competition' or 'illegal exercise of the profession'. (This no doubt explains why the intellectual field, with the permanent threat of casual essayism, is one of the key areas in which to grasp the logic of the struggles which pervade all fields.)

5 Only just over a third of the writers in the sample studied by Rémy Ponton had had any higher education, whether or not it led to a degree. See R. Ponton, 'Le champ littéraire de 1865 à 1905' (Paris: École des Hautes Études en Sciences Sociales, 1977), p. 43. For the comparison between the literary field and other fields, see C. Charle, 'Situation du champ littéraire', *Littérature*, 44 (1981), pp. 8–20.

6 This struggle can be observed as much in the literary field as in the artistic field (with the opposition between 'pure' art and 'bourgeois' art) and in each genre (with, for example, the opposition between avant-garde theatre and 'middle brow' boulevard theatre).

7 See R. W. Lee, *Ut pictura poesis: The Humanistic Theory of Painting* (New York: W. W. Norton, 1967); F. Bologna, *Dalle arte minori all' industrial design: storia di un' idealogia* (Bari: Laterza, 1972).

8 See D. Gamboni, 'Redon écrivain et épistolier', *Revue d'art* (1980), pp. 68–71, and 'Remarques sur la critique d'art, l'histoire de l'art et le champ artistique à propos d'Odilon Redon', *Revue suisse d'art et d'archéologie*, 2 (1982), pp. 57–63.

9    C. Charle, *La crise littéraire à l'époque du naturalisme* (Paris: Presses de l'École Normale Supérieure, 1979), p. 37.

10   J.-L. Fabiani, 'La crise du champ philosophique (1880–1914): contribution à l'histoire sociale du système d'enseignement', doctoral dissertation (Paris: École des Hautes Études Sciences Sociales, 1980), p. 100.

11   Ponton, 'Le champ littéraire de 1865 à 1905', p. 206. An exemplary expression of a field-effect converted into an explicit project can be seen in this declaration of Zola's: 'Anyway, if I have time, I will do what they want!' (J. Huret, *Enquête sur l'évolution littéraire* (Vanves: Thot, 1982), p. 160; first published Paris: Charpentier, 1891). In other words: I myself will perform the suppression of Naturalism, i.e. of myself, which my adversaries vainly seek to perform.

12   Cited by Fabiani, 'La crise du champ philosophique', p. 82.

13   Zola does not fail to point out this discrepancy between positional age and 'real' age: 'In their dallying with stupidities, with such futilities, at such a grave moment in the evolution of ideas, all these young people, all between thirty and forty, remind me of nutshells bobbing on Niagara Falls! The fact is, they have nothing beneath them but a gigantic, empty pretension!' (cited by Huret, *Enquête sur l'évolution littéraire*, p. 158).

14   See P. Lidsky, *Les écrivains contre la commune* (Paris: Maspero, 1970), pp. 26–7.

15   In every field, the dominant have an interest in continuity, identity and reproduction, whereas the dominated, the newcomers, are for discontinuity, rupture and subversion.

16   Divisions between generations therefore occur in accordance with the logic specific to the struggles which characterize each field (so that oppositions formed in the literary field cannot properly be extended to the whole social field – as was often done in late nineteenth-century France, i.e. at a time when the opposition between the generations tended to be generalized to the whole literary field. See R. Wohl, *The Generation of 1914* (Cambridge, Mass.: Harvard University Press, 1979).

17   V. Shklovsky, *Sur la théorie de la prose* (Lausanne: L'Age d'Homme, 1973), p. 24.

18   On the question of returns and Duchamp's approach to it, see 'The Production of Belief' (ch. 2 in P. Bourdieu, *The Field of Cultural Production* (Cambridge: Polity Press, 1993)).

19   The perception called for by a work produced in accordance with the logic of the field is a differential, distinctive perception, attentive to the differences, the deviations from what is normal, usual, *modal* at the moment in question, i.e. from other works, both contemporary and, especially, past ones – in short, a historical perception.

20   This was said in so many words by a Symbolist poet questioned by Huret: 'In all cases, I consider the worst Symbolist poet far superior to any of the writers enrolled under the banner of Naturalism' (Huret, *Enquête sur l'évolution littéraire*, p. 329). Another example, less forthright but closer to the experience which really inflects choices: 'At fifteen, nature tells a young man whether he is cut out to be a poet or should *be content with mere prose [la simple prose]*' (*ibid.*, p. 299, emphasis added). It is clear what the shift from poetry to the novel means for someone who has strongly internalized these hierarchies. (The division into castes separated by absolute frontiers which override real continuities and overlappings produces everywhere – e.g. in the relationships between disciplines, philosophy and the social sciences, the pure and applied sciences, etc. – the same effects, *certitudo sui* and the refusal to demean oneself, etc.)

21   The painters still had to win their autonomy with respect to the writers, without whom they would perhaps not have succeeded in freeing themselves from the constraints of the bureaucracies and academicism.

22   To those who seek to trace a direct relationship between any producers and the group from which they draw their economic support, it has to be pointed out that the logic of a relatively autonomous field means that one can use the resources provided by a group or institution to produce products deliberately or unconsciously directed against the interests or values of that group or institution.

23  It goes without saying that freedom with respect to institutions can never be truly institutionalized. This contradiction, which every attempt to institutionalize heresy comes up against (it is the antinomy of the Reformed Church), is seen clearly in the ambivalent image of institutional acts of consecration, and not only those performed by the most heteronomous institutions, such as academies (one thinks of Sartre's refusal of the Nobel Prize).

24  Although I realize that theoretical warnings count for little against the social drives which induce simplistic, apologetic or terroristic use of more-or-less scientific-seeming reference to 'father's occupation', it seems useful to condemn the inclination – in which the worst adversaries and acolytes too easily find common ground – to reduce the model that is proposed to the mechanical and mechanistic mode of thinking in which inherited capital (internalized in habitus, or objectified) determines the position occupied, which in turn directly determines position-takings.

25  *Social trajectory* or *constructed biography* is defined as the set of successive movements of an agent in a structured (hierarchized) space, itself subject to displacements and distortions, or, more precisely, in the structure of the distribution of the different kinds of capital which are at stake in the field, economic capital and the specific capital of consecration (in its different kinds). These movements, which define *social ageing*, are of two orders. They may be limited to one sector of the field and lie along the same axis of consecration, in which case ageing is marked by a positive, zero or negative accumulation of specific capital; or they may imply a change of sector and the reconversion of one kind of specific capital into another (e.g. the case of the Symbolist poets who moved into the psychological novel) or of specific capital into economic capital (in the case of shifts from poetry to the 'novel of manners' or the theatre or, still more clearly, to cabaret or serialized fiction).

26  A. Cassagne, *La Théorie de l'art pour l'art en France chez les derniers romantiques et les premiers réalistes* (Geneva: Slatkine Reprints, 1979), pp. 75ff. Originally published Paris, 1906.

27  E. de Goncourt and J. de Goncourt, *Manette Salomon* (Paris: Union générale d'éditions, 1979), p. 32.

28  The solidarity which is built up, within artistic groups, between the richest and the poorest is one of the means which enables some impecunious artists to carry on despite the absence of resources provided by the market.

29  See M. Rogers, 'The Batignolles Group: Creators of Impressionism', in M. C. Albrecht *et al.*, eds, *The Sociology of Art and Literature* (New York: Praeger, 1970).

30  Similarity of position, especially when defined negatively, is not sufficient to found a literary or artistic group, although it tends to favour rapprochement and exchanges. This was the case, for example, with the advocates of 'art for art's sake', who were linked by relations of esteem and sympathy without actually forming a group. Gautier received Flaubert, Théodore de Banville, the Goncourt brothers and Baudelaire at his Thursday dinner parties. The rapprochement between Flaubert and Baudelaire stemmed from the near simultaneity of their early works and their trials. The Goncourts and Flaubert much appreciated each other, and the former met Bouillet at Flaubert's home. Théodore de Banville and Baudelaire were long-standing friends. Louis Ménard, a close friend of Baudelaire, Banville and Leconte de Lisle, became one of the intimates of Renan. Barbey d'Aurevilly was one of Baudelaire's most ardent advocates. Whereas they were close acquaintances, these writers were little seen in high society since their high degree of professionalization limited their social intercourse (see Cassagne, *La Théorie de l'art pour l'art*, pp. 130–4).

31  'The Decadents did not mean to *sweep away* the past. They urged necessary reforms, conducted *methodically* and *prudently*. By contrast, the Symbolists wanted to *keep nothing* of our old ways and aspired to create an entirely new mode of expression' (E. Reynaud, *La Mêlée symboliste*, vol. 1 (Paris: La Renaissance du livre, 1918), p. 118, cited by J. Jurt, 'Symbolistes et Décadentes, deux groupes littéraires parallèles', mimeo (1982), p. 12 (emphasis added).

32    Ponton, 'Le champ littéraire de 1865 à 1905', pp. 299ff.; Jurt, 'Symbolistes et Décadentes', p. 12.

33    The opposition between Mallarmé and Verlaine is the paradigmatic form of an opposition which was gradually constituted and more and more strongly asserted through the nineteenth century – that between the professional writer, occupied full-time by his research and conscious of his mastery, and the amateur writer, a bourgeois dilettante who wrote as a pastime or hobby, or a frivolous, impoverished bohemian. At odds with the bourgeois world and its values, the professional writers, in the first rank of whom are the advocates of 'art for art's sake', are also set apart in countless ways from the bohemian sub-culture, its pretension, its incoherences and its very disorder, which is incompatible with methodical production. Flaubert must be cited: 'I maintain, and this should be a practical dogma for the artistic life, that one must divide one's existence into two parts: live like a bourgeois and think like a demi-god' (*Correspondence*, cited by Cassagne, *La Théorie de l'art pour l'art*, p. 307). And the Goncourt brothers: 'Literature is conceived only in silence and as it were in the sleep of the activity of the things and facts around one. Emotions are not good for the gestation of the imagination. One needs regular, calm days, a bourgeois state of one's whole being, a grocer's tranquillity, to give birth to the grand, the tormented, the poignant, the pathetic . . . Those who spend themselves in passion, in nervous agitation, will never write a book of passion' (*Journal*, cited by Cassagne, *La Théorie de l'art pour l'art*, p. 308). This opposition between the two categories of writers is no doubt the source of specifically political antagonisms, which were particularly manifested at the time of the Commune.

34    Cited by Cassagne, *La Théorie de l'art pour l'art*, p. 218.

35    Ponton, 'Le champ littéraire de 1865 à 1905', pp. 69–70.

36    An example of this is the case of Anatole France, whose father's unusual position as a Paris bookseller enabled him to acquire a social capital and a familiarity with the world of letters which compensated for his low economic and cultural capital.

37    Ponton, 'Le champ littéraire de 1865 à 1905', p. 57.

38    P. Vernois, 'La fin de la pastorale', in *Histoire littéraire de la France* (Paris: Éditions Sociales, 1977), p. 272.

39    Cited in *ibid.*, p. 272.

40    'As described by Champfleury (a Realist novelist, a friend of Courbet and Cladel), the Brasserie Allemande de Paris, where Realism emerged as a movement, was a Protestant village where there reigned rustic manners and a frank gaiety. The leader, Courbet, was a "journeyman", he went around shaking hands, he talked and ate a great deal, strong and stubborn as a peasant, the very opposite of the dandy of the 1830s and '40s. His behaviour in Paris was deliberately popular; he ostentatiously spoke patois, he smoked, sang and joked like a man of the people. Observers were impressed by the plebeian, domestic familiarity of his technique . . . Du Camp wrote that he painted "like a man polishing boots"' (M. Schapiro, 'Courbet et l'imagerie populaire', in *Style, artiste et société* (Paris: Gallimard, 1982), p. 293).

41    Cladel, cited by Ponton, 'Le champ littéraire de 1865 à 1905', p. 98. To assess how much the regionalist novel, the paradigmatic expression of one of the forms of the regionalist – and, more generally, populist – enterprise, derives from being the product of a negative vocation, one would have to compare systematically all those who ended up writing populist novels after such a trajectory with those who are exceptions, such as Eugène Le Roy, a minor civil servant in the Périgord who passed through Paris, author of *Le Moulin du Frau* (1895) and *Jacquou le Croquant* (1899), etc., and especially Émile Guillaumin, a sharecropper in the Bourbonnais and author of *La Vie d'un simple* (1904).

42    Schapiro, 'Courbet et l'imagerie populaire', p. 299.

43    *Ibid.*, p. 315ff.

44    Ponton, 'Le champ littéraire de 1865 à 1905', p. 73.

45    Dort, 'Vers un nouveau théâtre', p. 615.

46    *Ibid.*, p. 617. In terms of the same logic, Ponton ('Le champ littéraire de 1865 à 1905', pp. 80–2) observes that among the boulevard playwrights, directly subjected to the financial sanction of bourgeois taste, writers from the working classes or petite bourgeoisie are very strongly underrepresented, whereas they are more strongly represented in vaudeville, a comic genre which gives more scope for the easy effects of farcical or salacious scenes and also for a sort of semi-critical freedom, and that the authors who write for both boulevard theatre and vaudeville have characteristics intermediate between those of specialists in each genre.

47    S. Mallarmé, 'La musique et les lettres', in *Oeuvres complètes* (Paris: Gallimard (Pléiade), 1945), p. 647. On this text and the reading put forward by Heinrich Merkl, see Jurt, 'Symbolistes et Décadentes'.

## PART TWO

# From orality to literacy

# EDITORS' INTRODUCTION

The development of script traced back to Sumerian cuneiform and forward through the alphabet of the Phoenicians to those of the Greeks and the Romans, in which by and large this is being written, provides a fascinating history of the movement from speech to writing. Yet it is incomplete: not in the sense of a lack of self-sufficiency, although it does contain its own lacunae and cruces, but rather in its failure to take into account the social and cultural results of the technological changes it describes. In that, it resembles a history of printing compared to the more ambitious programme of book history outlined in the first part of this Reader. The use of the terms 'orality' and 'literacy' in this part, and adopted from the work of Walter Ong, itself attempts to indicate the wider perspective than that encapsulated in 'speech' and 'writing'.

Ong's approach spans past and present both in the sense of looking at historical evidence relating to the transition from orality to literacy and at recent anthropological and other studies of that transition in remoter parts of the globe, on the one hand, and in the sense of employing the anthropologist's toolbox to recreate the past, on the other. In doing so, Ong acknowledges the greater precision of the written – 'written words sharpen analysis, for the individual words are called upon to do more' – but its greater ability, in the absence of an interlocutor, to be ambiguous or deceitful. Hence the continuing oral nature of most legal systems where the cross-examination of witnesses remains a better guarantor of justice than scrutiny of written statements. Ong is clear that not only does the transition bring change in thought as well as new modes of written expression, but this change was not always received positively. He draws parallels with reactions to the use of calculators and others can be made with the growth of computer-mediated communication, what we termed in the Introduction the third revolution.

Chartier makes the same point about the spread of reading skills at a much later date than Ong's medieval European examples. Chartier stresses 'a persistent hostility to writing and its dissemination', a dissemination accelerated by the mass production of the printing press. The learned, and privileged, classes had a perhaps obvious antipathy to a phenomenon which challenged their status although the arguments could always be wrapped in an ersatz idealism: that printing produced multiple copies of faulty editions; that it issued heterodox works to undermine morality and society; and that knowledge spread in so facile a manner would be misunderstood and distorted. Müller adds to these objections a fifteenth-century concern for loss of interaction, 'such as had always characterized the medieval manuscript culture, even where it was not oriented toward oral forms of communication', and loss of longevity, guaranteed through the material characteristics of the individual manuscript as opposed to the decisions of printers as publishers. Antagonism came, moreover, from the unlettered classes as well, arising from the associations of writing with the law, with legally enforced duties and obligations, and with power whether legal or magical. Even a working-man's diary written as late as 1802 or 1803 can mention a work on black magic among his few references to books.

The relationship of writing to power is delineated by D. F. McKenzie in his discussion of the Treaty of Waitangi set in the context of Maori orality/literacy and British literacy/print culture. The missionaries developed a Maori alphabet so that an oral culture could read the Scriptures (while the Maoris wished to use their new tool to write letters) and encouraged printing so that copies of the Word of God could be circulated throughout New Zealand. C. A. Bayly recounts the entry of print into the rich and long-standing manuscript culture of nineteenth-century India. It is clear, from Bayly's description of the communication methods and networks available within the public sphere at that time as much as from McKenzie's analysis, that a simplistic, ameliorist model of progression from oral to literate to print has little validity. It should also make us wary of adding computer-mediated as the current culmination of such a movement.

Yet the conventional image of progress we hold in Western Europe and North America places printing at the heart of what has since been called 'the Enlightenment project' but which has its roots in the confluence of Humanism and Reformation. Eisenstein, in the extract reproduced here, exercises some caution in claiming that 'an increase in the output of old texts contributed to the formulation of new theories' but the general thrust of her work has been to strengthen that Whiggish, and Eurocentric, view of history.

# Chapter 8

# Walter Ong

## ORALITY AND LITERACY
## Writing restructures consciousness

### The new world of autonomous discourse

A deeper understanding of pristine or primary orality enables us better to understand the new world of writing, what it truly is, and what functionally literate human beings really are: beings whose thought processes do not grow out of simply natural powers but out of these powers as structured, directly or indirectly, by the technology of writing. Without writing, the literate mind would not and could not think as it does, not only when engaged in writing but normally even when it is composing its thoughts in oral form. More than any other single invention, writing has transformed human consciousness.

Writing establishes what has been called 'context-free' language (Hirsch 1977: 21–3, 26) or 'autonomous' discourse (Olson 1980), discourse which cannot be directly questioned or contested as oral speech can be because written discourse has been detached from its author.

Oral cultures know a kind of autonomous discourse in fixed ritual formulas (Olson 1980: 187–94; Chafe 1982), as well as in vatic sayings or prophesies, for which the utterer himself or herself is considered only the channel, not the source. The Delphic oracle was not responsible for her oracular utterances, for they were held to be the voice of the god. Writing, and even more print, has some of this vatic quality. Like the oracle or the prophet, the book relays an utterance from a source, the one who really 'said' or wrote the book. The author might be challenged if only he or she could be reached, but the author cannot be reached in any book. There is no way directly to refute a text. After absolutely total and devastating refutation, it says exactly the same thing as before. This is one reason why 'the book says' is popularly tantamount to 'it is true'. It is also one reason why books have been burnt. A text stating what the whole world knows is false will state falsehood forever, so long as the text exists. Texts are inherently contumacious.

### Plato, writing and computers

Most persons are surprised, and many distressed, to learn that essentially the same objections commonly urged today against computers were urged by Plato in the *Phaedrus* (Plato 1973: 274–7) and in the *Seventh Letter* against writing. Writing, Plato has Socrates say in the *Phaedrus*, is inhuman, pretending to establish outside the mind what in reality can be only in the mind. It is a thing, a manufactured product. The same of course is said of computers. Secondly, Plato's Socrates urges, writing destroys memory. Those who use writing will become forgetful, relying on an external resource for what they lack in internal resources. Writing weakens the mind. Today, parents and others fear that pocket calculators provide an external resource for what ought to be the internal resource of memorized multiplication tables. Calculators weaken the mind, relieve it of the work that keeps it strong. Thirdly, a written text is basically unresponsive. If you ask a person to explain his or her statement, you can get an explanation; if you ask a text, you get back nothing except the same, often stupid, words which called for your question in the first place. In the modern critique of the computer, the same objection is put, 'Garbage in, garbage out'. Fourthly, in keeping with the agonistic mentality of oral cultures, Plato's Socrates also holds it against writing that the written word cannot defend itself as the natural spoken word can: real speech and thought always exist essentially in a context of give-and-take between real persons. Writing is passive, out of it, in an unreal, unnatural world. So are computers.

*A fortiori*, print is vulnerable to these same charges. Those who are disturbed by Plato's misgivings about writing will be even more disturbed to find that print created similar misgivings when it was first introduced. Hieronimo Squarciafico, who in fact promoted the printing of the Latin classics, also argued in 1477 that already 'abundance of books makes men less studious' (quoted in Lowry 1979: 29–31): it destroys memory and enfeebles the mind by relieving it of too much work (the pocket-computer complaint once more), downgrading the wise man and wise woman in favor of the pocket compendium. Of course, others saw print as a welcome leveler: everyone becomes a wise man or woman (Lowry 1979: 31–2).

One weakness in Plato's position was that, to make his objections effective, he put them into writing, just as one weakness in anti-print positions is that their proponents, to make their objections more effective, put the objections into print. The same weakness in anti-computer positions is that, to make them effective, their proponents articulate them in articles or books printed from tapes composed on computer terminals. Writing and print and the computer are all ways of technologizing the word. Once the word is technologized, there is no effective way to criticize what technology has done with it without the aid of the highest technology available. Moreover, the new technology is not merely used to convey the critique: in fact, it brought the critique into existence. Plato's philosophically analytic thought, as has been seen (Havelock 1963), including his critique of writing, was possible only because of the effects that writing was beginning to have on mental processes.

In fact, as Havelock has beautifully shown (1963), Plato's entire epistemology was unwittingly a programmed rejection of the old oral, mobile, warm, personally interactive lifeworld of oral culture (represented by the poets, whom he would not allow in his Republic). The term *idea*, form, is visually based, coming from the same root as the Latin *video*, to see, and such English derivatives as vision, visible, or videotape. Platonic form was form conceived of by analogy with visible form. The Platonic ideas are voiceless, immobile, devoid of all warmth, not interactive but isolated, not part of the human lifeworld at all but utterly above and beyond it. Plato of course was not at all fully aware of the unconscious forces at work in his psyche to produce this reaction, or overreaction, of the literate person to lingering, retardant orality.

Such considerations alert us to the paradoxes that beset the relationships between the original spoken word and all its technological transformations. The reason for the tantalizing involutions here is obviously that intelligence is relentlessly reflexive, so that even the external tools that it uses to implement its workings become 'internalized', that is, part of its own reflexive process.

One of the most startling paradoxes inherent in writing is its close association with death. This association is suggested in Plato's charge that writing is inhuman, thing-like, and that it destroys memory. It is also abundantly evident in countless references to writing (and/or print) traceable in printed dictionaries of quotations, from 2 Corinthians 3:6, 'The letter kills but the spirit gives life' and Horace's reference to his three books of *Odes* as a 'monument' (*Odes* iii.30.1), presaging his own death, on to and beyond Henry Vaughan's assurance to Sir Thomas Bodley that in the Bodleian Library at Oxford 'every book is thy epitaph'. In *Pippa Passes*, Robert Browning calls attention to the still widespread practice of pressing living flowers to death between the pages of printed books, 'faded yellow blossoms/twixt page and page'. The dead flower, once alive, is the psychic equivalent of the verbal text. The paradox lies in the fact that the deadness of the text, its removal from the living human lifeworld, its rigid visual fixity, assures its endurance and its potential for being resurrected into limitless living contexts by a potentially infinite number of living readers (Ong 1977: 230–71).

## Writing is a technology

Plato was thinking of writing as an external, alien technology, as many people today think of the computer. Because we have by today so deeply interiorized writing, made it so much a part of ourselves, as Plato's age had not yet made it fully a part of itself (Havelock 1963), we find it difficult to consider writing to be a technology as we commonly assume printing and the computer to be. Yet writing (and especially alphabetic writing) is a technology, calling for the use of tools and other equipment: styli or brushes or pens, carefully prepared surfaces such as paper, animal skins, strips of wood, as well as inks or paints, and much more. Clanchy (1979: 88–115) discusses the matter circumstantially, in its western medieval context, in his chapter entitled 'The technology of writing'. Writing is in a way the most drastic of the three technologies. It initiated what print and computers only continue, the reduction of dynamic sound to quiescent space, the separation of the word from the living present, where alone spoken words can exist.

By contrast with natural, oral speech, writing is completely artificial. There is no way to write 'naturally'. Oral speech is fully natural to human beings in the sense that every human being in every culture who is not physiologically or psychologically impaired learns to talk. Talk implements conscious life but it wells up into consciousness out of unconscious depths, though of course with the conscious as well as unconscious co-operation of society. Grammar rules live in the unconscious in the sense that you can know how to use the rules and even how to set up new rules without being able to state what they are.

Writing or script differs as such from speech in that it does not inevitably well up out of the unconscious. The process of putting spoken language into writing is governed by consciously contrived, articulable rules: for example, a certain pictogram will stand for a certain specific word, or *a* will represent a certain phoneme, *b* another, and so on. (This is not to deny that the writer–reader situation created by writing deeply affects unconscious processes involved in composing in writing, once one has learned the explicit, conscious rules. More about this later.)

To say writing is artificial is not to condemn it but to praise it. Like other artificial creations and indeed more than any other, it is utterly invaluable and indeed essential for the realization of fuller, interior, human potentials. Technologies are not mere exterior aids but also interior transformations of consciousness, and never more than when they affect the word. Such transformations can be uplifting. Writing heightens consciousness. Alienation from a natural milieu can be good for us and indeed is in many ways essential for full human life. To live and to understand fully, we need not only proximity but also distance. This writing provides for consciousness as nothing else does.

Technologies are artificial, but – paradox again – artificiality is natural to human beings. Technology, properly interiorized, does not degrade human life but on the contrary enhances it. The modern orchestra, for example, is the result of high technology. A violin is an instrument, which is to say a tool. An organ is a huge machine, with sources of power – pumps, bellows, electric generators – totally outside its operator. Beethoven's score for his Fifth Symphony consists of very careful directions to highly trained technicians, specifying exactly how to use their tools. *Legato*: do not take your finger off one key until you have hit the next. *Staccato*: hit the key and take your finger off immediately. And so on. As musicologists well know, it is pointless to object to electronic compositions such as Morton Subotnik's *The Wild Bull* on the grounds that the sounds come out of a mechanical contrivance. What do you think the sounds of an organ come out of? Or the sounds of a violin or even of a whistle? The fact is that by using a mechanical contrivance, a violinist or an organist can express something poignantly human that cannot be expressed without the mechanical contrivance. To achieve such expression of course the violinist or organist has to have interiorized the technology, made the tool or machine a second nature, a psychological part of himself or herself. This calls for years of 'practice', learning how to make the tool do what it can do. Such shaping of a tool to oneself, learning a technological skill, is hardly dehumanizing. The use of a technology can enrich the human psyche, enlarge the human spirit, intensify its interior life. Writing is an even more deeply interiorized technology than instrumental musical performance is. But to understand what it is, which means to understand it in relation to its past, to orality, the fact that it is a technology must be honestly faced.

## What is 'writing' or 'script'?

Writing, in the strict sense of the word, the technology which has shaped and powered the intellectual activity of modern man, was a very late development in human history. *Homo sapiens* has been on earth perhaps some 50,000 years (Leakey and Lewin 1979: 141 and 168). The first script, or true writing, that we know, was developed among the Sumerians in Mesopotamia only around the year 3500 BC (Diringer 1953; Gelb 1963).

Human beings had been drawing pictures for countless millennia before this. And various recording devices or *aides-mémoire* had been used by various societies: a notched stick, rows of pebbles, other tallying devices such as the quipu of the Incas (a stick with suspended cords onto which other cords were tied), the 'winter count' calendars of the Native American Plains Indians, and so on. But a script is more than a mere memory aid. Even when it is pictographic, a script is more than pictures. Pictures represent objects. A picture of a man and a house and a tree of itself *says* nothing. (If a proper code or set of conventions is supplied, it might: but a code is not picturable, unless with the help of another unpicturable code. Codes ultimately have to be explained by something more than pictures; that is, either in words or in a total human context, humanly understood.) A script in the sense of true writing, as understood here, does not consist of mere pictures, of representations of things, but is a representation of an *utterance*, of words that someone says or is imagined to say.

It is of course possible to count as 'writing' any semiotic mark, that is, any visible or sensible mark which an individual makes and assigns a meaning to. Thus a simple scratch on a rock or a notch on a stick interpretable only by the one who makes it would be 'writing'. If this is what is meant by writing, the antiquity of writing is perhaps comparable to the antiquity of speech. However, investigations of writing which take 'writing' to mean any visible or sensible mark with an assigned meaning merge writing with purely biological behavior. When does a footprint or a deposit of feces or urine (used by many species of animals for communication – Wilson 1975: 228–9) become 'writing'? Using the term 'writing' in this extended sense to include any semiotic marking trivializes its meaning. The critical and unique breakthrough into new worlds of knowledge was achieved within human consciousness not when simple semiotic marking was devised but when a coded system of visible marks was invented whereby a writer could determine the exact words that the reader would generate from the text. This is what we usually mean today by writing in its sharply focused sense.

With writing or script in this full sense, encoded visible markings engage words fully so that the exquisitely intricate structures and references evolved in sound can be visibly recorded exactly in their specific complexity and, because visibly recorded, can implement production of still more exquisite structures and references, far surpassing the potentials of oral utterance. Writing, in this ordinary sense, was and is the most momentous of all human technological inventions. It is not a mere appendage to speech. Because it moves speech from the oral–aural to a new sensory world, that of vision, it transforms speech and thought as well. Notches on sticks and other *aides-mémoire* lead up to writing, but they do not restructure the human lifeworld as true writing does.

True writing systems can and usually do develop gradually from a cruder use of mere memory aides. Intermediate stages exist. In some coded systems the writer can predict only approximately what the reader will read off, as in the system developed by the Vai in Liberia (Scribner and Cole 1978) or even in ancient Egyptian hieroglyphics. The tightest control of all is achieved by the alphabet, although even this is never quite perfect in all instances. If I mark a document 'read', this might be a past participle (pronounced to rhyme with 'red') indicating that the document has been gone over, or it might be an imperative (pronounced to rhyme with 'reed') indicating that it is to be gone over. Even with the alphabet, extra-textual context is sometimes needed, but only in exceptional cases – how exceptional will depend on how well the alphabet has been tailored to a given language. . . .

### The onset of literacy

When a fully formed script of any sort, alphabetic or other, first makes its way from outside into a particular society, it does so necessarily at first in restricted sectors and with varying effects and implications. Writing is often regarded at first as an instrument of secret and magic power (Goody 1968b: 236). Traces of this early attitude toward writing can still show etymologically: the Middle English 'grammarye' or grammar, referring to book-learning, came to mean occult or magical lore, and through one Scottish dialectical form has emerged in our present English vocabulary as 'glamor' (spell-casting power). 'Glamor girls' are really grammar girls. The futharic or runic alphabet of medieval North Europe was commonly associated with magic. Scraps of writing are used as magic amulets (Goody 1968b: 201–3), but they also can be valued simply because of the wonderful permanence they confer on words. The Nigerian novelist Chinua Achebe describes how in an Ibo village the one man who knew how to read hoarded in his house every bit of printed material that came his way – newspapers, cartons, receipts (Achebe 1961: 120–1). It all seemed too remarkable to throw away.

Some societies of limited literacy have regarded writing as dangerous to the unwary reader, demanding a guru-like figure to mediate between reader and text (Goody and Watt 1968: 13). Literacy can be restricted to special groups such as the clergy (Tambiah 1968: 113–4). Texts can be felt to have intrinsic religious value: illiterates profit from rubbing the book on their foreheads, or from whirling prayer-wheels bearing texts they cannot read (Goody 1968a: 15–16). Tibetan monks used to sit on the banks of streams 'printing pages of charms and formulas on the surface of the water with woodcut blocks' (Goody 1968a: 16, quoting R. B. Eckvall). The still flourishing 'cargo cults' of some South Pacific islands are well known: illiterates or semi-literates think that the commercial papers – orders, bills of lading, receipts, and the like – that they know figure in shipping operations are magical instruments to make ships and cargo come in from across the sea, and they elaborate various rituals manipulating written texts in the hope that cargo will turn up for their own possession and use (Meggitt 1968: 300–9). In ancient Greek culture Havelock discovers a general pattern of restricted literacy applicable to many other cultures: shortly after the introduction of writing a 'craft literacy' develops (Havelock 1963; cf. Havelock and Herschell 1978). At this stage writing is a trade practiced by craftsmen, whom others hire to write a letter or document as they might hire a stone-mason to build a house, or a shipwright to build a boat. Such was the state of affairs in West African kingdoms, such as Mali, from the Middle Ages into the twentieth century (Wilks 1968; Goody 1968b). At such a craft-literacy stage, there is no need for an individual to know reading and writing any more than any other trade. Only around Plato's time in ancient Greece, more than three centuries after the introduction of the Greek alphabet, was this stage transcended when writing was finally diffused through the Greek population and interiorized enough to affect thought processes generally (Havelock 1963).

The physical properties of early writing materials encouraged the continuance of scribal culture (see Clanchy 1979: 88–115, on 'The technology of writing'). Instead of evenly-surfaced machine-made paper and relatively durable ball-point pens, the early writer had more recalcitrant technological equipment. For writing surfaces, he had wet clay bricks, animal skins (parchment, vellum) scraped free of fat and hair, often smoothed with pumice and whitened with chalk, frequently reprocessed by scraping off an earlier text (palimpsests). Or he had the bark of trees, papyrus (better than most surfaces but still rough by high-technology standards), dried leaves or other vegetation, wax layered onto wooden tables often hinged to form a diptych worn on a belt (these wax tablets were used for notes, the wax being smoothed over again for re-use), wooden rods (Clanchy 1979: 95) and other wooden and stone surfaces of various sorts. There were no corner stationery stores selling pads of paper. There was no paper. As inscribing tools the scribes had various kinds of styli, goose quills which had to be slit and sharpened over and over again with what we still call a 'pen knife', brushes (particularly in East Asia), or various other instruments for incising surfaces and/or spreading inks or paints. Fluid inks were mixed in various ways and readied for use into hollow bovine horns (inkhorns) or in other acid-resistant containers, or, commonly in East Asia, brushes were wetted and dabbed on dry ink blocks, as in water-color painting.

Special mechanical skills were required for working with such writing materials, and not all 'writers' had such skills suitably developed for protracted composition. Paper made writing physically easier. But paper, manufactured in China probably by the second century BC and diffused by Arabs to the Middle East by the eighth century of the Christian era, was first manufactured in Europe only in the twelfth century.

Longstanding oral mental habits of thinking through one's thoughts aloud encourages dictation, but so did the state of writing technology. In the physical act of writing, the medieval Englishman Orderic Vitalis says, 'the whole body labors' (Clanchy 1979: 90). Through the Middle Ages in Europe authors often employed scribes. Composition in writing, working out one's thought pen-in-hand, particularly in briefer compositions, was, of course, practiced to some extent from antiquity, but it became widespread for literary and other prolonged composition at different times in different cultures. It was still rare in eleventh-century England, and, when it occurred, even this late, could be done in a psychological setting so oral that we find it hard to imagine. The eleventh-century Eadmer of St Albans says that, when he composed in writing, he felt he was dictating to himself (Clanchy 1979: 218). St Thomas Aquinas, who wrote his own manuscripts, organizes his *Summa theologiae* in quasi-oral format: each section or 'question' begins with a recitation of objections against the position Thomas will take, then Thomas states his position, and finally answers the objections in order. Similarly, an early poet would write down a poem by imagining himself declaiming it to an audience. Few if any novelists today write a novel by imagining themselves declaiming it aloud, though they might be exquisitely aware of the sound effects of the words. High literacy fosters truly written composition, in which the author composes a text which is precisely a text, puts his or her words together on paper. This gives thought different contours from those of orally sustained thought. More will be said (that is, written) here later about the effects of literacy on thought processes.

## From memory to written records

Long after a culture has begun to use writing, it may still not give writing high ratings. A present-day literate usually assumes that written records have more force than spoken words as evidence of a long-past state of affairs, especially in court. Earlier cultures that knew literacy but had not so fully interiorized it, have often assumed quite the opposite. The amount of credence accorded to written records undoubtedly varied from culture to culture, but Clanchy's careful case history of the use of literacy for practical administrative purposes in eleventh- and twelfth-century England (1979) gives an informative sample of how much orality could linger in the presence of writing, even in an administrative milieu.

In the period he studies, Clanchy finds that 'documents did not immediately inspire trust' (Clanchy 1979: 230). People had to be persuaded that writing improved the old oral methods sufficiently to warrant all the expense and troublesome techniques it involved. Before the use of documents, collective oral testimony was commonly used to establish, for example, the age of feudal heirs. To settle a dispute in 1127 as to whether the customs dues at the port of Sandwich went to St Augustine's Abbey at Canterbury or to Christ Church, a jury was chosen consisting of twelve men from Dover and twelve from Sandwich, 'mature, wise seniors of many years, having good testimony'. Each juror then swore that, as 'I have received from my ancestors, and I have seen and heard from my youth', the tolls belong to Christ Church (Clanchy 1979: 232–3). They were publicly remembering what others before them had remembered.

Witnesses were *prima facie* more credible than texts because they could be challenged and made to defend their statements, whereas texts could not (this, it will be recalled, was exactly one of Plato's objections to writing). Notarial methods of authenticating documents undertake to build authenticating mechanisms into written texts, but notarial methods develop late in literate cultures, and much later in England than in Italy (Clanchy 1979: 235–6). Written documents themselves were often authenticated not in writing but by symbolic objects (such as a knife, attached to the document by a parchment thong – Clanchy 1979: 24). Indeed symbolic objects alone could serve as instruments transferring property. In *c.* 1130, Thomas de Muschamps conveyed his estate of Hetherslaw to the monks at Durham by offering his sword on an altar (Clanchy 1979: 25). Even after the Domesday Book (1085–6) and the accompanying increase in written documentation, the story of the Earle Warrenne shows how the old oral state of mind still persisted: before the judges in quo warranto procedures under Edward I (reigned 1272–1306), the Earle Warrenne exhibited not a charter but 'an ancient and rusty sword', protesting that his ancestors had come with William the Conqueror to take England by the sword and that he would defend his lands with the sword. Clanchy points out (1979: 21–2) that the story is somewhat questionable because of certain inconsistencies, but notes also that its persistence attests to an earlier state of mind familiar with the witness value of symbolic gifts.

Early charters conveying land in England were originally not even dated (1979: 231, 236–41), probably for a variety of reasons. Clanchy suggests that the most profound reason was probably that 'dating required the scribe to express an opinion about his place in time' (1979: 238), which demanded that he choose a point of reference. What point? Was he to locate this document by reference to the creation of the world? To the Crucifixion? To the birth of Christ? Popes dated documents this way, from Christ's birth, but was it presumptuous to date a secular document as popes dated theirs? In high technology cultures today, everyone lives each day in a frame of abstract computed time enforced by millions of printed calendars, clocks, and watches. In twelfth-century England there were no clocks or watches or wall or desk calendars.

Before writing was deeply interiorized by print, people did not feel themselves situated every moment of their lives in abstract computed time of any sort. It appears unlikely that most persons in medieval or even Renaissance western Europe would ordinarily have been aware of the number of the current calendar year – from the birth of Christ or any other point in the past. Why should they be? Indecision concerning what point to compute from attested the trivialities of the issue. In a culture with no newspapers or other currently dated material to impinge on consciousness, what would be the point for most people in knowing the current calendar year? The abstract calendar number would relate to nothing in real life. Most persons did not know and never even tried to discover in what calendar year they had been born.

Moreover, charters were undoubtedly assimilated somewhat to symbolic gifts, such as knives or swords. These were identifiable by their looks. And indeed, charters were quite regularly forged to make them look like what a court (however erroneously) felt a charter should look like (Clanchy 1979: 249, citing P. H. Sawyer). 'Forgers', Clanchy points out, were not 'occasional deviants on the peripheries of legal practice' but 'experts entrenched at the centre of literary and intellectual culture in the twelfth century'. Of the 164 now extant charters of Edward the Confessor, 44 are certainly forged, only 64 certainly authentic, and the rest uncertainly one or the other.

The verifiable errors resulting from the still radically oral economic and juridical procedures that Clanchy reports were minimal because the fuller past was mostly inaccessible to consciousness. 'Remembered truth was . . . flexible and up to date' (Clanchy 1979: 233). As has been seen in instances from modern Nigeria and Ghana (Goody and Watt 1968: 31–4), in an oral economy of thought, matters from the past without any sort of present relevance commonly dropped into oblivion. Customary law, trimmed of material no longer of use, was automatically always up to date and thus youthful – a fact which, paradoxically, makes customary law seem inevitable and thus very old (cf. Clanchy 1979: 233). Persons whose world view has been formed by high literacy need to remind themselves that in functionally oral cultures the past is not felt as an itemized terrain, peppered with verifiable and disputed 'facts' or bits of information. It is the domain of the ancestors, a resonant source for renewing awareness of present existence, which itself is not an itemized terrain either. Orality knows no lists or charts or figures.

Goody (1977: 52–111) has examined in detail the noetic significance of tables and lists, of which the calendar is one example. Writing makes such apparatus possible. Indeed, writing was in a sense invented largely to make something like lists: by far most of the earliest writing we know, that in the cuneiform script of the Sumerians beginning around 3500 BC, is account-keeping. Primary oral cultures commonly situate their equivalent of lists in narrative, as in the catalogue of the ships and captains in the *Iliad* (ii. 461–879) – not an objective tally but an operational display in a story about a war. In the text of the Torah, which set down in writing thought forms still basically oral, the equivalent of geography (establishing the relationship of one place to another) is put into a formulary action narrative (Numbers 33:16 ff.): 'Setting out from the desert of Sinai, they camped at Kibroth-hattaavah. Setting out from Kibroth-hattaavah, they camped at Hazeroth. Setting out from Hazeroth, they camped at Rithmah . . .', and so on for many more verses. Even genealogies out of such orally framed tradition are in effect commonly narrative. Instead of a recitation of names, we find a sequence of 'begats', of statements of what someone did: 'Irad begat Mahajael, Mehajael begat Methusael, Methusael begat Lamech' (Genesis 4:18). This sort of aggregation derives partly from the oral drive to use formulas, partly from the oral mnemonic drive to exploit balance (recurrence of subject–predicate–object produces a swing which aids recall and which a mere sequence of names would lack), partly from the oral drive to redundancy (each person is mentioned twice, as begetter and begotten), and partly from the oral drive to narrate rather than simply to juxtapose (the persons are not immobilized as in a police line-up, but are doing something – namely, begetting).

These biblical passages obviously are written records, but they come from an orally constituted sensibility and tradition. They are not felt as thing-like, but as reconstitutions of events in time. Orally presented sequences are always occurrences in time, impossible to 'examine', because they are not presented visually but rather are utterances which are heard. In a primary oral culture or a culture with heavy oral residue, even genealogies are not 'lists' of data but rather 'memory of songs sung'. Texts are thing-like, immobilized in visual space, subject to what Goody calls 'backward scanning' (1977: 49–50). Goody shows in detail how, when anthropologists display on a written or printed surface lists of various items found in oral myths (clans, regions of the earth, kinds of winds, and so on), they actually deform the mental world in which the myths have their own existence. The satisfaction that myths provide is essentially not 'coherent' in a tabular way.

Lists of the sort Goody discusses are of course useful if we are reflectively aware of the distortion they inevitably introduce. Visual presentation of verbalized material in space has its own particular economy, its own laws of motion and structure. Texts in various scripts around the world are read variously from right to left, or left to right, or top to bottom, or all these ways at once as in boustrophedon writing, but never anywhere, so far as is known, from bottom to top. Texts assimilate utterance to the human body. They introduce a feeling for 'headings' in accumulations of knowledge: 'chapter' derives from the Latin *caput*, meaning head (as of the human body). Pages have not only 'heads' but also 'feet', for footnotes. References are given to what is 'above' and 'below' in a text when what is meant is several pages back or farther on. The significance of the vertical and the horizontal in texts deserves serious study. Kerckhove (1981: 10–11 in proofs) suggests that growth in left-hemisphere dominance governed the drift in early Greek writing from right-to-left movement, to boustrophedon movement ('ox-plowing' pattern, one line going right, then a turn around a corner into the next line going left, the letters inverted according to the direction of the line), to *stoichedon* style (vertical lines), and finally to definitive left-to-right movement on a horizontal line. All this is quite a different world of order from anything in the oral sensibility, which has no way of operating with 'headings' or verbal linearity. Across the world the alphabet, the ruthlessly efficient reducer of sound to space, is pressed into direct service for setting up the new space-defined sequences: items are marked *a*, *b*, *c*, and so on to indicate their sequences, and even poems in the early days of literacy are composed with the first letter of the first word of successive lines following the order of the alphabet. The alphabet as a simple sequence of letters is a major bridge between oral mnemonic and literate mnemonics: generally the sequence of the letters of the alphabet is memorized orally and then used for largely visual retrieval of materials, as in indexes.

Charts, which range elements of thought not simply in one line of rank but simultaneously in horizontal and various criss-cross orders, represent a frame of thought even farther removed than lists are from the oral noetic processes which such charts are supposed to represent. The extensive use of lists and particularly of charts so commonplace in our high-technology cultures is a result not simply of writing, but of the deep interiorization of print (Ong 1958: 307–18, and *passim*), which implements the use of fixed diagrammatic word-charts and other informational uses of neutral space far beyond anything feasible in any writing culture.

## Some dynamics of textuality

The condition of words in a text is quite different from their condition in spoken discourse. Although they refer to sounds and are meaningless unless they can be related – externally or in the imagination – to the sounds or, more precisely, the phonemes they encode, written words are isolated from the fuller context in which spoken words come into being. The word in its natural, oral habitat is a part of a real, existential present. Spoken utterance is addressed by a real, living person to another real, living person or real, living persons, at a specific time in a real setting which includes always much more than mere words. Spoken words are always modifications of a total situation which is more than verbal. They never occur alone, in a context simply of words.

Yet words are alone in a text. Moreover, in composing a text, in 'writing' something, the one producing the written utterance is also alone. Writing is a solipsistic operation. I am writing a book which I hope will be read by hundreds of thousands of people, so I must be isolated from everyone. While writing the present book, I have left word that I am 'out' for hours and days – so that no one, including persons who will presumably read the book, can interrupt my solitude.

In a text even the words that are there lack their full phonetic qualities. In oral speech, a word must have one or another intonation or tone of voice – lively, excited, quiet, incensed, resigned, or whatever. It is impossible to speak a word orally without any intonation. In a text punctuation can signal tone minimally: a question mark or a comma, for example, generally calls for the voice to be raised a bit. Literate tradition, adopted and adapted by skilled critics, can also supply some extratextual clues for intonations, but not complete ones. Actors spend hours determining how actually to utter the words in the text before them. A given passage might be delivered by one actor in a shout, by another in a whisper.

Extratextual context is missing not only for readers but also for the writer. Lack of verifiable context is what makes writing normally so much more agonizing an activity than oral presentation to a real audience. 'The writer's audience is always a fiction' (Ong 1977: 53–81). The writer must set up a role in which absent and often unknown readers can cast themselves. Even in writing to a close friend I have to fictionalize a mood for him, to which he is expected to conform. The reader must also fictionalize the writer. When my friend reads my letter, I may be in an entirely different frame of mind from when I wrote it. Indeed, I may very well be dead. For a text to convey its message, it does not matter whether the author is dead or alive. Most books extant today were written by persons now dead. Spoken utterance comes only from the living.

Even in a personal diary addressed to myself I must fictionalize the addressee. Indeed, the diary demands, in a way, the maximum fictionalizing of the utterer and the addressee. Writing is always a kind of imitation talking, and in a diary I therefore am pretending that I am talking to myself. But I never really talk this way to myself. Nor could I without writing or indeed without print. The personal diary is a very late literary form, in effect unknown until the seventeenth century (Boerner 1969). The kind of verbalized solipsistic reveries it implies are a product of consciousness as shaped by print culture. And for which self am I writing? Myself today? As I think I will be ten years from now? As I hope I will be? For myself as I imagine myself or hope others may imagine me? Questions such as this can and do fill diary writers with anxieties and often enough lead to discontinuation of diaries. The diarist can no longer live with his or her fiction.

The ways in which readers are fictionalized is the underside of literary history, of which the topside is the history of genres and the handling of character and plot. Early writing provides the reader with conspicuous helps for situating himself imaginatively. It presents philosophical material in dialogues, such as those of Plato's Socrates, which the reader can imagine himself overhearing. Or episodes are to be imagined as told to a live audience on successive days. Later, in the Middle Ages, writing will present philosophical and theological texts in objection-and-response form, so that the reader can imagine an oral disputation. Boccaccio and Chaucer will provide the reader with fictional groups of men and women telling stories to one another, that is, a 'frame story', so that the reader can pretend to be one of the listening company. But who is talking to whom in *Pride and Prejudice* or in *Le Rouge et le noir*, or in *Adam Bede*? Nineteenth-century novelists self-consciously intone, 'dear reader', over and over again to remind themselves that they are not telling a story but writing one in which both author and reader are having difficulty situating themselves. The psychodynamics of writing matured very slowly in narrative.

And what is the reader supposed to make himself out to be in *Finnegans Wake*? Only a reader. But of a special fictional sort. Most readers of English cannot or will not make themselves into the special kind of reader Joyce demands. Some take courses in universities to learn how to fictionalize themselves *à la* Joyce. Although Joyce's text is very oral in the sense that it reads well aloud, the voice and its hearer do not fit into any imaginable real-life setting, but only the imaginative setting of *Finnegans Wake*, which is imaginable only because of the writing and print that has gone before it. *Finnegans Wake* was composed in writing, but for print: with its idiosyncratic spelling and usages, it would be virtually impossible to multiply it accurately in handwritten copies. There is no mimesis here in Aristotle's sense, except ironically. Writing is indeed the seedbed of irony, and the longer the writing (and print) tradition endures, the heavier the ironic growth becomes (Ong 1971: 272–302).

## Distance, precision, grapholects and magnavocabularies

The distancing which writing effects develops a new kind of precision in verbalization by removing it from the rich but chaotic existential context of much oral utterance. Oral performances can be impressive in their magniloquence and communal wisdom, whether they are lengthy, as in formal narrative, or brief and apophthegmatic, as in proverbs. Yet wisdom has to do with a total and relatively infrangible social context. Orally managed language and thought is not noted for analytic precision.

Of course, all language and thought is to some degree analytic: it breaks down the dense continuum of experience, William James's 'big, blooming, buzzing confusion', into more or less separate parts, meaningful segments. But written words sharpen analysis, for the individual words are called on to do more. To make yourself clear without gesture, without facial expression, without intonation, without a real hearer, you have to foresee circumspectly all possible meanings a statement may have for any possible reader in any possible situation, and you have to make your language work so as to come clear all by itself, with no existential context. The need for this exquisite circumspection makes writing the agonizing work it commonly is.

What Goody (1977: 128) calls 'backward scanning' makes it possible in writing to eliminate inconsistencies (Goody 1977: 49–50), to choose between words with a reflective selectivity that invests thought and words with new discriminatory powers. In an oral culture, the flow of words, the corresponding flood of thought, the *copia* advocated in Europe by rhetoricians from classical antiquity through the Renaissance, tends to manage discrepancies by glossing them over – the etymology here is telling, *glossa*, tongue, by 'tonguing' them over. With writing, words once 'uttered', outered, put down on the surface, can be eliminated, erased, changed. There is no equivalent for this in an oral performance, no way to erase a spoken word: corrections do not remove an infelicity or an error, they merely supplement it with denial and patchwork. The *bricolage* or patchwork that Lévi-Strauss (1966, 1970) finds characteristic of 'primitive' or 'savage' thought patterns can be seen here to be due to the oral noetic situation. Corrections in oral performance tend to be counterproductive, to render the speaker unconvincing. So you keep them to a minimum or avoid them altogether. In writing, corrections can be tremendously productive, for how can the reader know they have even been made?

Of course, once the chirographically initiated feel for precision and analytic exactitude is interiorized, it can feed back into speech, and does. Although Plato's thought is couched in dialogue form, its exquisite precision is due to the effects of writing on the noetic processes, for the dialogues are in fact written texts. Through a chirographically managed text couched in dialogue form, they move dialectically toward the analytic clarification of issues which Socrates and Plato had inherited in more 'totalized', non-analytic, narratized, oral form.

In *The Greek Concept of Justice: From Its Shadow in Homer to Its Substance in Plato* (1978), Havelock has treated the movement which Plato's work brought to a head. Nothing of Plato's analytic targeting on an abstract concept of justice is to be found in any known purely oral cultures. Similarly, the deadly targeting on issues and on adversaries' weaknesses in Cicero's orations is the work of a literate mind, although we know that Cicero did not compose his orations in script before he gave them but wrote down afterwards the texts that we now have (Ong 1967: 56–7). The exquisitely analytic oral disputations in medieval universities and in later scholastic tradition into the present century (Ong 1981: 137–8) were the work of minds honed by writing texts and by reading and commenting on texts, orally and in writing.

By separating the knower from the known (Havelock 1963), writing makes possible increasingly articulate introspectivity, opening the psyche as never before not only to the external objective world quite distinct from itself but also to the interior self against whom the objective world is set. Writing makes possible the great introspective religious traditions such as Buddhism, Judaism, Christianity, and Islam. All these have sacred texts. The ancient Greeks and Romans knew writing and used it, particularly the Greeks, to elaborate philosophical and scientific knowledge. But they developed no sacred texts comparable to the Vedas or the Bible or the Koran, and their religion failed to establish itself in the recesses of the psyche which writing had opened for them. It became only a genteel, archaic literary resource for writers such as Ovid and a framework of external observances, lacking urgent personal meaning.

Writing develops codes in a language different from oral codes in the same language. Basil Bernstein (1974: 134–5, 176, 181, 197–8) distinguishes the 'restricted linguistic code' or 'public language' of the lower-class English dialects in Britain and the 'elaborated linguistic code' or 'private language' of the middle and upper-class dialects. Walt Wolfram (1972) had earlier noted distinctions like Bernstein's between Black American English and standard American English. The restricted linguistic code can be at least as expressive and precise as the elaborated code in contexts which are familiar and shared by speaker and hearer. For dealing with the unfamiliar expressively and precisely, however, the restricted linguistic code will not do; an elaborated linguistic code is absolutely needed. The restricted linguistic code is evidently largely oral in origin and use and, like oral thought and expression generally, operates contextually, close to the human lifeworld: the group whom Bernstein found using this code were messenger boys with no grammar school education. Their expression has a formula-like quality and strings thoughts together not in careful subordination but 'like beads on a frame' (1974: 134) – recognizably the formulaic and aggregative mode of oral culture. The elaborated code is one which is formed with the necessary aid of writing, and, for full elaboration, of print. The group Bernstein found using this code were from the six major public schools that provide the most intensive education in reading and writing in Britain (1974: 83). Bernstein's 'restricted' and 'elaborated' linguistic codes could be relabeled 'oral-based' and 'text-based' codes respectively. Olson (1977) has shown how orality relegates meaning largely to context whereas writing concentrates meaning in language itself.

Writing and print develop special kinds of dialects. Most languages have never been committed to writing at all. But certain languages, or more properly dialects, have invested massively in writing. Often, as in England or Germany or Italy, where a cluster of dialects are found, one regional dialectic has developed chirographically beyond all others, for economic, political, religious, or other reasons, and has eventually become a national language. In England this happened to the upper-class London English dialect, in Germany, to High German (the German of the highlands to the south), in Italy to Tuscan. While it is true that these were all at root regional and/or class dialects, their status as chirographically controlled national languages has made them different kinds of dialects or language from those which are not written on a large scale. As Guxman has pointed out (1970: 773–6), a national written language has had to be isolated from its original dialect base, has discarded certain dialectal forms, has developed various layers of vocabulary from sources not dialectal at all, and has developed also certain syntactical peculiarities. This kind of established written language Haugen (1966: 50–71) has aptly styled a 'grapholect'.

A modern grapholect such as 'English', to use the simple term which is commonly used to refer to this grapholect, has been worked over for centuries, first and most intensively, it seems, by the chancery of Henry V (Richardson 1980), then by normative theorists, grammarians, lexicographers, and others. It has been recorded massively in writing and print and now on computers so that those competent in the grapholect today can establish easy contact not only with millions of other persons but also with the thought of centuries past, for the other dialects of English as well as thousands of foreign languages are interpreted in the grapholect. In this sense, the grapholect includes all the other dialects: it explains them as they cannot explain themselves. The grapholect bears the marks of the millions of minds which have used it to share their consciousnesses with one another. Into it has been hammered a massive vocabulary of an order of magnitude impossible for an oral tongue. *Webster's Third New International Dictionary* (1971) states in its Preface that it could have included 'many times' more than the 450,000 words it does include. Assuming that 'many times' must mean at least three times, and rounding out the figures, we can understand that the editors have on hand a record of some million and a half words used in print in English. Oral languages and oral dialects can get along with a small fraction of this number.

The lexical richness of grapholects begins with writing, but its fullness is due to print. For the resources of a modern grapholect are available largely through dictionaries. There are limited word lists of various sorts from very early in the history of writing (Goody 1977: 74–111), but until print is well established there are no dictionaries that undertake generalized comprehensive accounts of the words in use in any language. It is easy to understand why this is so if you think of what it would mean to make even a few dozen relatively accurate hand-written copies of *Webster's Third* or even of the much smaller *Webster's New Collegiate Dictionary*. Dictionaries such as these are light-years away from the world of oral cultures. Nothing illustrates more strikingly how it is that writing and print alter states of consciousness.

Where grapholects exist, 'correct' grammar and usage are popularly interpreted as the grammar and usage of the grapholect itself to the exclusion of the grammar and usage of other dialects. The sensory bases of the very concept of order are largely visual (Ong 1967: 108, 136–7), and the fact that the grapholect is written or, *a fortiori*, printed encourages attributing to it a special normative power for keeping language in order. But when other dialects of a given language besides the grapholect vary from the grammar of the grapholect, they are not ungrammatical: they are simply using a different grammar, for language is structure, and it is impossible to use language without a grammar. In the light of this fact, linguists today commonly make the point that all dialects are equal in the sense that none has a grammar intrinsically more 'correct' than that of others. But Hirsch (1977: 43–50) makes the further point that in a profound sense no other dialect, for example, in English or German or Italian, has anything remotely like the resources of the grapholect. It is bad pedagogy to insist that because there is nothing 'wrong' with other dialects, it makes no difference whether or not speakers of another dialect learn the grapholect, which has resources of a totally different order of magnitude.

# Chapter 9

# Roger Chartier

## THE PRACTICAL IMPACT OF WRITING

One of the most important developments of the modern era, according to Philippe Ariès, was the advent of written culture in Western society. The spread of literacy, the widespread circulation of written materials whether in printed or manuscript form, and the increasingly common practice of silent reading, which fostered a solitary and private relation between the reader and his book, were crucial changes, which redrew the boundary between the inner life and life in the community.

Between 1500 and 1800 man's altered relation to the written word helped to create a new private sphere into which the individual could retreat, seeking refuge from the community.

This development, however, as I will show, did not totally obliterate earlier practices, nor did it affect everyone who dealt with printed materials. Reading aloud, reading in groups or work or pleasure, did not cease with the arrival of silent and private reading. Different kinds of reading overlapped. But this should not cause us to lose sight of the fact that new models of behavior were being established, models that tell us a great deal about the process of privatization in the early modern period.

### Measuring literacy

Can the extent to which the written word penetrated Western societies in the early modern period be measured? Attempting to do so, historians have counted signatures on documents from parish records, notarial archives, the courts, and tax authorities; using these data they have estimated what proportion of the population consisted of people able to sign their own names. After lengthy debate, it is now widely accepted that, although this figure can be taken as a very rough estimate of a society's familiarity with writing, it cannot be interpreted directly as a measure of cultural advancement. In early modern societies, where the small fraction of children who attended school learned first to read and then to write, everyone who could sign his name could also read, but not everyone who knew how to read could sign his name.

Reprinted by permission of the Publisher from *A History of Private Life, Volume 3: Passions of the Renaissance*, Roger Chartier, translated by Arthur Goldhammer, Cambridge, Mass.: The Belknap Press of Harvard University Press, © 1989 the President and Fellows of Harvard College.

Furthermore, not all signers could actually write. For some, instruction in writing never went beyond learning how to sign their names; for others writing was a skill lost for want of practice, and the ability to sign was merely a relic of that lost skill. Paradoxically, the signature is the mark of a population that knows how to read but not necessarily how to write. It is impossible to estimate what fraction of the signers could actually write, and some people who could read never learned to sign their names. This does not mean that all the data concerning percentages of signers at different times and in different places are worthless. The figures constitute a kind of rough, composite index, which does not precisely measure the diffusion of either writing skills (which the percentages exaggerate) or reading skills (which they underestimate).[1]

## Numbers of readers

With this caveat in mind, it is clear from all the data that between 1500 and 1800 the percentage of signers rose sharply throughout Europe. (For convenience, we may refer to this percentage as the 'literacy rate', bearing in mind that it does not necessarily indicate the percentage of the population that could both read and write.) We possess sufficient data about three countries to permit generalizations on a national scale. In Scotland signatures collected for the National Covenant of 1638 (which affirmed the unity of the Presbyterian churches) and for the Solemn League and Covenant of 1643 (which promised Scottish support to the English Parliament, provided that it established the Presbyterian religion) reveal a literacy rate among males of 25 percent. A century later, signatures collected in the 1750s before the High Court of the Judiciary reveal rates of 78 percent for men and 23 percent for women; corrected to reflect differences between the social composition of the witness group and the general population, these figures suggest literacy rates of 65 and 15 percent, respectively.[2] In England signatures collected for the Protestation Oath of 1641 (an oath of allegiance to the 'true religion, reformed and Protestant') for the Vow and Covenant of 1643 (an oath of loyalty to Parliament), and for the Solemn League and Covenant of 1644 (which introduced Presbyterianism) indicate a male literacy rate of 30 percent. In the second half of the eighteenth century the marriage registers of the Church of England, which after 1754 required the signatures of both bride and groom, reflect the progress of the written word: 60 percent of the men signed in 1755 and in 1790, compared with 35 percent of the women in 1755 and 40 percent in 1790.[3] In France, finally, signatures of brides and grooms in the parish registers (recorded in almost all départements by schoolteachers enlisted for the purpose by Rector Maggiolo in 1877) reflect a century of progress: in 1686–1690, only 29 percent of men and 14 percent of women signed; in 1786–1790, 48 percent of men and 27 percent of women did.[4] Thus, over a period of a century and a half, male literacy rates rose by 40 percent in Scotland, 30 percent in England, and 19 percent in France.

In other countries, for which we lack the data to determine the national literacy rate, we find evidence of similar progress in specific cities or regions. In Amsterdam, for example, notarized betrothal agreements were signed by 85 percent of men and 64 percent of women in 1780, compared with 57 percent of men and 32 percent of women in 1630.[5] In Turin 83 percent of husbands and 63 percent of wives signed their marriage contracts in 1790, compared with 70 and 43 percent, respectively, in 1710. And in the province of Turin – that is, in the rural region governed by the city – progress was even more spectacular: the percentage of male signatories rose from 21 to 65, and of female signatories from 6 to 30.[6] In New Castile, in the jurisdiction of the inquisitorial court of Toledo, witnesses and accused (eight out of ten of whom were men and nearly one out of two a notable), 49 percent could sign their names, more or less, between 1515 and 1600, 54 percent between 1651 and 1700, and 76 percent between 1751 and 1817. The nature of the sample precludes using these figures as an indication of the literacy of the Castilian population as a whole, but the rising percentages suggest that literacy was making steady progress.[7]

The trend was similar in the American colonies. In New England, 61 percent of men signed their wills in 1650–1670, 69 percent in 1705–1715, 84 percent in 1758–1762, and 88 percent in 1787–1795.[8] For women, the comparable figures for the first three dates were 31, 41, and 46 percent, respectively. In Virginia, 50 percent of men signed their wills between 1640 and 1680, compared with 65 percent between 1705 and 1715 and 70 percent between 1787 and 1797.[9]

Thus, there was a widespread and often marked increase in the percentage of men and women able to sign their names, an increase that occurred regardless of the absolute level of literacy. In Protestant as well as Catholic countries, in countryside as well as cities, and in the New World as well as the Old, more and more people were familiar with writing. Large numbers of people acquired cultural skills that previously had been the exclusive possession of a minority. This is not to say that progress was uninterrupted. Although the literacy rate reveals a marked trend upward stretching over centuries, it was not without setbacks and recessions. In England the percentage of signers among witnesses before the ecclesiastical court of the diocese of Norwich shows temporary but significant declines. They affected those who reached their tenth year between 1580 and 1610, especially merchants, husbandmen, and yeomen; as well as the civil war generation, educated in the 1640s, where the decline among yeomen reached 20 percent; or in the period 1690–1710, which saw a particularly sharp decline in peasant literacy, especially among husbandmen.[10]

In Madrid the second half of the seventeenth century witnessed a similar decline in literacy: in 1650, 45 percent of testators signed their wills or declarations of poverty; between 1651 and 1700, this figure dropped to 37 percent.[11] The decline was more marked among men (68 to 54 percent) than among women (26 to 22 percent). Finally, in Provence the generations educated between 1690 and 1740 show no progress in literacy and in some areas suffered a sharp decline, to judge by the percentages of signatures on wills and marriage documents.[12] In general, literacy in Provence increased as it did everywhere else: between the end of the seventeenth century and the beginning of the nineteenth century, thirteen out of a sample of twenty communities doubled the percentage of signers. Yet this overall progress came in spite of lack of progress or even decline in the intervals between periods of significant advance, which in the case of Provence came between 1650 and 1680 and in the fifty or sixty years after 1740.

Reasons for the lack of progress, which varied from place to place, included deterioration of the schools, influx of less literate immigrants, or setbacks in the economy. The important point is that between 1500 and 1800 the progress of literacy was neither steady nor uninterrupted. It is this, perhaps, which distinguishes our period most sharply from the nineteenth century, when the advent of mass education inaugurated an era of steady improvement.

## Unequal skills

Although familiarity with writing increased, it was not shared equally. Certain inequalities stand out, probably the most glaring of all being the inequality between men and women. Everywhere the male literacy rate is higher than the female, with a gap between the two as high as 25 or 30 percent. Obviously women had less of a role to play in the world of the written word. But the figures do not give an accurate idea of differences in reading ability. In early modern societies learning to read was long considered a part of a girl's education; learning to write was not, for writing was held to be a useless and dangerous skill for women to acquire. In Molière's *Ecole des femmes*, Arnolphe is eager for Agnès to read so that she can absorb his 'Maxims for Marriage', but he succumbs to despair when he discovers that she knows how to write, especially to her beloved

Horace. Thus, for women even more than for men, the percentage of signers is an inadequate measure of the percentage of readers (especially in the lower classes).

Inequalities existed between people in different occupations and estates. In seventeenth-century rural England the ability to sign (measured by signatures of witnesses before the ecclesiastical courts) was closely correlated with work at social status. Nearly all clerics, notables, and important merchants knew how to write. Skilled artisans (goldsmiths, harness-makers, drapers) and yeomen could write in seven or eight out of ten cases. In most other trades, especially textiles and clothing, only about one in two could sign their names. Next came the village artisans and merchants (blacksmiths, carpenters, millers, butchers, and so forth), of whom only 30 to 40 percent could sign. At the bottom of the scale were building laborers, fishermen, shepherds, husbandmen, and agricultural workers, of whom at most one in four could sign their names.[13] With minor variations this example holds good throughout rural Europe, where the ability to sign one's name was largely determined by such factors as the degree of skill required by one's work and the degree of involvement in nonlocal markets.

In cities too the ability to write depended largely on occupation and status, but city dwellers were far in advance of their rural counterparts in absolute percentages. Consider early-nineteenth-century marriage records from the Emilia region of Italy.[14] In the five cities Piacenza, Parma, Reggio, Modena, and Bologna we find that 42 percent of grooms and 21 percent of brides were able to sign their names, whereas in the surrounding countryside the corresponding figures were, respectively, just 17 and 5 percent. The same is true in northern Europe: seventeenth-century London artisans and merchants were two to three times as literate as their rural counterparts, and domestic servants were two-and-a-half times as literate (in London, 69 percent signed, compared with only 24 percent in rural England).[15] This is one reason why the culture of the modern city was unique: large numbers of city dwellers knew how to write, and the ability to read and write was less unequally distributed than in the countryside.

All of these differences in access to the written word affected the process of privatization in the sixteenth, seventeenth, and eighteenth centuries. The ability to read was an essential prerequisite for certain new practices around which people built their private lives. Personal communion with a read or written text liberated the individual from the old mediators, freed him or her from the control of the group, and made it possible to cultivate an inner life. Solitary reading permitted the development of new forms of piety, which radically altered man's relation to the divine. The ability to read and write enabled people to relate to others and to the authorities in new ways. The greater a person's familiarity with writing, the more emancipated he was from traditional ways of life, which bound the individual tightly to his community and made him dependent on others to read and interpret the divine word and the commandments of his sovereign.

## The geography of literacy

Increasingly private ways of reading and relating changed the nature of European society, but at a different pace in each country. Broadly speaking, northern and northwestern Europe enjoyed higher rates of literacy than other areas. By the end of the eighteenth century 60 to 70 percent of the men in the more literate regions could sign their name: 71 percent in France north of the Saint-Malo–Geneva line, 61 percent in Austrian-dominated parts of the Low Countries,[16] 60 percent in England, 65 percent in Scotland. For women, the figures are 44 percent for northern and northeastern France, 37 percent in the Low Countries, and 40 percent in England. It is harder to gauge the literacy rate in other parts of Europe, where historians have done less research, but various signs indicate that it lagged well behind the rate of the more advanced regions. In Emilia, for instance, the *urban* signature rates were no higher than 45 percent for men and

26 percent for women in the early nineteenth century – a very late date. Hence there is every reason to believe that the literacy rate of the Italian population as a whole, counting peasants as well as city dwellers and the Mezzogiorno as well as the relatively advanced north, must have been lower, probably much lower, than that in northern Europe. In Hungary, in 1768, only 14 percent of the municipal magistrates in villages and towns could sign their names, and the percentage for the peasant population must have been even lower.[17] Finally, in Sweden, only 35 percent of conscripts in the 1870s knew how to write, which suggests that the literacy rate in the late eighteenth century must have been very low.

On the whole, however, northern and northwestern Europe was culturally more advanced than the rest of the continent: a crude contrast, but undoubtedly correct as far as it goes. Some corrections are called for, however. Between regions where the signature rate was as high as 30 percent in the late eighteenth century and regions where it was as low as 10 or 20 percent, there were transitional zones. Southern France, below the Saint-Malo–Geneva line, was one: on the eve of the Revolution, 44 percent of men and 17 percent of women signed their marriage papers.

Furthermore, even within the relatively backward zone, we can distinguish between areas where people could neither read nor write (as may have been the case in Italy and Hungary) and those where many people who could read were unable to write. In mid-eighteenth-century Sweden, for example, few people could write but 80 percent could read. With the promulgation of the Church Law of 1686, the Lutheran Church, backed by the state, had launched a campaign to teach people to read and see with their own eyes what God ordered and commanded through his sacred word. The parish clergy subsequently took charge of teaching reading. Periodically, parishioners were examined to test their reading skills and knowledge of the catechism, and those who could not read and did not know their catechism were prevented from receiving communion and marrying in the church. The campaign, which reached a peak of intensity between 1690 and 1720, left an enduring mark on the populations of Sweden and Finland, where everyone knew how to read (having been trained to do so by the clergy for religious purposes) but only a narrow elite knew how to write.[18]

Such a situation was probably not peculiar to Sweden. It may also have been true of Denmark, where the gap between reading and writing at the end of the eighteenth century seems to have been quite marked. It was surely true of Scotland, one of the most literate countries in Europe. According to evidence gathered in 1742 by the evangelical pastor of Cambuslang, a parish at the center of the religious revival then shaking the Church of Scotland, every man and woman in the parish claimed to be able to read, but only 60 percent of the men and 10 percent of the women said that they knew how to write.[19] Many said that they had learned to read in order to avoid the 'shame' of not being able to participate fully in religious assemblies. Thus, in some Protestant countries, the ability to read was universal, regardless of the 'literacy rate' measured by counting signatures.

## Writing and the Reformation

A high rate of literacy was not a necessary effect of Protestantism, however. In Germany, as early as the third decade of the sixteenth century, Luther abandoned his insistence that every Christian should know how to read the Bible. Instead he emphasized the importance of preaching and catechism, that is, the role of the pastor as teacher and interpreter of the holy text. In Lutheran states there was a marked difference between the education offered to the pastoral and administrative elites and popular religious instruction, which, being mainly oral and based on memorization, was quite compatible with illiteracy.[20] In the Rhineland, in the second half of the sixteenth century, religious examiners found that many people could recite texts that they did not understand and that they responded to questions with answers learned by heart and not always appropriate, proving that catechism classes taught formulas by rote and did not seek to foster a personal interpretation of the Bible.[21]

It was not until the so-called Second Reformation initiated by Pietism at the end of the seventeenth century that all the faithful were expected to learn what was in the Bible and develop a personal interpretation. To that end, Protestants first taught one another in religious conventicles. Later the government issued ordinances governing the course of instruction to be offered in the elementary schools. This changed the very status of the Bible. In sixteenth-century Germany it had been a book for pastors, students studying for the ministry, and parish libraries; by the early eighteenth century it had become a book for everyone, mass-produced and sold at a low price. This may account for the steep increase of literacy among German Pietists: in eastern Prussia the percentage of peasants capable of signing their name rose from 10 percent in 1750 to 25 percent in 1756 and to 40 percent by the end of the century.[22] Pietism, not Lutheranism, spread the ability to read in Germany.

## Medieval advances

The progress of literacy and diffusion of reading were major factors contributing to change in Western man's idea of himself and his relation to others. The magnitude of the phenomenon can be measured, however, only for the seventeenth and eighteenth centuries, because series of documents suitable for such techniques as counting signatures did not become available until the very end of the sixteenth century, and often much later. The cultural state of Europe in the late Middle Ages and even in the sixteenth century therefore remains largely unknown, and it is probably incorrect to assume that literacy rates were low everywhere and that only the clergy knew how to write. In Flanders, for example, various signs suggest that ordinary people could read, write, and count. In the cities 'Latinless' schools taught the basics to common folk. There were probably more than twenty of them in Saint-Omer in 1468, and Valenciennes, a town of 10,000 inhabitants, had twenty-four such schools in 1497. Another sign is the presence of texts on church frescoes and paintings. Still another is the high percentage of signatures – on the order of 70 percent – found in receipts of all sorts (for rents, supplies, and labor) collected by the accountants of the aldermen and hospitals of Saint-Omer in the fifteenth century. Many merchants and artisans seem to have been literate, and only laborers and haulers appear in the majority to have been unable to sign their names. In the countryside the situation was no doubt different, but the keeping of poor-table records, community and charity registers, and tax rolls suggests that writing was a widely shared ability, and the posting of tax rates suggests that at least some people could read them.[23]

Medieval Flanders was by no means unique in its ability to read and write. In Italian cities, as early as the fourteenth century, many people, even among the lower orders, were able to write. In Florence, in 1340, 45 to 60 percent of children between the ages of six and thirteen attended city elementary schools; since far more boys than girls attended school, the percentage of boys receiving an elementary education must have been very high.[24] In some places the ability to write was an accomplished fact by the end of the Middle Ages. Accordingly, the spectacular and widespread advances that occurred in the period 1600–1800 should not be taken to indicate that only a very few people knew how to read and write between 1400 and 1500.

## The rejection of writing

The progress made should not be allowed to obscure a persistent hostility to writing and its dissemination. Shakespeare dramatizes this resistance in *Henry VI*, Part 2 (whose quarto edition dates from 1594), in the treatment of Jack Cade's rebellion. In scene 2 of act 4 Cade and his men decide to kill 'all the lawyers' and for their first victim choose the clerk of Chatham. Their social animosity is fed by a threefold rejection of writing. First, writing is the medium in which the decisions of the authorities are couched. Cade's reference to 'parchment scribbled o'er' and sealed undoubtedly alludes to royal writs, which since the twelfth century had been used to record complaints submitted to the king and to convey decisions of the royal courts to local sheriffs. (Cade had been sentenced to having his hand burned for stealing livestock.) Second, writing was used to record the obligations of the poor, whence the reproach leveled against the clerk of Chatham: 'He can make obligations and write court-hand', which is to say, he records debts in the cursive script used in notarized documents. Third, writing was thought to have magic and evil powers. The clerk of Chatham has 'a book in his pocket with red letters in't', in other words, a book of witchcraft with rubrics or titles in red ink, possibly associated with his Jewishness, as indicated by his name, Emmanuel, whose epistolary significance is understood by Dick, one of the rebels: 'They use to write it on top of the letters.' The ability to write is thus a tool of the authorities, a method of domination, whether by law or magic, employed by the strong against the weak, hence the sign of a rejection of communal equality. Thus, Cade asks the clerk: 'Dost thou use to write thy name, or hast thou a mark to thyself, like an honest plain-dealing man?' The mark, which anyone can make, is proof of respect for man's original equality, whereas the signature, which sets apart those who know how to write, indicates rejection of the common rule.

In scene 7 the rebels, having gained control of London, give free rein to their hatred of written culture. They attempt to destroy the places where that culture is transmitted ('others to th'Inns of Court: down with them all'), its ancient monuments ('burn all the records of the realm'), its techniques of reproduction (Lord Say is accused of having constructed a paper mill and introduced printing), and its lexicon of description (another charge against Lord Say being that he is surrounded by men 'that usually talk of a noun and a verb, and such abominable words'). Against these oppressive and corrupting innovations Cade sets forth the claims of a traditional culture, based on speech and signs: 'My mouth shall be the parliament of England'. He thus alludes to the ancient conception of law, according to which its force stems from its oral proclamation. Instead of books and printed materials, Cade prefers the ancient practice of recording private debts by making notches on pieces of wood: 'the score and the tally'. In fact, Jack Cade's rebellion took place in 1449, twenty-seven years before the introduction of printing into England. In writing about a rebellion that occurred a century and a half earlier, Shakespeare was able to incorporate into his play the fundamental tension between two cultures: one increasingly based on recourse to the written word in both the public and the private spheres; the other based on nostalgic and utopian esteem for a society without writing, governed by words that everyone could hear and signs that everyone could understand. Whatever his intention in depicting a popular uprising as foolish and bloody and the rebels as dupes manipulated by others, it is clear that the underlying cause of the rebellion is hostility to writing, which is blamed for the upheavals that are transforming the society.

If Shakespeare depicted hostility to writing as a sentiment of the lower classes, that sentiment had a more literate counterpart in the rejection by the educated of printed books, a common reaction around the turn of the sixteenth century. In Venice, for example, a Dominican named Filippo di Strata proposed an argument against Gutenberg's invention that was accepted by a large part of the Venetian Senate. Printing, he maintained, was guilty on several counts: it corrupted texts, which were circulated in hastily manufactured, faulty editions composed solely for profit; it corrupted minds by making available immoral and heterodox works over which the ecclesiastical authorities had no control; and it corrupted knowledge, which was debased by being divulged to the ignorant. Whence the judgment: '*Est virgo hec penna, meretrix est stampificata*' (The pen is a virgin, the printing press a whore).[25]

More than a century later echoes of di Strata's argument can be heard in Lope de Vega's *Fuenteovejuna*, published in Madrid in 1619. In act 2, lines 892–930, a peasant, Barrildo, and a licentiate of the University of Salamanca, Leonelo, discuss the merits of printing. The learned Leonelo reveals his doubts about the usefulness of Gutenberg's invention. To be sure, it preserves valuable works and assures their wide distribution, but it also causes errors and absurdities to circulate, allows those who would ruin an author's reputation to usurp his identity and distribute nonsense in his name, and confuses people's minds with an overabundance of texts. Far from contributing to the progress of knowledge, printing may well have added to the sum of ignorance. When Barrildo says that the growing number of printed books has made it possible for every man to think of himself as a scholar, Leonelo curtly replies: '*Antes que ignoran màs*' (No, they are more ignorant than before).

The advent of written culture in the West had to contend with the persistent notion that dissemination of knowledge was tantamount to profanation. The growing number of those who could read and write and the proliferation of printed matter caused disarray among 'clerks' (lay as well as ecclesiastical), who had hitherto enjoyed a monopoly of the production and discussion of knowledge. In the Christian tradition, only clerics were authorized to interpret the secrets of God, nature, and the state. With the scientific revolution of the seventeenth century, the ancient taboos and limitations on access to knowledge were lifted, but only for a small minority, the *respublica litteratorum*, whose members were held to be the only people capable of pursuing knowledge without danger to religion, law, and order. At a time when Icarus and Prometheus became emblems of a knowledge without limits, people were also reminded that knowledge must remain the exclusive province of the new clerks: the intellectuals.[26]

Two motifs were indissolubly linked: the idea that the lower orders rejected written culture because they saw it as an instrument of domination and a threat to the social fabric, and the idea that the educated resisted appropriation by the vulgar of knowledge that had been theirs exclusively, hence also of the keys that gave access to that knowledge. Before the written word could find a place in Western society, it had to overcome both of these representations.

## Reading practices

### Silent reading

Between the sixteenth and eighteenth centuries, as growing numbers of people learned to read, new ways of reading became popular. The most novel of these, as Philippe Ariès has noted, was private reading in a quiet place away from other people, which allowed the reader to engage in solitary reflection on what he or she read. This 'privatization' of reading is undeniably one of the major cultural developments of the early modern era.

What conditions made it possible? First of all, people needed to acquire a new skill: the ability to read without pronouncing the words as they were read. Otherwise the reader remained subject to communal constraints while reading in a library, say, or a room where others were present. Silent reading also made possible the immediate internalization of what the reader read. Reading aloud was slow, laborious, and externalized; silent reading was faster, easier, and more immediate in its impact on the inner self. Apparently, during the Middle Ages, one group of readers after another mastered the technique of silent reading. The first were the copyists working in the monastic scriptoria. Then, around the middle of the twelfth century, scholars in the universities acquired the ability. Two centuries later the lay aristocracy learned to read silently. By the fifteenth century silent reading was the norm, at least for readers who also knew how to write and who belonged to segments of society that had long been literate. For others, who belonged to groups that slowly learned to read and for whom books remained strange, rare objects, the old way of reading no doubt remained a necessity. As late as the nineteenth century, neophytes and maladroit readers could be identified by their inability to read silently. In Labiche's play *La Cagnotte* (1864), the farmer Colladan replies to a person who loses patience when he reads a very private letter out loud: 'If I read out loud, it's not for you, it's for me . . . Whenever I don't read out loud . . . I don't understand what I'm reading.'

Silent reading opened new horizons for those who mastered it. It radically transformed intellectual work, which in essence became an intimate activity, a personal confrontation with an ever-growing number of texts, a question of memorization and cross-referencing. It made possible a more personal form of piety, a more private devotion, a relation with the sacred not subject to the discipline and mediation of the Church. The spirituality of the mendicant orders, the *devotio moderna*, and even Protestantism, all of which presuppose a direct relation between the individual and God, relied heavily on silent reading, which enabled at least some people to nurture their faith on private reading of spiritual books or the Bible itself. Finally, silent, secret, private reading paved the way for previously unthinkable audacities. In the late Middle Ages, even before the invention of the printing press, heretical texts circulated in manuscript form, critical ideas were expressed, and erotic books, suitably illuminated, enjoyed considerable success.[27]

Although the invention of printing was indeed a 'revolution' in that it made it possible to produce a large number of identical copies at a cost much lower than that of copying by hand (even at a time when print runs were small and printing costs quite high), it should not be credited with intellectual and psychological changes that were really the result of a new method of reading, regardless of whether the text was printed or manuscript. By the sixteenth century, the 'other revolution' – the revolution in reading – was already accomplished, although it had only recently made its impact felt on laymen and remained incomplete, since large numbers of readers who had not yet mastered writing were incapable of reading silently. There seems to have been a clear division between those for whom reading was a private act and those for whom it remained a communal act, perhaps even an act of class solidarity.

## More books for more readers

Did silent reading result in greater familiarity with books and a more prominent place for them in the home? The evidence is unfortunately imperfect, incomplete, and much criticized; we must rely primarily on inventories, generally compiled after a death, which described (to a limited extent) and estimated the value of an individual's possessions, including his books. One problem is that the presence of a book in an estate inventory does not imply that the book was read or even purchased by the deceased. Inventories also failed to include printed materials of little value, even though these might constitute the bulk of a person's reading, and of course omitted any valuable or dangerous books that might have been removed from the library beforehand. Such evidence, therefore, should not be relied upon for anything more than very general indications concerning, for instance, the presence of a particular book in the libraries of a particular class of society. Even more than in the case of signature rates, we must be very cautious in comparing data from different places, for the figures may be influenced by differences in notarial practices and in the composition of the populations for which estate inventories were compiled.

By the sixteenth century the evidence suggests that private individuals owned more books than ever before. In some places the percentage of book owners, both overall and by social class, remained constant, but the number of books owned increased. In Valencia, for example, books are mentioned in one out of three inventories between 1474 and 1550. The hierarchy of ownership remained stable: nine out of ten clerics owned books, as did three out of four members of the liberal professions, one out of two nobles, one out of three merchants, and only one out of ten manual laborers. Within each group the number of books in the average library increased. Between the end of the fifteenth century and the second quarter of the sixteenth century, the average physician's collection increased from 26 to 62 books; the average jurist's from 25 to 55; and the average merchant's from 4 to 10. As for artisans in the textile trade, who had generally owned only one book, the average 'library' now increased to 4 volumes.[28]

In sixteenth-century Florence the percentage of inventories compiled by the Magistrato de'pupilli in which books are mentioned remained quite low: 4.6 percent between 1531 and 1569, 5.2 percent between 1570 and 1608. (It had reached 3.3 percent between 1413 and 1453 but fell to 1.4 percent in the second half of the fifteenth century.) This percentage is much lower than that found in Valencia or Amiens (where, between 1503 and 1576, 20 percent of inventories mentioned books).[29] Was Italy backward in this respect? It is hard to say. We can, however, assert with confidence that, while the percentage of book owners increased very little, the proportion of books belonging to the largest libraries increased substantially. Libraries containing fewer than 6 volumes accounted for 55 percent of the total before 1570, but for only 31 percent after that date. Conversely, libraries with 51 to 100 volumes increased from 4.5 to 9 percent, and those with 101 to 200 volumes from 1 to 8 percent. Libraries with from 6 to 50 volumes, which had accounted for 38 percent of the total before 1570, rose to 47 percent afterward.[30]

A third possibility was an increase in the percentage of the population that owned books. In Canterbury, around the turn of the seventeenth century, inventories of men's estates indicate ownership of books in one out of ten cases in 1560, one out of four cases in 1580, one out of three cases in 1590, and nearly one out of two cases in 1620. A similar pattern has been noted in two smaller cities in Kent: Faversham and Maidstone. Here again, ownership of books depends strongly on social rank: between 1620 and 1640 in Canterbury 90 percent of men in the professions and 73 percent of nobles owned books, compared with only 45 percent of textile artisans, 36 percent of construction workers, and 31 percent of the city's yeomen. With such high percentages the three cities in Kent are not typical of England as a whole. In rural parishes books remained rare, even in the seventeenth century. Only 13 percent of inventories in Bedfordshire at the end of the second decade of the century and 14 percent of those from Middlesex between 1630 and 1690 mention the presence of books.[31]

Did private ownership of books increase between 1500 and 1800? Did growing familiarity with books contribute to the privatization characteristic of the period? The answers to these questions depend on location. Leading Europe in book ownership were the cities of the Protestant countries. In the middle of the eighteenth century, in the German Lutheran cities of Tübingen, Spire, and Frankfurt, books are mentioned in, respectively, 89, 88, and 77 percent of all inventories.[32] Compare this with Catholic France, whether in Paris, where only 22 percent of inventories in the 1750s mention books, or in provincial cities. (In nine cities of western France, the figure for 1757–1758 was 36 percent, and in Lyons in the second half of the eighteenth century it was 35 percent.)[33] Other Protestant countries were more like Germany, even largely rural countries like the United States. At the end of the eighteenth century, 75 percent of the inventories in Worcester County, Massachusetts, 63 percent in Maryland, and 63 percent in Virginia mention the presence of books.[34] These figures indicate marked progress compared with the previous century, where the figure in these same regions was about 40 percent.

## Protestant reading

Religion established an important difference with respect to book ownership. There is no more striking proof of this than a comparison of Catholic and Protestant libraries in the same city. In Metz, between 1645 and 1672, 70 percent of Protestant inventories mention books, compared with only 25 percent of Catholic ones. The gap remains wide, regardless of occupation: 75 percent of Protestant nobles owned books compared with only 22 percent of Catholic nobles; in the legal professions the figures are 86 and 29 percent; in the medical professions, 88 and 50 percent; for minor officers, 100 and 18 percent; for merchants, 85 and 33 percent; for artisans, 52 and 17 percent; for 'bourgeois', 73 and 5 percent; and for manual and agricultural laborers, 25 and 9 percent. Protestants owned more books than Catholics. Protestant professionals owned on the average three times as many books as their Catholic counterparts, and the ratio was the same for merchants, artisans, and minor officers. As for those classed as 'bourgeois', the libraries of the Calvinists were ten times as large as those of the Catholics.[35]

There were differences in the composition of libraries and in reading practices. In Lutheran countries all libraries, regardless of the social rank of the owner, were organized around a common set of religious books. In Rhenish cities this consisted of the Bible, pious books, manuals of preparation for communion and confession, and hymnals or *Gesangbücher*. The larger libraries had more titles and more different editions, but basically the same kinds of books. Differences in wealth and education were reflected not in these religious works but in the number and nature of profane books (which are found in just over a quarter of the libraries in the second half of the eighteenth century). Protestants thus developed a religious and cultural identity around a common set of books, used in connection with various religious exercises: Bible-reading, prayer, hymns, sermons, communion. Not all Protestant libraries were as homogeneous as these Lutheran ones, however. In seventeenth-century Metz, for example, apart from the Bible and psalms, titles and genres of books varied widely. The more puritanical Calvinist libraries resembled Lutheran ones, however, although they usually contained a smaller number of books.

In America reading and religion were inextricably intertwined, defining a culture based entirely on familiarity with the Bible.[36] Biblical stories were heard before they were read, since fathers or servants often read aloud to the entire family. In memoirs published in 1852, Joseph T. Buckingham, editor of Boston's first daily newspaper, recalls:

> For a number of years . . . I read every day [in the presence of his master and mistress] at least one chapter, and often two or three chapters in the Bible . . . I have no doubt that I read the Bible through *in course* at least a dozen times before I was sixteen years old, with no other omissions than the jaw-breaking chapters of the Chronicles. The historical parts I had read much oftener, and the incidents and the language became almost as familiar as the grace . . . said before and after meals — neither of which ever varied a word during . . . nine years.

In this culture the ability to read was taken for granted; from the moment the child first confronted the written word, he recognized texts that he had heard before and often memorized. Buckingham says:

> I have no recollection of any time when I could not read . . . In December, 1784, the month in which I was five years old, I went to a master's school, and, on being asked if I could read, I said I could read in the Bible. The master placed me on his chair and presented a Bible opened at the fifth chapter of Acts. I read the story of Ananias and Sapphira falling down dead for telling a lie. He patted me on the head and commended my reading.

Reading meant returning again and again to the same books — the Bible and a few others — which were transmitted from generation to generation. This practice, sometimes termed 'intensive' reading, had its radical exponents, such as the Quaker William Penn: 'Keep but few books, well chosen and well read, whether concerned with religious or civil subjects. Reading many books only takes the mind away from meditation. Much reading is an oppression of the mind'. The practice also had its methodological treatises. A sermon published in Boston in 1767 contains these recommendations:

> Be diligent in reading holy scripture. Every morning and every evening you must read a chapter of your Bible or a passage from a pious sermon, and when you read you must not scan the text and then set it aside. Better not to read at all than to read in that way. When you read, you must pay close attention to what you are reading, and when you have finished you must mull over what you have just read.[37]

Repeated reading of the same texts was the norm for American Protestants. In memoirs published in 1857, Samuel Goodrich, a writer and editor, says: 'In our family Bible it is recorded that he [my father] thus read that holy book through, in course, thirteen times, in the space of about five and twenty years.' The Bostonian Robert Keayne declared in his will: 'As my special gift to him [my son] my little written book in my closet upon I Cor. II, 27, 28, which is a treatise of the sacrament of the Lord's Supper . . . [It is] a little thin pocket book bound in leather, all written in my own hand, which I esteem more precious than gold, and which I have read over I think 100 and 100 times . . . I desire him and hope that he will never part with it as long as he lives'. Read and reread, religious texts inhabited the minds of the faithful, who drew from them not only spiritual comfort but a manner of speaking and writing and ways of organizing individual and communal life in accordance with the divine word. Consider the experiences of Joseph Crosswell, an itinerant preacher born in 1712 and converted during the Great Awakening:

> I know not when I have experienced greater consolation in reading the word of God. Blessed be its glorious and gracious Author. Sweetly regaled in the afternoon by the heavenly south breezes of the divine Spirit, whilst repeating scripture passages . . . I have this day repeated the whole book of Canticles by heart . . . Some enlivening about noon while passing through woods and repeating the last three chapters in the Canticles.

In America's Puritan culture we find the most radical privatization of reading. The book became the center of family life. People read for themselves and for others. They memorized passages, which by dint of frequent repetition became part of their everyday language. No doubt such diligence was quite rare, but practices were similar in other Protestant areas, even where the Calvinist and Puritan influence was small.[38]

## The library, retreat from the world

The book thus became the companion of choice in a new kind of intimacy. And the library, for those who could afford one, became the ideal place for retreat, study, and meditation. Consider, as one of many possible examples, the case of Montaigne. In 1579 he sold his post as *conseiller* with the Bordeaux parlement and went to Paris to oversee the printing of the works of his friend Etienne de La Boétie. The following year, upon returning to his château, he had painted on the walls of his library, 'a beauty among village libraries', this Latin inscription:

> In the year of Christ 1571, at the age of thirty-eight, Michel de Montaigne, long since bored with the slavery of parlement and public office but still vigorous, withdrew to lay his head on the breast of the learned Virgins in calm and security; he shall pass

the remaining days of his life there. Hoping that fate will allow him to perfect this dwelling, this sweet paternal retreat, he has consecrated it to his freedom, tranquillity, and leisure.

In the first place, then, the library was a retreat from the world, freedom enjoyed out of the public eye. Montaigne's description in the *Essays* (III:3) emphasizes its role as refuge: 'When at home I turn aside a little more often to my library', the most exposed room in the castle, 'which I like for being a little hard to reach and out of the way, for the benefit of the exercise as much as to keep the crowds away'.[39] Separated from the main building by a courtyard, the library is where he engages in the best of the 'three kinds of commerce', that of a man with his books, which is to say, with himself. Retreat does not mean seclusion or rejection of the world, however. Montaigne's library is a place from which one can see without being seen, which gives a kind of power to the person who retires there. Power over the household and its inhabitants: 'I turn aside a little more often to my library, from which at one sweep I command a view of my household. I am over the entrance and see below me my garden, my farmyard, my courtyard, and into most of the parts of my house.' Power over nature, which offers itself up to the eye: 'It offers rich and free views in three directions.' Power over the knowledge accumulated in the books that the eye takes in at a glance: 'The shape of my library is round, the only flat side being the part needed for my table and chair; and curving round me it presents at a glance all my books, arranged in five rows of shelves on all sides.' At a glance too Montaigne can take in the Greek and Latin sayings that have been painted on the beams, those taken from Stobaeus at the beginning of the retreat having been covered over later, in 1575 or 1576, by others taken from Sextus Empiricus and the Bible.

The tension between the desire to withdraw from the crowd while at the same time maintaining control over the world is probably symbolic of the absolute liberty made possible by commerce with books, hence of the possibility of complete self-mastery without constraint or supervision: 'There is my throne. I try to make my authority over it absolute, and to withdraw this one corner from all society, conjugal, filial, and civil.' The hours spent in the library are hours of withdrawal in two senses, which define the essence of privacy in the modern era: withdrawal from the public sphere, from civic responsibility, from the affairs of city and state; and withdrawal from the family, from the household, from the social responsibilities of domestic intimacy. In retreat, the individual is free, master of his time, of his leisure or study: 'There I leaf through now one book, now another, without order and without plan, by disconnected fragments. One moment I muse, another moment I set down or dictate, walking back and forth, these fancies of mine that you see here.' And dictate: note that the ancient method of composition, the writer speaking his words out loud as he walks and requiring the presence of a scribe, is not thought to be in contradiction with the sense of intimacy that comes from familiarity with the books of the library, which are close by and easy to leaf through.

The sense of power conferred by withdrawal into a library is depicted in other texts, such as Shakespeare's *The Tempest*, probably written between 1610 and 1613. Like Montaigne, Prospero preferred the privacy of his study to public affairs: 'Me, poor man, my library / Was dukedom large enough' (act I, scene 2, ll. 109–110). In exile, he thanks the person who allowed him to take some of his precious books: 'Knowing I lov'd my books, he furnish'd me, / From my own library, with volumes that / I prize above my dukedom' (act I, scene 2, ll. 166–168). But these familiar, cherished books, companions in solitude and misery, are also the instruments of a secret power, feared and fearsome. Knowing this, Caliban thinks that Prospero's power can be destroyed if his books are seized and burned: 'Remember, / First to possess his books; for without them / He's but a sot, as I am' (act 3, scene 2, ll. 83–85), and 'Burn but his books' (1. 87). Prospero himself associates books with his power: 'I'll to my book; / For yet, ere supper-time, I must perform / Much business appertaining' (act 3, scene 1, ll. 92–94). He also repudiates that power: 'And, deeper than did ever plummet sound, / I'll drown my book' (act 5, scene 1, ll. 56–57).

Thus there emerges a strange alliance between reading, that most private and hidden practice, and true, effective power, power far more effective than that of public office. The reading of books of magic (such as the *Books of Experiments* in sixteenth-century England or *the* nameless book of magic widely read in rural Aragon and Languedoc in the nineteenth century) became the paradigm for all reading, which had to be done in secret and which conferred upon the reader a dangerous power.[40]

## Reading becomes private

'Study: a place of retirement in ordinary homes where one can go to study or to find seclusion and where one keeps one's most precious goods. A room that contains a library is also called a study.' This definition, from Furetière's *Dictionary*, reveals the library's new status. It is no longer, or at any rate not always, an ostentatious room for receiving visitors, for 'show' as Pascal put it, but a place for keeping 'one's most precious goods', not only useful and rare books but one's own self. Privately owned books and the place where they were kept and consulted therefore commanded special attention.

Consider two contemporaries, Samuel Pepys (1633–1703) and John Locke (1632–1704). In the diary he kept from 1660 to 1669, Pepys, then Clerk of the Acts of the Navy Board and living in an apartment adjoining the offices of the Royal Navy, tells of his efforts to acquire, bind, and store books.[41] An assiduous client of bookstores (and not only so as to make free with the bookseller's wife) as well as an avid reader ('I know not how in the world to abstain from reading', he wrote on 18 March 1668, at a time when his eyesight had already suffered serious deterioration), he took upon himself the task of arranging his books (13 October 1660: 'Within all the afternoon, setting up shelfes in my study'), preparing a catalogue (4 February 1667: 'A little to the office and then to my chamber and there finished my catalogue of my books with my own hand, and so to supper and to bed, and had a good night's rest'), until, his eyesight almost gone, he asked his brother to finish the job (24 May 1669: 'To White Hall, and there all the morning, and thence home, and giving order for some business and setting my brother to making a catalogue of my books'). Wanting his books to look good, he made frequent trips to the binder (3 February 1665: 'My bill for the rebinding of some old books to make them suit with my study cost me, besides other new books in the same bill, £3; but it will be very handsome'). Pepys kept his money in his study and did business there, suggesting that this was one of the most private rooms in his house. On 11 December 1660, having discussed at the tavern the best ways to invest his money, he wrote: 'Up to my study, and there did make up an even 100l and sealed it to lie by. After that to bed.' On 18 July 1664 he returned home with a man who owed him money, 'and there he took occasion to owne his obligations to me, and did lay down twenty pieces in gold upon my shelf in my closett'.

John Locke, collector and scholar, marked each of his books with his personal stamp and organized his library so as to facilitate research. In 1691, after years of exile in the United Provinces, Locke returned to England and installed his library in two rented rooms in Sir Francis Masham's castle at Otes in Essex, twenty miles from London. With the aid of an assistant, he numbered each work (with a tag glued to the back of the binding and reproduced on the top plate inside). He then marked each number on sheets inserted into the *Catalogus impressorum* of the Bodleian, published by Hyde, which served as both an annotated bibliography and a catalogue of his own library; later he pasted his numbers in two somewhat less cumbersome catalogues. This effort made his library more usable, the catalogue numbers facilitating the task of finding books on the shelves, where they were arranged according to size in two ranks, with no order by subject.

Every book that came into Locke's library was carefully marked as his personal property. He placed his signature on the top plate of the binding, alongside the book's number. He underlined the final figures of the date on the title page, placed a line over the page number on the final page, marked the price he had paid for the book, usually on the eleventh page, and recorded the number, date, and pagination in his catalogues. While reading he made additional marks in at least some of his books. Pages were noted on the lower plate of the binding, and notes were sometimes written on inserted sheets. Locke also made symbolic notations (letters in italics, dots, dashes, plus and minus signs, initials) whose meaning is for the most part unclear. (Some of these signs seem to refer to the merits of the edition or text or to the presence of a second copy in the library.)

Locke's commerce with his books was thus a time-consuming occupation. He respected them, never writing or underlining on pages that contained text. They were his most intimate possessions and therefore demanded to be passed on to someone who would know how to make good use of them. In his will, Locke specified what was to become of his books: some were to go to Dame Damaris Masham, his host's second wife ('four folios, eight quartos, and twenty small books which she may choose among the books of my library'); others to Mr. Anthony Collins of the Middle Temple, a free-thinker and recent friend of Locke's; the bulk of the library, some 3,641 titles, was to be divided between his cousin Peter King and Francis C. Masham, Damaris Masham's only son, 'when he shall have attained the age of twenty-one years'.[42]

The presence of books became firmly linked to the habit of reading and privacy in seventeenth-century England. Estate inventories from Kentish towns show that they were less likely to be found in the hall, the most open room in the house, where guests were received, and more likely to be found in private areas such as the study (closet) or bedroom. (Between 1560 and 1600, 48 percent of books were found in the hall, compared with 39 percent between 1601 and 1640; the proportion of books found in more private rooms rose from 9 percent to 23 percent during the same interval.)

Books were found more often in the bedroom than in the 'study' or 'parlor', probably because it had become common to read before going to sleep. In Kent, for example, the wife of one yeoman in Otham was described by her maid in court documents as 'reading her book as she often did before going to bed'. This was Pepys's habit too, and in his diary we find frequent notations such as these from 1667: 'and so after supper to read, and then to bed' (1 May), and 'I to my book again, and made an end of Mr. Hooker's Life, and so to bed' (19 May).

Evening reading was not necessarily solitary. A couple might read together or to each other: 'I fell a-reading in Fuller's *History of Abbys* and my wife in *Grand Cyrus* till 12 at night; and so to bed' (7 December 1660). Sometimes they read the same books (poems of Du Bartas on 2 November 1662, Aesop's *Fables* on 24 May 1663), and sometimes (as on 2 November 1660) one read aloud to the other: 'In Paul's church-yard I called at Kirton's, and there they had got a mass book for me, which I bought and cost me twelve shillings; and, when I came home, sat up late and read in it with great pleasure to my wife, to hear that she was long ago so well acquainted with.' (Pepys's wife, Elisabeth Marchand, was the daughter of an exiled Huguenot and for a time had been a student at the Ursulines' school in Paris.)

Frequently Pepys ordered his valet to read to him, even before his eyesight had begun to deteriorate: 'I had the boy up tonight for his sister to teach him to put me to bed, and I heard him read, which he doth pretty well' (22 September 1660). Or again, on 9 September 1666: 'Anon to Sir W. Pen's to bed [after the London fire, Pepys had had to leave his damaged apartment], and made my boy Tom to read me asleep.' And on 25 December 1668: 'So home and to dinner alone with my wife, who, poor wretch! sat undressed all day till ten at night, altering and lacing of a noble petticoat: while I by her, making the boy read to me the Life of Julius Caesar, and Des Cartes' book of Musick, the latter of which I understand not . . . Then after supper I made the boy play upon his lute, which I have not done twice before since he come to me; and so, my mind in mighty content, we to bed.' Like the presence of the scribe in Montaigne's library, the presence of the 'boy' in Pepys's bedroom by no means spoils his intimacy with his book; reading could be a private without necessarily being a solitary pursuit.

By contrast, a person could enjoy a strictly private relation with his book outside the confines of the home. Pepys read at home in the evening, but he also read a great deal in various places around London. Sometimes he read while walking. On 18 November 1663: 'And so I walked to Deptford, where I have not been a very great while, and there paid off the Milford in very good order . . . After dinner came Sir W. Batten, and I left him to pay off another ship, and I walked home again reading of a little book of new poems of Cowley's, given my by his brother.' On 9 May 1666 he again went to Deptford: 'Walked back again reading of my Civill Law Book.' Then, on 17 August 1666: 'Down by water to Woolwich, I walking alone from Greenwich thither, making an end of the "Adventures of Five Hours", which when all is done is the best play that ever I read in my life.' Reading whiled away the hours while traveling the Thames by boat, as on 1 May 1666: 'Thence by water to Redriffe, reading a new French book my Lord Brouncker did give me today, L'histoire amoureuse des Gaules, being a pretty Libell against the amours of the Court of France.' Or, on 10 June 1667, as Pepys returns from Gravesend: 'So I homeward, as long as it was light reading Mr. Boyles book of Hydrostatickes, which is a most excellent book as ever I read . . . When it grew too dark to read, I lay down and took a nap, it being a most excellent fine evening.'

Silent reading created an air of intimacy that separated the reader from the outside world. Thus, even in the middle of the city, in the presence of other people, he might be alone with his book and his thoughts. Certain kinds of reading demanded more privacy, however. On 13 January 1668 Pepys 'stopped at Martins my bookseller, where I saw the French book which I did think to have had for my wife to translate, called L'escholle des Filles [attributed to Michel Millot and Jean l'Ange], but when I came to look into it, it is the most bawdy, lewd book that ever I saw, rather worse than putana errante [by Aretino], so that I was ashamed of reading in it'. His shame seems not to have lasted very long, since on 8 February he revisited the bookshop 'and bought that idle, roguish book, L'escholle des Filles; which I have bought in plain binding (avoiding the buying of a better bound) because I resolve, as soon as I have read it, to burn it, that it may not stand in the list of books, nor among them, to disgrace them if it should be found'. The next day finds him impatient to read this promising work: 'Up, and at my chamber all the morning and the office, doing business and also reading a little of L'escholle des Filles, which is a mighty lewd book, but yet not amiss for a sober man once to read over to inform himself in the villainy of the world.' And that evening, after dinner and an afternoon spent with friends and well lubricated by drink, he says: 'And then they parted and I to my chamber, where I did read through L'escholle des Filles; and after I had done it, I burned it, that it might not be among my books to my shame; and so at night to supper and then to bed.' In the pidgin he reserves for such occasions, he describes the effects of his reading: 'It did hazer my prick para stand all the while, and una vez to décharger.' Licentious reading material cannot be exposed to public view.

## Reading attire

The example of this seventeenth-century English reader shows that reading did indeed become a private activity, but in a variety of ways. By the eighteenth century the correlation of reading with privacy was firmly established, as though reading defined the limits of the inner life. Evidence for this can be seen in Chardin's painting The Amusements of Private Life. Commissioned in 1745 by

Louise Ulrique of Sweden to paint two works, one on 'Strict Education' and the other on 'Gentle, Insinuating Education', Chardin chose to paint two different subjects: a woman surprised while reading a book covered with colored paper resting on her knees, and a woman recording her household expenses. The diptych thus contrasts leisure time with time spent in the chore of family administration. The second painting was called *The Administrator* and the first, *The Amusements of Private Life*. The latter name was acquired early in the history of the work, because the Swedish ambassador to Paris used it in a letter dated October 1746, after the work was shown at the Salon; an engraving made in 1747 used the same name.[43] This is, so to speak, a pictorial synecdoche: the part (reading) stands for the whole (private life). A single practice, that of reading, stands for the whole range of private pleasures in the time left free after family chores and obligations.

In this portrait of a woman reading, contemporaries recognized a classic theme: the reading of romantic fiction. Consider two descriptions of the painting. In his *Reflections on Some Causes of the Present State of Painting in France* (1747), Lafont de Saint-Yenne saw it this way:

> He [Chardin] has given this year a piece that represents a pleasant but idle woman in the guise of a lady casually if fashionably dressed, with a rather striking face wrapped in a white bonnet tied under the chin, which hides the sides of her face. One arm lies on her lap, and her hand casually holds a brochure. Beside her, a little to the rear, is a spinning wheel set on a little table.

One year later, the painting, now referred to as *Amusements of the Tranquil Life*, was described in these terms in *Observations on the Arts and Some Paintings Shown at the Louvre in 1748*:

> It represents a woman nonchalantly seated in an armchair and holding in one hand, which rests on her lap, a brochure. From a sort of languor in her eyes, which gaze out toward a corner of the painting, we divine that she is reading a novel, and that the tender impressions it has made on her have set her dreaming of someone whom she would like to see arrive at any moment.

Thus, Chardin's painted act of reading is characterized in two ways: in terms of objects and in terms of postures. The objects situate the reader in a comfortable apartment, a setting of some wealth. The reader's armchair is a high-backed bergère with a thick cushion and stuffed armrests, which allow the chair's occupant to relax with feet raised on a small footstool. Other styles of furniture – the chaise longue and the duchesse – permitted the reader to stretch out and relax even more. The casual if fashionable clothing worn by the woman is a warm but lightweight indoor garment known as a *liseuse* – a dress for reading rather than for show or seduction. The book she holds in her hand is a 'brochure', a book that is not bound but held together by a paper cover. On a low cabinet in a corner of the room, several bound books, larger in size than this brochure, are ranged against the wall.

For the commentators, the woman's posture is one of abandonment: she sits 'nonchalantly' and 'casually' holds the brochure; her gaze is languorous. These signs suggest that she is reading a novel, which fills her mind with disturbing images and sentiments and arouses her senses. From this description a modern spectator has some difficulty recognizing Chardin's painting, which shows, seated in a comfortable but austere room, a woman who is not languid at all and whose eyes by no means convey emotional turmoil. In fact, the descriptions seem to refer to other paintings, to Baudoin's *Reading*, for instance, which depicts, in a highly eroticized representation, a young woman in a state of total abandonment. The comments reveal the power of an association between female reading and idleness, sensual pleasure, and secret intimacy. More than the painting, which is deliberately estranged from the *topos*, the commentators' remarks reveal how eighteenth-century men imagined the act of reading by women, which by then had become the quintessence of private activity. Without the painter's intrusion it would have remained shrouded in silence.

## The spoken text

In the eighteenth century the iconography of reading is exclusively female and secular, whereas previously it had been almost entirely male and religious – think of Rembrandt's readers, hermits and philosophers who have withdrawn from society in order to meditate over a book. Yet painting does not yield an exhaustive catalogue of early modern reading practices. Between 1500 and 1800 reading aloud, whether among friends or chance companions, was an essential ingredient of social life, even among the elite. Thus, the *corrector de la impresión* (editor of the revised edition) of *La Celestina*, published in Toledo in 1500 as *La Comedia de Calisto y Melibea*, specifies how it ought to be read in an octet that he appends to the work. It is entitled *Dice el modo que se ha de tener leyendo esta tragicomedia* (He indicates the manner in which this tragicomedy should be read). The *lector* (reader) to whom these instructions are addressed is advised to vary his tone, assume the part of every character, speak asides between clenched teeth (*cumple que sepas hablar entre dientes*), and make use of the *mil artes y modos*, the thousand ways and means of reading so as to capture the attention of his listeners, *los oyentes*.

Like the Latin and Humanist comedies, La Celestina was written to be read 'theatrically' but by a single voice before a limited if select audience. In a prologue added to the Saragossa edition of 1507, which alludes to contradictory opinions about the work, the author accounts for the diversity of opinions by invoking the conditions under which the work was read: 'So, when ten people gather to hear this comedy, in which, as is always the case, there are so many different humors, would anyone deny that there are grounds for disagreement about things that can be heard in so many different ways?' Ten listeners choose to come together to hear a text read aloud; the book becomes the center of a cultivated society of friends or acquaintances.

Along with *La Celestina*, other texts, particularly pastorals and novels, were favored for such gatherings, in which the written word was mediated by the spoken voice. Cervantes refers to this practice in *Don Quixote*, first by dramatizing, in chapter 32 of part 1, the reading of the *Curioso impertinente* by a priest to a small group of avid listeners gathered at an inn. And as title for chapter 66 of part 2 he chose: 'Which treats of that which he who reads will see and that which he will hear who listens to a reading of it.'[44]

In the seventeenth century people frequently listened to books read aloud. In the army in the field, such activity whiled away the time, strengthened friendships, and provided food for thought. As an ensign and, later, lieutenant in the Normandy Regiment between 1635 and 1642, Henri de Campion described in his *Memoirs* reading in the military:

> I had my books, which took up a portion of my wagon's load, and frequently spent
> time with them, sometimes alone but most of the time with three friends from the
> regiment, intelligent and studious men. The Chevalier de Sévigné, a Breton and captain
> of the corps, was one. He was by nature a studious man, had read widely, and from
> birth had always been at war or at court. Le Breuil-Marcillac, a Gascon, brother of
> the lieutenant colonel and my captain, was the third member of our group. He had
> studied until the age of twenty-eight, his parents having destined him for the Church,
> which he quit in order to take up the sword, having spent well his time in school and
> later at the Sorbonne. He was a mild man, accommodating, with nothing of the
> rudeness of military men. D'Almivar, from Paris, a lieutenant and my close friend,

was the fourth party to our studious commerce. He had a polished wit, was agreeable in conversations of all sorts, and quite sociable.

Reading, listening to, and arguing about books established a strong and lasting friendship among the four men:

> Those were the three men with whom I spent my hours of leisure. After reasoning together about the subjects that came up, without bitter dispute or desire on the part of one to shine at the expense of the others, one of us would read some good book aloud, and we would examine the finest passages in order to learn to live well and to die well, in accordance with morality, which was the principal subject of our study. Many people enjoyed listening to our discussions, which, I believe, were useful to them, for nothing was said that was not conducive to virtue. Since then I have found no society so comfortable or reasonable; it lasted seven years, during which I served in the Normandy Regiment.[45]

Thus, different ways of reading defined different but related social practices: solitary reading encouraged personal study and intellectual interchange; reading aloud, combined with interpretation and discussion of what was read, fostered friendship; and these friendly study groups could attract a wider audience, which benefited by hearing the texts read and discussed.

Similar 'convenient' and 'reasonable' societies existed in the cities. Before official academies came into being, people came together over books, which they lent to one another, discussed, examined, and read aloud. In 1700 a *petite académie* was founded in Lyons. Seven scholars and friends met in the home of one of their number: 'The place where we hold our meetings is the study of one of our academicians. There we gather amid five or six thousand volumes, which constitute a library as choice as it is large. That alone provides ready and agreeable assistance to our scholarly conferences' (letter from Brossette, one of the founders and an *avocat* at the court known as the *présidial*, to Boileau, 16 July 1700). Sometimes a friendly visit could lead to discussion of books. Laurent Dugas, president of the Cour des monnaies and one of the seven 'academicians', gives a number of examples of this in his correspondence. On 12 January 1719: 'Yesterday in my study I spent a good part of the evening with Father de Vitry and Father Follard, regent of rhetoric. I gave them chocolate. We spoke of M. de Cambrai and we argued about literature. Father de Vitry wanted to look at the new edition of Saint Clement of Alexandria, which the bishop of Oxford has published and which I own, to see if the editor remarked upon passages he had noted.' 27 March 1731: 'Cheinet spent the evening and had supper with me. We read some letters of Cicero and complained about the ignorance of the public, by which I mean the want of taste on the part of our young people, who amuse themselves reading new and often frivolous or superficial books and neglect the great models that might teach them to think well.' 23 March 1733: 'M. de La Font, gentleman-in-waiting to the queen, arrived and told me that he thought I would enjoy hearing a reading of a new work by M. de Voltaire entitled *The Temple of Taste*. If I were agreeable, however, we would await the return of my son who had gone that morning to Brignais and was expected at any moment. He arrived a half-hour later and took the role of reader. The reading lasted an hour and a half. My wife who came in at seven o'clock, heard three-quarters of it.' Thus, people listened to readings, read to each other, talked about books, and conversed in their libraries: all were common practices, which depended on the existence of readers who often read alone but who sometimes used books as the basis of social occasions.[46]

Travel provided another opportunity for reading. On 26 May 1668 Samuel Pepys returned from Cambridge to London:

Up by 4 a-clock; and by the time we were ready and had eat, we were called to the coach; where about 6 a-clock we set out, there being a man and two women of one company, ordinary people, and one lady alone that is tolerable handsome, but mighty well spoken, whom I took great pleasure in talking to, and did get her to read aloud in a book she was reading in the coach, being the King's Meditations [the meditations of Charles I prior to his execution]; and the boy and I to sing.

Here, reading is a way of establishing a temporary and friendly bond between traveling companions who had not known each other previously. An anonymous, ephemeral community is bound together by reading, conversation, and song, helping make the journey more agreeable for all. 'We dining all together and pretty merry', Pepys notes, recording the felicitous consequence of his initiatives.

Reading influenced privatization in several ways. It contributed to the emergence of a sense of self, as the reader scrutinized his own thoughts and emotions in solitude and secrecy. It was also a group activity, which made it possible 'to avoid both the boredom of solitude and the crush of the multitude', as Fortin de La Hoguette put it in his treatise *On Conversation*. There are numerous eighteenth-century images of these small groups bound together by reading. In 1728 Jean-François de Troy painted *Reading Molière*. In a rococo salon, at 3:30 according to the clock, five women and two men, comfortably seated on low armchairs, listen to one of the company reading a bound book, which he holds in his hands. The door is closed and a screen has been opened to protect the little group, gathered in a circle around the reader, from the rest of the world.

A year earlier Marivaux had written for the stage a play entitled *Love's Second Surprise*. One of the characters, Hortensius, is presented as a 'pedant' who has been hired by the marquise to direct her reading and read to her: 'Two weeks ago I took on a man to whom I have entrusted my library. I do not flatter myself that I will become a scholar, but I am eager to occupy my time. He reads me something every evening. Our readings are serious and reasonable. He establishes an order that instructs as it amuses me' (act 1, scene 7). But Hortensius' readings are not reserved for his mistress alone. The marquise invites her visitors, such as the chevalier in scene 8 of act 2: 'Chevalier, you are master if you wish to remain, if my reading pleases you.' In both the painting and the play, listening together by no means precludes private sentiments. De Troy suggests them through the play of glances: eyes meet, glances are averted, people avoid looking at one another. Marivaux has the chevalier react strongly against what he hears being read, which is a way of stating his incipient love for the ironic and flirtatious marquise.

## Family reading

Reading aloud was a way of structuring family life. Husband and wife read to each other. On 22 December 1667 Pepys's wife had taken to her bed: 'After dinner, up to my wife again, and who is in great pain still with her tooth and cheek; and there, they gone, I spent the most of the afternoon and night reading and talking to bear her company, and so to supper and to bed.' Three days later, on Christmas Day, she does the reading: 'And all the afternoon at home, my wife reading to me the history of the Drummer, of Mr. Monpesson, which is a strange story of spirits, and worth reading indeed.' Fathers and sons read to each other. Dugas of Lyons gives several examples: 'I spent considerable time with my son reading Greek and some odes of Horace' (22 July 1718); 'I read with my eldest son Cicero's *Treatise on Laws*, and with my second son I read Sallust' (14 September 1719); 'At night I play chess with my son. We start by reading a good book, that is, a book of piety, for half an hour' (19 December 1732).

Sometimes the entire family gathered around the reader, especially when the family was Protestant and the book the Bible. Protestant books of domestic instruction often described such compulsory reading. Justus Menius' *Oeconomia Christiana* shows, on the title page of the 1554 Regensburg edition, a father reading to his wife and children on his right and his servants in another corner of the room. On the table we see a heavy Bible, another, smaller book (perhaps the *Oeconomia* itself), a pair of eyeglasses, and a sandglass.[47] Although such Bible-reading was not always practiced in Protestant families, it is attested in a number of places from sixteenth-century Switzerland (where Felix Platter remembered from his youth that 'my father was in the habit, before we went to church, of reading the holy Bible and preaching from it') to eighteenth-century New England.

## Popular customs

Conviviality, family and domestic intimacy, and individual retirement were the three aspects of life in which books and reading played a major role – and not only for the educated elite. Among the lower classes too printed materials fulfilled a variety of functions, but those materials were seldom books. Those who could read well usually read aloud to others who read less well or not at all. This was true in the cities and in the fields, at work and at leisure, among strangers or fellow workers. Reading matter ranged from 'books of portraiture', that is, collections of models and patterns used in sixteenth-century workshops, to placards posted on city walls, from religious texts (as in Swabia, where peasants gathered in the late eighteenth century to listen to the reading of the Bible) to mass-circulation books such as those in France's '*Bibliothèque bleue*' or Blue Library, which were read in family gatherings or by people who shared a common life, such as early eighteenth-century shepherds in Lorraine, according to the testimony of Jamerey-Duval.[48]

In sixteenth- and seventeenth-century Spain, popular audiences gathered to hear a variety of works read aloud, novels of chivalry foremost among them. They were listened to by the common folk in the cities, according to Juan Arce de Otalora (1560): 'In Seville they say that there are artisans who, on holidays and in the evening bring a book and read it on the *Gradas*', that is, in front of the cathedral.[49] Peasants also listened, at least in *Don Quixote*, according to the chapter cited earlier (part 1, chapter 32). In describing the novels of chivalry that he keeps in his inn, the innkeeper says: 'As far as I can see, there is no better reading in the world. I myself have two or three of them along with some manuscripts, and they have been the very breath of life, not only to me, but to many others as well. For in harvest time the reapers gather here in large numbers on feast days, and there are always some among them who can read. One of them will take a book in his hands and thirty or more of us will crowd around and listen to him with so much pleasure that we lose a thousand gray hairs.'[50] Gathered to hear *Don Circongilio of Thrace* or *Felixmarte of Hircania*, the peasants and the innkeeper's family, including his daughters, never tire of listening: 'We could go on listening day and night', says the master of the house. Other texts suitable for reading aloud included the *pliegos sueltos* or *pliegos de cordel*. Related by format (quarto volumes of two to sixteen sheets) and poetic form (generally octosyllabic, assonant *romances*), these plays were written to be read aloud. Their titles, always similar in structure, could be shouted out by those who sold them, usually blind hawkers who belonged to confraternities; the texts lent themselves to being spoken or sung to a public that related to the written word by way of the ear rather than the eye.

The common folk also had other access to written literature. Between 1500 and 1800 writing insinuated itself into the majority of households in the form of printed materials on which people set a high emotional value because they were associated with important moments in the life of the family or individual. In certain dioceses marriage charters were part of the marriage ritual; the husband handed the charter to the wife, and its text and images served as reminders of the ceremony. Certificates were distributed to pilgrims as proof that they had completed their journey and accomplished their religious duty. Confraternities gave certificates attesting to membership and fidelity to a heavenly protector. Whether displayed on a wall or kept in a safe place, such documents, which always included images along with the text, could be deciphered in a variety of ways. They played a fundamental role as aids to memory and self-affirmation, thus helping to constitute a private life that was at once intimate and on exhibit.

## From reading to writing

Some common folk used their ability to write about themselves. The practice may have been more widespread than is suggested by the few surviving autobiographies, such as Jacques-Louis Ménétra's *Journal of My Life* and the writings of Louis Simon.[51] Ménétra, a Parisian glazier, began writing his journal in 1802 or 1803, based on fragments he had been accumulating since 1764. Simon in 1809 began writing 'the principal Events that happened in the Course of my life' in a 'book' (that is, a handwritten journal) inherited twenty-one years earlier from an uncle by marriage. The book opens with the century-old accounts of the uncle's uncle, who had been a wine merchant at La Flèche.

Ménétra and Simon had acquired the habit of writing long before beginning their memoirs. While touring France as a journeyman glazier, Ménétra used his writing skills for a variety of purposes, including keeping records for an organization of fellow journeymen known as the Devoir: 'I was accepted as a companion of the Devoir, and my fellow members asked me to recopy the roll of what they call Maître Jacques or the Devoir, and I was named Parisien le Bienvenu' [companions called one another by secret names]. He wrote to his family in Paris, especially his grandmother, asking for financial assistance. He dealt with the correspondence and kept the books for the widows who hired him. And he acted as secretary for his comrades in a dispute with the intendant of Bordeaux over the drawing of lots for the militia: 'They cast about for one of their number who could write. The Guyennois came looking for me, and I was the thirty-first companion [that is, he was added to the delegation of thirty chosen to negotiate with the authorities]. Thereafter I wrote the rules and counted up my fellow journeymen.' Through frequent letters he nourished the hopes of the widow in Nîmes who expected that he would return to marry her when his tour of France was complete and who in the mean time treated him most generously.

Louis Simon, a clothmaker from the village of La Fontaine, was esteemed for his ability to write. He was called upon to keep the books of the fabric and the town government and to draft the parish's grievances against the government. For him, the French Revolution was time spent – and wasted – writing: 'For I went three years without working because of the disturbances, and here they could only turn to me since I was the only one who knew how to write and who understood a little of affairs'.

In writing their accounts of their lives, both men made perhaps unwitting use of books they had read in the past. Young Louis Simon came to know the books in the local priest's library as well as those (no doubt from the Blue Library) sold by a hawker who had returned to the area: 'I spent my time enjoying the pleasure of playing instruments and reading all the books that I could obtain on ancient history, wars, geography, the lives of saints, the Old and New Testament, and other books sacred and profane. I also loved songs and psalms'. His writing bears traces of this half-scholarly, half-popular background.

Ménétra mentions few books (only the Bible, the *Petit Albert* [a book of black magic], and the works of Rousseau), but his reading and knowledge of contemporary literary forms shaped the retelling of his life, part real and part imaginary. Erotic novels had provided him with a repertory of ribald plots and characters (the nun who violates her vows, the noblewoman whose lust is insatiable, the girl who succumbs against her will but to her great satisfaction, and so on). The theater, which he loved, had taught him how to arrange the players in his little dramas so as to give himself the leading role, as in his encounter with Rousseau. Stories borrowed from widely circulated books give relief to his more commonplace adventures. Though not cited in the *Journal*, these texts served as so many mirrors, or rather prisms, by means of which Ménétra observed at his own life and then recomposed it to suit his desires, creating an embellished, idealized version.

The two men were very different. Simon sought to recapture through writing his beloved wife, who had died five years earlier, whereas Ménétra gazed admiringly upon his own past and attempted to assert his own culture, reflected in his deliberate refusal to abide by the ordinary rules of punctuation and spelling. The writings of both show that ordinary folk were familiar with writing, the written word, and books.

## Notes

1   My interpretation of signature rates therefore differs from that of Françoise Furet and Jacques Ozouf, *Lire et Ecrire. L'alphabétisation des Française de Calvin à Jules Ferry* (Paris: Minuit, 1977), I, 27. After examining, for 1866, signatures on marriage documents, conscripts' educational documents, and cultural data, they conclude that 'the ability to sign one's name corresponds to what we now call literacy, meaning the ability to read and write' and that 'there is a presumption in favor' of the hypothesis that the correlation between ability to sign and complete literacy is valid 'for earlier periods'.

2   Robert Allan Houston, 'The Literacy Myth? Illiteracy in Scotland, 1630–1760', *Past and Present* 96 (1982): 81–102.

3   See David Cressy, *Literacy and the Social Order. Reading and Writing in Tudor and Stuart England* (Cambridge: Cambridge University Press, 1980), pp. 62–103, for the oaths of 1641–1644, and R. S. Schofield, 'Dimensions of Illiteracy, 1750–1850', *Explorations in Economic History* 10 (1973): 437–454.

4   Michel Fleury and Pierre Valmary, 'Les progrès de l'instruction élémentaire de Louis XIV à Napoléon III d'après l'enquête de Louis Maggiolo (1877–1879)', *Population* 12 (1957): 71–93, and Furet and Ozouf, *Lire et Ecrire*.

5   Simon Hart, 'Onderzoek naar de samenstelling van de de bevolking van Amsterdam in de 17e en 18e eeuw, op grond van gegevnes over migratie, huwelijk, beroep en alfabetisme', *Geschrift ien Getal. Een keuze uit de demografisch-economisch en sociall-historische studiën op grond van Amsterdamse en Azzanse archivalia, 1600–1800* (Dordrecht, 1976), pp. 130–132.

6   M. R. Duglion, 'Alfabetismo e società a Torino nel secolo XVIII', *Quaderni Storici* 17 (May–August 1971): 485–509.

7   M.-C. Rodriguez and Bartolomé Bennassar, 'Signatures et niveau culturel des témoins et accusés dans les procès d'Inquisition du ressort du tribunal de Cordoue (1595–1632)', *Caravelle* 31 (1978): 19–46.

8   Kenneth A. Lockridge, *Literacy in Colonial New England: An Inquiry into the Social Context of Literacy in the Early Modern West* (New York: Norton, 1974).

9   Kenneth A. Lockridge, 'L'alphabétisation en Amérique, 1650–1800', *Annales ESC*, 1977, pp. 503–518.

10  Cressy, *Literacy*, pp. 157–174.

11  André Larquié, 'L'alphabétisation à Madrid en 1680', *Revue d'histoire moderne et contemporaine*, 1981, pp. 132–157, and 'L'alphabétisation des Madrilènes dans la seconde moitié du XVIIe siècle: stagnation ou évolution'? *Colloque 'Instruction, lecture, écriture en Espagne (XVIe–XIXe siècle)'* (Colloquium on Teaching, Reading, and Writing in Spain [16th–19th century]), Toulouse, 1982, mimeographed.

12  Michel Vovelle, 'Y a-t-il eu une révolution culturelle au XVIIIe siècle? A propos de l'éducation en Provence', *Revue d'histoire moderne et contemporaine*, 1975, pp. 89–141.

13  Cressy, *Literacy*, pp. 130–137, esp. table 6.8, p. 136.

14  Daniele Marchesini, 'La fatica di scrivere. Alfabestismo e sottoscrizioni matrimoniali in Emilia, Sette et Ottocento', in Gian-Paolo Brizzi, *Il Catechismo e la Grammatic* (Bologna: Il Mulino, 1985), II, 83–169.

15  Cressy, *Literacy*, pp. 124–125, 128.

16  Joseph Ruwet and Yves Wellemans, *L'An-alphabétisme en Belgique (XVIII–XIXe siècle)* (Louvain, 1978), p. 22.

17  Kalman Benda, 'Les Lumières et la culture paysanne dans la Hongrie du XVIIIe siècle', *Les Lumières en Hongrie, en Europe centrale et en Europe orientale*, proceedings of the 3rd Colloquium of Matrafüred (1975) (Budapest, 1977), pp. 97–109.

18  Egil Johansson, 'The History of Literacy in Sweden', in H. J. Graff, ed., *Literacy and Social Development in the West: A Reader* (Cambridge: Cambridge University Press, 1981), pp. 151–182.

19  T. C. Smout, 'Born Again at Cambuslang: New Evidence on Popular Religion and Literacy in Eighteenth-Century Scotland', *Past and Present* 97 (1982): 114–127 (which cites Markussen and Skovgaard-Petersen's study on Denmark).

20  Richard Gawthrop and Gerald Strauss, 'Protestanism and Literacy in Early Modern Germany', *Past and Present* 104 (1984): 31–35.

21  Bernard Vogler, *Vie religieuse en pays rhénan dans la seconde moitié du XVIe siècle (1556–1619)* (Lille, 1974), II, 796–799.

22  Rolf Engelsing, *Analphabetentum und Lektüre. Zur Sozialgeschichte des Lesens in Deutschland zwischen feudaler und industrieller Gesellschaft* (Stuttgart, 1973), p. 62.

23  André Derville, 'L'analphabétisation du peuple à la fin du Moyen Age', *Revue du Nord*, special issue, *Liber amicorum. Mélanges offerts à Louis Trénard*, nois. 261–262, April–September 1984, pp. 761–776.

24  Christiane Klapisch-Zuber, 'Le chiavi fiorentine di Barbalù: l'appredimento della lettura a Firenze nel XV secolo', *Quaderni Storici* 57 (1984): 765–792. The reason for the variation in the percentage of children in school has to do with varying estimates of the Florentine population in the period 1330–1340.

25  M. J. Lowry, *The World of Aldus Manutius. Business and Scholarship in Renaissance Venice* (Oxford: Basil Blackwell, 1979), pp. 26–41.

26  Carlo Ginzburg, 'High and Low: The Theme of Forbidden Knowledge in the Sixteenth and Seventeenth Centuries', *Past and Present* 73 (1976): 28–41.

27  Paul Saenger, 'Silent Reading: Its Impact on Late Medieval Script and Society', *Viator Medieval and Renaissance Studies*, 13 (1982): 367–414.

28  Philippe Berger, 'La lecture à Valence de 1747 à 1560. Evolution des comportements en fonction des milieux sociaux', *Livre et Lecture en Espagne et en France sous l'Ancien Régime*, colloquium of the Casa de Velázquez, ADPF, 1981, pp. 97–107.

29  André Labarre, *Le Livre dans la vie amiénoise du XVIe siècle. L'Enseignement des inventaires après décès, 1503–1576*. (Paris-Louvain: Nauwelaerts, 1971).

30  Christian Bec, *Les Livres des Florentins (1413–1608)*, ed. Leo S. Olschki (Florence, 1984), esp. pp. 91–96.

31  Peter Clark, 'The Ownership of Books in England, 1560–1640: The Example of Some Kentish Townfolk', in Lawrence Stone, ed., *Schooling and Society. Studies in the History of Education* (Baltimore: Johns Hopkins University Press, 1976), pp. 95–111.

32  Etienne Françoise, 'Livre, confession, et société urbaine en Allemagne au XVIIIe siècle: l'exemple de Spire', *Revue d'histoire moderne et contemporaine*, July–September 1982, p. 353–375.

33  For an overview of the French data, see Roger Chartier and Daniel Roche, 'Les pratiques urbaines de l'imprimé', in H.-J. Martin and Roger Chartier, eds., *Histoire de l'édition française* (Paris:

Promodis, 1984), vol. 2, *Le Livre triomphant, 1660–1830*, pp. 402–429, which uses, among other things, the work of Jean Quéniart on the cities of western France and that of Michel Marion on Paris.

34   R. A. Gross, 'The Authority of the Word: Print and Social Change in America, 1607–1880', paper presented to the colloquium Needs and Opportunities in the History of the Book in American Culture, Worcester, Mass., 1984, mimeographed.

35   Philip Benedict, 'Bibliothèques protestantes et catholiques à Metz au XVIIe siècle', *Annales ESC*, 1985, pp. 343–370.

36   David D. Hall, 'Introduction: The Uses of Literacy in New England, 1600–1850', in William L. Joyce *et al.*, eds., *Printing and Society in Early America* (Worcester, Mass.: American Antiquarian Society, 1983), pp. 1–47, from which the quotations that follow are taken.

37   The quotations in this paragraph have been retranslated from the French.

38   Rolf Engelsing, 'Die Perioden der Lesforschung in der Neuzeit. Das statistische Ausmass und die soziokulturelle Bedeutung der Lektüre', *Archiv für Geschichte des Buchwesens* 10 (1969): 945–1002, and *Der Bürger als Leser. Lesergeschichte in Deutschland, 1500–1800* (Stuttgart, 1974).

39   Michel Eyquem de Montaigne, *The Complete Essays of Montaigne*, trans. Donald M. Frame (Stanford: Stanford University Press, 1957), p. 629.

40   Daniel Fabre, 'Le livre et sa magie', in Roger Chartier, ed., *Pratiques de la lecture* (Marseilles: Rivages, 1985), pp. 182–206.

41   *The Diary of Samuel Pepys*, ed. Robert C. Latham and William Matthews, 9 vols. (Berkeley: University of California Press, 1970–1976).

42   John Harrison and Peter Laslett, *The Library of John Locke* (Oxford: Clarendon, 1971), 2nd ed., esp. Laslett, 'John Locke and His Books', pp. 1–65.

43   Concerning these two paintings, see the notices in the catalogue *Chardin, 1699–1779* (Paris: Editions de la Réunion des Musées Nationaux, 1979), pp. 278–283.

44   Miguel de Cervantes Saavedra, *Don Quixote de la Mancha*, trans. Samuel Putnam (New York: Modern Library, 1949), p. 943.

45   *Mémoires d'Henri de Campion* (Paris: Merure de France, 1967), pp. 95–96.

46   See *Correspondance littéraire et anecdotique entre M. de Saint-Fonds et le président Dugas* (Lyons, 1900), and Roger Chartier, 'Une académie avant les lettres patentes. Une approche de la sociabilité des notables lyonnais à la fin du règne de Louis XIV', *Marseille*, no. 101, *Les Provinciaux sous Louis XIV*, 1975, pp. 115–120.

47   Gerald Strauss, *Luther's House of Learning: Indoctrination of the Young in the German Reformation* (Baltimore: Johns Hopkins University Press, 1979), pp. 108–131, engraving p. 114.

48   David Sabean, 'Small Peasant Agriculture in Germany at the Beginning of the Nineteenth Century: Changing Work Patterns', *Peasant Studies* 7 (1978): 222–223. Valentin Jamerey-Duval, *Mémoires. Enfance et Education d'un paysan au XVIIIe siècle* (Paris: Le Sycomore, 1981), pp. 191–193. On the reading of Blue books, see Roger Chartier, 'Livres bleus et lectures populaires', *Histoire de l'édition française*, II, 498–511.

49   Cited by Maxime Chevalier, *Lectura y Lectores en la España de los siglos XVI γ XVII* (Madrid: Turner, 1976), p. 91.

50   Cervantes, *Don Quixote*, trans. Putnam, p. 275.

51   Jacques-Louis Ménétra, *Journal de ma vie* (Paris: Montalba, 1982); trans. by Arthur Goldhammer as *Journal of My Life* (New York: Columbia University Press, 1986). Anne Fillon, 'Louis Simon, étaminier 1741–1820 dans son village du haut Maine au siècle des Lumières', thesis, Université du Maine, 1982.

# Chapter 10

# Jan-Dirk Müller

## THE BODY OF THE BOOK
## The media transition from manuscript to print

### More durable than bronze

'Now I have created your image in marble, if you deign to receive favorably the verses already begun. Soon I will fix it in gold, in the Temple of Minerva, that is to say, in the pure hearts of scholars' (from a leaflet concerning the victory of Charles V over France (1525)). With these words, Viennese professor of rhetoric Johann Alexander Brassican recommended epigrams praising the government bureaucrats of Lower Austria in 1525. Verses, as hard as marble statues and eventually as valuable as gold, would recall the secretaries and councillors for all time, not only in a temple but everywhere in the hearts of the scholarly world. It is an old argument that memory preserved in writing is more permanent than any other monument. The elder Pliny already knew that immortality depended on the use of papyrus (*Nat. hist*. XIII, 21). The humanist panegyrists around 1500 believed they had immediate proof: the rediscovered writings of antiquity preserved the names of kings and senators, of generals and artists. Was it not reasonable to promise the same to one's own patron, especially insofar as he was only willing to support scholarly verses (and their authors) that immortalized his name?

The argument seemed convincing, and yet one important difference escaped notice: the altered communications situation and the change of the medium. The appeal of advertisements like Brassican's depended on a history in which select texts in single manuscripts were brought back to life after the passage of time. But what would happen if suddenly everywhere an army of writers engaged in the business of immortality? What if their texts no longer circulated in small groups as manuscripts, but were suddenly available everywhere in great numbers as printed leaflets? Technical reproduction might have seemed at first a chance to preserve writing for everyone and for all time, but it abolished traditional selection mechanisms that established what is worth knowing and preserving. Written and printed monuments ceased to be monuments capable of recalling memories.

Brassican promises monuments of solid materials, marble and gold, but delivers a few pages of printed paper, a material that is, as we know, perishable and hardly permanent. He promises a precious and desirable object, but his leaflet was of little value, and almost no one held on to it.

He promises a work of art that is unique or nearly so, having only a few replicas in a sacred site; but this kind of broadsheet has no particular place. Addressing virtually everyone, it concerns no one in particular. The place in the hearts of the scholarly world that was promised the Austrian bureaucrats was none too certain. Verses of praise and those praised were both fairly soon forgotten.

It is worthwhile to look from today's standpoint at the deep rift in the writing culture during the time of early print. The change wrought by the advent of print in the organization of knowledge and the social function of writing of that time was as drastic as the change wrought by the advent of electronic media today. I will not discuss the complex assumptions and consequences of book printing (see Eisenstein 1979) but will deal instead with a particular problem, the materiality of writing and its medium (marble, paper) and, along with this, the change in attitude toward time and duration and the change in perception of text and tradition. All these concepts are topics of contemporary discussion, yet in an entirely different sense. Classifieds announce the 'dematerialized' newspaper of the twenty-first century, and funeral orations are held in public for the book, that cumbersome object of information conveyance. The networking of all pieces of knowledge promises an immense acceleration of progress, that is to say, the irrelevance of anything that is old. Text is only the transitory product of the personal computer, between one proof and another. We cannot yet predict the continuing course of the process that was put in motion with the first technical revolution of writing culture. One should be cautious regarding historical parallels between the advent of printing and that of electronic media, and teleological assumptions proved to be wrong anyway, but the reactions of that time are telling insofar as they reflect certain conditions of modern writing culture in terms of resentments and exaggerated expectations, as well as the difficulty the established cultural system had in adjusting to these conditions.

## Reproduction and aura

Multiplication (*multiplicatio*) was one of the main points in the praise of the new invention (Widmann 1972: 253). But very soon the other side of the coin was discovered, the 'overabundance of writing' (*vile der gschrifft*), the fact that everything was printed with little concern for selection and correctness, 'for profit alone' (*alleyn vff gewynn*), and as a 'great scam' (*groß beschisß*). Books lost value everywhere (*nütz gelten überal*) along with them the scholars, who were now replaced by 'rude people' (*geburen*) (Brant 1968: chap. 103, vv. 77–78, 98–104). According to Brant, selection and refinement of the written tradition are taken away from the only competent faculty, scholars. Ecclesiastical and governmental control of writing grows more and more difficult (Schreiner 1984). If it were true, as the Parisian theologian Guillaume Fichet claimed around 1470, that everything that can be said or thought can be immediately written and preserved for posterity by movable type (Swierk 1972: 81), then the memory capacity of the cultural system would be overstressed and oblivion would be the result. Conrad Gesner asserts in 1545, after almost a hundred years of printing, that books disappear as quickly as they are produced. He demands the establishment of public libraries at least for the valuable old manuscripts, as the apparently unlimited possibilities of reproduction by print lead to arbitrariness and uselessness (Gesner 1966: 3r). The written word loses the 'aura' that it possessed in medieval culture as a guarantor of truth, as a vessel of arcane knowledge, even as a component of magical practices.

This trivialization of the written was counteracted from the beginning by the attempt to save the aura of the medium, artificial writing (*artificialiter scribere*). God Himself gave humankind the new invention, because the requirement for writing had surpassed the work capacity of the scribe to the point that science and the handing down of sacred truth were endangered. Now a printer could produce more pages in a single day than could a scribe in a whole year (see Swierk

1972: 81, for further examples). Early on the new art was called 'divina ars'. The colophon of Justinian's *Institutions* (1468) compares the inventors with the greatest artisans of the Old Testament, who built the tabernacle and the temple furnishings. 'Moses cannot complete the plan of the tabernacle, nor can Salomon complete the temple, without ingenious craftsmen. Thus, the one who is greater than Salomon (= Christ) creates anew Bezaleel and Hyram (i.e., Gutenberg) wishing to renew the Church' (Heidenheimer 1925: 109). What Bezaleel and Hyram contributed to the cult of Jehovah was accomplished by Gutenberg and Fust for the renewal of the Church by Christ. Books are tabernacles of God's truth: 'In libris posuisti procul dubio tabernaculum tuum' (Bury 1960: 16). If God is not Himself claimed to be the inventor, print is at least placed among the cultural technologies that humanity owes to mythical heroes (cf. Polidorus Vergilius 1502: xxxvii r/v). And if the product of the press is fleeting and subject to rapid deterioration, at least the more solid quality of the writing material is emphasized: not the brittle reed, stylus, or quill but brazen letters made for longevity (see Swierk 1972: 82, for further examples). In any case, such arguments could not conceal the fact that book printing did not create a new temple as a center of Christianity but instead decentralized the Christian world. Nor could they conceal that ordinary means of control of writing and criteria of relevance were shoved aside or subjected to the needs of the market.

Very early on, print separated itself from traditional centers of writing (bishops' seats, religious convents, and universities). It became a profit-oriented commerce that had to meet the varied and growing demand of a diverse and predominantly urban society with its antagonistic interests. Although at the end of the fifteenth century it was still possible for a bishop of Mainz to oblige the printers of a town like Frankfurt to subject themselves to censorship, in the long run an effective control of all production sites, not to mention those prints that could be exported, was far beyond the capabilities of any political institutions of the time. And no matter what was written about the durability of the press in comparison with the pen, its product was no longer the costly treasure that was preserved with care and passed on from generation to generation.

## Longevity of the codex versus longevity of the text

The notorious and curious words of Abbot Johannes Trithemius (1462–1516) in his *Praise of the Scribe* (*De laude scriptorum*, 1494) express how the nature of the written tradition changed along with the material characteristics of the medium. He reminds his Benedictine brethren of their duty to copy sacred books:

> The devotion of the scribe is more valuable than the office of the preacher because the admonition of the preacher disappears in time, but the message of the scribe lasts for many years. The preacher only speaks to those present, whereas the scribe also preaches to those in the future. . . . When the preacher dies, his work is finished; the scribe continues to be a teacher of morality even after his death.
>
> (Trithemius 1973: 58)

These are well-known arguments supported by quotations from Church Fathers and theologians. But are they not rendered obsolete by printing, which reproduces the sacred text much faster and for many more readers? The answer:

> Who is ignorant of the difference between writing [*scriptura*] and printing [*impressura*]? A manuscript, written on parchment, can last a thousand years. How long will print, this thing of paper [*res papirea*] last? It is quite a lot if it can last two hundred years in

a volume of paper [*in volumine papireo*]. . . . Actually, no matter how many books are printed, there will never be so many printed that one couldn't find something to copy that hasn't yet been printed. Hardly anyone will have access to all books or be able to buy them. But even if all the books in the world were printed, the devout scribe should never lessen his zeal. He should copy the usable prints and thereby give them longevity, since otherwise they would not last long. In so doing, the scribe grants stability to instable writings [*scripturis mutantibus*]. He gives value to those of little worth and longevity to those subject to deterioration. The devout scribe will always find a task by which he will do a great service. He is not restrained by external conditions like the printer. He is free and rejoices in his freely performed task. He is in no way inferior to the printer, and his zeal must not weaken because the other prints.

(Trithemius 1973: 62, 64)

D. Mertens (1983) has elucidated the background of this strange admonition. Trithemius is concerned with the reform of his order. It is therefore not a contradiction when elsewhere he praises printing and when he even benefits from its potential by giving his *Praise of the Scribe* to the press. He recognizes two main problems: selection and longevity. Not all manuscripts are printed and especially few from the Benedictine tradition (Mertens 1983: 92). Printing therefore does not encompass the entire stock of writing. Whatever is excluded has little chance of being passed on. A sufficient and standard demand must first exist in order for the effort to pay off. The rapid rise and fall of some shops and the number of business failures (see Chrisman 1982) testify to how the market corrects a publisher's bad decisions with brutal efficiency. The considerations that the printer must take into account are summarized by Trithemius as 'restrictive conditions' (*constringi sub conditione impressoris*). This he juxtaposes with the 'freedom' of the scribe. The opposition between the 'seven liberal arts' of the noble and the bound *artes mechanicae* of the artisan earning his living may be the background of this assertion. However, Trithemius also describes two ways in which texts of a past culture are handed down: extraneous conditions, and free and responsible decisions (the latter assuring results of a more durable nature). Above all, the longevity of the text is linked to writing material. 'Printing is a matter of paper and deteriorates quickly' (Trithemius 1973: 34). This is obviously a weak argument; it is based on false assumptions concerning the longevity of paper and disregards the possibility of printing on parchment – even if it is true that printing was done primarily on paper, that only the mass production of paper had allowed the development of the new technology, and that only texts of extraordinary subject matter sometimes were done on parchment (Mertens 1983). It is striking, however, that Trithemius is concerned less with the life of the text than with the life of the body of the text, that is, the individual codex. He therefore advocates the copying of prints, including his own *Praise of the Scribe*, onto parchment. This can only be understood in the framework of the manuscript culture. Jean Gerson, chancellor of the Sorbonne, made similar arguments around 1400: 'A piece of writing can last not just for a short time, but for 10, 100, or 1,000 years, and this not only by itself [*in se*] but also by the multiplication of the exemplars [*per multiplicationem exemplariorum*] that are copied from the original' (Gerson 1973: 425). Reproduction is the worse alternative because every copy is a variation if not a change of the original. A reduction of the steps of reproduction ensures the integrity of the text. Gerson criticizes the many incapable scribes and the many corruptions of texts. He recommends 'drinking' as closely to the 'source' of truth as possible, at the 'scripta veterum', this being the works of the ancients as well as the written texts. Hence, a text on parchment lasting a thousand years is more trustworthy than a chain of ten texts on paper, copied from each other, but each enduring only a short time (Gerson 1973: 428). Only the sound body of his book can guarantee the author a life after death. Otherwise the costs and labors of writing are lost.

## The book as body

Writing survives as a physically present object in the body of a book. If medieval culture is performance, the interaction of voice and bodies, as P. Zumthor (1987) demonstrates, then that culture also had a far more corporeal conception of writing than the age of the early print had. The comparison holds all the more true for the age of the ubiquitously available writing of electronic media. Writing not only is more permanent than speech, but also, strangely enough, has a stronger effect on the senses. This is in any case the opinion of Richard de Bury (1287–1345) in his famous *Philobiblon* (1345). Truth that appears – with Boethius – in thoughts, speech, or writing is most profitable in books:

> For the meaning of the voice [*virtus vocis*] perishes with the sound; truth latent in the mind [*mente latens*] is wisdom that is hid and treasure that is not seen; but truth which shines forth in books desires to manifest itself to every impressionable sense [*omni disciplinabili sensui*]. It commends itself to the sight when it is read, to the hearing when it is heard, and moreover in a manner to the touch, when it suffers itself to be transcribed, bound, corrected, and preserved.
>
> (de Bury 1960: 19)

Others add the sense of taste in the sampling and rumination of what is read. Compared with writing, thoughts lack a discursive partner (*socius*) and oral instruction does not affect the sense of sight. The written word, on the other hand, is the perfect teacher, a living partner, but without the failings of a person such as bad moods, tiredness, or infirmity and death. Always friendly and available to provide information, books 'are masters [*magistri*], who instruct us without rod or ferule, without angry words, without clothes or money. If you come to them they are not asleep; if you ask and inquire of them, they do not withdraw themselves; they do not chide if you make mistakes; they do not laugh at you if you are ignorant' (de Bury 1960: 21). Books are the teachers, not their authors. The conversation is held with books, not their authors. In them the author is present. This apparent presence is expressed in pictures of authors common in medieval manuscripts. The metaphor *accessus ad auctorem*, used as a typical medieval formula of introduction, expresses the same concept. That the author is conceived as present is shown in translations of Latin texts into the vernacular. Often the author does not appear as the speaker, as in modern translations, but the translator defers to the one to whom he gives a voice: 'Here Master X speaks and says . . .'

The metaphor of tradition or its loss speaks of books in terms of living beings. They, or actually the authors embodied in them, suffer in unworthy captivity, rot in cellars subjected to the bites of moths and roaches. Since the transmission of truth depends on the survival of the codices, they must be protected from decay. Nevertheless, they are mortal: 'But because all the appliances of mortal men with the lapse of time suffer the decay of mortality, it is needful to replace the volumes that are worn out with age by fresh successors, that the perpetuity of which the individual is by its nature incapable may be secured to the species' (de Bury 1960: 147). Longevity (*perpetuitas*) means a never-ending chain of mortal individuals – the books – in whom the species survives:

> For as the bodies of books [*librorum corpora*], seeing that they are formed of a combination of contrary elements, undergo a continual dissolution of their structure

[*suae compositionis*], so by the forethought of the clergy a remedy should be found, by means of which the sacred book paying the debt of nature may obtain a natural heir and may raise up like seed to its dead brother, and thus may be verified that saying of Ecclesiasticus: His father is dead, and he is as if he were not dead; for he hath left one behind him that is like himself.

(de Bury 1960: 147. Cf. Eccles. 30: 4)

To copy the ancients means to produce sons (*propagationes recentium filiorum*), to whom the office of the fathers (*paternum officium*) is transferred. The metaphors don't seem totally convincing: a procreation by clerics, with dark relationships (brother? son?). The understanding of tradition is nonetheless clear. Ecclesiasticus speaks of permanence and change in a traditional society. Such a society is made all the more stable as the elders successfully transmit their knowledge to their sons. The heritage of the past changes constantly because it must be passed on from one individual to another. Yet everything remains basically the same as it was and always has been, because the father lives on in the son and in the son's son. Likewise the author lives on in his descendants, his books (de Bury 1960: 18). Tradition seems to be a chain of generations. Communication with tradition is therefore not a hermeneutic problem because the substance of the old remains present in the descendant.

This concept of tradition begins to break apart in early humanism. It is one of the main points that the Reformation attacks. Of course, it was recognized before this that traditions can be distorted. This is not seen, however, as a historical–philological problem (as in the *ad fontes* principle of the humanists). Whatever changes also degenerates. Poor copies are bastards. Their nobility (Richard de Bury uses *generositas*, the English translation has 'purity of race') is ruined, as in a chain of mésalliances, by compilers, revisers, and (worst of all) translators for the laity. Reborn again from generation to generation they finally degenerate completely (*regeneratione multiplici renascentes degeneramus omnino*). Their true heritage is distorted: 'Ah! how often ye pretend that we who are ancient are but lately born, and try to pass us off as sons who are really fathers, calling us who have made you clerks the production of your studies' (de Bury 1960: 46, 47). The place in the chain of generations establishes nobility and the claim to truth: the authority of age.

## The chain of generations and the authentic text

Brother resembles brother and the son the father, but having a family resemblance is not the same as being identical. It is a fact that, in a manuscript culture, one copy will never be exactly the same as another. But this did not present problems as long as the authenticity of truth was granted by the 'purity' of the 'genetic heritage'. Transmission is therefore above all a moral problem. The permanence of truth depends on the scrupulous scribe and his care and not on a philological reconstruction of a corrupted text or on hermeneutic efforts to regain an obscured meaning. The truth remains the same in the generations and branches of the written text if the scribe is not lazy or a counterfeiter (and that means: an adulterer).

Textual corruption and textual variants, however, could be ignored less and less the more widespread the practice of copying became. The reform movements of the fifteenth century are not the last to criticize variants in sacred texts since they bring forth conflicts about articles of faith, differences in ecclesiastical discipline, and the religious cult. It therefore seemed necessary to Nicholas of Cusa to produce identical missals for all parishes of his diocese. This plan could have hardly been realized in the age of writing and was perhaps, as has been conjectured, based on ties between Cusa and early printers, since now liturgical books no longer needed to be renewed copy for copy but thanks to the new technology could be replaced all at once.

Yet the idea of the book as an individual within a family did not disappear right away. F. Geldner, an expert on early printing, has described an amazing example. In 1482/84, the bishop of Freising ordered liturgical texts to be meticulously proofread by a Bamberg printer. Evidently this was not done by comparing a sample with the written originals and then making the necessary corrections in the master form or transferring them from the sample to each other copy. Instead, it seems that each copy was compared individually with the written original. Only in this way, according to Geldner (1961: 102), do the payments for the proofreading make sense: 91 florins for 91 breviaries on parchment; 206 florins for 206 obsequies; 400 florins for 400 missals, and so on. The enormous sums as well as the exact correspondence between the numbers of copies and the numbers of forms paid support Geldner's thesis. Otherwise, the proofreading of the sample should have been much more expensive than each transferal of the (few) corrections onto the several copies, an operation requiring far less time. This odd investment is due to the old manuscript culture that required such individual proof, copy after copy. The result of a similar procedure, the proofreading of a printed missal 'word for word', seemed like a miracle to the bishop of Regensburg: 'And see, it was as if by a miracle of God that the text was found to correspond in order and arrangement in each letter, syllable, word, parts of speech [*orationibus*], punctuation [*punctis*], headings, and everything else that is necessary, in every copy [*in omnibus et per omnia*] to the originals of our church' (Geldner 1961: 104). Correspondence in every detail of every copy (!) was discovered where family resemblance was expected. Now an identical text existed beyond its material realizations. These curious cases, if Geldner has correctly interpreted them, show in an exemplary way how written communication can now be centrally controlled and how it detaches itself from a model of interaction between individuals.

## The chain of generations and the *Bibliotheca Universalis*

Concerning missals, the authoritative text is the result of careful selection and the decisions of the bishop. Such care was never granted in early printing. On the contrary, whatever manuscript happened to be available was chosen for print, and it was therefore left to chance what kinds of texts would experience the greatest distribution. As before, the chain of texts was simply expanded by one link that replaced the preceding one. The original was often destroyed for technical reasons; no matter: it had been replaced (Schottenloher 1931: 94). Humanist scholars and printers eventually opposed this practice (Widmann 1970: xliii). It was no longer sufficient simply to expand the chain; instead, the ever-growing inventory had to be looked through in order to produce the best text from the greatest number of prototypes. For the new philology, the single copies are but steps on the way to the ideal 'correct text', which is actually never attainable but must at least be attempted in some way by comparison and combination. Meaning is not eternally present in the materiality of the book but must first be reconstructed beyond the distance of tradition. If writing must now be collected and deciphered as a clue to a dim past, then historical understanding becomes a never-ending task for the future. Gesner discovers that the newer text, insofar as it is the result of careful philological efforts, is often better than the older text (the 'father'), in which the past seems to be present in its natural state (Gesner 1966: 4v). Historical perspective is inscribed in the new culture of writing from the beginning, even though reflection on it lags behind for two centuries.

The generation around 1550 realized a loss of tradition, even though printing seemed at first to secure everything that had been transmitted and was worthy of transmission (*quamuis enim ars typographica librorum conseruationi nata uideatur*; Gesner 1966: 3r). The loss of tradition manifests itself in the destruction of manuscripts. Nicolaus Mameranus states in 1550 that everybody stupidly trusts the first, best print, that is, the son who replaces the father, and hence accepts that old manuscripts, once printed, are sold, cut up, scraped clean, and then used for other purposes: 'The books are printed,' they say; 'isn't that enough?' Not at all, if one wants to establish the word of the author in its original state (*pristinam suam et nativam integritatem*), as Mameranus himself says in his edition of Paschasius Radpertus. To reestablish it, all available copies must be collected; 'the old exemplars must be preserved with holy zeal, and guarded as a treasure, even if they are printed a thousand times over' (Schottenloher 1931: 93–94).

Tradition is no longer considered as this or that codex, but as a whole. Its preservation requires new institutions. Mameranus demands, as do Conrad Gesner and Conrad Lycosthenes, that libraries be placed under public oversight via the nobility and government. The private availability of books, although a highly praised achievement of print (Lycosthenes 1551: p. b 1r), does not ensure survival (Gesner 1966: 3r). Gesner's endeavors aim beyond the simple preservation of manuscripts. His *Bibliotheca universalis* is no longer concerned with individual books but with the transmission of all writing, and it makes little difference to him if the listed titles are still extant or not since, if they are lost now, they could be rediscovered later. Like the more limited catalogues of Trithemius, his *Bibliotheca* is of an imaginary extension, no longer a stock placed here or there. Its place is the literary public as a whole. Scientific interests are no longer concerned with the individually available manuscript or print but with the abstract unity of text or tradition. The idea of a corporeal presence of books is no longer appropriate to such a concept. Writing finally loses any analogy to face-to-face interaction, such as had always characterized the medieval manuscript culture, even where it was not oriented toward oral forms of communication. Books can come to everyone, but they are no longer individuals in which the absent speaker is embodied. Their longevity is no longer dependent on their material characteristics but on the mechanisms of selection of society's new institutions that keep public and present what is fixed in writing.

## Final comment

The body of the book, in fact a metaphor, was in the manuscript culture a guarantor of the longevity of the word and of the presence of author and meaning. Writing naturally depends on material conditions even after the invention of print. But longevity is guaranteed no longer by the written 'monument' itself but rather by the numerous institutions that select the constantly growing reservoir of writings and allow them to become effective. Text and tradition are phenomena beyond the present available stock of books. The author and the meaning he is supposed to intend are sought behind what is written. The ties and analogies to situations involving oral communication are severed. How this process affects modern writing cannot be dealt with here. Today writing seems in any case to be losing its eminent position. The pictures, gestures, and sounds that supplement and replace it do not show a return to the medieval culture of performance (Zumthor 1987). Technically produced and disseminated, they only simulate the sensual presence that the medieval scribe still experienced in the book.

# Chapter 11

# Elisabeth Eisenstein

## DEFINING THE INITIAL SHIFT
## Some features of print culture

We should note the force, effect, and consequences of inventions which are nowhere more conspicuous than in those three which were unknown to the ancients, namely, printing, gunpowder, and the compass. For these three have changed the appearance and state of the whole world . . .

(Francis Bacon, *Novum Organum*, Aphorism 129)

To dwell on the reasons why Bacon's advice ought to be followed by others is probably less helpful than trying to follow it oneself. This task clearly outstrips the competence of any single individual. It calls for the pooling of many talents and the writing of many books. Collaboration is difficult to obtain as long as the relevance of the topic to different fields of study remains obscure. Before aid can be enlisted, it seems necessary to develop some tentative hypotheses relating the shift from script to print to significant historical developments.

  This task, in turn, seems to call for a somewhat unconventional point of departure and for a reformulation of Bacon's advice. Instead of trying to deal with 'the force, effect, and consequences' of a single post-classical invention that is coupled with others, I will be concerned with a major transformation that constituted a large cluster of changes in itself. Indecision about what is meant by the advent of printing has, I think, helped to muffle concern about its possible consequences and made them more difficult to track down. It is difficult to find out what happened in a particular Mainz workshop in the 1450s. When pursuing other inquiries, it seems almost prudent to by-pass so problematic an event. This does not apply to the appearance of new occupational groups who employed new techniques and installed new equipment in new kinds of workshops while extending trade networks and seeking new markets to increase profits made from sales. Unknown anywhere in Europe before the mid-fifteenth century, printers' workshops would be found in every important municipal center by 1500. They added a new element to urban culture in hundreds of towns.[1] To pass by all that, when dealing with other problems, would seem to be incautious. For this reason, among others, I am skipping over the perfection of a new process for printing with movable types and will not pause over the massive literature devoted to explanations of Gutenberg's invention.[2] Instead, I will begin where many studies end, after the first dated printed products had been issued and the inventor's immediate successors had set to work.

By the advent of printing then, I mean the establishment of presses in urban centers beyond the Rhineland during an interval that begins in the 1460s and coincides, very roughly, with the era of incunabula.[3] So few studies have been devoted to this point of departure that no conventional label has yet been attached to it. One might talk about a basic change in a mode of production, about a book revolution, or a media revolution, or perhaps, most simply and explicitly, about a shift from script to print. Will Durant refers to a 'typographical revolution'. Partly because it can be neatly coupled with the already well entrenched commercial revolution and also because it points to a major dimension of history which needs more attention, I believe 'communications revolution' best suits my purposes in this book. Whatever label is used, it should be understood to cover a large cluster of relatively simultaneous, closely interrelated changes, each of which needs closer study and more explicit treatment – as the following quick sketch may suggest.

First of all, the marked increase in the output of books and the drastic reduction in the number of man-hours required to turn them out deserve stronger emphasis. At present there is a tendency to think of a steady increase in book production during the first century of printing. An evolutionary model of change is applied to a situation that seems to call for a revolutionary one.

> A man born in 1453, the year of the fall of Constantinople, could look back from his fiftieth year on a lifetime in which about eight million books had been printed, more perhaps than all the scribes of Europe had produced since Constantine founded his city in A.D. 330.[4]

The actual production of 'all the scribes of Europe' is inevitably open to dispute. Even apart from the problem of trying to estimate numbers of books that went uncatalogued and then were destroyed, contemporary evidence must be handled with caution, for it often yields false clues to the numbers of books involved. Since it was customary to register many texts bound within one set of covers as but one book, the actual number of texts in a given manuscript collection is not easily ascertained.[5] That objects counted as one book often contained a varying combination of many provides yet another example of the difficulty of quantifying data provided in the age of scribes. The situation is similar when we turn to the problem of counting the man-hours required to copy manuscript books. Old estimates based on the number of months it took forty-five scribes working for Vespasiano da Bisticci to produce 200 books for Cosimo de Medici's Badia library have been rendered virtually worthless by recent intensive research.[6]

Thus the total number of books produced by 'all the scribes of Europe' since 330 or even since 1400, is likely to remain elusive. Nevertheless, some comparisons are possible and they place the output of printers in sharp contrast to preceding trends. 'In 1483, the Ripoli Press charged three florins per quinterno for setting up and printing Ficino's translation of Plato's *Dialogues*. A scribe might have charged one florin per quinterno for duplicating the same work. The Ripoli Press produced 1,025 copies; the scribe would have turned out one'.[7] Given this kind of comparison, it seems misguided to suggest that 'the multiplication of identical copies' was merely 'intensified' by the press.[8] Doubtless, hand-copying could be quite efficient for the purpose of duplicating a royal edict or papal bull.[9] Sufficient numbers of copies of a newly edited Bible were produced in the thirteenth century for some scholars to feel justified in referring to a Paris 'edition' of a manuscript Bible. To turn out one single whole 'edition' of any text was no mean feat in the thirteenth century, however. The one thirteenth-century scribal 'edition' might be compared with the large number of Bible editions turned out in the half century between Gutenberg and Luther. When scribal labor was employed for multiplying edicts or producing a whole 'edition' of scripture, moreover, it was diverted from other tasks.

Many valued texts were barely preserved from extinction; untold numbers failed to survive. Survival often hinged on the occasional copy being made by an interested scholar who acted as his own scribe. In view of the proliferation of 'unique' texts and of the accumulation of variants, it is doubtful whether one should refer to 'identical copies' being 'multiplied' before print. This point is especially important when considering technical literature. The difficulty of making even one 'identical' copy of a significant technical work was such that the task could not be trusted to any hired hands. Men of learning had to engage in 'slavish copying' of tables, diagrams and unfamiliar terms. The output of whole editions of sets of astronomical tables did not 'intensify' previous trends. It reversed them, producing a new situation which released time for observation and research.

The previous introduction of paper, it should be noted, did not have anything like a 'similar' effect, any more than did 'the organization of a regular trade in manuscript books'.[10] Paper production served the needs of merchants, bureaucrats, preachers and literati; it quickened the pace of correspondence and enabled more men of letters to act as their own scribes. But since the same number of man-hours was still required to turn out a given text, the increase in book production was sluggish and copies continued to be made at an irregular rate. Shops run by stationers or *cartolai* multiplied in response to an increasing demand for tablets, notebooks, prepared sheets and other supplies.[11] In addition to selling writing materials and school books as well as book-binding materials and services, some merchants also helped book-hunting patrons by locating valued works. They had copies made on commission and kept some for sale in their shops. But their involvement in the book-trade was more casual than one might think.

> The activities of the *cartolai* were multifarious, although they usually specialized in one or another branch of their trade. The preparation and selling of book materials and binding were probably their commonest occupations. Some *cartolai* were also illuminators or employed illuminators in their shops . . . Scribes who mostly had other occupations (they were often notaries or priests) seem usually to have worked at home or in their shops, on commission . . . Many of the *cartolai* especially those who specialized in the sale and preparation of book materials or in bindings were probably concerned little if at all, with the production or sale of manuscripts and (later) printed books, either new or secondhand . . .[12]

Even the retail book-trade that was conducted by Vespasiano da Bisticci, the most celebrated Florentine book merchant, who served prelates and princes and 'did everything possible' to attract patrons and make sales, never verged on becoming a wholesale business. Despite Vespasiano's unusually aggressive tactics in promoting sales and matching books with clients, he showed no signs of ever 'having made much money' from all his transactions.[13] He did win notable patrons, however, and achieved considerable celebrity as 'prince of publishers'. His shop was praised by humanist poets along lines which were similar to those used in later tributes to Gutenberg and Aldus Manutius.[14] His posthumous fame — achieved only in the nineteenth century after the publication of his memoirs and their use by Jacob Burckhardt — is perhaps even more noteworthy. Vespasiano's *Lives of Illustrious Men* contains a reference to the beautifully bound manuscript books in the Duke of Urbino's library and snobbishly implies that a printed book would have been 'ashamed' in such elegant company. This one reference by an atypical and obviously prejudiced bookdealer has ballooned into many misleading comments about the disdain of Renaissance humanists for vulgar machine-made objects. Thus the catalogue to the beautiful Morgan Library 1973 Exhibition on 'The Art of the Printed Book' asserts that the Medici [*sic*] 'considered newly printed books a degradation and would not allow them in their libraries'.[15] The same error was amplified by an article in *The New York Times*: 'The Medici and other Florentine Princes [*sic*] considered printing a degradation and barred it from their sacred manuscript libraries'.[16] Similar distortions, all emanating from Burckhardt's use of Vespasiano's *Lives*, have been multiplied and amplified in so many varying contexts that scholarly disclaimers cannot catch up with them.[17]

The need to make Renaissance bibliophiles and patrons into snobbish enemies of machine-made objects seems oddly compelling. Why else is the story so often told with no real hard evidence to support it and expanded to Florence with no supporting evidence at all? Actually, Florentine bibliophiles were sending to Rome for printed books as early as 1470. Under Guidobaldo da Montefeltro, the ducal library at Urbino acquired printed editions and (shamelessly or not) had them bound with the same magnificent covers as manuscripts. The same court also sponsored the establishment of an early press in 1482.[18] That Vespasiano was indulging in wishful and nostalgic thinking is suggested by his own inability to find sufficient support from princely patrons to persist in his exclusive trade. His chief rival in Florence, Zanobi di Mariano, managed to stay in business right down to his death in 1495. 'Zanobi's readiness to sell printed books – a trade which Vespasiano spurned – explains his survival as a bookseller in the tricky years of the late fifteenth century. Vespasiano dealing exclusively in manuscripts was forced out of business in 1478'.[19]

One must wait for Vespasiano to close shop before one can say that a genuine wholesale book trade was launched.

> As soon as Gutenberg and Schoeffer had finished the last sheet of their monumental Bible, the financier of the firm, John Fust, set out with a dozen copies or so to see for himself how he could best reap the harvest of his patient investments. And where did he turn first of all to convert his Bibles into money? He went to the biggest university town in Europe, to Paris, where ten thousand or more students were filling the Sorbonne and the colleges. And what did he, to his bitter discomfiture find there? A well organized and powerful guild of the book-trade, the Confrérie des Libraires, Relieurs, Enlumineurs, Ecrivains et Parcheminiers . . . founded in 1401 . . . Alarmed at the appearance of an outsider with such an unheard of treasure of books; when he was found to be selling one Bible after another, they soon shouted for the police, giving their expert opinion that such a store of valuable books could be in one man's possession through the help of the devil himself and Fust had to run for his life or his first business trip would have ended in a nasty bonfire.[20]

The story may be just as unfounded as the legend that linked the figure of Johann Fust with that of Dr Faustus.[21] The adverse reaction it depicts should not be taken as typical; many early references were at worst ambivalent.[22] The ones that are most frequently cited associate printing with divine rather than diabolic powers. But then the most familiar references come either from the blurbs and prefaces composed by early printers themselves or from editors and authors who found employment in print shops.[23] Such men were likely to take a more favorable view than were the guildsmen who had made a livelihood from manuscript books. The Parisian *libraires* may have had good reason to be alarmed, although they were somewhat ahead of the game; the market value of hand-copied books did not drop until after Fust was dead.[24] Other members of the *confrérie* could not foresee that most 'book-binders, rubricators, illuminators, and calligraphers would be kept busier than ever after early printers set up shop.[25] Whether the new art was considered a blessing or a curse; whether it was consigned to the Devil or attributed to God; the fact remains, that the initial increase in output did strike contemporary observers as sufficiently remarkable to suggest supernatural intervention. Even incredulous modern scholars may be troubled by trying to calculate the number of calves required to supply enough skins for Gutenberg's Bible.[26] It should not be too difficult to obtain agreement that an abrupt rather than a gradual increase did occur in the second half of the fifteenth century.

Scepticism is much more difficult to overcome when we turn from consideration of quantity to that of quality. If one holds a late manuscript copy of a given text next to an early printed one, one is likely to doubt that any change at all has taken place, let alone an abrupt or revolutionary one.

> Behind every book which Peter Schoeffer printed stands a published manuscript
> . . . The decision on the kind of letter to use, the selection of initials and decoration
> of rubrications, the determination of the length and width of the column, planning
> for margins . . . all were prescribed by the manuscript copy before him.[27]

Not only did early printers such as Schoeffer try to copy a given manuscript as faithfully as possible, but fifteenth-century scribes returned the compliment. As Curt Bühler has shown, a large number of the manuscripts made during the late fifteenth century were copied from early printed books.[28] Thus handwork and presswork continued to appear almost indistinguishable, even after the printer had begun to depart from scribal conventions and to exploit some of the new features inherent in his art.

That there were new features and they were exploited needs to be given due weight. Despite his efforts to duplicate manuscripts as faithfully as possible, the fact remains that Peter Schoeffer, printer, was following different procedures than had Peter Schoeffer, scribe. The absence of any apparent change in product was combined with a complete change in methods of production, giving rise to the paradoxical combination, noted above, of seeming continuity with radical change. Thus the temporary resemblance between handwork and presswork seems to support the thesis of a very gradual evolutionary change; yet the opposite thesis may also be supported by underlining the marked difference between the two different modes of production and noting the new features that began to appear before the fifteenth century had come to an end.

Concern with surface appearance necessarily governed the handwork of the scribe. He was fully preoccupied trying to shape evenly spaced uniform letters in a pleasing symmetrical design. An altogether different procedure was required to give directions to compositors. To do this, one had to mark up a manuscript while scrutinizing its contents.[29] Every manuscript that came into the printer's hands, thus, had to be reviewed in a new way — one which encouraged more editing, correcting and collating than had the hand-copied text.[30] Within a generation the results of this review were being aimed in a new direction – away from fidelity to scribal conventions and toward serving the convenience of the reader. The highly competitive commercial character of the new mode of book production encouraged the relatively rapid adoption of any innovation that commended a given edition to purchasers.[31] Well before 1500, printers had begun to experiment with the use 'of graduated types, running heads . . . footnotes . . . tables of contents . . . superior figures, cross references . . . and other devices available to the compositor' – all registering 'the victory of the punch cutter over the scribe'.[32] Title pages became increasingly common, facilitating the production of book lists and catalogues, while acting as advertisements in themselves.[33] Hand-drawn illustrations were replaced by more easily duplicated woodcuts and engravings — an innovation which eventually helped to revolutionize technical literature by introducing 'exactly repeatable pictorial statements' into all kinds of reference works.

The fact that identical images, maps and diagrams could be viewed simultaneously by scattered readers constituted a kind of communications revolution in itself. This point has been made most forcefully by William Ivins, a former curator of prints at the Metropolitan Museum.[34] Although Ivins' special emphasis on 'the exactly repeatable pictorial statement' has found favor among historians of cartography,[35] his propensity for overstatement has provoked objections from other specialists. Repeatable images, they argue, go back to ancient seals and coins; while *exact* replication was scarcely fostered by woodblocks which got worn and broken after repeated use. Here as elsewhere one must be wary of underrating as well as of overestimating the advantages of the new technology. Even while noting that woodcuts did get corrupted when copied for insertion in diverse kinds of texts, one should also consider the corruption that occurred when hand-drawn images had to be copied into hundreds of books. Although pattern books and 'pouncing' techniques were available to some medieval illuminators, the precise reproduction of fine detail remained elusive until the advent of woodcarving and engraving. Blocks and plates did make repeatable visual aids feasible for the first time. In the hands of expert craftsmen using good materials and working under supervision, even problems of wear and tear could be circumvented; worn places could be sharpened; blurred details refined and a truly remarkable durability achieved.[36]

It is not so much in his special emphasis on the printed image but rather in his underrating the significance of the printed text that Ivins seems to go astray. In his work the use of movable type is oddly described as 'little more than a way to do with a smaller number of proof readings'. A reference by Pliny the Younger to one thousand copies of a book being made in the second century A.D. is cited repeatedly as evidence that the duplicative powers of print were relatively feeble.[37] The incapacity of any two scribes (let alone one thousand) to produce identical copies while taking dictation is overlooked. Although he mentions in passing that 'the history of prints as an integrated series' begins with their use 'as illustrations in books printed from movable types'[38] Ivins' analysis elsewhere tends to detach the fate of printed pictures from that of printed books. His treatment implies that the novel effects of repeatability were confined to pictorial statements. Yet these effects were by no means confined to pictures or, for that matter, to pictures and words. Mathematical tables, for example, were also transformed. For scholars concerned with scientific change, what happened to numbers and equations is surely just as significant as what happened to either images or words. Furthermore, many of the most important pictorial statements produced during the first century of printing employed various devices – banderoles, letter-number keys, indication lines – to relate images to texts.[39] To treat the visual aid as a discrete unit is to lose sight of the connecting links which were especially important for technical literature because they expressed the relationship between words and things.

Even though block-print and letterpress may have originated as separate innovations and were initially used for diverse purposes (so that playing cards and saints' images, for example, were being stamped from blocks at the same time that hand illumination continued to decorate many early printed books), the two techniques soon became intertwined. The use of typography for texts led to that of xylography for illustration, sealing the fate of illuminator along with that of the scribe.[40] When considering how technical literature was affected by the shift from script to print, it seems reasonable to adopt George Sarton's strategy of envisaging a 'double invention; typography for the text, engraving for the images'.[41] The fact that letters, numbers and pictures were *all* alike subject to repeatability by the end of the fifteenth century, needs more emphasis. That the printed book made possible new forms of interplay between these diverse elements is perhaps even more significant than the change undergone by picture, number or letter alone.

Intellectual historians may find the new interplay between 'literate, figurative and numerate' forms of expression of particular interest.[42] Social historians also need to be alerted to the new interplay between diverse occupational groups which occurred within the new workshops that were set up by early printers. The preparation of copy and illustrative material for printed editions led to a rearrangement of all book-making arts and routines. Not only did new skills, such as typefounding and presswork, involve veritable occupational mutations;[43] but the production of printed books also gathered together in one place more traditional variegated skills. In the age of scribes, book-making had occurred under the diverse auspices represented by stationers and lay copyists in university towns; illuminators and miniaturists trained in special ateliers; goldsmiths and leather workers belonging to special guilds; monks and lay brothers gathered in scriptoria; royal clerks and papal secretaries working in chanceries and courts; preachers compiling books of sermons on their own; humanist poets serving as their own scribes. The advent of printing led to the creation of a new kind of shop structure; to a regrouping which entailed closer contacts among diversely skilled workers and encouraged new forms of cross-cultural interchange.

Thus it is not uncommon to find former priests among early printers or former abbots serving as editors and correctors.[44] University professors also often served in similar capacities and thus came into closer contact with metal workers and mechanics. Other fruitful forms of collaboration brought astronomers and engravers, physicians and painters together, dissolving older divisions of intellectual labor and encouraging new ways of coordinating the work of brains, eyes and hands. Problems of financing the publication of the large Latin volumes that were used by late medieval faculties of theology, law, and medicine also led to the formation of partnerships that brought rich merchants and local scholars into closer contact. The new financial syndicates that were formed to provide master printers with needed labor and supplies brought together representatives of town and gown.[45] As the key figure around whom all arrangements revolved, the master printer himself bridged many worlds.[46] He was responsible for obtaining money, supplies and labor, while developing complex production schedules, coping with strikes, trying to estimate book markets and lining up learned assistants.[47] He had to keep on good terms with officials who provided protection and lucrative jobs, while cultivating and promoting talented authors and artists who might bring his firm profits or prestige. In those places where his enterprise prospered and he achieved a position of influence with fellow townsmen, his workshop became a veritable cultural center attracting local literati and celebrated foreigners; providing both a meeting place and message center for an expanding cosmopolitan Commonwealth of Learning.

Some manuscript bookdealers, to be sure, had served rather similar functions before the advent of printing. That Italian humanists were grateful to Vespasiano da Bisticci for many of the same services that were later rendered by Aldus Manutius has already been noted. Nevertheless, the shop structure over which Aldus presided differed markedly from that known to Vespasiano. As the prototype of the early capitalist as well as the heir to Atticus and his successors, the printer embraced an even wider repertoire of roles. Aldus' household in Venice, which contained some thirty members, has recently been described as an 'almost incredible mixture of the sweat shop, the boarding house and the research institute'.[48] A most interesting study might be devoted to a comparison of the talents mobilized by early printers with those previously employed by stationers or manuscript bookdealers. Of equal interest would be a comparison of the occupational culture of Peter Schoeffer, printer, with that of Peter Schoeffer, scribe. The two seem to work in contrasting milieux, subject to different pressures and aiming at different goals. Unlike the shift from stationer to publisher, the shift from scribe to printer represented a genuine occupational mutation. Although Schoeffer was the first to make the leap, many others took the same route before the century's end.[49]

Judging by Lehmann-Haupt's fine monograph, many of Schoeffer's pioneering activities were associated with the shift from a retail trade to a wholesale industry which led the printer to turn peddler and to launch what soon became an annual book fair at Frankfurt. 'For a while the trade in printed books flowed within the narrow channels of the manuscript book market. But soon the stream could no longer be contained'. New distribution outlets were located; handbills, circulars and sales catalogues were printed and the books themselves were carried down the Rhine, across the Elbe, west to Paris, south to Switzerland. The drive to tap markets went together with efforts to hold competitors at bay by offering better products or, at least, by printing a prospectus advertising the firm's 'more readable' texts, 'more complete and better arranged' indexes, 'more careful proof reading' and editing. Officials serving archbishops and emperors were cultivated, not so much as potential bibliophiles, nor even as potential censors, but rather as potential customers, who issued a steady flow of orders for the printing of ordinances, edicts, bulls, indulgences, broadsides and tracts. By the end of the century, Schoeffer had risen to a position of eminence in the city of Mainz. He commanded a 'far-flung sales organization', had become a partner in a joint mining enterprise, and had founded a printing dynasty. His supply of types went to his sons upon his death and the Schoeffer firm continued in operation, expanding to encompass music printing, through the next generation.[50]

As the foregoing may suggest, there are many points of possible contrast between the activities of the Mainz printer and those of the Paris scribe. All need to be brought out more clearly when considering fifteenth-century trends. The movement of centers of book production from university towns, princely courts, patrician villas and monasteries to commercial centers; the organization of new trade networks and fairs; the new competition over lucrative privileges and monopolies; the new restraints imposed by official censors have been covered in special accounts.[51] But the implications of such changes need to be underlined so that they may be related to other concurrent developments. Competitive and commercial drives were not entirely absent among the stationers who served university faculties, the lay scribes who were hired by mendicant orders, or the semi-lay copyists who belonged to communities founded by the Brethren of the Common Life. But they were muted in comparison with the later efforts of Schoeffer and his competitors to recoup initial investments, pay off creditors, use up reams of paper, and keep pressmen employed. The manuscript bookdealer did not have to worry about idle machines or striking workmen as did the printer. It has been suggested indeed that the mere act of setting up a press in a monastery or in affiliation with a religious order was a source of disturbance, bringing 'a multitude of worries about money and property' into space previously reserved for meditation and good works. When one considers that such an event occurred in several places in the late fifteenth century, it seems to warrant more attention in studies of changes affecting late medieval religious life.[52]

We also need to hear more about the job-printing that accompanied book-printing. It lent itself to commercial advertising, official propaganda, seditious agitations and bureaucratic red tape as no scribal procedure ever had.[53] The very term 'avertissement' underwent an intriguing change. In the Low Countries, books copied during holy days in medieval scriptoria were regarded as specially consecrated. A note placed in the colophon designating holy-day work served as a warning (or 'avertissement') against sale.[54] Of course such a warning can be interpreted as indicating the commercialization of the manuscript book-trade. Books were being copied not just for the love of God but for sale, on all save holy days. But a different, more muted commercial theme was sounded by this kind of 'avertissement' than would be the case after presses were established.

As self-serving publicists, early printers issued book lists, circulars and broadsides. They put their firm's name, emblem and shop address on the front page of their books. Indeed, their use of title pages entailed a significant reversal of scribal procedures; they put themselves first. Scribal colophons had come last. They also extended their new promotional techniques to the authors and artists whose work they published, thus contributing to the celebration of lay culture-heroes and to their achievement of personal celebrity and eponymous fame. Reckon masters and instrument makers along with professors and preachers also profited from book advertisements that spread their fame beyond shops and lecture halls.[55] Studies concerned with the rise of a lay intelligentsia, with the new dignity assigned to artisan crafts or with the heightened visibility achieved by the 'capitalist spirit' might well devote more attention to these early practitioners of the advertising arts.

Their control of a new publicity apparatus, moreover, placed early printers in an exceptional position with regard to other enterprises. They not only sought ever larger markets for their own products; but they also contributed to, and profited from, the expansion of other commercial enterprises. What effects did the appearance of new advertising techniques have on sixteenth-century commerce and industry? Possibly some answers to this question are known. Probably others can still be found. Many other aspects of job printing and the changes it entailed clearly need further study. The printed calendars and indulgences that were first issued from the Mainz workshops of Gutenberg and Fust, for example, warrant at least as much attention as the more celebrated Bibles. Indeed the mass production of indulgences illustrates rather neatly the sort of change that often goes overlooked, so that its consequences are more difficult to reckon with than perhaps they need be.

In contrast to the changes sketched above, those that were associated with the consumption of new printed products are more intangible, indirect, and difficult to handle. A large margin for uncertainty must be left when dealing with such changes. Many of them also have to be left for later discussion because they involved prolonged, unevenly phased transformations which occurred over the course of several centuries. This seems especially true of those changes which are most commonly associated with the impact of printing: changes, that is, which hinge on the spread of literacy and which entail a variety of popularizing trends.

On the difficult problem of estimating literacy rates before and after printing, the comments of Carlo Cipolla seem cogent:

> It is not easy to draw a general conclusion from the scattered evidence that I have quoted and from the similarly scattered evidence that I have not quoted . . . I could go on to conclude that at the end of the sixteenth century 'there were more literate people than we generally believe' . . . I could equally conclude that 'there were less literate people than we generally believe' for in all truth one never knows what is it that 'we generally believe' . . . one could venture to say that at the end of the sixteenth century the rate of illiteracy for the adult population in Western Europe was below 50 percent in the towns of the relatively more advanced areas and above 50 percent in all rural areas as well as in the towns of the backward areas. This is a frightfully vague statement . . . but the available evidence does not permit more precision.[56]

Statements about literacy rates during the fourteenth and early fifteenth centuries are likely to be just as vague – perhaps even more so. In the absence of hard data, plausible arguments may be developed to support sharply divergent opinions and there is no way of settling the inevitable conflict between revolutionary and evolutionary models of change. Thus one may envisage a relatively swift 'educational revolution' in the sixteenth century, in which case, the effects produced by printing will loom large; or, one may instead describe a 'long revolution' which unfolds so slowly that these effects are completely flattened out.[57]

In view of the fragmentary evidence that is available and the prolonged fluctuations that were entailed, it would seem prudent to bypass vexed problems associated with the spread of literacy until other issues have been explored with more care. That there are other issues worth exploring – apart from the expansion of the reading public or the 'spread' of new ideas – is in itself a point that needs underlining (and that will be repeatedly underscored in this book). When considering the *initial* transformations wrought by print, at all events, changes undergone by groups who were already literate ought to receive priority over the undeniably fascinating problem of how rapidly such groups were enlarged.

Once attention has been focused on already literate sectors, it becomes clear that their social composition calls for further thought. Did printing at first serve prelates and patricians as a 'divine art' or should one think of it rather as the 'poor man's friend'? It was described in both ways by contemporaries, and probably served in both ways as well. When one recalls scribal functions performed by Roman slaves or later by monks, lay brothers, clerks and notaries, one may conclude that literacy had never been congruent with élite social status.[58] One may also guess that it was more compatible with sedentary occupations than with the riding and hunting favored by many squires and lords.[59] In this light, it may be misguided to envisage the new presses as making available to low born men, products previously used only by the high born. That many rural areas remained untouched until after the coming of the railway age seems likely. Given the large peasant population in early-modern Europe and the persistence of local dialects which imposed an additional language barrier between spoken and written words, it is probable that only a very small portion of the entire population was affected by the initial shift. Nevertheless within this relatively small and largely urban population, a fairly wide social spectrum may have been involved. In fifteenth-century England, for example, mercers and scriveners engaged in a manuscript book-trade were already catering to the needs of lowly bakers and merchants as well as to those of lawyers, aldermen, or knights.[60] The proliferation of literate merchants in fourteenth-century Italian cities is no less notable than the presence of an illiterate army commander in late sixteenth-century France.[61]

It would be a mistake, however, to assume that a distaste for reading was especially characteristic of the nobility, although it seems plausible that a distaste for Latin pedantry was shared by lay aristocrat and commoner alike. It also remains uncertain whether one ought to describe the early reading public as being 'middle class'. Certainly extreme caution is needed when matching genres of books with groups of readers. All too often it is taken for granted that 'low-brow' or 'vulgar' works reflect 'lower class' tastes, despite contrary evidence offered by authorship and library catalogues.[62] Before the advent of mass literacy the most 'popular' works were those which appealed to diverse groups of readers and not just to the plebes.

Divisions between Latin and vernacular reading publics are also much more difficult to correlate with social status than many accounts suggest. It is true that the sixteenth-century physician who used Latin was regarded as superior to the surgeon who did not, but also true that neither man was likely to belong to the highest estates of the realm. Insofar as the vernacular translation movement was aimed at readers who were unlearned in Latin, it was often designed to appeal to pages as well as apprentices; to landed gentry, cavaliers and courtiers as well as to shopkeepers and clerks. In the Netherlands, a translation from Latin into French often pointed away from the urban laity who knew only Lower Rhenish dialects and toward relatively exclusive courtly circles. At the same time, a translation into 'Dutch' might be aimed at preachers who needed to cite scriptural passages in sermons rather than at the laity (which is too often assumed to be the only target for 'vernacular' devotional works). Tutors trying to educate young princes; instructors in court or church schools; and chaplains translating from Latin in response to royal requests had pioneered in 'popularizing' techniques even before the printer set to work.

But the most vigorous impetus given to popularization before printing came from the felt need of preachers to keep their congregations awake and also to hold the attention of diverse outdoor crowds.[63] Unlike the preacher, the printer could only guess at the nature of the audience to which his work appealed. Accordingly, one must be especially careful when taking the titles of early printed books as trustworthy guides to readership. A case in point is the frequent description of the fifteenth-century picture Bible, which was issued in both manuscript and then blockbook form, as the 'poor man's' Bible. The description may well be anachronistic, based on abbreviating the full Latin title given to such books. The *Biblia Pauperum Praedicatorum* was not aimed at poor men but at poor preachers who had a mere smattering of Latin and found scriptural exposition easier when given picture books as guides.[64] Sophisticated analysts have suggested the need to discriminate between 'audiences' — that is, actual readership as determined by library catalogues, subscription lists and other objective data — and 'publics', the more hypothetical targets envisaged by authors and publishers, those to whom they address their works.[65] Given the tendency to cite titles or prefaces as evidence of actual readership, this distinction is worth keeping in mind.

> To arrive at valid conclusions . . . we must proceed with care and caution. Information on the spread of reading and writing . . . is limited and must be supplemented by analysis of the subject contents of the total production (in itself not an easy task); this in turn provides circumstantial evidence on the composition of the reading public: a cookbook . . . reprinted eight or more times in the xvth century was obviously read by people concerned with the preparation of food, the *Doctrinal des Filles* . . . a booklet on the behavior of young women, primarily by 'files' and 'mesdames.'

Such 'circumstantial evidence', however, is highly suspect. Without passing judgment on the audience for early cookbooks (its character seems far from obvious to me), booklets pertaining to the behavior of young ladies did not necessarily attract feminine readers and were probably also of interest to male tutors, or confessors, or guardians. As a later chapter suggests, the circulation of printed etiquette books had wide-ranging psychological ramifications; their capacity to heighten the anxiety of parents should not go ignored. Furthermore such works were probably also read by authors, translators and publishers of other etiquette books. That authors and publishers were wide-ranging readers needs to be perpetually kept in mind. Even those sixteenth-century court poets who shunned printers and circulated their verse in manuscript form[67] took advantage of their own access to printed materials. It has been suggested that books describing double entry bookkeeping were read less by merchants than by the writers of accountancy books and teachers of accountancy. One wonders whether there were not more playwrights and poets than shepherds who studied so-called *Shepherd's Almanacks*. Given the corruption of data transmitted over the centuries, given the false remedies and impossible recipes contained in medical treatises, one hopes that they were studied more by poets than by physicians. Given the exotic ingredients described, one may assume that few apothecaries actually tried to concoct all the recipes contained in early printed pharmacopeia, although they may have felt impelled to stock their shelves with bizarre items just in case the new publicity might bring such items into demand.[68] The purposes, whether intended or actual, served by some early printed handbooks offer puzzles that permit no easy solution. What was the point of publishing vernacular manuals outlining procedures that were already familiar to all skilled practitioners of certain crafts?[69] It is worth remembering, at all events, that the gap between shoproom practice and classroom theory was just becoming visible during the first century of printing and that many so-called 'practical' handbooks and manuals contained impractical, even injurious, advice.

While postponing conjectures about social and psychological transformations, certain points should be noted here. One must distinguish, as Altick suggests, between literacy and habitual book reading. By no means all who mastered the written word have, down to the present, become members of a book-reading public.[70] Learning *to read* is different, moreover, from learning by reading. Reliance on apprenticeship training, oral communication and special mnemonic devices had gone together with mastering letters in the age of scribes. After the advent of printing however, the transmission of written information became much more efficient. It was not only the craftsman outside universities who profited from the new opportunities to teach himself. Of equal importance was the chance extended to bright undergraduates to reach beyond their teachers' grasp. Gifted students no longer needed to sit at the feet of a given master in order to learn a language or academic skill. Instead they could swiftly achieve mastery on their own, even by sneaking books past their tutors – as did the young would-be astronomer, Tycho Brahe. 'Why should old men be preferred to their juniors now that it is possible for the young by diligent study to acquire the same knowledge'? asked the author of a fifteenth-century outline of history.[71]

As learning by reading took on new importance, the role played by mnemonic aids was diminished. Rhyme and cadence were no longer required to preserve certain formulas and recipes. The nature of the collective memory was transformed.

> In Victor Hugo's *Notre Dame de Paris* a scholar, deep in meditation in his study . . . gazes at the first printed book which has come to disturb his collection of manuscripts. Then . . . he gazes at the vast cathedral, silhouetted against the starry sky . . . 'Ceci tuera cela', he says. The printed book will destroy the building. The parable which Hugo develops out of the comparison of the building, crowded with images, with the arrival in his library of a printed book might be applied to the effect on the invisible cathedrals of memory of the past of the spread of printing. The printed book will make such huge built-up memories, crowded with images, unnecessary. It will do away with habits of immemorial antiquity whereby a 'thing' is immediately invested with an image and stored in the places of memory.[72]

To the familiar romantic theme of the Gothic cathedral as an 'encyclopedia in stone', Frances Yates has added a fascinating sequel. Not only did printing eliminate many functions previously performed by stone figures over portals and stained glass in windows but it also affected less tangible images by eliminating the need for placing figures and objects in imaginary niches located in memory theatres. The way was paved for a more thorough-going iconoclasm than any Christian church had ever known. 'The "Ramist man" must smash the images both within and without, must substitute for the old idolatrous art, the new image-less way of remembering through abstract dialectical order'.[73]

This line of argument dovetails neatly with Walter Ong's earlier studies of Ramism and print culture – perhaps too neatly in the judgment of some medieval scholars who see evidence in medieval manuscripts of those diagrammatic features which Ong reserves for the printed page.[74] But even if all parts of the argument are not deemed equally acceptable, the basic point still seems valid. Printing made it possible to dispense with the use of images for mnemonic purposes and thus reinforced iconoclastic tendencies already present among many Christians. Successive editions of Calvin's *Institutes* elaborated on the need to observe the Second Commandment. The favorite text of the defenders of images was the dictum of Gregory the Great that statues served as 'the books of the illiterate'.[75] Although Calvin's scornful dismissal of this dictum made no mention of printing, the new medium did underlie the Calvinist assumption that the illiterate should not be given graven images but should be taught to read. In this light it may seem plausible to suggest that printing fostered a movement 'from image culture to word culture', a movement which was more compatible with Protestant bibliolatry and pamphleteering than with the Baroque statues and paintings sponsored by the post-Tridentine Catholic Church.

Yet the cultural metamorphosis produced by printing was really much more complicated than any single formula can possibly express.[76] For one thing, the graven image became more, rather than less, ubiquitous after the establishment of print shops throughout Western Europe. For another thing, Protestant propaganda exploited printed image no less than printed word – as numerous caricatures and cartoons may suggest. Even religious imagery was defended by some Protestants, and on the very grounds of its compatibility with print culture. 'If graving were taken away we could have not printing', wrote Stephen Gardiner, putting the case for images against Nicholas Ridley in 1547. 'And therefore they that press so much the words of *Non facies tibi sculptile* . . . they condemn printed books, the original whereof is graving to make *matrices literarum*'.[77] A close study of two versions of sixteenth-century Dutch Bibles, one Protestant, the other Catholic, suggests that there was indeed a tendency for Protestants to deemphasize pictures and stress words; yet at the same time, they did engage in illustrating Bibles – a movement which Lutherans, at least, encouraged.[78] Luther himself commented on the inconsistency of iconoclasts who tore pictures off walls while handling the illustrations in Bibles reverently. Pictures 'do no more harm on walls than in books', he commented and then, somewhat sarcastically, stopped short of pursuing this line of thought: 'I must cease lest I give occasion to the image breakers never to read the Bible or to burn it'.[79]

If we accept the idea of a movement from image to word, furthermore, we will be somewhat at loss to account for the work of Northern artists, such as Dürer or Cranach or Holbein, who were affiliated with Protestantism and yet owed much to print. As Dürer's career may suggest, the new arts of printing and engraving, far from reducing the importance of images, increased opportunities for image makers and helped to launch art history down its present path. Even the imaginary figures and memory theatres described by Frances Yates did not vanish when their mnemonic functions were outmoded, but received a 'strange new lease on life'. They provided the content for magnificent emblem books and for elaborate Baroque illustrations to Rosicrucian and occult works in the seventeenth century. They also helped to inspire an entirely new genre of printed literature – the didactic picture book for children. Leipzig boys in Leibniz' day 'were brought up on Comenius' picture book and Luther's Catechism'.[80] In this form, the ancient memory images re-entered the imagination of Protestant children, ultimately supplying Jung and his followers with evidence that suggested the hypothesis of a collective Unconscious. Surely the new vogue for image-packed emblem books was no less a product of sixteenth-century print culture than was the imageless 'Ramist' textbook.

Furthermore, in certain fields of learning such as architecture, geometry or geography and many of the life sciences as well, print culture was not merely incompatible with the formula offered above; it actually increased the functions performed by images while reducing those performed by words. Many fundamental texts of Ptolemy, Vitruvius, Galen and other ancients had lost their illustrations in the course of being copied for centuries and regained them only after script was replaced by print. To think in terms of a movement going from image to word points technical literature in the wrong direction. It was not the 'printed word' but the 'printed image' which acted as a 'savior for Western science' in George Sarton's view. Within the Commonwealth of Learning it became increasingly fashionable to adopt the ancient Chinese maxim that a single picture was more valuable than many words.[81] In early Tudor England, Thomas Elyot expressed a preference for 'figures and charts' over 'hearing the rules of a science'[82] which seems worth further thought. Although images were indispensable for prodding memory, a heavy reliance on verbal instruction had also been characteristic of communications in the age of scribes. To be sure, academic lectures were sometimes supplemented by drawing pictures on walls; verbal instructions to apprentices were accompanied by demonstrations; the use of blocks and boards, fingers and knuckles were common in teaching reckoning and gestures usually went with the recitation of key mnemonics. Nevertheless, when seeking rapid duplication of a given set of instructions, words simply had to take precedence over other forms of communication. How else save by using words could one dictate a text to assembled scribes? After the advent of printing, visual aids multiplied, signs and symbols were codified; different kinds of iconographic and non-phonetic communication were rapidly developed. The fact that printed picture books were newly designed by educational reformers for the purpose of instructing children and that drawing was considered an increasingly useful accomplishment by pedagogues also points to the need to think beyond the simple formula: image to word.

As these comments may suggest, efforts to summarize changes wrought by printing in any one statement or neat formula are likely to lead us astray. Even while acknowledging that there was an increased reliance on rule books and less on rules of thumb, or that learning by reading gained at the expense of hearing or doing; one must also consider how printing encouraged new objections to bookish knowledge based on 'slavish' copying and how it enabled many observers to check freshly recorded data against received rules. Similarly, one must be cautious about assuming that the spoken word was gradually silenced as printed words multiplied or that the faculty of hearing was increasingly neglected in favor of that of sight. Surely the history of Western music after Gutenberg argues against the latter suggestion. As for the many questions raised by the assertion that print silenced the spoken word; a few are noted elsewhere in this chapter; all must be passed over here.

The purpose of this preliminary section has been simply to demonstrate that the shift from script to print entailed a large ensemble of changes, each of which needs more investigation and all of which are too complicated to be encapsulated in any single formula. But to say that there is no simple way of summarizing the complex ensemble is not the same thing as saying that nothing had changed. To the contrary!

Granted that some sort of communications revolution did occur during the late fifteenth century, how did this affect other historical developments? Since the consequences of printing have not been thoroughly explored, guidance is hard to come by. Most conventional surveys stop short after a few remarks about the wider dissemination of humanist tomes or Protestant tracts. Several helpful suggestions – about the effects of standardization on scholarship and science, for example – are offered in works devoted to the era of the Renaissance or the history of science. By and large, the effects of the new process are vaguely implied rather than explicitly defined and are also drastically minimized. One example may illustrate this point. During the first centuries of printing, old texts were duplicated more rapidly than new ones. On this basis we are told that 'printing did not speed up the adoption of new theories'.[83] But where did these new theories come from? Must we invoke some spirit of the times, or is it possible that an increase in the output of old texts contributed to the formulation of new theories? Maybe other features that distinguished the new mode of book production from the old one also contributed to such theories? We need to take stock of these features before we can relate the advent of printing to other historical developments.

## Notes

1    For estimate of numbers of printing offices and places of printing, see Lenhart, *Pre-Reformation Printed Books*, p. 7. For graphic presentation, see maps in Febvre and Martin, *L'Apparition*, p. 273, covering the two intervals: 1471 to 1480 and 1481 to 1500, and discussion in Hirsch's 1974 edition of *Printing, Selling*, p. x, concerning the updating of R. Teichl's more detailed rendering, 'Der Wiegendruck im Kartenbild'. Uhlendorf's 1932 article, 'The invention and spread of printing', has not been superseded as a brief suggestive treatment of possible socioeconomic factors contributing to the rapid spread of printing, and the clustering of early presses in certain centers. When one considers the massive literature devoted to shifts in trade routes during the early-modern era, it is remarkable how little work has been done on shifts in communications centers.

2   Stillwell, *The Beginning of the World of Books* offers useful guidance. See especially appendix A, pp. 75–87. Stillwell selects 1470 as a take-off point for the rapid spread of the new art (p. x).

3   That the age of incunabula should be extended to encompass the life-spans of the founders of early firms and hence to embrace the first few decades of the sixteenth century is persuasively argued by Steinberg, *Five Hundred Years*, pp. 15–17.

4   Clapham, 'Printing', p. 37. It is not clear whether Clapham takes 'all the scribes of Europe' to include those of Byzantium or not. If not, the statement becomes much more plausible.

5   The problematic and often composite nature of the medieval 'book' and the absence of any uniform conventions among medieval cataloguers who recorded them is discussed with many pertinent examples by E. P. Goldschmidt, *Medieval Texts*, pp. 95–101.

6   On the classic version derived from Vespasiano's *Lives*, see Burckhardt, *The Civilization of the Renaissance* I, part 3, chap. 3, p. 201. Doubts expressed by Ullman, *The Origin*, p. 132, have been thoroughly documented from surviving Fiesole accounts and mss. by de la Mare, 'Vespasiano', pp. 74–76 and appendix. (Her forthcoming study on 'Vespasiano and the Library of the Badia at Fiesole' to be published by the Warburg Institute will supply additional data.) She shows that Vespasiano obtained the books that filled the library by diverse methods, including the purchase of second-hand copies and reliance on other *cartolai*, and that the work took more than two years, encompassing an interval from 1461 until at least 1466–7. For recent use of the now discredited figures to estimate 'average' scribal output, see Burke, *Culture and Society*, p. 59.

7   De la Mare, 'Vespasiano', p. 207. The remarkable success of this 'uncommonly large edition' which was 'sold out in six years' when another printing took place is noted by Reynolds and Wilson, *Scribes and Scholars*, p. 130. According to Kristeller, 'Contribution of Religious Orders', p. 99, the Ripoli Press was 'one of the chief early presses in Florence'. In addition to the first edition of Ficino's Plato, which appeared in 1484, a 'Donatus' of 1476 and a *Book of Revelations* of 1478 are also noteworthy. The nuns of the Convent of San Jacopo di Ripoli, who ran the press, were 'the first women actually to print', according to Gies, 'Some Early Ladies', p. 1421. For basic work, see Nesi, *Il Diario della Stamperia di Ripoli*.

8   Harrington, 'The Production and Distribution', p. 3. This seems especially true when considering the fifty years before Gutenberg, when the system of the 'pecia' which had helped to speed duplication of large academic texts was no longer employed.

9   From conversation with Joseph Strayer, I learned that fourteenth-century French royal edicts were rapidly multiplied and distributed by a kind of 'chain letter' technique. At court, ten scribes were put to work producing ten copies each, some of which were carried by couriers to numerous provincial centers where the same procedure was repeated so that thousands of copies were quickly produced. See also evidence on Burgundian propaganda offered by Willard, 'The Manuscripts of Jean Petit'.

10  The 'enormous number' of manuscript copies of the Latin classics produced after the advent of paper is stressed by Kristeller, *Renaissance Thought*, pp. 14–15, who writes as a scholar concerned about the neglect of later Latin works and as an assiduous energetic investigator of Renaissance manuscript book lists. The compiler of *Iter Italicum* and *Latin Manuscript Books before 1600* is bound to be impressed by the remarkable output of copyists before print. Nevertheless, one must also make allowance for the fact that handmade copies, however 'enormous their number may seem, were still in very short supply compared to the number issued after printing. Paper was incapable of reducing the man-hours required for copying and hence could not achieve effects 'similar' to those produced by the press.

11  For a close-up view of the shop of an ordinary Florentine *cartolaio* who was engaged in binding books and selling writing materials rather than in procuring or producing bopks (although he kept some texts on hand for sale), see de la Mare, 'The Shop of a Florentine "cartolaio" in 1426'.

12  De la Mare, 'Bartolomeo Scala's Dealings', 240.

13  De la Mare, 'Vespasiano', pp. 95–7; 226.

14    See de la Mare, 'Vespasiano', pp. 108–9 for laudatory verses.

15    *Art of the Printed Book 1455–1955*, introduction by Joseph Blumenthal, p. 9. The same assertion was made on the label attached to entry no. 55 in this exhibition.

16    Shenker, 'Books as an Art Form Through Five Centuries', *The New York Times* (10 Sept., 1973), 2nd sect., p. 1.

17    See Burckhardt, *The Civilization of the Renaissance in Italy* I, p. 204 where Duke Federigo's shame is attributed to the idea of owning a printed book and Cardinal Bessarion's envoys when seeing a printed book in the house of Constantine Lascaris 'laughed at the discovery made among the barbarians in some German city'. Burckhardt's use of Vespasiano is discussed by Wieruszowski, 'Burckhardt and Vespasiano'.

18    Bühler, *Fifteenth Century Book*, p. 62; de la Mare, 'Vespasiano', p. 112; Moranti, *L'Arte Tipografia in Urbino*, p. 9.

19    De la Mare, 'Bartolomeo Scala's Dealings', p. 241.

20    Goldschmidt, *Gothic and Renaissance Bookbindings* I, 43–4.

21    By 1910, when the article for the eleventh edition of the Britannica was written, Phillips's, 'Faust', *Encyclopedia Britannica* X, 210, n. 1, could assert that 'the opinion, long maintained' of Faust and Fust being identical was 'now universally rejected'. Evidence showing that Fust was in Paris selling books in 1466 when he was killed by the plague suggests that the outcome of his first business trip did not discourage him from making a later one.

22    The ambivalence of scholars who cursed the errors made by careless printers much as earlier authors had cursed careless scribes is brought out by Bühler, *Fifteenth Century Book*, pp. 50–1, and by Hirsch, *Printing, Selling*, p. 48, n. 20. Early tributes to the 'divine' art are conveniently collected by Stillwell, *The Beginning of the World of Books*, appendix A: 2, pp. 88 ff. They often echo tributes to the labors of scribes – a topos that goes back at least to Cassiodorus and which was publicized by early printings of both Gerson's and Trithemius' *De Laude Scriptorum*

23    Gianandrea de' Bussi, a minor cleric, one-time private secretary to Nicholas of Cues and later Bishop of Aleria, helped to edit texts for Sweynheim and Pannartz (after they established the first press in Rome). In his dedicatory letter to Pope Paul II which appeared in the 1469 Roman edition of Saint Jerome's *Epistles* de' Bussi attributes the phrase 'divine art' ('Haec sancta ars') to Cusanus. Needless to say, early printers saw to it that the phrase received maximum exposure. A thoughtful essay on less well-publicized reactions – particularly some unpublished diatribes against early printing by a Dominican friar who had served as a copyist and reacted unfavorably to the Venetian press in the late fifteenth century – is contained in an article by Martin Lowry, 'Intellectuals and the Press in fifteenth century Venice' to appear in a forthcoming issue of the *Bulletin of the John Rylands University Library*.

24    De la Mare, 'Vespasiano', p. 113. On prices, see also Hirsch, *Printing, Selling*, pp. 68–73; Febvre and Martin, *L'Apparition*, chap. 4; Pettas, 'The Cost of Printing a Florentine Incunable'.

25    Of course, hindsight is required to show that technological unemployment was not severe, and fears, whether ultimately justified or not, may well have been aroused. On the new jobs created by printing, see Bühler, *Fifteenth Century Book*, pp. 25–7; Hirsch, *Printing, Selling*, pp. 48–9. In Florence the number of stationers' shops rose from twelve to thirty during the first half-century after the advent of the press. De la Mare, 'Vespasiano', p. 44.

26    See amusing speculations on sales of veal by Bühler, *Fifteenth Century Book*, p. 41.

27    Lehmann-Haupt, *Peter Schoeffer*, pp. 37–8.

28    Bühler, *Fifteenth Century Book*, p. 16. A detailed description of particular cases found in the Beinecke Library at Yale is offered by Lutz, 'Manuscripts Copied from Printed Books'.

29    Some Yale mss. marked up by early printers to be used as copy are noted by Lutz, 'Manuscripts Copied', p. 262, who also offers evidence of the irritation of a thirteenth-century scribe at a correction made by a bookdealer which destroyed the surface symmetry of two pages of a copy of a commentary by Thomas Aquinas.

30 For a pertinent example, see the account of the procedure used by Aldus Manutius' chief editor, Marcus Musurus, when preparing the printer's copy for the 1498 edition of Aristophanes' works. Reynolds and Wilson, *Scribes and Scholars*, pp. 132–3.

31 Lehmann-Haupt, *Peter Schoeffer*, pp. 53–4 contains relevant data.

32 Steinberg, *Five Hundred Years*, p. 28.

33 Steinberg, *Five Hundred Years*, p. 145. Along with many other authorities, both Steinberg (pp. 145 ff.) and Hirsch, *Printing, Selling*, p. 25 overstate the novelty of the title page when describing it as a purely post-print phenomenon. The Folger Library has a copy of Lorenzo Valla's *De Elegantiis Linguae Latinae* – Phillipps Ms 2966 (Folger 'v.a. 102') which is identified by A. M. de la Mare as being by the hand of a Veronese scribe: Cristoforo Schioppo. The name of the book's author, 'Lauretii Vallae', and part of the title are clearly placed on a single page as if engraved on a stone tablet. That this is by no means the only ms. 'title page' of its kind is attested to by Dr de la Mare. But the basic points made by Steinberg in his section on the title page are not really invalidated by his overlooking quattrocento humanist manuscripts and taking Northern ms. styles for his norm. Title pages did not become common and information contained in colophons did not get shifted until after print.

34 Ivins, *Prints and Visual Communication*. Some specific examples discussed by Ivins are treated in later discussion of scientific data collection and early field trips.

35 See e.g., Bagrow, *History of Cartography*, p. 89; Skelton, *Maps*, p. 12; Robinson, 'Map making', *Five Centuries of Map Printing*, p. 1. The illustrations (in this last mentioned work) of relevant tools and techniques are unusually clear and helpful.

36 Thus the second edition of Vesalius' *De Fabrica* profited from the sharpening of indistinct letters and lines by a Basel woodcarver using a fine knife. Woodblocks impressed only on moist paper and made of birchwood treated with hot linseed oil can remain unspoiled even after running off 3,000 to 4,000 copies, according to Willy Wiegand (who printed an edition of Vesalius' *Icones anatomicae* from old woodblocks in 1935). See Herrlinger, *History of Medical Illustration*, p. 113.

37 Ivins, *Prints and Visual Communication*, pp. 2, 11, 163.

38 Ivins, *Prints and Visual Communication*, p. 27.

39 See fascinating section on 'indication lines' in Herrlinger, *History of Medical Illustration*, pp. 54–60. I owe thanks to Karen Reeds for bringing this to my attention.

40 Questions pertaining to the relationship between block-printing and book-printing and to whether the block book preceded the invention and use of movable type have given rise to a massive controversial literature that cannot be examined here. To sample recent arguments see Musper, 'Xylographic Books', pp. 345–7 (esp. bibliography p. 347) and Lehmann-Haupt, *Gutenberg and the Master of the Playing Cards*. A close-up view of the overlap between hand illumination and early Mainz printing is offered by Vaassen, *Die Werkstatt der Mainzer Riesenbibel in Würzburg und Ihr Umkreis*. See review article by Labarre, 'Un Atelier Mayençais d'Enluminure vers 1450–1500'. For stimulating speculation relating changes in shop structure to new handbooks for illuminators, see Bober's review of *The Göttingen Model Book*.

41 Sarton, *Appreciation of Ancient and Medieval Science During the Renaissance 1450–1600*, p. xi.

42 I borrow these terms from Derek da Solla Price's article, 'Geometrical and Scientific Talismans'.

43 How the diverse skills of the punchcutter, matrix-maker and mold-maker got lumped under the heading of 'typefounder' is discussed by Harry Caster, *A View of Early Typography*, p. 92.

44 The widely varying social and occupational origins of early printers, extracted from biographical dictionaries such as those compiled by E. Voullième and Joseph Benzing for German-speaking regions, are indicated by Hirsch, *Printing, Selling*, pp. 18–23. A 'flocking of priests into printing' is noted on p. 22 and the numbers of priests and bishops involved in proof-reading, on p. 47. How a former monk and abbot abandoned his monastery to work full-time as an editor for Peter Schoeffer's early firm is noted by Lehmann-Haupt, *Peter Schoeffer*, p. 83, n. 6. A recent finely

detailed study of the Paris book-trade in the mid-sixteenth century confirms the impression of diverse backgrounds among those entering the trade: Parent, *Les Métiers du Livre*, pp. 175 ff. Parent also notes that publication of devotional literature was often supervised by a priest who was sent by a bishop to receive room and board from the printer (p. 122).

45   References to pertinent studies are given by Hirsch, *Printing, Selling*, p. 51. Bühler, *The University and the Press in 15th Century Bologna*, pp. 15–16 gives an example of a contract drawn up in 1470 to build and run a press for academic purposes. The complex arrangements that went into the printing for academic purposes of a massive commentary on Avicenna's *Canon* (comprising over a thousand double column large folio-sized pages of text) are described by Mardersteig, *Remarkable Story*.

46   He was such a protean figure that no one label such as 'printer' adequately designates his many-faceted role.

47   Mardersteig's *Remarkable Story* shows the printer, Petrus Maufer, coping with strikes and many other complications before triumphantly concluding the actual printing which began in May 1477 when the first reams of paper were delivered. From then until December 1, 1477 when the last sheet came off the press, 'not a working day was wasted'. Four hand presses had been in operation from daybreak to night-time without interruption, and 6,800,000 separate pieces of type had been procured and used. For general description of the complex working routines observed in most print shops during the first centuries after Gutenberg, McKenzie's article, 'Printers of the Mind', is unexcelled. A useful glimpse of Plantin's operational plan is given by Lotte and Wytze Hellinga, 'Regulations'. That routines were somewhat more orderly than either McKenzie or the Hellingas imply is suggested by K. I. D. Maslen and John Gerritsen, correspondence in *The Library* (June, 1975).

48   Martin Lowry, *The World of Aldus Manutius* (Oxford: Blackwell, 1979).

49   In sustaining a gradual evolutionary approach to the impact of printing, authorities on the history of the book naturally emphasize the stationer as the true precursor of the printer. Yet use of the term *scriptor* for *impressor* by printers showed that they considered themselves the successors not of stationers but of copyists. (See Hirsch, *Printing, Selling*, p. 19, n. 21.) It seems fair to say that early printers took over functions performed *both* by copyists *and* by stationers (or 'publishers') while diverging from both in significant ways.

50   See Lehmann-Haupt, *Peter Schoeffer, passim.*

51   Much of this is covered in detail by Febvre and Martin, *L'Apparition*, chap. 6, and is also well documented by Pollard and Ehrman, *The Distribution of Books*. Hirsch, *Printing, Selling*, pp. 63–4 points out how Schirokauer's (1951) study drastically underestimates the size of markets tapped by early printers.

52   Wytze Hellinga, 'Thomas A Kempis', 4–5.

53   Although Steinberg, *Five Hundred Years* (p. 22) stresses this aspect of Gutenberg's invention as the most far-reaching, it receives little attention from Febvre and Martin, *L'Apparition* because of their focus on 'the book'. 'Jobbing printing' was also, with one exception, omitted from the exhibition on 'Printing and the Mind of Man' assembled at the British Museum and at Earl's Court, July 16–27, 1963. See British Museum Catalogue (London, 1963) p. 8. Official printing for ecclesiastical and secular governments is discussed by Hirsch, *Printing, Selling*, pp. 52–3. It furnished an important part of Peter Schoeffer's output, according to Lehmann-Haupt, *Peter Schoeffer*, pp. 78–9.

54   See item 7, Catalogue of Exhibition held in the Royal Library of Brussels (Sept.–Oct. 1973): *Le Cinquième Centenaire de L'Imprimerie dans les Anciens Pays-Bas* (Brussels, 1973), pp. 11–12 and footnote reference to B. Kruitwagen, 'Her Schrijven op Feestdagen in de Middeleuwen'. One might compare this medieval approach to holy-day book making with the indignation of a member of the Royal Society at printing delays caused by 'the holy days sticking in the workman's hands', cited by Hill, book review, *English Historical Review* (1973).

55    Printed announcements of university lectures containing blurbs for pertinent books on sale are described by Hirsch, *Printing, Selling*, p. 51 and Parent, *Les Métiers*, p. 142.

56    Cipolla, *Literacy*, p. 60.

57    See Cipolla, *Literacy*, p. 52 where he discusses whether Lawrence Stone's concept of an 'educational revolution' in England is relevant to continental trends. In his article on 'Literacy and Education', p. 78, Stone underlines the importance of cheap paper and movable type whereas Williams, *The Long Revolution*, pp. 132–3 discusses the interval encompassed by Stone's 'educational revolution' without mentioning printing at all. On pp. 156–7, Williams mentions printing but traces the growth of the reading public back to the eighth century and beyond to Rome. When this approach is coupled with emphasis on the advent of a mass reading public after the steam press, the fifteenth-century typographical revolution is bound to recede. Williams does bring out the importance of printing as against writing in his brief study of *Communications*, p. 22. The topic is especially likely to be underplayed in connection with the history of education. See e.g. Talbott, 'The History of Education', where a survey of the literature shows printing to be omitted from among factors which 'triggered educational expansion' in early-modern England (p. 136).

58    The very term 'poor man's book' ('Liber Pauperum') goes back at least as far as the twelfth century in England where a Lombard master arranged a compilation of the Code and Digest for poor law clerks. Cf. Haskins, *The Renaissance of the Twelfth Century*, p. 211.

59    Thus in Richard Pace's celebrated anecdote about the early Tudor squire, who questioned the need to teach his sons how to read, hunting and hawking are opposed to armchair study.

60    Jacob, *The Fifteenth Century*, pp. 663–667. See also Adamson, 'The Extent of Literacy in England', 163–93; Bennett, *English Books and Readers 1475–1557*, p. 20; Parkes, 'The Literacy of the Laity'. Thrupp, *The Merchant Class*, p. 157 provides a useful table as well as relevant data.

61    See Renouard, *Etudes d'Histoire Médiévale*, I, pp. 419–26; Jeannin, *Merchants of the Sixteenth Century*, pp. 80–6; Sapori, *The Italian Merchant, passim*. Bec, *Les Marchands Ecrivains, passim*, has data on the numerous merchants who kept diaries as well as accounts.

62    Useful warnings on this point are offered by Natalie Z. Davis, 'Printing and the People'.

63    A thirteenth-century Dominican manual: *De Arte Predicandi* issued on 'how to sew a sermon together quickly' and how to appeal to special interest groups such as 'rich women in towns' or 'crowds at fairs' or 'young girls' is described by Murray, 'Religion among the Poor'.

64    James Strachan, *Early Bible Illustrations*, p. 7 raises the question of whether the abbreviated title *Biblia Pauperum* is appropriate or not.

65    This distinction, suggested by T. J. Clark in his study of Courbet is discussed in connection with problems posed by sixteenth-century 'popular' culture by Natalie Davis, 'Printing and the People'. It seems futile to try to restrict usage of terms already employed interchangeably in a large literature. I prefer the phrase: 'assumed public' (which is used by Davis elsewhere in the same article) since it is less likely to be misinterpreted.

66    Hirsch, *Printing, Selling*, p. 7.

67    Saunders, 'From Manuscript to Print', pp. 507–28.

68    On accountancy books, almanacs, pharmacopeia and other 'practical' guide-books see Natalie Davis, 'Printing and the People'.

69    In his *Speculum* review of *The Göttingen Model Book*, Harry Bober suggests that the detailed instructions for illumination contained therein (which included sixteen separate steps for painting one acanthus leaf) must have been aimed at a new group of untrained craftsmen mobilized by printers since scribal illuminators had no need of such a manual – any more than 'an experienced chef needs the numbered instructions on soup cans'. Even if this argument holds good for book-making, it still leaves open questions raised by other craft manuals in trades where there was no dramatic change in shop structure nor influx of neophytes. The purposes served by the early publication of vernacular booklets by the two German master masons: Matthias Roriczer

and Hans Schmuttermayer, for example, remain somewhat baffling, as I have learned from two articles by Shelby, 'The Education of Medieval English Master Masons', 1–26; 'The Geometrical Knowledge', 395–421, and correspondence with their author.

70  Altick, *The English Common Reader*, p. 31.

71  Jacobo Filippo Foresti, *Supplementum Chronicarum* (Venice, 1483) cited by Martin Lowry in his biography of Aldus.

72  Yates, *Art of Memory*, p. 131.

73  Yates, *Art of Memory*, p. 271.

74  In slide lectures given at Catholic University during the 1974 Medieval Academy Summer Institute program on 'The Archeology of the Book', Professor Richard H. Rouse of U.C.L.A. demonstrated graphically the frequent use of diagrams, brackets, cross-references, marginal guides and other devices in scribal compilations (especially in concordances and guides to patristic works) produced by medieval teachers and preachers.

75  Myron Gilmore, 'Italian Reactions to Erasmian Humanism', pp. 87–8.

76  Although Stone, 'Literacy and Education', p. 76 cites my preliminary 'Conjectures' as suggesting that the printed book caused Europe to move 'decisively from image culture to word culture' I am not convinced that this formulation is valid and regret any inadvertent implication that such a movement occurred. That Protestant bibliolatry and iconoclasm were more compatible with early print culture than Tridentine Catholicism was suggested in my article but that is a different matter than suggesting that European culture moved from image to word. For objections to the latter formulation, see paragraphs following this note in text above.

77  *The Letters of Stephen Gardiner*, pp. 258–9. I owe this reference and the one from Luther below to Margaret Aston, who is completing a major study of iconoclasm in Tudor England.

78  Hindman, 'The Transition from Manuscripts'. See esp. p. 205.

79  'Against the Heavenly Prophets in the Matter of Images and Sacraments', (1525), *Luther's Works*, XL 99–100. On Lutheran Bible illustration, see Ph. Schmidt, *Die Illustration der Lutherbibel 1522–1700*.

80  Yates, *Art of Memory*, pp. 134; 377. The magnificent Baroque engravings that made visible the elaborate memory systems developed in the sixteenth and seventeenth centuries may be sampled by examining almost any work by Robert Fludd. How much Comenius' *Orbis Pictus* (1658) owed to Campanella's *City of the Sun* and Rosicrucian manifestoes is noted by Yates, p. 377.

81  Sarton, *Appreciation*, pp. 91; 95. As is noted, the notion that the ancient Egyptians had compressed valuable data in each hieroglyph was believed by would-be decipherers of hieroglyphs until the nineteenth-century discovery of the Rosetta Stone.

82  See citation from the *Boke Called the Gouvernour* (1531) in Watson, *The Beginning of the Teaching of Modern Subjects in England*, p. 136.

83  Febvre and Martin, *L'Apparition*, pp. 420–1.

## References

Adamson, J. W. 'The Extent of Literacy in England in the Fifteenth and Sixteenth Centuries: Notes and Conjectures', *The Library*, 4th ser. x (1929) 163–93.

Altick, R. *The English Common Reader. A Social History of the Mass Reading Public 1800–1900* (Chicago, 1963).

Bagrow, Leo. *History of Cartography*, rev. and ed. R. A. Skelton (Cambridge, Mass., 1964).

Bennett, H. S. *English Books and Readers 1475–1557* (Cambridge, 1952).

Blumenthal, Joseph. Introduction. *Art of the Printed Book 1455–1955* (New York, 1973).

Bober, Harry. Review of *The Göttingen Model Book*, ed. H. Lehmann-Haupt, *Speculum* XLIX (April 1974) 354–8.

Bühler, Curt. *The Fifteenth Century Book, the Scribes, the Printers, the Decorators* (Philadelphia, 1960).

—— *The University and the Press in 15th Century Bologna*, Texts and Studies in the History of Medieval Education, vol. VII (South Bend, Indiana, 1958).

Burckhardt, Jacob. *The Civilization of the Renaissance in Italy*, tr. S. G. C. Middlemore, ed. B. Nelson and C. Trinkaus (2 vol. New York, 1958).

Burke, Peter. *Culture and Society in Renaissance Italy 1420–1540* (London, 1972).

Cipolla, Carlo M. *Literacy and Development in the West* (London, 1969).

Clapham, Michael. 'Printing', *A History of Technology* II *From the Renaissance to the Industrial Revolution*, ed. Charles Singer, E. J. Holmyard, A. R. Hall and Trevor Williams (4 vol. Oxford, 1957) 377–411.

Davis, Natalie Zemon. 'Printing and the People', *Society and Culture in Early Modern France: Eight Essays* (Palo Alto, California, 1975).

De la Mare, Albinia. 'Bartolomeo Scala's Dealings with Booksellers, Scribes and Illuminators, 1459–63', *Journal of the Warburg and Courtauld Institutes* XXXIX (1976) 237–45.

—— 'The Shop of a Florentine "cartolaio" in 1426', *Studi Offerti a Roberto Ridolfi* (Florence, 1973) 237–48.

—— 'Vespasiano and the Library of the Badia at Fiesole' to be published by the Warburg Institute. Forthcoming.

—— 'Vespasiano da Bisticci Historian and Bookseller' (unpublished doctoral dissertation, London University, 1965).

Febvre, Lucien and Martin, H.-J. *L'Apparition du Livre* (Paris, 1958).

Gardiner, Stephen. *The Letters of Stephen Gardiner*, ed. J. A. Muller (Cambridge, 1933).

Gies, Dorothy. 'Some Early Ladies of the Book Trade', *The Publishers Weekly* (Oct. 5, 1940).

Gilmore, Myron P. 'Italian Reactions to Erasmian Humanism', *Itinerarium Italicum*, ed. H. Oberman (Leiden, 1975) 61–115.

Goldschmidt, E. P. *Gothic and Renaissance Bookbindings* (2 vol. Amsterdam, 1967).

—— *Medieval Texts and Their First Appearance in Print* (London, 1943).

Harrington, J. H. 'The Production and Distribution of Books in Western Europe to the Year 1500' (unpublished dissertation, Columbia University, 1956).

Haskins, C. H. *The Renaissance of the Twelfth Century* (Cambridge, Mass., 1939).

Hellinga, Wytze. 'Thomas A Kempis – The First Printed Editions', *Quaerendo* IV (1974) 3–30.

Hellinga, Lotte and Wytze. 'Regulations Relating to the Planning and Organization of Work by the Master Printer in the Ordinances of Christopher Plantin', *The Library*, 5th ser. XXIX (March 1974) 52–61.

Herrlinger, Robert. *History of Medical Illustration from Antiquity to 1600*, tr. G. Fulton-Smith (New York, 1970).

Hill, Christopher. Book review, *English Historical Review* LXXXVIII (April 1973) 383–5.

Hindman, Sandra. 'The Transition from Manuscripts to Printed Books in the Netherlands: Illustrated Dutch Bibles', *In Navolging, Een bundel studies aangeboden aan C. C. de Bruin* (Leiden, 1975) 189–209.

Hirsch, Rudolf. *Printing, Selling, and Reading 1450–1550* (Wiesbaden, 1967; rev. edn, 1974).

Ivins, Jr., William M. *Prints and Visual Communication* (Cambridge, Mass., 1953).

Jacob, E. F. *The Fifteenth Century 1399–1485* (Oxford History of England) (Oxford, 1961).

Jeannin, Pierre. *Merchants of the Sixteenth Century*, tr. P. Fittingoff (New York, 1972).

Kristeller, Paul Oskar. *Iter Italicum: A Finding List of Uncatalogued Humanistic Mss* (2 vol. London and Leiden, 1963–67) I, preface, xi–xxviii.

—— *Latin Manuscript Books before 1600* (New York, 1965).

—— *Renaissance Thought: The Classic, Scholastic and Humanist Strains* (New York, 1961).

—— 'The Contribution of Religious Orders to Thought and Learning', *Medieval Aspects of Renaissance Learning: Three Essays*, ed. E. P. Mahoney (Durham, N.C., 1974) 95–159.

Kruitwagen, B. 'Het Schrijven op Feestdagen in de Middeleuwen', *Tijdschrift voor boek en bibliotheek wezen* V (1907) 97–120.

Labarre, A. 'Un Atelier Mayençais d'Enluminure vers 1450–1500', *Revue Français d'Histoire du Livre* IV (1974) 127–31.

Lehmann-Haupt, Hellmut. *Gutenberg and the Master of the Playing Cards* (New Haven, 1966).

—— *Peter Schoeffer of Gernsheim and Mainz* (Rochester, New York, 1950).

Lenhart, John M. *Pre-Reformation Printed Books: A Study in Statistical and Applied Bibliography* (Franciscan Studies no. 14) (New York, 1935).

Luther, Martin. 'Against the Heavenly Prophets in the Matter of Images and Sacraments' (1525), *Luther's Works*, ed. C. Bergendorff and H. T. Lehmann, XL (Philadelphia, 1958) 99–100.

Lutz, Cora E. 'Manuscripts Copied from Printed Books', *Essays on Manuscripts and Rare Books* (Hamden, Conn., 1975) 129–39.

McKenzie, D. F. 'Printers of the Mind: Some Notes on Bibliographical Theories and Printing House Practices', *Studies in Bibliography* XXII (Charlottesville, Va., 1969) 1–75.

Mardersteig, Giovanni. *The Remarkable Story of a Book Made in Padua in 1477*, tr. H. Schmoller (London, 1967).

Maslen, K. I. D. and Gerritsen, John. Correspondence, *The Library* XXX (June 1975) 81–94, 134–6.

Moranti, Luigi. *L'Arte Tipografia in Urbino* (Florence, 1967).

Murray, Alexander. 'Religion among the Poor in thirteenth-century France', *Traditio* XXX (1974) 287–324.

Musper, Heinrich T. 'Xylographic Books', *The Book Through Five Thousand Years*, ed. H. D. L. Vervliet (Brussels, 1972) 341–8.

Nesi, Emilia. *Il Diario della Stamperia di Ripoli* (Florence, 1903).

Parent, Annie. *Les Métiers du Livre à Paris au XVIe Siècle (1535–1560)* (Geneva, 1974).

Parkes, Malcolm B. 'The Literacy of the Laity', *The Medieval World*, ed. D. Daiches and A. Thorlby (*Literature and Western Civilization*, Vol. II) (London, 1972–6) 555–76.

Pettas, William. 'The Cost of Printing a Florentine Incunable', *La Bibliofila* LXXV (1973) 67–85.

Phillips, W. A. 'Faust', *Encyclopedia Britannica* X (28 vol. 11 edn, London, 1910–11) 210–11.

Price, Derek de Solla. 'Geometrical and Scientific Talismans', *Changing Perspectives in the History of Science: Essays in Honor of Joseph Needham*, ed. M. Teich and R. Young (London, 1973) 250–64.

Renouard, Yves. *Etudes d'Histoire Médiévale* (2 vol. Paris, 1968).

Reynolds, L. D. and Wilson, N. G. *Scribes and Scholars* (Oxford, 1968).

Robinson, Arthur H. 'Map Making and Map Printing', *Five Centuries of Map Printing*, ed. David Woodward (Chicago, 1975) 1–25.

Sapori, Armando. *The Italian Merchant in the Middle Ages*, tr. P. A. Kennen (New York, 1970).

Sarton, George. *Appreciation of Ancient and Medieval Science During the Renaissance 1450–1600* (New York, 1958, 2nd edn).

Saunders, J. W. 'From Manuscript to Print: A Note on the Circulation of Poetic Manuscripts in the Sixteenth Century', *Proceedings of the Leeds Philosophical and Literary Society* VI (May 1951) 507–28.

Schmidt, Ph. *Die Illustration der Lutherbibel 1522–1700* (Basel, 1962).

Shelby, Lon R. 'The Education of Medieval English Master Masons', *Medieval Studies* (Toronto) XXXII (1970) 1–26.

—— 'The Geometrical Knowledge of Medieval Master Masons', *Speculum* XLVII (July 1972) 395–421.

Shenker, Israel. 'Books as an Art Form Through Five Centuries', *The New York Times* (Sept. 10, 1973).

Skelton, R. A. *Maps: A Historical Survey* (Chicago, 1972).

Steinberg, S. H. *Five Hundred Years of Printing* (rev. edn, Bristol, 1961).

Stillwell, Margaret Bingham. *The Beginning of the World of Books 1450 to 1470. A Chronological Survey of the Texts Chosen for Printing . . . With a Synopsis of the Gutenberg Documents* (New York, 1972).

Stone, Lawrence. 'Literacy and Education in England 1640–1900', *Past and Present* 42 (Feb. 1969) 69–139.

Strachan, James. *Early Bible Illustrations: A Short Study* (Cambridge, 1957).

Talbott, John E. 'The History of Education', *Daedalus* 100 (Winter 1971) 133–51.

Teichl, R. 'Der Wiegendruck im Kartenbild', *Bibliothek und Wissenschaft* I (1964) 210–65.

Thrupp, Sylvia. *The Merchant Class of Medieval London (1300–1500)* (Ann Arbor, 1962).

Uhlendorf, B. A. 'The Invention and spread of printing till 1470 with special reference to social and economic factors', *The Library Quarterly* II (1932) 179–231.

Ullman, B. L. *The Origin and Development of Humanistic Script* (Rome, 1960).

Watson, Foster. *The Beginning of the Teaching of Modern Subjects in England* (London, 1909).

Wieruszowski, Helen. 'Burckhardt and Vespasiano', *Philosophy and Humanism: Essays in Honor of P. O. Kristeller*, ed. E. P. Mahoney (New York, 1976) 387–405.

Willard, C. C. 'The Manuscripts of Jean Petit's Justification: Some Burgundian Propaganda Methods of the Early Fifteenth Century', *Studi Francesi* 38 (1969) 271–80.

Williams, Raymond. *Communications* (London, 1962).

—— *The Long Revolution* (New York, 1966). **61**.

Yates, Frances. *The Art of Memory* (London, 1966).

# Chapter 12

# C. A. Bayly

## THE INDIAN ECUMENE
## An indigenous public sphere

The appearance of print added a powerful new weapon to the arsenal of debate within the ecumene. When Christian missionaries began to pour printed propaganda into north India, its guardians responded vigorously, initiating formal logical contests and written refutations.[1] Missionaries were often surprised by the vehemence with which not only the religious teachers, but also local officers, *thanadars* (superintendents) and kotwals,[2] engaged them in debate. These were not cowed victims of colonial power. These were trustees of a public doctrine which seemed under threat. Rev. C. B. Leupolt, for example, noted of a tour in the vicinity of Lucknow in 1837: 'The Molwee came according to appointment, with an immense retinue of Mussulmans, learned as well as unlearned, and sat outside the tent. He brought a man with pen, ink and paper to note down what was said.'[3] Vigorous responses in pamphlet and placard form often followed Christian attacks on the Prophet. Such works often contained covert critiques of the Company as a secular ruler and were not limited to doctrinal arguments over the veracity of the Koran and Bible. In the 1830s the Muslim police chief of Buxar, for example, revealed to a passing missionary that he had often put a stop to widow burnings within his jurisdiction and denounced the Company for cowardice in failing to confront the issue.[4]

In the Hindu world, too, the activities of Brahmins and ruling-caste men had long transcended their ascribed functions as priests and warriors. Brahmins filled a similar role to Sheikhs and Sayyids as local justiciars, counsellors, literary arbiters, astronomers and doctors. The late eighteenth and early nineteenth centuries saw continuing formal debates between different schools of the Hindu learned about scripture and philosophy.[5] But, faced with direct attacks on their spiritual clienteles by Christians, priestly Brahmins had now to defend, to rationalise, to preach and to grasp the new tools of publicity. Some missionaries resorted to physical violence and coercion, such as 'shaking' the fakirs out of their spiritual trance.[6] More often, they found themselves drawn into complex and inconclusive debates which raged around the nature of godhead, the age of the universe and the qualities of good kingship, so touching directly on the political realm and claims to truth of western science. In missionary memoirs we glimpse two Hindu philosophical traditions which engaged the spiritual invader with particular force. First, Advaita Vedantists vigorously asserted the oneness of creation, directly challenging the Christian assumption of the separation of God and his creatures. Secondly, the devotional bhakti tradition afforded ample resources for arguing back against the white man in an idiom which seemed superficially similar. When a missionary advanced on a Hindu priest affirming 'God is love', the priest put his hands on the missionary and responded – to the Christian's irritation – 'I love you.'[7] Hindu devotional love (*prem*) was here used against Christian love, to diminish the moral, physical and political distance between sahib and 'native'. A generation before the modernist Arya Samaj stepped in to defend ancient religion with print, north Indian Hindu scholars were employing their skills of logical debate to refute, rebuff or incorporate the missionaries. This was no simple Hindu 'reaction' to western 'impact'; instead, the headstrong westerners plunged into a torrent of controversy which had for centuries pitted Vaishnavite scholars against Buddhists and Jains, Siddhantists against the Puranas and devotional gurus against the orthodox. All these formally doctrinal issues, however, bore on the question of good kingship and social propriety.

## Speech and critical aesthetic comment

An important precondition for the development of this widespread debate on religion and politics was the flexibility and accessibility of the Hindustani or Urdu language itself (Urdu is used here to mean the more refined and Persianised form of the common north Indian language, Hindustani). Urdu came to impart to the discussions of the ecumene a popular character which was difficult when Arabic and Persian totally dominated them. The turn towards Urdu in the courts and camps of north India in the eighteenth and nineteenth centuries represented a deliberate populist strategy on the part of the elite. The emergence of Urdu was attested to by the work of indigenous grammarians as much as by the excellence of its poets. In the late eighteenth century Sirajuddin Ali Arzu, for instance, had critically edited earlier Persian works on Urdu. He argued that this was a true language and proposed a typology which ran from pure Sanskrit, through popular and regional variations of Hindustani to Urdu, which incorporated many loan words from Persian and Arabic.[8] His emphasis on the unity of languages reflected the view of the Sanskrit grammarians and also affirmed the linguistic unity of the north Indian ecumene. What emerged was a kind of register of language types which were appropriate to different conditions of man and society, and even to different times of the day and season.[9] There was a particular variant for the use of women, for court camp and army, for local officials and village registrar. Particular professions, sub-castes and even bands of criminals had their own argot. Sometimes the specific blend of language forms could be used to exclude and monopolise. This, for instance, was a claim commonly made about court and bazaar writers. But the abiding impression is of linguistic plurality running through the whole society and an easier adaptation to circumstances in both spoken and written speech.

Urdu / Hindustani itself had now taken on the character of the public tongue of the ecumene. It was a popular language spread by Sufi saints and Hindu devotees and a language of the court and a discerning literati. The best Urdu could be heard, it was said, at three places: in the court and army bazaar at Delhi, at the flower-sellers' market on the river Jumna, and at the tomb of the saint Shah Madar in Etah district, a resort of horse-sellers, harkaras, palankin-bearers and other common people.[10] Outside centres of high Urdu court culture some Muslims continued to use the Devanagari character. The devotional poetry of the fifteenth- and sixteenth-century Sufi teachers was as likely to be found in the Devanagari as in the Persian script. In the eighteenth century a Sufi teacher of Bihar, writing to the governor of Malwa on the duties of rulers, remarked that 'a king's familiarity with Hindi verses is also very necessary'.[11] According to the writer, the king should consult with 'saintly ascetics', not with 'worldly ulama [doctors of law]' and should espouse 'universal toleration'. Thus regional versions of Hindustani appear to have carried overtones of community and harmony.

The learned reached down to incorporate these more localised language cultures in order to broaden cultural community. Several sources remark on the difficulty of teaching in Arabic or even Persian. Mullahs had to resort to exaggerated mimes of the action when they read out passages from the Arabic or Persian scriptures. One British observer noticed that at Muslim assemblies in which the Fateha or declaration of faith and Arabic prayers were offered, 'the mullah gave the history of the saints', presumably the Shia martyrs, in Urdu 'to enable those present the better to understand it'.[12]

Poetic assemblies held in the court, in the houses of notables and in the shops of bazaar people, spread common standards of aesthetic judgement and common forms of language across the country. Urdu writing was not confined to a self-conscious realm of literature. Instead, it was a discourse among men of weight on matters of aesthetics, health, religion and politics. Aristocratic writers were honoured in this world, but their rank did not exempt their ideas, their forms of letter-writing or their calligraphy, from critical scrutiny.[13] The poet Mir is alleged to have ridiculed the Emperor Shah Alam for his poetry. The Emperor had claimed that he was such a good poet that he could dash off several poems while he was doing his ablutions in the morning; 'Yes, and they smell like it', said Mir.[14] Aesthetic issues could become more directly political. The debate between the advocates of Persian and those of Urdu had ethnic, class, and religious undertones.[15] Though they enjoyed the patronage of the royal family, by the 1840s the proponents of Urdu were often less consciously aristocratic than the champions of Persian and were more influenced by Indian forms.[16]

One literary form which reflected and perpetuated the memory of the ecumene was the *tazkirah*, or collective literary biography. Literature here went beyond poetry to topics as diverse as medicine and topography. Through such works literary lineages and styles of endeavour could be traced over many generations. Having one's name entered in a major tazkirah guaranteed some degree of literary immortality, and individuality. These collective biographies demonstrate the diverse origins of the people who were known to the Indian critical public. The models were Persian or central Asian forerunners, such as the biographies of the literary men and wits of Kashan, many of whom migrated to India in the thirteenth and fourteenth centuries.[17] Among the noted poets were sons of washermen, water-carriers, tailors, an 'occulist and chess-player', a 'talented man who gave himself up to profligacy', 'a great drunkard', and so on. Just as Islam was supposed to pay no attention to class in matters of faith, so in matters of style and literary excellence, men from humble backgrounds could achieve great fame.

In the 1840s Alois Sprenger carried out a detailed analysis of a number of literary biographies, including one of the Persian poets of Calcutta and Banaras, which paints a complex picture of social communication and the geography of the ecumene.[18] The literary men were often drawn from the old officers of the towns and qasbahs, such as the kazi and the King of Awadh's newswriter at Banaras.[19] As we have seen, the connection between political information systems and literary endeavour was very close. Others were dispersed remnants of the Delhi royal house, the Shahzadas of Banaras. Imperial family members who had been exiled or who had fled to Lucknow and Patna became the hubs of patterns of cultural patronage. Many of the people honoured worked in British government offices. They included residency munshis, clerks to the Calcutta Court of Appeal, clerks of the customs department at Banaras, and others in more lowly official positions who still cultivated Persian and Hindustani letters. The previously mentioned informant of the British, Ali Ibrahim Khan, was a prominent member of this group, and had written a collective biography of Persian poets.

People of poor background were not as evident here as in the Kashan list. Sprenger, however, listed many humbler authors in a comprehensive listing of tazkirahs, accounting for more than 1,800 literary people. Here, for instance, there were druggists,[20] a serving woman,[21] a Hazrat (one who had memorised the Koran) who kept an apothecary's shop in the Nakhas cattle market of Banaras,[22] a common writer,[23] a tailor skilled in *marsiyas* (lamentations on the Shia martyrs),[24] a Hyderabad 'dancing woman'[25] and many others. Hindus accounted for a small but significant percentage of the list. Most of these were from the Kashmiri Brahmin, Khattri or Kayastha communities and were traditionally associated with Persian and Urdu through Mughal service. There were, however, occasional entries for men of the Hindu commercial castes. One Eurasian even appeared: John Thomas, a 'soldier-like man',[26] son of George Thomas, who had founded a small state in Hariana at the end of the eighteenth century.

So it was not only men of power who participated in the literary activities of the ecumene. The egalitarian traditions of the Islamic lands and the community sensibilities of Indian cities encouraged ordinary artisans and people of the bazaars to aspire to eminence as poets or commentators. The form of the language was inclusive; it mirrored and even helped to stimulate the rapid social mobility which was characteristic of post-Mughal north India. Even women wrote and circulated poems.[27] In Lucknow, noblewomen, courtesans, musicians, dancers and other cultural performers from poor backgrounds achieved power in court and urban politics. This gravely offended evangelical Christian commentators and some later Indian purists, who saw corruption and decadence in what was actually striking social mobility.

## History, libraries and social memory

Alongside questions of public doctrine and literary aesthetics, 'history' and topography played an important role in maintaining the identity of the ecumene. History in the Indo-Muslim tradition was, as Peter Hardy has written, a protean form which merged into poetry, moral and political instruction, and theology.[28] Amir Khusrau's poetic and panegyric history of the fourteenth century began a tradition which still had its imitators in the eighteenth century when court historians rendered the deeds of the founders of the successor states into ornate Persian. More influential yet in our period was the historical work of Abul Fazl. The 'Ain' and the 'Akbarnamah' were read and discussed extensively by the literati of the successor states and the munshis of the British offices. Besides legitimating the divinely gifted status of the house of Timur, Abul Fazl's history was the philosophy of religious insight teaching by example. Valuing the divine revelation in all mature creeds, his picture of universal harmony, must have seemed particularly apposite to Muslim jurisconsults practising in an age when the 'tribe of Hindus' had achieved much influence in the state. Akbar's debates with his Hindu, Jain, Christian and Parsi subjects were viewed as a template of good government in the eighteenth century. They represented the strain of historical and moral philosophy which inspired Mirza Jan-i Janan to reaffirm the theology of Ibn-i Arabi, and the doctrine of the immanence of God, against the more exclusive doctrines of the Delhi theologians, Shah Waliullah and Shah Abdul Aziz. It inspired that archetypical denizen of the ecumene, Ghalib, to describe ecstatically the sight of the festival of lights, Diwali, at Banaras, 'the Mecca of India'.[29] Despite his earlier adherence to a purist creed, Sayyid Ahmad's description of Delhi diplays similar affection for the Hindu and Jain temples which had arisen in the city.[30]

This sense of the luminosity of place, and of the pleasures and ease of the erstwhile great and culturally diverse empire of Hindustan, was a compelling motif for much of the poetic-cum-historical work of the eighteenth and early nineteenth centuries. Hindus and Muslims, peasant and poet, were united in a wistful remembrance of what was and what might have been. This mode of elegiac historiography reached its fullest expression in the works of 'social poets' such as Sauda and Nazir who elaborated the form called *ashob sheher*,[31] 'bewailing the fallen greatness of the city', that is the civilisation of Mughal India. It also expressed itself in what is conventionally called 'history' (though the word *tarikh* does not quite mean history). A good example was the

'Araish-i-Mehfil' of Mir Sher Ali of Narnaul.[32] This writer had a family history typical of the military nobility of the eighteenth century. His father had been commander of the Nawab's Arsenal in Bengal. He himself moved between Delhi, Lucknow and Hyderabad, writing in Urdu under the patronage of Jawan Bakht, son of the Emperor Shah Alam. Late in his life he was introduced by Wellesley to Hasan Reza Khan and settled in Fort William College where he translated the Persian classic, 'Gulistan', under the superintendence of John Gilchrist. Drawing on the work of predecessors, notably Sujan Rai, Sher Ali wrote the history of the kings of Delhi from the Hindu period, described the customs of India's inhabitants, and the topography of each province. Though he recognised distress and decline, the overall tone seems to have been panegyric: 'All the inhabitants of Hindustan are capable, learned and clever and know merit'; the 'majority of grains have a delicious taste . . . rice is produced in a paradise on earth'.[33] There are descriptions of the excellence of palankins and other conveyances. He praises the beauty of Hindu women. He dilates on the feelings appropriate to the cycle of the Hindu months in a clear reference to the theory of *rasas* or essences which underlies Hindu aesthetics. But this was no more; after the Emperor Farrukhsiyar, corruption spread, Muhammad Shah became addicted to pleasure and 'the Empire became a sort of market'.[34] Poetry and panegyric in this tone persisted well into the nineteenth century. In 1849, for instance, Maharaja Apurva Krishna Bahadur wrote a historical epic 'The Conquerors of Hindustan' which praised the later Mughals.[35] The Empire had survived the wreck of its sister states, the Safavids and central Asian kingdoms, and even now, this work claimed, the Empire cast a glow like the setting sun. The writer apparently belonged to a family of the Sobha Bazaar, Calcutta, which had acquired its title by giving offerings to an indigent prince who was travelling around India with two mangy elephants.[36] The Anglo-Indian press ridiculed these poetic effusions, but they represent a continuing sense of cultural and political community and of criticism of the ruling powers, which remained strong until it was brutally terminated by the sack of Delhi in November 1857.

Libraries, or rather 'book houses' provided the resources from which this social memory in the fields of history, literature and theology was drawn. Indian libraries were no doubt highly unstable by European standards. Often they were built up out of patterns of princely gift-exchange[37] or plunder,[38] as annexes to royal treasuries. Royal and noble libraries were looted by their guardians as well as by external enemies.[39] Many Indian libraries were also exclusive. Temple libraries among Hindus and Jains were generally available only to priests; sacred knowledge was dangerous and had to be stored in safe places.[40] This literary memory, however, was neither negligible nor sealed off from the debates of the ecumene. The largest libraries comprised tens of thousands of volumes,[41] while many thousands of families had smaller collections amounting to a handful of manuscripts. There is some evidence, too, that a more specialist understanding of the library was developing among the elites even before the colonial period; in Jaipur, for example, Raja Jai Singh separated off a study collection from his treasury and this was used by the king and his officials in adjudications on religious and social issues.[42] Though never public, these collections could sometimes serve as a resource for the wider learned community. On occasion the Lucknow Royal Library was asked to produce a text when a controversy between the Muslim learned and Christian missionaries took place.[43] Scholars from outside princely families were allowed to see and copy texts. Sayyid Ahmad Khan, for example, was one person who was allowed to work in the Delhi Royal Library.[44]

## Communications and political debate

Historians agree that in the West the public sphere was a domain of communication given form by printed media and the market.[45] Evidently, this key component was lacking from the north Indian scene before the introduction of lithography in the 1830s and 1840s, but the reasons for this remain obscure. Politics may have played a part; several Indian rulers at the turn of the nineteenth century continued to discourage the use of the printing press because it threatened their authority.[46] Rather than being testimony to passivity and the absence of political debate, however, our evidence suggests exactly the opposite conclusion: that royal authority was already too fragile to support this further dissemination of ridicule and *lèse majesté*. This in turn points to a wider reason for the late start of printing. Indians had created a highly effective information order in which strategically placed written media reinforced a powerful culture of oral communication; printing in this sense was not needed until society itself began to change more radically under colonial rule. In the ecumene written media and oral communication complemented each other. Francis Robinson[47] has made a strong case for the dominance of oral exposition and importance of the physical presence of the reputed teacher within the pre-print culture of Islamic north India. Oral exposition, presence and memory were no doubt critical in philosophical debate, and among Hindus and Jains no less than among Muslims. They were also important in poetic and aesthetic discussion. Ghalib, for instance, is said rarely to have purchased a manuscript or book, as he committed to memory anything that he needed.[48] Written media were, nevertheless, an essential part of north Indian critical debate, and could create eddies and flurries of opinion distant from the immediate presence of their authors. Ghalib's proficiency as a letter-writer was as striking as his memory.

While the dismal picture conveyed by Europeans and by Indian reformers was of a society where the communication of knowledge was stunted by hierarchy, there is much evidence to the contrary. We have already noted the speed with which information from the northwest or from Persia was conveyed to Banaras. The combination of harkara information, newsletters and public recitations in bazaars or near the platform of the kotwal's station spread news very quickly across country. During the Nepal and Burma wars, during the Afghan and Sikh campaigns of 1838–52, and during the Multan revolt of 1848 anti-British information and rumour was determinedly spread by these means.[49] At the height of the Burma War, Malcolm warned that 'there was a dangerous species of secret war against our authority carried on by numerous tho' unseen hands – the spirit of which is kept up by letters, by exaggerated reports, by pretended prophecies, etc.'[50] Though, as late as 1836, Auckland discounted the influence of the indigenous press itself, he believed that news was still widely disseminated by newswriters and agents of powerful people in whose newsletters 'anything may be inserted . . . without scruple'.

The north Indian case indicates that critical debate within a broad political class could be spread through personal and institutional letter-writing, through placarding and public congregation. In Rajasthan and adjoining areas the bardic tradition and the written stories to which it gave rise also proved capable of carrying subversive political messages. James Tod noted the prevalence of 'licence' and satire, the dissemination of 'truths unpalatable' and 'the absence of all mystery and reserve with regard to public affairs'[51] in the Rajput principalities. All this gives a picture of a lively social and political debate whose existence was reluctantly acknowledged when colonial officials made disparaging references to 'bazaar rumour'.

A similar point was made by Garcin de Tassy on the basis of a lifetime's study of Hindustani literature. It was common to argue that politics and rational discourse had no part in a society dominated by fable. On the contrary, he argued, the western distinctions between politics, literature and history did not really apply. Many so-called 'fables' were strongly political in tone and 'Nous voyons, en effet, que la politique occupe le premier rang dans les fables orientales, et en forme le portion la plus importante . . .'[52] Here he mentions the famous 'Tota Kahani' or 'Tale of a Parrot'. Fables such as this, or the Panchatantra in its various forms, were highly pointed in their characterisation of human types and could be modified in oral presentations to refer to particular political situations. For instance one such story is a fable about diplomacy. A herd of deer hired a jackal to make a compact with a lion, but the jackal betrayed the deer to be eaten because he was the usual recipient of the lion's pickings.[53] This story must have seemed particularly timely in the savage politics of eighteenth century India.

In contemporary west Asia, political debate was carried on in smoking dens and coffee shops.[54] The same was true in India, though here druggists' stalls, selling betel nut, tobacco or medicaments,[55] and sweetshops[56] served as more important forums of gossip and news. In west Asia, again, more resolute protests were made by seizing control of that pre-eminently public place, the mosque, at a time just before the muezzin's call to prayer and making statements critical of the authorities from the minaret. The regularity of this procedure suggests that it was sanctioned by the community, and even reluctantly tolerated by rulers. In India, too, political demonstrations were made at or near mosques. The shrines of saints, or of deceased rulers popularly revered as just men, were also the venue of demonstrations – an indication of the relative importance for the subcontinent of tomb worship and Sufism in both elite and popular life. In Lucknow at the beginning of the nineteenth century, for example, 'oppressions' by the police chief of the city brought together thousands in the garden of the tomb of the late ruler, Shuja-ud Daulah. The crowd called out 'andhera! andhera!' 'darkness!, darkness!', that is 'tyranny!'[57] In other incidents, people affixed handbills to points on or near the Friday mosque or royal temple. We have already noticed the use of placards during the celebrated affair of the British Resident, James Achilles Kirkpatrick and the Hyderabad lady. Placards similarly denounced unpopular local Shia officials in Hyderabad,[58] announced changes of regime in Kathmandu,[59] and the onset of the Rebellion of 1857 in Lucknow. Pinning up critical poems in a mordant style, as well as passing them by word of mouth through the bazaar, appears to have been a political form as common as the pasquinade of Baroque Rome. Pasquino was the name given to a 'talking' classical statue near to the church of San Andrea della Valle. It has long been the practice to affix to it lampoons against the Pope or the authorities. Whereas in Rome, pasquinades were afforded legitimacy by the statuesque memorabilia of classical republicanism and ciceronian polemic, in India the tombs of just rulers or those Muslim saints, who had been appropriately unimpressed by the powers that be, served a similar purpose.

Political debates over a wider geographical area were carried on by the Indo-Muslim literati through recognised newsletters and also by private correspondence, still often delivered by covert indigenous postal systems. The literature associated with popular Sufi teachers sometimes contained critical comment on rulers, or on various ethnic groups.[60] Hindu sages crafted similar comments on contemporary politics. The poet Kavindracarya wrote verses in honour of the Emperor Shahjahan who had facilitated pilgrimage to Banaras.[61] They were recorded and used on later occasions when pilgrimage rights came under pressure. Shah Waliullah wrote letters to contemporary rulers urging a more strenuously Islamic policy.[62] Such epistles were, of course, destined for the readers of the wider critical ecumene; they were not 'private' letters.[63]

The practice of personal letter-writing also kept the ecumene informed. Figures for the early nineteenth century produced by the nascent British postal authorities suggest that even quite small towns produced a surprisingly large number of letters, perhaps as many as two hundred per annum per head for the literates and people who could afford to have letters written.[64] For men of the pen such as the poet Ghalib, letter-writing was viewed as a necessity of life. This was almost literally the case, because as much paper was spent by Ghalib and his correspondents discussing new remedies and the excellence of various physicians as on the diseases of the body politic.[65] Outside scholarly circles, most towns had substantial communities of bazaar writers acting for ordinary people who could pay them. Village schoolmasters also helped people communicate with their folk 'in distant parts'.[66] Most cities, again, supported large bodies of runners employed by private daks. After 1836, the British tried to suppress these in order to maximise postal revenue, but the impression is that many persisted clandestinely. 'Native intelligence' continued to move vigorously, transported by runners 'who shift their parcels at every sixteen or twenty miles' and never made unnecessary stops.[67]

As we have seen, the newsletters written from the courts of rulers all across the country were copied by hand in relatively limited numbers. As in the case of later printed newspapers which were read to large groups of people and handed around in the bazaar for several days, the information they purveyed seems to have become public property very quickly. Pages of newspapers were lent by one family to another.[68] Whole copies of newspapers were read out to crowds in the streets in the evening.[69] Professional newswriters moved between the world of the written newsletter and the printed newspaper. Some of these writers also kept lists of subscribers to whose houses they would repair daily in order to read the news from their own manuscript compilations.[70] A combination of these instruments could create a formidable blast of publicity even before the rise of the press. When in the early 1850s, the King of Delhi was maliciously reported to have become a Shia, a whole arsenal of written, lithographed and memorised refutations cannoned back. Ghalib, then poet laureate, was himself asked to write an ode in refutation.[71]

The ecumene was led by respectable men who could draw limits to the actions of government and also seek to impose their standards of belief and practice on the populace. Meanwhile, dense networks of social communication could bring butchers, flower-sellers, bazaar merchants and artisans into political debates and demonstrations. This has been thoroughly demonstrated by the many studies of the taxation riots and religious disputes of the early nineteenth century.[72] These events, however, are evidence of a continuing ecumenical critique; they should not be seen as sudden upsurges of resistance from tyrannised and voiceless subalterns. In 1779 in Lucknow, for instance, there was a celebrated debate between learned physicians who had newly arrived in town,[73] and resident savants who were trying to protect their livelihoods against the newcomers. The invasion of the new men was announced, according to the historian Mahomed Faiz Baksh, by a careful campaign of slander against existing 'doctors' in the city[74] (slander, of course, itself represents a kind of 'black public'). The conflict came to a head in a public debate. The ostensible subjects of the disputation were rival interpretations of an incident in early Islamic history – a revolt in AD 740 led by Ali Zaid. In fact, the two sides partly represented ethnic divisions, with Persians ranged against Indians. Alongside this there were political divisions, with the supporters of the Nawab and Warren Hastings ranged against partisans of the Begams of Awadh and other groups resisting the Awadh court and the British. The authority of texts and the spoken word were both in contention here.[75] Professional clerics contended with lay literati. Perhaps the most important aspect was the way in which the debate attracted the attention of the whole city with huge throngs of people of all persuasions, numbering more than 1,500, clustering around the house where the contest took place. Finally, order broke down amid Hogarthian scenes of rioting and revelry. As the chronicler wrote, 'It was a marvellous tumult and no-one knew what it was about . . . it ended at last, but for some time after it was much talked about and people composed ballads and wrote narratives about it'.[76]

Another example from the first months of British rule at Bareilly in 1804 revealed similar patterns. Fitzroy, a demented magistrate, had struck a Sayyid in a dispute over a garden. The cry went up 'A Seyud has been insulted and struck; our houses are about to be demolished . . .'. The Governor-General's agent, Archibald Seton, a prolix and learned Scotsman, feared that the 'Green Banner' was about to be raised and the paltry British occupying force in the city would be overwhelmed. To compromise the dispute, 'he went to the Mosque of Moftee Mahomed Ewuz, the most popular and respected Seyud at Barelli, from the purity of his conduct and the sanctity of his manners'.[77] As he entered the mosque, Seton took off his shoes and said to the swordsmen barring his way, 'Do you not see, my friends, that I am prepared to approach a sacred place and meet a holy man'. They respectfully parted and, according to Seton, 'I distinctly heard one of them say to the other "This gentleman is one of us." '[78] The honour of the community was restored by this act of contrition on the part of the Sahib, and, with the aid of two Muslim physicians and the Mufti, the wrong was compromised. The crowds retreated and Fitzroy was bundled out of town under restraint. This story illustrates the ecumene in action, its leading men acting to quell disputes in the same way as the Prophet had compromised the quarrels of the tribes of Arabia. Here the practice of politics and jurisconsultation was more striking than the 'resistance', for which some historians perennially search. However, resistance was indeed to come when the same Mahomed Ewuz took part in the house tax disturbances of 1816, and fled the city.[79] Faced with open resistance, the British authorities had a tendency to shoot first and consult the ecumene later.

Such standard patterns of political representation and debate embraced Hindus as well as Muslims. Several historians have given us analyses of the political movement at Banaras in 1810 against the new British system of house taxation, emphasising its popular character.[80] From our perspective what is striking is that a vigorous and effective public opinion could express itself in the public arena across the boundaries of caste and religion. Here the ecumene spoke in a Hindu idiom, though Muslims were also active. The protesters presented petitions against the asssessment as discrete communities. One particular market-gardener caste leadership sent a 'letter of righteousness' (*dharmapatra*) to mobilise its rural supporters, in what was probably an adaptation of the normal method of raising temple funds or seeking adjudication in cases of infringements of caste rules.[81] The action of the Banaras citizens was, however, carefully coordinated between groups. The demonstrators all took a common oath of resistance and congregated in a single spot. Petitions argued the case against taxation in terms of the sanctity of Banaras but also the past and present usage of 'the country of Hindoostan, preferable to the kingdom of the seven climes', acknowledging a sense both of charismatic place and of wider patria.[82] Ultimately, too, they accepted the good offices of the Maharaja of Banaras as an intermediary with the British. Abdul Kadir Khan and another 'faithful old government servant', Akbar Ali Khan, also played the part of intermediaries. Although one historian has denounced them as 'spies' for the British,[83] and they certainly worked to end the uprising, these men had high status within both communities. They continued to resemble the munshis and advisers of the eighteenth century rather than the police informers of the nationalist period.

Finally, one should beware of the assumption that, even in cases where religious communities were pitted against each other, rational argument and social communication was totally abandoned. A few months earlier than the house tax affair, Banaras had been convulsed by a riot between Hindus and Muslims over the status of a holy place. In this case the petitioners on the part of the Hindus argued from history and current information. All had been well in Banaras, they said, until the Emperor Aurangzeb had destroyed the harmony between the communities by demolishing a temple; but the Emperor was so powerful that the Hindus had 'necessarily submitted with patience'.[84] Now the Muslim weavers had become 'more bigotted' than Aurangzeb, and the Hindus were forced to respond. Showing an acute awareness of current affairs, they argued that Muslims should concentrate on protecting the holy places of the Middle East against the Arabian Wahhabis who had recently sacked them, killing, it appears, the agent in Iraq of the late Ali Ibrahim Khan.[85]

## Elite and mass in cultural performance

In addition to these set-piece demonstrations of discontent, strong political messages could be conveyed through cultural performance which linked elite and populace in enjoyment. Historians have been interested in recent years in the symbolism of festivals such as Ramlila, Holi or, amongst Muslims, Mohurrum and Id.[86] Well before the intervention of nationalist politicians at the end of the nineteenth century, these festivals had become the scene of attempts by magnates to claim new status or bodies of people attempting to assert cohesion or indentity. In this sense, the Ramlila festival, which increased in importance and size in most parts of north India in the eighteenth and nineteenth centuries, should itself be seen as a widening arena of public communication.[87] Garcin de Tassy listed many different types of popular literature for recitation at these festivals, including songs, chants, homilies and prayers, all of which could be used to promote cohesion and mutual knowledge.[88] These ranged from laments on the death of the Shia martyrs, through didactic treatises (*risalas*) to what he called, as early as the 1840s, 'national-musical' performances in Indian-owned premises in Calcutta and other cities.[89] This flexible range of media, part-written and part-oral, added up to a wide array of procedures for spreading information, subversion, parody and biting political comment.

A number of different styles stand out. The heroic ballads of warrior heroes conveyed not only tales of ancient valour but observations on right kingship and religious conduct. The 'Prithvi Raja ki Kahani' which told of the last Hindu king of Delhi was a kind of foundation-legend for the high-caste warrior communities. In its full version the story contained not only genealogical and epic material but observations on grammar, diplomacy and other useful arts. Peasants could sometimes be found who had exactly mastered the whole ballad.[90] These legends had a definite reactive and community dimension. The epic of Pabuji, for instance, was circulated throughout Rajasthan by travelling story-tellers with elaborate cloth panels depicting the hero's exploits. In it the Muslim ('Turk') Mirza Khan is anathematised as a cow-killer: 'Oh king of Patan, in your kingdom calves and white cows are slain; at daybreak are slain the frogs and peacocks of the gardens'.[91] Another type of popular story was the social comedy in which stereotyped members of different communities fall into conflict and farce. One typical version was the Punjabi *jhaggra* or *jhannau* in one of which an argument develops between a Khattri woman and a Jat woman'.[92] They embody respectively the merits of an acute businesswoman and a sturdy peasant. The Jat woman constantly ridicules the Khattri's assertion of caste superiority. Another version of popular communication was the didactic debate between pupil and master which was found both in the Sufi tradition and in its Hindu form. All these written media and their 'shadow' verbal forms could be used to propagate critical comment and debates on the conduct of both the rulers and society as a whole.

Alongside these, finally, should be placed the performances of wandering cultural specialists: bards, puppeteers, actors and jugglers. Bands of these artistes moved rapidly around India often from bases at the major pilgrimage places. They conveyed political and social messages which might originate in either the literate or the non-literate spheres. In Rajasthan and adjoining areas of the Agra Province, for instance, traditional bards (Bhats and Charans), singers of family pride and the heroic exploits of the Rajput rulers, introduced into their repertoire tales of the resistance of the Jats of Bharatpur against Mughal and British. Rather lower down the social scale, courtesans and prostitutes were famous purveyors of music and popular song. Some of their stock in trade were *ghazals*[93] or musical versions of poems which had been written by noted satirists, or even by popular and munificent rulers such as Nawab Asaf-ud Daulah of Awadh.[94] While the British garnered their fair share of sycophantic ditties, they were often the target of attack too. For decades after 1799, any European traveller who wandered into the red light district of Banaras was serenaded from the roof gardens of the courtesans' houses by songs praising the exploits of the deposed Nawab Vazir Ali, who had killed the British judge of Banaras and chief intelligence expert, George Cherry, during the abortive uprising of that year.[95]

Travelling puppet shows and theatrical performances also helped spread subversive political ideas. Thus, in the months before the Vellore mutiny of 1806, it was puppeteers that carried the message that Tipu Sultan's sons were about to regain their power, aided by the French. Several decades later an observer investigated the bodies of actors who took improvised comedies around north India to all the major festivals. Their plays were usually derived from Sanskrit originals but were burlesqued to include contemporary references. The Indians 'are devoted to the type of comedy which the *bazigars* [jugglers] perform at the great occasions, and which often contain political allusions'.[96] One group was attached to a body of irregular Indian cavalry, but was hired from time to time by rich magnates who wanted to entertain their guests. Captain Bevan recorded one such performance which satirised the proceedings in a British criminal court. In the drama the magistrate appeared whistling and striking his riding boots with a cane. The prisoner was brought in, but the magistrate paid no attention to him as he was flirting with a young Indian woman among the witnesses.[97] During the deposition he continued to make signs and leer at her. Finally, the bearer appeared saying '*tiffin taiyar hai*' ('tea is ready') and the magistrate got up. When the officers of the court asked what to do with the prisoner, he replied 'Dam [*sic*] his eyes, hang him'! This subversive assault on the white man's justice and lecherousness was, Bevan reported, greatly enjoyed both by the Indian troops and the British army officers present.

## The limits of the ecumene

The north Indian critical ecumene as we have described it spilled over the bounds of caste, community and sect; it encompassed a dialogue between elite and popular political culture. It stands as a reminder that Indian minds and Indian social life cannot be reduced to the behaviourist simplicities of hierarchy and segmentation. It takes us beyond the limited and monolithic concept of 'resistance' to the realm of political critique and intellectual history. Yet this is not to say that the ecumene was a seamless web. On the contrary, there were significant breaks and discontinuities in it. For example, while Hindu noblemen, poets and specialists took part in the wider debate and wrote in its languages, Persian and Urdu, the Brahmin establishments stood relatively aloof.[98] Ghalib could say that 'Benares was the Mecca of India', but it is difficult to imagine him participating in the pandits' ritual debates (*shastrarthas*) in the same way that Khattri Hindus participated in the Persian poetry circles. Even Ghalib had relatively few Hindu literary correspondents. In the case of one of the most prominent, Munshi Hargopal Tafta, it seems that the poet hoped to touch him for money;[99] elsewhere he says he employed 'bunya-language' (shopkeeper talk) with a leading Delhi banker.[100] As a token of the assimilative power of public doctrinal debate, some learned Hindus became Muslims, but the process did not take place in reverse even though poor and unlettered Muslims sometimes venerated Hindu deities.[101] Muslim scholars showed interest in the Hindu classics and literature, but learned Hindus do not seem to have analysed and critiqued the Islamic corpus until Dayananda Saraswati set out to ridicule it. Khairuddin Khan's debate with the Banaras pandits in the 1770s occurred precisely because he had heard that a rich Bengali 'held no communication whatever with Mussulmans, and avoided even the shadow of a Mahomedan'.[102] Ritual pollution created hairline fractures in cross-community debate. Khairuddin tried to reconcile the genealogy of Adam with the story of the Pandavas of the Hindu epics and some of the Brahmins went along with this. Even so, he asked in irritation, 'what do you know of the Mahomedan religion?'[103] An overlapping debate did not mean equal participation. In fact, when a critical public sphere using the newspaper finally emerged, these inequalities of participation were reinforced by the desire of editors to grasp and hold abstract constituencies of readers' opinions, now more distant from the face-to-face, or pen-to-pen, relations of the ecumene.

Amongst the less privileged, too, social and even economic discourse was still to some extent constricted within what was called the 'opinion of the caste', even if, as in the Peshwa's territories, the authorities intervened to adjudicate and advise.[104] Among the upper castes, extra-caste opinion and debate appears to have influenced these insider debates. So, for instance, social transgressions by an Agarwal banker might have been dealt with by the caste assembly, but it had severe repercussions within the wider multi-caste arena of the market and its rumours, since social and commercial credit were closely bound up. But nobody worried much about what went on amongst the leather workers or liquor distillers. Only bhakti devotion bridged these divides of status, and the sects were becoming increasingly respectable and market-centred in the eighteenth and nineteenth centuries.[105] The ecumene had always worked unevenly beneath the network of the most enlightened intelligentsia. In this, India was not qualitatively different from other societies with emergent public spheres.[106] Nevertheless, the ecumene did display a range of fractures which were widened by the powerful pressures of later colonial politics.

## Notes

1    Avril Powell, *Muslims and Missionaries in pre-mutiny India* (Richmond, 1993), pp. 43–75; *Church Missionary Record [CMR]*, I, 3, 1830, 59, 62; I, 6, 1830, 120–2, 133, 137; I, 10, 1830, 217–19.

2    e.g., the Sadr Amin and 'The chief native judge' near Lucknow refutes Christianity, *CMR*, 6, 7, 1836, 137–8; ditto, the office manager of the Collector of Ghazipur, *ibid.*, 9, 1, 1838, 15.

3    *CMR*, 7, 6, 1836, 139.

4    *The Missionary Register for MDCCCXXIV* [.] (London, 1824), April 1824, p. 195.

5    See, e.g., the description of a western Indian debate between Advaita Vedantists and their opponents, J. Howison, *European Colonies in Various Parts of the World* (London, 1834), II, 52–4.

6    C. B. Leupolt, *Recollections of an Indian Missionary* (London, 1856), p. 56.

7    e.g., *CMR*, 1, 6, 1830, 128; cf. *ibid.*, 131, 133; *ibid.*, 1, 10, 1830, 243; Leupolt, *Recollections*, p. 82; the missionaries displayed particular interest in Sadhs and Kabirpanthis, *ibid.*, 2,8, 1831, pp. 178–80; *Miss. Reg.*, April 1824, p. 314.

8    S. Kidwai, *Gilchrist and the 'Language of Hindostan'* (Delhi, 1972), pp. 88–9.

9    J. Majeed, 'The Jargon of Indostan – an exploration of jargon in Urdu and East India Company English' in P. Burke and R. Porter (eds) *Languages and Jargons* (Cambridge, Mass., forthcoming); D. Lelyveld, 'The fate of Hindustani: colonial knowledge and the project of a national language', in C. Breckenridge and P. van der Veer, *Orientalism and the Postcolonial Predicament* (New York, 1993), pp. 189–215.

10   E.B. Eastwick, tr., *The Bagh o Bahar* (Hertford, 1852), pp. 7–8, Munshi's preface; cf. W. Crooke, *Ethnographic Handbook of the North-western Provinces and Oudh* (Allahabad, 1887), p. 84, on 'Madari' palankin-bearers. But see also, A. Rai, *A House Divided. The Origins and Development of Hindi-Urdu* (Delhi, 1984), pp. 246–54, which notes the precolonial attempts to 'purify' Urdu of Sanskritic words; Surendra Gopal, *Patna in the Nineteenth Century. A socio-cultural profile* (Calcutta, 1982), pp. 60–79.

11   Askari, 'Mirat-ul-Muluk', *Indica* (Bombay, 1953), p. 31.

12   Westmacott, 'Travels', Westmacott Papers, Oriental and India Offices Collections, British Library, Ms. Eur C29 f. 183; *Friend of India*, 28 Feb. 1839.

13   A vivid picture of the world of the mushairah is given in Akhtar Qamber, *The Last Mushairah of Delhi* (Delhi, 1979).

14   R. Russell and K. Islam, *Three Mughal Poets. Mir, Sauda, Mir Hasan* (London, 1969) p. 6; cf. pp. 55–8; S. A. I. Tirmizi, *Persian Letters of Ghalib* (Delhi, 1969), p. xxiii.

15   Daud Rahbar (tr., ed.), *Urdu Letters of Mirza Asadu'llah Khan Ghalib* (Albany, New York, 1987), p. xxvii; Tirmizi, *Persian Letters of Ghalib*, p. xxviii–xxx.

16   cf. R. Russell and K. Islam, *Ghalib, 1797–1969*, I, *Life and Letters* (London, 1969), pp. 79–81.

17   A. Sprenger, *A Catalogue of the Arabic, Persian and Hindustani Manuscripts of the Libraries of the King of Oudh* (Calcutta, 1854), pp. 23ff.

18   *ibid.*, pp. 195–306; we have used the term ecumene to describe a *style* of communication but tazkirahs could be used to demonstrate the *geography* of social communication in the sense used

by Deutsch. The relative decline of literary and social comment in the western cities, Lahore, Delhi, etc. would be matched in the late eighteenth century by the rise of Lucknow, Banaras, Patna, Hyderabad and their associated qasbahs. Calcutta would become significant for Persian and Urdu scholarship.

19    *ibid.*, pp. 165–75.

20    *ibid.*, p. 207.

21    *ibid.*, p. 217.

22    *ibid.*, p. 234.

23    *ibid.*, p. 282.

24    *ibid.*, p. 289.

25    *ibid.*, p. 217.

26    *ibid.*, p. 299.

27    *LH* (J. H. Garcin de Tassy, *Histoire de la Littérature Hindouie et Hindoustanie*, 4 vols, reprint New York, 1970), I, 69–72; cf. Garcin de Tassy, 'Les femmes poetes de l'Inde', *Revue de l'Orient*, May 1854; Sprenger, *Catalogue of Libraries of Oudh*, p. 11.

28    P. Hardy, *Historians of Medieval India. Studies in Indo-Muslim Historical Writing* (London, 1960), pp. 122–31.

29    Tirmizi, *Persian Letters of Ghalib*, p. xxiii.

30    Sayyid Ahmad Khan, 'Asar-us Sanadid', trans. as 'Description des Monuments de Delhi en 1852', *Journal Asiatique*, Jan. 1861, 80, 87, 91, *passim*.

31    Fritz Lehman, 'Urdu Literature and Mughal Decline', *Mahfil*, 6, 2, 1970, pp. 125–31; Russell and Islam, *Three Mughal Poets*, pp. 1–68.

32    *LH*, I, 120–1.

33    *ibid.*, 127.

34    *ibid.*, 136.

35    'The Conquerors of Hindustan in Persian and English', *Delhi Gazette* cited *Friend of India*, 16 Dec. 1847; *ibid.*, 3 May 1849.

36    *Friend of India*, 3 May 1849.

37    I.A. Arshi, *Catalogue of the Arabic Manuscripts in Raza Library, Rampur*, 6 vols. (Rampur, 1963–77).

38    B. K. Datta, *Libraries and Librarianship of Ancient and Medieval India* (Delhi, 1970), p. 84.

39    Also note the lack of catalogues, A. Sprenger to H. Elliot, 25 Jun. 1847, Elliot Papers, Add 30,789, BL.

40    D.C. Dasgupta, *The Jaina System of Education* (Calcutta, 1944), pp. 36–40; John E. Cort, 'The Jain knowledge warehouses: traditional libraries in India', *Journal of the American Oriental Society*, 115, 1, 1995, 77–88.

41    Sprenger to Elliot, 25 Jun. 1847, Elliot Papers, Add. 30,789; cf. Sprenger, *Report of the Researches into the Muhammadan Libraries of Lucknow. Selections from the Records of the Government of India*, no. 28 (Calcutta, 1896) which records 6,000 volumes in the Topkhana Library and about 1,000 in the Farah Baksh; the private library of Sheikh Mahomed Hazin's family had 5,000 volumes, F. C. Belfour tr., *The Life of Sheikh Mohammed Ali Hayin written by himself* (London, 1830), p. 10; Datta, *Libraries*, pp. 69, 73, 85.

42    G.N. Bahura, 'Glimpses of historical information from manuscripts in the Pothikhana of Jaipur', in J.N. Asopa (ed.), *Cultural Heritage of Jaipur* (Jodhpur, 1982), pp. 104–5; cf. Arshi, *Rampur*, I, preface p. 1.

43    *Miss. Reg.*, Aug. 1826, p. 395.

44    C. W. Troll, *Sayyid Ahmad Khan. A Reinterpretation of Muslim Theology* (Delhi, 1978), p. 104.

45    Jurgen Habermas, *The Structured Transformation of the Public Sphere*, tr. T. Burgen (Cambridge, Mass.: Harvard University Press, 1992), pp. 57 ff.

46    e.g. the case in 1849 where the King of Awadh destroyed the Lucknow presses because they had displeased him, A. Sprenger, *A Catalogue of the Arabic, Persian and Hindustani Manuscripts in*

the *Libraries of the King of Oudh*, (Calcutta, 1854), p. vi, or an equivalent case in Punjab, Emmet Davis, *The Press and Politics in British West Punjab, 1836–47* (Delhi, 1983), p. 184.

47  F. Robinson, 'Technology and religious change. Islam and the impact of print', *MAS*, 27, i, 1993, 229–51.

48  Russell and Islam, *Ghalib*, I, 38.

49  *Englishman*, 12 Jan. 1835; material on Burma, etc.; Banaras 1852, E. A. Reade, *Contributions to the Banaras Recorder in 1852* (Banaras, 1858), fin., pp. 67–8.

50  Marginal note to Auckland's minute on the press, 8 Aug. 1836, Auckland Papers, Add. Mss. 37,709, f. 91b, BL

51  J. Tod, *Annals and Antiquities of Rajast'han, or the central and western Rajpoot states of India* (London, 1829–32, repr., 1950), Introduction, p. 16; cf. V.N. Rao, D. Shulman and S. Subrahmanyam, *Symbols of Substance. Court and State in Nayaka Period Tamilnadu* (Delhi, 1992), pp. 1–22 and passim.

52  *LH*, I, 10.

53  C. Bendall, 'The Tantrakhyana. A collection of Indian tales', *JRAS*, 2, 4, 1890, 484; cf. *The Panchatantra*.

54  Note by Prof. Halil Inalcik in author's possession.

55  An observation of Prof. Ravinder Kumar.

56  'Bankas and swindlers', *Delhi Gazette*, 18 Dec. 1839.

57  Muhammad Faiz Baksh, 'Tarikh-i Farah Baksh' entitled *Memoirs of Delhi and Faiyabad*, tr. W. Hoey, 2 vols (Allahabad, 1889) II, 285–7.

58  Mofussilite, 11 Feb. 1848 on 'Sunni–Shia disturbances at Hyderabad'.

59  'placards have been posted at Cathmandoo threatening destruction to several prominent chiefs and the Resident', the information was sent immediately to Banaras, 'the centre of information about Nepaul', *Delhi Gazette*, 20 Jan. 1841.

60  Askari, 'Mirat-ul-Muluk', *Indica*, pp. 44ff.

61  V. Raghavan, 'The Kavindrakalpalatika of Kavindracarya Sarasvati', *ibid.*, pp. 336–7.

62  S. A. A. Rizvi, *Shah Walli-allah and his Times* (Canberra, 1980), pp. 302–3.

63  cf. David Lelyveld, reported by S. Freitag, 'Introduction' *South Asia*, n.s., 14, 1, 1991, p. 9 and fn. 19.

64  'District Dawks', *Friend of India*, 18 Jul. 1850.

65  e.g., Ghalib to Nawab Alauddin Ahmad Khan, 15 Shaban 1298 (Feb. 1862), Rahbar, *Persian Letters of Ghalib*, pp. 25–6; same to Munshi Hargopal Tafta, nd. May (?) 1848, p. 57; same to Mirza Shahabuddin Abmad Khan, 24 Sept. 1861, p. 51; for the social networks in Ghalib's earlier correspondence, Tirmizi, *Ghalib*, pp. xiv, xxiii.

66  e.g., the case in Westmacott, 'Travels', Mss. Eur. C26, f. 173.

67  *Mofussilite*, 30 May 1848.

68  Rahbar, *Ghalib*, pp. 94, 205.

69  *Friend of India*, 4 April 1850.

70  Evidence of Chuni Lal, newswriter 'for the public', 'Trial of the King of Delhi', *PP*, 1859, 1st session, xviii, 84.

71  Rahbar, *Ghalib*, p. xxxiii.

72  See, K.H. Prior, 'The British administration of Hinduism in north India, 1780–1900', unpub. PhD thesis Cambridge University, 1990.

73  Juan R. I. Cole, *The Roots of North Indian Shi'ism in Iran and Iraq. Religion and State in Auradh, 1772–1859* (Berkeley, 1988), pp. 55–8.

74  Faiz Baksh, *Memoirs*, II, 44.

75  *ibid.*

76  *ibid.*

77  Seton to Wellesley, 22 Jan. 1804, Wellesley, Add. 13,577, BL.

78    *ibid.*, cf. Seton to Merrick Shawe, 10 Feb. 1804, Wellesley, Add. 13,577, BL.

79    Committee at Bareilly to Commrs, NWP, 3 July 1816, 27 and encls., BCJ, 25 Oct. 1816, 3, 132/48, OIOC; Rahman Ali, *Tazkirah-i Ulama-i Hind* (Lucknow, 1914), pp. 24–5.

80    R. Heitler, 'The Varanasi house-tax hartal of 1810–11', *IESHR*, 9, 3, 1972, 239–57; G. Pandey, *The Construction of Communalism in Colonial North India* (Delhi, 1990) pp. 24–50; S. Freitag, *Collective Action and Community. Public arenas and the emergence of communalism in north India* (Berkeley, 1989), pp. 19–52.

81    Actg Magt. to Govt, 8 Jan. 1811, Bengal Criminal Judl Procs., 8 Feb. 1811, 1, 130/28, OIOC.

82    Petition of Mohulla Seedhesree, Bengal Criminal Judl Procs., 5 Jan. 1811, 25, 130/27, OIOC.

83    Heitler, 'Hartal', p. 251; cf. Actg Magt. to Govt, 28 Jan. 1811, Bengal Crim. Judl, 8 Feb. 1811, 5, 130/28, OIOC.

84    'Memorial of the Hindoos of the City of Benares', 20 Nov. 1809, 'Disturbances at Benares', BC 365, OIOC; the British were peeved that another important old 'native informant', Bishambhar Pandit, had been involved in fomenting the Hindus.

85    *ibid.*

86    S. Freitag, *Culture and Power in Banaras. Community, performance and environment, 1800–1980* (Berkeley, 1989).

87    S. Pollock, 'Ramayana and political imagination in India', *Journal of Asian Studies*, 52, 2, 1993, 261–297.

88    *LH*, I, 24–50.

89    *LH*, I, 41.

90    *LH*, I, 382–5; *JRAS*, Aug. 1851, 192; this was a source for Tod, *Annals and Antiquities*.

91    J.D. Smith, *The Epic of Pabuji. A study in transcription and translation* (Cambridge, 1991), pp. 290–1.

92    D.J. Singh Johal, 'Historical significance of *Jhaggra Jatti te Katrani da*', in F. Singh and A.C. Arora (eds.), *Maharaja Ranjit Singh. Politics, Society, Economics* (Patiala, 1984), pp. 289–91; cf. S. Sagar, 'Social change and the *kissas* of the first half of the nineteenth century', *ibid.*, 292–301.

93    see A. Bansani, 'Ghazal', *Encyclopaedia of Islam*, 2nd. edn, II, 1036.

94    *LH*, I, 103–4.

95    Bholanauth Chunder, *The Travels of a Hindoo to various parts of Bengal and Upper India* (London, 1869), pp. i, 283; cf. *LH*, I, 103–4, on Asaf-ud Daulah; for the use of another *ghazal* in a contemporary dispute, Judge Banaras to Register Nizamat Adalat, 12 January 1813, Bengal Criminal Judicial, 12 July 1816, 18, 132/43, OIOC; for use of popular theatre in a political cause, de Tassy, *LH*, I, 24–5.

96    *LH*, I, 24; cf. 'Dramatic Amusements of the Natives of India', *Asiatic Journal*, n.s., 22, 1837, 25–34.

97    *ibid.*, 27.

98    'Mahommedan Festivals in India', *ibid.*, 16, 1835, 52.

99    Rahbar, *Ghalib*, p. 380, n. 1.

100    Ghalib to Nawab Husain Mirza, 29 Oct. 1859, *ibid.*, p. 207.

101    *LH*, I, 63–4.

102    Khairuddin Khan Illahabadi, ('Tuhfa-i-Taza', entitled *The Balwantnamah*, trans. F. C. Curwen (Allahabad, 1875), p. 87.

103    *ibid.*, p. 88. The Bengali eventually shook Khairuddin's hand and said, 'You are a pandit of my religion', but the author clearly took it as the victory of Muhammadan learning!

104    G.C. Vad (ed.), *Selections from the Satara Rajas' and the Peshwas' Diaries* (Bombay, 1907–11) makes it clear that the rulers' courts acted a role as a kind of 'public tribunal' for intra-caste disputes.

105    D. Gold, 'What the merchant-guru sold; social and literary types in Hindi devotional verse', *Journal of the American Oriental Society*, 112, 1, 1992, 22–36.

106    As is made clear by C. Calhoun (ed.), *Habermas and the Public Sphere* (Cambridge, Mass., 1992).

# Chapter 13

# D. F. McKenzie

## THE SOCIOLOGY OF A TEXT

### Orality, literacy and print in early New Zealand

As I am sure most of us have now come to understand, the discipline of bibliography cannot be limited to 'the study of books as physical objects', whether manuscript or printed. In at least three ways our subject is, ineluctably, evolving.

First, what it is now fashionable to call 'the impact of print' can only be measured of course in relation to a far older manuscript culture which print parallels and only in part displaces. But a serious historical concern with any manuscript culture, in its fullest ramifications, cannot be divorced from questions about the origins, social range, and different levels of literacy in that culture. And literacy, both as a concept and as an historically traceable phenomenon, is inseparable from a concern (both precedent and concurrent) with orality and the recording function of memory. We have only to think of, say, Homer, as an oral-memorial text, later made incarnate in manuscript and print, to see at once the impossibility of denying to bibliography any stage of the composition, dissemination, reception and descent of that text.

Orality, literacy and print can of course be so ordered as the primary, secondary and tertiary stages of a (perhaps misleadingly) progressive sequence in the history of civilization; and we may as bibliographers study them as distinct phases – each with its own 'impact' and forms of record – in the evolution of western society. But we must also, I think, recognize more frankly the diverse nature of each of those stages and their persistive interaction. There is nothing new in the observation that the words I am 'saying' to you now are written, indeed 'type'-written. I therefore 'speak' my 'book'. You 'hear' these letter-forms which only this 'I' can see – at least until they resurface in the silence of a reprint.

In other words, what we much too readily call 'the book' is a friskier and therefore more elusive animal than the words 'physical object' will allow. In such matters, social anthropologists have shown a lively interest in forms of evidence which we should all, I think, call 'bibliographical', since they relate to the telling, writing, reception and the distribution of 'texts'. In extending the definition of the word 'book' to include oral literature and quite elementary forms of written record, and in taking a more dynamic view of the social origin and functions of such texts, anthropologists working in non-European societies have much to teach us. As they well know, orality and literacy are not, after all, artefacts, but highly variable human conditions whose shaping force on the form and efficacy of 'texts' we cannot ignore. What, fundamentally, we study therefore is not so much the history of the book as the sociology of texts.

The second way in which I think bibliography must expand is, paradoxically, by heightening our sensitivity to the printed book as a physical form in order to refine our notions of the historicity of printed texts and our function in editing them. Specialists of type, paper, bindings and so on acknowledge the intrinsic interest for them of every physical element that goes to construct a book, yet few editors grant those physicalities of the book any textual or even contextual meaning. We practise 'textual criticism' as the meanings of words, and we study, discretely, 'book-trade history'. Occasionally a Charlton Hinman or a Peter Blayney will show how the deficiencies of a mechanical process negatively affect the choice or sequence (and therefore the symbolic import) of words. And so we seek to eliminate 'error' in the 'transmission' of 'texts'. Marshall McLuhan's catch-phrase 'the medium is the massage' makes the point in an equally negative way: the ideal (message) is *de*-formed (massage) in the process of being made manifest.

By contrast, once we acknowledge that the physical book as a whole is a rich complex of signs, each of which has its own human history and all of which unite to *create* the 'finished' book as a palpably articulated 'text' (to *form* it, not *de*-form it), then we enter an entirely new, more positive and, for me at least, more exciting phase of textual criticism. One thinks of Stanley Morison's *Politics and script* for the meanings he could give to letter forms as cultural witnesses. That example of a creatively interpretative mind addressing itself to the physical evidence makes it clear how the book as physical object becomes the book as expressive form. The inert materials of bark, clay, vellum or paper, script or type, ink, decoration, illustration, binding – we discover – were never really inert, never merely physical. For each and every one shared in a creative act, an expressive decision, within a definable historical context, to serve an author's intention, a bookseller's pocket, or an implied reader's comprehension of the 'text'. The book as physical object put together by craftsmen – as we all know – is in fact alive with the human judgements of its makers. It is not even in any sense 'finished' until it is read. And since it is re-creatively read in different ways by different people at different times, its so-called objectivity, its simple physicality, is really an illusion. But it is more directly the bibliographer's job to show editors (and historians) how rich an account of human behaviour the physical elements of a book may yield to those who *can* read all its signs and so recreate the historical dynamics of its making and reading. As such, even the book in its narrowest sense is evidence unrivalled in its complexity, its sharpness of focus, its ubiquity, and its capacity for successive reincarnations in response to changing human needs.

I turn now to my third and last general comment on the ways in which bibliography is bound to expand as a discipline. Until this century its restriction to the study of books as marks on paper or some other physical medium – stable, visible, palpable – was unavoidable. Its limitation to letter-forms, singly and in combination, mental and scribal or metal and printed, their design and production, packaging, dissemination, sale, resale, collection, counterfeiting, conservation or dismemberment, merely expressed the limited technology we then commanded to record and recover human behaviour. We now have a newer technology which permits us to record the sounds of words and music and images in motion. As these in turn parallel and in part displace the manuscript letter, printed book, and the static graphics of illuminator and engraver, our visible words must interact with the kinetic image and what W. J. Ong has called the 'secondary orality' of our electronic world.[1] If one thinks of the mutability of computer-stored information, it is clear that even some of our visible word-hoards share, by chance or design, the ephemerality of speech. Or to put it another (and in present company perhaps more acceptable) way, we as bibliographers must impart our skills to those whose professional concerns lie in sounds and moving images so that their work too shows the insights and affirms the values of the older discipline which we profess, in order responsibly to conserve the 'texts' of our own culture.

A future synthesis of bibliography as the study of the conception, mediation and reception of texts must enhance its power to interpret the past and expand its role in collecting, preserving, authenticating, accessing and interpreting the polymorphous texts of today and tomorrow. The new orthodoxy of '*histoire du livre*', as phrase and concept, describes much too limited a field but it is moving historians at least towards acknowledging a quite new centrality and status for the discipline of bibliography and its principal practitioner, the scholar-librarian as archivist, whether of manuscripts, print, film, disc or recorded sound.

Those points are not so remote as you might think from the topic I originally proposed, 'Two Early New Zealand Printers: William Colenso and R. Coupland Harding', for the careers of those two men span the movement in New Zealand from orality, through manuscript literacy to the introduction of printing and a full consciousness of the expressive resources of typography. Together with one crucial document, they offer a model from which to exemplify my larger argument.[2]

One hundred and forty-three years ago this month – on 6 February 1840 – forty-six Maori chiefs from the northern regions of New Zealand 'signed' a document written in Maori called '*Te Tiriti o Waitangi*', 'The Treaty of Waitangi'. In doing so, according to the English versions of that document, they ceded to Her Majesty the Queen of England 'absolutely and without reservation all the rights and powers of Sovereignty' which they themselves individually exercised over their respective territories. That act of assent became the substantive ground of British sovereignty over New Zealand.[3] Beneath a statue of Queen Victoria in my own city of Wellington, the European literacy myth implicit in that event of 1840 is complacently enshrined in the image of a Maori chief – as I say – 'signing' the treaty with quill pen. The reality, as William Colenso knew, and as we shall see as we meditate the sociology of that text, was different.

Twenty-five years earlier, the indigenous New Zealanders had been completely illiterate. They were a neolithic race with a wholly oral culture and their own body of myths. Not one of their myths, however, was so absurd as the European myth of the technologies of literacy and print as agents of change and the missionaries' conviction that what took Europe over two millenia to accomplish could be achieved – *had* been achieved – in New Zealand in a mere twenty-five years: the reduction of speech to alphabetic forms, an ability to read and write them, a readiness to shift from memory to written record, to accept a signature as a sign of full comprehension and legal commitment, to surrender the relativities of time, place and person in an oral culture to the presumed fixities of the written or printed word.[4] When Samuel Marsden bought 200 acres of land at Rangihoua in 1814 for the first mission station, he drew up a deed of conveyance and solemnly had the Maori chief 'sign' it by drawing on it a copy of his *moko* or facial tattoo pattern. The price was twelve axes, itself a potent symbol of the shift from a neolithic culture to the iron age, the de-afforestation of New Zealand and the pastoral economy to come. But the subtler, much more elusive and indeterminate technology was literacy.

Consider its stages. In 1815 Thomas Kendall, the first resident missionary, faced the problem of re-enacting one of the most momentous transitions in human history, the reduction of speech to its record in alphabetic form. Put like that, it sounds portentous, as in a literal sense it was. But just imagine the problems of trying to capture strange sounds alphabetically, the miracle that underlies all our printed books. When one early traveller recorded what he thought he heard as the Maori word for a paradise duck, he wrote *pooadugghiedugghie* (for *putangitangi*) and for the fantail *diggowaghwagh* (for *piwakawaka*), neither of which forms translates visually the aural beauty of the originals. The place-name *Hokianga* was rendered *Showkianga*, *Sukyanna*, *Jokeeangar*, *Chokahanga*. Another village, *Kerikeri*, was heard and rendered as *Kiddeekiddee*, *Muketu* as *Muckeytoo*. Those spellings are not only aurally inefficient, but to the English eye they appear crude and culturally primitive, thus reinforcing other such attitudes.[5]

The absence of a philology (let alone a grammar and syntax for a non-European language) made a rational orthography hard to devise. Yet until there was an orthography, the teaching of reading and writing was obviously impossible, and printing of course depended upon a standard set of letter forms. Kendall's first rough list of 1815 was revised and sent off to Samuel Lee, Professor of Arabic at Cambridge. Kendall and two Maori chiefs, Hongi and Waikato, joined him there in 1820, and together they produced *A grammar and vocabulary of the language of New Zealand*. It was printed later that year by R. Watts, printer to the Church Missionary Society in London. Kendall, unlike Marsden, was determined that Maori should not be anglicized; *c*, *q* and *x* were dropped for a start, but the *Grammar* at that stage still included letters for non-Maori sounds thought necessary for foreign words — *f*, hard *g*, *j*, *v*, *z* — and so it still ran to five vowels, eighteen consonants, and one digraph *ng* (as in Ngaio Marsh). It included sample sentences such as 'the performance of the white man is good, the performance of the white man is exceeding good', but linguistically at least the performance of the white man still left room for improvement. Should stress marks be included, how should long vowels be distinguished (by macron or doubling?),[6] were all remaining letters really needed (since greater simplicity would enhance its efficacy)?

In the next ten years — by 1830 — the alphabet was in fact reduced to five vowels and nine consonants, with only two forms remaining unsettled, *h* and *w*. There were attempts to indicate a palatal *h* by adding an apostrophe (as in *H'ongi*) and the voiced *w* (pronounced rather like *f* ), again by an apostrophe or by the combination *wh*. Colenso, as printer, argued for the doubling of long vowels (to avoid special sorts), the simple *h* (to avoid the troublesome Greek-style apostrophe), and a digammic *v* for *wh* (to avoid setting two letters where one would do) although *wh* was confirmed in 1842.[7] By then the foreign consonants plus *b*, *d*, *l*, *s* and *y* had been dropped and foreign words were rendered in Maori forms: so 'missionary' became *mihanere*, 'governor' *kawana*; I leave you to guess *komite*. Those decisions about letter forms were typographically efficient but culturally explosive, for by giving English words a Maori semblance they disguised their quite different conceptual import. But, clearly, the first great book printed in New Zealand, Colenso's Maori New Testament of 1837, is inconceivable without this prior shift from acoustics to optics, the visualization of sound in a simplified and standardized alphabet, and the human motivations at work in bringing it about. Today the Maori language is written with the five vowels, and ten consonants *h*, *k*, *m*, *n*, *p*, *r*, *t*, *w*, *g*, *wh*.

The pre-print years of its evolution (1815–30) were also those in which the missionaries made a tentative start to teach reading and writing. The decision to teach those skills in the vernacular had long since been settled elsewhere; in Bengal, for example, it generated a remarkable renaissance in the indigenous culture.[8] It also seemed an efficient policy. English was difficult to master and would have split the population; a universal conversion of parent and child, of old and young, was only conceivable if they were bound together by a common speech within which the new learning could pass quickly, unimpeded by language barriers. More than that, the missionaries were all too well aware that English would give the Maori access to the worst aspects of European experience. By containing them culturally within their own language, they hoped to keep them innocent of imported evils. By restricting them further to the reading of biblical texts and vocabulary, they limited the Maori to knowledge of an ancient middle-eastern culture; at the same time the missionaries enhanced their familiar pastoral role morally and politically as interpretative guides, a point I shall come back to when discussing the Treaty of Waitangi. In 1833 William Williams wrote that 'A reading population, whose only book is the Word of God, cannot fail to make a great moral change in the face of the country, as soon as that Word begins to take effect'.[9] And in 1842, when he should have known better, William Puckey rejoiced that the Maori, 'having no other books to read but Scripture and productions from Scripture, their pursuits must all be of a sacred nature'.[10] Such a vision implied that priority be given to the translation of the Scriptures into Maori. This ideological bias was reinforced by doctrinal strife in 1839–40, just when the policy should have been relaxed but when the Church Missionary Society faced competition from Bishop Pompallier's Catholic mission and press.[11] To study Colenso's printed output is simply to look at the expression of those policies.

The naïvety there is now patent, but is also present in the programme to teach reading and writing in the mission schools. The enthusiastic reports back to London of the remarkable desire of the Maori to learn to read, the further stimulation of that interest through native teachers, the intense and apparently insatiable demand so created for books, formed the cumulative pressure to supply the one instrument thought essential to give instant and local effect to universal literacy as the principal means to personal salvation. I mean of course printing.

But what was the reality? Kendall set up the first school with thirty-three pupils in 1816, but it was not until the early 1830s that numbers were at all significant. There is almost complete accord in the reports, not only that the schools were effective but that the Maori achieved literacy with the greatest of ease. Of another school it was said in 1829: 'Not six years ago they commenced the very rudiments of learning: now, many of them can read and write their own language, with propriety, and are complete masters of the First Rules of Arithmetic'.[12] A visitor to one mission in 1833 noted:

> I was not prepared to find, among a people who had previously no written language, so many who had benefitted from the instruction given in our Mission Schools . . . [In the Boys' School] I observed all ranks and ages, Chiefs and subjects, old and young, bound and free, receiving and communicating instruction, with a degree of decorum and regularity which would have reflected credit on a school of the same kind in England. Catechisms, reading, spelling, writing on slates from dictation, and cyphering, formed the employment of the upper classes, while the lowest were engaged in learning the alphabet and forming letters . . . [In the Girls' School] The senior classes read remarkably well, and write equally from dictation on slates . . . Men of hostile tribes, even, now lay aside their antipathies, and unite for instruction, disregarding the person of a teacher, even if a slave, and valuing instruction even from a child.[13]

The highly literate rhetoric of that description is itself revealing: the writer, a Captain Jacob, transforms the school's routines into a vision of the society he wishes to see evolving, one indeed better than his own. Of the mission station at Waimate he remarked:

> The writing of the senior classes was really better than that of most school-boys in England; and what struck me much, it was remarkably free from orthographical mistakes; which can only be accounted for from the simplicity of their language, each letter of which admits but one simple sound. Here also I observed Chiefs and subjects, freemen and slaves, all incorporated into classes.[14]

Hobbs, writing in January 1833, noted:

> For this long time past it has become fashionable for the young people to try to learn to read . . . Such is the wish of many of the Natives to learn to read, that on several occasions they have brought pigs, which would weigh from fifty to an hundred pounds, and offered them as payment for a book, consisting of sacred portions of the Scriptures, and the Liturgy of the Church of England.[15]

The impression is also given by the missionary reports that once the rudiments were known, many a Maori pupil would go off and teach others:

In every village there are several of the Natives who can read and write: and a School is established among them by the Natives themselves, where a number are taught to read and write; and old and young are taught their Catechism. Their desire for books is very great.[16]

. . . many of the Natives, who are living at a distance, manifest a great desire for instruction; and with very little assistance from us, they are learning to read and write; and their efforts have so far been crowned with success that they know some of the letters of the alphabet and can write them.[17]

. . . there are many villages where Schools are conducted entirely by the Natives, and some of them making considerable proficiency in reading and writing. The day is not far distant, when the people generally will be able to read for themselves, in their own tongue, the wonderful works of God.[18]

But such reports are essentially anecdotal and less informative as objective accounts (though historians have treated them as such) than they are as expressions, at worst, of wishful thinking or, at best, of a readiness to define literacy, and therefore later the effective impact of printed texts, at a level far below that demanded by the social changes to which the Maori were being exposed.[19] It is as if the very notion of literacy itself compelled a heightened language of self-approval and infinite promise. Victims of their own myths, the missionaries found what they wanted to find, and reported what they knew their London committee wished to hear. Marsden, Williams, Hadfield and Pompallier were intelligent men, but what could they have understood by the words 'reading' and 'writing' for them to say:

The natives . . . were carrying in their hands, the Litany, and the greater part of the Church Service, with their Hymns, written in their own language. The Church Service, as far as it has been translated, they can both read and write with greatest ease.[20]

I was much pleased to find, that wherever I went I found some who could read and write. The Church Service had been translated into the Native language, with the Catechism, Hymns, and some other useful pieces. They are all fond of reading; and there are many who have never had an opportunity of attending the schools who, nevertheless, can read. They teach one another in all parts of the country.[21]

What 'teaching one another' might have meant is suggested by Henry Williams:

One young man began to ask the meaning of letters. I wrote them down for him, and in half an hour he knew them all, and was teaching several outside. Numbers of others came until I had no paper left of any description on which to write a copy. At length they brought small pieces, to have the letters written for them, and about 200, old and young, were soon employed teaching and learning the letters with the greatest possible interest. [Next morning] the boys brought their papers for me to hear them their letters and asked what they were to learn next.[22]

Vast numbers learn to read and write who do not attend school, by possessing themselves of a book or part of a book, and spelling it over until they are fully acquainted with every word in it.[23]

They easily learn to read and write without the necessity of constant teaching. It is only necessary to give them a few leaflets of easy reading, and to write some characters on bits of slate to enable them to read and write their own language within three months.[24]

By comparison, R. K. Webb, in *The British working-class reader*, says that at the Borough Road School, London, in the early nineteenth century, it took twelve months to teach a child to read, and between three and four years to write well and calculate.[25] A more realistic account of the nature of Maori literacy is that given by Fairburn in 1838:

> There is scarcely a petty tribe now to be met with, where there are not some who can write and read. I mention this more particularly, as it must sound strange to an English ear to be told that we have met with many of the self-taught Natives who could write on a slate or paper so as to make their wants known, while they could not read a single line from the book. Their habits of idleness . . . are in some respects favourable to their learning to read. Since they have got books among them, they make use of them, I have not the smallest doubt, in the way of amusement, in teaching each other; it seems to have superseded their once favourite game of Draughts.[26]

That at least suggests the minimal competence achieved by many so-called 'readers'.

If we reflect that the teaching of elementary reading is primarily oral/aural, not visual, because it involves the pronouncing and repetition of letters, syllables and words (a practice reinforced where there are few books, fewer texts, and group teaching), we can appreciate how oral repetition from memory might masquerade as reading; and the Maori – used to an oral tradition – had a most retentive memory.[27] The interconnection is evident in Kemp's report of 1832: 'For want of more Translations of the Scriptures, the Natives are almost at a stand: some have committed to memory all that has been printed: I hope this will soon be remedied by more being printed'.[28] Or Williams in 1832: 'We feel the want of books for the Natives very greatly: what they at present possess, they, generally, know by heart'.[29] Other specific reports have their general interest:

> The Natives manifest a strong desire to learn to read the Scriptures . . . Wherever I go amongst the Natives, I hear portions of the Catechism repeated. One Native, who, though he cannot read, has learned a considerable part of the Catechisms, puts the Questions to those around him; and then he and the others repeat the answers.[30]

> [I] visited a tribe in which the only teaching was done by a Maori who had learned to read at Paihia and, returning to his village, read the Scriptures to his countrymen. Before this time they were in the habit of meeting, and repeating from memory, the Confession and Lord's Prayer, not any one being able to read.[31]

> My attention was called . . . to a blind man reading the Scriptures . . . He came to me some time since, and requested that I would let him have a complete book. I asked of what use a book would be to him, as he was blind. He replied that it would be of great use; for though he could not see, he could hear; and by possessing one he could let others read to him, until he should see it with his heart . . . I [later] saw the poor fellow lying on the ground with his book open before him, as though he was pondering over its contents, repeating aloud verse by verse.[32]

'Poor fellow'? The memorized text of course makes one a living library in a way the read book cannot. Repetition of the catechism – known by *heart*, not read by *eye* – was after all the higher proof of conversion. Simply to illustrate the illusory nature of the presumed shift from orality to literacy, I quote Sir Apirana Ngata, writing on 'The Maori and Printed Matter' as late as 1940:

> The people preferred to hear the matter, whether written or printed, read to them. Not only did this relieve the labour of spelling out words, syllable by syllable, but it was closer than mute transference through the eye to what they had been accustomed to: it was nearer the old-time narrative of adept raconteurs, or of poetical and priestly reciters. More than that, the genius of the race preferred education through the ear, conveyed by artists in intonation and gesticulation . . . The printed matter indeed achieved a limited popularity, but for every one who owned a copy of the Scriptures and Church Liturgy or Rawiri, there were in my boyhood days still fifty or more content to listen to and memorize the words which were read out of the printed books by the ministers, teachers, or lay-readers.[33]

If reading, the passively receptive and more easily acquired art, could be so easily evaded, what of writing? This was the active counterpart of reading, a personally expressive skill, but one much harder to acquire and inhibited by the primitive nature, cost and scarcity of quills, ink and paper. Just as the oral element in reading persisted to limit the full and easy visual perception of texts, so too a reliance on writing and readiness to use it could only grow slowly from a long acquaintance with documents.[34] Oral witness held its primacy over written evidence for centuries in Europe; to have expected a non-literate people to reverse that disposition within a decade was unrealistic, and to presume that it has yet happened would be a mistake.[35]

The main use of literacy to the Maori was not reading books for their ideas, much less for the access they gave to divine truths, but letter writing. For them, the really miraculous point about writing was its portability; by annihilating distance, a letter allowed the person who wrote it to be in two places at once, his body in one, his thoughts in another. It was the spatial extension, not the temporal permanence, of writing that become politically potent in gathering the tribes and planning a war a decade and more later.[36] Historical time, defined by dated and legally binding documents, represented a much more profound challenge to an oral culture used to reshaping its past traditions to accord with present needs. It is a challenge that is still resisted.

On a journey in 1833 Williams received several letters which had been sent on to him and his Maori attendants and he records the reaction of other Maori who had not seen letters before:

> This was an interesting particular for the people of the place, as they were thus enabled to see the nature and value of written characters, by the testimony of these their countrymen. Our boys seemed to look for, and read over *their* letters, with as much pleasure as we did *ours*, to the delight of all around; they repeated them aloud, to the admiration of their auditors, who were struck with wonder at hearing, as they described it, 'a book speak': for though they expect that a European can perform an extraordinary thing, yet they cannot understand how it is that a New Zealand youth can possess the same power.[37]

In the early 1830s we see the hesitant beginnings of letter writing in written requests for baptism, proving (as William Yate put it) that 'the heart of the sanguinary and untutored New Zealander is as the heart of the civilized and polished Englishman'.[38] The originals of course were in Maori.

I, Pahau, am now writing a Letter to you. Perhaps you will not be pleased with it, and send it back; and then, perhaps, my heart will be sad, and I shall cry. Now, then, I am going to write to you. Read it first, from the top to the bottom, on this side and on that side, before you say 'Nonsense', and throw it away from you and tear it to pieces. Now, Mr Yate, listen to what I am going to say upon this paper. I have been thinking and thinking about what I am going to write; and now I am thinking you will shut your ears, and will not listen to me. This is what I am going to write: – Remember, that if you say 'Nonsense', it was you who said we were to put down our wishes in a book.[39]

Another letter begins, in a vein reminiscent of Caxton: 'My ink is not good, my paper dirty, and I am altogether ashamed'.[40] Yet another, from husband and wife: 'There are many mistakes in our two's Letter: and Mary says, "Do not send it: wait and talk when he comes to Kerikeri"'.[41]

Untutored New Zealanders? These writers – the manuscript makers – were the literate élite in Maori, not draught-players turned scribblers but those trained to readiness for baptism. The effective use of letters for political purposes was many years away. Nor did printing of itself become a re-expressive tool for the Maori until the late 1850s.[42] When it did so – in Maori newspapers – the essential motives, the effective contextual forces, were economic, political and military, not religious. *He wahine, he whenua, e ngaro ai te tangata* – by women, and by land, men perish. The forcing issue for the Maori, then as now, was land. Only when literacy began to serve that supreme social interest could it be significantly achieved. Its roots in the texts of an alien religion were inevitably shallow, despite the technology of printing.

But for the missionaries, printing was the great hope. 'We feel very much the want of a Printing Press, to work off some copies of portions of Scripture, which could be read by several natives now with us', Davis had written to the Church Missionary Society in 1827.[43] In 1828 Williams wrote: 'We want a printer, and a printer we must have'.[44] The plea to the Church Missionary Society was twice repeated in 1829. When the long-sought-after press did arrive, it was an anticlimax, proving that technology in itself is nothing without a human mind and dedicated skill to make it work in a context where it matters. In 1830, William Yate brought a small press from Sydney, and a fifteen-year-old James Smith to help him. Neither Yate nor Smith had any professional competence.

In his journal for September 1830 Yate noted that, in printing off a few hymns in the native language, 'we succeeded beyond our most sanguine expectations'. These were the first items ever printed in New Zealand. 'We thank you for the Press', he wrote back to London, 'and have no doubt but that, with the blessing of God, it will be an instrument of great good in this Land. You will perceive by a copy of a Hymn forwarded by this conveyance, that we shall be able, in a short time, to manage it'.[45] Others took his tone. Kemp reported that 'The Schools will receive great benefit from the Press, for we shall be able to get portions of the Scriptures printed, as they are wanted'.[46] No copy of their Hymns is known to survive but Yate and Smith also printed a small catechism in Maori, both extant copies of which testify to the printers' gross incompetence in planing the type, locking the forme, and making ready. Writing of a new translation a year later, Yate faced facts: 'We shall not . . . be able to print it here'.[47]

Henry Williams, two years after that first experiment, told his masters:

You have sent us out a Printing Press of a certain description and a specimen of its production has been sent to you, accompanied with many expressions of delight – but these were first feelings excited by the novelty of the work: there stands the poor thing enshrined in cobwebs as an exciter for further expectations and desires.

> It has been examined by a printer of some experience who said he would not possess
> it as a gift . . . Had we something respectable, our work would be more so than it is
> at present.[48]

As the Maori proverb says (one later recorded by Colenso), 'even a little axe, well used, brings
plenty of food'. But with Yate as food gatherer, the missionaries starved. Defeated in his own
efforts, Yate returned to Sydney the following year to supervise the printing of what, when it
arrived, he described as 'the most valuable cargo that ever reached the shores of New Zealand' –
1800 copies of a book containing eight chapters of Genesis and almost half the New Testament.[49]
On receiving these books in 1833, Williams wrote home: 'I hope our good friends in London will
see in time the necessity of allowing a press and a printer. The book contains 250 pages and abounds
in typographical errors, not less . . . than two to a page. It must not be offered without correction.
So much for colonial work'.[50] In 1836 Colenso was even less complimentary about this early Australian export to New Zealand: 'poor things, they reflect no credit on the printer, less on the binder,
and still less on the editor – it has been computed that there are not less than 1000 errors in the
work'.[51] Yate's ignominious effort in 1830 deprived William Colenso of the honour of being literally
New Zealand's first printer, a New Zealand Caxton, as Coupland Harding was later to call him.

William Colenso, a cousin of the bishop of that name, was born in Penzance in 1811 and
on 3 September 1826 was bound for six years to a local printer, John Thomas.[52] While still in his
time he read his first paper to the Penzance Natural History and Antiquarian Society (on Phoenician
trade with west Cornwall) and compiled a history of Penzance, *The ancient and modern history of
the Mounts*, which was printed and published by Thomas in 1831. In October 1833 he moved to
London and found work with Richard Watts and Son, Crown Court, Temple Bar, printers to the
Church Missionary Society and the British and Foreign Bible Society.[53] Some anonymous articles
he wrote for the religious serial *The Pilot* came for printing to Watts who recognized Colenso's
handwriting. This led to an introduction to Dandeson Coates, lay secretary to the Society, just as
the New Zealand missionaries were again supplicating for a press. Commissioned as printer by
the Society and preparing to leave for New Zealand in 1834, Colenso wrote in his diary: 'In addition
to Satan's temptations at having no interest in Jesus he assails me with "You are going abroad, and
are unfit for the work"'. In fact there was none fitter. Colenso arrived at Paihia in the north of
New Zealand on 30 December 1834. The next day, he records, 'Numbers of Natives came to see
me – and when they found I was a Printer were quite enraptured – crying out *Pukapuka*'. Saturday
3 January 1835 was, as he wrote to Coates,

> A memorable epoch in the annals of New Zealand – I succeeded in getting the Printing
> Press landed. I was obliged to unpack it on board, but, I am happy to say, it is all safe
> on shore. Could you, my dear Sir, but have witnessed the Natives when it was landed,
> they danced, shouted, and capered about in the water, giving vent to the wildest
> effusions of joy. Enquiring the use of this, and the place of that, with all the eagerness
> for which uncivilized nature is celebrated. Certes, they had never seen such a thing
> before! I trust soon to be able to get it to work. May the father of Mercies . . . grant
> me strength and ability to work it for His Glory! May it be instrumental, under His
> blessing, in bringing thousands to the Cross of our Immanuel! – and of sending away
> that Sombre pall of darkness and gloom, which 'the Prince of the power of the Air'
> has so long successfully wrapped around the inhabitants of these islands.[54]

In fact, getting the Stanhope ashore had been far from easy and lest the parcels of type be seized
for making musket balls it could not be unpacked until safely landed. Most revealing, however,

for what it implies about the symbolic power of 'the press' as distinct from the realities of using one, is Colenso's list of necessary articles which he found to be absolutely wanting:

> For the information of Printers I will just set down a few of them; though I almost fear my relation will scarcely be believed. There was no wooden furniture of any kind, nor quoins, . . . no galleys, no cases, no leads of any size, no brass rule, no composing-sticks, (save a private one of my own that I had bought two years before in London, a most fortunate circumstance!) no inking table, no potash, no lye-brushes, no mallet and shooter, no roller-irons and stock, though there was a massy cast-iron roller mould, and . . . no imposing-stone nor page-cord; and, worst of all, actually *no printing paper!!*[55]

Colenso found a local joiner who made him a few galleys, a small inking table, some furniture and quoins, although he complained that these last 'were wretched things (partly owing to the want of proper and seasoned wood,)' and gave him 'an enormous amount of labour, vexation and trouble'. The joiner also made him

> two or three pairs of type-cases for the printing office after a plan of my own. For as the Maori language contained only 13 letters (half the number in the English alphabet), I contrived my cases so, as to have both Roman and Italic characters in the *one* pair of cases; not distributing the remaining 13 letters (consonants) used in the compositing of English, such not being wanted . . . Such an arrangement proved to be a very good one while my compositing was confined to the Maori language only; but when I had any English copy to compose it was altogether the reverse! then I had to pick out the discarded English consonants as required from their lots put up in paper parcels. Fortunately this occurred but rarely; except at the time of the Treaty of Waitangi (1840), when I had necessarily much printing work to do for the Government of the Colony; and having no extra cases, was obliged to place the letters required in little lots on tables, and on the floor![56]

With the press in place and the type disposed, it was agreed that as all parties, European and Maori, wished to see something printed, the missionaries should supply some writing paper, that the first sheet from the press should be in Maori from the New Testament, and that it should be small. The Epistles to the Ephesians and Philippians was chosen. Colenso set it up, and on 17 February 1835 pulled proofs of what he then thought was the first book printed in New Zealand, 'the printing office being filled with spectators to witness the performance'. On 21 February,

> twenty-five corrected copies were printed and stitched and cut round for the Missionaries; their wives kindly furnishing a few sheets of pink blotting-paper from their desks wherewith to form coloured paper covers for these tracts; which, of course, had first to be pasted on to stronger paper. This little book was in post 8vo., Long-Primer type, and consisted of 16 pages in double columns. For leads I was driven to the miserable substitute of pasting paper together, and drying and cutting it up! . . . And not being able to manufacture a roller, I was obliged to do my best with a small makeshift 'ball' of my own contriving.[57]

Knowing nothing of Yate's earlier efforts, Colenso wrote home to Coates:

This 'first fruits' of the New Zealand Press, which the Lord hath pleased to allow me to begin and complete, is very much liked by the Natives. – May it, being the 'Word of God', be the means of making thousands 'wise unto Salvation' – and the preface, as it were, to a more glorious diffusion of Gospel light over these benighted lands.[58]

On 19 May he printed what was indeed the first English book, eight pages octavo, a report of the New Zealand Temperance Society. Given the later history of New Zealand's licensing laws, it was a prophetic start.

Earlier that year, on 23 March, having heard that supplies of paper and more equipment for him had reached Sydney, he began setting his one great work, the complete Maori New Testament. It was a demy-octavo, set in small Pica, and running to 356 pages. He pulled the first sheets of a run of 5,000 copies on 23 June 1836. The Maori pressmen he later employed and paid 3s. a week were soon disenchanted by 'the many disagreeables inseparable from this new and wonderful art of printing', as Colenso put it, but on two subsequent occasions he was able to secure the help of some American sailors who had trained as pressmen before going to sea. Of the second pair he wrote:

> The wages I paid these two men were, at first, the same as to the two former pressmen, 5/- per day; but after a short time, at their own request, their pay was altered to 25 cents, or 1/- each per 'token', (10 quires = ½-ream,) besides which, as they could not be always at press-work, they were paid 12 cents, or 6d per hour for other work connected with the Printing-office and Binding-room, and Warehouse, – as, in drying, and pressing, and folding the sheets, &c.; but would never do anything in the way of distributing type, and even if a letter should be drawn out, or be broken in their working-off the forms, (which sometimes though rarely did happen,) they would not, or more properly could not well, replace it; and spoiled paper (if any) they had to pay for, – which, however, did not amount to much. Upham worked alone at Press for a period of six months, after his companion left, (always a disagreeable and slow process for *one* person,) and, of course, from that time he was paid 2/- per 'token'. He was a very good and trusty pressman, and kept the 'colour' well up, and his rollers, &c., in nice working order.[59]

Colenso records that when the book was finished, in December 1837, 'the demand for copies became great beyond expression, from all parts of New Zealand', and finding it impossible to bind them fast enough he sent off lots of 500 at a time to Sydney to have them done (poorly done, as he later complained). Since the Maori were said to value more highly any article they paid for than one given to them free, the books were sold at 4s. each. As evidence of interest and demand, Colenso makes the incidentally valuable point (distinguishing reading from writing) that 'as not many of the principal Maori Chiefs or their sons could then write, many of them travelled on foot and barefooted to Paihia, from very great distances, to obtain a copy'. William Jowett, responding as clerical secretary of the Church Missionary Society to Colenso's expressed wish for ordination, advised him to turn his thoughts

> to the peculiarly useful (and therefore honourable) department which you *do* occupy. The sight of that New Testament in the Native language, which you have been privileged to carry through the Press, is such a sight as fills my heart with indescribable joy. Think now to what great ends it is capable of becoming instrumental . . . it will,

moreover, help the fixing of the language; and schoolbooks, and many other books, will grow out of it. No doubt the spirit of GOD will use this sword.[60]

There is one excellent point in Jowett's response to which I shall return, but here I just wish to note again the ecstatic tone which belies both the actual achievement and the future promise of literacy.

How many Maori could read before Colenso arrived? In 1833 Yate had estimated that some 500 in the north could do so. In 1834, Edward Markham ventured 'not less then ten Thousand people that can Read, write and do sums in the Northern end of the Island'.[61] Refining such impressionism by apparently objective fact, one historian turns to the presumed demand for and effects of printing: between January 1835 and January 1840 Colenso printed 3,500,000 pages of religious material, and in 1840 produced over 2,000,000 more – figures as ignorantly impressionistic (though true) as Yate's and Markham's.[62] Added to the further information that Colenso's New Testament was reprinted in London in 1841, 1843 and 1845 (each time in 20,000 copies), it reinforces the missionary notion of widespread literacy and the immense impact of print. On those figures, by 1845 there was at least one Maori New Testament for every two Maori people in New Zealand. Colenso felt confident to write in his journal in 1840:

> Here I may be permitted to remark the Press has been an inst[rument] of very great good in this land . . . Howr. partial it may be supposed I am in my opinion, I believe (and that belief too is deduced from what I have seen and heard on the spot) that the press has been more effective (under God) as an instr[ument] of good among this people during the last 5 yrs. than the whole body of miss[ionaries] put together.

As Colenso's Day- and Waste-Book, paper-book, and ledger all survive, we can detail everything he printed for the years 1836–43. In terms of *histoire-du-livre* econometrics we can say exactly what his output was; but instead of using figures like three and a half million and two million *pages*, we as bibliographers would see that from January 1835 to January 1840 he printed only 16 items, set up in type only 34.15 sheets, and printed in all only 145,775 perfected sheets in five years. The New Testament alone accounted for 22.5 of those 34.15 sheets and 122,500 of the 145,775 perfected sheets. In 1840, he printed 11 items, involving 18.875 sheets and 89,313 perfected sheets. One book, the Psalms, accounted for a third of the setting and two-thirds of the presswork.

If this technical view of Colenso's output checks us slightly, what other evidence is there of reception? It is well known that people in an oral society, seeing books for the first time, often treat them as ritual objects.

> Many people who know not a letter wish to possess themselves of a copy of the translated Scriptures because they consider it possesses a peculiar virtue of protecting them from the power of evil spirits.[63]

At an early church service,

> Many of [the Maori] thought it highly proper that they should be armed with books. Is might be an old ship's almanac, or a cast-away novel, or even a few stitched leaves of old newspapers.[64]

The book was given a totemic power of warding off not only evil spirits: in 1836 it was said that a Maori fighting party had refused to storm a *pa* (a fortified village) because of a printed Bible inside it and contented themselves with a blockade.[65] In 1839 Taylor recorded seeing Maori with mission books (or at least odd leaves from them) rolled up and thrust through holes in the lobes of their ears.[66] Books were also useful for making roll-your-own cartridges. One book so used was Milner's *Church history*, thus giving a slightly different sense to the phrase 'the church militant'.[67] Colenso picked up such a cartridge in which the paper came from II Samuel and bore the words from chapter 19, v. 34: 'How long have I to live?'[68] Markham said his servants melted down his pewter spoons in 1834 to make musket balls of them, 'and the first Volume of my Voltaires, 'Louis 14. et 15'. torn up and made Cartridges of them'.[69] A proper use, perhaps, in Voltaire's view?

As the number of New Testaments disseminated was reaching saturation point (one to every two Maori) in the early 1840s – just when the impact of printing should have been at its height – we find Selwyn noting 'A general complaint in all parts of the country, that the schools are not so well attended as heretofore'. He remarked 'a growing indifference to religion, and a neglect of the opportunities for instruction'.[70] Another missionary comments that 'We have gained a very large portion of this people but we have no hold on their children'.[71] By 1844, Hadfield could say at last

> It appears every year more evident that our present system of conveying instruction to these people is wholly inadequate to their present wants; they have been brought to a certain point, and we have no means of bringing them beyond that.[72]

What we have here is not only disillusionment about the actual extent to which literacy of the most elementary kind had been achieved, but a clear example of the way in which even the most sophisticated technology (print) will fail to serve an irrelevant ideology (an alien religion).[73] For the missionaries and their great instrument of truth had failed lamentably to equip the Maori to negotiate their rights with the Pakeha in the one area that really mattered to them – land. Nor was it merely a failure in creating literacy in Maori. In 1844 almost no Maori spoke (let alone read) English. In that year a settler said he had met only two who did so.[74] Selwyn had recognized the need to break away from the old policy and in 1843 produced the first primer to help Maori read English. Colenso followed up in 1872 on a Government commission with *Willie's first English book*, 'Written for young Maoris who can read their own Maori Tongue and who wish to learn to read the English Language'. For all his piety, however, Colenso saw the need for another innovation too: 'in order to the greater and more general use of the work, all words and sentences of a strictly religious nature have been purposely omitted'.

Historians have too readily and optimistically affirmed extensive and high levels of Maori literacy in the early years of settlement, and the role of printing in establishing it. Protestant missionary faith in the power of the written word, and modern assumptions about the impact of the press in propagating it, are not self-evidently valid, and they all too easily distort our understanding of the different and competitively powerful realities of societies whose cultures are still primarily oral. Yet, as Jowett told Colenso when congratulating him on completion of the Maori New Testament, printing had helped to fix the Maori language – albeit in one dialect and with some dangerous neologisms. Colenso himself was later to make the point that the oral memory, as a faculty, too easily absorbed and perpetuated the new and corrupt words born of settlement and trade, taking up the simpler and degenerate forms used by the settlers.[75] Had it not been for the missionaries and Colenso's printing, the language as it was at an early stage of European contact might well have been irretrievably lost.

I wish now to focus on one test of the missionaries' efforts to teach literacy in the 1830s, one test of Colenso's effect after five years' printing, one example of a 'text' which offers textual and contextual problems, one case-study to prove that bibliography is an explosive subject. I return to the Treaty of Waitangi. (The name, by the way, means 'the waters of lamentation'.) *An authentic and genuine history of the signing of the Treaty of Waitangi* was written at the time by Colenso although it was not printed until 1890.

On the morning of 30 January 1840 Colenso printed in Maori one hundred copies of a circular letter inviting Maori chiefs in the northern area to meet at Waitangi on 5 February. An English draft of the treaty (a composite version by three men, Governor Hobson, Freeman and Busby) had been cobbled together by the 3rd and was given to Henry Williams on the 4th to translate into Maori. The first English draft, the foul papers as it were, has not survived.[76] Williams's translation was discussed with the chiefs on 5 February; alterations were made and the revised Maori version copied on to parchment that night by Richard Taylor. The original copy of that revised Maori version has not survived. The fair copy of it, made on parchment the previous night, was presented to the chiefs next day, 6 February, for their signatures. It is this document in Maori, a revised version of a translation into Maori made from a composite English draft no longer extant, which is the Treaty of Waitangi. But its textual complexities do not end there.

Governor Hobson also sent abroad, either to Sydney or London, five English versions of the Treaty. There are minor differences in three of them, but the other two bear a different date, differ from the others in the wording of their preamble, and differ critically from each other in the second article. Comparison shows that the extant Maori version, the actual Treaty as signed by the chiefs on 6 February, is not a translation of any one of these five English versions, nor is any of the English ones a translation from the Maori. They must therefore descend, with greater or less accuracy and no authority, from the first full English draft, now lost, and made before the Maori translation in its first and revised forms. One English version sent to the Secretary of State was endorsed by Williams, who said it was 'as Literal a translation of the Treaty of Waitangi as the Idiom of the Language will admit of'. This cannot have been true, but a comparable disregard for strict textual accuracy in our own day has led to the inclusion of one of the unauthoritative English versions as a Schedule to the Waitangi Day Act (1960).[77] There are other complications of textual authority deriving from the fact that names were added to the Treaty over the next seven months, thirty-nine such names being found on an English copy which the signatories, being illiterate, could not have read even if they had known the language.

That last example puts at its most extreme my argument about the non-literate state of the nation in 1840 after ten years of intensive teaching and five years of proselytic printing. But even if we confine ourselves to the Maori text, how literate were the signatories? As Cressy has said, 'only one type of literacy is directly measurable – the ability or inability to write a signature' and because the evidence of signatures or marks is, in Schofield's words, 'universal, standard and direct', it has come to displace the merely anecdotal, subjective, inescapably impressionistic evidence hitherto accepted by historians.[78] Applying this test to the Treaty of Waitangi, what do we find? The number of signatories is in fact uncertain; estimates vary from 512 to 541 and, in the manner common to many societies with mass illiteracy, many of the names given were written out by the government clerk on behalf of the chief concerned. On my count the highest possible number of personal signatures, as distinct from crosses or *moko*-patterns, is seventy-two.[79] Could the Maori in the commemorative plaque *read* what he was signing in even the most literal way? Even if he could do that, the odds are heavily loaded against his knowing how to *write* even his own name.

In any case, whose 'Maori' was it? Of course it was not indigenous Maori but missionary Maori, specifically Williams's English Protestant missionary Maori, learnt from the distinctive dialect of the Ngapuhi tribe. Not only the concepts but many of the words, for all their Maori form, were English.

Before the document was signed, Hobson explained, with Williams translating, that if the chiefs did sign the Queen would protect them. In an important sense this was true: many Maori wanted the British to establish some legal authority over their own unruly European settlers and traders and incidentally by their authority to inhibit inter-tribal strife. Busby, in a half truth, said the Governor had not come to take away their land but to secure them in the possession of what they held. But Te Kemara called his bluff and asked for the return to him of the very land on which they were standing. Rewa, eloquent but sad, added, 'I have no lands now – only a name, only a name!' Kawiti rejected Hobson's plan: 'We are free'. Hakiro supported him: 'We are not thy people. We are free'. Tareha: 'No, we only are the chiefs, the rulers. We will not be ruled over. What, thou a foreigner up, and I down! Thou high, and I, Tareha, the great chief of the Ngapuhi tribes, low! No, never, never'. With a flair for the dramatic, he held a canoe paddle high in the air to deride Hobson's intolerable ambition. Tareha, says Colenso, was also clothed in a filthy piece of coarse old floor matting simply to ridicule Hobson's supposition that New Zealanders needed the extraneous aid of clothing, &c, from foreign nations.[80]

For the Maori present, the very form of public discourse and decision-making was *oral* and confirmed in the consensus not in the document. In signing the treaty, many chiefs made complementary oral conditions which were more important than (and certainly in their own way modified) the words on the page. For the illiterate, the document and its implications were meaningless; for the merely literate, the ability to sign one's name was a trap. At the end of the first day, as Hobson went to his boat, an elderly chief rushed in front of him and looked staringly and scrutinizingly, says Colenso, into the Governor's face. Having surveyed it, he exclaimed in a shrill, loud and mournful voice, '*Auee! he koroheke! Ekore e roa kua mate*'. Colenso was reluctant to translate but on being pressed did so: 'He says, "Alas! an old man. *He* will soon be dead!"' – and he was, but the document lived on.

The next day, 6 February (now celebrated as a public holiday), some three to four hundred Maori were, in Colenso's words, 'scattered in small parties according to their tribes, talking about the treaty, but evidently not understanding it'. But Hobson wanted to make an end. Colenso's report runs:

The Native chiefs were called on in a body to come forward and sign the document. Not one, however, made any move nor seemed desirous of doing so till Mr. Busby, hitting on an expedient, proposed calling them singly by their names as they stood in *his* (private) list, in which list the name of Hoani Heke (known, too, to be the most favourable towards the treaty) happened to be the first – at least, of those who were this day present. On his being called by name to come and sign, he advanced to the table on which the treaty lay. At this moment I, addressing myself to the Governor, said, –

'Will your Excellency allow me to make a remark or two before that chief signs the treaty'?

The Governor: 'Certainly, sir'.

Mr. Colenso: 'May I ask your excellency whether it is your opinion that these Natives understand the articles of the treaty which they are now called upon to sign? I this morning' –

The Governor: 'If the Native chiefs do not know the contents of this treaty it is no fault of mine. I wish them fully to understand it . . . They have heard the treaty read by Mr. Williams'.

Mr. Colenso: 'True, your Excellency; but the Natives are quite children in their ideas. It is no easy matter, I well know, to get them to understand – fully to comprehend a document of this kind; still, I think they ought to know somewhat of it to constitute its legality . . . I have spoken to some chiefs concerning it, who had no idea whatever as to the purport of the treaty'.

Mr. Busby here said, 'The best answer that could be given to that observation would be found in the speech made yesterday by the very chief about to sign, Hoani Heke, who said, "The Native mind could not comprehend these things: they must trust to the advice of their missionaries"'.

Mr. Colenso: 'Yes; and that is the very thing to which I was going to allude. The missionaries should do so; but at the same time the missionaries should explain the thing in all its bearings to the Natives, so that it should be their very own act and deed. Then, in case of a reaction taking place, the Natives could not turn round on the missionary and say, "You advised me to sign that paper, but never told me what were the contents thereof"'.

The Governor: 'I am in hopes that no such reaction will take place'.

So Colenso gave up, having expressed his conscientious feeling and discharged what he felt strongly to be his duty. Then forty-six chiefs, anxious to get home, played this new game and put their marks on the parchment. They included chiefs who had declaimed *against* signing; but (as Colenso records of one of them) 'Marupu, having made his mark (as he could neither read nor write) shook hands heartily with the Governor' and left.

To pursue the sociology of that text one stage further: in all the English versions of the treaty the chiefs 'cede to Her Majesty the Queen of England, absolutely and without reservation, all the rights and powers of Sovereignty'. The question here is what the English meant and the Maori understood by the word 'Sovereignty'. Did it mean that the chiefs gave up to the Crown their personal power and supreme status within their own tribes, or was it only something more mundanely administrative, like 'governorship'? In fact the word used by Henry Williams to translate 'Sovereignty' was precisely that: *kawanatanga*, a transliteration of 'Governor' (*kawana*) with a suffix to make it abstract. Such was his translation for the order of morning service: 'that all our doings may be ordered by thy governance'. What he significantly omitted in translating the 'Sovereignty' which the Maori were being asked to surrender was the genuine Maori word *mana*, meaning personal prestige and the power that flowed from it, or even the word *rangatiratanga*, meaning chieftainship. He had used both words in translating Corinthians chapter 15, v. 24 with its references to the 'kingdom of God' and 'all authority and power'. By choosing not to use either *mana* or *rangatiratanga* to indicate what the Maori would exchange for 'all the Rights and Privileges of British subjects', Williams muted the sense, plain in English, of the treaty as a document of political appropriation.[81] The status of their assent is already questionable enough, but had any Maori heard that he was giving up his *mana* or *rangatiratanga* he could never have agreed to the treaty's terms. Williams's Maori version of Hobson's composite English one set the trap which King Lear fell into when (in a version published in 1608) he said to Albany and Cornwall:

> I doe inuest you iointly in my powre,
> Preheminence, and all the large effects
> That troope with Maiestie, . . .
>     onely we still retaine
> The name and all the addicions to a King

where 'addicions' implies the attributes of ultimate personal prestige and authority.

There are other textual problems created by the versions. In the second article the word *rangatiratanga* does appear in a context which (in Maori) seeks to assure the chiefs of the *rangatiratanga* or 'full possession of their lands, their homes and all their possessions'. Four of the five English versions, however, spell out that provision to read 'full, exclusive and undisturbed possession of their Lands and Estates, Forests, Fisheries and other properties which they may collectively or individually possess'. Although technically the English version has no textual authority, its explicit references to forests and fisheries have become a matter of great import and Maori today have found good reason to plead the intention of the English versions against the more limited wording of the Maori one.[82] Even more significantly, indeed tragically, the English versions of the second article also require the chiefs to 'yield to Her Majesty the exclusive right of Pre-emption over such lands as the proprietors thereof may be disposed to alienate, at such prices as may be agreed upon'. Williams's Maori version omitted to spell out and thereby legitimate under the treaty the Crown's *pre-emptive* right to purchase Maori land. As a consequence, the English versions have been taken to bestow legality on the actions of successive Governments, while the Maori version seems morally to justify the deep sense of grievance still widely suffered over Maori land issues.[83] Once more, Colenso, writing to the Church Missionary Society, did not 'for a moment' suppose that the chiefs were aware that 'by signing the Treaty they had restrained themselves from selling their land to whomsoever they will', and cited one Maori who, although he had signed the treaty, had since offered land for sale privately. On being told that he could not do that, he replied: 'What? Do you think I won't do what I like with my own'?[84]

From a European point of view, one conditioned to accept and apply evidence as 'literally' true or false, the English versions of the treaty have proved a potent political weapon in legitimating government of the Maori, even though standards of textual and historical truth also deriving from European traditions oblige us to acknowledge the Maori one as the only authoritative document, that which states the terms and bears the written marks of assent. From a Maori point of view, the truth is not so confined, and signatures bear no absolute authority. For the Maori, as I have already indicated, the 'text' was the consensus arrived at through discussion, something much more comprehensive than the base document or any one of its extant versions. Williams later defended himself, saying that he had explained the text *orally*; but only the documents survive, and successive Governments have chosen the English ones to act on when these best served their ends. At a later treaty meeting, Mohi Tawhai said that 'the sayings of the Pakeha float light, like the wood of the *whau* tree, and always remain to be seen, but the sayings of the Maori sink to the bottom like stone'.[85] Manuscript and print, the tools of the Pakeha, persist, but words which are spoken fade as they fall.

Print is still too recent for the Maori. Oral traditions live on in a distrust of the mere document, and in a refusal by many young Maori to accept political decisions based on it. Pakeha and Maori versions of the past continue to collide. During a Russian scare in the 1880s the Government of the day pre-empted the purchase of Maori land at Bastion Point, a fine site overlooking Auckland harbour. When a more recent Government proposed to resell it for luxury housing, it was occupied for several months by Maori protesters. In my mind's eye, I can still read the vivid television news pictures of police and military vehicles as they moved in to evict the squatters. To bring my own report right up to date, and allow print its complementary role, I cite an item from a Wellington newspaper of 7 February 1983:

> 99 protesters were arrested as riot-equipped police took strong precautions at the Waitangi Day celebrations at Waitangi to prevent recurrence of last year's violence and fire-bombing.

As such moments literacy defines itself for many as a concordat of sword and pen, of politics and script indeed.

In the reports Colenso has left us, he shows his perception of the complex relationships of oral witness, text, print and political and economic power. For us, the texts in context quickly deconstruct and lose their 'literal' authority – no book was ever bound by its covers. Pakeha [i.e. Europeans] continue to assume 'Sovereignty' where radical Maori persist in believing that nothing so sacred as *mana* has ever been ceded under the treaty, that Maori sovereignty was, and is, intact.

But must the story end there, in a conflict of irreconcilable versions? In terms of a sociology of the text, it is impossible to regard the Maori version as complete, although it carries the highest authority, nor the English ones as authoritative, although they are far more explicit. Like many dramatic texts, each has been born, here maimed and deformed, of the pressures of context. In the rarefied world of textual scholarship, it would now be commendably scholarly to deny any possibility of conflation, any notion that 'the text' of the Treaty of Waitangi is anything other than its distinct historical versions. And yet, as the Maori always knew, there is a real world beyond the niceties of the literal text and in that world there is *in fact* a providential version now editing itself into the status of a social and political document of power and purpose. The physical versions and their fortuitous forms are not the only testimonies to intent: implicit in the accidents of history is an ideal text which history has begun to discover, a reconciliation of readings which is also a meeting of minds. The concept of an ideal text as a cultural and political imperative is not imposed *on* history but derives *from* it and from an understanding of the dynamics of bibliography as a study of the meanings 'books' make.

Lest that seem too dangerous, too messianic a mission, let me call W. W. Greg back from the shades to which he has latterly been consigned and ask him to repeat his crisply perceptive comment that many editors, declining to conflate, abdicate and 'produce, not editions of their author's works at all, but only editions of particular authorities for those works'.[86] To illustrate a principle of textual criticism operative in the real world which implies the concept of an ideal text that the versions have failed fully to express, one might cite legal opinion on the interpretation of treaties. For example, there is recent judicial authority that treaties and other judicial documents should be interpreted in the spirit in which they are drawn and taking into account the surrounding circumstances. In the case of bilingual treaties, there is ample authority for the view that the two or more versions should help one another, so that one may be interpreted by reference to another. In New Zealand, under the Treaty of Waitangi Act, an advisory tribunal was recently set up and directed by Government 'to determine the meaning and effect of the Treaty as embodied in the two [*sic*] texts' and '*to decide* issues raised by differences between them'. As a motion towards the higher criticism it recognizes clearly the *social* inutility of a clutter of versions as distinct from the social value of a harmonized text. The Waitangi Tribunal, however, affirmed an even higher principle:

> A Maori approach to the Treaty would imply that its *wairua* or spirit is something more than a literal construction of the actual words used can provide. The spirit of the Treaty transcends the sum total of its component written words and puts narrow or literal interpretations out of place.[87]

I myself cannot help but see texts, their distinct versions, their different physical modes, and their comprehension in social contexts – in a word, the sociology of texts – as the substance of bibliography. The book, in all its forms, enters history only as an evidence of human behaviour, and it remains active only in the service of human needs.

Colenso died in 1899 at the ripe old age of eighty-eight, thirty-six hours after penning his last letter to Coupland Harding, the man who might have completed our model by transplanting us from the level of mere printing to the fine controls of typography and the book as an expressive form. Colenso left to Harding two hundred pounds for his son, William Colenso Harding, and all his printing materials, including 'my sole composing-stick – with which I did so much work both in England and in New Zealand'. Harding was a worthy recipient and was later to note: 'It was in this stick that the Maori New Testament of 1837 was set, and also the Treaty of Waitangi – Truly, a venerable relic'.[88]

## Notes

*Presidential address to The Bibliographical Society 15 February 1983.* This paper was originally announced as 'Two early New Zealand printers: William Colenso and R. Coupland Harding', but the range of material precluded all but a brief reference (and that mainly a succession of slides) to Harding's work. A few passages omitted when the paper was first read have been restored and the final section revised. The footnotes, a literal sub-text, embody suggestions made both before and after its delivery. I am particularly indebted to A. G. Bagnall, Alexandra Barratt, Simon Cauchi, Barney Cohn, Kathleen Coleridge, Tamsin Donaldson, Penelope Griffith, Harvey Graff, Ross Harvey, Michael Jackson, Dorothy V. Jones, Iain Lonie, Jane McRae, Paul McHugh, David and Rosamond McKitterick, Robert Rosenthal, Marshall Sahlins and Ian Willison.

1    See Walter J. Ong, *Orality and literacy: the technologizing of the word* (London, 1982).
2    Denis McQuail and Sven Windahl, *Communication models* (London, 1982), p. 2, have a useful summary of the advantages of models.
3    I have consulted the treaty documents as reproduced in *Facsimiles of the Declaration of Independence and the Treaty of Waitangi*, edited by H. H. Turton (Wellington, 1877; reprinted 1960). I am most grateful to Paul McHugh for his legally informed endorsement of my claim that Maori assent to the treaty became the substantive ground of British sovereignty over New Zealand. There is, however, a body of opinion which regards the treaty as having had no effect and British sovereignty as arising rather from the occupation and settlements of lands inhabited by uncivilized native peoples.
4    The phrases 'European myth of . . . literacy and print as agents of change' and 'from memory to written record' allude to Harvey Graff's *The literacy myth: literacy and social structure in the nineteenth-century city* (New York, 1979), to Elizabeth L. Eisenstein's *The printing press as an agent of change: communications and cultural transformations in early modern Europe*, 2 vols (Cambridge, 1979), and to M. T. Clanchy's *From memory to written record: England 1066–1307* (London, 1979).
5    William Colenso, *Fifty years ago in New Zealand. A commemoration; a jubilee paper; a retrospect: a plain and true story* (Napier, 1888), p. 27. Edward Markham, writing in 1834, took a different view, criticizing what he saw as an over-simplified orthography because it obscured regional and dialect differences, 'Thus making the Language poorer instead of enriching it': *New Zealand or reminiscences of it*, edited by E. H. McCormick (Wellington, 1963), p. 62. The circumstances surrounding the reduction of spoken languages to their first alphabetic or syllabic forms seem to have received little attention. Judith Binney, *The legacy of guilt* (Auckland, 1968), pp. 177–85, discusses Kendall's work in the Maori language; see also Johannes Andersen, 'The Maori alphabet', in *A history of printing in New Zealand 1830–1940*, edited by R. A. McKay (Wellington, 1940), pp. 57–74. Joyce Banks, of the National Library of Canada, is currently working on the Cree syllabary (which is still in use). Tamsin Donaldson, 'Hearing the first Australians', in *Seeing the First Australians*, edited by Ian Donaldson and Tamsin Donaldson (Sydney, 1984), looks at the motives underlying nineteenth-century attempts at writing down two Australian languages, Ngiyampaa and Wiradjuri, and at the effects of European assumptions on the forms these writings took.

6    The length of vowels is an important discriminator of meanings in Maori: kākā is a parrot; kăkā a garment, fibre or stalk; kākă is red-hot; kākă a bittern or, as adjective, poisoned-by-the-tutu. Practice in indicating long vowels still varies.

7    *Fifty years ago.* pp. 24–27, 47–49.

8    See David Kopf, *British orientalism and the Bengal renaissance: the dynamics of Indian modernization 1773–1833* (Berkeley and Los Angeles, 1969). A distinction must be drawn, of course, between reviving in print an already literate culture, as in Bengal, and capturing the current forms of an oral culture in all its diversity and levels of textual authority: see Bruce Biggs, 'The translation and publishing of Maori material in the Auckland Public Library', *Journal of the Polynesian Society*, 61 (1952), 177–91.

9    Letter of 1 October 1833, *Missionary Register* (November 1834), 513. William Brown, *New Zealand and its aborigines* (London, 1845), p. 101, had been told 'the natives would only learn every species of vice through the medium of the English language'.

10    Letter of 6 June 1842, cited by C. J. Parr, 'A missionary library, printed attempts to instruct the Maori, 1815–1845', *Journal of the Polynesian Society*, 70 (1961), 429–50 (p. 445).

11    Woon to the Wesleyan Mission Society 24 November 1838: 'The press will be a mighty engine in exposing the errors [of the Papists'] system', *Wesleyan Mission Notices*, n.s. 9 (September 1839), 142. Henry Williams 2 December 1840: '[we need] a vigorous effort at this time to meet the present demand for books before the Papists come forward with their trash', cited by Parr, 'A missionary library', p. 447. The Roman Catholic mission arrived in 1838, its main press (a Gaveau) on 15 June 1841.

12    G. Clarke, *Missionary Register* (December 1829), 372.

13    William Jacob, 13 March 1833, *Missionary Register* (January 1834), 60.

14    *Ibid.*, p. 61.

15    *Missionary Register* (February 1834), 119.

16    G. Clarke, 4 June 1833, *Missionary Register* (December 1833), 550.

17    William Puckey, 6 January 1835, *Missionary Register* (July 1836), 155.

18    G. Clarke, 12 February 1833, *Missionary Register* (October 1833), 468.

19    The most useful accounts of literacy among Maori in the early period are C. J. Parr, 'A missionary library', loc. cit., and 'Maori literacy 1843–1867', *Journal of the Polynesian Society*, 72 (1963), 211–34; and Michael D. Jackson, 'Literacy, communications and social change', in *Conflict and compromise: essays on the Maori since colonization*, edited by I. H. Kawharu (Wellington, 1975), pp. 27–54. Related studies are G. S. Parsonson, 'The literate revolution in Polynesia', *Journal of Pacific History*, II (1967), 39–57, and Gérald Duverdier, 'La pénétration du livre dans une société de culture orale: le cas de Tahiti', *Revue Française d'Histoire du Livre* n.s. 1 (1972), 27–51. Parr's thoroughness in noting so many primary references to Maori reading and writing in the 1830s and 1840s has greatly eased my own search, and I have found Jackson s admirable discussion most pertinent to my own because it is specifically concerned to examine Maori social change from the useful vantage point of literacy (p. 28). Michael Jackson also directed me to Manfred Stanley's 'Technicism, liberalism, and development: a study in irony as social theory', in *Social development: critical perspectives* (New York, 1972), 274–325, a suggestive discussion of the philosophical implications of technology for social structure and (if proleptically and only implicitly) *histoire du livre*.

Nevertheless I argue that early missionaries and recent historians have alike misread the evidence for Maori literacy. If it ceases to be true of the 1840s, the conventional view of the rapid attainment of literacy by the Maori in the 1830s must be wrong: a literacy with any potency for social change is not skin-deep. Having accepted the missionaries' euphoric accounts of the 1830s, Parr asks of the 1840s: 'What happened? Where were the self-appointed teachers, the hundred mile journeys to obtain books and instruction, the eager learners of letters, the crowded day schools of only a dozen years before'? ('Maori literacy', p. 221). The answer is at least partly that Maori 'literacy' of the 1830s is a chimera, a fantasy creation of the European mind. Although few Maori are today, in the simplest functional sense, illiterate, the written and printed word is not the mode which they habitually use. The question is therefore an even more fundamental one than whether or not the Maori failed to become fully literate in the 1830s, or why the missionaries failed to teach them full literacy. It is, rather, why has the Maori 'failed' to become literate at all? Or, to shift the burden of guilt, what is it about literacy and books that makes these technologies so inadequate to cope with the complex realities of a highly civilized social experience which the Maori know but which the literate mind too readily and reductively perhaps tries to capture in the book?

20   Marsden, 14 March 1830, *Missionary Register* (January 1831), 58.

21   Marsden, February 1837, *Missionary Register* (April 1838), 137.

22   *The life of Henry Williams*, edited by H. Carleton (Wellington, 1948), p. 137.

23   Hadfield, 22 July 1840, cited by Parr, 'A missionary library', p. 438.

24   J. F. B. Pompallier, *Early history of the Catholic Church in Oceana* (Auckland, 1888), p. 47.

25   (London, 1955), p. 17. Illiteracy was probably high among British working-class settlers. My own paternal grandfather was illiterate, signing both his marriage certificate and his will with a cross; and my paternal grandmother, like many a Maori chief and medieval king, 'wrote' her letters by dictation.

26   30 April 1836, *Missionary Register* (July 1839), 348.

27   See Duverdier, 'La pénétration', pp. 41–42, and William Ellis, *Polynesian researches, during a residence of nearly eight years in the Society and Sandwich Islands*, 2 vols (London, 1829), I, 492–93, II, 20. Duverdier draws most of his material from Ellis.

28   January 1832, *Missionary Register* (September 1832), 406.

29   6 July 1832, *ibid.* (May 1833), 243.

30   C. Baker, 26 December 1831, *ibid.* (September 1832), 407.

31   Fairburn, 30 April 1838, *ibid.* (July 1839), 348.

32   Henry Williams, 29 August 1834, *ibid.* (November 1835), 258.

33   In McKay, *A history of printing in New Zealand*, pp. 48–49.

34   This point is well made by Clanchy, *From memory to written record*.

35   Among those who currently affirm Maori rights and protect Maori *mana*, those more conciliatory towards European attitudes stress the complimentary ease and speed with which Maori are said to have become literate, those less conciliatory and more radical the supreme importance of the oral tradition and virtual irrelevance of the European 'book'. In practice, the oral mode rules. By compelling those who speak eloquently to substitute a mode in which they are less fluent, literacy can function insidiously as a culturally *regressive* force. Such at least is how many Maori experience it.

    As Jane McRae reminds me, there are few Maori writers and very few who write in Maori, but the tradition of oral composition and exposition continues, it is the only tradition with 'literary structures or styles, and the 'sound' text is usually all there is to be read. Even within University Departments of Maori Studies, the book is suspect. Manuscripts and printed texts in libraries, publications by Europeans on Maoridom, are seldom consulted; oral etiquette, debate and transfer of knowledge on the *marae* or meeting ground are what matter. Such conditions encourage the spontaneous, orally improvised, dramatic recreation of shared stories or themes and an evolutionary concept of texts; the fixed text, catching in print an arbitrary moment in the continuum of social exchange, demands a different sense of history and its own literal re-play.

36   Jackson, 'Literacy, communications, and social change', p. 38; see also A. Buzacott, *Mission life in the islands of the Pacific* (London, 1866), pp. 66–67.

37   *Missionary Register* (September 1834), 418–19.

38   *Ibid.* (April 1832), 192.

39    *Ibid.*, Letter 6.

40    *Ibid.*, Letter 7.

41    *Ibid.* (October 1834), 460. See also *Letters to the Rev. William Yate from natives of New Zealand converted to Christianity* (London, 1836).

42    See W. J. Cameron, 'A printing press for the Maori people', *Journal of the Polynesian Society*, 67 (1958), 204– 10; and Johannes Andersen, 'Maori printers and translators', in McKay, *A history of printing in New Zealand*, pp. 33– 47. An official Government newspaper, *Te Karere o Nui Tireni*, later *Te Karere Maori*, had been printed in Maori from 1842 to 1846 and doubtless established an early role for this medium.

43    Cited by Parr, 'A missionary library', p. 432.

44    *Ibid.*

45    July and September 1830, *Missionary Register* (January 1831), 67.

46    *Ibid.*

47    28 April 1831, *ibid.* (March 1832), 150.

48    6 July 1832, Letters of Henry Williams, vol. II (1830–38), typescript in the Auckland Institute and Museum.

49    *An account of New Zealand* (London, 1835), p. 232.

50    *Life of Henry Williams*, p. 185.

51    Letter to Dandeson Coates, 9 January 1836.

52    A. G. Bagnall and G. S. Petersen, *William Colenso; printer, missionary, botanist, explorer, politician; his life and journeys* (Wellington, 1948) is the standard life. Colenso's journals and his correspondence with the Church Missionary Society are in the Hocken Library, Dunedin; his Day- and Waste-book, Paper-book and printing-house ledger are in the Alexander Turnbull Library, Wellington; his correspondence with Coupland Harding is in the Mitchell Library, Sydney; his personal memorandum book, kept while he worked for Watts and travelled to New Zealand, and his will, are in the Hawkes Bay Museum and Art Gallery. An edition of his printing-house records and a thorough study of his work as a printer remains to be done. R. Coupland Harding has written three brief accounts: 'New Zealand's first printer', *The Inland Printer*, 7 (1889–90), 504 –06; 'Relics of the first New Zealand press', *Transactions and Proceedings of the New Zealand Institute*, 32 (1900), 400–04; 'William Colenso: some personal reminiscences', *The Press* (Christchurch), 27 February 1899. Harding also printed several of Colenso's papers, including *Fifty years ago in New Zealand*. See also H. Hill, 'The early days of printing in New Zealand: a chapter of interesting history', *Transactions and Proceedings of the New Zealand Institute*, 33 (1901), 407–26; and Johannes Andersen, 'Early printing in New Zealand', in McKay, *A history of printing in New Zealand*, pp. 1–31. The fate of Colenso's Stanhope press is unknown; his Columbian is probably that now in the Dominion Museum, Wellington; his table model foolscap Albion (Hopkinson and Cope No. 1964, dated 1845) is in the Hawkes Bay Museum and Art Gallery.

53    Colenso's memorandum book for this time details his wages and the way in which they were made up for composing, correction, altering heads, share of 'fat', or reduced by candle fine and error in casting (the last cost him 16*s*. 4*d*.), along with other sharply observed features of an early nineteenth-century printing house.

54    Colenso Papers, Hocken Library.

55    *Fifty years ago*, p. 6. Writing to Coupland Harding on 31 December 1890, Colenso recalled Williams's first encounter with practical printing: 'Mr. W., evidently, had never seen Type-setting before: he was often in the Pg. Office, & well do I remember his Exclamation of pleasing surprize on seeing a line spaced out in cpg. stick – "he had often wondered how is was done to have all the lines of equal length"'.

56    *Fifty years ago*, p. 7.

57    *Ibid.*, p. 9.

58    16 March 1835, Colenso Papers, Hocken Library; also *Missionary Register* (July 1836), 164.

59    *Fifty years ago*, p. 19.

60    17 December 1838, reprinted in *Fifty years ago*, pp. 21–22.

61    For Yate, see Eric Ramsden, *Marsden and the missions* (Sydney, 1936), p. 28; for Markham, *New Zealand or recollections of it*, p. 55. Sensing that the figure he had heard might be optimistic, Markham qualified it in a note: 'For fear of exaggeration [*sic*] say 8000'.

62    Harrison M. Wright, *New Zealand, 1769–1840: Early years of western contact* (Cambridge, Mass., 1959), p. 53. Wright's figures are calculated from the tables (titles, formats, edition quantities) supplied by Colenso in *The Missionary Register* (1840), p. 512, and (1841), p. 519. To keep the comparative base I have used the same source, but a more exact calculation would have to include a few jobbing items excluded from Colenso's reports but included in his ledger.

63    Richard Davis, 10 November 1832, cited by Wright, p. 176.

64    G. Clarke, *Early life in New Zealand* (Hobart, 1903), p. 31.

65    Whiteley, 22 December 1836, cited by Parr, 'A missionary library', p. 445.

66    28 April 1839, ibid.

67    *Life of Henry Williams*, p. 60.

68    *Fifty years ago*, p. 42.

69    *New Zealand or recollections of it*, p. 32.

70    15 June 1843, cited by Parr, 'Maori literacy', p. 212.

71    Thomas Chapman, 28 March 1846, *ibid.*, p. 213.

72    Cited by Parr, 'A missionary library', p. 446.

73    As Stanley writes, 'Physical machinery [sc. books?] cannot 'make' men do anything. People act or fail to act on the basis of their interpretations of the world around them, interpretations embodied in language, institutions, and social organization. The physical world created by human innovative effort reflects – in the forms of material objects – human assumptions, values, desires, and aspirations' ('Technicism, liberalism, and development', p. 279). The first part is true of Maori resistance to literacy, the second of the missionaries in the value they imparted and imputed to the book. Paradoxically the Maori is very sensitive to (because suspicious of) the very form of a book, and gives an expressive intention to features which a European takes for granted as mere 'accidentals' and has virtually ceased to see. For example, in a review of Michael King's *Maori – a photographic and social history* (Auckland, 1983), Keri Kaa questions the very depiction of corpses: 'The pictures of the tupapaku (corpses) I found most disturbing . . . My initial reaction was to ask: Whose Nanny is that? Whose Mother is that? Do their mokopuna [children] mind about their taonga [precious heirlooms] being displayed for all the world to see?' And again 'There is a strange combination of pictures on page 35. At the top of the page is a picture of a tangi [funeral], underneath it one of a woman cooking. Anyone who understands the concepts of tapu and noa [lifting of tapu] would appreciate that the two should never be mixed by being placed together *on a page*'. (my italics) *The New Zealand Listener*, 24 September 1983, p. 99.

74    Brown, *New Zealand and its aborigines*, p. 99. Augustus Earle, *Narrative of a residence in New Zealand*, edited by E. H. McCormick (Oxford, 1966), pp. 133–34, wrote: 'I cannot forbear censuring the missionaries, inasmuch as they prevent the natives, by every means in their power, from acquiring the English language'. See also J. S. Polack, *Manners and customs of the New Zealanders*, 2 vols (London, 1840), II, 147: '[The Maori] take much delight in speaking the English language, and had the Missionaries chosen to have taught the children this tongue, what an immense store of able works could at once have been put into the hands of the native youth, instead of a few imperfect translations on one subject, that may teach mechanical devotion, but can never mentally illuminate the native mind'.

75    'On nomenclature', in *Three literary papers* (Napier, 1883), p. 9. In this paper Colenso also discusses the orthography of place names on maps and in school geographies, raising many of the issues

recently dramatized by Brian Friel in his play *Translations* (1981). See also, H. W. Williams, 'Reaction of the Maori to the impact of civilization', *Journal of the Polynesian Society*, 44 (1935), 216–43, esp. 234–35.

76    Some drafts survive: one by Hobson of the preamble; one in the hand of Freeman, Hobson's secretary, of the three articles and another version of the preamble; a fair copy of a draft by James Busby. Bus they do not themselves constitute the English text given to Williams to translate. Although Colenso provides an unrivalled account of the treaty occasion, by far the most perceptive analysis of the texts and their implications is that of R. M. Ross, 'Te Tiriti o Waitangi: texts and translations', *New Zealand Journal of History*, 6 (1972), 129–67. The account I give of the relationship of the texts is based wholly on Ross.

77    To add insult to injury, the Maori text printed as the first schedule to the Act contains, in the second article, numerous misprints.

78    It is also the most reductive form of 'literacy' test. See David Cressy, *Literacy and the social order: reading and writing in Tudor England* (Cambridge, 1980), p. 53; and R. S. Schofield. 'The measurement of literacy in pre-industrial England', in *Literacy in traditional societies*, edited by Jack Goody (Cambridge, 1968), p. 319.

79    The treaty is supplemented and ultimately constituted by a collection of sheets subscribed in different parts of the country between 6 February and 3 September 1840. Fig. 2(a) [omitted] shows part of a declaration of their independence of all foreign powers that had been subscribed on 28 October 1835 by thirty-four chiefs, of whom only four signed their own name. In the next four years a further eighteen chiefs subscribed, of whom only three signed their own names. Most such signatures appear to have been written with difficulty. In later times some Maori who could in fact write their names preferred to use their *moko* as giving documents a more sacred sign of approval.

80    Graphic as it is, Colenso's account of the Maori speeches understandably does scant justice to the originals. As he wrote much later, 'Some of the New Zealanders were truly natural orators, and consequently possessed in their large assemblies great power and influence. This was mainly owing to their tenacious memories, to their proper selection from their copious and expressive language; skilfully choosing the very word, sentence, theme, or natural image best fitted to make an impression on the lively impulsive minds of their countrymen . . . the orator's knowledge of their traditions and myths, songs, proverbs and fables was ever to him an inexhaustible mine of wealth . . . All the people well knew the power of persuasion – particularly of that done in the open air – before the multitude' (*The New Zealand Exhibition* (Wellington, 1865); section on 'Ethnology: On the Maori races of New Zealand', pp. 70–71). What Hobson was up against may be judged from his letter of 17 February 1840, reporting the Hokianga meeting at which he had sought further subscriptions to the treaty: 'The New Zealanders are passionately fond of declamation, and they possess considerable ingenuity in exciting the passions of the people. On this occasion all their best orators were against me, and every argument they could devise was used to defeat my object' (Facsimiles, p. [x]). Maori orators, it should be noted, often enjoyed playing devil's advocate. Colenso vividly recounts the anger of Te Kemara ('eyes rolling . . . extravagant gestures and grimace'), but adds: 'And yet it was all mere show – not really intended; as was not long after fully shown, when they gave their evidence as to the fair sale, &c., of their lands before the Land Commissioners, I myself acting as interpreter'.

    All quotations here and below relating to the discussion and signing of the treaty on 5 and 6 February are taken from Colenso's own eye- and ear-witness report, *The authentic and genuine history of the signing of the Treaty of Waitangi* (Wellington, 1890), principally pp. 32–33. Written immediately after the events described, it was read and its accuracy confirmed by James Busby who was also present.

81    I do not impute to Williams any will to deceive the Maori by his choice of terms. Attempts to establish a legal basis for the control of British subjects in New Zealand by extra-territorial

jurisdiction had proved unsuccessful. Furthermore, unless Britain formally secured sovereignty, neither Britain nor the Maori could establish an exclusive claim to the islands as against claims that might be made by other European powers. (The Declaration of Independence of 1835 was a device to establish the chiefs' collective territorial rights and forestall an imminent French claim.) In furthering both concerns, however dubious the exact legal status of the treaty, the British Government was anxious to secure Maori assent and genuinely hopeful that British sovereignty would not disrupt Maori life. Nevertheless, cultural and linguistic suppositions on both sides, compounded by European assumptions about literacy and the status of documents, frustrated that hope and later (if then still unforeseen) patterns of immigration destroyed it. Williams certainly shows himself, at that critical time, to have been less sensitive than Colenso to Maori modes of understanding. As Claudia Orange has made clear to me, Maori understanding of the Treaty was undoubtedly formed by their sense that the independence (the *rangatiratanga*) they had affirmed in 1835 and reaffirmed by further subscriptions as late as 1839, was not nullified by the Treaty. One document did not supersede the other: they lived together, one complementing the other.

82   Fishing rights have again become a matter of contention in this century, most recently in 1983 when the then Government proposed to direct into the sea effluent from a synthetic petrol plant at Motunui. The subsequent *Report, findings and recommendations of the Waitangi Tribunal on an application . . . on behalf of the Te Atiawa Tribe in relation to fishing grounds in the Waitara district* (Wellington, 1983) includes a valuable résumé of many textual issues raised by the present paper.

83   Sir Apirana Ngata's literal translation from the Maori of the second article reads: 'The Queen of England confirms and guarantees to the Chiefs and Tribes and to all the people of New Zealand the full possession of their lands, their homes and all their possessions, but the chiefs assembled and all other chiefs yield to the Queen the right to alienate such lands which the owners desire to dispose of at a price agreed upon between the owners and person or persons appointed by the Queen to purchase on her behalf' (*The Treaty of Waitangi: an explanation*, Christchurch, 1950, p. 7).

84   Lesser begun 24 January 1840, cited by Bagnall and Petersen, pp. 93–94. Again I acknowledge the kind help of Paul McHugh. The Crown's pre-emptive right to extinguish the native title had been long practised in colonizing overseas territories and was most vigorously affirmed in the Royal Proclamation of 1763 which was seen as protecting North American Indian lands from unscrupulous appropriation. The English land law assumption that all rights to land derive from a grant by the Crown clearly did not apply to new territories, where the aboriginal title rested at law, not upon a grant from the Crown, but (exceptionally) upon the Crown's recognition of aboriginal rights. To the British mind, however, it was unthinkable that aboriginal and heathen notions of title should control the form of land transfers to British settlers, and so the pre-emptive right was adopted as a way of converting Crown-recognized title into Crown-derived title. From the British point of view, it was undoubtedly seen as preventing the chaos which must have followed from the operation of a mixed system, and at the same time (if fairly administered) as protecting the Maori from land-jobbers. One has to concede that neither Hobson nor Williams could have communicated the full import of 'pre-emptive' to those who were asked to assent to the treaty, but by so simplifying the issue in his translation of the second article into Maori, Williams again showed less readiness than did Colenso to penetrate 'the Native mind' and 'explain the thing in all its bearings . . . so that it should be their very own act and deed'. One might be accused of arguing from hindsight were it not for Colenso's contemporary insight.

85   Cited by Ross, op. cit., p. 152, from British Parliamentary Papers, 1845, XXXIII, 108, p. 10. Despite the transience of the spoken word, there is a wealth of Maori speech in manuscripts still to be studied. Some are *tapu* and unable to be consulted, but the written transcripts of

evidence delivered in Maori land courts are a rich source of information about language and forms of oral witness to land rights as declaimed in court. Elsdon Best records that when he was secretary to the Land Commission, an old man recited 406 songs for him from memory, a genealogy which took three days to recite and included over 1400 persons in proper sequence, and much other evidence on the occupation of certain lands: *The Maori school of learning: its objects, methods and ceremonies* (Wellington, 1923), p. 5.

86  'The rationale of copy-text', in *Collected papers*, edited by J. C. Maxwell (Oxford, 1966), p. 384.

87  *Report* pp. 52–63; the immediate quotation is on p. 55. As indicated in note 35 above, an oral culture will generate, not a fixed text, but a variety of versions which have their local and topical value in giving life to the *wairua* of the 'text' which comprehends and transcends them all. As it is so pertinent to my larger argument, I have here incorporated opinion from the Waitangi Tribunal's report, although neither the report nor the circumstances which occasioned it existed when this paper was delivered. Treaties are likely to become a more frequently used resource, not only for ethnohistorical studies, but for concepts of text in complex political, linguistic and cultural contexts, for their mixed modes of oral and written discourse, for their synchronic and diachronic dimensions, for their continuing human implications (they are not exactly dramatic fictions), and for the forcing circumstances which compel the law to offer what are essentially editorial judgements. David R. Miller of the Newberry Library tells me that the microfilming of 9,552 Iroquois treaty documents has been almost completed and that an associated study has just been published: *The history and culture of Iroquois diplomacy: an interdisciplinary guide to the treaties of the Six Nations and League* (Syracuse, 1983). The value of treaties as texts for analysis of diplomacy as a matter of cultural as well as political contact is well demonstrated in Dorothy V. Jones's *Licence for empire: colonisation by treaty* (Chicago, 1983). A. S. Keller, O. J. Lissitzyn, and F. J. Mann, *Creation of rights of sovereignty through symbolic acts, 1400–1800* (New York, 1938) remains a convenient historical summary of European attitudes and practice.

88  Letter to G. Robertson, 1 March 1899: Mitchell MS AC 83/4.

## PART THREE

# Commodifying print: Books and authors

# EDITORS' INTRODUCTION

The establishment of print as a major form of social communication in the centuries following the Gutenberg print revolution, meant also the development of print as a commodity and textual production as a profession. Demands for books created a demand for authors to write and produce them. But what exactly is meant by 'authorship' has been subject to debate and changing interpretation in critical circles over recent years. Questions about and examinations of the notion of the author are at the heart of this part's extracts. Roland Barthes's oft-quoted 'Death of the Author' set the tone in the 1960s for upturning previous assumptions about the role of the author in the formation of texts. His point, as of that in Michel Foucault's response, was to attempt to shift critical emphasis from author-centred enquiry to reader-based analysis.

Decentering and decoupling the author from texts was not a new concept: elevating the common reader to ultimate creator of textual meaning was. But as Foucault was clear to point out, eliminating the authorial role completely from the textual production equation was not satisfactory. 'Authorship' was a cultural formation inseparable from the commodification of literature: literary reputation could and did shape cultural responses to texts in a manner not accounted for by Barthesian analysis. Subsequent developments in book history studies have expanded and developed critical thinking regarding these matters. Thus Mark Rose's empirically situated piece, which establishes that the struggle over authorship as a concept can be located in the creation of literary property under copyright legislation in Britain in the eighteenth century, itself a product of national struggle between the Scots and the English.

Copyright legislation allowed authors legal rights to be recognized as originators and therefore owners of a specific commodity (in this case text). It formed the basis for a new profession and industry to develop exponentially in the eighteenth century, one that combined the manufacture and distribution of cultural commodities with an affirmation of the author (rather than as before the printer/bookseller) as the original source of such material. John Brewer's piece traces the resulting development of the literary marketplace in eighteenth-century Britain. These changes in social and cultural networks of literary production laid the groundwork for the full-fledged emergence of authorship as a respected and lucrative profession in the industrially driven and print-literate world of nineteenth-century Western Europe and North America.

An example of the incorporation of such matters into revisionist analyses of authorial concepts is Jane Tompkins's 1985 *Sensational Designs: The Cultural Work of American Fiction: 1790–1860*, a portion of which is reproduced here. Tompkins's contrast of the New York based Sophie Warner's waning cultural significance with Nathaniel Hawthorne's emerging literary reputation (the latter achieved as a result of cultural and social networks embedded in mid-nineteenth-century New England), very clearly illustrates the manner in which authorial reputation and textual readings could shift according to changing cultural conditions. As Tompkins points out, how both authors emerged into or disappeared from cultural visibility and the literary marketplace can be traced to the specific social, literary and economic circumstances in which they were read and produced. John Sutherland's piece provides a contrasting view of authorial identity and activity in Victorian Britain. His detailed empirical study of 878 novelists offers insight into the vastness of the infrastructure which by the late nineteenth century had developed to support and produce textual material for cultural consumption.

With such appraisals has come recognition that book history studies now needs to take into account the economic imperatives governing textual production. The work of James L. W. West III illustrates, for example, the manner in which twentieth-century American authors such as F. Scott Fitzgerald maximized earnings through manipulation of literary markets and diverse print outlets such as modern mass-circulation magazines and film and radio. N. N. Feltes's piece rounds off the section with a strongly Marxist perspective on textual production, offering a case study of E. M. Forster that highlights the links between commercial interests, changing marketplaces, business practices and textual production in the wake of the Net Book Agreement brokered by British publishers at the turn of the twentieth century.

# Chapter 14

# Roland Barthes

## THE DEATH OF THE AUTHOR

In his story *Sarrasine* Balzac, describing a castrato disguised as a woman, writes the following sentence: '*This was woman herself, with her sudden fears, her irrational whims, her instinctive worries, her impetuous boldness, her fussings, and her delicious sensibility*.' Who is speaking thus? Is it the hero of the story bent on remaining ignorant of the castrato hidden beneath the woman? Is it Balzac the individual, furnished by his personal experience with a philosophy of Woman? Is it Balzac the author professing 'literary' ideas on femininity? Is it universal wisdom? Romantic psychology? We shall never know, for the good reason that writing is the destruction of every voice, of every point of origin. Writing is that neutral, composite, oblique space where our subject slips away, the negative where all identity is lost, starting with the very identity of the body writing.

No doubt it has always been that way. As soon as a fact is *narrated* no longer with a view to acting directly on reality but intransitively, that is to say, finally outside of any function other than that of the very practice of the symbol itself, this disconnection occurs, the voice loses its origin, the author enters into his own death, writing begins. The sense of this phenomenon, however, has varied; in ethnographic societies the responsibility for a narrative is never assumed by a person but by a mediator, shaman or relator whose 'performance' – the mastery of the narrative code – may possibly be admired but never his 'genius'. The author is a modern figure, a product, of our society insofar as, emerging from the Middle Ages with English empiricism, French rationalism and the personal faith of the Reformation, it discovered the prestige of the individual, of, as it is more nobly put, the 'human person'. It is thus logical that in literature it should be this positivism, the epitome and culmination of capitalist ideology, which has attached the greatest importance to the 'person' of the author. The *author* still reigns in histories of literature, biographies of writers, interviews, magazines, as in the very consciousness of men of letters anxious to unite their person and their work through diaries and memoirs. The image of literature to be found in ordinary culture is tyrannically centred on the author, his person, his life, his tastes, his passions, while criticism still consists for the most part in saying that Baudelaire's work is the failure of Baudelaire the man, Van Gogh's his madness, Tchaikovsky's his vice. The *explanation* of a work is always sought in the man or woman who produced it, as if it were always in the end, through the more or less transparent allegory of the fiction, the voice of a single person, the *author* 'confiding' in us.

Though the sway of the Author remains powerful (the new criticism has often done no more than consolidate it), it goes without saying that certain writers have long since attempted to loosen it. In France, Mallarmé was doubtless the first to see and to foresee in its full extent the necessity to substitute language itself for the person who until then had been supposed to be its owner. For him, for us too, it is language which speaks, not the author; to write is, through a prerequisite impersonality (not at all to be confused with the castrating objectivity of the realist novelist), to reach that point where only language acts, 'performs', and not 'me'. Mallarmé's entire poetics consists in suppressing the author in the interests of writing (which is, as will be seen, to restore the place of the reader). Valéry, encumbered by a psychology of the Ego, considerably diluted Mallarmé's theory but, his taste for classicism leading him to turn to the lessons of rhetoric, he never stopped calling into question and deriding the Author; he stressed the linguistic and, as it were, 'hazardous' nature of his activity, and throughout his prose works he militated in favour of the essentially verbal condition of literature, in the face of which all recourse to the writer's interiority seemed to him pure superstition. Proust himself, despite the apparently psychological character of what are called his *analyses*, was visibly concerned with the task of inexorably blurring, by an extreme subtilization, the relation between the writer and his characters; by making of the narrator not he who has seen and felt nor even he who is writing, but he who *is going to write* (the young man in the novel – but, in fact, how old is he and who is he? – wants to write but cannot; the novel ends when writing at last becomes possible), Proust gave modern writing its epic. By a radical reversal, instead of putting his life into his novel, as is so often maintained, he made of his very life a work for which his own book was the model; so that it is clear to us that Charlus does not imitate Montesquiou but that Montesquiou – in his anecdotal, historical reality – is no more than a secondary fragment, derived from Charlus. Lastly, to go no further than this prehistory of modernity, Surrealism, though unable to accord language a supreme place (language being system and the aim of the movement being, romantically, a direct subversion of codes – itself moreover illusory: a code cannot be destroyed, only 'played off'), contributed to the desacrilization of the image of the Author by ceaselessly recommending the abrupt disappointment of expectations of meaning (the famous surrealist 'jolt'), by entrusting the hand with the task of writing as quickly as possible what the head itself is unaware of (automatic writing), by accepting the principle and the experience of several people writing together. Leaving aside literature itself (such distinctions really becoming invalid), linguistics has recently provided the destruction of the Author with a valuable analytical tool by showing that the whole of the enunciation is an empty process, functioning perfectly without there being any need for it to be filled with the person of the interlocutors. Linguistically, the author is never more than the instance writing, just as *I* is nothing other than the instance saying *I*: language knows a 'subject', not a 'person', and this subject, empty outside of the very enunciation which defines it, suffices to make language 'hold together', suffices, that is to say, to exhaust it.

The removal of the Author (one could talk here with Brecht of a veritable 'distancing', the Author diminishing like a figurine at the far end of the literary stage) is not merely an historical fact or an act of writing; it utterly transforms the modern text (or – which is the same thing – the text is henceforth made and read in such a way that at all its levels the author is absent). The temporality is different. The Author, when believed in, is always conceived of as the past of his own book: book and author stand automatically on a single line divided into a *before* and an *after*. The Author is thought to *nourish* the book, which is to say that he exists before it, thinks, suffers, lives for it, is in the same relation of antecedence to his work as a father to his child. In complete contrast, the modern scriptor is born simultaneously with the text, is in no way equipped with a being preceding or exceeding the writing, is not the subject with the book as predicate; there is no other time than that of the enunciation and every text is eternally written *here and now*. The fact is (or, it follows) that *writing* can no longer designate an operation of recording, notation, representation, 'depiction' (as the Classics would say); rather, it designates exactly what linguists, referring to Oxford philosophy, call a performative, a rare verbal form (exclusively given in the first person and in the present tense) in which the enunciation has no other content (contains no other proposition) than the act by which it is uttered – something like the *I declare* of kings or the *I sing* of very ancient poets. Having buried the Author, the modern scriptor can thus no longer believe, as according to the pathetic view of his predecessors, that this hand is too slow for his thought or passion and that consequently, making a law of necessity, he must emphasize this delay and indefinitely 'polish' his form. For him, on the contrary, the hand, cut off from any voice, borne by a pure gesture of inscription (and not of expression), traces a field without origin – or which, at least, has no other origin than language itself, language which ceaselessly calls into question all origins.

We know now that a text is not a line of words releasing a single 'theological' meaning (the 'message' of the Author-God) but a multi-dimensional space in which a variety of writings, none of them original, blend and clash. The text is a tissue of quotations drawn from the innumerable centres of culture. Similar to Bouvard and Pécuchet, those eternal copyists, at once sublime and comic and whose profound ridiculousness indicates precisely the truth of writing, the writer can only imitate a gesture that is always anterior, never original. His only power is to mix writings, to counter the ones with the others, in such a way as never to rest on any one of them. Did he wish to *express himself*, he ought at least to know that the inner 'thing' he thinks to 'translate' is itself only a ready-formed dictionary, its words only explainable through other words, and so on indefinitely; something experienced in exemplary fashion by the young Thomas de Quincey, he who was so good at Greek that in order to translate absolutely modern ideas and images into that dead language, he had, so Baudelaire tells us (in *Paradis Artificiels*), 'created for himself an unfailing dictionary, vastly more extensive and complex than those resulting from the ordinary patience of purely literary themes'. Succeeding the Author, the scriptor no longer bears within him passions, humours, feelings, impressions, but rather this immense dictionary from which he draws a writing that can know no halt: life never does more than imitate the book, and the book itself is only a tissue of signs, an imitation that is lost, infinitely deferred.

Once the Author is removed, the claim to decipher a text becomes quite futile. To give a text an Author is to impose a limit on that text, to furnish it with a final signified, to close the writing. Such a conception suits criticism very well, the latter then allotting itself the important task of discovering the Author (or its hypostases: society, history, psyché, liberty) beneath the work: when the Author has been found, the text is 'explained' – victory to the critic. Hence there is no surprise in the fact that, historically, the reign of the Author has also been that of the Critic, nor again in the fact that criticism (be it new) is today undermined along with the Author. In the multiplicity of writing, everything is to be *disentangled*, nothing *deciphered*; the structure can be followed, 'run' (like the thread of a stocking) at every point and at every level, but there is nothing beneath: the space of writing is to be ranged over, not pierced; writing ceaselessly posits meaning ceaselessly to evaporate it, carrying out a systematic exemption of meaning. In precisely this way literature (it would be better from now on to say *writing*), by refusing to assign a 'secret', ultimate meaning, to the text (and to the world as text), liberates what may be called an anti-theological activity, an activity that is truly revolutionary since to refuse to fix meaning is, in the end, to refuse God and his hypostases – reason, science, law.

Let us come back to the Balzac sentence. No one, no 'person', says it: its source, its voice, is not the true place of the writing, which is reading. Another – very precise – example will help to make this clear: recent research (J.-P. Vernant[1]) has demonstrated the constitutively ambiguous nature of Greek tragedy, its texts being woven from words with double meanings that each character understands unilaterally (this perpetual misunderstanding is exactly the 'tragic'); there is, however, someone who understands each word in its duplicity and who, in addition, hears the very deafness of the characters speaking in front of him – this someone being precisely the reader (or here, the listener). Thus is revealed the total existence of writing: a text is made of multiple writings, drawn from many cultures and entering into mutual relations of dialogue, parody, contestation, but there is one place where this multiplicity is focused and that place is the reader, not, as was hitherto said, the author. The reader is the space on which all the quotations that make up a writing are inscribed without any of them being lost; a text's unity lies not in its origin but in its destination. Yet this destination cannot any longer be personal: the reader is without history, biography, psychology; he is simply that *someone* who holds together in a single field all the traces by which the written text is constituted. Which is why it is derisory to condemn the new writing in the name of a humanism hypocritically turned champion of the reader's rights. Classic criticism has never paid any attention to the reader; for it, the writer is the only person in literature. We are now beginning to let ourselves be fooled no longer by the arrogant antiphrastical recriminations of good society in favour of the very thing it sets aside, ignores, smothers, or destroys; we know that to give writing its future, it is necessary to overthrow the myth: the birth of the reader must be at the cost of the death of the Author.

## Note

1   Cf. Jean-Pierre Vernant (with Pierre Vidal-Naquet), *Mythe et tragédie en Grèce ancienne*, Paris 1972 esp. pp. 19–40, 99–131.

# Chapter 15

# Michel Foucault

## WHAT IS AN AUTHOR?

The coming into being of the notion of 'author' constitutes the privileged moment of *individualization* in the history of ideas, knowledge, literature, philosophy, and the sciences. Even today, when we reconstruct the history of a concept, literary genre, or school of philosophy, such categories seem relatively weak, secondary, and superimposed scansions in comparison with the solid and fundamental unit of the author and the work.

I shall not offer here a sociohistorical analysis of the author's persona. Certainly it would be worth examining how the author became individualized in a culture like ours, what status he has been given, at what moment studies of authenticity and attribution began, in what kind of system of valorization the author was involved, at what point we began to recount the lives of authors rather than of heroes, and how this fundamental category of 'the-man-and-his-work criticism' began. For the moment, however, I want to deal solely with the relationship between text and author and with the manner in which the text points to this 'figure' that, at least in appearance, is outside it and antecedes it.

Beckett nicely formulates the theme with which I would like to begin: '"What does it matter who is speaking," someone said, "what does it matter who is speaking".' In this indifference appears one of the fundamental ethical principles of contemporary writing (*écriture*). I say 'ethical' because this indifference is not really a trait characterizing the manner in which one speaks and writes, but rather a kind of immanent rule, taken up over and over again, never fully applied, not designating writing as something completed, but dominating it as a practice. Since it is too familiar to require a lengthy analysis, this immanent rule can be adequately illustrated here by tracing two of its major themes.

First of all, we can say that today's writing has freed itself from the dimension of expression. Referring only to itself, but without being restricted to the confines of its interiority, writing is identified with its own unfolded exteriority. This means that it is an interplay of signs arranged less according to its signified content than according to the very nature of the signifier. Writing unfolds like a game (*jeu*) that invariably goes beyond its own rules and transgresses its limits. In writing, the point is not to manifest or exalt the act of writing, nor is it to pin a subject within language; it is, rather, a question of creating a space into which the writing subject constantly disappears.

The second theme, writing's relationship with death, is even more familiar. This link subverts an old tradition exemplified by the Greek epic, which was intended to perpetuate the immortality of the hero: if he was willing to die young, it was so that his life, consecrated and magnified by death, might pass into immortality; the narrative then redeemed this accepted death. In another way, the motivation, as well as the theme and the pretext of Arabian narrative – such as *The Thousand and One Nights* – was also the eluding of death: one spoke, telling stories into the early morning, in order to forestall death, to postpone the day of reckoning that would silence the narrator. Scheherazade's narrative is an effort, renewed each night, to keep death outside the circle of life.

Our culture has metamorphosed this idea of narrative, or writing, as something designed to ward off death. Writing has become linked to sacrifice, even to the sacrifice of life: it is now a voluntary effacement which does not need to be represented in books, since it is brought about in the writer's very existence. The work, which once had the duty of providing immortality, now possesses the right to kill, to be its author's murderer, as in the cases of Flaubert, Proust, and Kafka. That is not all, however: this relationship between writing and death is also manifested in the effacement of the writing subject's individual characteristics. Using all the contrivances that he sets up between himself and what he writes, the writing subject cancels out the signs of his particular individuality. As a result, the mark of the writer is reduced to nothing more than the singularity of his absence; he must assume the role of the dead man in the game of writing.

None of this is recent; criticism and philosophy took note of the disappearance – or death – of the author some time ago. But the consequences of their discovery of it have not been sufficiently examined, nor has its import been accurately measured. A certain number of notions that are intended to replace the privileged position of the author actually seem to preserve that privilege and suppress the real meaning of his disappearance. I shall examine two of these notions, both of great importance today.

The first is the idea of the work. It is a very familiar thesis that the task of criticism is not to bring out the work's relationships with the author, nor to reconstruct through the text a thought or experience, but rather to analyze the work through its structure, its architecture, its intrinsic form, and the play of its internal relationships. At this point, however, a problem arises: What is a work? What is this curious unity which we designate as a work? Of what elements is it composed? Is it not what an author has written? Difficulties appear immediately. if an individual were not an author, could we say that what he wrote, said, left behind in his papers, or what has been collected of his remarks, could be called a 'work'? When Sade was not considered an author, what was the status of his papers? Were they simply rolls of paper onto which he ceaselessly uncoiled his fantasies during his imprisonment?

Even when an individual has been accepted as an author, we must still ask whether everything that he wrote, said, or left behind is part of his work. The problem is both theoretical and technical. When undertaking the publication of Nietzsche's works, for example, where should one stop? Surely everything must be published, but what is 'everything'? Everything that Nietzsche himself published, certainly. And what about the rough drafts for his works? Obviously. The plans for his aphorisms? Yes. The deleted passages and the notes at the bottom of the page? Yes. What if, within a workbook filled with aphorisms, one finds a reference, the notation of a meeting or of an address, or a laundry list: Is it a work, or not? Why not? And so on, ad infinitum. How can one define a work amid the millions of traces left by someone after his death? A theory of the work does not exist, and the empirical task of those who naively undertake the editing of works often suffers in the absence of such a theory.

We could go even further: Does *The Thousand and One Nights* constitute a work? What about Clement of Alexandria's *Miscellanies* or Diogenes Laertius's *Lives*? A multitude of questions arises with regard to this notion of the work. Consequently, it is not enough to declare that we should do without the writer (the author) and study the work itself. The word *work* and the unity that it designates are probably as problematic as the status of the author's individuality. . . .

It is not enough, however, to repeat the empty affirmation that the author has disappeared. For the same reason, it is not enough to keep repeating (after Nietzsche) that God and man have died a common death. Instead, we must locate the space left empty by the author's disappearance, follow the distribution of gaps and breaches, and watch for the openings that this disappearance uncovers.

First, we need to clarify briefly the problems arising from the use of the author's name. What is an author's name? How does it function? Far from offering a solution, I shall only indicate some of the difficulties that it presents.

The author's name is a proper name, and therefore it raises the problems common to all proper names. (Here I refer to Searle's analyses, among others.[1]) Obviously, one cannot turn a proper name into a pure and simple reference. It has other than indicative functions: more than an indication, a gesture, a finger pointed at someone, it is the equivalent of a description. When one says 'Aristotle', one employs a word that is the equivalent of one, or a series, of definite descriptions, such as 'the author of the *Analytics*', 'the founder of ontology', and so forth. One cannot stop there, however, because a proper name does not have just one signification. When we discover that Rimbaud did not write *La Chasse spirituelle*, we cannot pretend that the meaning of this proper name, or that of the author, has been altered. The proper name and the author's name are situated between the two poles of description and designation: they must have a certain link with what they name, but one that is neither entirely in the mode of designation nor in that of description; it must be a *specific* link. However – and it is here that the particular difficulties of the author's name arise – the links between the proper name and the individual named and between the author's name and what it names are not isomorphic and do not function in the same way. There are several differences.

If, for example, Pierre Dupont does not have blue eyes, or was not born in Paris, or is not a doctor, the name Pierre Dupont will still always refer to the same person; such things do not modify the link of designation. The problems raised by the author's name are much more complex, however. If I discover that Shakespeare was not born in the house that we visit today, this is a modification which, obviously, will not alter the functioning of the author's name. But if we proved that Shakespeare did not write those sonnets which pass for his, that would constitute a significant change and affect the manner in which the author's name functions. If we proved that Shakespeare wrote Bacon's *Organon* by showing that the same author wrote both the works of Bacon and those of Shakespeare, that would be a third type of change which would entirely modify the functioning of the author's name. The author's name is not, therefore, just a proper name like the rest.

Many other facts point out the paradoxical singularity of the author's name. To say that Pierre Dupont does not exist is not at all the same as saying that Homer or Hermes Trismegistus did not exist. In the first case, it means that no one has the name Pierre Dupont; in the second, it means that several people were mixed together under one name, or that the true author had none of the traits traditionally ascribed to the personae of Homer or Hermes. To say that X's real name is actually Jacques Durand instead of Pierre Dupont is not the same as saying that Stendhal's name was Henri Beyle. One could also question the meaning and functioning of propositions like 'Bourbaki is so-and-so, so-and-so, etc.' and 'Victor Eremita, Climacus, Anticlimacus, Frater Taciturnus, Constantine Constantius, all of these are Kierkegaard.'

These differences may result from the fact that an author's name is not simply an element in a discourse (capable of being either subject or object, of being replaced by a pronoun, and the like); it performs a certain role with regard to narrative discourse, assuring a classificatory function. Such a name permits one to group together a certain number of texts, define them, differentiate them from and contrast them to others. In addition, it establishes a relationship among the texts. Hermes Trismegistus did not exist, nor did Hippocrates – in the sense that Balzac existed – but the fact that several texts have been placed under the same name indicates that there has been established among them a relationship of homogeneity, filiation, authentication of some texts by the use of others, reciprocal explication, or concomitant utilization. The author's name serves to characterize a certain mode of being of discourse: the fact that the discourse has an author's name, that one can say 'this was written by so-and-so' or 'so-and-so is its author', shows that this discourse is not ordinary everyday speech that merely comes and goes, not something that is immediately consumable. On the contrary, it is a speech that must be received in a certain mode and that, in a given culture, must receive a certain status.

It would seem that the author's name, unlike other proper names, does not pass from the interior of a discourse to the real and exterior individual who produced it; instead, the name seems always to be present, marking off the edges of the text, revealing, or at least characterizing, its mode of being. The author's name manifests the appearance of a certain discursive set and indicates the status of this discourse within a society and a culture. It has no legal status, nor is it located in the fiction of the work; rather, it is located in the break that founds a certain discursive construct and its very particular mode of being. As a result, we could say that in a civilization like our own there are a certain number of discourses that are endowed with the 'author function', while others are deprived of it. A private letter may well have a signer – it does not have an author; a contract may well have a guarantor – it does not have an author. An anonymous text posted on a wall probably has a writer – but not an author. The author function is therefore characteristic of the mode of existence, circulation, and functioning of certain discourses within a society. . . .

Up to this point I have unjustifiably limited my subject. Certainly the author function in painting, music, and other arts should have been discussed, but even supposing that we remain within the world of discourse, as I want to do, I seem to have given the term 'author' much too narrow a meaning. I have discussed the author only in the limited sense of a person to whom the production of a text, a book, or a work can be legitimately attributed. It is easy to see that in the sphere of discourse one can be the author of much more than a book – one can be the author of a theory, tradition, or discipline in which other books and authors will in their turn find a place. These authors are in a position which we shall call 'transdiscursive'. This is a recurring phenomenon – certainly as old as our civilization. Homer, Aristotle, and the Church Fathers, as well as the first mathematicians and the originators of the Hippocratic tradition, all played this role.

Furthermore, in the course of the nineteenth century, there appeared in Europe another, more uncommon, kind of author, whom one should confuse with neither the 'great' literary authors, nor the authors of religious texts, nor the founders of science. In a somewhat arbitrary way we shall call those who belong in this last group 'founders of discursivity'. They are unique in that they are not just the authors of their own works. They have produced something else: the possibilities and the rules for the formation of other texts. In this sense, they are very different, for example, from a novelist, who is, in fact, nothing more than the author of his own text. Freud is not just the author of *The Interpretation of Dreams* or *Jokes and Their Relation to the Unconscious*; Marx is not just the author of the *Communist Manifesto* or *Das Kapital*: they both have established an endless possibility of discourse.

Obviously, it is easy to object. One might say that it is not true that the author of a novel is only the author of his own text; in a sense, he also, provided that he acquires some 'importance', governs and commands more than that. To take a very simple example, one could say that Ann Radcliffe not only wrote *The Castles of Athlin and Dunbayne* and several other novels, but also made possible the appearance of the Gothic horror novel at the beginning of the nineteenth century; in that respect, her author function exceeds her own work. But I think there is an answer to this objection. These founders of discursivity (I use Marx and Freud as examples, because I believe them to be both the first and the most important cases) make possible something altogether different from what a novelist makes possible. Ann Radcliffe's texts opened the way for a certain number of resemblances and analogies which have their model or principle in her work. The latter contains characteristic signs, figures, relationships, and structures which could be reused by others. In other words, to say that Ann Radcliffe founded the Gothic horror novel means that in the nineteenth-century Gothic novel one will find, as in Ann Radcliffe's works, the theme of the heroine caught in the trap of her own innocence, the hidden castle, the character of the black, cursed hero devoted to making the world expiate the evil done to him, and all the rest of it.

On the other hand, when I speak of Marx or Freud as founders of discursivity, I mean that they made possible not only a certain number of analogies, but also (and equally important) a certain number of differences. They have created a possibility for something other than their discourse, yet something belonging to what they founded. To say that Freud founded psychoanalysis does not (simply) mean that we find the concept of the libido or the technique of dream analysis in the works of Karl Abraham or Melanie Klein; it means that Freud made possible a certain number of divergences – with respect to his own texts, concepts, and hypotheses – that all arise from the psychoanalytic discourse itself. . . .

To conclude, I would like to review the reasons why I attach a certain importance to what I have said.

First, there are theoretical reasons. On the one hand, an analysis in the direction that I have outlined might provide for an approach to a typology of discourse. It seems to me, at least at first glance, that such a typology cannot be constructed solely from the grammatical features, formal structures, and objects of discourse: more likely there exist properties or relationships peculiar to discourse (not reducible to the rules of grammar and logic), and one must use these to distinguish the major categories of discourse. The relationship (or nonrelationship) with an author, and the different forms this relationship takes, constitute – in a quite visible manner – one of these discursive properties.

On the other hand, I believe that one could find here an introduction to the historical analysis of discourse. Perhaps it is time to study discourses not only in terms of their expressive value or formal transformations, but according to their modes of existence. The modes of circulation, valorization, attribution, and appropriation of discourses vary with each culture and are modified within each. The manner in which they are articulated according to social relationships can be more readily understood, I believe, in the activity of the author function and in its modifications than in the themes or concepts that discourses set in motion.

It would seem that one could also, beginning with analyses of this type, reexamine the privileges of the subject. I realize that in undertaking the internal and architectonic analysis of a work (be it a literary text, philosophical system, or scientific work), in setting aside biographical and psychological references, one has already called back into question the absolute character and founding role of the subject. Still, perhaps one must return to this question, not in order to reestablish the theme of an originating subject, but to grasp the subject's points of insertion, modes of functioning, and system of dependencies. Doing so means overturning the traditional problem, no longer raising the questions: How can a free subject penetrate the substance of things and give it meaning? How can it activate the rules of a language from within and thus give rise to the designs which are properly its own? Instead, these questions will be raised: How, under what conditions, and in what forms can something like a subject appear in the order of discourse? What place can it occupy in each type of discourse, what functions can it assume, and by obeying what rules? In short, it is a matter of depriving the subject (or its substitute) of its role as originator, and of analyzing the subject as a variable and complex function of discourse.

Second, there are reasons dealing with the 'ideological' status of the author. The question then becomes: How can one reduce the great peril, the great danger with which fiction threatens our world? The answer is: one can reduce it with the author. The author allows a limitation of the cancerous and dangerous proliferation of signification, within a world where one is thrifty not only with one's resources and riches, but also with one's discourses and their significations. The author is the principle of thrift in the proliferation of meaning. As a result, we must entirely reverse the traditional idea of the author. We are accustomed, as we have seen earlier, to saying that the author is the genial creator of a work in which he deposits, with infinite wealth and generosity, an inexhaustible world of significations. We are used to thinking that the author is so different from all other men, and so transcendent with regard to all languages that, as soon as he speaks, meaning begins to proliferate, to proliferate indefinitely.

The truth is quite the contrary: the author is not an indefinite source of significations which fill a work; the author does not precede the works; he is a certain functional principle by which, in our culture, one limits, excludes, and chooses; in short, by which one impedes the free circulation, the free manipulation, the free composition, decomposition, and recomposition of fiction. In fact, if we are accustomed to presenting the author as a genius, as a perpetual surging of invention, it is because, in reality, we make him function in exactly the opposite fashion. One can say that the author is an ideological product, since we represent him as the opposite of his historically real function. (When a historically given function is represented in a figure that inverts it, one has an ideological production.) The author is therefore the ideological figure by which one marks the manner in which we fear the proliferation of meaning.

In saying this, I seem to call for a form of culture in which fiction would not be limited by the figure of the author. It would be pure romanticism, however, to imagine a culture in which the fictive would operate in an absolutely free state, in which fiction would be put at the disposal of everyone and would develop without passing through something like a necessary or constraining figure. Although, since the eighteenth century, the author has played the role of the regulator of the fictive, a role quite characteristic of our era of industrial and bourgeois society, of individualism and private property, still, given the historical modifications that are taking place, it does not seem necessary that the author function remain constant in form, complexity, and even in existence. I think that, as our society changes, at the very moment when it is in the process of changing, the author function will disappear, and in such a manner that fiction and its polysemous texts will once again function according to another mode, but still with a system of constraint – one which will no longer be the author, but which will have to be determined or, perhaps, experienced.

All discourses, whatever their status, form, value, and whatever the treatment to which they will be subjected, would then develop in the anonymity of a murmur. We would no longer hear the questions that have been rehashed for so long: Who really spoke? Is it really he and not someone else? With what authenticity or originality? And what part of his deepest self did he express in his discourse? Instead, there would be other questions, like these: What are the modes of existence of this discourse? Where has it been used, how can it circulate, and who can appropriate it for himself? What are the places in it where there is room for possible subjects? Who can assume these various subject functions? And behind all these questions, we would hear hardly anything but the stirring of an indifference: What difference does it make who is speaking?

## Note

1   *Ed.*: John Searle, *Speech Acts: An Essay in the Philosophy of Language* (Cambridge, Eng.: Cambridge University Press, 1969), pp. 162–74.

# Chapter 16

# Mark Rose

## LITERARY PROPERTY DETERMINED

At one level, the literary-property question was a legal struggle about the nature of property and how the law might adapt itself to the changed circumstances of an economy based on trade. At another, it was a contest about how far the ideology of possessive individualism should be extended into the realm of cultural production. At still another, it was a commercial encounter, played out in the form of a national contest between England and Scotland, in which a deeply entrenched business establishment was challenged by outsiders. The complex layering of the literary-property struggle generated a number of intriguing contradictions, among them that it was in the name of the liberal value of 'property' – and authorial property no less – that the London booksellers were defending a monopolistic system with roots in the medieval guild culture. Their principal challenger was a scrappy and determined Scottish businessman, 'who saw a new and lucrative opening in the bookselling trade, and availed himself of it' (Gray 182).

Alexander Donaldson's career as a bookseller began in 1750 in Edinburgh shortly after the determination of *Millar v. Kinkaid* in the Court of Session. After this decision was announced, Donaldson, according to his own account, took counsel from both Scottish and English lawyers who confirmed him in his opinion that copyright was limited to the statutory term. Thereupon he went into the bookselling business in a large way, specializing in inexpensive reprints of standard works whose copyright term had expired, including according to the *Eighteenth-Century Short Title Catalogue* works by Defoe, Fielding, Gay, Locke, Milton, Pope, Shakespeare, Swift, Thomson, and Young. Donaldson prospered, and his house and shop became something of a center for literary Scotsmen, among them the young James Boswell who, together with his friend Andrew Erskine, published an anthology of contemporary Scottish poems with Donaldson. Eventually Donaldson started a journal, the biweekly *Edinburgh Advertiser*, which also did very well.

For many years after their unsuccessful appeal of *Millar v. Kinkaid*, the great London booksellers ignored Donaldson and the other Scots. But then in the late 1750s and early 1760s they took up their campaign to establish the common-law copyright and to drive the Scottish reprint business out of England. In 1763 Donaldson responded by boldly opening his own shop in London, where he sold his books at 30–50 percent under the usual London prices. Samuel Johnson, for one, was incensed. Boswell reports that Johnson, who held the London booksellers in high regard, 'was loud and violent against Mr. Donaldson', saying that it had always been understood by the trade that 'he, who buys the copy-right of a book from the authour, obtains a perpetual property' (*Life* 1:438, 439). A barrage of harassing Chancery lawsuits followed the opening of the shop. Donaldson retaliated by publishing *Some Thoughts on the State of Literary Property Humbly Submitted to the Consideration of the Public* in which he threatened to sue for damages caused by 'unlawful combination, whereby the *London* booksellers have conspired to beat down all opposition, and to suppress the sale of every book reprinted in the other parts of the united kingdom' (10).

Despite having to contend with what he later, in his petition against the Bookseller's Relief Bill of 1774, termed 'the united force of almost all the eminent booksellers of London and Westminster' (*Petitions and Papers* 10), Donaldson was determined to keep his reprint business – from which he was making a fortune, despite his legal expenses. In 1765, after the aborted decision in *Tonson v. Collins*, Donaldson succeeded in getting dissolved two injunctions against him for publication of James Thomson's poems. Sounding much like his predecessor Lord Hardwicke in *Tonson v. Walker* a dozen years earlier, Lord Chancellor Northington, who heard the arguments in *Osborne v. Donaldson* (1765) and *Millar v. Donaldson* (1765), remarked that the issue of the common-law right was 'a point of so much difficulty and consequence, that he should not determine it at the hearing, but should send it to law for the opinion of the judges'. Northington said that 'he desired to be understood as giving no opinion on the subject'. He added, however, that he thought it might be 'dangerous to determine that the author has a perpetual property in his books, for such a property would give him not only a right to publish, but to suppress too' (*ER* 28:924). Probably Donaldson would have welcomed taking the question further, as Northington invited – it was, he said, 'his fixed purpose that the law should be finally settled in the Supreme Court of the kingdom' (*Petitions and Papers* 10) – but neither Osborne nor Millar wished to pursue the issue. Instead, Millar took action against Robert Taylor of Berwick upon Tweed, again in connection with Thomson's *The Seasons*, and thus began the landmark case of *Millar v. Taylor*.[1] . . .

Andrew Millar died in June 1768 while *Millar v. Taylor* was pending. A year later, after the momentous King's Bench decision, Millar's copyrights were put up for sale by his estate, and Thomas Becket and a group of other London printers and stationers purchased the rights in *The Seasons* and a number of other Thomson poems for £505. In January 1771 the new proprietors of Thomson, armed with the King's Bench decision, filed a bill in Chancery against Donaldson and his brother John, with whom he was associated in connection with the 1768 edition of *The Seasons*. An injunction was granted, and in November 1772 it was made perpetual in a hearing before Lord Chancellor Apsley who, as he explained later at the time of Donaldson's appeal, was merely affirming the decree as a matter of course, pursuant to the decision in *Millar v. Taylor*. Simultaneously, John Hinton's case against Donaldson over *Stackhouse's Bible*, initiated in the Court of Session just before the start of Becket's action in Chancery, was making its way to a decision. On 27 July 1773 the Court of Session rendered its decision in favor of Donaldson, and with this precedent in hand to offset *Millar v. Taylor*, Donaldson appealed the Chancery injunction to the House of Lords. It was time to achieve his 'fixed purpose' of seeing the law of literary property settled by Britain's highest court.

*Donaldson v. Becket*, then, represented both an appeal of *Millar v. Taylor*, to which Donaldson was not a party, and an attempt to secure a confirmation of the Court of Session's decision in *Hinton v. Donaldson*. Sir James Burrow's report of *Millar v. Taylor*, entitled *The Question Concerning Literary Property Determined by the Court of King's Bench*, had been brought out the previous spring while the Scottish case was impending.[2] In order to make available a comparable account of *Hinton v. Donaldson*, Donaldson's old friend James Boswell, who was one of the junior counselors in the case, 'worked up his notes' and persuaded 'several of the judges to revise their opinions freely for the benefit of peers and posterity' (Brady 88). Boswell's *Decision of the Court of Session upon the Question of Literary Property*, published by Donaldson in an elegant edition, appeared according to an advertisement in the *Morning Chronicle* on February 1774, just in time for the opening of the appeal three days later. . . .

On 22 February the peers voted to overturn the Chancery injunction, and in Scotland the reaction was tumultuous: 'Great rejoicing in Edinburgh upon victory over literary property: bonfires and illuminations' (Ross 143). In England, at least among those connected with the London book trade, the reaction was also intense. A paragraph that appeared in the *Morning Chronicle* and in a number of other places after the decision claimed that a vast amount of property had been annihilated:

> By the above decision of the important question respecting copy-right in books, near 200,000 l. worth of what was honestly purchased at public sale, and which was yesterday thought property is now reduced to nothing. The Booksellers of London and Westminster, many of whom sold estates and houses to purchase Copy-right, are in a manner ruined, and those who after many years industry thought they had acquired a competency to provide for their families now find themselves without a shilling to devise to their successors.
>
> (*Morning Chronicle* 23 Feb. 1774)

Whether the London booksellers' panic was justified is doubtful – they were by no means ruined by the decision – but the note of desperation that marks their utterances is probably sincere enough. The works of Shakespeare, Bacon, Milton, Bunyan, and others, all the great properties of the trade that the booksellers had been accustomed to treat as private landed estates, were suddenly declared open commons.

In 1774 the House of Lords decided cases by a general vote of the peers, lawyers and laymen alike. Great weight was usually given to the opinions of the lawyers, but the practice of lay peers not being recognized when the House of Lords sat as a court had not yet been instituted. In important cases such as *Donaldson v. Becket*, however, the twelve common-law judges of the realm – the judges of King's Bench, Common Pleas, and the Exchequer – would be summoned to the House to hear the arguments of counsel and to give their advice on matters of law, after which the peers would debate the issue and vote.

The arguments in *Donaldson* were made by lawyers who had been involved in the literary-property question for years. . . . After the arguments, which added little of substance to what Sir James Burrow called this 'old and often-litigated question' (*ER* 98:201), Lord Chancellor Apsley put three questions to the judges. First, did the author have a common-law right to control the first publication of his work? Second, did the author's right, if it existed, survive publication? Third, if the right survived publication, was it taken away by the statute? To these questions Charles Pratt, Lord Camden, who was a former chief justice of Common Pleas, a lord chancellor, and the major opponent of perpetual copyright in the House of Lords, added two more. Did the author or his assigns have the sole right to a composition in perpetuity by the common law? Was this right in any way restrained or taken away by the statute? Insofar as they repeat the substance of the second and third of the original questions, Camden's questions were redundant, but he was trying to remind the judges and peers that the case was not just one of authors' rights but of booksellers', and that the issue was copyright in perpetuity.

The opinions of the judges, delivered one by one over the course of three days, were divided. On the first question, the judges divided 8 to 3 in support of the author's right. On the second, the vote was 7 to 4, again in support of the author's right. There is, however, a puzzle connected with the vote on the third question. According to both the *Journal of the House of Lords* and the standard legal and historical references, the vote on this question was 6 to 5 against the author's right – that is, the majority of the judges were of the opinion that the statute took away the author's right. But contemporary newspaper and other accounts give good reason to believe that the clerk of the House of Lords made an honest error in recording the opinion of one of the judges. Most likely the tally was 6 to 5 in favor of the common-law right surviving the statute. Note that only eleven judges voted: Lord Mansfield remained silent. James Burrow explained that Mansfield, whose opinion was well known, abstained 'from reasons of delicacy' since the case was in effect an appeal from his own court (*ER* 98:262). Had Mansfield voted, the tally would have been a substantial seven to five in favor of the common-law right surviving the statute. But the judges' opinions were only advisory; the final decision would be made by vote of the entire House; and in *Donaldson* the floor debate appears to have been very important.

Any issue thrown into the House of Lords was always in danger of becoming entangled in a network of personal and political rivalries. Lord Mansfield was the acknowledged champion of the common-law right. Lord Camden, who opened the debate with a speech of an hour and a half together with a motion that the Chancery decree against Donaldson be reversed, was Mansfield's 'lifelong political opponent' (Holdsworth, *History* 12:306). Camden, a Chathamite Whig, differed from Mansfield on most matters and had clashed with him many times before, most recently and bitterly in December 1770 when the issue was the rights of juries in cases of seditious libel. In that affair Camden directly challenged Mansfield to defend his opinion in a debate in the House of Lords, but Mansfield, to the dismay of some, refused.[3] Before the *Donaldson* appeal came on for debate, Camden had been inactive in the House of Lords for several years, but now he rose to challenge his old antagonist. Given their acrimonious history, it is hard to avoid the suspicion that part of Camden's purpose in leading the attack on the common-law right was a desire to embarrass Mansfield by having the peers repudiate his determination in *Millar v. Taylor*. . . .

As early as 16 February, after the first group of four judges had read their opinions, the *Public Advertiser* reported that Mansfield would not give his opinion as a judge but would speak later as a peer. On 22 February, after all the judges had spoken, the *Advertiser* repeated that Mansfield would speak as a peer. Camden's speech plainly called for a response, but, contrary to all expectation, Mansfield was silent. 'As Lord Mansfield had so warmly taken the Respondents side of the question on the determination in the Court of King's Bench between Miller and Taylor in 1769, it was yesterday much wondered at that his Lordship did not support his opinion in the H. of Peers'. So reported the *Morning Chronicle* on 23 February. The London booksellers, who had counted on Mansfield as their strongest bulwark in the House of Lords, felt betrayed and they were furious:

> It was his duty to have given an opinion on one side or other, and the neglecting to
> do so, was a manifest breach of his duty. Judges are paid by the public, and should
> render those services attendant on their office; and I should be glad to see a law passed
> to oblige them to a strict performance of their duty.
>
> (*Edinburgh Advertiser* 29 April 1774)

Why was Mansfield silent? The situation was reminiscent of Camden's challenge over jury rights four years earlier. Whatever it was that impelled him to keep his peace then – lack of courage or, more likely, lack of spirit for further bruising conflict – perhaps restrained him again. His opinion on literary property was a matter of public record, and it had been supported by a majority of the judges. If the House of Lords were inclined to overturn the Chancery decree and thereby declare that literary property was not perpetual, probably nothing he could say would materially affect the outcome.

Lord Camden was followed in the debate by Lord Chancellor Apsley, who had issued the original injunction and now delivered the *coup de grâce* to perpetual copyright by seconding the motion to overturn his own decree. He had made the decree, Apsley said, entirely as a matter of course pursuant to the judgement in *Millar v. Taylor*, and he viewed the action merely as a step toward a final determination of the copyright question in the House of Lords. As for the substance of the matter, he saw no precedents that could support the respondents in their argument. Moreover, he said he had evidence in the form of original letters from Dean Swift showing that the sense of Parliament was against the common-law right at the time of the Statute of Anne.[4] So his opinion was with the appellants. Three other peers spoke – Lord Lyttleton, who supported perpetual copyright as an encouragement to authors; the Bishop of Carlisle, who believed that literary property was limited to the statutory term, though the statute was defective and needed revision; and Lord Effingham, who thought perpetual copyright a danger to constitutional rights – and then the question was called. Eighty-four peers were present for the vote, an extraordinary show of interest (*LJ* 34:33).[5] Although Cobbett reports that the vote was 22 to 11 in favor of reversing the Chancery decree (17:1003), neither the *Journal of the House of Lords* nor the contemporary newspapers indicate a formal division of the House, and the *Public Advertiser* explicitly says there was no division (23 Feb. 1774). Most likely the decision was by simple voice vote. As Donaldson's newspaper reported, undoubtedly with some exaggeration about the unanimity of the House, Lord Chancellor Apsley desired 'all who were for reversing the judgment, to say Content, and such as were of a different opinion to say, Not: Nothing was heard but the word Content' (*Edinburgh Advertiser* 1 March 1774).

In voting as they did against the perpetual right, the Lords went against the judges, whose vote on the third question was 6 to 5–7 to 5 if Mansfield were counted – in favor of the common-law right surviving the statute. There is no great mystery about why they did so: the House of Lords had long been antipathetic to the London booksellers' monopolies, and the outcome in *Donaldson v. Becket* was consistent with the House's previous treatment of copyright questions. But on what basis did the peers make their determination? What understanding of the nature of copyright did they adopt? Were they persuaded that there never was a common-law right? Or did they believe that there was but that it ended with publication? Or that it was taken away by the statute? Were they persuaded by Lord Camden's argument that common-law determinations had to be founded on solid written authorities, or were they more influenced by the position associated with Joseph Yates that ideas could not in the nature of things be treated as property? Some peers may have voted on the basis of a legal theory, but many others, I suspect, were less concerned with the basis than with the result. Thus the peers gave an answer to the literary-property question, but they did not provide a rationale. 'It is more satisfactory . . . to convince by reason, than merely to silence by authority', Blackstone had said in the course of arguments in *Tonson v. Collins* (*ER* 96:182). But what the House of Lords did in *Donaldson v. Becket* was finally no more than to declare by authority that copyright henceforth would be limited in term.[6] . . .

A year before the decision in *Donaldson v. Becket*, Samuel Johnson, we recall, 'descanted on the subject of Literary Property' at dinner, coming down on the side of limited copyright. So he was reasonably satisfied with the result in *Donaldson*, though he thought the present copyright term too short. In a letter dated 7 March 1774, probably written at the request of the bookseller William Strahan to use in lobbying for the booksellers' relief bill, Johnson called the Lords' decision 'legally and politically right'. On the one hand, the author had a natural right to the profits of his work; on the other, it was wrong that a useful book should become 'perpetual and exclusive property';

therefore the author must purchase the protection of society by resigning 'so much of his claim as shall be deemed injurious or inconvenient to Society'. Johnson recommended an extension of the present two fourteen-year terms to a single one of the author's lifetime plus thirty years. This would in most cases yield a total term of about fifty years, which would be 'sufficient to reward the writer without any loss to the publick' (*Johnsonian Miscellanies* 2:444–445).

Johnson understood the decision in *Donaldson* as a compromise between the author's claim and the broader needs of society, but the peers themselves had articulated no such theory. As we have seen, they simply resolved the practical question of perpetuity. This was sufficient for the needs of the moment, but in the longer run it was necessary to make some sense of their vote, to reach some understanding as to the theory of copyright behind the limited term. What developed in the years after 1774 was a belief that *Donaldson* represented a compromise along lines similar to those that Johnson articulated, a belief that the decision curtailed the author's right without rejecting it entirely.

This understanding of *Donaldson* was made possible by the way the case was reported by James Burrow, whose excellent law reports were, and still are, regarded as authoritative. At the time of *Donaldson* it was technically a crime to print an account of a case on appeal in the House of Lords. *Donaldson* had of course been widely reported in the press, and in fact shortly after the decision two full reports were published as pamphlets under the titles *The Cases of the Appellants and Respondents in the Cause of Literary Property* and *The Pleadings of the Counsel Before the House of Lords in the Great Cause Concerning Literary Property*. But Burrow held an official position as Master of the Crown Office; so when he gave notice of *Donaldson* as part of his account of *Millar v. Taylor* in his 1776 collection of King's Bench reports, he discreetly limited himself to printing the record as it appeared in the *Minute Book* of the House of Lords. Like the *Minute Book*, Burrow gave the questions and the judges' votes, but no account of their speeches. At the conclusion he added a tally, a comment about Lord Mansfield, and a note about the reversal:

> So that of the eleven Judges, there were eight to three, upon the first question; seven to four, upon the second; and five to six, upon the third.
>
> It was notorious, that Lord Mansfield adhered to his opinion; and therefore concurred with the eight, upon the first question; with the seven, upon the second; and with the five, upon the third. But it being very unusual, (from reasons of delicacy,) for a peer to support his own judgment, upon an appeal to the House of Lords, he did not speak.
>
> And the Lord Chancellor seconding Lord Camden's motion 'to reverse; the decree was reversed.'
>
> (*ER* 98:262)

In presenting the tally for the third question as 5 to 6 against the author's right, Burrow perpetuated the error of the clerk of the House and made it appear as if the reversal followed as a matter of course from the judges' vote. Moreover, his suppression of Lord Camden's and Lord Chancellor Apsley's speeches made it seem as if the author's common-law right was not seriously challenged; on the contrary, he conveyed the impression that the determination in *Donaldson* consisted of a solid affirmation of the author's right, followed by a narrow decision that perpetuity was taken away by the statute.[7] This representation was a distortion in a number of respects. In fact only a single judge, Henry Gould of Common Pleas, had held that there was a common-law right impeached by the statute. (The others had either held that there was no common-law right – or at any rate none that survived publication – or that it was not taken away by the statute.) But even so it had much to recommend it, for it made it possible to suppose that, even if perpetual copyright had been rejected, still an author had a natural right to property in his work. Thus some years later in *Beckford v. Hood* (1798), the King's Bench found that *Donaldson* did not take away a plaintiff's right to sue at common law during the statutory term (*ER* 101:1164–68), and by the early nineteenth century Robert Maugham was able to state bluntly in his important *Treatise on the Laws of Literary Property* (1828) that in *Donaldson* 'it was determined by the House of Lords that the common law right was merged in the statute' (27).[8]

In the eighteenth-century debates themselves, the copyright issue had nearly always been framed in terms of absolutes: either authors had a common-law right or they did not. But if copyright was seen as a kind of compromise, then it became possible to reconsider the length of the copyright term, as Johnson had done. In 1814 a revised statute extended the copyright term to twenty-eight years after publication or the author's lifetime, whichever was longer, but this seemed paltry to those such as Robert Southey or William Wordsworth, who objected to any limitation. 'The question is simply this,' Southey said in his 1819 *Quarterly Review* essay: 'upon what principle, with what justice, or under what pretext of public good, are men of letters deprived of a perpetual property in the produce of their own labours, when all other persons enjoy it as their indefeasible right – a right beyond the power of any earthly authority to take away?' (211–212). And in a letter to J. Forbes Mitchell dated 21 April 1819, Wordsworth asked 'why the laws should interfere to take away those pecuniary emoluments which are the natural Inheritance of the posterity of Authors' (*Letters* 3:535).

In 1837 Thomas Noon Talfourd, a friend of Wordsworth's and an author as well as a member of Parliament, opened a campaign for revision of the copyright act. Talfourd reminded Parliament that a majority of the judges in *Donaldson* determined that an author had a perpetual common-law right. In principle, he saw 'no reason why authors should not be restored to that inheritance which, under the name of protection and encouragement, has been taken from them'. Nevertheless, because copyright had long been treated as a matter of compromise between those who denied the author's right altogether and 'those who think the property should last as long as the works which contain truth and beauty live', he would 'rest satisfied with a fairer adjustment of the difference than the last act of Parliament affords' (8).

The term that Talfourd proposed – the author's lifetime plus sixty years – drew opposition from the book trade, most notably from Thomas Tegg, who specialized in cheap reprints, and this roused Wordsworth to action.[9] The poet addressed some fifty letters to individual members of Parliament urging them to support Talfourd's bill. He declined to present his own petition. 'I am loth to think so unfavourably of Parliament as to deem that it requires petitions from authors as a ground for granting them a privilege, the justice of which is so obvious', he wrote to Talfourd on 18 April 1838 in a letter intended as a 'public declaration' of his sentiments on the copyright bill and in which he reasserted his conviction that the author's right should be perpetual (*Prose Works* 3:313). But, in fact, personal petitions from authors were necessary to overcome the opposition. In 1839 Wordsworth, Southey, Thomas Carlyle, and Hartley Coleridge as well as other literary figures submitted petitions to Parliament (*CJ* 94:237); finally, under the stewardship of Lord Mahon, Parliament passed the Copyright Act of 1842, which lasted until the twentieth century. This provided a term of the author's lifetime plus seven years or forty-two years from publication, whichever was longer – a resolution not far off from what Johnson had proposed in 1774.

Let us note a striking reversal. In the eighteenth century the proponents of perpetual copyright were the booksellers. By the early nineteenth century, however, the trade had adjusted to the limited copyright term, and many had a vested interest in it; it was authors such as Southey and Wordsworth who were now claiming that their rights should be perpetual.[10] *Donaldson v. Becket* is conventionally regarded as having established the statutory basis of copyright, and of course it did. But given the way Donaldson came to be understood, perhaps it should be simultaneously regarded as confirming the notion of the author's common-law right put forward by Mansfield and Blackstone.

## Notes

1   Millar did not charge Taylor with printing the books, only with publishing, exposing them to sale, and selling them in England, and indeed the *Eighteenth-Century Short Title Catalogue* lists no editions of *The Seasons* with Taylor's imprint. Possibly the books involved were printed by Donaldson, who had issued *The Seasons* in 1761 shortly after the statutory copyright expired, and a two-volume set of Thomson's complete *Poetical Works* in 1763.

2   In the preface to *The Question Concerning Literary Property* Burrow notes that the Scottish account of *Millar v. Taylor* – *Speeches or Arguments of the Judges of the Court of King's Bench in the Cause of Millar against Taylor* – was both 'full of Faults' and 'in Every Body's Hands' and that therefore 'Some whom I have long known, and whose Friendship I am proud of' urged him to prepare his own report as a separate publication. Burrow's 'Preface', dated 5 April 1773, suggests that his book was published in time for the Court of Session to read before ruling on *Hinton v. Donaldson* in July. In any event, the book was available and widely advertised the following winter at the time of the appeal to the House of Lords.

3   This famous episode involved Mansfield's instructions to the jury in *Rex v. Woodfall*, which concerned the Junius letters. Mansfield had instructed the jury only to consider whether Woodfall had printed the letters, not whether the letters themselves were libelous, which he reserved as a point of law. According to one opinion, Mansfield in not responding to Camden's challenge showed an 'equal want of courage and of self-possession' (Fifoot 46). But perhaps Mansfield, as Holdsworth suggests, refused to rise to the bait because he was beginning to weary of political strife (*History* 12:475). The episode is recounted in Cobbett 16:1302–22, as well as in Eeles 113—114.

4   I have not been able to identify any such letters.

5   For comparison, sixty-eight peers heard the king's speech from the throne on 13 January 1774, the opening day of the session. Fifty-six peers were present on 4 February, the opening day of the arguments of counsel, and approximately the same number for the later days of argument. Seventy-four peers were present on 15 February, the first day that the judges' opinions were heard, and sixty-five on the two later days of opinions, 17 and 21 February.

6   Howard Abrams suggests that the lords 'grounded their decision on the position that copyright had never existed as a right at common law' (1157). This was the position both of Lord Camden, who made the motion to reverse the decree, and of Lord Chancellor Apsley, who seconded it. But Camden's and Apsley's speeches, important as they were, cannot be regarded as the equivalent of a modern majority opinion. Many lay peers perhaps deferred to Camden and Apsley on the technical legal issues, though there was always the contrary opinion of Lord Mansfield to give pause to any lay peer who was seeking a legal authority to follow. As Whicher remarked some years ago, the House of Lords overturned the ruling in *Millar v. Taylor*, but 'when we ask what doctrine, precisely, the lords preferred to that which they thus cast aside, Clio (that coy muse) simply shrugs' (126).

7   Josiah Brown's subsequent account in the seventh volume of his *Reports of Cases, Upon Appeals and Writs of Error, in the High Court of Parliament* (1783) would not correct this impression. Brown's report includes a summary of the cases of the appellants and respondents as well as the questions put to the judges, but it does not give the substance of the judges' opinions or say anything about the floor debate. Unlike Burrow, Brown gives only the vote on the question of whether the statute impeached the common-law right. Five of the judges were in favor of the perpetuity or common-law right, he reports, and six were opposed whereupon it was ordered that the

decree be reversed (*ER* 1:837–849). The fuller report of the case in the seventeenth volume of *Cobbett's Parliamentary History* was not published until 1813 and was less cited than Burrow and Brown. On the development of the interpretation of *Donaldson v. Becket* see Whicher, esp. 130, and Howard Abrams, esp. 1164–66. Both Whicher and Abrams emphasize the crucial role of Burrow's and Brown's reports.

8    This tradition of interpretation continues to the present day. In *Copinger and Skone James on Copyright*, the standard modern British treatise, Burrow's report is cited and we are told in terms similar to those in Maugham that it was 'held by the majority of the judges that the common law right which an author had to copyright in his works became merged in the statutory right conferred by the Copyright Act' (5).

9    On Wordsworth's involvement in the campaign that led to the copyright act of 1842, see Zall, Moorman 551–555, and the commentary in Owen and Smyser 3: 303–306. On Tegg and the resistance to Talfourd's proposal, see Zall 134–135, and Feather, 'Publishers and Politicians, Part II' 48–50.

10    Moreover by the nineteenth century the notion of the author's right might be internalized by a writer. Susan Eilenberg points out the frugality of Wordsworth's style, his characteristic blurring of the distinction between the verbal and the material, his literary territoriality and resentment of plagiarism and remarks that Wordsworth's 'attitude towards his poems sometimes resembled that of a landowner towards his lands' (357). Part of Wordsworth's concern with copyright was his interest in providing an estate for his family, but the obsessiveness of his concern suggests that psychological factors were also at work. The length of the copyright term was linked to the length of an author's life. Eilenberg argues, then, that Wordsworth's campaign can also be understood as associated with a fear of death and annihilation: to reform copyright was for him 'to secure a refuge from oblivion' (369).

## References

Abrams, Howard B. 'The Historic Foundation of American Copyright Law: Exploding the Myth of Common Law Copyright', *Wayne Law Review* 29 (1983): 119–191.

Forbes, Gray, W. 'Alexander Donaldson and His Fight for Cheap Books', *Juridical Review* 38 (1926): 180–202.

Boswell, James. *The Life of Johnson*. 1799. Ed. George Birkbeck Hill, rev. L. E. Powell. Oxford: Clarendon, 1934–1964. 6 vols.

Brady, Frank. *James Boswell: The Later Years 1769–1795*. New York: McGraw, 1984.

Cobbett, William. *Parliamentary History of England*. London, 1806–1820. 36 vols.

Copinger, Walter Arthur, and E. P. Skone James. *Copinger and Skone James on Copyright*. 12th ed. London: Sweet, 1980.

Eeles, Henry S. *Lord Chancellor Camden and His Family*. London: Philip Allan. 1934.

Eilenberg, Susan. 'Mortal Pages: Wordsworth and the Reform of Copyright'. *ELH* 56 (1989): 351–374.

*English Reports* [*ER*]. Ed. A. Wood Renton. London: Stevens, 1900–1932. 178 vols.

Feather, John. 'Publishers and Politicians: The Remaking of the Law of Copyright in Britain, 1775–1842. Part I: Legal Deposit and the Battle of the Library Tax. Part II: The Rights of Authors'. *Publishing History* 24 (1988): 49–76; 25 (1989): 45–72.

Fifoot, C. H. S. *Lord Mansfield*. Oxford: Clarendon, 1936.

Holdsworth, Sir William. *A History of English Law*. 1938. London: Methuen and Sweet & Maxwell, 1966. 16 vols.

Johnson, Samuel. *Johnsonian Miscellanies*. Ed. George Birkbeck Hill. Oxford: Clarendon, 1907. 2 vols.

*Journal of the House of Commons* [*CJ*].

*Journal of the House of Lords* [*CH*].

Maugham, Robert. *A Treatise of the Laws of Literary Property*. London, 1828.

Moorman, Mary. *William Wordsworth: The Later Years*. Oxford: Clarendon, 1965.

*Petitions and Papers Relating to the Bill of the Booksellers Now Before the House of Commons*. London, 1774. Rpt. *The Literary Property Debate: Eight Tracts 1764–1774*. Ed. Stephen Parks. New York: Garland, 1975.

Ross, Ian Simpson. *Lord Kames and the Scotland of his Day*. Oxford: Clarendon, 1972.

*Some Thoughts on the State of Literary Property Humbly Submitted to the Consideration of the Public*. London, 1764. Rpt. *The Literary Property Debate: Eight Tracts 1764–1774*. Ed. Stephen Parks. New York: Garland, 1975.

Southey, Robert. 'Inquiry into the Copyright Act'. *Quarterly Review* 21 (Jan 1819): 196–213.

Talfourd, Thomas Noon. *A Speech Delivered by Thomas Noon Talfourd, Sergeant at Law, in the House of Commons*. London, 1837.

Whicher, John F. 'The Ghost of *Donaldson v. Beckett*'. *Bulletin of the Copyright Society of the U.S.A.* 9 (1961–62): 102–151, 194–229.

Wordsworth, William. *Letters of William and Dorothy Wordsworth*. 2nd ed. Ed. E. de Selincourt. Oxford: Clarendon, 1967–1988. 7 vols.

Wordsworth, William. *The Prose Works of William Wordsworth*. Ed. W. J. B. Owen and Jane Worthington Smyser. Oxford: Clarendon, 1974. 3 vols.

Zall, Paul M. 'Wordsworth and the Copyright Act of 1842'. *PMLA* 70 (1955): 132–144.

# Chapter 17

# John Brewer

## AUTHORS, PUBLISHERS AND THE MAKING OF LITERARY CULTURE

Samuel Richardson (1689–1761), printer, sometime publisher and best-selling novelist, is best remembered as the author of three extremely long epistolary novels – *Pamela* (1740), *Clarissa* (1747–8) and *Sir Charles Grandison* (1753–4) – which brought him international fame and fortune in his middle age. Somewhat improbably, this pious, sober and sententious man, who travelled little and could hardly have been more English, was inundated with praise from French *philosophes* and German critics. Denis Diderot, in his hyperbolic *Éloge de Richardson* (1761), compared Richardson to Moses, Homer, Euripides and Sophocles, composing the most effulgent of the many panegyrics which sprang from the European press.

Richardson rose to literary splendour from the humblest beginnings. The son of a rural joiner, he was able by dint of hard work, good luck and astute connections, to make a comfortable fortune in the printing trade. Even before fame was thrust upon him in the 1740s he had attained a prosperity that contrasted with the poverty of his youth. He was the beneficiary, as both printer and author, of the remarkable transformation in British publishing that occurred between the late seventeenth and late eighteenth centuries.

When Richardson published his first novel, *Pamela*, he was more than fifty years old; by then there were few byways of publishing he did not know. He had worked as a proof corrector and as a hack, writing prefaces and compiling indexes; he had printed newspapers and conduct books and won the lucrative contract to be official printer to the House of Commons. He had worked for booksellers and published books on his own account. From his presses had rolled not only the finely printed folio *Journals of the House of Commons*, weighty tomes that only a successful printer at the peak of his trade could produce, but also the ephemera – handbills, advertisements and trade cards – that earned the daily bread of the humble jobbing printer.

In his early years, when he had little capital or clout, Richardson was often hired by a bookseller to print part of a work. He was a craftsman for hire, a cog in the publishing machine. To act on his own behalf, to escape the control of the booksellers who dominated publishing, he had to take risks. Printing the work of such government opponents and Jacobites as Francis Atterbury, the banished former Bishop of London, and Philip, Duke of Wharton, the mad-cap rake and sometime drinking companion of the exiled Stuart Pretender, invited the hostility of the authorities and the threat of arrest; but it was also profitable and helped the young printer to make his mark.

But as Richardson prospered in the 1730s, he grew more prudent, avoiding controversy and diversifying his business to include newspaper and government work. He bought a share in the *Daily Gazetteer*, a paper which he printed, and began the profitable business of printing parliamentary bills and reports, work that in its best year grossed him nearly £600. He also printed literary works, including James Thomson's famous poem *The Seasons* and several editions of Daniel Defoe's *Tour Through the Whole Island of Great Britain*, which he re-edited to include his own material.

Richardson's career as a printer followed the path laid down in his first published work, the advice book *The Apprentice's Vade Mecum: or, Young Man's Pocket Companion*: it took him by dint of industry and virtue from the margins of his trade to the centre of his profession. Like Hogarth's Tom Goodchild in *The Industrious and Idle Apprentice*, Richardson married his master's daughter; and though, unlike Tom, he never became Lord Mayor, he did achieve high office, being elected Master of the Company of Stationers in 1753.

Yet none of Richardson's experience and success prepared him for the remarkable chain of events that followed the publication of his first novel. *Pamela*, the moralistic story of a servant girl whose determined defence of her sexual virtue is rewarded by genteel marriage, was a runaway best-seller in 1740. Within a year of its appearance it had gone through five editions, been pirated and parodied, notably in Henry Fielding's *Shamela*, dramatized on the London stage by Henry Giffard and put into verse by George Bennett.

*Pamela*'s popularity was not confined to Britain. North American editions appeared in New York, Philadelphia and Boston. The novel swept Europe, being translated into French, Italian, Dutch, German, Swedish, Russian, Spanish and Portuguese. Voltaire and the Italian dramatist Carlo Goldoni wrote plays based on *Pamela*'s plot. Today when we think of an eighteenth-century novelist we think of Daniel Defoe and Henry Fielding, perhaps of Tobias Smollett or Laurence Sterne; in eighteenth-century Europe the English novelist was almost synonymous with Samuel Richardson.

Richardson's second novel was also a blockbuster. *Clarissa* appeared seven volumes, devoting more than a million words to the conflict between the rake Lovelace and the virtuous heroine Clarissa Harlowe, a struggle which ends with their deaths. It was not a book for plot lovers – as Dr Johnson remarked, 'if you would read Richardson for the story, your impatience would be so much fretted that you would hang yourself. But you must read him for the sentiment' – nor was it a quick read. But *Clarissa* followed its predecessor on to the bookshelves of Europe, being translated into German, French, Russian, Italian and Portuguese.

The success of Richardson's first two novels lay in his portrayal of female virtue under duress. His growing band of admirers – which included a coterie of literary and genteel women – urged him to create a comparable male portrait. Richardson complied in his last novel *Sir Charles Grandison*. Though *Grandison* never achieved the success of his earlier fiction, male virtue proving less popular than its female equivalent, the novel was such a hot publisher's item that copies of its sheets were stolen from Richardson's press and spirited off to Dublin; an Irish edition appeared before its author and printer had published his own in London. . . .

The success of his epistolary fiction transformed Richardson from a prosperous printer into a literary lion. He was inundated with fan mail, flooded with suggestions for his plots, and deluged with praise and criticism. His circle of acquaintance grew to include the bluestockings Mrs Mary Delany, Hester Chapone and Elizabeth Carter. Dr Johnson became a good friend, who may have borrowed money from Richardson but more than paid back his debt in the hard currency of critical acclaim. Johnson repeatedly lauded Richardson at the expense of Henry Fielding – 'Sir, there is more knowledge of the heart in one letter of Richardson's, than in all "Tom Jones" ' – and enshrined the novelist's prose in his *Dictionary*, including ninety-seven citations from *Clarissa*, almost double that of any other work by a living author.

In the 1750s Richardson looked back on his life and proudly remarked, 'Twenty years ago I was the most obscure man in Great Britain, and now I am admitted to the company of the first characters of the Kingdom'. If he had chosen to travel, he would have also graced the drawing rooms of Europe. The publishing industry had served him well; when he died in 1761 he left an enviable literary legacy and a comfortable fortune of £14,000. Richardson liked to imagine that his success as printer and author was the result of his exceptional moral probity and ferocious industry. But it was also a sign of the remarkable transformation of the publishing business that had taken place in his lifetime and was to continue into the nineteenth century.

In 1689, the year of Richardson's birth and the first year after the Glorious Revolution had toppled James II, the English press was still far from free. Controls, enshrined in the Licensing Act of 1662 and reinforced in the new charter that the Stationers' Company had been granted in 1684, were designed to ensure that the government could monitor publications and that the Stationers' Company could maintain a monopoly of commercial publishing throughout England. This compact between a government anxious to suppress dissent and a guild determined to retain control of the book trade was secured by three provisions that tightly bound the press: prior government censorship of all publications; mandatory entry of all published works in the Registers of the Stationers' Company; and limitation of the printing trade to twenty master printers. . . .

The lapse of the Licensing Act in 1695 – something of a legislative accident – finally removed the major legal constraints on the expansion of the press, but it did not entirely eliminate government control or create a completely free market. Censorship before publication ended, but laws against blasphemy, obscenity and seditious libel were frequently enforced. . . .

Numerous taxes, including duties on paper, printed matter and advertisements, created a system of fiscal regulation that could also be used against printers and publishers. And periodic though not very effective attempts were made to regulate the distribution of the press. In 1782, for instance, hawkers and street vendors were prevented from hiring out newspapers rather than selling them, a common means of increasing their circulation. But with the lapse of the Licensing Act and the consequent end of the system that registered all printed material with the Stationers' Company, and in the absence of a registry of printing presses (not required until 1799 in reaction to the French Revolution), it was impossible for the government to exercise any systematic control of publishing. Sporadic intervention, no matter how heavy-handed, was not the same as continuous policing. . . .

In the year of Richardson's birth printing and publishing had been a collection of trades, dominated by a powerful guild and confined to a few streets and lanes in the city of London. Printing presses clattered in Aldersgate Street, Bartholomew Close, Whitefriars and St John's Lane; book- and printsellers displayed their wares on stands and in shops that clustered in Little Britain, around St Paul's Churchyard and near Temple Bar; and trade publishers' premises were concentrated near Stationers' Hall on Warwick Lane and Paternoster Row. Business thrived but was confined to a community in which nearly everyone was personally acquainted and in which a short walk was all that was necessary to complete a deal.

Nearly 100 years later the publishing industry was so diverse, complex and dispersed that the bookseller John Pendred brought out the first guide to English publishing, *The London and Country Printers, Booksellers and Stationers Vade Mecum* (1785). Pendred's world extends far beyond the confines of St Paul's Churchyard and Paternoster Row. His account of the metropolitan trade lists nearly 650 businesses engaged in thirty-two different occupations. In this highly specialized world, stationers and booksellers outnumbered printers, who were enumerated alongside engravers, map-, music- and printsellers, bookbinders, paper-, card- and board-makers, typefounders and warehousemen. Fancy booksellers listed their premises in Oxford Street, Piccadilly, Berkeley Square and on Pall Mall; engravers worked in the artists' quarter of Covent Garden as well as in the fashionable West End, and printers and publishers were scattered all over the city.

But the most important part of the guide was concerned not with London at all but with the provinces. For one of Pendred's main purposes was to provide the London trade with valuable information about how to exploit provincial advertising and distribution networks. When he listed the forty-nine country newspapers printed in thirty-four towns, he gave two crucial pieces of information: the names of newspaper owners and the addresses of their London agents. Booksellers could thus place advertisements in the provincial press through London agents, or they could contact the proprietors directly in order to exploit the distribution network they had established. What had begun as a London trade had become a national business.

The world of eighteenth-century publishing is best understood as an expanding maze or labyrinth, and it offered the potential author many entrances and numerous routes to eventual publication, each full of hazards, pitfalls and dead ends. Presided over by the Cerberus-like figure of the bookseller, the maze was not difficult to enter but easy to get lost in, and the author needed both guides and a map. Richardson was an exception, for he knew the ways of publishing intimately, could print his books himself, and had good working relations with the booksellers, notably John Osborn and Charles Rivington, whose request that he write a book of morally instructive letters was the inspiration for his first novel. But few authors were either so fortunate or so well informed.

Still, the number and variety of authors who embarked on the journey into print was quite remarkable. . . .

The crucial vehicle was the periodical press. Any aspiring author seeking fame, fortune or just the pleasure of seeing their words in print could send their work to a magazine proprietor, and many a career began with such an unsolicited contribution. Elizabeth Rowe, who became a successful author of pious verse much admired by Protestant Nonconformists, had her earliest poems published anonymously in John Dunton's *Athenian Mercury* in the 1690s. Lady Wortley Montagu's first publication was an essay in Addison and Steele's *Spectator*. And *Felix Farley's Bristol Journal* was the means by which Thomas Chatterton launched his brief, tragic career as poet and forger of medieval documents. . . . What brought them all to the periodical press was the unparalleled opportunity it offered to get into print. . . .

Periodicals also made possible a career dedicated solely to writing. Magazine proprietors were inundated with unsolicited material, some of which came gratis, and the growing competition among the magazines meant that the demand for material exceeded supply. The professional author stepped into the breach with essays, reviews, poems and criticism that enlivened and enlightened the public; publication enabled him to earn a living. By the 1760s he could contribute to more than thirty London periodicals; by the end of the century there were more than eighty. . . .

By the middle of the century, in large part because of the expansion of this periodical press, a small but growing band of professional writers was established in London. These authors, personified in the shambling, eccentric but indomitable figure of Samuel Johnson, were still outnumbered by amateur and occasional writers from every walk of life, for the very circumstances that had made professional authorship possible had also enormously increased the number of dilettante writers in print. But the inconspicuousness of professional authors was not entirely attributable to their low numbers. They laboured under a more severe handicap, often suffered by new figures on the social landscape: they did not fit into prevailing ideas about how the literary world was constructed.

Fifty years earlier the tribe of authors had been conventionally divided into two radically different camps. There were those who wrote to edify, amuse and instruct but who shunned monetary reward and there were those who wrote for money. In the former view writing was a 'liberal' pursuit, the occupation of persons of enlarged views and unbiased vision. Writing for money not only reduced authorship to a mechanical trade but subverted the value of the work. . . .

Commentators considered these authors as shackled and imprisoned by their trade. As James Ralph put it in his eloquent defence in 1758, 'there is no Difference between the Writer in his Garret, and the Slave in his Mines; but that the former has his Situation in the Air, and the latter in the Bowels of the Earth: Both have their Tasks assigned them alike: Both must drudge *and* Starve; neither can hope for Deliverance. The compiler must compile; the Composer must compose on; sick or well; in spirit or out'. Hack work provided only enough to avoid destitution. Pay was poor. A reviewer at mid-century, for example, would receive a standard fee of two guineas for writing eighty pages of reviews. . . .

How was the author to escape the double-bind which James Ralph so clearly identified? The author's dilemma, Ralph pointed out, was that he was damned if he did take the money, and poor if he didn't:

A Man may plead for Money, prescribe or quack for Money, preach and pray for Money, marry for Money, fight for Money, do any thing within the Law for Money, provided the Expedient answers, without the least imputation.

But if he writes like one inspired from Heaven, and writes for Money, the Man of *Touch*, in the right of *Midas* his great Ancestor, enters his Caveat against him as a Man of *Taste*; declares the two Provinces to be incompatible; that he who aims at Praise ought to be starved; and that there ought to be so much draw-back upon Character for Every Acquisition in Coin . . . [The author] is laugh'd at if poor; if, to avoid that curse, he endeavours to turn his Wit to Profit, he is branded as a Mercenary.

Ralph's dyspeptic diatribe against professions that purported to be liberal but that were tainted with mammon reveals his frustration; he has no alternative vision that would place the professional author in a new setting. How could the writer be paid but respectable? This was the essential question.

The answer was slow in formulation and grew out of two related debates, one about artistic value, the other about intellectual property. The former focused on the high-minded issue of creativity, the latter on the prosaic question of copyright; both helped to formulate and clarify the notion of the author as creator of a unique property which he owned by virtue of a singular, imaginative act.

The liberal criterion of what made authorship legitimate was social. Financial independence, the eighteenth-century equivalent of Virginia Woolf's '£500 a year and a room of one's own', produced good writing; the marketplace produced trash. Against this claim, Johnson and his allies argued that the ability to produce valuable literature was nor determined by economic conditions but was rather a matter of individual ingenuity and originality. Literature was less a matter of uncovering and revealing traditional 'natural' truths than of creating an original – that is, new – literary artifact. This emphasis on creativity was not novel – it can be found in the work of the classical critic Longinus, and the notion of originality had a long history. But the association of creative genius with originality had never before been made so forcefully. 'The highest praise of genius', wrote Johnson in his *Life of Milton*, 'is original invention'.

Originality distinguished the true author from the hack. Both might be paid, both embark on projects suggested and financed by booksellers, like most of Johnson's major works, but an author had creative powers that the compiler and pastiche writer lacked. Above 'the drudges of the pen' and the 'manufacturers of literature' Johnson identified the few who 'can be said to produce, or endeavour to produce, new ideas, to extend any principle of science, or gratify the imagination with any uncommon train of images or contexture of events'.

The emphasis on originality and novelty, introducing as it did a new hierarchy of literary endeavour, underscored the special relationship that the author bore to his text. If a work was original it was also unique, the distinctive consequence of a writer's imagination. Each text bore the distinctive impress of its author's mind. In emphasizing the singularity of literary work, writers like Johnson threw the personality and character of the author into sharp relief. Literary criticism became more than an assessment of a work's conformity to a set of conventions and rules; it also set out to show how each individual author shaped a particular work. . . .

By the late eighteenth century the professional author, the creator of unique works of literature, had become a recognizable type, distinguishable from both the liberal writer and the hack. His creativity not only shaped what he wrote but conferred on him a public authority to explain how it should be interpreted and how it differed from earlier writing. As in Johnson's case, the creative author was inclined to become the historical critic, concerned to reveal literary tradition in order to establish his own place in literary history.

Even if the author fabricated and fashioned literary works, there was still the question of what right he had to own them. It is one of the great ironies of this period that the establishment of an author's rights in his literary property should have been achieved largely with the help his old enemy, the bookseller. . . .

How then was a writer to be ennobled and how was he or she to retain the title? Establishing the legitimacy of the idea of professional authorship did not secure the careers and status of *individual* writers, which depended on how effectively each could exploit the resources and opportunities of the literary system. The author's first task was to seek entry into the labyrinth of publishing. Without the resources of a Horace Walpole and despite the opportunities afforded by the periodical press, the writer almost certainly needed to procure the services of a bookseller. Only such a commercial middleman had the resources necessary to produce and distribute books. . . .

Whether the writer approached a bookseller in person or solicited support through importunate correspondence, the author's reception was rarely warm, occasionally tepid and often cold. The arrogance and hauteur of the bookseller, brilliantly captured in Thomas Rowlandson's pen and wash drawing *The Bookseller and the Author* (1780–4) was an authorial cliché and longstanding grievance. Still, Rowlandson's sneering bookseller, whose corpulent prosperity contrasts with the cringing emaciated figure of the imploring author, is a caricature. Though there were booksellers like Edmund Curll who abused their position and the writers they employed, most members of the trade were prudent, honest and conservative men of business who faced problems that many authors were eager to avoid. The bookseller bore the risk of publication and needed to make a profit. He was inundated with manuscripts, many of which lacked merit or commercial value. The sheer volume of material made it hard for him to discriminate, to pick out the work that would prove a success. He might claim, as James Ralph put it, to know 'best what Assortment of Wares will best suit the Market', but he knew that literary innovation was exceptionally chancy. It was much less risky to publish and trade in the copyrights of established figures. Only the most adventurous booksellers preferred an unknown living author to a dead literary monument.

How, then, was the hapless writer to overcome the bookseller's reluctance to help him into print? One of the best stratagems was to appeal to the personal interests and sympathies of the publisher. Though Rowlandson, like many embittered authors, depicted booksellers as venal monsters and ruthless profit-seeking entrepreneurs, most held certain subjects and certain causes close to their heart. Jacob Tonson loved Whiggery and *belles-lettres*; John Wilkie admired conservative works on politics and religion; John Newbery and William Darton specialized in children's literature and Robert Dodsley in poetry. Authors needed to know booksellers. The more specialized or controversial the work, the more important it was to find the right publisher. John Millan would have been delighted to publish a manuscript on British antiquities that would have made most booksellers blanch, while the radical bookseller Joseph Johnson was willing to publish tracts that many others thought too hot to handle.

Such booksellers were intent not upon the ruthless maximization of profit but upon combining their cultural, social, religious and political interests with making a respectable living. They saw themselves, as Johnson, a man not prone to flattery, described them, as 'modern patrons of literature'. For though the historical cliché has emphasized their exploitation of authors, the historical record reveals many of them to have treated their clients and employees with a patience and charity which some writers barely deserved. . . .

The bookseller was first and foremost a businessman, but this did not mean that he had no regard for authors and their works, any more than the professional author had no regard for the content of his work as long as it turned a profit. Both bookseller and author shared in the balancing act between pecuniary reward and intellectual interest that gave eighteenth-century publishing much of its energy. Yet the liberal tradition of writing, which was so concerned to deny the legitimacy of writing for money, died hard, even amongst those who became professional authors. In their eyes the bookseller remained a dangerous and dubious figure, essential to their livelihood but a constant reminder of the pact they had made with mammon.

When the would-be author approached a bookseller he still needed to allay the under-standable anxieties of someone who knew how risky it was to back a literary tyro. Reassurance took two forms. First, the author could secure the support of someone whose critical acumen would vouch for the value of the work and whose public endorsement would help its sales. The best friend an aspiring author could have was someone already experienced in the ways of Grub Street. For all the personal rivalries and bitter quarrels that rent the community of authors, many of their number heeded the advice of Johnson and of James Ralph that writers should stand together, going to considerable lengths to help their brother scribblers. . . .

Johnson enjoyed his role as literary patron and played it with gusto. Though, as Hester Piozzi complained, he said 'very contemptuous things of our sex', he helped a number of female poets and novelists into print, notably Anna Williams, Frances Burney and Charlotte Lennox. Such was his enthusiasm for Lennox's writing that he induced fellow members of the Ivy Lane Club to throw an all-night party to celebrate the birth of her 'first literary child'. At times passion got the better of his judgement. Johnson was an early and ardent supporter of William Lauder's attacks on Milton. Lauder, a Scottish classicist and Jacobite schoolmaster who had lost a leg after being hit by a golfball, castigated Milton as a feeble and politically misdirected plagiarist. Johnson, who had little sympathy for Milton's politics, wrote prefaces for Lauder's work and urged it on the booksellers.

But how was an unknown writer to meet the likes of Johnson? It was best to join one of the many informal coteries and circles which made up literary London. Some of these associations, like Johnson's Club, were only open to members and the occasional guest. But, as we have seen, throughout the period writers frequented coffee houses and taverns which were open to anyone who could pay the reckoning. In these informal surroundings an introduction or witty remark could lead to acquaintance, and acquaintance to friendship with an established author or critic whose circle of influence might include booksellers, newspaper proprietors and the literary managers of magazines. Fellow authors could rarely offer financial support (except, perhaps, for the occasional short-term loan) but had something far more valuable – influence and connections, the power to mobilize the resources that the aspiring author so desperately needed. Authors, then, were not only producers of literature but also among its most important patrons.

The support of a colleague made an author's work more credible to a bookseller, but it only marginally reduced the latter's financial risk. Risk reduction could be achieved in one of two ways: by getting someone else to bear the costs of publication, or by guaranteeing a number of sales by organizing a subscription of purchasers prior to publication. Both methods required the support of literary patrons.

The question of patronage was and remains a vexed one. For much of the eighteenth century authors had two contradictory complaints about the patronage of literature. On the one hand, they regretted the demise of what was vaguely imagined as an ideal past in which kings, nobles and gentlemen supported literary endeavour of the highest quality. Such nostalgia, rampant early in the century, was a hankering for a world that authors never had, and was in large part a hostile reaction to the growth of commercial publishing and a political response to the Hanoverian regime. Many writers, especially those who aspired to gentility and literary high-mindedness, were appalled by the growing trade in literary commodities. And many of them – notably the Scriblerian circle that included Pope, Swift, Arbuthnot and Gay – were also politically opposed to George I and George II, resentful of their exclusion from royal patronage, and conscious of the court's declining importance as a centre of literary largesse.

Other authors were happy to see patrons fade away, however, and wished good-riddance to a putative golden age of patronage. The old relations between patron and client had, in the eyes of many, created a form of literary prostitution. Gentlemen, wrote the poet Charles Churchill, 'kept a bard, just as they keep a whore'. Henry Fielding's use of the whoring metaphor in his *Author's Farce* differed only slightly: 'Get a patron,' one of his characters advises, 'be pimp to some worthless man of quality, write panegyrics on him, flatter him with as many virtues as he has vices.' In the politically charged climate of eighteenth-century England, reliance on a private individual, even the patronage of the monarch, was deemed incompatible with the independent requirements of modern authorship. A professional writer, it was felt, should be servant to no one but the public. His work should not reflect the etiolated taste of a sybaritic aristocrat but rest on the firmer foundation of public approval. . . .

In the complex and often fraught relations between patron and authorial client the balance of power slowly but irreversibly shifted in favour of the writer. Because authors increasingly had the alternative resources of a commercial literary world, they became less dependent on individual largesse. This did not make them any less eager to secure aristocratic support, but what they wanted was not, on the whole, the rather demeaning place of the household servant, but money – underwriting an edition, paying for its production costs – and, most important of all, someone to talk up their books in polite society. The influential cleric who 'went from Coffee-house to Coffee-house, calling upon all men of taste to exert themselves in rescuing one of the greatest geniuses that ever appeared from obscurity' helped James Thomson every bit as much as Lords Talbot and Lyttelton. For what a writer most needed was reputation; from this all else, including financial independence, followed.

The greatest service, then, that a patron, whether aristocratic or not, could render an author was to laud his or her abilities, to praise the writer's work in fashionable society. Johnson's famous denunciation of Lord Chesterfield – 'Is not a Patron, my Lord, one who looks with unconcern on a Man struggling for Life in the water, and when he has reached ground encumbers him with help' – complained not about the noble lord's failure to fund the *Dictionary* (which was financed, after all, by the booksellers) or about his financial niggardliness to its author, who received a meagre

£10 for dedicating its plan to him. What irked Johnson was Chesterfield's failure during the *Dictionary*'s seven-year gestation to provide 'one Act of assistance, one word of encouragement, or one smile of favour'. He should have been supporting the project, praising its aim and author in the literary circles and genteel drawing rooms he frequented. His job was not to commission a work nor to house and feed its author – acts that would have compromised authorial independence – but to encourage and orchestrate its praise. Chesterfield's meagre contribution to Johnson's enterprise showed that he knew what he was supposed to do. He wrote two short letters puffing the *Dictionary* in the newspaper *The World* in November and December 1754. It was a gesture, but Johnson felt that for seven years' labour it was not enough.

The shifting role of the patron from commissioner and controller of literary work to its promoter, consumer and distributor was best epitomized by the practice of book subscription which increased as the nature of patronage changed. The number of subscription volumes rose rapidly between the late seventeenth century and the 1730s, levelled off until the 1760s, and spurted again during the last two decades of the century. Poems, sermons, music, histories, medical and advice manuals, biography, theology, mathematics, husbandry and, by the end of the century, even novels and plays were published in this way.

The object of subscription was to secure down-payments on and promises to purchase a book before its publication. This ensured that production and distribution costs were covered before a work went to press, an arrangement that pleased the booksellers because it cut risks and could promise large profits. Authors solicited some subscribers by getting job printers to produce proposals and by hawking their wares in the drawing rooms and at the assemblies of the great. But the booksellers and authors' friends handled many more. Richardson printed numerous subscription editions and helped to organize the 1730 subscription editions of James Thomson's *The Seasons*, printing proposals and taking down-payments and orders at his shop. Johnson was an inveterate organizer of subscriptions for those he admired or whom he found in distress. He spent more than fifteen years helping to organize a subscription to Anna Williams's *Miscellanies in Prose and Verse*, which eventually appeared in 1766. The blind Miss Williams, who for many years lived in Johnson's house, earned over £300 as a result of Johnson's benevolence. His efforts on behalf of Charlotte Lennox, the success of whose novel, *The Female Quixote*, did not prevent her from falling into penury, were no less assiduous though much less successful. Numerous proposals he wrote for her in the 1770s all came to nothing. . . .

Subscription publication brought together the interests of author, patron and bookseller. For the author it helped to get into print works such as expensive and scholarly tomes which might otherwise never have been published. It was the main means of publishing a collected volume or volumes of a single author's works in either prose or verse. A well-managed subscription could also prove sufficiently popular and profitable to secure an author's financial independence. The subscriptions to Pope's works freed him from what he viewed as the clutches of the booksellers; the 1,200 subscribers to Elizabeth Carter's *All the Works of Epictetus* earned her almost £1,000, enabling her to devote the rest of her life to her bluestocking literary interests. From the subscriber's point of view it was an opportunity to patronize and to be seen to support an author without the difficulties that attended a more personal relationship between patron and client. For the publisher, not only was there a reduced risk but the chance of additional sales through the network of retail booksellers, encouraged by the publicity provided by a list of distinguished subscribers.

# Chapter 18

# Jane Tompkins

## MASTERPIECE THEATER

## The politics of Hawthorne's literary reputation

Because modern commentators have tended to ignore the context within which nineteenth-century authors and critics worked, their view of the criticism that was written on *The Scarlet Letter* in the nineteenth century has failed to take account of the cultural circumstances that shaped Hawthorne's novel for his contemporaries. They evaluate this criticism as if it had been written about the same text that they read, and so produce accounts of that criticism that are unrelated to the issues with which it was actually engaged. For example, three modern scholars of Hawthorne criticism all find George Loring's reply in 1850 to an attack on *The Scarlet Letter* that had appeared in the *North American Review* one of the ablest contemporary discussions of the novel.[1] It is not hard to see why these critics think so highly of Loring's defense. His essay is written in answer to a religious attack on the novel which argues that *The Scarlet Letter* is unchristian because it presents its adulterous heroine in a sympathetic light, sees 'devils and angels [as] alike beautiful', deals with a 'revolting' subject whose 'ugliness' is unredeemed by Hawthorne's 'wizard power over language' and is manifestly untrue to the realities of 'God's moral world'.[2] Because Loring's essay sets itself up in opposition to what seems to the modern critics a narrowly based doctrinal attack, they find the defense admirable. When Loring says, for example, that without sorrow and sin 'virtue cannot rise above innocency', it looks as if he has acknowledged the complex nature of moral problems as the twentieth century views them.[3] When he says that those who think 'vice stands at one pale and virtue at another' betray a 'want of sympathy' which 'the experience of our own temptation should remove', Loring seems to be acknowledging the existence of 'the dark underside of the psyche' with which so much modern criticism has been preoccupied.[4] When he writes that 'in casting [Hester] out, the world had torn from her all the support of its dogmatic teachings, . . . and had compelled her to rely upon that great religious truth which flows instinctively around a life of agony, with its daring freedom', the modern critic discerns a celebration of human individuality and an affirmation of the heroic struggle for personal freedom at all costs.[5]

But Loring's review of *The Scarlet Letter* does not escape the confines of religious controversy; on the contrary, his argument with the reviewer for the *North American* is mounted on specifically doctrinal grounds. . . .

Loring's interpretation of *The Scarlet Letter* arises from the theological controversy (which was also a power struggle) then raging within the New England churches.[6] The very shape of his disagreement with the reviewer for the *North American* shows that the text these critics argued over had been structured by a set of interests and beliefs that we can reconstruct but no longer hold. It is just as impossible for a twentieth-century critic to argue, as Loring does, that the story of Hester's sin demonstrates the existence of a certain 'spot' in the human soul as it would have been for a Transcendentalist to read it, along with Charles Feidelson, as demonstrating the 'anti-conventional impulse . . . inherent in symbolism.[7] This is not simply because each critic looks at the text from a different point of view or with different purposes in mind, but because *looking* is not an activity that is performed outside of political struggles and institutional structures, but arises *from* them.

One such structure is the machinery of publishing and reviewing by means of which an author is brought to the attention of his audience. The social and economic processes that govern the dissemination of a literary work are no more accidental to its reputation, and indeed to its very nature, as that will be perceived by an audience, than are the cultural conceptions (of the nature of poetry, of morality, of the human soul) within which the work is read. The conditions of dissemination interpret the work for its readers in exactly the same way as definitions of poetry in that they flow from and support widely-held – if unspoken – assumptions about the methods of distribution proper to a serious (or non-serious) work. The fact that an author makes his or her appearance in the context of a particular publishing practice rather than some other is a fact about the kind of claim he or she is making on an audience's attention and is *crucial* to the success of the claim. Hawthorne's debut as a novelist illustrates this proposition rather strikingly.

In 1970, C. E. Frazer Clark, Jr., published an article that revealed some little-known facts surrounding the publication of *The Scarlet Letter*.[8] Clark observed that despite Hawthorne's habit of referring to himself as 'the most unpopular author in America', he was much better known than he himself was aware. His satires and sketches had been pirated liberally by newspapers up and down the Eastern seaboard; notices, advertisements, and reviews of his work had regularly appeared in the periodical press. And so, when Hawthorne lost his job as surveyor of customs at Salem, it caused a furor in the local papers.[9] The press took up the case of political axing not because such events were so extraordinary – nothing could have been more common with a change of administrations – but because Hawthorne was already newsworthy. This publicity attracted the attention of James T. Fields, shortly to become New England's most influential publisher, who until then had not printed a word of Hawthorne's, but whose business instincts now prompted him to visit Salem on the off-chance that Hawthorne might have something ready for the press. Hawthorne, as it happened, did have something on hand which, very reluctantly, he gave to Fields. It was a story which Fields encouraged him to turn into a novel – novels being more marketable than short fiction. Hawthorne took this suggestion and prefaced the story with an introductory essay on his stint in the customs house to help achieve the desired length. As Fields suspected, Hawthorne's first book to appear after the customs house fiasco sold remarkably well: the advance publicity had guaranteed that *The Scarlet Letter* would be a success.

Encouraged by the attention paid to his novel, and prodded by the ever-vigilant Fields, who saw an opportunity to capitalize on the reputation so recently enlarged, Hawthorne, who until then had not been a prolific writer, turned out two more novels in rapid succession. These received a great deal of favorable attention from well-placed reviewers, with the result that, two years after the publication of *The Scarlet Letter*, Hawthorne was being referred to as a classic American writer – and has been so identified ever since. But the success of *The Scarlet Letter* and of the subsequent novels becomes fully explicable only within a larger frame of reference than the one Clark's essay supplies.

By the 1840s Irving's reputation had sagged and Cooper had alienated large portions of the reading public and the critical establishment with his attacks on American manners and his unpopular political stands. America needed a living novelist whom it could regard as this country's answer to Dickens and Thackeray, a novelist who represented both what was essentially American and what was 'best' by some universal criteria of literary value. Hawthorne seemed well-suited for the role, since, as almost every critic emphasized, his work made use of characteristically American materials. Hawthorne's feel for the humbler aspects of the American scene made him attractive both as an interpreter of 'spiritual laws' that know no nationality and as a spokesman for the democratic way of life. These qualities, however, as I have suggested, were shared equally by novelists like Warner and Stowe who, if anything, outdid him in this respect. What finally distinguished Hawthorne from his popular rivals was his relation to the social and institutional structures that shaped literary opinion; these associations ultimately determined the longevity of his reputation. The parallel but finally divergent careers of Hawthorne and Warner illustrate dramatically how important belonging to the right network was as a precondition for long-standing critical success.

The circle of well-educated, well-connected men and women who controlled New England's cultural life at mid-century thought of themselves as spiritually and culturally suited to raise the level of popular taste and to civilize and refine the impulses of the multitude. Any writer whom they chose as a model of moral and aesthetic excellence, therefore, had to be someone whose work had not already been embraced by the nation at large, but had been initially admired only by the discerning few. Longfellow formulates the prevailing view of Hawthorne as a writer for a cultivated minority in his review of the second edition of *Twice-told Tales*:

> Mr. Hawthorne's . . . writings have now become so well known, and are so justly appreciated, by all discerning minds, that they do not need our commendation. He is not an author to create a sensation, or have a tumultuous popularity. His works are not stimulating or impassioned, and they minister nothing to a feverish love of excitement. Their tranquil beauty and softened tints, which do not win the notice of the restless many, only endear them the more to the thoughtful few.[10]

The 'thoughtful few' to whom Longfellow refers are the people who controlled New England's cultural life before the Civil War. Once Hawthorne's work had been published by Ticknor and Fields, New England's most prominent publisher; once it had been reviewed by E. P. Whipple, a member of Fields' coterie and one of the most influential contemporary reviewers; and had become the subject of long discussions in the *Christian Examiner* and the *North American Review*, periodicals whose editors, in Sydney Ahlstrom's words, 'alone constitute . . . a hall of fame of the New England flowering'; Hawthorne had gained a place in a socio-cultural network that assured his prominence because its own prominence was already an established and self-perpetuating fact.[11]

Lewis Simpson has characterized this group of literary and intellectual men who took the nation's spiritual welfare as their special charge as the 'New England clerisy'.[12] Simpson traces its beginnings in the passage from a theological to a literary clergy in the early years of the nineteenth century, using the career of Joseph Stevens Buckminster, a precocious young theology professor at Harvard, to exemplify the broadening of ecclesiastical authority to include general cultural matters, and especially literature. Buckminster and his associates, who founded the *Monthly*

*Anthology*, America's most serious literary journal at the time, spoke of literature as a 'commonwealth' with its own 'government', that along with church and state fought for civilization against barbarism.[13] As a result of their activity, Simpson writes, 'the image in the New England mind of the old theocratic polity begins to become the image of a literary polity. . . . The *Respublica Christiana* . . . becomes the *Respublica Litterarum*.'[14] The metaphor of the state as a means of conceptualizing literary activity is important because it suggests the need for centralized leadership and control in cultural affairs: the choice of proper reading matter was not something that could be left to the 'restless many', but rightly belonged to the 'thoughtful few' whose training and authority qualified them as arbiters of public taste. The formation of a literary canon in the nineteenth century was not a haphazard affair, but depended on the judgment of a small group of prominent men, the members of the Anthology Society – clergymen, professors, businessmen, judges, and statesmen – who conceived of their task as a civic and moral duty. The power they had to determine who would be read and who would not is dramatically illustrated by the career of Richard Henry Dana, Sr., whose ardent admiration for the English Romantic poets drew scathing criticism from the Boston literati. He failed to be elected to the editorship of the *North American* (the direct descendant of the *Monthly Anthology*), and thereafter refused to contribute to it. When his essays and tales, his long poem, and the collected edition of his poems and prose elicited only a cool response from reviewers, he simply withdrew from the world, devastated by its failure to recognize his genius.[15]

This fate did not befall Nathaniel Hawthorne because he had been taken up by the second generation of the New England clerisy, whose power to shape literary opinion had been inherited from the first through an interlocking network of social, familial, political, and professional connections. William Tudor, an active member of the Anthology Society, the *Monthly Anthology*'s editorial board, became the founding editor of the *North American Review*. John Kirkland, another of the Society's original members, became president of Harvard. Alexander Everett, another member, later a minister to Spain, also went on to edit the *North American*, as did Edward Everett, who had studied German at Göttingen with George Ticknor, both of them original members of the Anthology Society. Ticknor, who preceded Longfellow as Professor of Modern Languages at Harvard, was the cousin of William Ticknor, of Ticknor and Fields, who became one of Hawthorne's lifelong friends. William Emerson, pastor of the First Church of Boston, who edited the *Monthly Anthology* for two years before the Society took over, was Ralph Waldo Emerson's father.[16]

Joseph Buckminster's father had strenuously opposed the liberal theological tendencies of his son, just as the Unitarians of Buckminster's era and beyond would oppose the radical theorizing of Emerson and his circle; but the authority to speak on spiritual and cultural issues passed smoothly down from father to son undiminished by doctrinal differences. The men who thus assumed the role of cultural spokesmen at mid-century – Longfellow, Holmes, Lowell, Whittier, and Emerson – were particularly powerful since by then Boston had become the literary center of the nation.[17] These were the men whom Caroline Ticknor records as gathering to socialize at the Old Corner Bookstore, as Ticknor and Fields was familiarly known.[18] These were the men who in 1857 'all agreed to write for the *Atlantic* and . . . made it immediately . . . the most important magazine in America'.[19] These were the men who, as Sophia Hawthorne left the cemetery after her husband's funeral, stood with bared heads as the carriage passed.[20]

It is hard to overestimate the importance of Hawthorne's connections with these men who outlived him by a score of years and who launched the periodical that would dominate literary activity in the United States for the rest of the nineteenth century. When William Dean Howells returned to Boston in 1866, he became assistant editor of the *Atlantic Monthly* under James T. Fields (Hawthorne's publisher), who had taken over the editorship from Lowell (Hawthorne's good friend). Howells, whom Hawthorne had helped get his start by introducing him to Emerson, took over the editorship from Fields in 1871, and George Persons Lathrop, Hawthorne's son-in-law, became an assistant editor.[21] Lathrop would publish the first full-length study of Hawthorne, which Howells' close friend, Henry James, would challenge three years later in *his* full-length study. This touched off a critical controversy – notably in an essay by Howells – over whether Hawthorne was an idealist or a realist, so that it was Hawthorne whose texts critics used to argue the merits of literary realism in the 80s and 90s.[22] Meanwhile, several friends published poems commemorating Hawthorne's death; relatives, friends, and associates printed their reminiscences; Sophia published excerpts from Hawthorne's journals; and other admirers wrote pieces with titles such as 'The Homes and Haunts of Hawthorne'.

But most important in assuring Hawthorne's continuing presence in the cultural foreground was James T. Fields. Fields, wanting to make good on his investment, followed his former practice of putting out anything he thought would pique the public's interest in his author and managed to produce eleven posthumous editions of Hawthorne's work between 1864 and 1883. This meant, twenty years after he was dead, that Hawthorne was still being reviewed as a live author. Osgood, the successor to Fields, pushed this strategy further by adding Hawthorne to his 'Little Classics' series, and in 1884, Houghton Mifflin, the successor to Osgood, capped it off by publishing *The Complete Works of Nathaniel Hawthorne* in twelve volumes edited by his son-in-law. Finally, Houghton Mifflin reinforced the image by including Hawthorne in two more series: 'Modern Classics' and 'American Classics for the Schools'. In 1883, the academic establishment put its imprimatur on what the publishers had done. In that year, Yale allowed English literature students for the first time to write their junior essays on 'Hawthorne's Imagination' – the only topic on the list that concerned an American author. Consequently, Hawthorne's texts were 'there' to be drawn upon for ammunition in the debates over the question of realism that raged during the 1880s. By the end of the century, as Edwin Cady observes in his survey of Hawthorne criticism, 'a minor critic might well have doubted his respectability if he failed to cite Hawthorne whether in praise of or attack against any writing in question'.[23]

The prominence of Hawthorne's texts in the post-Civil War era is a natural consequence of his relation to the mechanisms that produced literary and cultural opinion. Hawthorne's initial connections with the Boston literati – his acquaintance with Longfellow at college, his residence next door to Alcott and a half mile from Emerson (his son and Emerson's nephew roomed together at Harvard), his marrying a Peabody, becoming fast friends with Ticknor and Lowell, being published by the indefatigable Fields, socializing with Duyckinck and Whipple – these circumstances positioned Hawthorne's literary production so that it became the property of a dynastic cultural elite which came to identify itself with him.[24] The members of this elite could not fail to keep Hawthorne's reputation alive since it stood for everything they themselves stood for. America's literary establishment, no less than James T. Fields (who was part of it), had an investment in Hawthorne. In short, the friends and associates who outlived Hawthorne kept his fiction up-to-date by writing about it, and then *their* friends took over. Consequently, when the next generation of critics – Howells, James, and their contemporaries – came of age, they redefined his work according to the critical tastes of the new era. And so when the century turned, it seemed appropriate that a volume of Hawthorne criticism should appear in 1904 celebrating the hundredth anniversary of his birth. And 'by then', writes Edwin Cady, 'figures like George Woodberry, William Peterfield Trent, and Paul Elmer More had come to maturity', who, with their 'Arnoldian . . . neo-humanism' would 'project Hawthorne toward the present century's Age of Criticism'.[25]

During the same period, Warner's critical reputation dwindled to nothing. Whereas critics writing before the Civil War had discussed her work alongside that of Hawthorne, Brockden Brown, Cooper, Irving, Longfellow, and Stowe, by the 70s they had ceased to take her novels seriously as literature and finally stopped reviewing them altogether. Under the pressure of new conditions, Warner's work, like Hawthorne's, came to be redefined. The circumstances that created each author's literary reputation were of the same *kind* in either case – that is, they consisted of the writer's relation to centers of cultural domination, social and professional connections, blood relations, friendships, publishing history, and so on – but in Warner's case the circumstances were negative rather than positive.

Warner's connections – such as they were – sprang from New York rather than Boston, which at this particular period put her at a geographical disadvantage. Unlike Hawthorne, Warner had not lived in Concord, did not know Emerson and his circle, was not published by Fields, had not known Longfellow at college, had not roomed with a former President of the United States whose campaign biography she would write and who would get her a consulship when she needed money. Rather, she had been forced by her father's financial failure in the 1830s to retire to an island in the Hudson River where the family owned property, and where, along with her maiden sister, she wrote novels to earn a living. The Warners' poverty and their resulting social isolation affected both what they wrote and the way their work was perceived by contemporary audiences. As a consequence of their social isolation, the Warners threw themselves into church-centered activities and became extremely devout followers of the Reverend Thomas Skinner – a New Light Presbyterian who preached the importance of faith over doctrine in religious conversion. They considered the novels and stories they wrote their best means of doing the Lord's work and – since they had to – of supporting themselves. These conditions (at one point their house was in receivership and creditors took their furniture away) determined not only what they wrote, but how much, how fast, for what kind of audience, and for which publishers.[26] Though they had started out with G. P. Putnam, a large commercial publisher in New York whose founder had been a friend of their father, in the 1860s they gave most of what they wrote to Robert Carter, a highly respected religious publisher who could guarantee a certain number of sales. The audience for religious books was large, stable, and provided an outlet for the Warners that answered their need both to win souls and to have bread on the table. Thus, at a time when changes in the economic and social environment created the context within which literary realism flourished, the Warner sisters guaranteed that their novels would be read as religious rather than literary discourse, labeled with Carter's imprint and with titles – 'Stories on the Lord's Prayer', 'A Story of Small Beginnings', 'The Word' – more reminiscent of tract society pamphlets than of high art.

Given a different cultural milieu, these conditions of production might have guaranteed the Warner sisters lasting fame. If the religious views that characterized the attacks on *The Scarlet Letter* in the 1850s had dominated literary criticism after the war, Hawthorne would have done well to experience a religious conversion and switch to Carter, too. But the moral impulse behind American criticism, which had been evangelical and religious in the ante-bellum years, evolved during the 70s and 80s into a concern for the material conditions of social life. Novels which had previously appeared to contain superb renditions of American character and homely scenes imbued with universal human truths, now seemed to be full of idealized characters, authorial didacticism, and an overt religiosity that marked them as morally false and artistically naive. Warner's work became identified with an outmoded piety and a discredited Romanticism that assured its swift disappearance from the critical scene. It is not that critics suddenly discovered limitations they had previously failed to notice, but that the context within which the work appeared had changed the nature of the work itself. If Warner had had the kinds of connections that kept Hawthorne's works in the public eye, had commanded the attention of influential publishers, editors, and reviewers, her early novels might have remained critically viable as they came to be recast according to the prevailing standards. And in that case *The Wide, Wide World* might have been passed down to us as one of the benchmarks of American literary realism.[27] But when she died in 1885, there were no famous men at her funeral to write poems in her memory for the *Atlantic Monthly* or for Harvard Phi Beta Kappas to hear. She had no publisher whose commercial interests lay in bringing out posthumous editions of her work, whose friends would write retrospective evaluations of her career. There were no surviving relatives whose connections would allow them to publish excerpts from her journals in prestigious places, no son to write three volumes of reminiscences, no son-in-law to write a full-length critical study and then go on to edit her complete works in twelve volumes.

What these facts demonstrate is that an author's relation to the mechanisms by which his or her work is brought before the public determines the status of that work in the world's eyes. Hawthorne's canonization was the result of a network of common interests – familial, social, professional, commercial, and national – that, combined, made Hawthorne a literary and cultural artifact, a national possession. The same combination of circumstances in reverse reconstituted Warner's best-selling novels as ephemera that catered to the taste of a bygone age. Nor was there a conspiracy involved in keeping Hawthorne's reputation green while Warner's withered. By attributing the canonical status of Hawthorne's work to factors other than its 'intrinsic' merit, I do not mean to suggest that the merits that critics and editors discerned in that work were not real, that they promoted work they believed was worthless or mediocre, or that they deliberately ignored work they believed was good. On the contrary, although a mixture of motives was bound to be present in any individual decision to publish or write about Hawthorne's work – friendship, family feeling, commercial gain, professional advancement – these motives are not distinguishable from a belief in Hawthorne's genius and the conviction that his novels were great works of art. For that conviction is itself a contextual matter; that is, it does not spring from a pure, unmediated perception of an author's work on the part of his admirers and supporters (a kind of perception which, as I argued earlier, is never possible), but is determined by the situation in which they encounter it. The circumstances surrounding Hawthorne's texts in the 70s and 80s – literary, cultural, social, economic, and institutional – presented that work to its readers in such a way that it possessed the marks of greatness. Indeed, Hawthorne's work had by that time become one of the touchstones by which literary excellence could be defined, for canonical texts themselves become the bearers of the particular tradition of quality of which they are the exemplars. To put it another way, the fact that an author's reputation depends upon the context within which his or her work is read does not empty the work of value; it is the context – which eventually includes the work itself – that creates the value its readers 'discover' there. Their reading is an activity arising within a particular cultural setting (of which the author's reputation is a part) that reflects and elaborates the features of that setting simultaneously.

At this point, someone might object that while my description of the way Hawthorne's reputation came into being may support the foregoing account of how Hawthorne's texts were constructed, it does not really furnish grounds for making claims about literary works in general. What about Melville, some readers may ask; how did his work come to be appreciated in the twentieth century if there were no relatives and friends, no critical establishment, working to keep it in the public eye? Conversely, why did Longfellow, who had all of the social and institutional advantages I have ascribed to Hawthorne, lose his place in the canon while Hawthorne maintained his? The cases of Melville and Longfellow, though they differ from Hawthorne's at the particular level, are in principle exactly the same. It is not that their work, unlike Hawthorne's, has been judged on its intrinsic merits, but rather that it has been constituted by a changing series of interpretive frames. These authors' fluctuating reputations (Longfellow is now on the verge of a revival) further illustrate how changing definitions of literary value, institutionally and socially produced, continually refashion the literary canon to suit the culture's needs.

# Notes

1   George Bailey Loring, *Massachusetts Quarterly Review*, 3 (September 1850), p. 484–500, as reprinted in *Hawthorne: The Critical Heritage*, ed. Joseph Donald Crowley (New York: Barnes & Noble, 1970), pp. 168–175. The critics in question are Bertha Faust; Joseph Donald Crowley; and Bernard Cohen, ed., *The Recognition of Nathaniel Hawthorne* (Ann Arbor: University of Michigan Press, 1969).

2   Anne W. Abbott, in *Hawthorne*, ed. Crowley, pp. 165, 166.

3   Loring, in *The Recognition of Nathaniel Hawthorne*, ed. Bernard Cohen (Ann Arbor: University of Michigan Press, 1969), p.48.

4   Loring, in *The Recognition of Hawthorne*, ed. Cohen, p. 48; Henry Nash Smith's characterization of Hawthorne's subject matter in 'The Scribbling Women and the Cosmic Success Story', *Critical Inquiry*, 1 (September 1974), p. 58.

5   Loring, in *Hawthorne*, ed. Crowley, p. 173.

6   For the main outlines of the controversy, see Conrad Wright, 'Introduction', *A Stream of Light, A Sesquicentennial History of American Unitarianism*, ed. Conrad Wright (Boston: Unitarian Universalist Association, 1975).

7   Charles Feidelson, Jr., *Symbolism and American Literature* (Chicago: University of Chicago Press, 1953), p. 15.

8   C. E. Frazer Clark, Jr., 'Posthumous Papers of a Decapitated Surveyor: *The Scarlet Letter* in the Salem Press', *Studies in the Novel*, 2 (1970), pp. 395–419.

9   What happened was that Hawthorne, who had gotten the job through the influence of his old college friends and not through local connections or service to the party, lost his post when the Whigs took office. Because he was accused, in the process, of using his office for partisan ends, he became angry enough to stir up his friends on his behalf – hence the heated exchanges in the Salem and Boston papers. See George Woodberry, *Nathaniel Hawthorne* (Boston: Houghton Mifflin, 1902), pp. 163–177, and Arlin Turner, *Nathaniel Hawthorne, A Biography* (New York: Oxford University Press, 1980), pp. 177–187.

10  Longfellow, *North American Review*, 56 (April 1842), pp. 496–499, as reprinted in *Hawthorne*, ed. Crowley, p. 83.

11  Sydney E. Ahlstrom, *A Religious History of the American People* (New Haven: Yale University Press, 1972), p. 398. Ahlstrom's account of the emergence of Unitarianism is instructive for understanding, the literary history of the period.

12  Lewis P. Simpson, *The Man of Letters in New England and the South* (Baton Rouge: Louisiana State University Press, 1973).

13  Simpson, p.22.

14  Simpson, p. 22.

15  Robert E. Spiller *et al.*, eds., *Literary History of the United States*, 3rd ed., rev. (London: Macmillan, 1963), pp. 286–287.

16  Francis Luther Mott, *A History of American Magazines, 1850–1865* (Cambridge, Mass.: Harvard University Press, 1957) (1930), I, pp. 253–255.

17  Mott, *American Magazines* (1957), II, p. 32.

18  Caroline Ticknor, *Hawthorne and His Publisher* (Boston: Houghton Mifflin, 1913), p. 7.

19  Mott, *American Magazines* (1957), II, pp. 33, 494, 496.

20  Turner, pp. 392–393.

21  *Literary History*, ed. Spiller, p. 888; Mott, *American Magazines* (1957), II, pp. 493 ff.

22  Edwin Cady, ' "The Wizard Hand': Hawthorne, 1864–1900', in *Hawthorne Centenary Essays*, ed. Roy Harvey Pearce (Columbus: Ohio State University Press, 1964), pp. 324 ff.

23  Cady, p. 331.

24  Much of this interesting social information is contained in Julian Hawthorne, *The Memoirs of Julian Hawthorne*, ed. Edith Garrigue Hawthorne (New York: Macmillan, 1938).

25    Cady, p. 334.

26    Anna Warner, *Susan Warner* (New York: G. P. Putnam Sons, 1909), p. 126.

27    Henry James, writing in *The Nation* in 1865, says that in its depiction of rural scenes *The Wide, Wide World* is superior to the realism of Flaubert. But later in the review he expresses exactly that critical doctrine which would eventually disqualify Warner's fiction from serious consideration as art. In reviewing *The Schönberg-Cotta Family*, he says that novels written for both parents and children, 'frequently contain . . . an infusion of religious and historical information, and they in all cases embody a moral lesson. This latter fact is held to render them incompetent as novels; and doubtless, after all, it does, for of a genuine novel the meaning and the lesson are infinite; and here they are carefully narrowed down to a special precept'. (*The Nation* [September 14, 1865], pp. 344–345). It is interesting to compare James' comment with Brownson's review of *The Scarlet Letter* attacking the novel for failing to be Christian and moral enough.

# Chapter 19

# John Sutherland

## THE VICTORIAN NOVELISTS
## Who were they?

### I

Awareness of Victorian fiction as an industry is uncommon, even at the level of parenthesis or historical backing to scholarly discussion of canonical texts. And generalizations about 'the Victorian novel' (which are common enough) are often hobbled by their being restricted in range of reference to the dozen writers designated 'major' by the *New Cambridge Bibliography of English Literature* – writers whose extraordinary literary distinction renders them necessarily unrepresentative. Despite fifty years of intense, academically-sponsored research into the form, we still make do with only the sketchiest sense of the infrastructure of Victorian fiction – how the bulk of it was produced; who originated, reproduced, distributed and consumed the product. For most critics, commentators and readers, the Victorian novel is something that appears quite magically on the library shelf, or in the 'Literary Classics' section of the bookshop, found, as it were, under the gooseberry bush, the fruit of Dickens's 'genius' or George Eliot's 'moral sensibility' or Thackeray's 'satire' or Henry James's 'art'.

Statistics are an initial area of vagueness. In his monumental *Nineteenth-Century Fiction, A Bibliographical Catalogue* (5 vols, 1982–86), R. L. Wolff estimates that there are some 42,000 published Victorian novels of which – aiming at completeness – he contrived to collect 7,000. The annual statistics of the trade journal the *Publisher's Circular*, 1837–1901, suggest that total book production rose annually from 2,000 to 8,000 new titles over the Victorian period, and that the proportion of fiction concurrently rose from around 12 per cent to about 25 per cent (the increase being largely explained by the recruitment of new reading publics, particularly after the Education Act of 1870). Assuming exponential progressions for both figures over the 64 years, one arrives at a probable total output of around 50,000 novels. But exactness is impossible, given the fuzzy borders of fiction where it shades into religious-tract, educational and ephemeral periodical reading matter. Around 50,000 is, however, at this stage, a good ball-park figure to start from. When the promised 'History of the Book in Britain' project has done its work we shall know more precisely.[1]

This chapter is concerned less with bibliometrics than with the human infrastructure of Victorian fiction, namely the novelists, those largely invisible masses that Dickens called 'my fellow labourers'. Given an average output of 17 novels per novelist (for the justification of this figure, see below), a work-force of around 3,500 may be hazarded. Given an average working life for novelists of around 32 years (see below again), and the fact that many novelists qualify with only work of fiction, it is a fair guess that two such working forces would populate the period, with the necessary chronological overlaps and a progressive upward scaling to take account of the production increase over the 64 years. At the end of the century, Walter Besant (in his capacity as founder of the Society of Authors) reckoned that there were some 1,200 novelists at work, of whom 200 were entirely self-supporting by their writing. This seems somewhat on the low side and may be biased (especially as regards the self-supporting figure) by Besant's ineradicable gloom about the treatment of the creative writer by philistine English culture. But it is roughly in line with my estimates if one adds the amateurs and one-novel wonders who would have been beneath Besant's notice.

Most of these estimated 3,500 Victorian novelists will never emerge from the obscurity of the statistical mass. Even the most exhaustive investigations can turn up no worthwhile biographical (or sometimes even reliable bibliographical) data. The cult of anonymous authorship which persisted well into the late Victorian period is an often impenetrable screen. Another source of obscurity is the sheer human insignificance of the very minor Victorian novelist. In personal terms, they were of no more consequence than the cabby who drove Dickens to the *All the Year Round* office, or the chambermaid who cleaned the room at the 'Priory', where George Eliot wrote *Felix Holt, the Radical*.

I would guess that some bio-bibliographical profile (dates of birth, death, career details, marital status, total number of novels published) can be readily retrieved for about 1,200 Victorian novelists. For another purpose than this chapter, I have gathered such material on some 878 of them. These represent authors whose records lie close enough to the surface for one to discover salient facts using the resources of the British Library.[2] It is, I think, probably the largest database yet assembled. (The *New Cambridge Bibliography of English Literature*, for instance, has entries on under 200; this will probably be rectified in the third *Cambridge Bibliography*, currently in production.) A lifetime's work could probably turn up a few hundred more, but the majority of Victorian novelists have, I suspect, sunk for ever without trace.

As a sample, 878 cases out of 3,500 is more than substantial enough for statistical analysis, if the sample is not too skewed. But, one must assume, it is manifestly skewed in favour of the 'noteworthy' writer. To have left any record is, in itself, a mark of egregiousness. If the condition of the Victorian novelist is obscurity, to be known is to be in some degree exceptional and to be at all famous (either to one's contemporaries or posterity) is to be a very rare bird indeed. Nevertheless, with the necessary qualifications, 878 novelists is a solid starting point. What I intend to do here is make some preliminary interrogation of this data with the hope of arriving at a set of initially serviceable generalizations about the Victorian novelist, *en masse*.

## II

Close up, the corps of Victorian novelists is bewildering in its variety and diversity. All Victorian life seems to be there: from servants, errand-boys and criminals to High-Court judges, generals, admirals, bishops, prime ministers and marquises. In the general catalogue they may, like Macbeth's dogs, be cleped novelists, but what rational points of congruence can one find, say, between the following pair?

LENNOX, Lord William [Pitt] (1799–1881). Born at Winestead Abbey in Yorkshire, Lennox was the fourth son of the fourth Duke of Richmond. His godfather was William Pitt and one of his cousins was Charles James Fox. While still a thirteen-year-old boy at Westminster school, he was gazetted to a cornetcy. He then joined Wellington's staff as an aide-de-camp, remaining in the post until three years after Waterloo. He missed the battle itself, though in Brussels his mother threw the ball for him which is commemorated in Thackeray's *Vanity Fair*, Byron's *Childe Harold* and Charles Lever's *Charles O'Malley*. If not the author of good literature himself, Lennox was the cause of good literature in others. Lennox sold his commission in 1829, and served as a Whig MP from 1832 to 1834. He was, however, more interested in sport (particularly flat racing) and literature than in public service. The young lord went on to write extensively for the journals and was the author of fashionable novels, which hit the taste of the day but which look very feeble to the modern eye. In his later years, he was a sadly broken-down figure willing to hire himself out for lectures on the theme of 'Celebrities I have known'. Nonetheless his volumes of reminiscences, published in the late 1870s, are lively. His fiction includes: *Compton Audley*, (1841), *The Tuft Hunter* (1843), *Percy Hamilton* (1851), *Philip Courtenay* (1855), *The Adventures of a Man of Family* (1864). There are thirteen novels by Lennox deposited in the British Library.

LEVY, Amy (1861–89). Levy was born at Clapham into a cultured and orthodox Jewish family who actively encouraged her literary talents. She was educated at Brighton, and at Newnham College Cambridge, where she was the first Jewish girl to matriculate. At university in 1881 Levy's first volume of poems was published. Entitled *Xantippe* (after Socrates' fabled shrew of a wife) the work indicated her feminist sentiments. The details of Levy's subsequent life are tantalisingly mysterious. She may have taught, or even have worked in a factory from idealistic motives. She was a friend of Olive Schreiner and of the socialist novelist Clementina Black. Her novel *Reuben Sachs* (1888) is the story of a sexually unscrupulous politician. Its depiction of Jewish life in London as grossly materialistic caused a furore, and was widely taken as a race libel, as was Julia Frankau's similarly anti-Semitic *Dr Philips* (1887). Levy's subsequent novel, *Miss Meredith* (1889) was less tendentious. It is the story of an English Governess, who falls in love with the son of the Italian household where she is employed. Its lightness of tone suggests that it may have been written some time before actual publication. Levy also wrote the shorter fiction *The Romance Of A Shop* (1888), in which four sisters set up their own business. A prey to melancholy, Levy committed suicide by suffocating herself with charcoal fumes shortly after correcting her fifth and last volume of poems for the press. There are three novels of Levy's deposited in the British Library.[3]

Both these are, in their ways (more particularly in their failures), fascinating and instructive cases. Lennox, if we confuse fact and fiction, was actually *there* when George Osborne made his reckless proposal to Becky Sharp on the night before Waterloo. In fact, as the central figure of that actual ball, he survives for posterity only as one of the far background props in its most famous fictional representations. The pathos of his hawking himself around London as a kind of raree show or literary Prufrock is a parable on the treacherous evanescence of fame. And his career is a powerful reminder of the rule that interesting lives do not, inevitably, make for interesting novels. Lennox's is not, of course, a harrowing end, as is Levy's, even in the starkly skeletal form of a dictionary entry. Her Roman death (accompanied by the final act of literary duty) is an almost unbearably poignant indictment of the cruelty of the sensitive Victorian novelist's lot.

Regarding Levy and Lennox as co-professional writers ('two Victorian novelists'), what can one reasonably claim that they had in common, other than that both lived in nineteenth-century England and wrote what the generic record calls fiction? Clearly, the differences make more sense than the similarities. And the main difference I would draw attention to is that Levy began writing early in life as a direct (almost reflexive) career option. Lennox, by contrast, came to novel writing late and indirectly. He ricocheted into it from an earlier, more promising career in the military (cut short by an inconvenient declaration of peace) and from his clear incompetence in fulfilling his expected class destinies in Parliament (possibly due to the equally inconvenient Reform Bill of 1832). This ricochet route into novel writing is, I suggest, a typical male pattern. The direct route into authorship that Levy followed is, by contrast, typically female. In many ways, the archetypal female novelist is Daisy Ashford (1881–1972), who began writing at the age of nine and had four novels complete by the age of thirteen, when she was packed off to convent school, never to write fiction again. The archetypal male novelist, by contrast, would be William de Morgan (1839–1917) who began life as an art student, worked with William Morris, rediscovered medieval techniques for staining glass, set up a successful ceramics factory at Fulham and retired in 1905. In his retirement, aged 65, he began a successful career writing Victorian (in all but date) novels with *Joseph Vance* (1906). He was initially encouraged to write by his wife, who was worried by his depressed state of mind. De Morgan followed this bestseller with five more, and left two works of fiction incomplete at the time of his death. At its bluntest, one may say that men tended to have lived, loved and worked before writing fiction, women often the other way round.

This is not to say that women could not turn their hand to fiction late in life, if they had to; more particularly if it was the only way they could put bread on the family table. One can cite, for instance, the case of Mrs Trollope (1779–1863) who, finding herself let down by her bankrupt husband in the early 1830s, set to at the age of 55 and wrote 35 sprightly works of fiction to keep the Trollopes in middle-class respectability. As resourceful was Amelia Barr (1831–1919), whose husband dragged her off to America and then died of yellow fever (together with three of his daughters), leaving the widow Barr on the streets of New York with $5 in her purse and three surviving daughters to support. At the age of 54, Mrs Barr set to and went on to write 64 popular novels (among them *Remember The Alamo*, 1888, elements of which resurfaced in the 1960s John Wayne movie). A sizeable band of these resourceful ladies can be assembled who, had the wolf not been at the door, would never have put pen to paper, and certainly not in their grandmotherhood.

Something that one may deduce as having been shared professionally by Amy Levy and William Lennox is a sense of guilt and shame. It must have been wormwood for Lennox to pocket his paltry guineas for lecturing on the celebrities he, anything but a celebrity, had known. What the guilt was that drove Levy to suicide one can only guess. But clearly the male, Lennox, was more able to survive than was the female, Levy. This is a pattern one sees elsewhere in the ranks of the profession. Suicide is uncommon, but pseudonyms and anonymity, for instance, were often used to mask shame at being a novelist. Thus Julia Wedgwood (1833–1914, an offspring of the Wedgwood–Darwin dynasty) wrote one of her two novels anonymously and one pseudonymously (as 'Florence Dawson'). Evidently her first (*Framleigh Hall*, 1858) was written without her father's knowledge; her second (*An Old Debt*, 1859) was published only after he gave her his patriarchal imprimatur, having read and censored the manuscript. Thereafter, parental disapproval inhibited Julia Wedgwood from writing fiction altogether. Hugh Stowell Scott (1862–1903) ran into similar paternal opposition. His father, a prosperous shipowner in Newcastle upon Tyne, decreed that his son should follow the family business. Ostensibly dutiful, young Hugh complied. But secretly he began writing and publishing novels, at first anonymously, then under the pseudonym 'Henry Seton Merriman' (the overtones of hedonistic release implicit in this pen name – 'the merry man' – are striking). The difference between Scott and Wedgwood is that he did not finally crumple into filial silence. He went on to write 18 bestselling works of fiction. (He also turned his duplicity to good effect in later life by serving as one of the early clandestine agents of the British secret service.) This greater resolution and independence of the male novelist in the face of the stigma attached to writing fiction is generally borne out by mass survey.

Skimming the bio-bibliographies of 878 Victorian novelists yields any number of suggestive primary observations. Not least, the inadequacy of the term 'novelist', implying as it does both someone who merely wrote a novel and someone who devoted their life to (and won their bread by) fiction. It is said that the Eskimo has twenty words for snow. It would be useful to have a similarly discriminating sub-vocabulary for 'Victorian novelist'. As it is loosely applied, the term can legitimately cover someone like Grace Kimmins ('Sister Grace of the Bermondsey Settlement', 1870–1954), whose philanthropy expressed itself primarily in charitable work in the East End, and who in furtherance of that work wrote one successful novel with a purpose, *Polly Of Parker's Rents* (1899). 'Victorian novelist' equally covers the similarly philanthropic, but exclusively literary Miss Evelyn Everett-Green (1856–1932) who has no less than 254 works of fiction deposited in the British Library (many written for the Religious Tract Society). It is hard to imagine that given a 24-hour day and a 76-year life-span Everett-Green ever had time to do anything but write fiction. If quantity means anything, she was a novelist of a quite different stamp from one-shot Grace Kimmins.

A feature that stands out from a cursory scanning of the 878 bio-bibliographical capsules is the clear link between novel writing and certain historical conjunctions. Sea captains in the 1830s, for instance, were recruited in large numbers into the profession (the names of Marryat, Howard, Chamier, Barker, Glascock, and Neale come to mind). Clearly peace, half-pay, and national nostalgia for the Great Victorious War all played a part. But so too did the training and discipline of the officer's life at sea, which was quite different from that of the land-based soldier. Naval service in the early nineteenth century entailed long periods of boredom unmitigated by drink or women. And, unlike their military counterparts, naval commanders were expected to write as a central part of their duty, keeping the log-book being a daily ritual (soldiers, by contrast, were notoriously illiterate). This state of affairs holds up only to the mid-1850s after which (following Crimean reforms) soldiers became better penmen (and more of them wrote novels). With the advent of steam, sailors had less time to spin yarns, in both senses of the term. Apart from the 1830s and 1840s, sea captains rarely feature as active novelists.

Another fact that strikes the casually enquiring eye is the dynastic effect of the great Victorian novelist on those around him/her, particularly close relatives. Thus, for instance, Thackeray had one daughter, Anne Thackeray Ritchie, who went on to be a considerable novelist in her own right. His other daughter was the first wife of Leslie Stephen, father of Virginia Woolf. The woman with whom Thackeray had his (possibly) adulterous love affair in 1851, Jane Octavia Brookfield, went on after 1868 (Thackeray dying in 1863) to write 4 novels. And her son, Arthur Brookfield, went on in his turn to write 5 novels. A Thackeray cousin, Blanche Ritchie, wrote a novel and so did her husband, Francis Warre Cornish (both narratives were pseudo-Thackerayan in tone). To have 6 novelists clustered so closely around a major novelist is a much higher than chance rate. The same clustering phenomenon is found among the Trollopes. There is Anthony, who wrote 47 novels, his mother Frances Milton who wrote 35, his sister Cecilia who before dying of consumption wrote one, a couple of cousins who wrote about a dozen between them. Finally there was Anthony's brother Thomas Adolphus, who wrote 20 novels, and Thomas's second wife, Frances Eleanor Trollope, who wrote 60-odd. Altogether, Trollopes accounted for some 170 Victorian novels, or

0.3 per cent of the Victorian total. Add his present-day descendant, Joanna Trollope, and the total on the dynastic scoreboard soars out of sight.

Frances Eleanor Trollope's maiden name was Ternan, and she was the sister of Dickens's mistress, Ellen Ternan. Dickens's son Charles Jr did not write novels (although he commissioned many, as the editor in succession to his father on *All The Year Round*). But Angela Dickens, Charles Jr's daughter (1863–1946), went on to write nine novels (all noticeably morbid in tone) and she was aunt (I believe) to the twentieth-century novelist, Monica Dickens. Dickens's daughter Kate married Charles Allston Collins, author of two novels and brother of Wilkie, author of 30. Altogether, this Dickens constellation accounts for some 60 Victorian novels.

Charles Kingsley wrote 10 novels of the first rank. Only slightly less far behind in critical standing was his brother Henry Kingsley, with 20. A daughter of Charles, Mary St Leger, whose married name was Harrison and whose pen-name was 'Lucas Malet', wrote 12 novels. A younger sister, Charlotte (married name 'Chanter') wrote a bestseller, *Over The Cliffs*, in 1860. Altogether, this Kingsley constellation accounts for 45 works of Victorian fiction, all of very high literary quality. Of the 11 children of Frederick Marryat, 4 daughters and one son wrote Victorian novels, running up a family score of around 100 titles.

One could follow these genealogical, or free-masonic, connections much further than I have done here. But it is clear that one of the main predisposing factors to writing Victorian novels was to have a close relative, or intimate acquaintance, who wrote Victorian novels.

## III

Looking at individual cases is delightful, yielding the same kind of pleasure as turning over the pages of old photograph albums. And clearly enough it is instructive as well as perplexing to get to know the personnel behind the novels. But I want now to move to quantitative and more systematic analysis of my 878 cases. The questions to which initial answers are sought are: (1) How many Victorian novelists were seriously professional, and how many were amateur or sideline novelists? (2) Given the fact that Victorian fiction was unique in being a profession/industry/hobby in which males and females took part in equal numbers, is there any observable difference in the ways in which men and women were drawn or recruited into writing novels? Put more simply – what made the Victorian a Victorian novelist, and was the process different for men and women?

For multi-factorial research about 40 different fields can be covered by my data, including such factors as class origin, education, religious background, illness or handicap at significant periods of life, career activities, marital status, and so on. For my purposes here, I have collected responses on the following questions: (1) When was s/he born, and when did s/he die? (2) How many novels did s/he write? (3) At what age did s/he start writing? (4) Was there a career previous to writing novels?

Novel writing, I have said, was unique in Victorian society in being a public and professional activity open both to middle-class men and middle-class women on more or less equal terms. Nevertheless, given the social role forced on them, women naturally tended to be more of a modestly submerged component than their male partners. There was clearly more inhibition on women revealing themselves in the public activity of publication, hence they made more use of the pseudonymity and anonymity conventions afforded by the profession. Revealingly enough, their pseudonyms tended to be sexually neutral, or transsexual as in the following: 'John Oliver Hobbes' (Pearl M. T. Craigie), 'George Egerton' (Mrs Chavelita Bright), 'G. E. Brunefille' (Lady Colin Campbell), 'Lucas Malet' (Mary St Leger Harrison), 'Lucas Cleeve' (Adelina Kingscote), 'Cecil Adair' (Evelyn Everett-Green), 'Leslie Keith' (Grace Johnston), 'Michael Fairless' (Margaret Barber), 'Maxwell Gray' (Mary Tuttiett), 'John Law' (Margaret Harkness), and, most famously,

Currer, Ellis, and Acton Bell (the Brontë sisters). The process is almost entirely one-way. Although men often used pseudonyms, for a variety of reasons, I have discovered only one male using even a vaguely female pen-name, the obscure nautical novelist Alexander Christie (1841–95), who wrote as 'Lindsay Anderson', an amalgamation of his mother's and his wife's maiden names.

The total of 878 yields 566 men and 312 women. As I suggest above, I imagine this is a function of greater reticence about declaring identity among women writers. Altogether, these 878 authors account for 15,490 fiction titles. At first glance, this looks like an impressively large fraction of the 50,000-or-so hypothetical total. But it needs to be qualified. Given the fact that Victorian authors were, regrettably enough, not all born in 1837 and overlap both ends of the period, the 15,490 figure should in prudence be reduced by as much as a third. The graph in Figure 19.1 shows the birthdates of the 878 novelists, from 1790 to 1870. Many of those born at the very end of the period continued writing, in some cases up to the mid-twentieth century. Demographically, the sample reveals no great surprises. The average life expectancy of the male novelist was 66; the female novelist slightly longer, at 68.5 years. The average length of writing career (first novel to death) was 29.9 years for men, and 35.2 years for women. The average age of starting to write was 36 for the male novelist, 33 for the female. (Given the difficulty of determining when a writer actually broke into print, I suspect this figure should be adjusted downwards by about 5 years.)

The per-author lifetime total breaks down to 17.6 novels per writer. Sexually, women novelists averaged 21 titles against men's 15.7. This is a high amount in all categories and suggests that the practice of fiction was thoroughly professionalized. At an average payment of around £250, 16–21 novels would make a useful contribution to a life's income and in many circumstances would constitute its bulk. Given the average career lengths, it gives a novel for every 24 months of professional activity. But the per-author output figures rise even higher if one breaks them down. Thus:

878    (100%)     wrote 1 novel or more       (15,490 titles, or 100%)
553    (63%)      wrote 5 novels or more      (14,542, or 93%)
400    (45.5%)    wrote 10 novels or more     (13,352, or 86%)
212    (24%)      wrote 20 novels or more     (10,651, or 68.7%)

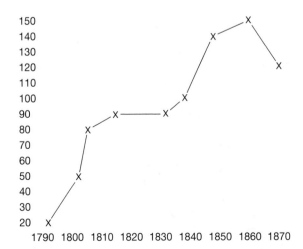

*Figure 19.1*    Birthdates of Victorian novelists

| 141 | (16%) | wrote 30 novels or more | (8,883, or 57.3%) |
|---|---|---|---|
| 95 | (10.8%) | wrote 40 novels or more | (7,277 or 46.9%) |
| 67 | (7.6%) | wrote 50 novels or more | (5,992, or 38.6%) |
| 45 | (5%) | wrote 60 novels or more | (4,159, or 30.7%) |
| 29 | (3.3%) | wrote 70 novels or more | (3,713, or 23.9%) |
| 24 | (2.7%) | wrote 80 novels or more | (3,344, or 21.5%) |
| 19 | (2.1%) | wrote 90 novels or more | (2,932, or 18.9%) |
| 18 | (2%) | wrote 100 novels or more | (2,837, or 18%) |

It is evident from this sample that Victorian fiction was largely the product of a relatively small, active component within a fairly large loosely participatory community (i.e. 7 per cent producing a third of all titles). It is evident too that the canonical novelists could make do on smaller than average outputs (Dickens 15, Gaskell 15, Thackeray 9, Eliot 10) because their work was rewarded more highly than average. And Anthony Trollope, with his 47 fiction titles, is not – given the production rates of the profession – as fertile a writer as commonly believed. Almost half of all Victorian novels seem to have been produced by authors clocking up 40 or more titles.

I have not analysed the class backgrounds in the sample, or other predisposing factors such as higher education. But the prior, or concurrent profession field throws up interesting results. Among the male novelists, all but 57 can be allocated at least one (and in many cases more than one) previous or other gainful line of work. In over half the cases, these are lines of work in which the embryo Victorian novelist has not notably succeeded. The principal stepping-stones to a Victorian man's writing fiction were as follows:

| | |
|---|---|
| Law (predominantly service at the bar) | 110 |
| Journalism | 82 |
| Business, civil service | 75 |
| Church | 57 |
| Army | 50 |
| Teaching | 37 |
| Navy | 21 |
| Medicine | 21 |
| Manual, menial | 17 |
| Book trade | 11 |
| Total = | 481 |

The dominance of law as an entry point into novel writing is the striking feature here. Put simply, one in five (male) Victorian novelists was a lawyer, and in the vast majority of cases a failed barrister. 'Called to the Bar but never practised' is thus the commonest prelude to a career in writing novels. And if one adds lawyer fathers (or, for women, lawyer husbands) the coincidence of a training in law with the Victorian novel is even more pronounced. Nor is it just hacks who turned from law to fiction. Among the great novelists one can cite are: Thackeray (failed barrister), Dickens (articled as a solicitor's clerk in Gray's Inn), Blackmore (called to the Bar but never practised), Stevenson (studied law at Edinburgh), Charles Reade (called to the Bar but never practised), Meredith (articled to a solicitor for a while), Wilkie Collins (called to the Bar but never practised), Harrison Ainsworth (studied law at the Inner Temple).

Some reasons for the law–fiction link may be guessed at. To read for the English Bar, it is necessary to have family money, contacts and (usually) an Oxbridge education. To practise at the Bar was, and is, a top job and one from which the working classes are generally excluded. And, for complex reasons, the British aristocracy have never encouraged younger sons to follow law, directing them instead to the army and the Church. None of this is, however, a convincing explanation of the wide bridge connecting Victorian law and Victorian fiction. A more likely factor is the closeness of the Inns of Court to Fleet Street – journalism often being the transitional stage between law and writing novels. But geographically, some of the main teaching hospitals are even nearer Fleet Street. Yet failed doctors did not drift into novel writing in anything like the same numbers as young lawyers.

The critical factor was, presumably, the peculiar nature of legal training. Reading for the Bar centres on two activities: (1) reading, self-evidently; (2) dining; the law, even more than Parliament, being one of the best clubs in London with the difference that taking dinner a certain number of times is obligatory on trainee barristers. Moreover, the study and practice of law is punctuated by absurdly long vacations. Young doctors, especially during internship, are routinely overworked for 50 weeks of the year. And they do not just read up their professional expertise, which is largely a matter of manual and interpersonal skills. Unlike the newly-qualified doctor, the young barrister emerged from his training without any clear next step. He waited, hopefully, for briefs. Often they were slow in coming. Typically, in this awkward interval, the lawyer would marry, incurring new debts. And typically, in this interval, the drift to writing would occur. Finally, although it is a hard link to discern, there is probably an affinity between the mentalities of jurisprudence and Victorian fiction, shaped as both were by the study of individual cases and the canons of (poetic) justice.

Only 32 of the 312 women can be given alternative professional, business or trade activities. Those with no other vocational attribution than 'married woman' or 'spinster' hugely predominate:

| | |
|---|---|
| Married women | 167 |
| Spinsters | 113 |
| Journalists | 9 |
| Teachers or governesses | 8 |
| Actresses or artists | 6 |
| Doctors or nurses | 4 |
| Book trade | 4 |
| Business | 1 |
| Total = | 312 |

Not surprisingly, perhaps, the Victorian spinster author was the most productive single category of writer, with an average output of 24 titles.

These findings are very preliminary, and in many cases simply confirm what common sense would anyway suggest. And even where the conclusions are instructive (as in the male-professional and female-amateur finding), they should be treated with some caution. The principal uncertainty can be expressed as a question: do the 878 cases examined mirror the profession, or are they a superstructure of the most successful practitioners self-selected by being that much better than the rest? Granted the sample is probably unrepresentative, but it is less unrepresentative than the invariable dozen or so novelists who furnish the staple material for the study of 'Victorian fiction' in higher education. Beneath that elite handful my 878 novelists form a reasonably sound and now fairly visible foundation. Beneath these 878 is a still invisible sub-stratum (of several thousands) composed, one suspects, of failures, rank amateurs, third-rate hacks and utter nonentities. Some future literary archaeological tool will have to be devised to investigate these lower reaches.

## Notes

1   This project is being undertaken by a team of scholars, under the general editorship of D. F. McKenzie. Simon Eliot's *Some Patterns and Trends in British Publishing, 1800–1919* (London, 1994) supersedes some of my comments here.

2   The purpose for which the material was collected was *The Longman Companion to Victorian Fiction* (London, 1988).

3   These entries, and 876 like them, will be found in the *Longman Companion*.

# Chapter 20

# James L. W. West III

## THE MAGAZINE MARKET

> It's all a question of how much a writer can stand to compromise
> — Elizabeth Nowell to Vardis Fisher (1935)

During the 1880s and 1890s, modern mass-circulation magazines came into being in the United States. For the author they provided an important outlet for work and a major source of income. Before 1880, serious authors had only a few respectable magazines in which they could publish – *Scribner*'s, *Harper*'s, the *Century*, and three or four others. Such magazines were usually allied with book publishing firms and addressed a relatively well-educated and genteel audience. They tended, in editorial philosophy, to pattern themselves after such British models as *Blackwood*'s, the *Edinburgh Review* and the *Fortnightly*. In the 1890s and early 1900s, however, editors and publishers like Frank Munsey, S. S. McClure, John Brisben Walker, Edward Bok, and George Horace Lorimer began to produce mass-circulation magazines for a vast middle-to-lowbrow American readership that hitherto had not been addressed successfully. Advances in printing technology – especially in the reproduction of illustrations – made it possible to manufacture visually attractive magazines in huge printing runs and to price them at fifteen cents or a dime, well within reach of these new audiences. During this same period, America was making the final transition from a largely agricultural economy to a predominantly industrial one. Urbanization, growth in average income, better public education, and an increase in leisure time combined to produce a ready audience for magazines that published popular fiction and articles of general interest. During the first half of the twentieth century the American author could publish stories and serialize novels in an unprecedented number and variety of such magazines.

The great boom in national retailing and the growing importance of brand names made mass-circulation magazines the ideal advertising medium for American business. Indeed, it was the partnership between advertising and magazines that made possible the enormous growth of the periodical industry in the United States. Magazine publishers could sell their magazines for less than production costs and still take substantial profits from advertising revenues. Magazine publishers thus became intermediaries between specific groups of businessmen and homogeneous groups of readers. A publisher had to devise an editorial philosophy that would appeal to a particular body of readers and acquire material to fit that philosophy. Then space had to be sold to advertisers who wanted to present their products to that segment of the retail market. Almost every magazine was designed for a well-defined public, large or small, within the total population. As a consequence, the magazine publisher came to be a dealer both in reading matter and in consumer groups.

The great success of magazines such as the *Saturday Evening Post*, *Ladies' Home Journal*, *Redbook*, *Munsey's*, *Collier's*, *Woman's Home Companion*, the *Delineator*, *Cosmopolitan*, *McCall's*, *Liberty*, the various McClure publications, and many other magazines opened up high-paying markets for fiction writers and began to make the services of a good literary agent indispensable. Agents became brokers between magazines and authors, guiding writers to editors who could use their work and introducing editors to authors whose writing would fit the needs of their magazines. Not coincidentally, advertising agencies began to spring up in New York and in other publishing centers at about this time. Such agencies facilitated dealings at another 'interface': they brought businesses in touch with magazines that would reach their particular markets, helped these businesses with copy-writing and layout, and carried out elementary experiments in market analysis.[1]

The important role played by advertising in the magazine industry had an effect on content. A magazine like the *Smart Set*, which addressed a limited and sophisticated readership, could afford to be risqué or controversial because it charged a high price per copy and did not court advertising from name-brand national firms. The drawback for the author was that the *Smart Set* and other magazines of its kind paid low fees – from one hundred to four hundred dollars for a short story and even less for nonfiction. Writers who wanted to publish in mass-circulation magazines and enjoy the financial rewards and wide exposure of such publication had to be ready to tailor their work for those markets. That usually meant turning out a relatively bland product. Much of the material in mass-circulation magazines was written to order. Experienced authors like John P. Marquand and Eric Ambler would receive specific instructions from editors about subject matter, structure, tone, and length. The editor might even dictate the point of the article, story, or poem; the author would write to these specifications for an agreed-upon price, negotiated by the agent.

One writer who worked well within this system was Booth Tarkington, who for over thirty years received top prices for his short fiction and serials from national magazines – particularly from the *Saturday Evening Post*. The editorial philosophy of the *Post* was pro-business and pro-success. The hero of a typical *Post* story used his inborn resourcefulness to overcome difficulties and to achieve high standing in business and fulfillment in love. This philosophy originated in the personal beliefs of George Horace Lorimer, editor of the magazine, who liked to call himself 'The Old Hard-Boiled Self-Made Merchant'. Few deviations from pattern were allowed in the *Post* and an author had to be willing to conform in order to publish there.[2]

Most of the stories Tarkington submitted to the *Post* were readily and even enthusiastically accepted, and Lorimer regularly raised Tarkington's story fee in order to bind him more securely to the magazine. By 1939, Tarkington's price had reached four thousand dollars per story. The self-effacing Gentleman from Indiana was so embarrassed by Lorimer's generosity that he asked, in January 1939, to have his price *cut* – a suggestion that Lorimer laughed down. Tarkington sometimes had to alter his work for the *Post*, however. Political themes, for example, were *verboten*: the *Post* returned Tarkington's story 'Ripley, Try to Be Nice' in April 1939 because 'it is patent anti-New Deal propaganda and we have burnt our fingers on propaganda stories'. Tarkington removed the political references and sold the manuscript to the *Post* on a second try.[3]

Near the end of his life, Tarkington's fiction – heretofore relentlessly upbeat – began to take on slightly darker tones. His novel *The Man of the Family* was turned down for serialization by the *Post* in February 1940 because fiction editor Adelaide W. Neall thought it 'very depressing reading, and it is the fact that it is depressing up to the end that makes us doubt it as a serial for a popular magazine'. For almost the first time in the long history of his dealings with the *Post*, Tarkington was moved to protest. Correspondence followed with Neall about such subjects as 'reality' and 'life', but she was not persuaded. 'I am not prepared to argue with you when you say that none of our lives has a happy ending', she wrote him. Then she added with incontrovertible commercial logic: 'Isn't that perhaps why people want to read stories that suggest that perhaps some of the characters are going to find happiness?' Tarkington gave in and by early March 1940 was revising his serial. He still retained his imaginative facility and his knack for compromise; on 18 March, Neall accepted the revised novel for publication. In her congratulatory letter she told Tarkington, with no apparent irony: 'We have all been admiring the seemingly effortless skill with which you have repaired the weaknesses – from a serial point of view – in MAN OF THE FAMILY.' Neall was not quite finished with the novel, however. When she sent galleys to Tarkington in April, she directed that he cut 'hells or damns or other swear words', all of which she had queried in the margins. He could have a few, she noted, but only a few.[4]

Even a willingness to compromise would not always guarantee a sale, especially if the material in a prospective serial involved a woman of doubtful moral behavior. Zona Gale's novel *Light Woman* dealt with an actress who refused to marry the man with whom she had been living because, after the fashion of the time, she was opposed to the idea of marriage. The manuscript had another drawback as well – it contained a suicide. *Ladies' Home Journal* turned down *Light Woman* in 1934 as did *Cosmopolitan*, even after Gale had offered to change her ending and have her heroine marry the man. Edwin Balmer at *Redbook* stalled, then asked for a new ending; Gale rewrote her conclusion, but Balmer still rejected *Light Woman*. Through Paul Revere Reynolds the novel was offered in succession to *Woman's Home Companion*, *Pictorial Weekly*, *Harper's*, *Scribner's*, *McCall's*, the *Delineator*, *Collier's*, and even the *New York Herald Tribune*, which sometimes printed first-run serials. At that point, Reynolds gave up and returned the manuscript to Gale, who, through a friend, played a long shot and sent the novel to *Liberty*. That magazine, to Gale's great relief, bought the serial rights. Gale had learned a hard lesson about the kind of behavior expected of heroines in popular magazine fiction.[5]

Money from the magazines was extremely important to writers before 1940. Indeed, they often made a good deal more from serial rights than from book royalties. Between 1919 and 1936, F. Scott Fitzgerald earned some $225,784 for his magazine fiction as opposed to only $66,588 for his novels. Theodore Dreiser, in the early 1920s, was still relying heavily on fees for magazine work to meet his day-to-day expenses. Dreiser was by then in his early fifties and was the author of five novels, including *Sister Carrie*, *Jennie Gerhardt*, and *The Financer*, but those books brought him little in the way of dependable income. And Edith Wharton, to take one final example, left Scribners for Appleton in part because the latter house offered more profitable arrangements for serializing her novels in magazines.[6] Serial money, collected in advance, could make it possible to complete a book. A dependable writer whose work was in demand could often contract for serial rights on the basis of a manuscript that was only about one-fourth complete. If an editor liked the finished chapters and the accompanying synopsis of the rest of the story, the magazine would buy the serial rights for a stated figure, payable in installments. An advance of perhaps one-third of the money would be made initially. The author lived on these funds while composing subsequent chapters and collected further checks as later chapters were delivered against specific deadlines. Often the early chapters were running in the magazine before the final chapters had been composed. When these last chapters were delivered, the author received the remainder of the money and was free to begin revising the novel for book publication.

Frequently, however, the author had to pay an artistic price for serial publication. Some novels lend themselves more readily to serialization than others: an episodic story with a chronologically arranged plot, for example, can easily be presented in coherent segments over a five- or six-month period. On the other hand, a novel written within a twenty-four-hour time frame or a narrative with frequent flashbacks and dislocations in chronology will not appear to best advantage in monthly installments. *A Farewell to Arms*, for example, is a relatively straightforward narrative; it was a simple matter for *Scribner's Magazine* to serialize the book in six segments from May to October of 1929. *Tender Is the Night*, by contrast, has a complex time frame and employs a major flashback sequence that takes up the middle third of the book. By splitting this three-part novel into four installments, *Scribner's Magazine* made the potentially confusing narrative structure quite difficult to follow. Fitzgerald was convinced that most reviewers of *Tender* had read it as a serial and that they had gotten a negative first impression of the book in that medium.

Authors who were interested in selling serial rights obviously needed to write their novels with serialization in mind from the beginning, taking care to structure the narrative in installments suitable for monthly magazine publication. James Boyd's first novel, a historical adventure about the Revolutionary War entitled *Drums*, had not been written in this fashion, however, and Robert Bridges, editor of *Scribner's Magazine*, turned it down for magazine publication in 1924 because of Boyd's technique of delineating character. 'The very excellence of your method which reproduces the character through a succession of episodes, rather than through the development of a strong story, seems to me to stand in the way of that impelling interest which is necessary in a serial', wrote Bridges to the young author. In composing subsequent novels, Boyd took care to tailor his manuscripts for the serial market. For example, when he sent the first installment of *Roll River* to Maxwell Perkins ten years later, he noted: 'The action is sustained, and the break is logical. I have an idea that the succeeding installments will not only be briefer but more rapid in movement and therefore satisfactory from a serialization standpoint'.[7]

Concessions to taste and decorum also had to be made. *Scribner's Magazine* had to persuade Hemingway to omit numerous words and lines from *A Farewell to Arms* because they were judged too strong for magazine presentation.[8] Pregnancy, even within wedlock, was a delicate subject: Fitzgerald's 1926 novella 'The Rich Boy' was made fit for appearance in *Redbook* by a bumbling editor who removed from the text, without Fitzgerald's permission, all references to the character Paula Hagerty's swollen shape during her pregnancy. One can imagine the confusion in readers' minds when Paula dies in childbirth a few pages later, without its having been mentioned that she is with child. By 1939 Fitzgerald had learned to anticipate such problems. While drafting *The Last Tycoon*, he realized that some of his material would be potentially censorable. He wrote Kenneth Littauer, editor of *Collier's*, that he would compose the central seduction scene two ways: 'Now we have a love affair between Stahr and Thalia, an immediate, dynamic, unusual, physical love affair – and I will write it so that you can publish it. At the same time I will send you a copy of how it will appear in book form somewhat stronger in tone.'[9]

Some authors saw serialization as undignified. Ellen Glasgow, who was much concerned about her literary reputation, all but forbade her agent Paul Revere Reynolds from offering serial rights for her novels to mass-circulation magazines.[10] More business-minded authors simply saw serialization as a source of additional income. In answer to a query from agent Carl Brandt about a serial feeler from England, John P. Marquand sent a simple two-word telegram: 'HOW MUCH?' An author, however, often lost some control over the text in return for serial money. After purchasing North American serial rights to Marquand's *Point of No Return* for sixty thousand dollars, *Ladies' Home Journal* made it clear to Brandt that some cutting and editorial rewriting might be done. 'It is understood', they wrote, 'that we must of necessity be the final judges as to what goes into the magazine.'[11] Even when novels had been written to specifications, authors could end up with maimed texts, especially if they were not close enough to New York to oversee publication. In 1921, English novelist Arnold Bennett wrote angrily from London to Eric Schuler of the Authors League that the *Delineator* had butchered the first four serial installments of *Mr. Prohack*, a one-hundred-thousand-word novel that he had written for the magazine, as directed, in seven installments of some fourteen thousand words each. From the first four installments, totaling fifty-seven thousand words, the *Delineator* had cut more than twenty-six thousand words. Bennett was furious, but there was nothing he could do.[12] A year later, Fitzgerald's second novel, *The Beautiful and Damned*, was treated similarly by Carl Hovey at *Metropolitan Magazine*. Fitzgerald was unhappy, but the only satisfaction he received was in seeing the uncut text published in book form by Scribner's after the serial run was over.[13]

Authors who wrote regularly for mass-circulation magazines sometimes found themselves typecast by previous material. After the great success of her two-volume *Early Life of Abraham Lincoln* in 1900, Ida Tarbell found that there was virtually no way she could *stop* writing about Lincoln, so insistent were magazine editors that she do follow-up articles on incidents from his life that she had not treated in her biography. People who had known Lincoln or had observed him would contact her with requests that she write up this or that incident; sometimes Tarbell would pay a percentage of her magazine fee to the source of the material. She probably could have made her way easily for the rest of her career by manufacturing little else but spin-off articles on Lincoln, but she very much wanted to work with different material. So eager was she to write on other subjects that she proposed to Reynolds a lengthy article on 'the rise of the hookless fastener' – to us, the zipper. It was a 'rather long and dramatic story', she assured him.[14]

Stephen Vincent Benét's short story 'The Devil and Daniel Webster', published first in the *Saturday Evening Post* on 24 October 1936, brought wide notice to its author and was quickly anthologized in numerous high school textbooks. The story was also adapted for radio and the movies; later a stage play and a television production were mounted. Benét found a ready market thereafter for short fiction based on incidents in American history, but eventually he tired of the material. He complained in a letter to his agent, Carl Brandt, and asked that Brandt try to interest magazine editors in something else. Brandt, however, did not seem to understand the problem: 'I am much interested in the spread of your patriotic writing', he wrote Benét. 'In all seriousness, I don't see how you can get out of it or think you should.'[15] Still, Benét felt trapped by his own success with 'Daniel Webster'.

Something similar happened to William Faulkner in his dealings with *Scribner's Magazine* during the early 1930s. Faulkner sold a cut-down version of 'Spotted Horses' to *Scribner's* in February 1931 and thereafter had difficulty selling them anything else for a time, so determined were they to have another Flem Snopes story. K. C. Crichton, assistant editor of the magazine, wrote Faulkner, 'We regret that it has not been possible to accept more of the stories you have offered us, but on Flem Snopes we are clear. He is our character and we think that in your hands he will become one of the great characters of literature'. Faulkner was probably flattered, but unfortunately for *Scribner's* he had found a higher-paying market for his Flem Snopes material – the *Saturday Evening Post*. In the meantime he sent other stories to *Scribner's*, including 'Rose of Lebanon', 'Idyll in the Desert', and 'All the Dead Pilots', but all were turned down. 'We have become so hipped on the thought of Flem Snopes', wrote Crichton, 'that we are confining all our prayers in the hope that George Horace Lorimer will be struck with lightning just at the time those pieces of yours reach him.'[16]

Fitzgerald must have felt similarly trapped in 1937 when, down on his luck and living in a seedy hotel in Tryon, North Carolina, he was desperately attempting to manufacture amusing love stories, in his old style, for the *Post*. Fitzgerald was heavily in debt to Charles Scribner's Sons, his publisher, and to Harold Ober, his literary agent. He had been in debt before – indeed it was almost a perpetual condition for him after 1920 – but he had always been able to rescue himself by writing short fiction for the *Post* and other mass-circulation magazines. In fact he had even tried to have himself declared 'virtually an employee' of the *Post* in 1932 for income tax purposes.[17] By 1937, however, Fitzgerald had lost the knack of turning out salable material for the popular fiction market. This situation was caused in part by his inability to write convincingly about his prototypical Fitzgerald heroine.Young, beautiful, and willfully independent, she had been a feature of nearly all of his magazine fiction since 1919. By 1937, however, Fitzgerald was no longer much interested in her, and his repeated attempts to recreate her in his post-1935 stories were unsuccessful. These stories are puzzling: the familiar matter of his earlier *Post* fiction is there, but the manner is lacking. The heroines are curiously diminished versions of their more engaging, vital sisters from Fitzgerald's earlier stories. As a working author, however, he had to meet the demands of his market, which, as he interpreted it, still wanted his heroine.

In March 1937, living in the Tryon hotel, the weary Fitzgerald began a story of young love entitled 'A Full Life'. The manuscript opened with an improbable incident in which his heroine, named Gwen Davis, donned an inflatable flying suit and floated out the window of a Manhattan skyscraper. This was to be the first occurrence of a motif Fitzgerald wanted to work into the story, a motif of flying and falling. Gwen flies and falls first from the skyscraper window, later from the deck of an ocean liner, and finally from a circus cannon. Had he been able to inject his writing with a suitably light tone, Fitzgerald might have brought off this little fantasy, but as one reads through the surviving draft of the story, one sees that his heart was not in the work. Plotting is artificial, characters are wooden, and motivations are unclear.

About midway through the draft, Fitzgerald apparently realized what was happening and, in disgust, worked a freakish detail into the story. He quite literally filled his heroine with dynamite. Gwen leaves her childhood home because she does not want to 'raise the roof'. Later she marries the son of a gunpowder manufacturer because she has 'always belonged to him'. Still later she becomes a circus daredevil who makes her living by being shot from a cannon. Gwen's performing name is symptomatic of Fitzgerald's dislike for her: he dubs her 'The Human Shell' – and indeed she is an empty character. Discouraged by his inability to bring his dynamite-filled heroine to life and tired of trying to manufacture yet another light romance for the *Post*, Fitzgerald made a macabre private gesture in his manuscript. He blew Gwen up. The explosion killed a man standing next to her and was heard as far away as New York City. This grisly little tale reveals much about Fitzgerald's state of mind during his famous Crack-Up period. He felt victimized by his previous success, locked into writing one kind of story about one type of character – a heroine about whom he no longer cared.[18]

Many authors of novels and short fiction chafed under the formal and structural limitations imposed on them by mass-circulation magazines. They disliked the simplistic, undeviating pattern of the 'formula' story: it began typically with action or dialogue in order to capture the attention of a reader paging through an issue; it was rigidly plotted and moved relentlessly toward an artificial climax; and it ended with a 'final suspiration', often faintly saccharine in tone, usually in the advertising pages at the rear of the magazine'.[19] Some writers (Sherwood Anderson, for example) could not adapt to these limitations. Other authors – Fitzgerald, Faulkner, and Dreiser among them – learned to work more or less within the formula and eventually turned out some very good short fiction for the big-audience slicks. Writing for high-paying magazines, however, was not a predictable business. Editors and staff readers changed with some frequency at the various magazines, and editorial requirements fluctuated. Writing for the magazines took patience, adaptability, and a thick skin. There was no sheet of dos and don'ts for prospective authors to follow; length, subject matter, tone, language, plot, characterization – all had to be negotiated by a complicated system of trial and error, inference and suggestion, submission, rejection, and re-submission. The work could be frustrating, but the potential financial rewards were large. In fact, most American authors before World War I saw the magazine market as virtually their only source of big money. After the war, however, different ways of publishing one's work, or adapting it to other media, began to emerge. Books could be serialized or abridged or distributed through book clubs or reprinted as paperbacks; story material could be adapted for presentation on the radio, stage, screen, or lecture circuit. Even translation rights could yield significant amounts of money for some books. The author set about tapping these new sources of income and learning how to exploit the full earning potential of what was now beginning to be called a 'literary property'.

## Notes

1 Theodore Peterson, *Magazines in the Twentieth Century*, 2d ed. (Urbana: University of Illinois Press, 1964), chaps. 1–5; James Playsted Wood, *Magazines in the United States*, 2d ed. (New York: Ronald Press, 1956), chaps. 9–11, 13, 20–21.

2 John Tebbel, *George Horace Lorimer and the* Saturday Evening Post (Garden City, N.Y.: Doubleday, 1948); 'George Horace Lorimer', in James Playsted Wood, *The Curtis Magazines* (New York: Ronald Press, 1971). In 1901–2, Lorimer wrote an extraordinarily popular epistolary series for the *Post* entitled 'Letters from a Self-made Merchant to His Son' – hence the sobriquet. Also see Bernard Berelson and Patricia J. Salter, 'Majority and Minority Americans: An Analysis of Magazine Fiction', *Public Opinion Quarterly* 10 (1946): 168–90; and Patricke Johns-Heine and Hans H. Gerth, 'Values in Mass Periodical Fiction, 1921–1940', *Public Opinion Quarterly* 13 (1949): 105–13.

3 Adelaide W. Neall (*Post* fiction editor) to Tarkington, 17 April 1939, Tarkington Papers, Princeton University, Princeton, N.J. Literary feuding was also not allowed. In March 1930, Sherwood Anderson sent an article on cotton-mill workers to John Hall Wheelock at *Scribner's Magazine*. The manuscript, entitled 'Labor and Sinclair Lewis', was in part an attack on the author of *Main Street* for his satirical portraits of life in small American towns. Wheelock found Anderson's treatment of Lewis too vehement and personal and required Anderson to rewrite in order to direct his criticisms more generally against a group of anti-small-town writers. (Wheelock to Anderson, 19 March 1930, Scribner Archive, Princeton University, Princeton, N.J.)

4 Neall to Tarkington, 12 and 19 February, 18 March, and 22 April 1940, Tarkington Papers, Princeton University, Princeton, N.J.

5 Zona Gale files, P. R. Reynolds Papers, Butler Library, Columbia University, New York, esp. Reynolds to Gale, 6 September 1934.

6 *As Ever, Scott Fitz – Letters between F. Scott Fitzgerald and His Literary Agent Harold Ober, 1919–1940*, ed. Matthew J. Bruccoli and Jennifer McCabe Atkinson (Philadelphia: Lippincott, 1972), p. xviii; Thomas P. Riggio's introduction to Dreiser's *American Diaries, 1920–1926*, ed. Thomas P. Riggio *et al.* (Philadelphia: University of Pennsylvania Press, 1982), p. 15; Charles A. Madison, 'Charles Scribner and Edith Wharton', in *Irving to Irving: Author–Publisher Relations, 1800–1974* (New York: Bowker, 1974), pp. 140–41

7 Bridges to Boyd, 13 May 1924; Boyd to Perkins, 20 March 1934, Scribner Archive. In his letter to Perkins, refers to *Roll River* by its working title, 'The Dark Shore'.

8 Michael S. Reynolds, *Hemingway's First War: The Making of* A Farewell to Arms (Princeton: Princeton University Press, 1976), chap. 3.

9 James L. W. West III and J. Barclay Inge, 'F. Scott Fitzgerald's Revision of "The Rich Boy"', *Proof* 5 (1976): 133; Fitzgerald to Littauer, 29 September 1939, *Correspondence of F. Scott Fitzgerald*, ed. Matthew J. Bruccoli and Margaret M. Duggan (New York: Random House, 1980), p. 547.

10 James B. Colvert, ed., 'Agent and Author: Ellen Glasgow's Letters to Paul Revere Reynolds', *Studies in Bibliography* 14 (1961): 177–96.

11 Marquand to Brandt (cable), 7 December 1948; Hugh M. Kahler (*Ladies' Home Journal*) to Carl Brandt, 21 September 1948, Marquand Collection, Beinecke Library, Yale University, New Haven, Conn.

12   Bennett to Schuler, 14 October 1921, Authors League file, Henry Holt Papers, Princeton University, Princeton, N.J.

13   See Arthur Mizener, *The Far Side of Paradise*, rev. ed. (Boston: Houghton Mifflin, 1965), p. 158.

14   Tarbell to Reynolds, 22 August 1927, P. R. Reynolds Papers.

15   Brandt to Benét, 27 June 1941, Benét Collection, Beinecke Library, Yale University, New Haven, Coon.

16   Crichton to Faulkner, 23 July and 6 August 1931, in James B. Meriwether, ed., 'Faulkner's Correspondence with *Scribner's Magazine*', *Proof* 3 (1973): 268–69.

17   Fitzgerald to Ober, ca. 21 April 1932, *As Ever Scott Fitz–*, pp. 190–93.

18   See James L. W. West III, 'Fitzgerald Explodes His Heroine', *Princeton University Library Chronicle* 49 (1988): 159–65.

19   Henry Seidel Canby, 'Free Fiction', *Atlantic Monthly* 116 (July 1915): 60–68.

# Chapter 21

# N. N. Feltes

## ANYONE OF EVERYBODY
## Net books and *Howards End*

In her book on Mudie's Library, Guinevere Griest's answer to her own question, 'Who killed the three-decker?' is neither precise nor satisfying. She rightly dismisses the proud claims of individuals, of George Moore or his publisher, Henry Vizetelly, or of other publishers who had independently issued single-volume novels in the 1890s, but she then cites only 'years of economic pressure' before shifting her attention completely: 'What is remarkable about the end of the three-volume form is the completeness and rapidity of its disappearance.'[1] Royal Gettmann, in the other extended study of the sudden disappearance of novels in the three-volume format, is more specific in assigning a cause – 'the three-decker was bound to disappear because it had ceased to be profitable to the libraries'[2] – but he then becomes too engrossed in the 'pounds, shillings and pence' of Mudie's diminishing profits (257–58). Gettmann's analysis is based on the account books and correspondence of the house of Bentley, so that his explanations tend often to elaborate Bentley's own, or those given in the letters from Mudie. At the end of the chapter on the three-decker he does allude to wider circumstances, to 'confusion and uncertainty', 'bewilderment and paralysis' in publishing, remarking ambiguously that the abolition of the old form meant, in effect, that 'the publisher for the moment could not call the tune or that he was forced to call a new one' (262). But he does not escape the individual publisher's vantage point enough to question what that 'tune', old or new, might be. To think through the death of the three-decker novel we again need a more relational, a dialectical point of view, not least because, as Gettmann admits,

> actually the 'nineties was not a bad time for publishers, as may be seen from the number of other new firms which came into existence and flourished at this time – Edward Arnold, Methuen and Company, John Lane, and Duckworth and Company. (263)

. . .

The signs of confusion were everywhere in the publishing industry from the mid-80s. The era of 'free trade in books', inaugurated in 1852 by the defeat of the London Booksellers' Committee's attempt to regulate retail prices, had been a period of intense retail price competition, as booksellers discounted new books directly to the public. Indeed, because of this, by 1890, when the London Booksellers' Society was founded, 'the complete collapse of retail bookselling' seemed imminent.[3] At the same time, the circulating libraries' profits were diminishing because the number of novels published (and the space required to stock three-deckers) was increasing faster than the subscription lists, a pressure that was increased as the publishers more often hurried the date of reprinting at a low price.[4] Individual authors such as George Moore demanded that novels be issued at 'a purchaseable price', so that they might appeal directly to the public, while authors organized into the Society of Authors in 1883, a move which was thought to be provocative, 'trade union' behavior.[5] The Education Act of 1870 had obviously changed the conditions of publishing, as did the Berne Convention on international copyright in 1887 and the American 'Chace Act' of 1891:

> The decline of the three-decker from the mid-eighties until its death in the mid-nineties is well known to have resulted from differences between British publishers, booksellers, circulating libraries and the Authors' Society. But it is not altogether fanciful to detect a contributory cause in American copyright law. After 1891 the British publisher was naturally reluctant to go to the expense of printing three volumes at home of a novel which had also to be manufactured as a single volume in America.[6]

From the point of view of the production of books those are but contributions or responses to the larger, conjunctural crisis; the prevailing arrangement, the relations of production and distribution, were clearly blocking realization of the potential for the production of commodity-texts. The crisis entailed changing the system while retaining control; the problem was who was to inherit control of the production of books, and the answer, of course, was the capitalist publishers. . . .

In 1895 the Associated Booksellers of Great Britain and Ireland was founded (succeeding the London Booksellers) 'to support . . . the principle of a net price for books'.[7] The Publishers' Association was formed in the same year, and by 1899 the Net Book Agreement had been adopted by the two associations and by the Society of Authors and went into effect the next year.[8] The Net Book Agreement had established a new, consensual 'terms of trade'; Frederick Macmillan proudly referred to it in 1924 as 'the Magna Charta of the book trade'.[9]

But if the Net Book Agreement was the book trade's Magna Carta, the 'Book War' was its war of liberation, the struggle by which the new publishing structure established itself ideologically. That controversy from 1906 to 1908 over the practices of the *Times* Book Club both clarified the new terms which the agreement had instituted and showed that they could be defended publicly, that the new ideological consensus was one which not even the *Times* could subvert. The *Times* had been in financial difficulty in the early 1900s: for several years neither its sales, the amount of advertising, nor its profits had grown. Moberly Bell, its editor, believed that it had become impossible to make the *Times* pay, both because he believed that it was increasingly difficult to make even an ordinary newspaper pay and because the *Times* 'was neither an ordinary newspaper nor produced in ordinary conditions'.[10] In 1898, assisted by two American entrepreneurs, Bell had attempted to boost circulation by marketing a cheap reprint of the ninth edition of the *Encyclopaedia Britannica* in installments. When this scheme proved profitable, the same promoters founded the *Times* Book Club, a subscription system in which a 'discount subscriber' to the *Times* might borrow any book, three volumes at a time, delivered and collected without charge anywhere in London. Also, and this was the real issue of the 'Book War', the subscriber-member was entitled to purchase at a large discount any book previously borrowed.[11] Clearly, this promise to discount 'unspoilt' copies a few weeks after publication side-stepped the Net Book Agreement; as a publishers' pamphlet argued, 'a "spoiled" copy is everywhere recognized as a copy which . . . cannot be sold as a new or fresh copy', and 'an "unspoilt" copy is, therefore, equivalent to a new copy'.[12] Edward Bell, the president of the Publishers' Association, stated their case:

> It is obvious that such announcements were calculated to divert custom from the regular dealers in new books, and in the case of net books, amounted to an evasion, if not an actual infringement of the Net Book Agreement.[13]

The *Times*, of course, tried to define the terms of the struggle in its own interest:

> Fifty-four years ago the publishers attempted, by restrictions on trade, to maintain the high prices then charged for books, and to create for their own profit a firm and permanent monopoly, to be maintained at the expense of the public.
>
> Today the publishers . . . are trying to control not only the price of new books, but the price of second-hand books.[14]

But the prices were no longer 'high', and the issue was no longer perceived as 'monopoly'; the new terms of trade constituted by the Net Book Agreement seemed untouched by the *Times*' charges that while they did not formally constitute a trust they nevertheless allowed the publishers to be 'so solidly organized that they act as against all outsiders with the unanimity and precision of a trust'.[15] 'Exclusive dealing' was the term helpfully suggested by the judge in the libel case which so undermined the position of the *Times* and its Book Clubs.[16] The Booksellers' Association and the Society of Authors[17] sided with the publishers, and when Lord Northcliffe secretly bought the *Times* in 1908 he quickly sued for peace. The settlement not only reasserted the Net Book Agreement 'without any modification', but added a provision for a 'close time' on Book Club copies, six months on net books and three months on subject books, during which they might not be sold as 'second-hand'. Thus ended, as Frederick Macmillan recalls, 'in a manner most satisfactory to me and to publishers in general, one of the most remarkable quarrels in the annals of the Book Trade'.[18] The satisfactory result was to establish the Net Book Agreement definitively as the 'terms of trade', and thus to allow the victorious publishers fully to explore the possibilities in these newly structured relations of production and distribution of books.

But what had happened in the book trade was simply what had happened generally in the production and distribution of commodities at the turn of the century. The end of the last and the beginning of the new century, says a standard history of the subject, 'saw a decisive change from competitive to associative organization in almost every trade in Britain', as a new form of monopolist organization established itself in retail trade associations like the Publishers' Association. This was 'merely a continuation of the development of cartels and trusts in British industry',[19] in the same way that the Net Book Agreement transformed the hegemony of the three-decker/lending library arrangement by concentrating control in the hands of publishers. The purpose of the agreement (indeed, the 'kernel' of all trade associations' policy) was 'to eliminate certain phases of competition by imposing on their members certain regulations of trading',[20] that is, to eliminate 'underselling' by enforcing net prices for books. But the practices of retail price maintenance have a more direct bearing on our understanding of publishing practice following the Net Book Agreement. Hermann Levy discusses the way that manufacturers, given 'general agreement about price levels and certain trading conditions', are now constantly faced with the need to devise 'new methods of securing [their] retailing customers', and a primary means is that extension of the principle of a *patent* which creates 'branded goods', to be sold at advertised (or in the publishers' term, 'net') prices.[21] . . .

But in the new 'direct' arrangement, control has passed the publishers; 'the key to the situation', writes another commentator, 'lies in the manufacturer's hands'.[22] The practice of 'branded goods' permits manufacturers not only to 'discipline price cutters'[23] but, more importantly, directly 'to capture the retailer's customers' by creating what these economic historians call 'consumer insistence': 'it is this "consumer insistence" which is intended to create the quasi-monopoly value of the brand'.[24] Thus, while publishing may be 'a type of business distinct from others in many respects',[25] in many other respects it is very similar, these practices of retail price maintenance generally explaining the early distinction between 'net' and 'subject' books, the dynamics of book production under the Net Book Agreement, and the reasons for finally including, in 1914, novels among net books. Since the economics of the 'branded article' conform fundamentally with 'the necessities of modern mass distribution in general',[26] in book publishing the 'branded article' may be seen as a translation of the function of 'class' categories in the 'new journalism', interpellating 'consumer insistence' from a 'class' of 'unknown customers'. The translation, the ideological categories, and the practices specific to book production may be seen only occasionally in the few historical studies, but quite vividly in publishers' notices in the trade journals of the 1890s and early 1900s. . . .

In 1894, the *Bookseller*, responding in 'Trade Gossip' to letters to the *Times* about net book prices, was again to specify 'the application of the system to certain select classes of books, especially those published at a high price, or which appeal only to a limited class of readers'.[27] Macmillan's choice of net books in those early months was clearly to some extent dictated by those considerations; but their very first choice for a net book had been intended from the start to test a more subtle possibility. 'It was important that the book chosen should be a good one', Frederick Macmillan recalled,

> because if the first net book did not sell, its failure would certainly be attributed to its *netness* and not to its quality. It so happened that in the spring of 1890, we had in preparation a book on *The Principles of Economics*, by Professor Alfred Marshall, the well-known economist and then Professor of Political Economy at the University of Cambridge. There was little doubt that this book would at once take a leading place in the literature of Economics, and it suggested itself as a most appropriate subject for the experiment we wished to try.[28]

Here we have the beginning of an experiment in selling books as a new kind of 'branded goods'; rather than appealing to a known, limited market for a commodity-book, with Mrs. Oliphant's *Royal Edinburgh*, say, or to the market for gilt edges and morocco bindings, Macmillan is here testing an assumed 'quality', a 'reputation-value', as a way of interpellating the 'unknown' reader prepared to buy a commodity-text. Books advertised as 'net' in these first years appear to be of these two types: either they are the sort of books which booksellers could not sell generally, on abstruse topics or in special formats or bindings, or they are books which by some sort of 'reputation-value' may be hoped to interpellate an unspecified 'class' of unknown readers. Thus 'net' books might be either commodity-books or commodity-texts; 'subject' books remained commodity-books, subject ultimately to a bookseller's persuasion and blandishment, as well as discount. But it was the possibility of extra profit which was opened up in the 'net' category which publishers were to explore and exploit directly.

To assert, then, that 'at first the net system was only applied to high priced books, especially books selling at more than 6 *s.*,' is inaccurate, but more importantly it is an assertion which arises out of 'free market' assumptions, based on the simple efficacy of 'demand'. The net system was at first applied only to high-priced books, Russi Jal Taraporevala writes, 'presumably because the demand for these books was considered by publishers to be relatively inelastic':

> Hence the increase in price, due to 'netting', was not expected to reduce total sales substantially. On the other hand cheaper books, for which the demand was presumably thought to have been more elastic, came within the net system only in its later years.[29]

The problematic of a presumed elasticity/inelasticity of 'demand' only obscures the dynamics of the net book system; from the point of view of the production of books (rather than 'demand'), the publishers may be seen to have eventually so expanded net books as sophisticated 'branded goods' that 'demand' became a controlled effect of production. The 'reputation-value' at the core of 'branded goods' lay in an author's name, as with the 'well-known' Professor Marshall, interpellating unknown readers of commodity-texts, creating a new audience, although ideologically it might be explained as 'satisfying a demand'. Publishers were now in a position in the economic structure to undertake in a controlled way the creation of the kinds of mass audiences which the different careers of Charles Dickens and Charles Knight, seventy-five years earlier, had shown to be accessible to a new literary mode of production, by exploiting systematically the power of a commodity-text to interpellate an infinity of unknown subjects. Neither an author, a printer, nor a bookseller could afford

> to take the risk of promoting books . . . on the scale that was now necessary. Older publishing houses . . . rose to greater prominence, and new ones . . . soon achieved leading positions in the book trade.[30]

Hence 'the mad quest for the golden seller' that Henry Holt described in 'The Commercialization of Literature' in 1905, 'the mad payment to the man who has once produced it, and the mad advertising of doubtful books in the hope of creating the seller'.[31] . . .

The particular forms of 'modernization' I have been analyzing are not merely new 'marketing techniques' but rather a necessary extension of the transformation of the relations of production which constituted fully capitalist book publishing. The process initiated in 1890 by Frederick Macmillan, explored in his own list and expanded to those of other publishers, was precisely the 'emerging deciding dividing' process of which Williams writes. It arrives (in passing, of course), as net books become increasingly the rule, in increasingly integrated, confident, standardized, and masculine structures of capitalist control, 'masculine' not only because of the list of agents (Macmillan, John Murray, William Heinemann, or Edward Arnold) but also because of the patriarchal necessity of control, of centralized, purposeful planning (sometimes described as 'risk-taking') in the production of commodity-texts. For the disruptions in the form of the novel were produced by these transformations of the relations of novel production; if 'the parting of the ways' (Williams's chapter heading in *The English Novel*) may be described on an ideal level as the separating of psychological from sociological fiction, from the point of view of production the separation was determined in the last instance by those very forces which determined the separation of 'net' from 'subject' books. Even new novels, until 1914 usually sold subject to discount, could not entirely escape 'netness', those forces determining the overall net/subject structure, for the whole production process, as well as each sector of it, was inevitably in an overdetermined relationship to the 'visibly altering world', the 'quite fundamental changes in the economic situation', such as scientific management and the revival of capital export, which were producing also the new unionism, the crisis in the London housing market and in the growth of the suburbs, and, in 1903, the Women's Social and Political Union.[32]

Edward Arnold was one of the first of the new names in publishing in the nineties; although the firm became noted for publishing the standard school books required after the Education Act, fiction was 'not uncommon under this imprint' early in the century.[33] Forster came to Arnold with *A Room with a View* in 1908. His first two novels had been published by William Blackwood. Forster had sent a short manuscript entitled 'Monteriano' to *Blackwood's Magazine* in 1905 and, as he wrote to his mother, Blackwood offered to publish it in volume form:

> the terms they offer are not at all good – I have written trying to do better, and meantime am trying to find out whether Blackwoods as *publishers* are a good firm, as though I dont mind much about money it's important to be in the hands of people who will advertise you well. Methuen and Heinemann are the firms I should have naturally tried first. The title has to be changed, which is very sad, but I see their point of view.[34]

Blackwood's point of view was that the name 'Monteriano' would be detrimental to the sale of the book; a friend of Forster's suggested 'Where Angels Fear to Tread' and Blackwood agreed that the change would improve the novel's 'already slight chances of success'.[35] Forster remained with Blackwood for *The Longest Journey* (1907) but switched to Arnold with *A Room With a View*; the reasons for the change are unknown.[36] In March 1909 Forster sent Arnold a synopsis and 'a rough draft' of thirty chapters of *Howards End*.[37] Oliver Stallybrass, the editor of the Abinger Edition of the novels, notes that the firm's readers and Arnold himself were bothered by Helen's sexual encounter with Leonard Bast, perhaps having that episode in mind when they suggested shortening the novel. A month later, when the novel was in proof, Forster indicated to Arnold some agreement about Helen:

> I was much struck by your original criticism, and tried to do what I could, but the episode had worked itself into the plot inextricably. I hope however that the public may find the book convincing on other counts.[38]

Edward Arnold published *Howards End* on 18 October 1910, 6 *s.*, crown 8vo., in 2,500 copies with further impressions of 1,000, 3,000 and 2,500 copies in November 1910, and 1,000 more in December; 9,959 copies were sold.[39] P. N. Furbank describes the novel's reception: 'The book hit the note of the time. . . . For the first time the word "great" was bandied about . . . ', and he quotes the *Daily Mail* reviewer's emphasis on the novel's 'coherence and connectedness', saying that 'only connect' might be Forster's motto 'not only for his book but for his method of work':

> the fitting of the perception of little things with the perception of universal things; consistency, totality, *connection*. Mr. Forster has written a *connected novel*.[40]

Clearly one 'note of the time' which *Howards End* hit is indicated by the appreciation in the contemporary press for the injunction to 'connect', a note which paradoxically seems timeless, given the attention paid by later critics to Forster's concern with 'the relationships, and the possibility of reconciliation, between certain pairs of opposites'. . . .

This vision of connectedness is presented metaphorically again and again in *Howards End*, as when the narrator demonstrates the 'wisest course' for showing a foreigner England: to stand on the summit of the final section of the Purbeck Hills, 'then system after system of our island would roll together under his feet', and as Forster directs 'the trained eye' to these systems, the reason fails, like a wave on the Swanage beach; the imagination swells, spreads and deepens, until it becomes geographic and encircles England. (164–65)

Yet such a vision, such imagination, is not accessible to the lower-middle-class Leonard Bast – in a moment of despair Leonard realizes 'to see life steadily and to see it whole was not for the likes of him' (52) – nor was it available to a calculating businessman, 'who saw life more steadily, though with the steadiness of the half-closed eye' (320). Margaret Schlegel, on the other hand, believing that it is impossible to see 'modern life' steadily, had chosen 'to see it whole' (158). The novel's 'patient synoptic comment' is here vague and ambiguous, the imaginative vision which is its theme being finally only 'an impossible, yet heroic, effort to "see life steadily and see it whole",'[41] which echoes both wistfully and a little shrilly in the defensive naiveté of its final words:

> 'The field's cut'! Helen cried excitedly – 'The big meadow! We've seen to the very end, and it'll be such a crop of hay as never'! (340)

But if Helen's outburst embodies the thematic uncertainty in *Howards End*, ignored or accepted by contemporary and later critics alike, its language, as in the final utterance, also embodies a more profoundly historical contradiction, in the novel's interpellation of its reader-subject. We, too, have 'seen to the very end', of *Howards End*; but, then, who are 'we'? The novel asks this question, historically crucial, on several levels, some of them more self-reflexive than others. 'Who's "we"?' Henry Wilcox asks his son, 'My boy, pray, who's "we"?' (281) and Wilcox is himself later asked by Margaret, as he is attempting to ensure her personal loyalty, 'Who is "we"?' (301). But in 1910 that question was central for the novelist too; it had a determinate historical weight. For while *Howards End* was published by Arnold 'subject to discount', Longman, Chatto, and others were already publishing new fiction 'net', in various formats and prices.[42] Forster was inevitably implicated in that continuing project to establish the new structures of net-book publishing; in 1909 he had joined with other authors in an undertaking 'not to publish an edition of any novel first published at the price of 6 *s*. in a cheap form at any time within two years from the date of its first publication'.[43] And whether a novel was published 'net' or 'subject', the reading audience as a whole was being reconstituted by the relations of production we have discussed. A novelist might not necessarily be attempting to interpellate a mass audience, but as the relations of production moved ever more towards that possibility it became increasingly difficult for a novelist to imagine who or where another, more specific audience might be. In *Howards End* this difficulty, the determinate presence of the Net Book Agreement, registers itself in the awkward indeterminacy of the narrator's indefinite pronouns, 'we' and 'one'.

The characters in *Howards End* most often use the indefinite 'we' in a conventional way, 'in general statements in which the speaker includes those whom he addresses, his contemporaries, his fellow countrymen, or the like' (*OED*), as in Mrs. Munt's 'what *we* are doing in music' (33), or sometimes by asserting a specifically upper-middle-class 'we', as when she wonders if the Wilcoxes are 'our sort' (6). Similarly, within the created Schlegel world, 'one knows what foreigners are' (12), 'one' being 'anyone of everybody, including (and in later language often specially meaning) the speaker himself' (*OED*); thus Mrs. Wilcox gently rebukes her son: 'one doesn't ask plain questions' (19). But, outside the Schlegel/Wilcox world, the narrator's 'we' or 'one' is far less confident. It may include the speaker, fellow countrymen, and the like, but the 'like' may shift uneasily to include unknown reader/subjects. The narrator's 'we' is often clearly English, as when the London railway termini are described as 'our' gates to the provinces (9)' or when 'two members of our race' play at 'Capping Families' (18). But while 'we' are also occasionally clearly upper-middle-class – 'we' visit the country on weekends, and 'we' look back with disquietude to the 'elder race' which once lived there (266) – the interpellation of that class is often undercut, complicated by a not-quite-assured irony which in its uncertainty acknowledges values and subjects more inclusive and urgent than class-values and class-subjects. Leonard Bast's flat in Camelia Road contains a photograph of 'a young lady named Jacky' which had been taken 'at the time when young ladies named Jacky were often photographed with their mouths open'. Jacky's photograph and smile are condescended to further, but then the tone is disrupted just as the narrator moves directly to enlist the reader:

> Take my word for it, that smile was simply stunning, and it is only you and I who will be fastidious, and complain that true joy begins in the eyes, and that the eyes of Jacky did not accord with her smile, but were anxious and hungry. (46)

Who, indeed, constitute the 'you and I' here, revised from the 'you or I' of the manuscript precisely to be inclusive?[44] The narrator is, at first, still ironical about the 'stunning smile', then, as 'you and I' is introduced, 'fastidious' (and still more ironically 'captious' in the manuscript [43]), but then erases 'our' ironic privilege by admitting it, as 'we' contradictorily acknowledge the anxiety and hunger. At a moment like this the text's 'we', the 'everybody' which includes 'anybody', tries jerkily to expand to include even nobodies like Jacky. . . .

   This effort which the text of *Howards End* so often makes tentatively to open up the narrator's 'we', or the indefinite 'one', to an 'anyone' of a determinedly inclusive 'everybody', is much more historically specific than being merely 'the fag-end of Victorian liberalism'.[45] It is the effort which the new literary mode of production demands of 'net' books, but also of 'subject' books (like most novels in 1910), as the new literary market is itself 'produced'. For while Forster assuredly did not set himself in 1909–10 to write a best-seller in *Howards End*, he nevertheless equally surely wrote within a determinate structure of book production, developed over the preceding twenty years, which enabled publishers to use the new means of production to produce commodity-texts. The 'bestsellerism' and 'bestsellerdom' to which John Sutherland refers are but ideological labels for the full development in capitalist book production of that internal drive towards 'total commercial rationalization' and the 'hectic change and turnover' in which capitalism realizes its 'general formula'.[46] Sutherland finds 'good historical reasons' why the modern novel is 'necessarily tied to the wheels of progressive technology, commercial management and the dictatorship of the consumer'.[47] I have denied the 'dictatorship' of the consumer, insisting instead on the control of the capitalist publisher, but otherwise I have detailed the material conditions of Sutherland's necessities and traced that historical process in a text, not even of a best-seller, but of *Howards End*. For the audience of the old, hegemonic literary mode of production had disappeared with the three-decker; readers were being reagglomerated as 'consumers' of commodity-texts by the new, rampant, fully capitalist literary mode of production, with the publishers' sway stretching past the bookseller to 'capture the retailer's customers'. And because these powerful lines of control extended themselves through the production process the interpellated subject was also transformed. Whatever Forster's political or social 'liberalism', whatever its placement within Edwardian ideology generally, the reader addressed by *Howards End*, that novel's peculiarly indistinct interpellated subject, was inevitably determined by these material relations of its production. In the ambiguity of its constructed reader-subject *Howards End* bears the impress of its historical mode of production, encodes within itself, in the ways we have seen, its own record of 'how, by whom and for whom it was produced.'[48]

## Notes

1   Guinevere L. Griest, *Mudie's Circulating Library and the Victorian Novel* (Bloomington: Indiana University Press, 1970), 209–11.

2   Royal A. Gettmann, *A Victorian Publisher: A Study of the Bentley Papers* (Cambridge: Cambridge University Press, 1960), 257.

3   W. G. Corp, *Fifty Years: A Brief Account of the Associated Booksellers of Great Britain and Ireland, 1895–1945* (Oxford: Basil Blackwell, 1945), 3; see also David Stott, 'The Decay of Bookselling', *Nineteenth Century* 36 (1894): 932–38.

4   Arthur Waugh, *A Hundred Years of Publishing* (London: Chapman and Hall, 1930), 192; Griest, *Mudie's*, 169–70.

5   Gettmann, *Victorian Publisher*, 256; Griest, *Mudie's*, 189; John Goode has analyzed the place of the Society of Authors in the 'more mystified ideology of literary production' in 'The Decadent Writer as Producer', in *Decadence and the 1890s*, ed. Ian Fletcher (London: Edward Arnold, 1979), 117–21.

6   Simon Nowell-Smith, *International Copyright Law and the Publisher in the Reign of Queen Victoria* (Oxford: Clarendon Press, 1968), 82.

7   W. G. Corp, *Fifty Years*, 5; the London Booksellers' Society had already, in 1894, submitted to selected publishers a memorial supporting net prices. Russi Jal Taraporevala, *Competition and Control in the Book Trade, 1850–1939* (Bombay: D.B.T. Taraporevala and Sons, 1969), 36.

8   R. J. L. Kingsford, *The Publishers' Association, 1896–1946* (Cambridge: Cambridge University Press, 1970), 5–17.

9   Frederick Macmillan, *The Net Book Agreement 1899 and the Book War 1906–1908* (Glasgow: Robert Maclehose, 1924), 30.

10  [Anon.], *The History of the Times*, vol. 3, *The Twentieth Century Test, 1884–1912* (London: The Times, 1947), 441.

11  *The History of the Times*, 443–48.

12  [Anon.], *'The Times' and the Publishers* (London: privately printed for the Publishers' Association, 1906), 11–12, 7.

13  Edward Bell, 'The *Times* Book Club and the Publishers' Association, an Account of the "Book War" of 1906–1908', in Macmillan, *The Net Book Agreement*, 31.

14  [Anon.], *Publishers and the Public: Reprinted From the Times of 1852* (London: The Times, 1906), Note, 1.

15  [Anon.], *The History of the Book War: Fair Book Prices Versus Publishers' Trust Prices* (London: The Times, 1907), 36.

16  *John and A. H. Hallam Murray v. Walter and Others* (London: printed for private circulation, John Murray, 1908), 84.

17  The *Times* attacked novelists as 'the curled darlings of the fiction market [who] came forth from the lotos-land through the looking-glass where they dwell withdrawn from the vulgar battle of commerce, or emerged from the vapourous private Utopias wherein they excogitate phosphorescent millenniums'. *The History of the Book War*, 32.

18  Macmillan, *The Net Book Agreement*, 75, 77.

19  Hermann Levy, *Retail Trade Associations. A New Form of Monopolist Organization in Britain* (London: Kegan Paul, Trench, Trubner and Co., 1942), 20, 7.

20  *Ibid.*, 5.

21  *Ibid.*, 63–64.

22  B. S. Yamey, 'The Origins of Retail Price Maintenance: A Study of Three Branches of the Retail Trade', *EJ* 62 (1952): 528.

23  Yamey, 'Origins', 527–28.

24  Levy, *Retail Trade Associations*, 67, 70.

25   *Ibid.*, 15.

26   *Ibid.*, 71.

27   *The Booksellers*, 444 (6 November 1894): 1021.

28   Macmillan, *The Net Book Agreement*, 14.

29   Taraporevala, *Competition and Control*, 54.

30   B. W. E. Alford, 'Business Enterprise and the Growth of the Commercial Letterpress Printing Industry, 1850–1914', *Business History* 7 (1965): 4.

31   Henry Holt, 'The Commercialization of Literature', *Atlantic Monthly* 96 (1905): 599; the Americans had been listing 'best sellers' since 1895. Alice Payne Hackett, *70 Years of Best Sellers: 1895–1965* (New York: R. R. Bowker, 1967), 2.

32   Maurice Dobb, *Studies in the Development of Capitalism*, 2d ed. (London: Routledge and Kegan Paul, 1963), 313; Asa Briggs, 'The Political Scene', in *Edwardian England, 1901–1914*, ed. S. Nowell-Smith (London: Oxford University Press, 1964), 82; E. J. Hobsbawm, *Industry and Empire* (Harmondsworth: Penguin, 1968) 191.

33   F. A. Mumby and Ian Norrie, *Publishing and Bookselling*, 5th ed. rev. (London: Cape, 1974), 279, 347.

34   Oliver Stallybrass, Editor's Introduction, *Where Angels Fear To Tread*, Abinger ed. (London: Arnold, 1975), xi; *Selected Letters of E. M. Forster*, ed. Mary Lago and P. N. Furbank (London: Collins, 1983), 1: 67.

35   Stallybrass, Editor's Introduction, *Angels*, xii; Lago and Furbank, *Letters*, 1: 84 n. 2.

36   Forster may have decided that 'as *publishers*', Blackwood was not 'a good firm', for although he 'didn't mind much about money', Blackwood's terms for *Angels* were 'really no money at all' (Lago and Furbank, *Letters*, 1: 71); on the other hand, Forster may have been uneasy with Blackwood's very public Toryism, or his own company among the 'chief Blackwood's writers', who in 1904 included, besides Joseph Conrad, 'Zack', Sydney Grier, Mary Skrine, Beatrice Harraden, Storer Clouston, etc. F. D. Tredrey, *The House of Blackwood, 1804–1954* (Edinburgh: Blackwood, 1954), 193.

37   Oliver Stallybrass, Editor's Introduction, *Howards End*, Abinger ed. (London: Arnold, 1973), xii; Edward Arnold had been the reader for *Murray's Magazine* who had refused *Tess of the D'Urbervilles* in 1889 'virtually on the score of its improper explicitness'. R. L. Purdy, *Thomas Hardy: A Bibliographical Study* (Oxford: Clarendon Press, 1968), 73.

38   Stallybrass, Editor's Introduction, *Howards End*, xiii.

39   B. J. Kirkpatrick, *A Bibliography of E. M. Forster*, 2d rev, imp. (London: R. Hart-Davies, 1968), 29; Derek Hudson, 'Reading', in *Edwardian England*, ed. Nowell-Smith, 315.

40   P. N. Furbank, *E. M. Forster: A Life* (London: Secker and Warburg, 1977), 1: 188–89.

41   Frederick L. Crews, *E. M. Forster: The Perils of Humanism* (Princeton, N.J.: Princeton University Press, 1962), 34.

42   *The Booksellers*, 96, n.s. (28 October 1910): 52.

43   *The Author* 19, 9 (1 June 1909): 241.

44   Oliver Stallybrass, ed., *The Manuscripts of Howards End*, Abinger ed. (London: Arnold, 1973), 43; hereafter referred to as 'manuscript'.

45   E. M. Forster, 'The Challenge of Our Time', *Two Cheers for Democracy*, Abinger ed., ed. Oliver Stallybrass (London: Arnold, 1972), 54.

46   John Sutherland, *Bestsellers* (London: Routledge and Kegan Paul, 1981), 8; 'the valorization of value takes place only within this constantly renewed movement. The movement of capital is therefore limitless'. Karl Marx, *Capital*, trans. B. Fowkes (Harmondsworth: Penguin, 1976), 1: 253.

47   Sutherland, *Bestsellers*, 21.

48   Terry Eagleton, *Criticism and Ideology* (London: New Left Books, 1976), 48.

## PART FOUR

# Books and readers

# EDITORS' INTRODUCTION

Reception, or to be more accurate the study of reading and reading practices, was once upon a time the Cinderella of book history. However, the agenda set out by Robert Darnton in his 'First Steps Toward a History of Reading' has been taken up by the scholarly community and the survey he offers of work up to that point has been built on and extended in new directions (Darnton 1990: 154–87). Darnton called for further research into a history of reader response: 'comparing readers' accounts of their experience with the protocols of reading in their books and, when possible, with their behaviour'.

We are now, in Darnton's terms, exploring the 'whys' and 'hows' of the history of reading as much as the 'who', 'what', 'where' and 'when'. The sources for this history remain fertile and problematic: the archival material, including booksellers' lists, library records and state registers, offers generalized data which can be used to ascertain patterns and trends which may or may not be localized; and the personal material, including letters, diaries and autobiographies, offers presentations of the reading self which can provide cautious insights into the individual's reading habits and practices. Richard Altick's account of reading in Britain from the late fifteenth until the eighteenth century illustrates the richness and density to be derived from this material as well as alerting us to the need to recreate the *mentalité* of the culture under review – the 'why' and the 'how'.

Darnton's 'how' includes both the paratextual elements of the printed word (a theme developed by McGann and Genette) and the nature of the act of reading itself. The latter theme was the subject of the school of reader-response criticism which emerged from Germany in the 1970s and in which Wolfgang Iser was the predominant figure. Iser restored the reader to the centre of the act of reading, a position from which a blinkered focus upon the author's 'intentions' and the structures of the text had dislodged him/her. Within Iser's model of reading, the reader becomes an active and creative participant in the creation of meaning from the text. This model might seem then to underline the importance of the historical since it follows that different readers at different periods will derive different meanings from their reading. That different readers will, in fact, arrive at remarkably similar meanings and that a single reader may change his/her view of a text over time are central concerns of Stanley Fish. Fish, although by no means 'of the school of' Iser, reiterates the key point of the reader-response model that the meaning of the text does not exist independently of the reader and the reader's contribution, reflecting his/her experience, to its creation. He extends the model by offering the concept of 'interpretive communities' to account for similarities, if not sameness, in both the way of reading of groups of individuals and the meaning they derive individually from a text.

This notion has proved important in allowing the historian of reading to move from data about individuals to conclusions about audiences – to attempt to refute Darnton's assertion that 'the experience of the great mass of readers lies beyond the range of historical research'. Jonathan Rose moves the focus of inquiry from the individual to the individual as member of an 'audience' to examine how texts affect the lives and intellectual development of the 'common', that is, non-professional, reader. Where Janice Radway had undertaken this for contemporary readers of romance novels, Rose sets out to undertake historical research without the obvious benefit of direct access to the readers themselves. Radway herself exploits archival material, as well as 'real-time' interviews and observation, to clarify the nature of the selection process for the Book-of-the-Month Club and the role of the Club in creating, relating to and reinforcing an 'interpretive community' of middle-class and aspiring middle-class readers. Where the Book-of-the-Month Club achieved this in a positive manner, the negative means of creating an 'interpretive community' by signalling what will not be read by its members, or the children of its members to be more precise, provides Kate Flint with a key element in her profile of the woman reader in the nineteenth century.

# Chapter 22

# Wolfgang Iser
## INTERACTION BETWEEN TEXT AND READER

Central to the reading of every literary work is the interaction between its structure and its recipient. This is why the phenomenological theory of art has emphatically drawn attention to the fact that the study of a literary work should concern not only the actual text but also, and in equal measure, the actions involved in responding to that text. The text itself simply offers 'schematized aspects'[1] through which the aesthetic object of the work can be produced.

From this we may conclude that the literary work has two poles, which we might call the artistic and the aesthetic: the artistic pole is the author's text, and the aesthetic is the realization accomplished by the reader. In view of this polarity, it is clear that the work itself cannot be identical with the text or with its actualization but must be situated somewhere between the two. It must inevitably be virtual in character, as it cannot be reduced to the reality of the text or to the subjectivity of the reader, and it is from this virtuality that it derives its dynamism. As the reader passes through the various perspectives offered by the text, and relates the different views and patterns to one another, he sets the work in motion, and so sets himself in motion, too.

If the virtual position of the work is between text and reader, its actualization is clearly the result of an interaction between the two, and so exclusive concentration on either the author's techniques or the reader's psychology will tell us little about the reading process itself. This is not to deny the vital importance of each of the two poles – it is simply that if one loses sight of the relationship, one loses sight of the virtual work. Despite its uses, separate analysis would only be conclusive if the relationship were that of transmitter and receiver, for this would presuppose a common code, ensuring accurate communication since the message would only be traveling one way. In literary works, however, the message is transmitted in two ways, in that the reader 'receives'

Acknowledgement to Princeton University Press for permission to reprint Wolfgang Iser, 'Interaction between Text and Reader' from Susan K. Suleiman and Inge Crossman, eds, *The Reader in the Text: Essays on Audience and Interpretation*, New Jersey: Princeton University Press, 1980, pp. 106–119. Copyright © 1980 by Princeton University Press. Reprinted by permission of Princeton University Press.

it by composing it. There is no common code – at best one could say that a common code may arise in the course of the process. Starting out from this assumption, we must search for structures that will enable us to describe basic conditions of interaction, for only then shall we be able to gain some insight into the potential effects inherent in the work. . . .

An obvious and major difference between reading and all forms of social interaction is the fact that with reading there is no *face-to-face-situation*.[2] A text cannot adapt itself to each reader it comes into contact with. The partners in dyadic interaction can ask each other questions in order to ascertain how far their images have bridged the gap of the inexperienceability of one another's experiences. The reader, however, can never learn from the text how accurate or inaccurate are his views of it. Furthermore, dyadic interaction serves specific purposes, so that the interaction always has a regulative context, which often serves as a *tertium comparationis*. There is no such frame of reference governing the text–reader relationship; on the contrary, the codes which might regulate this interaction are fragmented in the text, and must first be reassembled or, in most cases, restructured before any frame of reference *can* be established. Here, then, in conditions and intention, we find two basic differences between the text–reader relationship and the dyadic interaction between social partners.

Now, it is the very lack of ascertainability and defined intention that brings about the text–reader interaction, and here there is a vital link with dyadic interaction. Social communication arises out of the fact that people cannot experience how others experience them, and not out of the common situation or out of the conventions that join both partners together. The situations and conventions regulate the manner in which gaps are filled, but the gaps in turn arise out of the inexperienceability and, consequently, function as a basic inducement to communication. Similarly, it is the gaps, the fundamental asymmetry between text and reader, that give rise to communication in the reading process; the lack of a common situation and a common frame of reference corresponds to the 'no-thing', which brings about the interaction between persons. Asymmetry and the 'no-thing' are all different forms of an indeterminate, constitutive blank, which underlies all processes of interaction. With dyadic interaction, the imbalance is removed by the establishment of pragmatic connections resulting in an action, which is why the preconditions are always clearly defined in relation to situations and common frames of reference. The imbalance between text and reader, however, is undefined, and it is this very indeterminacy that increases the variety of communication possible.

Now, if communication between text and reader is to be successful, clearly the reader's activity must also be controlled in some way by the text. The control cannot be as specific as in a *face-to-face-situation*, equally it cannot be as determinate as a social code, which regulates social interaction. However, the guiding devices operative in the reading process have to initiate communication and to control it. This control cannot be understood as a tangible entity occurring independently of the process of communication. Although exercised *by* the text, it is not *in* the text. This is well illustrated by a comment Virginia Woolf made on the novels of Jane Austen:

> Jane Austen is thus a mistress of much deeper emotion than appears upon the surface. She stimulates us to supply what is not there. What she offers is, apparently, a trifle, yet is composed of something that expands in the reader's mind and endows with the most enduring form of life scenes which are outwardly trivial. Always stress is laid upon character. . . . The turns and twists of the dialogue keep us on the tenterhooks of suspense. Our attention is half upon the present moment, half upon the future. . . . Here, indeed, in this unfinished and in the main inferior story, are all the elements of Jane Austen's greatness.[3]

What is missing from the apparently trivial scenes, the gaps arising out of the dialogue – this is what stimulates the reader into filling the blanks with projections. He is drawn into the events and made to supply what is meant from what is not said. What is said only appears to take on significance as a reference to what is not said; it is the implications and not the statements that give shape and weight to the meaning. But as the unsaid comes to life in the reader's imagination, so the said 'expands' to take on greater significance than might have been supposed: even trivial scenes can seem surprisingly profound. The 'enduring form of life' which Virginia Woolf speaks of is not manifested on the printed page; it is a product arising out of the interaction between text and reader.

Communication in literature, then, is a process set in motion and regulated, not by a given code, but by a mutually restrictive and magnifying interaction between the explicit and the implicit, between revelation and concealment. What is concealed spurs the reader into action, but this action is also controlled by what is revealed; the explicit in its turn is transformed when the implicit has been brought to light. Whenever the reader bridges the gaps, communication begins. The gaps function as a kind of pivot on which the whole text–reader relationship revolves. Hence, the structured blanks of the text stimulate the process of ideation to be performed by the reader on terms set by the text. There is, however, another place in the textual system where text and reader converge, and that is marked by the various types of negation which arise in the course of the reading. Blanks and negations both control the process of communication in their own different ways: the blanks leave open the connection between textual perspectives, and so spur the reader into coordinating these perspectives and patterns – in other words, they induce the reader to perform basic operations *within* the text. The various types of negation invoke familiar and determinate elements or knowledge only to cancel them out. What is cancelled, however, remains in view, and thus brings about modifications in the reader's attitude toward what is familiar or determinate – in other words, he is guided to adopt a position *in relation* to the text.

In order to spotlight the communication process we shall confine our consideration to how the blanks trigger off and simultaneously control the reader's activity. Blanks indicate that the different segments and patterns of the text are to be connected even though the text itself does not say so. They are the unseen joints of the text, and as they mark off schemata and textual perspectives from one another, they simultaneously prompt acts of ideation on the reader's part. Consequently when the schemata and perspectives have been linked together, the blanks 'disappear'.

If we are to grasp the unseen structure that regulates but does not formulate the connection or even the meaning, we must bear in mind the various forms in which the textual segments are presented to the reader's viewpoint in the reading process. Their most elementary form is to be seen on the level of the story. The threads of the plot are suddenly broken off, or continued in unexpected directions. One narrative section centers on a particular character and is then continued by the abrupt introduction of new characters. These sudden changes are often denoted by new chapters and so are clearly distinguished; the object of this distinction, however, is not separation so much as a tacit invitation to find the missing link. Furthermore, in each articulated reading moment, only segments of textual perspectives are present to the reader's wandering viewpoint.

In order to become fully aware of the implication, we must bear in mind that a narrative text, for instance, is composed of a variety of perspectives, which outline the author's view and also provide access to what the reader is meant to visualize. As a rule, there are four main perspectives in narration: those of the narrator, the characters, the plot, and the fictitious reader. Although these may differ in order of importance, none of them on its own is identical to the meaning of the text, which is to be brought about by their constant intertwining through the reader in the reading process. An increase in the number of blanks is bound to occur through the frequent subdivisions of each of the textual perspectives; thus the narrator's perspective is often split into that of the implied author's set against that of the author as narrator. The hero's perspective may be set against that of the minor characters. The fictitious reader's perspective may be divided between the explicit position ascribed to him and the implicit attitude he must adopt to that position.

As the reader's wandering viewpoint travels between all these segments, its constant switching during the time flow of reading intertwines them, thus bringing forth a network of perspectives, within which each perspective opens a view not only of others, but also of the intended imaginary object. Hence no single textual perspective can be equated with this imaginary object, of which it forms only one aspect. The object itself is a product of interconnection, the structuring of which is to a great extent regulated and controlled by blanks.

In order to explain this operation, we shall first give a schematic description of how the blanks function, and then we shall try to illustrate this function with an example. In the time flow of reading, segments of the various perspectives move into focus and are set off against preceding segments. Thus the segments of characters, narrator, plot, and fictitious reader perspectives are not only marshaled into a graduated sequence but are also transformed into reciprocal reflectors. The blank as an empty space between segments enables them to be joined together, thus constituting a field of vision for the wandering viewpoint. A referential field is always formed when there are at least two positions related to and influencing one another – it is the minimal organizational unit in all processes of comprehension,[4] and it is also the basic organizational unit of the wandering viewpoint.

The first structural quality of the blank, then, is that it makes possible the organization of a referential field of interacting textual segments projecting themselves one upon another. Now, the segments present in the field are structurally of equal value, and the fact that they are brought together highlights their affinities and their differences. This relationship gives rise to a tension that has to be resolved, for, as Arnheim has observed in a more general context: 'It is one of the functions of the third dimension to come to the rescue when things get uncomfortable in the second'.[5] The third dimension comes about when the segments of the referential field are given a common framework, which allows the reader to relate affinities and differences and so to grasp the patterns underlying the connections. But this framework is also a blank, which requires an act of ideation in order to be filled. It is as if the blank in the field of the reader's viewpoint had changed its position. It began as the empty space between perspective segments, indicating their connectability, and so organizing them into projections of reciprocal influence. But with the establishment of this connectability the blank, as the unformulated framework of these interacting segments, now enables the reader to produce a determinate relationship between them. We may infer already from this change in position that the blank exercises significant control over all the operations that occur within the referential field of the wandering viewpoint.

Now we come to the third and most decisive function of the blank. Once the segments have been connected and a determinate relationship established, a referential field is formed which constitutes a particular reading moment, and which in turn has a discernible structure. The grouping of segments within the referential field comes about, as we have seen, by making the viewpoint switch between the perspective segments. The segment on which the viewpoint focuses in each particular moment becomes the theme. The theme of one moment becomes the background against which the next segment takes on its actuality, and so on. Whenever a segment becomes a theme, the previous one must lose its thematic relevance[6] and be turned into a marginal, thematically vacant position, which can be and usually is occupied by the reader so that he may focus on the new thematic segment.

In this connection it might be more appropriate to designate the marginal or horizontal position as a vacancy and not as a blank; blanks refer to suspended connectability in the text, vacancies refer to non-thematic segments within the referential field of the wandering viewpoint.

Vacancies, then, are important guiding devices for building up the aesthetic object, because they condition the reader's view of the new theme, which in turn conditions his view of previous themes. These modifications, however, are not formulated in the text – they are to be implemented by the reader's ideational activity. And so these vacancies enable the reader to combine segments into a field by reciprocal modification, to form positions from those fields, and then to adapt each position to its successor and predecessors in a process that ultimately transforms the textual perspectives, through a whole range of alternating themes and background relationships, into the aesthetic object of the text. . . .

To sum up, then, the blank in the fictional text induces and guides the reader's constitutive activity. As a suspension of connectability between textual perspective and perspective segments, it marks the need for an equivalence, thus transforming the segments into reciprocal projections, which in turn organize the reader's wandering viewpoint as a referential field. The tension that occurs within the field between heterogeneous perspective segments is resolved by the theme-and-background structure, which makes the viewpoint focus on one segment as the theme, to be grasped from the thematically vacant position now occupied by the reader as his standpoint. Thematically vacant positions remain present in the background against which new themes occur; they condition and influence those themes and are also retroactively influenced by them, for as each theme recedes into the background of its successor, the vacancy shifts, allowing for a reciprocal transformation to take place. As the vacancy is structured by the sequence of positions in the time flow of reading, the reader's viewpoint cannot proceed arbitrarily; the thematically vacant position always acts as the angle from which a selective interpretation is to be made.

Two points need to be emphasized: (1) we have described the structure of the blank in an abstract, somewhat idealized way in order to explain the pivot on which the interaction between text and reader turns; (2) the blank has different structural qualities, which appear to dovetail. The reader fills in the blank in the text, thereby bringing about a referential field; the blank arising in turn out of the referential field is filled in by way of the theme-and-background structure; and the vacancy arising from juxtaposed themes and backgrounds is occupied by the reader's standpoint, from which the various reciprocal transformations lead to the emergence of the aesthetic object. The structural qualities outlined make the blank shift, so that the changing positions of the empty space mark out a definite need for determination, which the constitutive activity of the reader is to fulfill. In this sense, the shifting blank maps out the path along which the wandering viewpoint is to travel, guided by the self-regulatory sequence in which the structural qualities of the blank interlock.

Now we are in a position to qualify more precisely what is actually meant by reader participation in the text. If the blank is largely responsible for the activities described, then participation means that the reader is not simply called upon to 'internalize' the positions given in the text, but he is induced to make them act upon and so transform each other, as a result of which the aesthetic object begins to emerge. The structure of the blank organizes this participation, revealing simultaneously the intimate connection between this structure and the reading subject. This interconnection completely conforms to a remark made by Piaget: 'In a word, the subject is there and alive, because the basic quality of each structure is the structuring process itself'.[7] The blank in the fictional text appears to be a paradigmatic structure; its function consists in initiating structured operations in the reader, the execution of which transmits the reciprocal interaction of textual positions into consciousness. The shifting blank is responsible for a sequence of colliding images, which condition each other in the time flow of reading. The discarded image imprints itself on its successor, even though the latter is meant to resolve the deficiencies of the former. In this respect the images hang together in a sequence, and it is by this sequence that the meaning of the text comes alive in the reader's imagination.

## Notes

This essay contains a few ideas which are dealt with more comprehensively in my book *The Act of Reading: A Theory of Aesthetic Response* (The Johns Hopkins University Press: Baltimore, 1978).

1    See Roman Ingarden, *The Literary Work of Art*, trans. George G. Grabowicz (Evanston, III., 1973), pp. 276ff.

2    E. Goffman, *Interaction Ritual: Essays on Face-to-Face Behavior* (New York, 1967).

3    Virginia Woolf, *The Common Reader: First Series* (London, 1957), p. 174. In this context, it is well worth considering Virginia Woolf's comments on the composition of her own fictional characters. She remarks in her diary:

> I'm thinking furiously about Reading and Writing. I have no time to describe my plans. I should say a good deal about *The Hours* and my discovery: how I dig out beautiful caves behind my characters: I think that gives exactly what I want; humanity, humour, depth. The idea is that the caves shall connect and each comes to daylight at the present moment.
>
> (*A Writer's Diary: Being Extracts from the Diary of Virginia Woolf*,
> ed. Leonard Woolf (London, 1953), p. 60)

The suggestive effect of the 'beautiful caves' is continued in her work through what she leaves out. On this subject, T. S. Eliot once observed:

> Her observation, which operates in a continuous way, implies a vast and sustained work of organization. She does not illumine with sudden bright flashes but diffuses a soft and placid light. Instead of looking for the primitive, she looks rather for the civilized, the highly civilized, where nevertheless something is found to be left out. And this something is deliberately left out, by what could be called a moral effort of the will. And, being left out, this something is, in a sense, in a melancholy sense, present.
>
> ('T. S. Eliot "Places" Virginia Woolf for French Readers', in *Virginia Woolf:
> The Critical Heritage*, ed. Robin Majumdar and Allen McLaurin
> (London, 1975). p. 192)

4    See Aron Gurwitsch, *The Field of Consciousness* (Pittsburgh, 1964), pp. 309–75.

5    Rudolph Arnheim, *Toward a Psychology of Art* (Berkeley and Los Angeles, 1967), p. 239.

6    For a discussion of the problem of changing relevance and abandoned thematic relevance, See Alfred Schütz, *Das Problem der Relevanz*, trans. A. v. Baeyer (Frankfurt am Main, 1970), pp. 104ff., 145ff.

7    Jean Piaget, *Der Strukturalismus*, trans. L. Häfliger (Olten, 1973), p. 134.

# Chapter 23

# E. Jennifer Monaghan

## LITERACY INSTRUCTION AND GENDER
## IN COLONIAL NEW ENGLAND

Hanna Newberry, the most prominent mortgage-holder in Windsor, Connecticut, for most of the second quarter of the eighteenth century, was unable to sign the many documents to which she affixed her name. Instead, she subscribed her mark, the initials HN. Her case illustrates, according to Linda Auwers, 'the widespread fact of female illiteracy among women born in the seventeenth century and the difficulty in relating literacy to social class'.[1]

Literacy historians have used signatures and marks as indicators of, respectively, the literacy and illiteracy of ordinary people in the seventeenth and eighteenth centuries in Europe and America.[2] For colonial New England, the best-known study remains that by Kenneth Lockridge, who tabulated the signatures/marks made on over three thousand wills. He found that the proportion of males able to sign their own wills increased from 60 percent in the 1660s to 85 percent by 1760 and to almost 90 percent by 1790. Female signing rates were much lower throughout the entire period. Some 31 percent of the women signed their wills before 1670; this average increased, but only to 46 percent by the 1790s.[3] Three later studies have found a higher rate of signing than Lockridge did, in part by using deeds and other sources in addition to wills, so accessing a larger or less decrepit population.[4] One of these is the study cited above by Auwers, who allocated her signers/markers into birth cohorts and found that the proportion of women in Windsor who could sign their own names to deeds rose from 27 percent for the cohort born between 1650 and 1669 to 90 percent for the 1740–49 cohort.[5]

The equation of literacy possession with signing rests on the assumption that signing ability is roughly equivalent to fluent reading. As reading was taught before writing, the argument runs, the ability to write (as indicated by a signature) also indicates the ability to read. Carl Kaestle has recently summarized the arguments for and against this position, and – after warning us that the relationship between signing and reading may vary by gender, class, place, and period – finally suggests that signature counts indicate roughly the 'minimum number of people who were minimally literate'.[6]

Reprinted from Cathy N. Davidson, ed., *Reading in America: Literature and Social History*, pp. 53–80. © 1989 Johns Hopkins University Press. Reprinted with permission of the Johns Hopkins University Press.

Although scholars have varied in their interpretations of what a signature implies, there has been more general agreement about the mark: it has been viewed as a valid indicator of illiteracy. Lockridge's figures have therefore contributed to the widely held belief that in New England and elsewhere females were dramatically less literate than males throughout the colonial period, reaching roughly half the literacy level of males.

Several scholars, however, including Lockridge himself, have raised the possibility that some people – particularly women – could read but not write. Margaret Spufford and Victor Neuburg have provided examples of this in the context of seventeenth- and eighteenth-century England.[7] The thesis of the present study is that this was also true of colonial New England. When we examine the contexts in which literacy instruction was conducted, paying close attention to the role played by gender, it will become apparent that the mark cannot be considered an infallible indicator of illiteracy, particularly in the seventeenth century.

The evidence to be presented is qualitative in nature, scattered, and fragmentary; it is also skewed toward the seventeenth century. Further research will be necessary to see if the conclusions to be drawn will stand. Nonetheless, the bits and pieces of the puzzle seem to form a remarkably coherent picture across time and place. In order to support my contention, I first discuss how reading and writing were taught and by whom, then turn to examine how the colonists themselves viewed literacy from the legal and economic standpoints. Next follows an elaboration of the relationship between schooling and gender. Basic to the entire discussion is the concept that literacy was considered by the colonists to comprise a deliberately imparted set of skills, taught in ways that were both widely accepted and precise.

## The reading curriculum

The colonial reading curriculum was, of course, brought over to the new continent, along with so much else, from England. The seventeenth-century curriculum followed the outline sketched by John Locke, who in 1693 characterized it as the 'ordinary road of the Hornbook, Primer, Psalter, Testament, and Bible'.[8]

There is plenty of evidence that the colonists followed this 'ordinary road' in the early days of settlement and throughout the seventeenth century. The hornbook formed the novice's introduction to reading. Its name derived from its single page (originally covered with transparent protective horn), which was tacked onto a little wooden paddle. It presented the alphabet, the first few lines of the syllabarium (*ab eb ib ob ub*), and the Lord's Prayer. Often mentioned in the same context as primers, hornbooks turn up here and there in the sources over the course of the seventeenth century, and advertisements for primers and both gilt and plain hornbooks have been found in Philadelphia newspapers as late as 1760.[9] The hornbook was used in dame schools – private schools for small children run by a woman in her own home – as the child's first 'text'. Samuel Sewall mentioned one in just such a context. He recorded in his diary on April 27, 1691, that he had sent his little son Joseph, not yet three years old, to school (obviously for the first time). 'This afternoon had Joseph to school to Capt. Townsend's Mother's, his cousin Jane accompanying him, carried his Horn-book.'[10]

Hornbooks were apparently never manufactured on American soil, but were all imported.[11] Primers, the next step in the reading curriculum, were also imported into the colonies from very early on. They must have been a standard item in any village store. One example of their widespread availability is documented for New Haven, in 1645 – only seven years after it was founded as a separate colony. That year, a Captain Turner was accused by Mistress Stolion before the New Haven Colony Court of having reneged on a deal in which he had promised to give her two cows in exchange for six yards of cloth. Not to be outdone, the captain accused Mrs. Stolion in turn of price gouging: he claimed that 'she sold primmers at 9*d* [nine pence] apeece which cost but 4*d* here in New England'.[12]

Primers were such essential texts for instruction in both reading and religion, however, that their publication on American presses is documented early in the colonial adventure. The oldest extant American primer was composed by John Eliot as part of his efforts to convert the Massachuset Indians. Written in the Massachuset dialect of the Algonquian language and published in 1669 on the Cambridge, Massachusetts, press, the primer admirably sums up, in its title, the dual role it, like the hornbook, played in both reading and religious instruction. The English version reads, *The Indian Primer; or, the Way of Training up of Our Indian Youth in the Good Knowledge of God, in the Knowledge of the Scriptures and in an Ability to Read*.[13]

Primers as a genre became a publishing staple in New England and the middle states as presses increased in number. The *New England Primer*, the most famous of colonial textbooks, has a publishing history that runs from 1690, when it was already in its second impression, to long after the American Revolution. (Its sales up to 1830 have been estimated at between six million and eight million copies.) It contained several pages of instructional material, presenting the syllabarium and words of increasing length, from monosyllables to words of six syllables. Its popularity was enhanced by the inclusion of a catechism.[14] In addition to the *New England Primer*, there were numerous other primers in the marketplace.[15]

The next text in both the religious and reading curriculum was the Psalter (the Book of Psalms). Psalters too were extensively printed on American presses. They were generally published without the addition of any reading instructional material, but we do know of one 1760 Philadelphia edition that indicated that it had been 'Improved by the addition of a variety of lessons in spelling. . . . Likewise, rules for reading. . . . The whole being a proper introduction, not only to learning, but to the training of children in the reading of the holy scriptures in particular.'[16]

One incident that revealed the Psalter's status as a reading instructional text occurred in the context of writing instruction. John Proctor, master of the town-financed North Writing School in Boston from 1731 to 1743, was summoned in 1741 before the Boston selectmen to answer what seems to have been a parental complaint: he was accused of having refused to admit boys from 'Families of low Circumstances' to his school. Proctor replied that he had 'refus'd none of the Inhabitants Children, but such as could not Read in the Psalter'.[17] Clearly, the Psalter was being used as a kind of minimum competency test of reading ability.

The final two stages in the reading curriculum consisted of mastering first the New Testament and then the entire Bible (both Old and New Testaments). Because it was illegal to print these on American presses (John Eliot's *Indian Bible* being a specialized exception), English Bibles were imported until after the American Revolution.

The use of the Scriptures as the climax of the reading curriculum is well known. Two seventeenth-century instances occur in the records of New Haven. The first illustrates the seventeenth-century assumption that reading instruction was supposed to have begun before a child entered the town school. The job description for a New Haven schoolmaster, hired in 1651, was to 'perfect male chilldren in the English, after they can reade in their Testament or Bible, and to learne them to wright', and to bring them on to Latin, if he could.[18] The second involved a school for girls. That same year, the daughter of a Captain How was brought before the New Haven Court and charged with misconduct that included speaking in a blasphemous way of the Scriptures. The girl's mother claimed that her daughter had picked up some of her bad habits at 'Goodwife Wickams', where she went to school. Witnesses testified that they had seen the girl look in a Bible, turn over a leaf, and say that 'it was not worth reading'. It is not too far-fetched to assume that young Miss How had reached the stage of reading the Bible at her school.[19]

Not included in Locke's characterization of the 'ordinary road' was the spelling book. In a major pedagogical shift that cannot be documented here in any detail, the spelling book was introduced into schools, perhaps fairly early in the eighteenth century, as an important beginning text for reading instruction.[20] In the rise of the speller we see the demands of religious content taking second place to the requirements of methodology, in a continuation of a process begun when the first alphabet was added to the primer.[21]

Spelling books as a genre appear at least as early as Edmund Coote's *The English Schoole-Maister*, published in London in 1596, and reprinted fifty-four times by 1737.[22] Moreover, spellers were printed very early on colonial presses: an unidentified speller came off Stephen Daye's press in Cambridge, in the Bay Colony in about 1644.[23] It was not, however, until the eighteenth century that the speller's ascendancy as a school text began. An important clue to its popularity is the frequency with which English spellers were reprinted on American presses. (Unlike primers, some of which reflected colonial circumstances, American spellers were all reproduced verbatim from English copies until after the American Revolution.) When Benjamin Franklin in 1747 reprinted Thomas Dilworth's *A New Guide to the English Tongue*, he ushered onto the American scene a spelling book that would enjoy tremendous popularity in the second half of the eighteenth century ('the nurse of us all', as one user put it), until ousted by Noah Webster's speller after 1783.[24]

The name 'spelling book' was a reflection of the prevailing methodology: spelling was the key to reading. After mastering the letters of the alphabet, the novice reader's next task was to spell out, orally, syllables and words (broken into syllables) from the printed page. Spelling books incorporated exactly the same methodology – the alphabetic method – as primers did. Although some spellers included secular content, a key difference between primers and spellers was that the latter presented the reading curriculum in a more elaborate and systematic fashion. The tables of words were greatly increased in number and were followed by 'lessons' – reading material based in part on vocabulary already introduced.[25]

One key aspect of the alphabetic method was that reading instruction was conducted entirely orally, without requiring the child to write. Progress in learning to read could therefore be gauged simply by listening to the child's oral spelling. As Edmund Coote had put it in the 1596 preface to his speller, the purchaser of his book could sit at the loom or needle, 'and neuer hinder thy worke, to heare thy scholers, after thou hast once made this little booke familiar vnto thee'.[26]

Comprehension was virtually ignored, pedagogically speaking. It would probably be fairer to say that comprehension of the text was assumed. After all, the seventeenth-century reading curriculum was in essence a course in Christianity: the texts used were basic to the religion itself. Not until the spelling books of the eighteenth century would any reference be made to such matters as how easily a child could learn the material.

In sum, the task of the reading teacher throughout the entire colonial period was clearly laid out. Both methodology and content were agreed upon; the curriculum was, in effect, standardized. Moreover, no qualifications for teaching reading were necessary other than being able to read oneself. Not only did the child not write in the course of learning to read; the teacher did not need to know how to write either.

## The reading teacher

Because the task of the reading teacher was so well defined and was considered, rightly or wrongly, to be easy, the teaching of reading was more often than not considered to be a female province. In the context of family education, it is significant that in those rare cases when we know who taught the child to read at home, it is the mother who is singled out. A pious mother was particularly motivated to teach her child to read. The Boston minister Increase Mather (father of Cotton Mather) was born in Dorchester, Massachusetts, in 1639, nine years after the town was founded. He wrote that he 'learned to read of my mother' whom he described as a 'very Holy praying woman'. (Significantly, it was his father who taught him to *write*.) Richard Brown, born in 1675, also had a 'pious and prudent' mother, who endeavored to instill in him 'the principals of Religion and Holiness'. After 'she had caused me to read well at home, she sent me to school'.[27]

It appears, however, that early in the colonial period children began attending a school to learn to read, either as well as, or instead of, learning from their mothers. Such schools were called dame schools or reading schools. The dame school is well documented for England in the seventeenth and eighteenth centuries.[28] A woman would take small children, both boys and girls, into her own home for a few hours. We even know of one two-year-old girl who drowned on her way to school.[29] While no doubt the dame's major contribution was to afford an overworked mother a few hours of respite from her three- and four-year-olds, ostensibly her purpose was to introduce her charges to reading. In fact, some dame schools taught a substantial amount of reading. John Barnard, born in 1681, recalled that when he was less than six years old his schoolmistress 'made me a sort of usher, appointing me to teach some children that were older than myself, as well as smaller ones; and in which time I had read my Bible through thrice'.[30]

The dame, or reading, school was not funded by the town, but was a private venture. It represented, of course, a most useful source of income for a woman. We meet women as paid teachers of reading in unexpected contexts. The Commissioners of the United Colonies of New England, who disbursed monies sent over from England for missionary work among the Indians, not only employed a woman to teach the Indians to read, but even gave her a raise. As their letter said, in 1653, 'The wife of William Daniell of Dorchester hath for this three yeares last past bestowed much of her time in teaching severall Indians to Read and that shee hath onely Receiued the summe of six pounds towards her paines; [we] thought fitt to allow her nine pounds more for the time past.'[31]

Women are notoriously invisible in colonial records. Even though most townships (Boston, for instance) required private schoolteachers to obtain permission from the town before they were allowed to teach, private women teachers do not appear in the Boston records until the 1730s. In the seventeenth century, therefore, most of our evidence comes from those rare cases in which women teachers were involved with the law, as happened to Goodwife Wickam of New Haven. One can only guess how many women must have earned a few pennies a week as private teachers of reading throughout that century. As we shall see, in the following century women would be called upon to ply their skills in the public arena as well.

## Writing instruction

Writing was defined, in the colonial context, as penmanship.[32] In only a few respects did writing instruction resemble reading instruction. Just as 'good' reading was considered to be accurate oral reading, so 'good' writing seemed to be viewed entirely in terms of fine letter formation. Composition seems rarely to have been discussed at all. Similarly, mastery was to be attained by rote and repetition: by the careful reproduction by the learner of the 'copy' set for him by the writing master. As was the case in reading instruction, mastery of the individual letters of the alphabet was the first step in the writing curriculum. Later the learner would copy, five or six times, pithy moral sentences, and then work up to copying poems or texts reproduced by the master from the traditional copybooks such as George Bickham's *The Universal Penman* (1743).[33]

In other respects, however, the contrast between the teaching of the two literacy skills could hardly have been greater. Writing was considered a craft, subject to all the limitations of access that that implied. The gender bias implicit in the term 'penmanship' was not fortuitous: writing was largely a male domain. This was particularly true as it related to the gender of the instructor: men taught writing. The writing master, analogous to the scribe of earlier times, was the possessor of a fairly arcane skill. The most telling evidence that his knowledge was considered specialized was that he had usually had to attain it through the apprenticeship route.[34]

Moreover, unlike textbooks for reading instruction, which were early reproduced on American presses, the texts for writing instruction were, for technical reasons, not reprinted on American presses but imported. Although the successful reproduction of different kinds of 'hands' (scripts) had been made much easier by the invention of copperplate engraving, engraving not only was costly but demanded a great deal of skill; in fact, the best engraving was undertaken by penmen themselves. (George Bickham, for instance, personally engraved the work of some twenty-five masters for his *Universal Penman*.) The closest Americans came to reproducing scripts was in a text like George Fisher's *The Instructor: or, Young Man's Best Companion*, which included a few pages of scripts in its American versions from 1748 on. Not until after the American Revolution would there be copy books penned by Americans and printed on American presses.[35]

Again unlike reading texts, which could be purchased in any colony for mere pennies and were probably in most households, copybooks were costly to purchase and the prized possessions of the writing master. It was clearly not to the best interests of the profession to encourage the notion that anyone could learn from a book, rather than from a person.[36] Writing, in short, unlike reading, was considered a specialized skill, and colonial access to instructional writing texts was far more limited than access to reading texts.

What penmanship was used for, however, was even more important, in terms of who would be taught to write, than its aspect as a specialized skill. Writing was a male job-related skill, a tool for ministers and shipping clerks alike. When the Boston town meeting voted in 1682 to open a town writing school, Bostonians were acknowledging the importance of Boston as a thriving commercial and mercantile center. Hundreds of boys a year passed through the three writing schools that Boston had established by 1720. They mastered the English round hand that had become the international script for commerce, routing the old secretary hand of the seventeenth century.[37] At a time when all clerical and bookkeeping work was a male stronghold, every young man with business aspirations needed to know how to form a legible script. Writing was also, of course, useful for rural concerns. Farmers who wanted to sell surplus produce needed to write in order to keep accounts. Penmanship was therefore both a hallmark of the well-educated and the servant of commerce.

## Sequence of instruction

The order, then, of the different components of the literacy curriculum followed the sequence implicit in the 'three R's', a term still glossed today as 'reading, 'riting, and 'rithmetic'. There is nothing accidental about this universally agreed-upon phrase: its wording faithfully reflects the actual order of instruction during the colonial period. Reading instruction preceded, and was independent of, writing instruction. That this was possible was a function of its methodology – reading instruction was, as we have seen, conducted entirely orally. Arithmetic, which involved the endless writing of rules and examples, in turn presupposed the mastery of writing.[38]

It may be difficult for the modern reader/writer to believe reading instruction could be conducted without having the child write. A few examples will have to suffice. In 1660, a master in New Haven was asked whether he had seen to his apprentice's education, as he was legally obliged to do. He responded that the apprentice 'could read pretty well, and that he was now learning to write'. Two years later, one William Potter, who had been accused of (and was subsequently hanged for) the crime of bestiality, was asked by the New Haven Court if he had been educated. 'He answered, well, and was taught to reade'. Had he also been taught to write, he would undoubtedly have said so.[39]

A century later, in 1762, Samuel Giles of New York City advertised his private writing and arithmetic instruction at his evening school. After stating firmly that teaching small children the rudiments had taken up too much of his time, he said that 'for the Future, no Children will be taken but such as have already been taught to Read, and are fit for Writing'. Finally, there is an advertisement that appeared in a Boston newspaper in 1755. In it, the advertiser promised to teach 'persons of both sexes from twelve to fifty years of age, who never wrote before, to write a good hand in five weeks, at one hour per day, at his house in Long Lane'.[40]

## Literacy and the law

The Dissenters who had made their way over hazardous seas to settle in New England saw themselves as part of a literate culture. At a time when paper itself was precious and scarce, the meticulous records of the early town secretaries stand as a self-explanatory tribute to a new settlement's belief in the power of the written word to safeguard its new laws.

The greater importance placed by colonial Americans on the ability to read rather than to write is well exemplified by the legislation passed in 1642 by the colony of Massachusetts. Religious and political motives are explicit in this law; economic motives are implicit. The law empowered the colony's elected representatives, the selectmen, to inquire into the 'calling and implyment' of all children, 'especially of their ability to read and understand the principles of religion and the capitall lawes of this country'. Children who were not being trained to a skill or taught to read were liable to be removed from their parents and apprenticed to someone else for such instruction.[41] While the provisions in the law for 'putting out' indigent children to apprenticeship were borrowed from English precedents, the educational provisions were unique to the colonies. As Lawrence Cremin has put it, the statute was part of 'a vigorous legislative effort to increase the political and economic self-sufficiency of the colony'.[42]

The Massachusetts law that required that children be taught to read was quickly replicated by other colonies. Connecticut passed such a provision in 1650, New Haven (then a separate colony) in 1655, New York in 1665, Plymouth in 1671, and Pennsylvania in 1683.[43] The colony of New Haven was unusual in adding, in 1660, a writing requirement to the law. Significantly, only one of the sexes was to be taught this skill: 'To the printed law, concerning the education of children, it is now added, that the sonnes of all the inhabitants within this jurisdiction, shall (vnder the same penalty) be learned to write a ledgible hand, so soone as they are capable of it.'[44] The only other colony to require writing initially was Pennsylvania, which in its 1683 ordinance mandated that parents and guardians should ensure that children 'may be able to read the Scriptures and to write' by the age of twelve.[45]

The 1642 law on reading was taken seriously by at least several Massachusetts townships. When the Dorchester selectmen called in Timothy Wales and his sons in 1672, they examined the boys and found that they were unable to read. The following year Salem conducted its own investigation, found several families in violation of the law, and initiated – although it may not have carried out – the process of finding persons to whom the children could be apprenticed.[46] Watertown, Massachusetts made a particularly consistent effort over successive decades to keep parents up to the mark. The first recorded Watertown inspection occurred in 1661. Upon surveying their fellow townsmen to see whether they fulfilled the law that required 'the knowledg of God and excerising reading to the advancing of Catachising', the selectmen discovered that four families, with eighteen children among them, had failed in this respect. All the families were poor (so providing an early example of a correlation between poverty and illiteracy).[47]

Successive versions of what came to be called the Massachusetts Poor Laws continued to authorize the removal of children, without the consent of their parents, if the parents were considered unable to maintain them. A 1703 supplement to earlier acts reaffirmed the need to provide apprentices with an education by stipulating that the masters should provide 'for the instructing of children so bound out, to read and write, if they be capable'. Clearly, as both sexes could be apprenticed, both sexes were to be taught reading and writing. However, it turned out that the legislators had not intended this. In 1710, an amendment was passed that altered the order to, 'males to read and write, females to read'. The act was repeated in the same form once a decade until 1741, when the requirement of 'cyphering' was added to the regulations for males. Finally, in 1771, the legislation was changed once again, and the legislation for children apprenticed under the Poor Laws now stipulated, 'males, reading, writing, cyphering; females, reading, writing'.[48]

In other words, it was not until 1771 that Massachusetts considered the ability to write to be a minimal educational necessity for girls. This is particularly significant because the whole purpose of apprenticing these children was to provide them with a skill with which they could eventually support themselves, so as not to be a burden on the town like their indigent parents. Boys needed to be able to write, girls did not.

## Literacy and employment

If legislation on involuntary apprenticeship reveals that children's gender made a difference to the kind of literacy instruction they were required to receive, so too do the terms of apprenticeship agreements that were completely voluntary. In a study of apprenticeship in seventeenth-century Massachusetts, Judith Walter identified 267 apprentices, of whom 32 were girls. For only 31 of all the apprentices was some kind of educational provision specified. For boys, the indenture usually stipulated that the boy be taught to read, write and cipher. James Chichester, for example, when apprenticed at the age of ten, was to be sent to school 'until he can write a leagable hand'. The 1658 indenture of Hopestill Chandler, who was being apprenticed to a blacksmith, required that he be taught to read the Bible and 'to write enough to keep book for his trade'. In contrast, the educational provisions made in 1674 for Sarah Joye of Salem were that she be taught her catechism, and 'to read English, [and] the capital laws of the country', while Sarah Braibrok of Watertown was apprenticed in 1656 to a couple who were to teach her 'to reade the English Tongue' and provide her with religious instruction. In not one case does Walter report finding a writing provision for female apprentices.[49]

The explanation lies in colonial perceptions of the function of writing. Writing was a job-related skill. Because girls were being trained not to hold jobs, but to be successful homemakers, penmanship was an irrelevant acquisition for them. The skill that corresponded, for girls, to what writing was for boys was the ability to sew. In the study just cited, Walter identified some forty different crafts and trades that the boys were to learn during their apprenticeships. There was no indication, however, that girls were to learn anything other than housewifery and, in two cases, sewing or knitting and spinning.[50]

Further evidence on the relationship between jobs and literacy comes from court rulings. In 1655, the Hartford Court ordered the administrators of Thomas Gridley's estate to educate his children, 'learning the sons to read and write, and the daughters to read and sew well'. The next year, the same court interpreted the provisions of Thomas Thomson's will that related to education as follows: 'the sons shall have learning to write plainly and read distinctly in the Bible, and the daughters to read and sew sufficient for the making of their ordinary linen'.[51]

More evidence of sewing as the advanced skill to be acquired by girls in lieu of writing is provided by contemporary records from across the Atlantic. They are particularly instructive because both sexes were being educated in the same institution. Orphaned or needy children between the ages of five and fifteen were admitted to the Great Yarmouth Children's Hospital, which was in effect a charitable workhouse. The master of the hospital was expected to see to the children's education, and kept a register of their educational attainments upon entering and leaving the hospital. David Cressy has tabulated the notes in the hospital register on 132 boys and 85 girls admitted to the hospital between 1698 and 1715. The register reveals that several boys were taught to write before they left the hospital. In contrast, 'none of the girls reached the stage of writing', according to Cressy. Their 'highest achievement was to sew well and to read in the testament or Bible'.[52]

The fact that none of the girls was taught to write should, however, surely be interpreted differently. As eleven of the girls were already in either their Testament or Bible on entering the hospital, they were as ready as the thirty-six boys, similarly prepared, for further instruction. That not even these relatively accomplished readers were taught to write suggests that writing instruction was withheld from them because of their gender, not because they had not 'reached the stage of writing'. Mary Clark, for instance, had entered the hospital at the age of nine with the comment, 'can't read at all'. Four years later, she was characterized as reading 'in her testament but indifferently and hath gone through her sampler'.[53] If girls were to form letters, it would be through the medium of thread, not ink.

No wonder Anne Bradstreet, whose first book of poetry appeared in London in 1650, felt that she was incurring odium by stepping outside the role prescribed by society for women, in exchanging her needle for a pen:

> I am obnoxious to each carping tongue
> Who says my hand a needle better fits,
> A Poets pen all scorn I should thus wrong,
> For such despite they cast on female wits.[54]

Nor should gender restrictions on writing instruction be considered simply a seventeenth-century feature. Apprenticeship indentures for sixty poor children 'put out' by the Newbury selectmen between 1743 and 1760 reveal precisely the same differentiation. Forty-nine boys were apprenticed to learn a range of skills from blacksmithing to making periwigs. The eleven girls, however, were to learn only 'women's work' or 'housewifery'. All the apprentices were promised reading instruction, but only the boys were to be taught writing and arithmetic.[55]

There are several cases in which masters of apprentices were hauled into court for not fulfilling their educational obligations toward their apprentices. We have already noted the New Haven master who in 1660 was brought to court for his alleged failure to teach his apprentice his craft, and who was examined on how much literacy education his apprentice had received. A telling instance is provided about a century later by John Adams. In 1761, Adams remarked on the case of Daniel Prat, 'a poor, fatherless Child' who was suing his master, Thomas Colson. The terms of the apprenticeship had required Colson to teach Prat to read, write, and cipher, and to teach him the trade of a weaver. He had done none of these. Adams felt strongly that Prat, as a child without a male parent, was to be favored in the case, 'Because the English Law greatly favours Education. In every English Country, some sort of Education, some Acquaintance with Letters, is necessary, that a Man may fill any station whatever'.[56]

From the earliest days of settlement, then, and throughout the colonial period, the colonists expected that all children ought to be able to read, no matter how low their station or how poor their circumstances.

## Schooling and gender

As we have seen, in 1642 the Bay Colony had legislated reading without any mention of either schools or writing. Five years later, in striking contrast, a new law mentioned writing and schoolmaster in the same breath: in 1647, Massachusetts passed its first schooling law. Every township of over fifty families was required to engage a master to 'teach all such children as shall resort to him to write and reade', while towns of over a hundred families were to provide a (Latin) grammar school.[57]

The relationship between writing instruction and schooling is exemplified by Watertown, Massachusetts, which constructed its first schoolhouse in 1649 and soon thereafter hired Richard Norcross as its first schoolmaster. The job description spelled out that he was responsible 'for the teaching of Children to Reed and write and soe much of Lattin . . . as allso if any of the said towne, haue any maidens, that haue a desire to learne to write that the said Richard, should attend them for the Learning off them; as allso that he teac[h]e such as desire to Cast acompt'.[58] The clear implication of this wording is that girls would attend the school only if they wished to learn writing and arithmetic. Obviously, they were supposed to have learned to read at home.

Norcross's contract is also an example of the ambiguity of the word 'children'. To modern ears, the word indicates children of both sexes. In the colonial period, there was a strict separation of roles in the home and workplace by gender, and it was the males who held all the positions of responsibility and power.[59] Male children, therefore, were the prime targets of any town's educational efforts. As a result of this bias, the word 'children' meant, in effect, male children, even though it always retained its broader meaning of children of both sexes. (In discussions of Boston schools, for example, the town records habitually refer to the students of their free schools as 'children'. Yet free schooling in the Boston system was restricted to males until 1789.)[60]

While 'reading' is indeed included in Norcross's job description, as we saw earlier, children were supposed to have mastered initial reading before they reached the town school. The school was expected to 'perfect' them in reading, not introduce them to it. Moreover, girls were often not admitted to town schools, particularly if such schools had any aspirations toward teaching Latin (the hallmark of the true grammar school). The rules and regulations of the Hopkins Grammar School, opened by New Haven in 1684, are a case in point. They insisted that 'noe Boyes be admitted into the said Schoole for the learning of English Books, but such as have ben before taught to spell their letters well and begin to Read, thereby to perfect theire right Spelling, and Reading, or to learne to write, and Cypher . . . and that all others either too young and not instructed in letters and spelling, and all Girles be excluded as Improper and inconsistent with such a Grammer Schoole'.[61']

Walter Small, in his study of some two hundred schools in the colonial period, reported finding only seven schools that definitely admitted girls, and another five that might have. The school in Rehoboth, Massachusetts, was among the seven. In 1699, Robert Dickson contracted with the Rehoboth selectmen 'to do his utmost endeavor to teach *both sexes* of boys and girls to read English and write and cast accounts'. Similarly, Deerfield, in northwestern Massachusetts, obviously allowed girls to enter its town school in 1698, because it warned parents that all heads of families with children between the ages of six and ten, whether male or female, should pay a poll tax to the school, 'whether they send such children or not'. Five years later the town made a similar motion, but this time changed the ages of admission. Families of 'boys from four to eight, and girls from four to six years old', were to pay their proportion of ten pounds for the ensuing year.[62] (The shorter timespan for girls suggests that they were to leave school at the point when they were supposed to be able to read, having reached the age for the instruction in writing that they would not receive.)

The comparatively late dates at which these and similar provisions were enacted is significant: they suggest that on the boundaries of settlement, as the seventeenth century drew to a close, the town school had two characteristics. In the first place, it did not attempt any education fancier than the three R's, and in the second, it chose not to restrict its education to boys. Indeed the experience of the frontier settlement of Hatfield may prove, with further research, to be characteristic. From 1695 to 1699 there were no girls in Hatfield's town school; in 1700 there were four girls and forty-two boys during the winter term; nine years later there were sixteen girls in a total of sixty-four schoolchildren.[63]

Nevertheless, there were many towns that stood firm against the admission of girls to the master's school throughout the entire seventeenth and even the eighteenth century. Farmington, Connecticut, for example, voted in 1686 to devote twenty pounds to a town school, 'for the instruction of all such children as shall be sent to it, to learn to read and write the English tongue'. Some parents of daughters, it seems, interpreted this too broadly, for the following year the town issued a clarification: 'all such children as shall be sent is to be understood only *male* children that are through their horning book [hornbook]'. Small found many instances of town schools – Salem, Medford, Haverhill, Gloucester, Hingham, and Charlestown – that, shortly before or even well after the American Revolution, were only just beginning to open their doors to girls. And in these cases, the girls were being admitted only for a couple of hours a day (presumably for writing instruction). As one witness put it, remembering his schooling in Lynn, Massachusetts, 'In all my school days which ended in 1801, I never saw but three females in public schools, and they were there only in the afternoon to learn to write'.[64]

## School dames

A new feature in colonial town schooling can be detected as the seventeenth century drew to a close: the towns' formal sponsorship of women to teach reading. One presumes that private dame-school instruction had continued for decades in New England; after 1670, however, we see towns actively seeking female teachers to teach reading to small children. These women were paid a few pennies per week per child, and substantially less than their male colleagues.

Walter Small collected numerous references to such 'school dames'. Among Massachusetts towns, Woburn paid ten shillings to two women in 1673, and the same sum to another in 1686. Cambridge reported in 1680 that 'For English, our school dame is Goodwife Healy; at present but nine scholars.' Two years later, Springfield made an agreement with Goodwife Mirick that, in order to 'encourage her in the good work of training up of children and teaching children to read', she should have three pence per child per week.[65]

After 1700, mention of school dames increases. Small found references to them in records running from 1700 to 1730 for, among others, Waterbury and Windsor in Connecticut, and for Weymouth, Lexington, Charlestown, Salem, and Falmouth, all in Massachusetts. A few of these, as was the case for Charlestown, only involved the town in paying women for the instruction of poor children who could not otherwise attend school. But increasingly, as the eighteenth century wore on, there seems to have been a definite shift in the direction of employing women to teach reading on a regular basis, in specific parts of town, with funds allocated for that purpose from the town treasury. Framingham had voted as early as 1713 to appoint selectmen to 'settle school dames in each quarter of the town'. Worcester in 1731 decided that, because small children could not walk to the school in the center of town, up to five school dames should be hired 'for the teaching of small children to read' and placed in different parts of the town. Wenham, two years later, made an arrangement with its schoolmaster that permitted him to delegate some of his teaching responsibilities to others: he was to be 'allowed to teach little children to read by suitable women, in the several parts of the town, that he shall agree with, by the approbation of the selectmen; also to teach to write by another man in another part of town'.[66]

Marriage was no obstacle for a woman in teaching reading. In fact, there were those who taught for almost the whole of their adult lives. When Abigail Fowler died in Salem, Massachusetts, in 1771, her death was reported affectionately: 'Widow Abigail Fowler, a noted school dame, finished her earthly labors. She was in her 68th year, and began to teach children before she was 18, and continued so to do till her decease, with the exception of a few years after she was married.'[67]

The reason for the towns' new eagerness to employ women seems to have been the continuing failure of parents to carry out their legal responsibility to teach their children to read. For example, at the turn of the century Marblehead undertook a survey on the number of boys who could not read, and who could therefore not be admitted to the master's school. The town found a total of 122 such boys.[68]

Note that there were children who still read too poorly for the master's school despite the fact that standards for admission appear to have been lowered in many schools as the decades progressed. Whereas, formerly, schoolmasters had expected children to be in their Psalter or Bible (still the case in Boston's three elite writing schools, as the incident with John Proctor revealed), now the admission requirement was only, for the New Haven grammar school in 1684, to 'have been taught to spell the letters well and begin to Read', or, for Farmington, Connecticut, two years later, that boys should be through their hornbook.

For many women, the chance to earn money from the town must have been most welcome. Others, as the eighteenth century lengthened, were able to use newspapers successfully to advertise their private literacy instruction.

## Conclusion

The arguments made up to this point are as follows:

1.   Reading was considered easy to teach, and reading instruction unaccompanied by writing instruction was the province of women, both at home and at school (private or town-sponsored). Texts for reading instruction were cheap and easy to obtain.
2.   Writing was considered a craft, difficult to teach and taught by men. Texts for writing instruction were comparatively expensive and difficult to obtain.
3.   Reading instruction preceded, and was independent of, writing instruction. Instruction in reading was conducted orally, by means of the oral alphabet method.
4.   Because reading was considered to be important for religious, political, and economic reasons, legislation was passed that required it of all children.
5.   Because writing was considered a job-related skill, society only required that it be taught to boys.
6.   Writing was one of the key components of the curriculum of the town schools, which were taught by men and in many cases restricted to boys. Girls won access to some, but by no means all, of the masters' schools from the 1690s on.
7.   Towns began to employ women (school dames) to teach reading to small children of both sexes from the 1680s on.

These statements generate further conclusions:

8.   Because reading was required to be taught, and because people could and did learn to read without also learning to write, we cannot assume that all those – particularly women – who only marked documents were totally illiterate.

9. However, because educational standards in New England were raised over time, marks have to be interpreted in context.

In the seventeenth century, class, gender, and rural location all militated against obtaining writing instruction. In terms of class, the children whose apprenticeships have been mentioned above were at the bottom of the social heap, as were the orphans admitted to the Great Yarmouth Children's Hospital. Even at this low social level, it is clear that boys were offered both reading and writing instruction, but girls were only expected to know how to read and sew. If such girls could not sign when grown women, it was because no one had ever taught them to write.

Of course, then as now, low social class combined with poverty often correlated with illiteracy in reading as well as writing. It is surely no coincidence that the eighteen children found to be unable to read in Watertown in 1661 all came from impoverished families, and that the boys who could not read the Psalter, and who were therefore refused admittance to one of the Boston writing schools in 1741, were the children of 'Families of low Circumstances'.

As we would also expect, high social standing, when combined with an urban setting, was able to erase the restrictions on female access to writing instruction. In cities, the daughters of the higher ranks learned to write because their parents sent them off for private instruction. In Boston, for instance, even in the seventeenth century, girls were taught by private entrepreneurs like the writing master who taught Hannah Sewall (wife of Samuel Sewall) to write. In the eighteenth century, girls could also learn from publicly financed town masters who taught fee-paying female students 'out of hours'.[69] The fact that during the early colonial period rural women, even when wealthy, signed at a lower rate than urban women is surely to be explained by the exclusion of girls from the town school and the relative paucity of private male teachers in rural areas. But in cities, private teachers abounded: at least twenty private writing masters have been documented for Boston during the colonial period.[70]

It is the girls of modest social standing, however, who are of the most importance to my argument. Even in the seventeenth century access to reading instructional materials was easy, and the teaching of reading was considered a female domain. There is every reason to believe that reading at some level was taught widely to girls by women, whereas writing, for a long time considered a male teaching preserve, was not.

Around the turn of the century, several strands were coming together, all of them favoring increasing education in general, and female education in particular. One that should not be ignored is domestic tranquility, bought at considerable cost to both whites and Indians. King Philip's short but bloody war, 1675 to 1676, spelled the end of the political and military power of the Indians. Slaughter and disease had thinned their ranks, and surviving Indian communities passed into obscurity.[71] The colonists were therefore freer to concentrate less on defense and more on such matters as education.

As we have seen, after 1680 women were increasingly incorporated into town educational systems, hired for their skill in teaching beginning reading. (Such women would have had to be taught to write, for they needed to be able to keep school records.) Girls were also winning access to some of the masters' town schools, and so to writing instruction.

There are several other factors that no doubt made their contribution, although proof of these lies beyond the scope of this essay. For instance, eighteenth-century instructional texts in reading improved, thanks to the advent of the spelling book. Similarly, the switch from the secretary hand of the seventeenth century to the eighteenth-century round hand would appear to have made penmanship easier. There were also political changes: some colonies began to put teeth into their education laws. The expansion during the course of the eighteenth century in the availability of secular reading material, including chapbooks and, at the end of the century, novels, was undoubtedly significant.

These speculations aside, it is still possible to take a fresh look at the supposed illiteracy of those who made marks instead of signatures. First, a comment on the mark itself. When we talk today about making a 'mark' on a document, what springs to mind is the traditional X. That is not, however, how most colonists marked documents. When the information is available, marks often turn out to be initials, like the HN used by Hanna Newberry. These initials indicate, at the least, an acquaintance with the alphabet.[72]

We can now reinterpret some of the detailed information provided by Auwers for Windsor, Connecticut. What puzzled Auwers was that she found no correlation between social class and the signatures ('literacy') of Windsor women born before 1690: many rich women, like Hanna Newberry, only made marks. We can now explain this as a function of gender, which impeded access to writing instruction. Surely Hanna could read: her socioeconomic status alone makes it very unlikely that she would have been truly illiterate.

Windsor forms a useful example in other ways. In 1717 the town employed its first school dame: Sarah Stiles was hired to teach reading in the summer; schooling opportunities improved.[73] The dramatic increase that Auwers found in the percentage of women able to sign their names, as the decades passed, suggests that the right of girls to write in Windsor had been permanently won by the 1740s.

And what of the female will-markers in Lockridge's study, cited so often in defense of claims of massive female illiteracy in colonial New England? The figures from these women are misleading, I believe, in several respects. For one, as Lockridge is the first to point out, the sample of females is small, representing under 15 percent of his total sample and only 5 percent of the population he was investigating.[74] Just as important is the fact that wills were Lockridge's only source. Some women may have been able to sign but chose not to. People often make their wills late in life, and when a mark was as legal as a signature, initialing a will if you were old and ill may have seemed more appealing than struggling to sign. Auwers's study, for instance, identified thirty-one women who had affixed their names to both deeds and wills. Eight of these (26 percent) signed their deeds but marked their wills, only one did the reverse. (This could also be interpreted, with Auwers, as evidence of the marginality of female signing skill.)[75] We can speculate that no stigma would have attached to a woman who chose not to sign her name. In contrast, because society increasingly expected them to write, men by the early eighteenth century might have felt more deeply about the social cachet attached to signing.[76] Even more important is the age at which a person subscribed his or her will. A mark in the 1760s may represent the absence of writing instruction as much as forty or fifty years earlier.

Be that as it may, it is, in any case, likely that many of Lockridge's female will-markers could read, at least to some extent. Further research, ideally using Linda Auwers's birth cohort approach, is likely to produce evidence of higher female signing rates in the eighteenth century similar to those found by Auwers and, later in the century, William Gilmore.[77]

How well could someone read who could read but not write? The colonists themselves were aware that there were differing levels of literacy. Experience Mayhew, a pastor on Martha's Vineyard, discussed in 1727 the literacy of the Christian Indians who could read books published in their own language; he said that such Indians read and wrote only at the 'rate that poor Men among the English are wont to do'.[78] The literacy of nonwriters fits the profile of 'traditional literacy' that David D. Hall has sketched, of readers who approached print with reverential deliberation.[79] Probably, many nonwriters read familiar material without too much trouble. This would have been particularly true of the Scriptures: the advantage was that ministers, heads of households, and other family members were constantly reading from them aloud. Nonwriters would also have been able to decipher writings such as the notes – like those asking for information on strayed animals – that were so often tacked onto the doors of meeting houses.[80] They surely could not, however, as Cathy N. Davidson points out, have been able to read the works of John Locke.[81]

On the other hand, we should not underestimate the pleasure that even a limited reading ability can bring. For a colonial woman, reading must have provided one of the very few sources of satisfaction that was not dependent upon others. In virtually all of the roles identified by Laurel Thatcher Ulrich, whether as housewife, deputy husband, consort, mother, mistress of servants, or neighbor, a woman was looking out for the welfare of others.[82] When she was reading, she was doing something for herself. Above all, if she were a Christian (another of the roles posited by Ulrich), her reading would have been an important and meaningful part of her private devotions.[83] For those who were called upon to teach reading to others, their reading ability transformed itself into a measure of independence. These were small treasures of the mind and spirit that we should not despise.

There is no reason to suppose that the conclusions drawn here for New England are very different from those to be drawn for other parts of colonial America – except, perhaps, for the South, where male tutors on plantations taught children of both genders to read and write. A poem penned by a judge in Philadelphia at the end of the seventeenth century shows that differentiation of schooling by gender was not exclusive to New England:

> Here are schools of divers sorts,
> To which our youth daily resorts,
> Good women, who do very well
> Bring little ones to read and spell,
> Which fits them for writing, and then,
> Here's men to bring them to their pen,
> And to instruct and make them quick
> In all sorts of arithmetick.[84]

## Notes

This research was supported in part by grant no. 6-64048 from the PSC-CUNY Research Award Program of the City University of New York.

1    Linda Auwers, 'Reading the Marks of the Past: Exploring Female Literacy in Colonial Windsor, Connecticut', *Historical Methods* 13 (1980): 209.

2    See Carl F. Kaestle's summary of literacy studies in 'The History of Literacy and the History of Readers', in *Review of Research in Education*, vol. 12, ed. Edmund W. Gordon (Washington, D.C., 1985), 11–53.

3    Kenneth A. Lockridge, *Literacy in Colonial New England: An Enquiry into the Social Context of Literacy in the Early Modern West* (New York, 1974), 128 n. 4, 13, 38–42, 140 n. 57.

4    Auwers, 'Reading the Marks of the Past'; and Ross W. Beales, Jr., 'Studying Literacy at the Community Level: A Research Note', *Journal of Interdisciplinary History* 9 (1978): 93–102. The largest study to date is that by William Gilmore, who surveyed 10,467 documents dated between 1760 and 1830 from the Upper Connecticut Valley, and found almost universal male signing levels by the 1770s, while female signing began at two-thirds in the late 1770s and rose thereafter: William J. Gilmore, *Elementary Literacy on the Eve of the Industrial Revolution: Trends in Rural New England, 1760–1830* (Worcester, Mass. 1982), 98, 114.

5    Auwers, 'Reading the Marks of the Past', 204–5.

6    Kaestle, 'History of Literacy and the History of Readers', 21.

7    E.g. *ibid.*, 21, 29; Margaret Spufford, *Small Books and Pleasant Histories: Popular Fiction and Its Readership in Seventeenth-Century England* (Cambridge, 1981), 22, 27, 29, 34–35; Victor E. Neuburg, *Popular Education in Eighteenth-Century England* (London, 1971), 55, 93; Geraldine Jonçich Clifford, 'Buch und Lesen: Historical Perspectives on Literacy and Schooling', *Review of Educational Research* 54 (1984): 474–75 and Gerald F. Moran and Maris A. Vinovskis, 'The Great Care of Godly Parents: Early Childhood in Puritan New England', in *History and Research in Child Development*, ed. Alice Boardman Smuts and John W. Hagen, *Monographs of the Society for Research in Child Development* 50, nos. 4–5 (1985): 34. Lockridge himself raises the possibility several times in *Literacy in Colonial New England*, 14, 109, 127, 134 n.26, but rejects it for the purpose of his analysis, 38.

8    James L. Axtell, ed., *The Educational Writings of John Locke: A Critical Edition with Introduction and Notes* (London, 1968), 260; and Lawrence A. Cremin, *American Education: The Colonial Experience, 1607–1783* (New York, 1970), 277. I would like to acknowledge here my indebtedness to Professor Cremin's bibliography.

9    George A. Plimpton, *The Horn book and Its Use in America* (Worcester, Mass., 1916). Plain and gilt hornbooks were listed in the book inventories of a Boston bookseller in 1700: Worthington C. Ford, *The Boston Book Market, 1679–1700* (rpt. New York, 1972), 177–78.

10   Quoted in Andrew W. Tuer, *History of the Horn Book* (1897; rpt. New York, 1979), 133.

11   Plimpton, *Hornbook and Its Use in America*, 9.

12   Charles J. Hoadly, ed., *Records of the Colony and Plantation of New Haven, from 1638 to 1649* (Hartford, Coon., 1857), 176. For ease of reading, I have silently expanded all the abbreviations in this and other quotations (e.g., 'yᵉ,' 'yᵗ,' and 'Testamᵗ' appear as 'the', 'that', and 'Testament'), but have preserved the spelling, punctuation, and capitalization of the originals.

13   John Eliot, *The Indian Primer . . .* (Cambridge, Mass., 1669).

14   Paul L. Ford, *The New-England Primer: A History of Its Origin and Development with a Reprint of the Unique Copy of the Earliest Known Edition* (New York, 1897); and Richard L. Venezky, 'A History of the American Reading Textbook', *Elementary School Journal* 87, no. 3 (1987): 249. For a discussion of *The New England Primer* as the vehicle for a set of metaphors on Christian obedience, see David H. Watters, '"Spake as a Child": Authority, Metaphor and *The New-England Primer*', *Early American Literature* 20 (1985–86): 193–213.

15   Charles F. Heartman, *American Primers, Indian Primers, Royal Primers, and Thirty-Seven Other Types of Non-New-England Primers Issued Prior to 1830* (Highland Park, N.J., 1935).

16   Quoted in Nila Banton Smith, *American Reading Instruction* (Newark, Del., 1965), 17–18.

17   Boston, Registry Department, *Records Relating to the Early History of Boston*, vol. 15, *A Report of the Record Commissioners of the City of Boston, Containing the Records of Boston Selectmen, 1736 to 1742* (Boston, 1886), 288.

18   Franidin B. Dexter, ed., *New Haven Town Records, 1649–1662* (New Haven, Coon., 1917), 97. Similarly, the Reverend Peter Thacher wrote of a new student in 1680 that he was 'to perfect him in reading, and to teach him to write'; quoted in David D. Hall, 'The Uses of Literacy in New England, 1600–1850', in *Printing and Society in Early America*, ed. William L. Joyce *et al.* (Worcester, Mass., 1983), 24.

19   Dexter, *New Haven Town Records*, 88.

20   For spelling books in Britain, see Neuburg, *Popular Education*, 64–91; R. C. Alston, *A Bibliography of the English Language from the Invention of Printing to the Year 1800*, vol. 4, *Spelling Books* (Bradford, England, 1967); and Ian Michael, *The Teaching of English: From the Sixteenth Century to 1870* (Cambridge, 1987). For spelling books in the American colonies, see Raoul N. Smith, 'Interest in Language and Languages in Colonial and Federal America', *Proceedings of the American Philosophical Society* 123 (1979): 36–38.

21    Venezky, 'History of the American Reading Textbook', 248.

22    William R. Hart, 'The English Schoole-Maister (1596) by Edmund Coote: An Edition of the Text with Critical Notes and Introductions', diss., University of Michigan, 1963, 8.

23    Robert F. Roden, The Cambridge Press, 1638–1692: A History of the First Printing Press Established in English America, Together with a Bibliographical List of the Issues of the Press (New York, 1905), 36.

24    E. Jennifer Monaghan, A Common Heritage: Noah Webster's Blue-Back Speller (Hamden, Coon., 1983), 31–34; quotation, 26. There were seventy-six editions of Dilworth by 1801, of which forty-three were printed before 1787: Smith, 'Interest in Language and Languages', 36.

25    Monaghan, Common Heritage, 33–34; and Smith, American Reading Instruction, 25–31.

26    Edmund Coote, The English Schoole-Maister (London, 1596), A3; in Hart, 'The English Schoole-Maister', 129.

27    M. G. Hall, ed., The Autobiography of Increase Mather (Worcester, Mass., 1962), 278; Richard Brown is quoted in James Axtell, The School upon a Hill: Education and Society in Colonial New England (New Haven, Conn., 1974), 174–75. Cf. Hall, 'The Uses of Literacy', 25; and M. T. Clanchy, 'Learning to Read in the Middle Ages and the Role of Mothers', Studies in the History of Reading, ed. Greg Brooks and A. K. Pugh (Reading, England, 1984), 33–39.

28    Spufford, Small Books, 35–36; J. H. Higginson, 'Dame Schools', British Journal of Educational Studies 22, no. 2 (1974): 166–81; and D. P. Leinster-MacKay, 'Dame Schools: A Need for Review', British Journal of Educational Studies 24, no. 1 (1976): 38–48; cited in Joan N. Burstyn, 'Women in the History of Education', paper presented at the annual meeting of the American Educational Research Association, Montreal, April 1983.

29    Axtell, School upon a Hill, 176.

30    'Autobiography of the Rev. John Barnard', Collections of the Massachusetts Historical Society 3, no. 5 (1836): 178. Cf. 'The Commonplace Book of Joseph Green', Publications of the Colonial Society of Massachusetts 34 (1943): 236.

31    David Pulsifer, ed., Records of the Colony of New Plymouth, in New England. Acts of the Commissioners of the United Colonies of New England, vol. 2, 1653–1679 (Boston, 1859), 106.

32    E. Jennifer Monaghan and E. Wendy Saul, 'The Reader, the Scribe, the Thinker: A Critical Look at the History of American Reading and Writing Instruction', in The Formation of School Subjects: The Struggle for Creating an American Institution, ed. Thomas S. Popkewitz (New York, 1987), 88.

33    George Bickham, The Universal Penman, Engraved by George Bickham, London 1743 (New York, 1954). For the writing curriculum, see E. Jennifer Monaghan, 'Readers Writing: The Curriculum of the Writing Schools of Eighteenth-Century Boston', Visible Language 21, no. 2 (1987): 167–213.

34    Ray Nash, American Writing Masters and Copybooks: History and Bibliography through Colonial Times (Boston, 1959), 13.

35    George Fisher, The Instructor; or, American Young Man's Best Companion, 30th ed. (Worcester, Mass., nd.); and Nash, American Writing Masters and Copybooks, 25–34.

36    At least one copybook, however, proclaimed (in 1656) that it was Set forth for the benefit of poore Schollers, where the Master hath not time to set Copies: see Nash, American Writing Masters and Copybooks, 21–22.

37    Monaghan, 'Readers Writing'.

38    Cremin, American Education, 501–3; Patricia Cline Cohen, A Calculating People: The Spread of Numeracy in Early America (Chicago, 1982), 120–22.

39    Dexter, New Haven Town Records, 438; and Charles J. Hoadly, ed., Records of the Colony or Jurisdiction of New Haven, from May 1653, to the Union, Together with the New Haven Code of 1656 (Hartford, Coon., 1858), 443.

40    Robert F. Seybolt, The Evening School in Colonial America (Urbana, Ill., 1925), 23; advertisement quoted in Walter H. Small, Early New England Schools (Boston, 1914), 317.

41   Nathaniel B. Shurtleff, ed., *Records of the Governor and Company of the Massachusetts Bay in New England*, vol. 2, *1642–1649* (Boston, 1853), 6–7.

42   Cremin, *American Education*, 125.

43   *Ibid.*

44   Hoadly, *Records of the Colony or Jurisdiction of New Haven, from May 1653, to the Union*, 376.

45   Quoted in Cremin, *American Education*, 125.

46   Dorchester Antiquarian and Historical Society, *History of the Town of Dorchester, Massachusetts* (Boston, 1859), 223–24; and Salem, Massachusetts, *Town Records of Salem, Massachusetts*, vol. 2, *1659–1680* (Salem, Mass., 1913), 180.

47   Watertown, Massachusetts, *Watertown Records Comprising the First and Second Books of Town Proceedings* (Watertown, Mass., 1894), 71. Subsequent inspections occurred in 1665, 1670, 1672, 1674, 1679, 1680, and later: *ibid.*, 86, 104, 113, 121, 137, 145.

48   Robert F. Seybolt, *Apprenticeship and Apprenticeship Education in Colonial New England and New York* (New York, 1917), 46–47.

49   Judith Walter, 'Apprenticeship Education and Family Structure in Seventeenth Century Massachusetts Bay', M.A. thesis, Bryn Mawr College, 1971, 33–34, 42–43.

50   *Ibid.*, 34.

51   Walter H. Small, 'Girls in Colonial Schools', *Education* 22 (1902): 534.

52   David Cressy, *Literacy and the Social Order: Reading and Writing in Tudor and Stuart England* (Cambridge, 1980), 30–34; quotation, 34.

53   *Ibid.*, 34. For girls taught only reading and sewing in England, see Spufford, *Small Books*, 34–35.

54   Quoted in Thomas Woody, *A History of Women's Education in the United States* (1929; rpt. New York, 1966), I: 132.

55   Laurel Thatcher Ulrich, *Good Wives: Image and Reality in the Lives of Women in Northern New England, 1650–1750* (New York, 1982), 43–44.

56   L. H. Butterffield, ed., *Diary and Autobiography of John Adams*, vol. I, *Diary 1755–1770* (Cambridge, Mass., 1961), 219.

57   Shurtleff, *Records of the Governor and Company of the Massachusetts Bay*, 2: 203.

58   *Watertown Records Comprising the First and Second Books*, 18, 21.

59   Lyle Koehler, *A Search for Power: The 'Weaker Sex' in Seventeenth-Century New England* (Urbana, Ill., 1980).

60   See, for example, the proposal in 1682 to open a free school for the 'teachinge of Children to write & Cypher': Boston, Registry Department, *Records Relating to the Early History of Boston*, vol. 7, *A Report of the Record Commissioners of the City of Boston, Containing the Boston Records from 1660 to 1701* (Boston, 1881), 158.

61   *American Journal of Education* 4 (1857): 710.

62   Small, 'Girls in Colonial Schools', 532–33. Small used primary sources such as town records for his study, but did not document his sources. Where I have been able to crosscheck them, I have found them accurate.

63   *Ibid.*, 533.

64   *Ibid.*, 533–37; quotations, 533–34.

65   *Early New England Schools*, 168, 165.

66   *Ibid.*, 165–70; quotations, 179, 168, 170.

67   *Ibid.*, 169.

68   *Ibid.*, 167.

69   Robert F. Seybolt, 'Schoolmasters of Colonial Boston', *Publications of the Colonial Society of Massachusetts* 27 (1928): 137; for an example of female instruction by a writing master, see Alice Morse Earle, ed., *Diary of Anna Green Winslow: A Boston School Girl of 1771* (1894; rpt. Williamstown, Mass., 1974), 12, 92–94.

70   Seybolt, 'Schoolmasters of Colonial Boston'.

71   William C. Sturtevant, ed.,*Handbook of North American Indians*, vol. 15, *Northeast*, ed. Bruce G. Trigger (Washington, D.C., 1978), 177.

72   For initials as marks, see, for example, Joseph Underwood's V in 1684 as his mark set to an agreement to teach his male apprentice to read and write: *Watertown Records Comprising the First and Second Books*, 129.

73   Auwers, 'Reading the Marks of the Past', 204.

74   Lockridge, *Literacy in Colonial New England*, 128.

75   Auwers, 'Reading the Marks of the Past', 207.

76   I am indebted to Ross W Beales, Jr., for this insight.

77   Auwers, 'Reading the Marks of the Past'; and Gilmore, *Elementary Literacy on the Eve of the Industrial Revolution*.

78   Experience Mayhew, *Indian Converts: Or, Some Account of the Lives and Dying Speeches of a Considerable Number of the Christianized Indians of Martha's Vineyard, in New-England* (London, 1727), xxiii.

79   Hall, 'The Uses of Literacy', 21–24. Hall emphasizes the role played by memorization and recitation in learning to read.

80   See, for example, the complaint in 1687 about such notes: Watertown, Massachusetts, *Watertown Records Comprising the Third Book of Town Proceedings and the Second Book of Births Marriages and Deaths to End of 1737* (Watertown, Mass., 1900), 31.

81   Cathy N. Davidson, *Revolution and the Word: The Rise of the Novel in America* (New York, 1986), 59.

82   Ulrich, *Good Wives*, 9–10.

83   Charles E. Hambrick-Stowe, *The Practice of Piety: Puritan Devotional Disciplines in Seventeenth-Century New England* (Williamsburg, Va., 1982), 157–61.

84   Quoted in Carl Bridenbaugh, *Cities in the Wilderness: The First Century of Urban Life in America, 1625–1742* (1938; rpt. Oxford, 1971), 283–84.

# Chapter 24

# Kate Flint

## READING PRACTICES

### Reading, prohibition and transgression

Not all accounts of reading are untroubled. Numerous narratives of prohibitions, warnings, and censorship are told, which amount to a substantial body of evidence about the control exercised within some families, particularly concerning the ideas and emotions which were considered suitable for girls to encounter. Such accounts of transgression provide sites for the writer's own assertion of individuality, measures of the distance she has travelled from her family background and the ideological assumptions of her parents, even siblings. Julia Kristeva may claim that the adolescent is one of those mythic figures which has the function of distancing us from certain of our faults by reifying them in the form of someone who has not yet grown up,[1] but the role of the figure of the adolescent reader in many of these writings is to problematize the idea of fault. A symbolic action against family or against dominant social beliefs is not so much distanced from the time of writing as highlighted; presented as an incident which helps form the recognition and assertion of individual identity which leads directly towards the self-confidence necessary for the writing of published autobiography.

Sometimes, these instances of rebellious reading took place in carefully chosen social contexts, like Marie Corelli (b. 1855) deliberately startling her governess with quotations from *Don Juan*,[2] or Mrs Benson, wife of the Headmaster of Wellington College, scandalizing his friends by letting her children read George Eliot, and thrusting *Adam Bede* into the hands of clergymen's wives telling them not to mind being seen reading it.[3] Sometimes they were private ones, like Jean Curtis Brown and her friend Lucy consuming the forbidden magazine *Home Chat*, borrowed from the kitchen on the cook's night out.[4] But the impact of the transgressive act was not necessarily dependent on breaching obvious moral imperatives or crossing class boundaries. It could signify a different form of assertion: access into the domain of parental property. Joan Evans, later to become a historian of medieval art and a well-known Ruskin scholar, was brought up in the 1890s in a house full of books, most of them dating from the early and mid-century: she could claim that she was more familiar with life in England between 1810 and 1850 than with anything happening in her own time. Yet despite the freedom of her access to the fiction, of Scott and Thackeray, she was aware that she lacked poetry, of which there was little in the house other than the well-bound wedding presents, belonging to her mother, kept in a glass-fronted bookcase in the drawing room:

> One of my few conscious naughtinesses after I had attained the age of perception was to steal into the drawing-room, when I knew my parents were safe in London, open the case, and take deep delicious draughts of verse. Tennyson and Matthew Arnold are all the sweeter for being read in secret.[5]

Controls over what was, or was not, considered suitable reading focused around certain specific issues. Some of these controls were generically determined, demonstrating, especially, the distrust of novels. 'Lucas Malet', daughter of Charles Kingsley (b. 1852), told a reporter that 'novels were practically forbidden at Eversley Rectory', and that she was not allowed to read even so safe a writer as Charlotte Yonge until she was twenty. Despite the fact that she had the run of Kingsley's library, where she read history, philosophy, and the poets, 'novels were not within my reach', and she never recollects having seen her father open a novel.[6] This is perhaps not entirely surprising, given the attitudes towards women as readers of fiction which her father professed outside the home. In 'Nausicaa in London: Or, The Lower Education of Woman', written in 1879, for example, he paints a particularly dismal picture of the unhealthy modern girl, stunted, pallid, subsisting on tea and bread and taking a novel from the library as her stimulus.[7] On the other hand, Kingsley was not entirely consistent, recognizing elsewhere that women may have needs in their reading which can be met through fiction. He defended his habit of inserting pieces of information into his own novels on the ground that many readers enjoyed them, especially intelligent women who were starved of opportunities for serious discussion.[8] Kingsley's novels themselves, incidentally, were not immune from censure: Edward Pusey considered *Hypatia* 'a work not fit to be read by our wives and our sisters'.[9]

There are plentiful further examples of fiction being regarded with qualified disapproval. Mary Paley Marshall, for example, one of Newnham's first students, recalls her father in the 1860s reading aloud *The Arabian Nights*, *Gulliver's Travels*, the *Iliad* and *Odyssey*, Shakespeare, and, above all, Scott's novels, but she never understood why – unless it was the more pronounced 'religious tone' in Scott – which meant that his novels were allowed whilst Dickens's were forbidden: 'I was grown up before I read *David Copperfield* and then it had to be in secret.[10] But it is impossible to arrive at any sound generalizations. Dorothy McCall (b. c.1884) recalls that *The Heart of Midlothian* was the one book in her father's library which she and her siblings were forbidden to read: 'he immured it in his dressing room, where we took our baths at night. It was a gentleman's agreement, and we behaved like gentlemen, and never looked inside it'.[11] On the other hand, Julia Grant, leaving for boarding-school for the first time in 1877, was bought a copy of the same novel by her father at the railway station, for reading on the journey'.[12] And Anne Thackeray's (b. 1837) memories serve to remind us that what an adult might find unsuitable was in any case often unintelligible to a child: she could not 'imagine how little Em'ly ever was so stupid as to run away from Peggotty's enchanted houseboat'.[13]

The combination, here, of reference to Scott's aura of religiosity on the one hand, and on the other to *David Copperfield*, the novel of Dickens's most commonly considered *risqué*, points to the two most common areas in which familial control was exercised: sexuality and religion. First, sexuality. Like McCall's family, Maurice Baring's sisters were not allowed to read *The Heart of Midlothian* 'which was not, as they said, for the J.P. (jeune personne)'.[14] Frequently forbidden, too, was George Eliot's *Adam Bede*. Whilst Lucy Caroline Lyttelton's grandmother only left out one chapter of this new novel about which 'the world raves . . . a heart-rending book, with its stern true moral of the irrevocableness of sin' when she was reading it aloud to her grandchildren,[15] as late as the 1890s, Harriet Shaw Weaver's mother was shocked when she came upon her adolescent daughter reading *Adam Bede*: the story in part of a girl who had given birth to and disposed of an illegitimate child, written by a woman who herself lived unmarried, with a man. Weaver was sent immediately to her room, and the local vicar was asked to call in order to explain the book's unsuitability. This incident was to remain painful to her for fifty years, since it epitomized, for her, the forthcoming conflict between loyalty to her family and her championing of individual liberties.[16] Slightly less surprisingly, given its content, Yeats forbade his sisters to read George Moore's *A Mummer's Wife*: a proscription which led Susan Mitchell, who lived with the family, to 'gulp . . . guilty pages of it' as she went to bed.[17] Mary Butts's (b. 1890) mother warned her solemnly against the cupboard in her father's room:

> I was not to look at the books in the cupboard. It was full of dreadful books. Books, she went on to explain, that only men read, and she wished indeed that my father would not read them. But I was always to remember that men were different. Also it seemed that even God would have to try specially hard to forgive Daddy for reading some of the books that were in there.

These works included books by Ronsard, Guy de Maupassant, Defoe, Balzac, and Stendhal. On her father's death, Butts's mother ceremoniously burnt the offending texts on a funeral pyre, paying no concern to their potential financial, let alone literary value, so shocked was she by what she knew, or presumed, of their contents: 'Little square old books, the noble pages of Burton in their gold and black, their delicate engravings of fabulous princesses. French memoirs, with their portraits of Ninon and the Dubarry and the great Pompadour'.[18]

It was not only the young who could be presumed to be corrupted, or to think themselves corrupted, by what they read. A letter from Elizabeth Barrett Browning to Arabel Barrett tells of a sixty-year-old woman who believed that her morals had been injured by reading *Aurora Leigh* and that her character would be in danger if it were to become known that she had looked at the poem.[19] Josephine Butler recalled the publication of Elizabeth Gaskell's *Ruth* in 1853 and the voicing of double standards to which it gave rise in Oxford University circles:

> A moral lapse in a woman was spoken of as an immensely worse thing than in a man; there was no comparison to be formed between them. A pure woman, it was reiterated, should be absolutely ignorant of a certain class of evils in the world, albeit those evils bore with murderous cruelty on other women. One young man seriously declared that he would not allow his own mother to read such a book as that under discussion – a book which seemed to me to have a very wholesome tendency, though dealing with a painful subject. Silence was thought to be the great duty of all on such subjects.

This formed one among a growing list of iniquities which led Butler into 'revolt against certain accepted theories in Society'.[20] Gaskell herself recorded how one close Chapel associate of her family 'has forbidden his wife to read it',[21] and expressed to Anna Jameson her sorrow and surprise 'how very many people – good kind people – and *women* infinitely more than men, really & earnestly disapprove of what I have said & express that disapproval at considerable pain to themselves, rather than allow a "demoralizing laxity" to go unchecked'.[22]

Readers more willing to confess to their assertions of independence explicitly indicate how prohibition and censorship in themselves, unsurprisingly, led to inquisitiveness and transgression. These were presented as crucial acts in the development of their consciousness which they could look back to, in some cases, with gratitude. Lady Frances Balfour, for example, was brought up in a highly literary environment: her father and mother both read poetry aloud (she particularly recollected her mother repeating 'How well Horatius kept the bridge in the brave days of old') and at home she listened to Gladstone reading Latin and Italian. The book 'on which my youth was nourished', however, was *Uncle Tom's Cabin*, the plot of which served as an analogy for the liberation of her own bonds of thought and experience. She was forbidden to read the second volume of this 'but human nature cannot be denied, and of course I read it . . . It did its work! A woman's pen, under Divine inspiration touched the iron fetters, the rivets fell apart and "the slave where'er he cowers" went free'.[23] Netta Syrett recalls how when a pupil at North London Collegiate School, aged about thirteen, Miss Buss confiscated Lemprière's *Classical Dictionary* on the grounds that it was a 'clumsy book' which she did not wish her to read:

> Up to that moment in perfect innocence (if anyone had been so unwise as to set it)
> I could have passed an examination in the stories of the gods and goddesses, sexual
> vagaries and all, for I looked upon these as part of the general incomprehensiblity of
> grown-up people. But when the book was removed I never rested till I knew, at least
> dimly, why I was not allowed to keep it in my possession.[24]

Autobiographies and letters certainly show that many girls picked up what they knew about sex from what they read, and the patchiness of this knowledge is a vindication in itself for the campaign that greater straightforward information about sex should be given to girls, whether directly by their mothers or, if this proved too intimate and embarrassing, through the written word. H. M. Swanwick, in the late 1870s, absorbed what she could from any available scientific books and medical journals, and puzzled over the Bible, Shakespeare, Chaucer, La Fontaine. Forbidden *David Copperfield*, *Bleak House*, *The Heart of Midlothian*, and *The Vicar of Wakefield*, she read them none the less, 'and my attention was sharpened by the prohibition'. She:

> must have been still a child when I rebelled against the common morality of the day
> in I regard to responsibility in sex relations. These little Em'lys and Hetties and Olivias
> and Effies – by what divine law was it decreed that they must for ever live a life of
> abject penitence or, better still, die?[25]

When she was lent Dante Gabriel Rossetti's poems by a friend, 'Jenny', which takes a prostitute for its subject-matter, came as a welcome antidote.

The degree to which girls could be protected from 'unsuitable' material could be taken to ridiculous lengths. Mary Stocks (b. 1891) recorded how her Aunt Tiddy made great efforts to preserve her and her siblings from 'indelicacy':

> In Tennyson's poem, 'The Revenge', which was among those she read to us, occurs
> the line: 'Bearing in her womb that which left her ill-content'. Over the word 'womb'
> Aunt Tiddy stuck a narrow strip of paper. My family still cherishes the tattered volume
> of Tennyson showing the marks from which the strip was surreptitiously removed
> by us to satisfy a curiosity very natural in the young.[26]

Dora Russell, at Sutton High School during the first decade of the twentieth century, knew 'nothing whatever about sex': she was not aided in any attempt at self-instruction by the fact that books on anatomy and physiology in the school library had 'certain dangerous pages stuck fast together'.[27]

In her biography of Marie Stopes, Ruth Hall indicates that prior to the birth-control reformer's marriage, her only sexual knowledge came from reading Browning, Swinburne, and – ignoring her mother's advice – Shakespeare's sonnets and 'Venus and Adonis', with the addition of novels, and 'the only book on sex that she had read before her marriage', Edward Carpenter's *Love's Coming of Age*. This last figures frequently in her letters. Certainly Carpenter believes that young people should be informed about sex, should be told how 'intoxicating, indeed, how penetrating – like a most precious wine – is that love which is the sexual transformed by the magic of the will into the emotional and spiritual', and that the young of both sexes should not be kept 'in ignorance and darkness and seclusion from each other'[28] but he includes virtually no physiological detail to support his rhapsody.

Some girls obtained straightforward practical information about sexual matters from standard household reference books. Vera Brittain's far from bookish home contained, in addition to the yellow-back novels which formed the main staple of her early reading, a volume entitled *Household Medicine*: 'the treatment of infectious diseases left me cold, but I was secretly excited at the prospect of menstruation; I also found the details of confinement quite enthralling'. She added the knowledge thus gained to other sources, recalling 'that intensive searching for obstetrical details through the Bible and such school-library novels as *David Copperfield* and *Adam Bede* which appears to have been customary almost everywhere among the adolescents of my generation'. None the less, she went into wartime nursing a relative innocent, only learning the details of venereal disease – the 'hidden plague' of newspaper reports – when she had to nurse a case in 1917; her knowledge of Army doctors and nurses, 'derived entirely from the more idealistic poems of Kipling', in no way helping her to understand her colleagues' suggestive language and furtive manœuvrings.[29] Other women add a small number of further texts to this catalogue of sources. The Viscountess Rhondda mentions *Midshipman Easy* as an enabling text, presumably because of the presence of the illegitimate child of Jack Easy's wet-nurse, and the general post-Fielding-and-Smollett stress on physical functions. Cicely Hamilton, the suffragette and actress, claimed that she learnt 'what are sometimes called "the facts of life" . . . fairly early from the Bible'.[30] Hamilton's autobiography also indicates how it was possible to come across potentially controversial material and read it undetected – even under the guise of approval – when she tells how she found a dusty copy of Eugene Sue's *Juif Errant* in a cupboard and, with the aid of a dictionary, read it from cover to cover. The fact that 'it contained episodes which those in authority would probably consider unsuitable for juvenile reading' only adding to her enjoyment, for, in this educational context, 'there were only smiles of approval when I was seen with a French book in my hand . . .'.[31]

Despite the considerable furore in the press concerning both sensation and the so-called 'New Woman' fiction, and the undesirable degree of explicitness on sexual matters which these genres were criticized for offering, and despite, too, the number of copies of such novels in circulation, few women noted that they made much of an impact. An exception is provided by Dr Elizabeth Chesser, recollecting Glasgow in the 1890s, at a time when the onerous duties of the daughters of professional men stretched to dusting the drawing-room and washing the aspidistras. She contrasts the atrophy inherent in this lifestyle with reading 'extraordinary "modern" sexual novels . . . in open drawers which were shut on the approach of adult footsteps', or hidden under the mattresses.[32] Maud Churton Braby recalls the excitement Grant Allen's *The Woman Who Did* aroused when she was a schoolgirl, 'and my acute disappointment when it was forcibly commandeered from me by an irate governess who apparently took no interest in these enthralling subjects'. But she claims that despite the temporary enthusiasm kindled by this and other fictions in precocious and impressionable girls, that the eventual lure of 'the Ring, the Trousseau, and the House of My Own' almost inevitably won out.[33]

It is worth while bearing in mind, despite all the testimony to the furtive but fascinated searches for sexual information entered into by many of the women who look back at their adolescence, that others of them remained unenlightened, despite the breadth of their reading. Nor did they necessarily resent this fact: they represent themselves as having had other priorities. Mary Hamilton (b. 1884), looking back at her time at Newnham, recalls that during her second year, Matthew Arnold was left open on the mantelpiece, to remind her of the vanity of human wishes and the essential loneliness of the heart. Even being in love, for her, 'expressed itself almost exclusively in highly spiritual and mental terms; although I had always been allowed, nay encouraged, to read omniverously, I remained blankly ignorant about sex and its manifestations, even the most normal ones'. She refers here to the lesbian relationships within her college which, looking retrospectively, she could recognize, but which, she said, she would not remotely have been able to comprehend at the time. An intense concern for politics, she said, made up for ignorance about sex.[34] There is a clear sense, here, of a young woman, proud of her educational achievements and intellectual interests, separating herself off – unconsciously at the time, consciously in later life – from the concerns of those whom she did not regard as privileged enough to share the same exalted mental space.

As this memory hints, not all prohibitions were based around preserving the 'innocence' of the young woman in relation to sexual matters, nor was sexuality the area with which the young woman's mind was necessarily the most consciously concerned. A variety of anxieties centred around the reading of religious works, or works which might cause the young woman to query important Christian tenets, or to find religion disturbing rather than affirmative. Elizabeth Sewell and her sister were given a volume of Cardinal Newman's sermons by an Oxford friend of their brother William, 'but it was with the caution that there were two sermons which it was better for us not to read'. Whilst the prohibition was ultimately lifted, this was only when the friend had made up his mind that the girls were not likely to have their minds disturbed by the new teaching.[35] Laura Knight, in 1899, was mystified by being forbidden Foxe's *Book of Martyrs*: 'Just the sort of horrors I would love to read about – or so I imagined', having been used to enjoying Edgar Allen Poe, the more gruesome parts of *The Ingoldsby Legends*, and the *Boy's Own Paper*, bought with her weekly penny for helping with the housework.[36] And older women, too, could be disturbed by the tone and content of works which queried their religious beliefs. Fanny Kemble (b. 1809), for example, recalled how 'extremely disagreeable' Chambers's *Vestiges of the Natural History of Creation* was to her, although the knowledge that it dealt with facts, not fiction, gave it 'a thousand times more interest than the best of novels for me'.[37]' Mary Howitt wrote to her daughter concerning Harriet Martineau and Henry Atkinson's 'new *infidel* book' *Letters on the Laws on Man's Social Nature and Development* (1851): first telling her that the volume was making such an excitement that it was always out from the London Library when she sent for it, and then, with disgust, noting that 'It is to my mind the most awful book that was ever written by a woman. It made me sick and ill to hear them talk of Jesus as a mere clever mesmerist'.[38]

But such disquiet and revulsion are predictable enough. More interesting, from the point of view of the individual's development, are those writers who, when they remember being frightened or unsettled by what they read, frequently indicate that a girl's perception of what texts might or might not be advisable differed from that of adults: troubling effects could not invariably be guarded against. Margaret Cole claimed that the only reading which was forbidden her was Bram Stoker's *Dracula*, Poe's *Tales of Mystery and Imagination*, and *What a Young Mother Ought to Know*, plus 'trashy magazines', but maintained that she read 'all that was forbidden' anyway. Whilst the motherhood manual was an obvious target for prohibition because of the explicitly sexual material it concerned, the more deliberately frightening material is introduced by her in the context of what *actually* disturbed her. Thus Cole writes that she was scared by Uncle Remus, by a series of American picture stories called the Golliwog books, and by a book of noble deeds, principally rescues from shipwrecks and burning houses: 'Even today I cannot read the words "blind alley" without a faint reminiscent shudder born of a story, whose details have entirely forgotten, of people fleeing from a burning building into a blind alley with the flames at their heels'.[39] On occasion, the experience of disturbance could derive from texts disapproved of by parents. For example, in the early 1870s, the ten-year-old Annabel Huth Jackson 'was terribly frightened by the episode of the mad woman tearing the wedding veil' in *Jane Eyre*, although the existence of this incident alone was doubtless insufficient to explain Jackson's mother's horror when she learnt her daughter had read the book.[40] But as many reminiscences, including Cole's, show, the reading which frightened rarely involved the reading material about which parents expressed direct apprehension. Margaret Campbell ('Marjorie Bowen'), for example, was particularly scared by a book – she believes one of Thackeray's novels – which 'had a yellow paper cover of a howling negro running along in terror while a man shot at him', and by Wordsworth's 'Lucy Gray';[41] Winifred Peck claims to have been 'terrified' by a book routinely figuring as a Sunday School prize, Wood's *Natural History*;[42] Janet Courtney remembers 'as a special terror' Scott's White Lady of Avenel in *The Monastery*,[43] and Cicely Hamilton, who had read all of Scott by the time she was eleven, wrote that one of his short stories, 'The Tapestry Chamber':

> was a disturber of my rest for years. So too was an illustrated version of *The Ingoldsby* Legends; I remember the peculiar horror inspired by a devil, arrayed in Elizabethan garb, who danced up the room with a lady and *never came down again!* And the even greater horror inspired by the Dun Horse ridden by Exciseman Gill, with hell-fire streaming from its nostrils!'[44]

These instances act as reminders, too, that not all disturbing effects were necessarily linked to gender expectations, nor, in any explicit way, to the gendered experiences of the reader.

## Notes

1   Julia Kristeva, 'The Adolescent Novel', in John Fletcher and Andrew Benjamin (eds), *Abjection, Melancholia and Love: The Work of Julia Kristeva* (1990), 8.

2   Bertha Vyver, *Memoirs of Marie Corelli* (1930), 19–20.

3   Amy Cruse, *The Victorians and their Books* (1935), 278.

4   Jean Curtis Brown, *To Tell My Daughter* (1948), 67.

5   John Evans, *Prelude and Fugue: An Autobiography* (1964), 17

6   'Lucus Malet' (Mary St Leger Harrison), interviewed by Sarah A. Tooley, 'Some Women Novelists', *Woman at Home*, 5 (1897), 187.

7   Charles Kingsley, 'Nausicaa in London: Or, The Lower Education of Woman', *Health and Education* (1879), 82.

8   See Brenda Colloms, *Charles Kingsley: The Lion of Eversley* (1975), 130.

9   Quoted by Cruse, *The Victorians and their Books*, 275.

10   Mary Paley Marshall, *What I Remember* (1947), 7.

11   Dorothy McCall, *When That I Was* (1952), 118.

12   Julia M. Grant, Katherine H. McCutcheon, and Ethel F. Sanders, *St Leonards School 1877–1927* (1927), 164.

13   Anne Thackeray Ritchie, *Chapters from Some Memoirs* (1894), 78.

14   Maurice Baring, *The Puppet Show of Memory* (1922), 49.

15   *Diary of Lady Frederick Cavendish*, i. 83.

16 Jane Lidderdale and Mary Nicholson, *Dear Miss Weaver: Harriet Shaw Weaver 1876–1961* (1970), 33.

17 Susan L. Mitchell, *George Moore* (Dublin, 1916), 43.

18 Mary Butts, *The Crystal Cabinet: My Childhood at Salterns* (1937), 102, 111. For Butts and her treatment of the past, see Patrick Wright, *On Living in an Old Country: The National Past in Contemporary Britain* (1985), 93–134.

19 Elizabeth Barrett Browning to Arabel Barrett (19 Feb. 1857), Berg collection, New York Public Library.

20 Josephine E. Butler, *Recollections of George Butler* (Bristol and London, 1893), 96.

21 Elizabeth Gaskell, letter to Eliza Fox (?early Feb. 1853), *The Letters of Mrs Gaskell*, ed. J. A. V. Chapple and Arthur Pollard (Manchester, 1966), 223.

22 Elizabeth Gaskell, letter to Anna Jameson (7 Mar. 1853), *Letters*, 226.

23 Lady Frances Balfour, *Ne Obliviscaris: Dinna Forget*, 2 vols. (1930), i. 89.

24 Netta Syrett, *The Sheltering Tree* (1939), 20. Syrett's *The Victorians* (1915), a novel which draws considerably on her own childhood, gives considerable space to the importance played by reading in an adolescent girl's life.

25 H. M. Swanwick, *I Have Been Young* (1935), 83–4.

26 Mary Stocks, *My Commonplace Book* (1970), 12.

27 Dora Russell, *The Tamarisk Tree: My Quest for Liberty and Love* (1975), 24.

28 Edward Carpenter, *Love's Coming of Age* (Manchester, 1896), 11, 102.

29 Vera Brittain, *Testament of Youth* (1933, repr. 1983), 26, 48, 49.

30 Cicely Hamilton, *Life Errant* (1935), 4.

31 *Ibid.* 17.

32 Elizabeth Sloan Chesser, MD, in Countess of Oxford and Asquith (ed.), *Myself When Young, by Famous Women of To-Day* (1938), 81.

33 Maud Churton Braby, *Modern Marriage and How to Bear it* (1909), 6, 8.

34 Mary Agnes Hamilton, *Remembering My Good Friends* (1944), 46–7.

35 Sewell, *Autobiography*, 65.

36 Laura Knight, *Oil Paint and Grease Paint* (1936), 7; idem, *The Magic of a Line* (1965), 56. Angela Brazil, on the other hand, was considerably disturbed by the pictures in the work, especially the final one which showed a half-charred body falling out of lurid flames. The disturbance worked at two levels, stimulating both physical revulsion and self-doubt: 'At night when I lay awake in the dark I saw those fearful pictures, and not the least of their horror was the persuasion that I had not the stuff in me so make a martyr'. *My Own Schooldays* (1925), 164.

37 Frances Anne Kemble, *Records of Later Life*, 3 vols (1882), iii. 242.

38 Margaret Howitt (ed.), *Mary Howitt: An Autobiography* (1889), 67, 69.

39 Cole, *Growing up into Revolution*, 11.

40 Jackson, *A Victorian Childhood*, 58.

41 Margaret Campbell, in Oxford and Asquith, *Myself When Young, by Famous Women of To-Day*, (1938), 44, 48.

42 Peck, *A Little Learning*, 34. John George Wood published a large number of volumes on natural history: most probably she refers to his *Natural History Book for Children*, 3 vols (1861–3).

43 Courtney, *Recollected in Tranquillity*, 25.

44 Hamilton, *Life Errant*, 4.

# Chapter 25

# Jonathan Rose

## REREADING THE ENGLISH COMMON READER
## A preface to a history of audiences

As a genre, the working-class autobiography originates around 1800 – here too the reading revolution marked a watershed, when common readers began to write about themselves. And they are often wonderfully forthcoming about their reading experiences – not only what they read, but how they comprehended and reacted to their reading.

These sources open up a new scholarly frontier. They will make possible a third generation of reading history – a history of audiences, which would reverse the usual perspective of intellectual historiography. It would first define a mass audience, then determine its cultural diet, and ultimately measure the collective response of that audience not only to particular works of literature, but also to education, religion, art, and any other cultural activity. Whereas reception histories have generally traced the responses of professional intellectuals (literary and social critics, academics, clergymen), audience histories would focus on the common reader – defined as any reader who did not read books for a living. The British working-class reader happens to be my subject, but this essay offers general encouragement and advice for the study of common readers in all classes and all nations. It illustrates some of the questions a history of audiences could tackle, and points out the methodological problems it may involve.

Although autobiographies will probably prove to be the richest sources for a history of audiences, they must be used with caution and balanced against other materials. Memoirists are not entirely representative of their class (whatever that class may be), if only because they were unusually articulate. Autobiographies were produced in every one of the several British working classes, ranging down to tramps and petty criminals, but a disproportionate number were written by skilled workers and especially the self-employed. Only one in ten nineteenth-century workers' memoirs were written by women, and the whole sample is skewed to the political left: the

Jonathan Rose, 'Rereading the English Common Reader: A Preface to a History of Audiences', *Journal of the History of Ideas*, 53 (1992), 47–70. © The Journal of the History of Ideas, Inc. Reprinted with permission of The Johns Hopkins University Press, 1992.

twentieth-century volume of the Burnett-Vincent-Mayall bibliography lists many more Communists than Conservatives.[1]

We also must bear in mind that an autobiographer (like any other 'nonfiction' writer) is liable to forget, misremember, remember selectively, embellish, invent, and rearrange events in the interest of creating an engaging story. The uncertainties are especially troublesome in the case of common readers, since we usually have no other sources to check their memoirs against. Flora Thompson's *Lark Rise* (1939) – perhaps the most widely read of all working-class memoirs, cited by every important historian of Victorian rural life – has been compared with parish, poor law, school, legal, and census records; and there are just enough discrepancies to give one a moment's pause.[2] To crosscheck and augment the data gleaned from memoirs, a historian of audiences could look to library records, reader surveys, the reports of educational bodies, and oral history projects.[3] It is not Micawberish to suggest that, if we look deliberately enough, we may stumble on a documentary gold mine – such as the Lenin Library archive of N. A. Rubakin, a popular educator in late Czarist S Russia who corresponded with eleven thousand readers.[4]

A history of audiences could supply tests for the various theories of reading offered by phenomenological, deconstructionist, semiotic, reader-response, and Marxist critics. Already, it is becoming evident that many of these theories do not square with the praxis of reading, especially in connection with the provocative issue of canon formation. Do the 'great books' embody universal moral values, psychological insights, and aesthetic standards; or do they represent an arbitrary cultural hierarchy imposed upon the masses by the ruling classes? Hayden White has argued that 'the comic strip cannot be treated as *qualitatively* inferior to a Shakespeare play or any other classic text'.[5] Janice Radway, who has recently moved on from Harlequin Romances to the Book-of-the-Month Club, asserts that critics have no right to dismiss the latter as 'middlebrow'. If literature professors insist on drawing such prejudiced distinctions, that, Radway concedes, is 'understandable', so long as they do it in the privacy of the classroom; but they must recognize that Book-of-the-Month Club books 'might be valuable to others because they perform functions more in keeping with their own somewhat different social position, its material constraints, and logical concerns'.[6]

Similarly, Barbara Herrnstein Smith (past president of the Modern Language Association) insists that 'The endurance of a classic canonical author such as Homer . . . owes not to the alleged transcultural or universal value of his works but, on the contrary, to the continuity of their circulation in a particular culture.' They survive only because they have been 'repeatedly cited and recited, translated, taught and imitated, and thoroughly enmeshed in the network of intertextuality that continuously *constitutes* the high culture of the orthodoxly educated population of the West'. The classics are irrelevant to people who have not received an orthodox Western education, Smith asserts. It is an undeniable 'fact that Homer, Dante, and Shakespeare do not figure significantly in the personal economies of these people, do not perform individual or social functions that gratify their interests, *do not have value for them*'. It is also unquestionably a 'fact that other verbal artifacts (not necessarily "works of literature" or even "texts") and other objects and events (not necessarily "works of art" or even artifacts) have performed and do perform for them the various functions that Homer, Dante, and Shakespeare perform for us'.[7]

Here Radway and Smith fall into the error that Radway herself so rightly showed up in *Reading the Romance*: they dogmatize enormously about the sociology of reading without bothering to study actual readers. They really do not know what functions Homer, Book-of-the-Month Club selections, comic books, or any other verbal artifacts perform for their respective audiences. Moreover, their theories cannot explain autodidacts like Will Crooks, the Edwardian Labour Member of Parliament. Growing up in extreme poverty in East London, Crooks stumbled across a copy of the *Iliad*, and was dazzled:

What a revelation it was to me! Pictures of romance and beauty I had never dreamed of suddenly opened up before my eyes. I was transported from the East End to an enchanted land. It was a rare luxury for a working lad like me just home from work to find myself suddenly among the heroes and nymphs of ancient Greece.[8]

According to Barbara Herrnstein Smith, this should not have happened. Crooks was not orthodoxly educated, and he was not particularly enmeshed in the network of intertextuality that includes classical literature. All the same, Homer spoke to him – and that is about as radical a transcultural leap as one can imagine. Smith claims that we respond to a great book only because it tends to '*shape and create* the culture in which its value is produced and transmitted and, for that reason, to perpetuate the conditions of its own flourishing'.[9] If she wants to defend that argument, she will have to explain how the *Iliad* created the culture of the East End – without using italics as a substitute for evidence.

She will also have to account for other accomplished proletarian classicists: for example, Thomas Cooper, the Chartist shoemaker who authored one of the best-known workers' autobiographies, and Tom Barclay, Leicester's intellectual bottle-washer.[10] Of course, such autodidacts were hardly typical of the British working class, but they did constitute a fairly substantial minority. In her 1907 sociological study *At the Works*, Lady Bell estimated that one out of eight working-class households in Middlesbrough included someone who 'read books that are absolutely worth reading', and three out of ten families were 'fond of reading'. A decade later Arnold Freeman, a settlement house warden, interrogated 408 Sheffield workers and classified twenty to twenty-six percent of them as intellectually 'well-equipped'.[11]

Throughout the Victorian period and well into the twentieth century, the British working class maintained a vital autodidact culture that, quite independently of ruling-class cultural hegemony, found inspiration in the canonical works of Western culture. The literary diet of worker-intellectuals was sometimes suggested by clergymen, settlement house residents, university-bred instructors in continuing education classes, and periodicals like *Cassell's Popular Educator*. Usually, however, they were introduced to books by friends, schoolmates, teachers, workmates, or relatives – that is, by other members of the working class. Peter Miles has shown how Robert Tressell's socialist novel *The Ragged-Trousered Philanthropists* (1914) was disseminated by word-of-mouth and by simply passing along battered copies of the book.[12] The same process of grassroots cultural transmission brought *Hamlet* and *The Origin of Species* to the workers.

'Until now intellectual history has chosen to account for the dissemination of ideas and values by the easy trickle-down hypothesis', observes William Gilmore. 'Its foundation assumption is that the dissemination of ideas, and hence of reading, and of specific types of reflection, proceeded in a hierarchical two-step fashion, from elites to the masses and from "high" to "popular" culture.' But as Gilmore illustrates, books and ideas were actually diffused through a web of cultural institutions and personal networks that were often created and controlled by common readers, who recognized 'high culture' even when no professors were there to point it out to them.[13] In 1815 Vermont's Windsor District had not quite thirty college graduates among a population of seventeen thousand, mostly farmers and workers; but within a few years the area could boast ten lending libraries, two debating societies, several series of public lectures, a theater club, a music society, and a lyceum.[14]

Similarly, by the early twentieth century South Wales was served by a network of Miners' Institutes – worker-run adult education centers offering libraries, evening classes, lectures, and theatrical productions. Will Jon Edwards remembered discussions of Shakespeare, Darwin, Marx, and Herbert Spencer down in the pits. At times he heard some fairly incisive literary criticism: 'Meredith is a poet who sings with a harp', one collier observed; 'Kipling is a nobody who sings what he can sing with a mouth-organ although he does talk of tambourines'.[15] This is not to imply that there was a seminar down every mineshaft: you had to gain admission to the right pit. Walter Haydn Davies recalled that, at his mine,

> The conveyor face down the Number 2 Pit was a university, the surface of Number 1 Pit a den of grossness. Night after night in this Alma Mater, well-read intelligent, clean minded men discussed the burning topics of the day, the changing religious trend, the theory of evolution, the nature of spiritualism, Christian Socialism, Communism and all the other isms that then did abound. The ideas expressed by Charles Darwin, R.J. Campbell, Sir Oliver Lodge, Keir Hardie, Ramsay Macdonald, Karl Marx, Noah Ablett were treasured in their minds as well as in the books they carried in their pockets.

Incidentally, it was no anomaly that Walter Haydn Davies was named after a classical composer; that was a custom that reflected the musical culture in which Welsh miners were steeped. 'In fact', he remembered, 'in one family there was a Handel, Haydn, Elgar, Verdi, Joseph Parry, Caradog, Mendy (short for Mendelssohn) and an unforgettable Billy Bach, together with an only daughter Rossini (called Rosie for short)'.[16]

As David Vincent demonstrated, the autodidact usually directed his own reading in a highly idiosyncratic and random manner, somehow managing to discover the classics on his own.[17] He might, like young Manny Shinwell, pick up Dickens, Meredith, Hardy, Keats, Burns, Darwin, Huxley, Kant, and Spinoza from rubbish heaps and tuppenny second-hand bookstalls.[18] Like George Howell, the Victorian bricklayer and trade unionist, he could grope his way through the canon 'on the principle that one poet's works suggested another, or the criticisms one led to comparisons with another. Thus: Milton–Shakespeare; Pope–Dryden; Byron–Shelley; Burns–Scott; Coleridge–Wordsworth and Southey, and later on Spenser–Chaucer, Bryant–Longfellow, and so on through a numerous class of writers'[19] Working people often made a point of reading the books their employers warned them not to read: that was how Flora Thompson discovered Byron's *Don Juan*.[20] Far from following hegemonic lines laid down by cultural elites, workers were so independent in their choice of books as to provoke endless hand-wringing among the university-educated. Even Arnold Freeman, who dedicated his life to working-class education, despaired over what he considered to be the unsystematic reading patterns revealed in his 1918 survey.[21]

A concise summary may be found in a 1906 survey of the first large cohort of Labour Members of Parliament. The 51 MPs were asked to name the books and authors that had influenced them most, and 45 of them responded as follows:

17   John Ruskin
16   Charles Dickens
14   The Bible
13   Thomas Carlyle
12   Henry George
11   Walter Scott
10   John Stuart Mill
 9   William Shakespeare
 8   Robert Burns, John Bunyan
 6   Alfred Lord Tennyson, Giuseppe Mazzini
 5   Charles Kingsley, T. B. Macaulay, James Russell Lowell

4    Adam Smith, William Cobbett, Sidney and Beatrice Webb, W. M. Thackery, J. R. Green,
     Charles Darwin, Henry Drummond

Interestingly, only two MPs mentioned Karl Marx, while five cited at least one of the ancient Greeks or Romans. Granted, the 45 respondents were all politicians, all male, and all on the leftward half of the political spectrum; if our sample had been more representative of the working class, the above list would have included more literature and less politics and economics. Generally, Victorian working-class intellectuals read more American literature and less Greek and Roman literature than their middle-class counterparts.[22]

However, with the exception of Henry Drummond and the Webbs (who may have involved copyright problems) every one of the authors listed above would be included in Everyman's Library, the series of shilling classics launched by J. M. Dent just after this survey was conducted. In other words, the writers cited by these MPs were nearly all canonical, as that term was defined by a major publisher in 1906. Rarely did these men refer to newspapers, the novels of Harrison Ainsworth, or anything commonly labelled 'popular culture'. Five of the forty-five respondents made no pretense to intellectual culture, asserting (a bit defensively) that they had been educated in 'the school of life'. Beyond that, there is no real basis for what Barbara Herrnstein Smith calls 'the fact that other verbal artifacts (not necessarily "works of literature") . . . have performed and do perform for them the various functions that Homer, Dante, and Shakespeare perform for us'. When they were asked what had inspired them to create a new social order, these men pointed to a selection of 'great books'.

A history of audiences could put some sorely needed discipline into the study of popular culture – and it might begin by abolishing the term 'popular culture' as vague and misleading. Morag Shiach has shown that, for as long as intellectuals have discussed 'popular' or 'folk' or 'mass' culture, they have never been able to offer any firm and unslippery definitions of those categories.[23] In attempting such a definition, Ray B. Browne, the dean of American popular culture studies, manages to contradict himself several times in the space of two sentences:

> Popular Culture is the culture of the people, of *all* the people, as distinguished from a select, small elite group. It is also the dominant culture of minorities – of ethnic, social, religious, or financial minorities – simply because their way of life is, by and large, not accepted into the elite culture of the dominant group.[24]

Popular culture, then, is the culture of all the people *and* of minorities. This would presumably include nearly all culture except that of the British working class, which was neither the whole population nor a minority within it. It excludes any 'small elite group', though that is by definition a minority, and rentier intellectuals would certainly qualify as a 'financial minority'. Students of popular culture create this kind of muddle when they try to sort all culture and all audiences into two bins: 'high culture' and social elites are tossed together into one category, while all culture that is not 'high' is labelled 'popular' and is assumed to have a mass audience. Even when great books clearly have a mass readership, they are usually excluded from popular culture monographs: Jeffrey Brooks appreciates that Maxim Gorky and Leonid Andreev were 'genuinely popular' writers, and that Leo Tolstoy was the author most highly regarded among Red Army soldiers, but Brooks deliberately puts them aside to concentrate on cheap tales of romance and banditry.[25]

Ray Browne cannot account for the Victorian workers who attended Shakespearean drama, or for the Victorian aristocrats who frequented boxing matches. A growing number of cultural historians, however, are discovering that what we call 'high' and 'popular' culture can both spill across class lines.[26] A history of audiences would follow Roger Chartier in avoiding 'the simple opposition of *populaire* versus *savant*';[27] rather than start off with that kind of false antithesis, it would reconstruct the cultural diet of a given audience. The term 'popular culture' is only meaningful as a quantitative measure of the audience – applying, say, to any novel that sells over a million copies. 'High culture' is not its polar opposite, but rather a qualitative measure of the work – the best that is known and thought in the world, leaving open the question of whose criteria we are following. Given those definitions, it is clear that some culture (such as *Sons and Lovers*) is both popular and high, and some culture (such as Victorian pornography) is neither.

However we define it, high culture is clearly not enjoyed exclusively by social elites. British working-class autobiographers generally drew a clear distinction between 'improving' literature and 'light' or 'low' literature; I have yet to find a single one who defended the latter as anything more than a good read. Though George Acorn grew up in poverty in late Victorian East London, he recalled that, even as a boy, he had 'some appreciation of style' and a sense of literary hierarchies, 'tackling all sorts and conditions of books, from "Penny Bloods" to George Eliot'. He was sophisticated enough to understand that a gifted writer could draw on the conventions of trash literature and work them into a near-classic – in this case *Treasure Island*, which he discerningly characterized as 'the usual penny blood sort of story, with the halo of greatness about it'.[28]

This is not to say that working-class autodidacts were as hostile to gutter literature as late Victorian educators and clergymen, who loudly warned that penny dreadfuls were encouraging juvenile delinquency.[29] In fact a few proletarian autobiographers did admit that Dick Turpin stories inspired them to commit petty thefts,[30] but the following comment is far more typical: '[My] budding love of literature . . . I trace to an enthusiastic reading of Penny Dreadfuls which, so far from leading me into a life of crime, made me look for something better.'[31] The key word here is 'better'. Where middle-class critics reviled penny dreadfuls as dangerous trash, workers read them as harmless trash, perhaps even delightful trash – but trash all the same.

Many cultural historians – most recently John Springhall – read penny dreadfuls with an eye to discerning whether they 'reinforce rather than subvert the existing social and political structures'.[32] Literary critics and journalists commonly subject all sorts of texts, from Hardy novels to cigarette ads, to that kind of political examination; but their efforts may be misdirected on two counts. First, they usually overlook the possibility that these texts were politically innocuous; Springhall fails to consider that penny dreadfuls may have only entertained their readers and exercised the reading habit, which is what working-class autobiographers generally suggest. Second, this and most other exercises in cultural studies founder on the receptive fallacy.[33] As James Smith Allen presumes, 'Because literature was recreated by historical audiences, the world view expressed by the novel may well have involved the beliefs of the readers themselves, who were the most enthusiastic about a particular work. In fact the more popular the work, the more likely this is.'[34] In fact because literature was *re*created by historical audiences, and may have been recreated in a fashion quite unlike anything envisioned by the author or the critic, the world view of the novel does not necessarily equal the beliefs of the reader, no matter how popular the work may be. We cannot even assume that popular fiction does not offend its readers: Janice Radway's interviewees were often repelled by the violence and brutal sexuality they found in some romance novels. The reaction of one of those romance fans should serve as a salutary reminder to all cultural historians: one possible reader response is to toss the text in the garbage bin.[35]

Hayden White, then, is quite wrong to conclude that 'Every text, grand or humble, is seen to be equally representative, equally interpretive of its proper milieu.'[36] We may not treat any text as representative of any reader without that reader's authorization. In his day the sensational novelist G. W. M. Reynolds outsold Charles Dickens, but in their memoirs Victorian working people repeatedly call on Dickens to represent them, not Reynolds. Dickens, they recall, was an honored name in their home;[37] and even in the most extreme poverty, they could be touched and comforted by a cast-off copy of *David Copperfield*.[38] They saw something of themselves in Jo the crossing-sweeper[39] or had learned to pick pockets like the Artful Dodger.[40] They had attended a school like Dr. Blimber's Academy[41] or Dotheboys Hall.[42] They recalled that bad actors in cheap theaters were treated just like Mr. Wopsle in *Great Expectations*;[43] and East End readers praised *A Tale of Two Cities* for transporting them out of a 'confused kitchen, that reeked still of fish and chips . . . , to France and the Revolution'.[44]

Above and beyond that, Dickens played a critically important role in making the British working classes articulate. He supplied a fund of allusions, characters, tropes, and situations that could be drawn upon by people who were not trained to express themselves on paper. In 1869 the *Dundee, Perth, and Forfar People's Journal*, which had a huge circulation among Scottish workers, sponsored a Christmas story competition: readers submitted more than a thousand entries (about one for every hundred subscribers) and many of them clearly reflected the influence of *A Christmas Carol*.[45] Cotton operative Joseph Burgess was so deeply shocked by the death of Dickens that he was driven, almost unconsciously, to compose a poem, and that began his long career as a labor poet and journalist.[46] We find the daughter of a Dudley shoe repairer beginning her reminiscences as David Copperfield began his ('I am born'), and a Devonshire farm boy could point to the tale of 'The Convict's Return' from *The Pickwick Papers* to affirm the importance of writing a biography of a 'homely and ordinary life'.[48] Clearly, Dickens provided working people with the inspiration and the generic literary conventions they needed to tell their own stories.

G. W. M. Reynolds did not have that kind of impact. Except for an occasional dismissive comment, his novels are rarely mentioned by working-class memoirists.[49] Equally 'popular' texts do not necessarily have equal influence: some transform the lives of their readers, whereas others are consumed like literary chewing gum, leaving no taste behind. Properly done, a history of audiences could teach us to make that kind of distinction.

Of course, even the most ephemeral literature can leave a mark on the consciousness. Joseph Burgess traced his optimistic turn of mind to a blackface minstrel song he once heard in Manchester:

> I will live as long as I can, ha! ha!
> Or I'll know de reason why,
> For as long as dere's breff in pore old Jeff,
> Dis nigger will never say die, ha! ha![50]

Henry Coward, who rose from poverty to become an eminent Sheffield choir conductor, launched his ascent when he read the following in a scrap of newspaper: '"Men may be divided into two classes, leaders and followers, and any one who has the equipment for leadership – brains and power of control – will never lack followers if the cause is a just and reasonable one." Eureka! Eureka! I had found my niche'.[51]

These autobiographies, however, suggest that this is all 'low' culture can do: it can communicate simple formulas. The *Iliad*, in contrast, did not transmit any pat 'message' to Will Crooks, but it did something far more radical and valuable: it revealed a world outside of the East End, it introduced him to new standards of beauty, it aroused desires and dissatisfactions, it explosively expanded the range of his imagination, it inspired him to recreate his world. That kind of epiphany recurs again and again in working-class autobiographies, and it is usually produced by canonical literature, not by any odd verbal artifact. For Arthur Harding, an East End pickpocket, the magical book was *The Decline and Fall of the Roman Empire*.[52] And it was a 'serious novel' that liberated housemaid Edith Hall from the cultural hegemony imposed by the popular press of the 1920s, when

*Punch* and other publications of that kind showed cartoons depicting the servant class as stupid and 'thick' and therefore fit subjects for their jokes. The skivvy particularly was revealed as a brainless menial. Many of the working-class were considered thus and Thomas Hardy wrote in *Tess of the D'Urbervilles* that 'Labouring farm folk were personified in the newspaper press by the pitiable dummy known as Hodge . . .' and it was in this book that Hardy told the story of Tess, a poor working girl with an interesting character, thoughts and personality. This was the first serious novel I had read up to this time in which the heroine had not been of 'gentle birth' and the labouring classes as brainless automatons. This book made me feel human and even when my employers talked at me as though I wasn't there, I felt that I could take it; I knew that I could be a person in my own right.[53]

The crucial difference between middle-class and working-class autobiographers, according to Regenia Gagnier and Nan Hackett, is that the latter present themselves less as individuals than as members of a class, 'social atoms' among the masses.[54] That is true up to a point – but only to the point where the proletarian memoirist describes the book that made all the difference, the book that conferred a sense of identity, mastery, and possibility on the reader. In that respect a history of audiences could provide as good a test as any for identifying 'great books'. These are the books that do what *Tess* did for Edith Hall – they burst the boundaries of the mind, and they have a record of doing that for a broad range of audiences, representing different classes, cultures, and generations.

In an attempt to rehabilitate forgotten nineteenth-century novelists like Harriet Beecher Stowe, Jane Tompkins has argued that their books must be judged not by modernist aesthetic criteria but according to the 'kind of work the text is doing within its particular milieu'.[55] When we look to readers' memoirs, however, it becomes apparent that the quality of work done by canonical and noncanonical texts is very different. In the 1890s Elizabeth Bryson, the daughter of a Dundee factory worker, did indeed find the story of *Uncle Tom's Cabin* quite gripping. *Sartor Resartus*, however, was nothing less than a 'miracle': it incited 'the exciting experience of being kindled to the point of explosion by the fire of words'.[56]

Likewise, as a Tyneside hospital worker in the 1920s, Catherine McMullen enjoyed Elinor Glyn's *The Career of Catharine Bush*, in which a common girl prepares for marriage into the aristocracy by studying Lord Chesterfield's letters to his son. But Glin's novel was valuable to Miss McMullen mainly because it induced her to visit the public library and read Lord Chesterfield: he was the author who transformed her life.

Now here (to anticipate a possible objection) Barbara Herrnstein Smith might step in and claim vindication. Catherine, one could argue, read Chesterfield's letters not because they were intrinsically great literature but because they were cited in some trashy novel. That is how upper-class cultural hegemony seduces the poor working girl: it ensnares her in a web of intertextuality.

My first response is that (as noted earlier) working people can recognize great literature when they see it. Winifred Albaya once picked up an old *Strand* magazine and was wonderfully impressed by a story set in an industrial town like Sheffield, where she was growing up. Only years later did she learn that the story, 'Tickets Please', was by D. H. Lawrence.[57] Second, while Smith's theories may explain why Catherine McMullen read Lord Chesterfield, they do not account for the emancipating power of the book. Inspired by its vision of aristocratic splendor ('I would see myself beautifully gowned going down a marble staircase on the hand of Chesterfield'), she became (as Catherine Cookson) an immensely successful author of novels about poor but plucky Northern girls. Even more importantly, she recalled, Lord Chesterfield brought her for the first time into a public library:

And here began my education. With Lord Chesterfield I read my first mythology. I learned my first real history and geography. With Lord Chesterfield I went travelling in the world. I would fall asleep reading the letters and awake around three o'clock in the morning, my mind deep in the fascination of this new world, where people conversed, not just talked. Where the brilliance of words made your heart beat faster. . . . Dear, dear Lord Chesterfield. Snob or not I owe him much.[58]

Marxist critics have long contended that classic literature can persuade workers like Catherine to accept social hierarchies and distract them from the business of correcting social injustice. Indeed, Chris Baldick and Terry Eagleton have argued that English literature was established as an academic discipline partly for the purpose of social control:

Since literature, as we know, deals in universal human values rather than in such historical trivia as civil wars, the oppression of women or the dispossession of the English peasantry, it could serve to place in cosmic perspective the petty demands of working people for decent living conditions or greater control over their own lives, and might even with luck come to render them oblivious of such issues in their high-minded contemplation of eternal truth and beauties. . . . Instead of working to change such conditions . . . you can vicariously fulfill someone's desire for a fuller life by handing them *Pride and Prejudice*.[59]

That might have been the intention of some critics and educators, but did literature actually have such a narcotizing effect on the workers? How then do we explain the fact that another great fan of Lord Chesterfield's letters was the ultra-radical agitator Richard Carlile?[60] While serving respective prison sentences, T. A. Jackson read Jane Austen worshipfully; J. T. Murphy devoured Conrad and Macaulay; and Manny Shinwell was consoled by Shakespeare, Walter Scott, Dickens, Hardy, Keats, Shelley, and Tennyson. All three of these proletarian Marxist intellectuals survived the great books with their ideological loyalties intact.[61] Canonical literature tended to spark insurrections in the mind of the working-class reader and was more likely to radicalize than mollify him. In Arnold Freeman's Sheffield survey, the population of worker-intellectuals was not identical with the radical activists, but the two groups overlapped very closely. Robert Roberts recalled that the most militant socialists in Edwardian Salford, the workers who most persistently challenged prevailing conservative ideologies, were the 'readers of Ruskin, Dickens, Kingsley, Carlyle, and Scott'.[62] At the same time Jewish anarchists in London's East End were sponsoring popular lectures on *Hamlet*, *Gulliver's Travels*, and Beethoven's Ninth Symphony because they believed that kind of acculturation was essential to political liberation.[63]

This brings us to a corollary of the receptive fallacy: even when working people read books approved and provided by the governing classes, there was no guarantee that they would read those texts as their patrons wished. *Pilgrim's Progress* was a staple of prison and Sunday School libraries, but nascent Chartists like John James Bezer read it as a radical political allegory:

My own dear Bunyan! if it hadn't been for you, I should have gone mad, I think, before I was ten years old! Even as it was, the other books and teachings I was bored with [in Sunday School], had such a terrible influence on me, that somehow or other, I was always nourishing the idea that 'Giant Despair' had got hold of me, and that I should never get out of his 'Doubting Castle'. Yet I read, ay, and *fed* with such delight as I cannot *now* describe – though I think I could *then*. Glorious Bunyan, you too were a 'Rebel', and I love you *doubly* for *that*. I read you in Newgate, – so I could, I understand, if I had been taken care of in Bedford jail, – your books are in the library of even your Bedford jail. Hurrah for progress![64]

Even an author with a conservative message could be turned to radical uses by working-class activists. When Walter Scott was first published, he was denounced as a reactionary by Thomas Wooler and Richard Carlile,[65] but among the first Labour MPs he ranked near the top of the charts. George Howell read *The Wealth of Nations* as a critique rather than a defense of capitalists: 'Adam Smith, with that clear insight and accurate knowledge of life which he so eminently possessed, pointed out that combinations among masters, either directly or tacitly, enabled them to fix the price of labour or to regulate it'.[66] The land nationalizers inspired by Thomas Spence likewise appropriated John Locke as their champion. After all, Locke had discovered a natural right to property, and had postulated that all land was held in common in the 'state of nature': for the Spenceans, the communalization of land followed logically from those Premises.[67] This does not necessarily mean that C. B. Macpherson was wrong to conclude that Locke 'provides a moral foundation for bourgeois appropriation';[68] but a history of audiences would remind us to ask, 'Provides for whom?' Until we can answer that question, we should foreswear the critical habit of pronouncing that texts reinforce or subvert existing social and political structures.

Literary theorists have debated endlessly whether the reader writes the text or the text manipulates the reader. A history of audiences could lead us out of this deadlock by revealing the interactions of specific readers and texts. Already, a pattern is emerging from Carlo Ginsberg's study of a sixteenth-century Italian miller, Margaret Spufford's work on seventeenth-century English peasant readers, Ned Landsman's recent article on popular responses to Presbyterian preachers in eighteenth-century Scotland, Richard Altick's nineteenth-century English common readers, and my own research into twentieth-century students in a British adult education program. Spufford was 'startled' to find laborers and peasants reading and discussing Scripture with striking critical independence. They were, she concluded, 'far from being the docile material which their ministers no doubt desired'. Landsman also found that 'the laity possessed a rather remarkable capacity to integrate seemingly disparate beliefs and actively forge their own understandings of the delivered message and create their own religious symbols', all of which could be quite unlike anything their preachers intended to convey.[69] We have all independently discovered what Roger Chartier calls 'appropriation': the power of an audience – even at the bottom of the social pyramid – to transform received messages, rendering those messages 'less than totally efficacious and radically acculturating.[70]

Literary theorists may argue, as an epistemological question, whether texts have any fixed meaning; but intellectual historians hardly need to be told that, in practice, all readers are editors – often ruthless and insensitive editors. The Jacques Derrida who worried that wantonly deconstructive criticism 'would risk developing in any direction at all and authorize itself to say almost anything'[71] might have been shocked to learn what common readers can do to texts. They create their own meanings, they mistake the 'unmistakable', they read very selectively. The same workingmen who drew inspiration from Ruskin's social criticism, for instance, were apparently baffled by his art criticism. Regarding the latter 'I was frankly a philistine', wrote Frederick Rogers, a bookbinder and self-taught Elizabethan scholar, 'and in this I undoubtedly expressed the feelings of the . . . workmen who had read his books'.[72] Likewise, several of the autodidacts who embraced Karl Marx frankly confessed that they could hardly understand him.[73]

We must be equally careful not to underestimate the common reader's level of comprehension. Jonathan Culler states a general postulate that has become a commonplace among reader-response critics: 'Literary works may be quite baffling to those with no knowledge of the special conventions of literary discourse'.[74] That sounds logical, but readers ignorant of the appropriate literary conventions sometimes read difficult works anyway, and thereby manage to puzzle out those conventions. One Edwardian bootmaker's daughter recalled finding her father's Shakespeare in the attic, 'and I tried to kind of get out the plots in my mind, from reading the dialogue, . . . and I didn't ever get them outright, but it was a good help to me, wasn't it, trying to get by myself'. Clearly it was a great help: she expanded her vocabulary and later entered a teacher training college, where she performed in productions of *Twelfth Night* and *Electra*.[75]

Richard Altick recognized that common readers who had not learned the literary conventions of the Bible could still read it as a simple collection of stories.[76] As a boy W. E. Adams enjoyed *Pilgrim's Progress*, *Gulliver's Travels*, and the *Arabian Nights* on the same level: 'The religious meaning of the first, the satirical meaning of the second, and the doubtful meaning of the third were, of course, not understood. The story was the thing – the trials of Christian, the troubles of Gulliver, the adventures of Aladdin'.[77] George Acorn may have read George Eliot at age nine, but 'solely for the story. I used to skip the parts that moralized, or painted verbal scenery, a practice at which I became very dextrous'.

That kind of editing, Acorn added, was a defense mechanism that working people had to develop against

> the flood of goody-goody literature which was poured in upon us. Kindly institutions sought to lead us into the right path by giving us endless tracts, or books in which the comparative pill of religious teaching was clumsily coated by a mild story. It was necessary in self-defense to pick out the interesting parts, which to me at the time were certainly not those that led to the hero's conversion, or the heroine's first prayer:[78]

A striking illustration of this selective reading is the working-class response – or rather, nonresponse – to imperialist propaganda. Patrick Dunae and others have argued that a whole generation of boys were converted to imperialism by the novels of G. A. Henty and similar forms of indoctrination. 'At school, in church groups, in recreational associations – at almost every turn boys were exposed to the imperial idea': that undeniable fact leads Dunae to the conclusion that 'in the late nineteenth and early twentieth century most British youths were acutely aware of their imperial heritage. They could scarcely have been otherwise'.[79]

They certainly could have been otherwise. The majority of those youths were working-class, and they seem to have been acutely unaware of their empire. Although John MacKenzie has shown that imperialist propaganda saturated textbooks, popular literature, and later the cinema, he fails to prove that this message got through to its intended audience.[80] The memoirs of Robert Roberts, Willie Gallacher, and Harry Pollitt all document workers' indifference to the empire, except for brief and exceptional outbursts of jingoism during the First World War.[81] Roberts reports that the same people who rushed to the colors in August 1914 would have considered it a disgrace to join the army in peacetime. Royal jubilees were celebrated as national, not imperial, holidays: 'One felt the coming together of a whole country for a day of contentment and freedom'. Schoolchildren might well be imperialists on Empire Day, having been taught 'a lot of inconsequential facts on India [and] parts of Africa, . . . all ruled over by Edward the Peace-maker (pacemaker, my father called him)'. But, Roberts emphasizes, 'Except in periods of national crisis or celebration, industrial labourers, though Tory, royalist and patriotic, remained uninterested in any event beyond the local, horse racing excepted.'[82]

That last point is confirmed by the very titles of workers' autobiographies: *A Sheffield Childhood*, *My Dorset Days*, *Newlyn Boyhood*, *Memories of Old Poplar*, *Salford Boy*, *Ancoats Lad*, *A Man of Kent*, *A Love for Bermondsey and Its People*, *In a Lancashire Street*, *36 Stewart Street*, *Bolton*, *Lark Rise*.

The scope of these memoirs is almost entirely local. There lies one of the most telling silences in workers' memoirs: they not only fail to express imperialist sentiments, they scarcely mention the empire. Many autobiographers, including several future socialists, do recall that they enjoyed reading Hentyesque stories;[83] but they did not therefore become imperialists. Apparently they did not even notice the ideological freight carried by these tales, which were read purely as adventure stories, in which India or Africa was simply an exotic backdrop, not a territory the reader wanted to spend his life policing.

A history of audiences, then, will have to take into account not only the concrete messages that readers pick up from texts, but also the degree of credulity, involvement, and critical distance that readers bring to those texts. Semioticians call this dimension of audience response 'suture', which has been defined by Jacques Alain-Miller as 'the relation of the subject to the chain of its discourse'.[84] Roger Chartier, for example, has tried to fix the relation of readers to the roguery stories published in seventeenth- and eighteenth-century France. He concludes that because these stories combined documentary effects with parody, they may have suspended the reader somewhere between credulity and incredulity:

> Belief in what is read is thus accompanied by a laugh that gives it the lie; the readers' acceptance is solicited, but a certain distance shows literature for what it is. . . . This delicate balance permits multiple readings that fluctuate between a persuasion by literal interpretation and an awareness of and amusement at the parody. . . . Thus the reader could simultaneously know and forget that fiction was fiction.[85]

Perhaps he could, but how do we know that? Lacking more direct evidence of audience involvement, Chartier tries to infer it from an analysis of texts and of editorial decisions made by the publishers; the method is ingenious, but it does not avoid the receptive fallacy. Most students of suture construct their theories on still shakier foundations: Kaja Silverman, for instance, tells us with great assurance what perspectives Hitchcock's film *Psycho* 'obliges' the audience to assume, without interrogating any actual viewer. In this area George Acorn was a superior sociologist: he observed audiences at the Edwardian counterpart of *Psycho* and the roguery tale – 'lurid, streaky melodrama, in which the villain always vowed to steep his hands in the hero's gore' – and found that their involvement with the narrative ran the complete gamut:

> 'Look out!' an overwrought galleryite would shout, ''e's going to stab her with a knife'. Or when the poisoned cup was offered to the handsome hero, the action of the play would be delayed by voices anxiously bidding him not to drink it. 'Shut up, Fathead!' some grumpy old chap would say to the nearest possessor of one of those voices; ''ow can the play go on if he don't get drugged? Besides, the 'ero's bahnd to win in the end, ain't he?'[86]

Where Chartier and Silverman assume that all audiences have the same relation to a given narrative, Acorn appreciated that individual theatergoers might be 'sutured' very differently. Where Chartier concluded that his readers simultaneously believed and disbelieved, Acorn found his audience sharply divided between the totally credulous and the contemptuously incredulous. Silverman asserts that suture involves 'passive insertions into pre-existing discursive positions', in which the audience 'permits itself to be spoken by the film's discourse'; but part of Acorn's audience quite aggressively tried to insert itself into the narrative and seize control of the discourse, while another section (including Acorn) was wholly divorced from the play and sneered at all its clanking machinery. Anyone who doubts that the common reader can manipulate the text should consider the case of a Victorian actor who, having died an elaborately melodramatic stage death, was loudly urged by his working-class audience to 'Die again!' – and did so.[87]

Given that these audiences were so obstreperous and even dictatorial, the term 'suture' should be scrapped as misleading, since it suggests that the reader is helplessly stitched into the narrative. We should instead be asking questions about the degree of audience *involvement*, which may have been quite active. We might also ask why Silverman and so many other literary theorists habitually treat that audience as a passive vessel, but that is another question for another essay. A brief answer would be that, in a democratic society, this assumption is attractive to both extremes of the political spectrum, because it rationalizes their failure to win broad popular support: they *would* enjoy that support, if only the masses were not somehow manipulated by the media. Thus cultural studies monographs and the House Un-American Activities Committee have both tried to expose the devilishly subtle political messages embedded in Hollywood movies, and for essentially the same reason.

There is no denying that films and books can be manipulative; but it should be equally obvious that we cannot know whether or when they succeed without somehow questioning the audience. Many literary critics today are understandably anxious to present themselves as sociologists rather than mere belletrists: they are concerned not with what texts mean, but with what texts do, as Stanley Fish has put it.[88] I would reply that it is equally worthwhile to ask what texts do, what texts mean, and which texts are the best texts; my point is that literary criticism cannot answer the first of these questions, while a history of audiences might. In that sense, the reader is outside the text.

## Notes

1   John Burnett, David Vincent, and David Mayall (eds), *The Autobiography of the Working Class: An Annotated, Critical Bibliography* (3 vols, New York, 1984–89) For scholars who want to investigate upper- and middle-class readers, the potential sample is even larger, more than 6000 entries in William Matthews, *British Autobiographies* (Hamden, Conn., 1968).

2   Barbara English, 'Lark Rise and Juniper Hill: A Victorian Community in Literature and in History', *Victorian Studies*, 29 (1985), 7–35. Joel Wiener likewise corrected the autobiography of Chartist William Lovett in *William Lovett* (Manchester, 1989), 2.

3   For example, much information on popular reading can be extracted from the oral history project on family, work, and community in Britain before 1918, conducted by Paul Thompson and Thea Vigne and housed at the University of Essex.

4   Jeffrey Brooks, *When Russia Learned to Read: Literacy and Popular Culture, 1861–1917* (Princeton, 1988).

5   Hayden White, 'Method and Ideology in Intellectual History: The Case of Henry Adams', Dominick LaCapra and Steven L. Kaplan (eds), *Modern European Intellectual History: Reappraisals and New Perspectives* (Ithaca, 1982), 307–8.

6   Janice Radway, 'The Book-of-the-Month Club and the General Reader: On the Uses of "Serious" Fiction', *Critical Inquiry*, 14 (1988), 518–19.

7   Barbara Herrnstein Smith, *Contingencies of Value: Alternative Perspectives for Critical Theory* (Cambridge, Mass., 1988), 52–53.

8   George Haw, *The Life Story of Will Crooks, MP* (London, 1917), 22.

9   Smith. *Contingencies*, 50.

10  Thomas Cooper, *The Life of Thomas Cooper* (London, 1882), 5, 33, 59–60; Tom Barclay, *Memoirs and Medlies: The Autobiography of a Bottle-Washer* (Leicester, 1934), 19–20.

11  Naturally, Lady Bell and Mr. Freeman were following their subjective Edwardian upper- and middle-class definitions of culture, and Freeman's was a bit generous: he classified as 'well-equipped' some workers who were thoroughly respectable but had few intellectual interests.

On the other hand, Lady Bell tended to err on the side of restrictiveness: she found that a quarter of working-class families read only novels, and she wrote them all off as culturally deprived. Lady [Florence] Bell, *At the Works* (London, 1907), ch. 7. [Arnold Freeman], *The Equipment of the Workers* (London, 1919), ch. 3.

12   Peter Miles, 'The Painter's Bible and the British Workman: Robert Tressell's Literary Activism', Jeremy Hawthorn (ed.), *The British Working-Class Novel in the Twentieth Century* (London. 1984), 2–10.

13   William J. Gilmore, *Reading Becomes a Necessity of Life: Material and Cultural Life in Rural New England 1780–1835* (Knoxville, 1989) 163.

14   *Ibid.*, 103, 289.

15   Will Jon Edwards, *From the Valley I Came* (London, 1956), 46–48, 67.

16   Walter Haydn Davies, *The Right Place – The Right Time* (Llandybie, 1972), 64–66, 101–5.

17   David Vincent, *Bread, Knowledge and Freedom: A Study of Nineteenth-Century Working Class Autobiography* (London, 1981), ch. 6.

18   Emanuel Shinwell, *Conflict without Malice* (London, 1955), 24–25.

19   George Howell, draft autobiography, Bishopsgate Institute, vol. B, b/4, f. 4.

20   Flora Thompson, *Lark Rise to Candleford* (Harmondsworth, 1987), 414–15.

21   Freeman, *Equipment*, ch. 3. A similar observation is made in Bell, *At the Works,* ch. 7.

22   'The Labour Party and the Books That Helped to Make It', *Review of Reviews*, 33 (1906), 568–82.

23   Morag Shiach, *Discourse on Popular Culture* (Cambridge, 1989).

24   Ray B. Browne, 'Popular Culture – New Notes Toward a Definition', Christopher G. Geist and Jack Nachbar (eds), *The Popular Culture Reader* (3rd ed.; Bowling Green, 1983), 13.

25   Brooks, *Russia Learned to Read*, xvi, 33.

26   See John E. Toews, 'Intellectual History after the Linguistic Turn: The Autonomy of Meaning and the Irreducibility of Experience', *American Historical Review*, 92 (1987), 883–85.

27   Roger Chartier, *The Cultural Uses of Print in Early Modern France*, tr. Lydia G. Cochrane (Princeton, 1987), 3–8.

28   One might doubt Acorn's claim that he appreciated all that at age nine, but he had certainly reached that level of understanding by young adulthood, when he wrote his autobiography. George Acorn, *One of the Multitude* (London, 1911), 49–50.

29   Patrick A. Dunae, 'Penny Dreadfuls: Late Nineteenth-Century Boys' Literature and Crime', *Victorian Studies*, 22 (1979), 133–50.

30   J. H. Howard, *Winding Lanes* (Caernarvon, nd.), 27; Peter Donnelly, *The Yellow Rock* (London, 1950), 31–32.

31   Alfred Cox, *Among the Doctors* (London, 1950), 17.

32   John Springhall, '"A Life Story for the People"? Edwin J, Brett and the London "Low-Life" Penny Dreadfuls of the 1860s', *Victorian Studies*, 33 (1990), 225.

33   Lately, a few investigators in this field have come to recognize that fallacy. See Anne Beezer, Jean Grimshaw, and Martin Barker, 'Methods for Cultural Studies Students', David Punter (ed.), *Introduction to Contemporary Cultural Studies* (London, 1986), 97, 109–113.

34   James Smith Allen, 'History and the Novel: *Mentalité* in Modern Popular Fiction', *History and Theory*, 22 (1983), 248–49.

35   Radway, *Romance*, 63–76.

36   White, 'Method and Ideology', 282.

37   Charles H. Welch, *An Autobiography* (Banstead, 1960), 33.

38   Acorn, *Multitude*, 28–35.

39   Thomas McLauchlan, *The Life of an Ordinary Man* (np., 1979), 51.

40   Arthur Harding, *East End Underworld: Chapters in the Life of Arthur Harding*, ed. Raphael Samuel (London, 1981), 47, 74–75.

41   Alfred Gilchrist, *Naethin at A'* (Glasgow, nd.), 14.

42 John Sykes, *Slawit in the 'Sixties* (London, 1926), 23–29.

43 Thomas Wright, *Some Habits and Customs of the Working Classes* (London, 1867), 166.

44 Elizabeth Flint, *Hot Bread and Chips* (London, 1963), 163.

45 William Donaldson, *Popular Literature in Victorian Scotland* (Aberdeen, 1986). 32.

46 Joseph Burgess, *A Potential Poet? His Autobiography and Verse* (Ilford, 1927). 33.

47 Nora Hampton, 'Memories of Baptist End, Netherton, Dudley in the Period 1895–1919', TS, Brunel Univ. Library, p. 1.

48 Richard Pyke, *Men and Memories* (London, 1948), 9.

49 Interestingly, the radical journalist W. E. Adams anticipated in 1903 that changing literary standards might bring about Reynolds's rehabilitation: 'With the taste for sensation and salacious details which the modern novelist and modern dramatist have cultivated, it is not at all unlikely that he would . . . [be] admitted to the hierarchy of fiction'. But as Adams reviled all the Emile Zolas of contemporary literature, that hardly constituted an endorsement. W. E. Adams, *Memoirs of a Social Atom* (New York, 1968) 102–8, 233–34, ch. 57.

50 Burgess, *Potential Poet*, 70–72.

51 Henry Coward, *Reminiscences of Henry Coward* (London, 1919), 42.

52 Harding, *East End Underworld*, 274.

53 Edith Hall, *Canary Girls and Stockpots* (Luton, 1977), 39–40.

54 Regenia Gagnier, 'Social Atoms: Working-Class Autobiography, Subjectivity and Gender', *Victorian Studies*, 30 (1987), 335–63. Nan Hackett, *XIX Century British Working-Class Autobiographies: An Annotated Bibliography* (New York, 1985).

55 Jane Tompkins, *Sensational Designs: The Cultural Work of American Fiction 1790–1860* (New York, 1985), 38. See Chapter 18 of this Reader.

56 Elizabeth Bryson, *Look Back in Wonder* (Dundee, 1967), 71, 80–82 124–25.

57 Winifred Albaya, *A Sheffield Childhood* (Sheffield, n.d.), 40–41.

58 Catherine Cookson, *Our Kate* (London, 1969), 158–60.

59 Terry Eagleton, *Literary Theory: An Introduction* (Minneapolis, 1983), 22–27; Chris Baldick, *The Social Mission of English Criticism 1848–1932* (Oxford, 1983), 63–67.

60 Joel H. Wiener, *Radicalism and Freethought in Nineteenth-Century Britain: The Life of Richard Carlisle* (Westport, Conn., 1983), ch. 4.

61 T. A. Jackson, draft autobiography, Marx Memorial Library, 364; J. T. Murphy, *New Horizons* (London, 1941), 216; Shinwell, *Conflict*, 72–73.

62 Robert Roberts, *The Classic Slum: Salford Life in the First Quarter of the Century* (London, 1990), 177–79.

63 William J. Fishman, *East End Jewish Radicals 1875–1914* (London, 1975), 266.

64 John James Bezer, 'The Autobiography of One of the Chartist Rebels of 1848', David Vincent (ed.), *Testaments of Radicalism: Memoirs of Working Class Politicians 1790–1885* (London, 1977), 167.

65 Paul Thomas Murphy, '"Imagination Flaps Its Sportive Wings": Views of Fiction in British Working-Class Periodicals, 1816–1858', *Victorian Studies*, 32 (1989), 341–53.

66 George Howell, *The Conflicts of Capital and Labour* (2nd ed., London 1890), ch. 4.

67 Malcolm Chase, *The People's Farm: English Radical Agrarianism 1775–1840* (Oxford, 1988), 143, 181.

68 C. B. Macpherson, *The Political Theory of Possessive Individualism: Hobbes to Locke* (Oxford, 1964), 194–221.

69 Ginzberg, C. *The Cheese and The Worms*, xiv–xxi, 41–50; Spufford, *Small Books*, xvii, 30–34; Ned Landsman, 'Evangelists and Their Hearers: Popular Interpretation of Revivalist Preaching in Eighteenth-Century Scotland', *Journal of British Studies*, 28 (1989), 120–49; Altick, *Common Reader*, 255–56; Jonathan Rose, 'The Workers in the Workers' Educational Association, 1903–1950', *Albion*, 21 (1989), 591–608.

70    Chartier, *Cultural Uses of Print*, 3–8.

71    Jacques Derrida, *Of Grammatology*, tr. Gayatri Chakravorty Spivak (Baltimore, 1976), 158.

72    Frederick Rogers, *Life, Labour and Literature* (London, 1913), 61–62.

73    Shinwell, *Conflict*, 25–28.

74    Culler, 'Prolegomena', 49.

75    University of Essex Oral History Archive, 'Family, Work and Community Life Before 1918', interview 21.

76    Altick, *Common Reader*, 255–56.

77    Adams, *Memoirs*, 100–101.

78    Acorn, *Multitude*, 49–50.

79    Patrick A. Dunae, 'Boys' Literature and the Idea of Empire, 1870–1914', *Victorian Studies*, 24 (1980), 105–21.

80    John M. MacKenzie, *Propaganda and Empire: The Manipulation of British Public Opinion, 188–1960* (Manchester, 1984), 254.

81    William Gallacher, *Revolt on the Clyde: An Autobiography* (London, 1936), 18–19; Harry Pollitt, *Serving My Time: An Apprenticeship in Politics* (London, 1940), 85–87.

82    Roberts, *Classic Slum*, 140–44, 162–63, 179–82.

83    John Lanigan, 'Thy Kingdom *Did* Come', TS in Brunel University Library, 22, 63; William Holt, *Under a Japanese Parasol* (Halifax, 1933), 111–12; John Allaway in Ronald Goldman (ed.), *Breakthrough: Autobiographical Accounts of the Education of Some Socially Disadvantaged Children* (London, 1968), 7–9; James Griffiths, *Pages from Memory* (London, 1969), 11–12; John Edwin, *I'm Going – What Then?* (Bognor Regis, 1978), 89.

84    For a theoretical discussion of suture, see Kaja Silverman, *The Subject of Semiotics* (New York, 1983), ch. 5.

85    Chartier, *Cultural Uses of Print*, 335–36.

86    Acorn, *Multitude*, 134–36.

87    Thomas Wright, *Habits and Customs*, 165.

88    Stanley Fish, *Is There a Text in This Class?* (Cambridge, Mass., 1980), 3. See Chapter 27 in this Reader.

# Chapter 26

# Richard Altick

## THE ENGLISH COMMON READER

## From Caxton to the eighteenth century

**I**

William Caxton set up his printing press in Westminster at a fortunate moment in history. Already the great cultural revolution with which his name is associated was under way. Though most Englishmen still depended upon their ears for their share of the common cultural heritage, or upon their ability to interpret the pictures and statuary they saw in the churches, by 1477 there were substantial hints that in the future the art of reading would have a greater role in their lives. The demand for manuscripts was increasing. Caxton had not yet begun business when John Shirley, a dealer in manuscripts, started to lend out copies of the works of such authors as Chaucer and Lydgate in a sort of primitive circulating-library arrangement. In fifteenth-century inventories and wills, too, one finds mention of books, as if the rising class of country gentlemen and city merchants felt that the possession of a few manuscript volumes would provide them with a certain cachet.[1] The demand threatened soon to exceed the supply – unless, as actually happened, a means were discovered of duplicating books so that, instead of but a single manuscript, there could be hundreds and even thousands of printed copies.

We do not know how large the literate public was in Caxton's time, or in the century that followed. Only a few unsatisfactory scraps of evidence survive. Of 116 witnesses before the consistory court in 1467–76, some 40 per cent were recorded as literate.[2] In 1533 Sir Thomas More said that 'farre more than fowre partes of all the whole divided into tenne coulde never reade englishe yet',[3] an obscure statement which may possibly be interpreted as implying a literacy rate of 50 per cent or so. In 1547, on the other hand, Stephen Gardiner, Bishop of Winchester, observed that 'not the hundredth part of the realme' could read.[4] One modern estimate is that in Shakespeare's London between a third and a half of the people were literate.[5] It is at least certain that the growing commercial life of the nation required men of the merchant class to read and write English in order to transact business, keep records, and interpret legal documents. Some guilds set literacy as a condition of membership. Even women were becoming literate, and servants as well, if their circumstances required and permitted it.[6] Indeed, a recent historian has asserted that in Elizabethan times 'there was a higher level of literacy among women than at any other time until the later nineteenth century'.[7]

Opportunities for education, at least to the extent of learning to read the vernacular, increased in the fifteenth and sixteenth centuries and were available to a fairly wide diversity of classes. A youth from even the lowest stratum of freemen had always had the chance of following Chaucer's clerk to the university as a mendicant student. The ideal of extending education to the 'poor' was affirmed in the foundation statutes of the grammar schools. The phase *pauperes et indigentes scholares* in such statutes, it appears, was not simply designed to insure to the school the legal privileges of a charitable institution but means that boys of relatively humble station (say the equivalent of the modern lower-middle class) really were enrolled in some numbers.

No longer, in any event, was education limited, as it had been in the Middle Ages, to those destined for the religious life. Even if the prospects were that they would take up their father's occupation, the children of small tradesmen, farm laborers, and domestic servants had some opportunity to learn to read English. For them, by Henry VIII's time, were provided petty schools, ABC schools, and song schools for the training of choirboys.[8]

These schools were all under the control of the church, and it used to be thought that Henry VIII's expropriation of ecclesiastical property, some of the income from which had been earmarked for teaching purposes, dealt a severe blow to English education. Today, however, it is believed that the dissolution of the churchly establishments did not interfere too much, at least in the long run, with the spread of learning. In time, new schools sprang up to replace those that were wiped out. A favorite practice among those who profited by the nation's prosperity was to endow grammar (that is, classical) schools. Almost every town of any size had at least one such school; in 1600 there were about 360 of them.[9] In addition, many noblemen and other large landowners founded and supported schools for the children of the neighborhood. Some of these were limited to elementary instruction; others, like the one at Stratford-on-Avon which Sir Hugh Clopton re-endowed in 1553, provided an excellent Latin education.

Therefore, since there was as yet little sign of the social exclusiveness that later was to reserve grammar-school and university education largely for children of noble or gentle birth, it was possible for bright boys from the artisan and tradesman class to acquire a thorough schooling. This is suggested by the number of Elizabethan writers who sprang from that station. To mention only a few: Peele was the son of a salter; Marlowe, of a cobbler; Munday, of a draper; Chettle, of a dyer; Herrick, of a goldsmith; Gabriel Harvey, of a ropemaker; Donne, of an ironmonger.[10]

A classical education was, however, the lot of only a minority of those who went to school at all. More numerous were the boys who received an abbreviated education in primary or petty schools. These schools were open not only to those destined to go on to the Latin curriculum but also to those who would begin their apprenticeship immediately after learning to read. While parish clergymen still could be found teaching children their letters, by the middle of the sixteenth century the church's monopoly over elementary education was forever ended. From the humble hand-laborer in a remote parish teaching a few pupils the ABC's, to the professional schoolmaster in the town, laymen became teachers. Their 'private adventure' schools made literacy available to a wide range of society. In addition, a growing number of craft guilds established schools for their members' children.

By the latter part of the sixteenth century the people who could read only English had become so numerous as to require more and more books to be printed in the vernacular. Contemporary writers, apologizing for their use of what was still considered an inferior language, frequently alluded to the 'unskilfull', the 'unacquainted with the latine tounge', the 'unlettered', who nevertheless should share in the age's knowledge. The very fact that this was the great age of translations proves the existence of a sizable audience who knew only English. The translator of a Latin theological work in 1599 remarked that he 'brought into the artificer's shop, [that] which was before in the studies and closets of the learned alone'.[11]

In the country, where most of the people lived, the proportion of literates probably was much smaller than in the towns, partly because there were fewer schools, partly because the conditions of rural life made illiteracy less of a handicap. Most cottagers were wholly indifferent to education, or could not spare their children from labor in field or cottage for even a year or two. Furthermore, by no means all the children who learned to read ever exercised their talent in later life. The boys soon went to the plow or the craftsman's shop, and the girls (of whom there were at least a sprinkling in some of the ABC schools) to the spinning wheel and the rearing of families; and having neither books nor any necessity for them, they lost such small gift as they had once possessed.

When all allowances have been made, however, it seems likely that in the Tudor and Stuart eras the ability to read was more democratically distributed among the English people than it would again be until at least the end of the eighteenth century. But, since there is a vital distinction between the simple possession of literacy and its active, continual exercise, it does not follow that the reading public in the late sixteenth and early seventeenth centuries was either as large or socially as diversified as the apparent extent of literacy in the nation might suggest. Books were not easy to acquire. Their production was artificially limited in several ways. One was the restriction on the number of printers. In 1586, partly to satisfy the printers already in business and partly to ease the ecclesiastical authorities' alarm over the spread of controversial and polemic books, the Star Chamber forbade the establishment of any new press until a vacancy occurred among the already existing ones (twenty-two commercial presses, in addition to the Queen's Printer and the two university presses).[12] Again, to make work for the increasing number of journeymen and apprentices, the Stationers' Company in 1587 limited to 1,250 or 1,500 the number of copies of a book that could be produced from one setting of type, although, in the interests of public morality and enlightenment, 'grammers, Accidences, prymers, and Catechisms' were allowed four impressions annually, of 2,500 to 3,000 copies each.[13] How prices would have been affected had a printer been free to issue as many copies as he foresaw a sale for, we can only speculate.

The book trade was also restricted, at the expense of the reader, by 'privilege' – the vested right accorded to certain booksellers in the printing and sale of specified categories of books. As early as 1559 such patents had been granted, and although in the 1580s some individual patentees transferred their monopolies to Stationers' Company, the practice continued unabated to the end of the Queen's reign. Her successors, James I and Charles I, between them allowed forty-three new patents.[14] The effect this monopoly had upon prices is illustrated by the fact that the London booksellers sold *Aesop's Fables* at 4d. a sheet[15] and Ovid's Epistles at 8d., while in Cambridge the same books, issued by the university press (which was unaffected by 'privilege'), cost respectively 3d. and 5d. a sheet. The university authorities bitterly resented the refusal by members of the Stationers' Company to sell these cheaper books, and in 1621 they obtained a royal injunction against the company's boycott of the Cambridge edition of Lily's *Grammar*.[16] Thus, although there might be a brisk demand for books of a certain kind, the number available was limited to those that the privileged bookseller desired or was able to produce in his own shop. There could be no competition and no healthy multiplication of such books.

The crescendo of public events in the first part of the seventeenth century, as well as the spread of the reading habit on other grounds among the middle class, increased the demand for books. Gradually the Tudor restrictions were lifted, and the market became better supplied. When the Court of the Star Chamber was abolished in 1641, the number of London printers ceased to be limited, and by 1660 there were about sixty printing houses in the city. Although the Licensing Act of 1662 reaffirmed the old regulation, it was for the most part ineffectual.[17] The day when the availability of books could be governed by that kind of maneuver was past, and in the future the government would have to find other ways of regulating the press.

In 1635, the restrictions on the number of copies to be issued from a single setting of type were liberalized to 1,500 or 2,000 for ordinary books, and to 3,000 for books in brevier type and 5,000 in nonpareil.[18] These ceilings were probably adequate for the market. In 1652, during a squabble between members of the Stationers' Company, one party alleged that the usual impression of a book was 1,500 copies, while the other asserted that the figure was too high.[19] Apart from staple items like almanacs (Partridge's *Anglicus* sold 13,500 in 1646, 17,000 in 1647, and 18,500 in 1648) and Lily's imperishable *Grammar* (20,000 copies a year in mid-century), a book would have had to be very popular indeed to sell as many as 5,000 copies in two years, as did the combined edition of Quarles's *Emblems and Hieroglyphikes* in 1639–40.[20] *Paradise Lost* sold 1,300 copies in two years. No edition, according to Milton's agreement with his bookseller, was to consist of more than 1,500 copies.[21] Our information on the prices of new books in the sixteenth and seventeenth centuries is sketchy.[22] In the earlier part of the sixteenth century, the average cost of a book was between two and three sheets for a penny.[23] On this basis, in 1520, Luther's *De potestate papae* cost 3*d.*, the ABC's a penny or 2*d.*, broadside ballads a halfpenny, Christmas carols 1*d.* or 2*d.*, and the book of Robin Hood, 2*d.*[24] In 1541, by royal proclamation, the price of Coverdale's Great Bible was fixed at 10*s.* unbound, 12*s.* bound.

Debasement of the coinage resulted in the doubling of commodity prices between 1540 and 1550, and books shared in the inflation. The cost of a psalter rose from 10*d.* in 1548 to 2*s.*4*d.* in 1563. But after this increase, the prices of books remained remarkably constant down to 1635, despite another 100 per cent rise in the general price index during that period. In the golden age of Elizabethan literature, Holinshed's *Chronicles* cost £1 6*s.* bound, *Euphues* 2*s.* unbound, Camden's *Britannia* 2*s.*6*d.*, North's *Plutarch* 14*s.* bound, Spenser's *Shepheardes Calender* 1*s.*, Sidney's *Arcadia* 9*s.* bound, and Hakluyt's *Voyages* 9*s.* unbound. Quarto plays, such as Shakespeare's, were 4*d.* or, more usually, 6*d.*[25]

During the Elizabethan and Jacobean periods, therefore, books were not too expensive when compared with other commodities. But that does not mean that they were easily accessible to a great many would-be readers, for one of the basic facts of English economic history at this time is that wages lagged far behind prices. The ordinary man could afford only the cheapest of books, and not many of these. When an unbound copy of Hamlet was selling for 6*d.*, master artisans and handicraftsmen in London – carpenters, joiners, cobblers, smiths – earned about 16*d,* a day. Shopkeepers made about the same. Thus a man who had seen *Hamlet* at the Globe and wanted to read it at his leisure would have had to spend between a quarter and a half of his day's earnings. With that same sixpence he could have bought two dinners or gone back to the Globe (if he were content to stand in the pit) for six more performances.[26]

Even professional men, who would have been more likely to be habitual readers, did not have enough money to buy many books. An ordinary clergyman made between £10 and £20 a year, which means that the purchase of Sidney's *Arcadia* or Hakluyt's *Voyages* would have required the sacrifice of one or two whole weeks' income. A schoolmaster, making, say, £6 9*s.* a year, would have had to spend the equivalent of about three weeks' income.[27]

About 1635, for a reason not yet clear, book prices rose by some 40 per cent.[28] Incomes, however, were rising as well, so that books were relatively no more expensive by the Restoration than they had been in Shakespeare's time. In 1668 folios, meant for the wealthy trade, were priced from 5*s.* to 16*s.*, the majority from 7*s.* to 10*s.* Most newly published books in octavo, the commonest size, ranged from 1*s.* to 4*s.* bound. Unbound plays were regularly published at 1*s.*, and sermons, controversial pamphlets, accounts of trials, and other 'timely' items of restricted length as a rule were 6*d.* The smallest books (12mo) usually were 1*s.*6*d.*[29] During this general period (there were, of course, variations from year to year) butter sold for 6*d.* a pound, coffee 3*s.* a pound, sugar 6*d.* a pound, and canary wine 7*s.* a gallon.[30] Pepys laid out 24*s.* for a 'nightgown' (i.e., dressing robe) for his wife, and 2s. for a pair of kid gloves. Admission to the gallery of a theater where Nell Gwyn was playing cost 12d. or 18d., although a citizen out on the town might pay as much as 2s.6d. to go into the pit.[31] In 1688 the average income of lesser clergymen was estimated at a little less than a pound a week; that of farmers, 16s.4d.; of shopkeepers, 17s.4d.; and of artisans and handicraftsmen, 14s.7d.[32]

Between this time and the first quarter of the eighteenth century, book prices again rose. Whatever the strictly economic reasons behind the increase, it was also a natural development in a period when the reading public was contracting instead of expanding. The demand for books, like the writing of them, was limited to a narrower social group. Whether the higher prices charged for books were a contributory cause or merely a symptom of the change, we cannot tell. But as the seventeenth century drew to a close, it is at least plain that books were dearer and readers were fewer.

Books, then, were the possession chiefly of the more prosperous members of the middle class in the sixteenth and seventeenth centuries, as well as of that permanent nucleus of well-educated upper-class readers whose existence will be constantly assumed, though seldom mentioned, in this volume. Among them were the keepers of fair-sized shops and master artisans who, like Simon Eyre in Dekker's comedy *The Shoemaker's Holiday*, had achieved the dignity of being employers of labor. Here and there, members of the class carried their bookishness to the point of becoming collectors on a modest scale. As early as 1575 a London mercer, writing to another, described the library of one Captain Cox, a Coventry mason. Eighty years later we find an undersheriff of London giving up his office to be free to make his daily round of the bookstalls, and a turner in Eastcheap lining his 'studdy' with books.[33]

Since the printing trade was concentrated in London and transportation and communication were still primitive, there was little commerce in books in the provinces. Only occasionally are books mentioned in yeomen's wills. Most men of that class seem to have read little, or in any event to have owned so few books that it was not worthwhile to include them in the inventories of their personal effects.[34]

## II

The people of the Tudor and Stuart eras read books for reasons which would have made excellent sense to their Victorian descendants. John Stuart Mill, in his inaugural address at the University of St. Andrews in 1867, spoke of 'the two influences which have chiefly shaped the British character since the days of the Stuarts: commercial money-getting business, and religious Puritanism'. These influences affected reading tastes in Milton's time as profoundly as in Mill's. Their tendency was to discourage popular interest in most forms of imaginative literature. 'Business', said Mill, 'demanding the whole of the faculties, and whether pursued from duty or the love of gain, regarding as a loss of time whatever does not conduce directly to the end; Puritanism, which looking upon every feeling of human nature, except fear and reverence for God, as a snare, if not as partaking of sin, looked coldly, if not disapprovingly, on the cultivation of the sentiments'.[35]

Protestantism, in the phrase of Élie Halévy, is a 'book religion'.[36] From the time it began to transform English life in the sixteenth century it laid emphasis upon the practice of private reading. With the appearance in 1540 of the Great Bible (Coverdale's revised translation), the first English Bible to be authorized by the Crown, Henry VIII ordered a copy to be placed in every church. 'Every body that could', wrote Strype, the early biographer of Cranmer, 'bought the book, or busily read it, or got others to read it to them, if they could not themselves; and divers more elderly people learned to read on purpose. And even little boys flocked among the rest to hear portions of the holy Scripture read. . . . When the King had allowed the Bible to be set forth to be read in all churches, immediately several poor men in the town of Chelmsford in Essex . . . bought the New Testament, and on Sundays sat reading it in the lower end of the Church.'[37] But this novel freedom to read the Bible was short-lived. In 1543 the Reformed Parliament forbade it to all women (except those of high birth), artificers, apprentices, journeymen, servingmen, husbandmen, and laborers – an evidence of the social distribution of literacy even at that early date.

However, with the accession of Mary, though the practice of displaying Bibles in the churches was condemned, no attempt was made to interfere with individual reading. Under Elizabeth I, Bibles were restored to the churches, and the idea that men had to be 'authorised and licensed' to read Scripture for themselves was quietly dropped.[38] But only under the Puritans did Scripture become the veritable foundation of Christian faith, achieving, along with the surrounding literature of religion, a place in men's lives that was inconceivable in pre-Reformation England.

It was not, however, only the Protestant, and especially the Puritan, emphasis upon private Bible-reading as a way to religious truth and thus to personal salvation which stimulated the spread of reading. The religious controversies that reached a climax in the Civil War played their part as well. They reached into the minds, and even more the passionate emotions, of great numbers of ordinary people, who were as stirred by them as later generations would be by purely political furor. And the controversies were carried on by floods of tracts and pamphlets, arguments and replies and rejoinders and counterrejoinders – printed matter which found a seemingly limitless market among all classes that could read.[39] With the establishment of the Commonwealth, 'everybody with views to express, from Milton down to the most insignificant crank or fanatic, took a hand'.[40] The London bookseller George Thomason collected some 23,000 books and pamphlets printed between 1641 and 1662.

On the secular side of life, men's interest in books stemmed from motives strikingly prophetic of nineteenth-century utilitarianism. Readers were increasingly concerned to obtain books of practical guidance and information.[41] With the simultaneous spread of a new economy, which required a degree of knowledge unnecessary under the old feudal system, and of a humanism which brought vast new areas of worldly interest to men's attention, books became instruments of utility. Through them, men could learn the things they needed to know as businessmen and functionaries in civil government and could share in the humane learning of the Renaissance. Reading was inextricably associated with 'improvement', with cultivation of the prudential virtues and the more easily acquired amenities of conduct. The books most in request were those which either showed the way to a morality acceptable in the eyes both of God and of Mammon or brought the ideals of humanistic conduct down to the level of the common man. Thus – to adopt the categories described in Louis Wright's encyclopedic account of middle-class reading in the age – the demand was for handbooks of improvement, lessons in diligence and thrift, instruction in domestic relations, guides to godliness, popularized histories (always with useful lessons), translations, travel books, and books on science,

These were the books that the sober, ambitious citizen read. Other kinds were available, as we shall note in a moment; but, though they might be admitted to a Simon Eyre's shelf, they owed their presence there to stealth or rationalization, or both. For the spirit of the time was strongly against books of any lighter quality than the types just mentioned. Over the whole age, affecting even those who were staunchest in their allegiance to orthodox Anglicanism, hung the fervent Puritan opposition to polite letters as un-Christian, frivolous, and demoralizing. From the 1580s to the Root and Branch petition of 1640, which attacked the prevalence of 'lascivious, idle, and unprofitable Books and Pamphlets, Play-Books and Ballads', the Puritan divines ceaselessly denounced the reading of books which offered no more than idle entertainment. We shall hear their voices again – though the rhetorical splendor of Puritan pulpit utterance will be sadly missing

— when we look into the effect of evangelicalism, the neo-Puritanism of the industrial age, upon the reading habits of the nineteenth century.

Even the courtesy books, interpreters of humanistic standards of conduct to the middle-class citizen, frowned upon the reading of plays and romances. At best, reading was only a minor one among the many polite activities one might pursue; but if one did read, it should always be with at least a moderately serious purpose.[42]

But the demands of the imagination and the feelings are too strong to be consistently denied. At their disposal always is man's inexhaustible talent for rationalization, and the extent to which it was employed is suggested by the popularity of lighter forms of literature – jestbooks, chapbooks, ballads, and the fiction that Thomas Nashe and Thomas Deloney devised expressly for the common reader. Usually the Elizabethan or Jacobean reader could find a plausible reason for dipping into such dubious books. The reading of jestbooks could be, and was, justified on the ground that they were pills to purge melancholy and thus (since the Elizabethans were firm believers in psychosomatic medicine) could improve one's physical health. Similarly, because the reading of history was recommended as perfectly safe and useful, it was possible to take up with a clear conscience any book, however fantastic, that had the word 'history' displayed on its title page.[43] Thus innumerable chapbooks and debased romances found their way into the hands of pious purchasers. Nor did the factual truth of the travel books have to be scrutinized too carefully. So long as they had an air of genuineness – so long as their authors did not candidly admit that they were spinning tales – they could be read as improving literature, no matter how outrageous their romancing. In such ways as these the reading regimen of the sixteenth- and seventeenth-century public had, despite its surface appearance of austerity, a full seasoning of imagination and escapism.[44]

Even among the strictest of Puritans, whose reading dealt exclusively and unambiguously with the concerns of the soul, imaginative stimulation and satisfaction were by no means lacking. The Bible is unequaled, among all the books of the world, for the variety and splendor of its imaginative and emotional appeal. Between a single pair of covers it offers the cosmic dramas of creation and the Last Judgment, the human pathos of Ruth and the tragedy of Samson; the wars of the Hebrews, the destruction of the Babylonians, the simple charm of the nativity story, the wonder of the miracles, the supreme climax of the Crucifixion and the Resurrection.

Furthermore, as William Haller has pointed out in his study of Puritanism, the Puritan preachers offered in their sermons, which in printed form had a wide circulation, a very acceptable substitute for the forbidden drama. 'They were to discover that their listeners . . . took a livelier interest in sin itself than in its categories, in the psychology of spiritual struggle than in the abstract analysis of moral behavior or even the satirical exposure of vice and folly. . . . So they set out to describe the warfare of the spirit, to portray the drama of the inner life, to expound the psychology of sin and redemption'.[45] Between the Bible itself, and such works as Foxe's *Book of Martyrs*, and these exceedingly dramatic presentations of the conflict of good and evil, the reading hours of even the most rigorous Puritans were seldom dull.

Of another segment of the reading public, which had few such scruples as affected the book choice of the sober middle class, we have little record except that of the books it preferred. This was the lowest stratum of the literate population: the casual, unpurposeful readers, those who, in the phrase of Heming and Condell's dedication in the 1623 Shakespeare folio, 'can but spell'. It was among these people – apprentices, common laborers, peasants, rivermen, and the rest – that the printers of broadside ballads and chapbooks found their chief market. The ballads were the precursors of a later era's sensational newspapers: never was a celebrated highwayman executed or a catastrophe visited upon a hapless town but the event was described in crude language and cruder woodcuts. They were, as well, the poor man's history: John Aubrey's nurse could recite the whole chronicle of England, from the Conquest to Charles I, in ballads.[46] The chapbooks, vulgarized versions of old chivalric tales, were his fiction – as Milton put it, 'the countryman's *Arcadias*, and his *Monte Mayors*'.[47]

This popular printed literature ran as a continuous thread, however seldom seen in the formal historical records, from Elizabeth's time to Victoria's. The descendants of Autolycus were to be found trudging with their packs along every rural road; in the end they would be acquiring fresh stock from the thriving establishment of Jemmy Catnach in London's unsavory Seven Dials. The fact that ballads and chapbooks did not vanish from the English scene until the advent of penny periodicals is assurance enough that the tradition of reading among the poor, in town and country, never wholly disappeared.

But the size of this public fluctuated with the vicissitudes of popular education, and we cannot know how large it was, in Tudor times or later. Though it is pleasant to envision the Elizabethan cottage with its faded and tattered ballads on the wall, and the cottager crouching over the feeble fire spelling out the words of a chapbook of Sir Thopas or an account of a late horrid crime and the ensuing visitation of justice on the malefactor, it would be a mistake to imagine that reading had any but the most incidental place in the life of the masses. For most of them – the fact is inescapable – were illiterate; and, impressive though the spread of reading was among the middle class in these first centuries of printing, it made little headway among the humble in either town or country. Their life still was lived according to the immemorial pattern. The recreations that occasionally lightened their hard lives were those which had been traditional centuries before Caxton – the rude games, the maypole dances, the harvest celebrations, and the other festivals that marked the progress of the seasons. Songs and stories were handed down by word of mouth from generation to generation, with never a page of print intervening. The life of the imagination and the feelings was still attuned to the ear rather than to the eye. The popular tradition, rich in folk heroes and broad humor and proverbial wisdom and memorable events, a strange and fascinating mixture of local legend and the lore of the Bible and the classics and medieval tale, was part of the very soil, and there was as yet no need for the printed word to supplant it.

## Notes

1    Bennett, 'The Author and His Public in the Fourteenth and Fifteenth Centuries', pp. 19–23. This and the other studies by Bennett (see References) are the fullest sources for the reading public in Caxton's time and the first century afterward.
2    Sylvia L. Thrupp, *The Merchant Class of Medieval London, 1300–1500* (Chicago, 1948), p. 156.
3    Quoted by Adamson, 'Literacy in England in the Fifteenth and Sixteenth Centuries', p. 45.
4    Bennett, *English Books and Readers*, p. 28.
5    Albert C. Baugh, *A History of the English Language* (New York, 1935), p. 246.
6    Bennett, 'The Author and His Public', pp. 18–19.
7    A. L. Rowse, *The England of Elizabeth: The Structure of Society* (1950), p. 503.
8    Material on Tudor and Stuart schools has been derived from Adamson's article (n. 3 above); Curtis, *History of Education in Great Britain*, chap. ii; Wright, *Middle-Class Culture in Elizabethan England*, chap. iii; Rowse, *The England of Elizabeth*, chap. xii; and general histories of the period. These draw upon specialized earlier studies of the subject, notably those by A. F. Leach.
9    Rowse, p. 496.
10   Wright, pp. 17–18.
11   Richard F. Jones, *The Triumph of the English Language* (Stanford, Calif., 1953), pp. 36 ff.
12   Plant, *The English Book Trade*, p. 83.
13   Ibid., pp. 92–93. Occasionally a printer evaded this regulation by setting aside his types after the legal maximum of copies had been struck off, and then reusing them after a prudent interval for a 'new edition'. But type was too scarce to make this a frequent procedure.

14   *Ibid.*, pp. 100–14.

15   A 'sheet' is a piece of paper one side of which is printed in a single operation. After both sides have been printed, it is folded once or several times to form one unit of the prospective book. The practice of selling books at retail in individual sheets – that is, a small section at a time – was a common means of 'cheapening' literature during the nineteenth century.

16   S. C. Roberts, *A History of the Cambridge University Press* (Cambridge, 1921), pp. 34–38.

17   Plant, pp. 84–85.

18   *Ibid.*, p. 93; W. W. Greg, *Some Aspects and Problems of London Publishing between 1550 and 1650* (Oxford, 1956), p. 16.

19   Communication by Alcuin Shields, O.F.M., *Times Literary Supplement*, February 22, 1952, p. 141.

20   Stanley Gardner, *Times Literary Supplement*, March 7, 1952, p. 173. This letter and an accompanying one by H. John McLachlan provide much information, garnered from contemporary sources, on the number of copies printed at a single impression in the seventeenth century.

21   David Masson, *The Life of John Milton* (1894), VI, 510, 628.

22   Only after the Restoration did booksellers begin to adopt fixed prices; until then, they asked whatever the customer could be induced to pay. Hence such figures as we have for the period before 1660 are for individual transactions, and they may or may not represent the average selling price. Nor are the records always clear as to whether the price given is for a volume in its bound or unbound state. Binding could as much as double the price of a book.

23   Bennett, *English Books and Readers*, p. 233.

24   *The Day-Book of John Dorne, Bookseller in Oxford, A.D. 1520*, ed. F. Madan, *Collecteana*, Ser. 1, Part III (Oxford Historical Society, 1885).

25   Johnson, 'Notes on English Retail Book-Prices, 1550–1640' (the most detailed survey of the subject, as Bennett's *English Books and Readers* is for the period just preceding); Plant. p. 240.

26   Alfred Harbage, *Shakespeare's Audience* (New York, 1941), pp. 55–62. J. E. Thorold Rogers, *A History of Agriculture and Prices in England* [*1259–1793*] (Oxford, 1866–1902), Vols. V and VI, gives masses of figures for sixteenth- and seventeenth-century wages and commodity prices. The prices, unfortunately, are almost always wholesale; very few retail prices are available. Figures for London wages are only approximate, since few city wages for these centuries are known to economic historians. They are reckoned on the assumption that the pay scale in London was at least a third higher than in the country. It may sometimes have been double the country rate.

27   Plant, p. 42.

28   Johnson, p. 93.

29   Based on advertised prices for books published in 1668–69: *Term Catalogues, 1668–1709*, ed. Edward Arber (1903–1906), I, 1–7.

30   From household accounts of the Russell family at Woburn: Gladys S. Thomson, *Life in a Noble Household, 1641—1700* (1937), pp. 137, 166–67, 198. This volume gives hundreds of figures for food, clothing, and other expenses in the middle and late seventeenth century.

31   Pepys, *Diary*, under dates of September 7 and 8, 1667, and January 1, 1667/68. Pepys's entries for April 13–17, 1668, contain many records of everyday expenses such as cab fare and meals.

32   Gregory King's estimate of the annual incomes of the various classes of society; frequently reprinted, e.g., in G. N. Clark, *The Later Stuarts* (Oxford, 1934), p. 25.

33   Wright, *Middle-Class Culture*, pp. 76 n., 84–85. On other Elizabethan book collectors, see Phoebe Sheavyn, *The Literary Profession in the Elizabethan Age* (Manchester, 1909), pp. 150–51, and Raymond Irwin in *Library Association Record*, LVI (1954), 195–201.

34   Sheavyn, p. 149; Mildred L. Campbell, *The English Yeoman under Elizabeth and the Early Stuarts* (New Haven, 1942), pp. 266–68.

35 *Inangural Address Delivered to the University of St. Andrews* (1867), p. 89.

36 *History of the English People in 1815*, p. 457.

37 Quoted by David Daiches, *The King James Version of the English Bible* (Chicago, 1941), pp. 38–59.

38 *Ibid.*, *passim*.

39 David Mathew, *The Social Structure in Caroline England* (Oxford, 1948), p. 95.

40 Esmé Wingfield-Stratford, *The History of British Civilization* (1928), I, 563.

41 Bennett, 'Caxton and His Public', *passim*.

42 See John E. Mason, *Gentlefolk in the Making* (Philadelphia, 1935).

43 Wright, pp. 102–103, 301.

44 Pepys permitted himself to read Helot's *L'Escole des Filles* before throwing it into the fire on the ground that, though it was a 'mighty lewd book', yet it was 'not amiss for a sober man once to read over to inform himself in the villainy of the world' (*Diary*, entry for February 9, 1667/68). The rationalization is thoroughly in the spirit of his class and time.

45 William Haller, *The Rise of Puritanism* (New York, 1938), pp. 32–33.

46 *Aubrey's Brief Lives*, ed. O. L. Dick (1949), p. xxix.

47 *Areopagitica*.

# Chapter 27

# Stanley Fish

## INTERPRETING THE *VARIORUM*

### Undoing the case for reader-response analysis

The assumptions to which I stand opposed – the assumption that there *is* a sense, that it is embedded or encoded in the text, and that it can be taken in at a single glance – are, in order, positivist, holistic, and spatial, and to have them is to be committed both to a goal and to a procedure. The goal is to settle on a meaning, and the procedure involves first stepping back from the text, and then putting together or otherwise calculating the discrete units of significance it contains. My quarrel with this procedure (and with the assumptions that generate it) is that in the course of following it through the reader's activities are at once ignored and devalued. They are ignored because the text is taken to be self-sufficient – everything is *in* it – and they are devalued because when they are thought of at all, they are thought of as the disposable machinery of extraction. In the procedures I would urge, the reader's activities are at the center of attention, where they are regarded not as leading to meaning but as *having* meaning. The meaning they have is a consequence of their not being empty; for they include the making and revising of assumptions, the rendering and regretting of judgments, the coming to and abandoning of conclusions, the giving and withdrawing of approval, the specifying of causes, the asking of questions, the supplying of answers, the solving of puzzles. In a word, these activities are interpretive – rather than being preliminary to questions of value, they are at every moment settling and resettling questions of value – and because they are interpretive, a description of them will also be, and without any additional step, an interpretation, not after the fact but of the fact (of experiencing). It will be a description of a moving field of concerns, at once wholly present (not waiting for meaning but constituting meaning) and continually in the act of reconstituting itself.

As a project such a description presents enormous difficulties, and there is hardly time to consider them here;[1] but it should be obvious how different it is from the positivist-formalist project. Everything depends on the temporal dimension, and as a consequence the notion of a mistake, at least as something to be avoided, disappears. In a sequence where a reader first structures the field he inhabits and then is asked to restructure it (by changing an assignment of speaker or realigning attitudes and positions) there is no question of priority among his structurings; no one of them, even if it is the last, has privilege; each is equally legitimate, each equally the proper object of analysis, because each is equally an event in his experience.

The firm assertiveness of this paragraph only calls attention to the questions it avoids. Who is this reader? How can I presume to describe his experiences, and what do I say to readers who report that they do not have the experiences I describe? Let me answer these questions or rather make a beginning at answering them in the context of an example from Milton's *Comus*. In line 46 of *Comus* we are introduced to the villain by way of a genealogy:

> Bacchus that first from out the purple grape,
> Crushed the sweet poison of misused wine.

In almost any edition of this poem, a footnote will tell you that Bacchus is the god of wine. Of course most readers already know that, and because they know it, they will be anticipating the appearance of 'wine' long before they come upon it in the final position. Moreover, they will also be anticipating a negative judgment on it, in part because of the association of Bacchus with revelry and excess, and especially because the phrase 'sweet poison' suggests that the judgment has already been made. At an early point then, we will have both filled in the form of the assertion and made a decision about its moral content. That decision is upset by the word 'misused'; for what 'misused' asks us to do is transfer the pressure of judgment from wine (where we have already placed it) to the abusers of wine, and therefore when 'wine' finally appears, we must declare it innocent of the charges we have ourselves made.

This, then, is the structure of the reader's experience – the transferring of a moral label from a thing to those who appropriate it. It is an experience that depends on a reader for whom the name Bacchus has precise and immediate associations; another reader, a reader for whom those associations are less precise will not have that experience because he will not have rushed to a conclusion in relation to which the word 'misused' will stand as a challenge. Obviously I am discriminating between these two readers and between the two equally real experiences they will have. It is not a discrimination based simply on information, because what is important is not the information itself, but the action of the mind which its possession makes possible for one reader and impossible for the other. One might discriminate further between them by noting that the point at issue – whether value is a function of objects and actions or of intentions – is at the heart of the seventeenth-century debate over 'things indifferent'. A reader who is aware of that debate will not only *have* the experience I describe; he will recognize at the end of it that he has been asked to take a position on one side of a continuing controversy; and that recognition (also a part of his experience) will be part of the disposition with which he moves into the lines that follow.

It would be possible to continue with this profile of the optimal reader, but I would not get very far before someone would point out that what I am really describing is the intended reader, the reader whose education, opinions, concerns, linguistic competences, and so on make him capable of having the experience the author wished to provide. I would not resist this characterization because it seems obvious that the efforts of readers are always efforts to discern and therefore to realize (in the sense of becoming) an author's intention. I would only object if that realization were conceived narrowly, as the single act of comprehending an author's purpose, rather than (as I would conceive it) as the succession of acts readers perform in the continuing assumption that they are dealing with intentional beings. In this view discerning an intention is no more or less than understanding, and understanding includes (is constituted by) all the activities which make up what I call the structure of the reader's experience. To describe that experience is therefore to describe the reader's efforts at understanding, and to describe the reader's efforts at understanding is to describe his realization (in two senses) of an author's intention. Or to put it another way, what my analyses amount to are descriptions of a succession of decisions made by readers about an author's intention – decisions that are not limited to the specifying of purpose but include the specifying of every aspect of successively intended worlds, decisions that are precisely the shape, because they are the content, of the reader's activities.

Having said this, however, it would appear that I am open to two objections. The first is that the procedure is a circular one. I describe the experience of a reader who in his strategies is answerable to an author's intention, and I specify the author's intention by pointing to the strategies employed by that same reader. But this objection would have force only if it were possible to specify one independently of the other. What is being specified from either perspective are the conditions of utterance, of what could have been understood to have been meant by what was said. That is, intention and understanding are two ends of a conventional act, each of which necessarily stipulates (includes, defines, specifies) the other. To construct the profile of the informed or at-home reader is at the same time to characterize the author's intention and vice versa, because to do either is to specify the *contemporary* conditions of utterance, to identify, by becoming a member of, a community made up of those who share interpretive strategies.

The second objection is another version of the first: if the content of the reader's experience is the succession of acts he performs in search of an author's intentions, and if he performs those acts at the bidding of the text, does not the text then produce or contain everything – intention *and* experience – and have I not compromised my antiformalist position? This objection will have force only if the formal patterns of the text are assumed to exist independently of the reader's experience, for only then can priority be claimed for them. Indeed, the claims of independence and priority are one and the same; when they are separated it is so that they can give circular and illegitimate support to each other. The question 'do formal features exist independently'? is usually answered by pointing to their priority: they are 'in' the text before the reader comes to it. The question 'are formal features prior?' is usually answered by pointing to their independent status: they are 'in' the text before the reader comes to it. What looks like a step in an argument is actually the spectacle of an assertion supporting itself. It follows then that an attack on the independence of formal features will also be an attack on their priority (and vice versa), and I would like to mount such an attack in the context of two short passages from *Lycidas*.

The first passage (actually the second in the poem's sequence) begins at line 42:

> The willows and the hazel copses green
> Shall now no more be seen,
> Fanning their joyous leaves to thy soft lays.

It is my thesis that the reader is always making sense (I intend 'making' to have its literal force), and in the case of these lines the sense he makes will involve the assumption (and therefore the creation) of a completed assertion after the word 'seen', to wit, the death of Lycidas has so affected the willows and the hazel copses green that, in sympathy, they will wither and die (will no more be seen by *anyone*). In other words, at the end of line 43 the reader will have hazarded an interpretation, or performed an act of perceptual closure, or made a decision as to what is being asserted. I do not mean that he has done four things, but that he has done one thing the description of which might take any one of four forms – making sense, interpreting, performing perceptual closure, deciding about what is intended. (The importance of this point will become clear later.) Whatever he has done (that is, however we characterize it), he will undo it in the act of reading the next line, for here he discovers that his closure, or making of sense, was premature and that he must make a new one in which the relationship between man and nature is exactly the reverse of what was first assumed. The willows and the hazel copses green will in fact be seen, but they will not be seen by Lycidas. It is he who will be no more, while they go on as before, fanning their joyous leaves to someone else's soft lays (the whole of line 44 is now perceived as modifying and removing the absoluteness of 'seen'). Nature is not sympathetic, but indifferent, and the notion of her sympathy is one of those 'false surmises' that the poem is continually encouraging and then disallowing.

The previous sentence shows how easy it is to surrender to the bias of our critical language and begin to talk as if poems, not readers or interpreters, did things. Words like 'encourage' and 'disallow' (and others I have used in this essay) imply agents, and it is only 'natural' to assign agency first to an author's intentions and then to the forms that assumedly embody them. What really happens, I think, is something quite different: rather than intention and its formal realization producing interpretation (the 'normal' picture), interpretation creates intention and its formal realization by creating the conditions in which it becomes possible to pick them out. In other words, in the analysis of these lines from *Lycidas* I did what critics always do: I 'saw' what my interpretive principles permitted or directed me to see, and then I turned around and attributed what I had 'seen' to a text and an intention. What my principles direct me to 'see' are readers performing acts; the points at which I find (or to be more precise, declare) those acts to have been performed become (by a sleight of hand) demarcations *in* the text; those demarcations are then available for the designation 'formal features', and as formal features they can be (illegitimately) assigned the responsibility for producing the interpretation which in fact produced them. In this case, the demarcation my interpretation calls into being is placed at the end of line 42; but of course the end of that (or any other) line is worth noticing or pointing out only because my model *demands* (the word is not too strong) perceptual closures and therefore locations at which they occur; in that model this point will be one of those locations, although (1) it need not have been (not every line ending occasions a closure) and (2) in another model, one that does not give value to the activities of readers, the possibility of its being one would not have arisen.

What I am suggesting is that formal units are always a function of the interpretative model one brings to bear; they are not 'in' the text, and I would make the same argument for intentions. That is, intention is no more embodied 'in' the text than are formal units; rather an intention, like a formal unit, is made when perceptual or interpretive closure is hazarded; it is verified by an interpretive act, and I would add, it is not verifiable in any other way. This last assertion is too large to be fully considered here, but I can sketch out the argumentative sequence I would follow were I to consider it: intention is known when and only when it is recognized; it is recognized as soon as you decide about it; you decide about it as soon as you make a sense; and you make a sense (or so my model claims) as soon as you can.

Let me tie up the threads of my argument with a final example from *Lycidas*:

> He must not float upon his wat'ry bier
> Unwept . . .                                                                 (13–14)

Here the reader's experience has much the same career as it does in lines 42–44: at the end of line 13 perceptual closure is hazarded, and a sense is made in which the line is taken to be a resolution bordering on a promise: that is, there is now an expectation that something will be done about this unfortunate situation, and the reader anticipates a call to action, perhaps even a program for the undertaking of a rescue mission. With 'Unwept', however, that expectation and anticipation are disappointed, and the realization of that disappointment will be inseparable from the making of a new (and less comforting) sense: nothing will be done; Lycidas will continue to float upon his wat'ry bier, and the only action taken will be the lamenting of the fact that no action will be efficacious, including the actions of speaking and listening to this lament (which in line 15 will receive the meretricious and self-mocking designation 'melodious tear'). Three 'structures' come into view at precisely the same moment, the moment when the reader having resolved a sense unresolves it and makes a new one; that moment will also be the moment of picking out a formal pattern or unit, end of line/beginning of line, and it will also be the moment at which the reader, having decided about the speaker's intention, about what is meant by what has been said, will make the decision again and in so doing will make another intention.

This, then, is my thesis: that the form of the reader's experience, formal units, and the structure of intention are one, that they come into view simultaneously, and that therefore the questions of priority and independence do not arise. What does arise is another question: what produces *them*? That is, if intention, form, and the shape of the reader's experience are simply different ways of referring to (different perspectives on) the same interpretive act, what is that act an interpretation *of*? I cannot answer that question, but neither, I would claim, can anyone else, although formalists try to answer it by pointing to patterns and claiming that they are available independently of (prior to) interpretation. These patterns vary according to the procedures that yield them: they may be statistical (number of two-syllable words per hundred words), grammatical (ratio of passive to active constructions, or of right-branching to left-branching sentences, or of anything else); but whatever they are I would argue that they do not lie innocently in the world but are themselves constituted by an interpretive act, even if, as is often the case, that act is unacknowledged. Of course, this is as true of my analyses as it is of anyone else's. In the examples offered here I appropriate the notion 'line ending' and treat it as a fact of nature; and one might conclude that as a fact it is responsible for the reading experience I describe. The truth I think is exactly the reverse: line endings exist by virtue of perceptual strategies rather than the other way around. Historically, the strategy that we know as 'reading (or hearing) poetry' has included paying attention to the line as a unit, but it is precisely that attention which has made the line as a unit (either of print or of aural duration) available. A reader so practiced in paying that attention that he regards the line as a brute fact rather than as a convention will have a great deal of difficulty with concrete poetry; if he overcomes that difficulty, it will not be because he has learned to ignore the line as a unit but because he will have acquired a new set of interpretive strategies (the strategies constitutive of 'concrete poetry reading') in the context of which the line as a unit no longer exists. In short, what is noticed is what has been *made* noticeable, not by a clear and undistorting glass, but by an interpretive strategy.

This may be hard to see when the strategy has become so habitual that the forms it yields seem part of the world. We find it easy to assume that alliteration as an effect depends on a 'fact' that exists independently of any interpretive 'use' one might make of it, the fact that words in proximity begin with the same letter. But it takes only a moment's reflection to realize that the sameness, far from being natural, is enforced by an orthographic convention; that is to say, it is the product of an interpretation. Were we to substitute phonetic conventions for orthographic ones (a 'reform' traditionally urged by purists), the supposedly 'objective' basis for alliteration would disappear because a phonetic transcription would require that we distinguish between the initial sounds of those very words that enter into alliterative relationships; rather than conforming to those relationships, the rules of spelling make them. One might reply that, since alliteration is an aural rather than a visual phenomenon when poetry is heard, we have unmediated access to the physical sounds themselves and hear 'real' similarities. But phonological 'facts' are no more uninterpreted (or less conventional) than the 'facts' of orthography; the distinctive features that make articulation and reception possible are the product of a system of differences that must be *imposed* before it can be recognized; the patterns the ear hears (like the patterns the eye sees) are the patterns its perceptual habits make available.

One can extend this analysis forever, even to the 'facts' of grammar. The history of linguistics is the history of competing paradigms, each of which offers a different account of the constituents of language. Verbs, nouns, cleft sentences, transformations, deep and surface structures, semes, rhemes, tagmemes – now you see them, now you don't, depending on the descriptive apparatus you employ. The critic who confidently rests his analyses on the bedrock of syntactic descriptions is resting on an interpretation; the facts he points to *are* there, but only as a consequence of the interpretive (man-made) model that has called them into being.

The moral is clear: the choice is never between objectivity and interpretation but between an interpretation that is unacknowledged as such and an interpretation that is at least aware of itself. It is this awareness that I am claiming for myself.

## Interpretive communities

It seems then that the price one pays for denying the priority of either forms or intentions is an inability to say how it is that one ever begins. Yet we do begin, and we continue, and because we do there arises an immediate counterobjection to the preceding pages. If interpretive acts are the source of forms rather than the other way around, why isn't it the case that readers are always performing the same acts or a sequence of random acts, and therefore creating the same forms or a random succession of forms? How, in short, does one explain these two 'facts' of reading? (1) The same reader will perform differently when reading two 'different' (the word is in quotation marks because its status is precisely what is at issue) texts; and (2) different readers will perform similarly when reading the 'same' (in quotes for the same reason) text. That is to say, both the stability of interpretation among readers and the variety of interpretation in the career of a single reader would seem to argue for the existence of something independent of and prior to interpretive acts, something which produces them. I will answer this challenge by asserting that both the stability and the variety are functions of interpretive strategies rather than of texts.

Let us suppose that I am reading *Lycidas*. What is it that I am doing? First of all, what I am not doing is 'simply reading', an activity in which I do not believe because it implies the possibility of pure (that is, disinterested) perception. Rather, I am proceeding on the basis of (at least) two interpretive decisions. (1) that *Lycidas* is a pastoral and (2) that it was written by Milton. (I should add that the notions 'pastoral' and 'Milton' are also interpretations; that is, they do not stand for a set of indisputable, objective facts; if they did, a great many books would not now be getting written.) Once these decisions have been made (and if I had not made these I would have made others, and they would be consequential in the same way), I am immediately predisposed to perform certain acts, to 'find', by looking for, themes (the relationship between natural processes and the careers of men, the efficacy of poetry or of any other action), to confer significances (on flowers, streams, shepherds, pagan deities), to mark out 'formal' units (the lament, the consolation, the turn, the affirmation of faith, and so on). My disposition to perform these acts (and others; the list is not meant to be exhaustive) constitutes a set of interpretive strategies, which, when they are put into execution, become the large act of reading. That is to say, interpretive strategies are not put into execution after reading (the pure act of perception in which I do not believe); they are the shape of reading, and because they are the shape of reading, they give texts their shape, making them rather than, as it is usually assumed, arising from them. Several important things follow from this account:

(1) I did not have to execute this particular set of interpretive strategies because I did not have to make those particular interpretive (pre-reading) decisions. I could have decided, for example, that *Lycidas* was a text in which a set of fantasies and defenses find expression. These decisions would have entailed the assumption of another set of interpretive strategies (perhaps like that put forward by Norman Holland in *The Dynamics of Literary Response*) and the execution of that set would have made another text.

(2) I could execute this same set of strategies when presented with texts that did not bear the title (again a notion which is itself an interpretation) *Lycidas, A Pastoral Monody*. I could decide (it is a decision some have made) that *Adam Bede* is a pastoral written by an author who consciously modeled herself on Milton (still remembering that 'pastoral' and 'Milton' are interpretations, not facts in the public domain); or I could decide, as Empson did, that a great many things not usually considered pastoral were in fact to be so read; and either decision would give rise to a set of interpretive strategies, which, when put into action, would *write* the text I write when reading *Lycidas*. (Are you with me?)

(3) A reader other than myself who, when presented with *Lycidas*, proceeds to put into execution a set of interpretive strategies similar to mine (how he could do so is a question I will take up later), will perform the same (or at least a similar) succession of interpretive acts. He and I then might be tempted to say that we agree about the poem (thereby assuming that the poem exists independently of the acts either of us performs); but what we really would agree about is the way to write it.

(4) A reader other than myself who, when presented with *Lycidas* (please keep in mind that the status of *Lycidas* is what is at issue), puts into execution a different set of interpretive strategies will perform a different succession of interpretive acts. (I am assuming, it is the article of my faith, that a reader will always execute some set of interpretive strategies and therefore perform some succession of interpretive acts.) One of us might then be tempted to complain to the other that we could not possibly be reading the same poem (literary criticism is full of such complaints) and he would be right; for each of us would be reading the poem he had made.

The large conclusion that follows from these four smaller ones is that the notions of the 'same' or 'different' texts are fictions. If I read *Lycidas* and *The Waste Land* differently (in fact I do not), it will not be because the formal structures of the two poems (to term them such is also an interpretive decision) call forth different interpretive strategies but because my predisposition to execute different interpretive strategies will produce different formal structures. That is, the two poems are different because I have decided that they will be. The proof of this is the possibility of doing the reverse (that is why point 2 is so important). That is to say, the answer to the question 'why do different texts give rise to different sequences of interpretive acts?' is that *they don't have to*, an answer which implies strongly that 'they' don't exist. Indeed, it has always been possible to put into action interpretive strategies designed to make all texts one, or to put it more accurately, to be forever making the same text. Augustine urges just such a strategy, for example, in *On Christian Doctrine* where he delivers the 'rule of faith' which is of course a rule of interpretation. It is dazzlingly simple: everything in the Scriptures, and indeed in the world when it is properly read, points to (bears the meaning of) God's love for us and our answering responsibility to love our fellow creatures for His sake. If only you should come upon something which does not at first seem to bear this meaning, that 'does not literally pertain to virtuous behavior or to the truth of faith', you are then to take it 'to be figurative' and proceed to scrutinize it 'until an interpretation contributing to the reign of charity is produced'. This then is both a stipulation of what meaning there is and a set of directions for finding it, which is of course a set of directions – of interpretive strategies – for making it, that is, for the endless reproduction of the same text. Whatever one may think of this interpretive program, its success and ease of execution are attested to by centuries of Christian exegesis. It is my contention that any interpretive program, any set of interpretive strategies, can have a similar success, although few have been as spectacularly successful as this one. (For some time now, for at least three hundred years, the most successful interpretive program has gone under the name 'ordinary language'.) In our own discipline programs with the same characteristic of always reproducing one text include psychoanalytic criticism, Robertsonianism (always threatening to extend its sway into later and later periods), numerology (a sameness based on the assumption of innumerable fixed differences).

The other challenging question – 'why will different readers execute the same interpretive strategy when faced with the "same" text?' – can be handled in the same way. The answer is again that *they don't have to*, and my evidence is the entire history of literary criticism. And again this answer implies that the notion 'same text' is the product of the possession by two or more readers of similar interpretive strategies.

But why should this ever happen? Why should two or more readers ever agree, and why should regular, that is, habitual, differences in the career of a single reader ever occur? What is the explanation on the one hand of the stability of interpretation (at least among certain groups at certain times) and on the other of the orderly variety of interpretation if it is not the stability and variety of texts? The answer to all of these questions is to be found in a notion that has been implicit in my argument, the notion of *interpretive communities*. Interpretive communities are made up of those who share interpretive strategies not for reading (in the conventional sense) but for writing texts, for constituting their properties and assigning their intentions. In other words, these strategies exist prior to the act of reading and therefore determine the shape of what is read rather than, as is usually assumed, the other way around. If it is an article of faith in a particular community that there are a variety of texts, its members will boast a repertoire of strategies for making them. And if a community believes in the existence of only one text, then the single strategy its members employ will be forever writing it. The first community will accuse the members of the second of being reductive, and they in turn will call their accusers superficial. The assumption in each community will be that the other is not correctly perceiving the 'true text', but the truth will be that each perceives the text (or texts) its interpretive strategies demand and call into being. This, then, is the explanation both for the stability of interpretation among different readers (they belong to the same community) and for the regularity with which a single reader will employ different interpretive strategies and thus make different texts (he belongs to different communities). It also explains why there are disagreements and why they can be debated in a principled way: not because of a stability in texts, but because of a stability in the makeup of interpretive communities and therefore in the opposing positions they make possible. Of course this stability is always temporary (unlike the longed for and timeless stability of the text). Interpretive communities grow larger and decline, and individuals move from one to another; thus, while the alignments are not permanent, they are always there, providing just enough stability for the interpretive battles to go on, and just enough shift and slippage to assure that they will never be settled. The notion of interpretive communities thus stands between an impossible ideal and the fear which leads so many to maintain it. The ideal is of perfect agreement and it would require texts to have a status independent of interpretation. The fear is of interpretive anarchy, but it would only be realized if interpretation (text making) were completely random. It is the fragile but real consolidation of interpretive communities that allows us to talk to one another, but with no hope or fear of ever being able to stop.

In other words interpretive communities are no more stable than texts because interpretive strategies are not natural or universal, but learned. This does not mean that there is a point at which an individual has not yet learned any. The ability to interpret is not acquired; it is constitutive of being human. What is acquired are the ways of interpreting and those same ways can also be forgotten or supplanted, or complicated or dropped from favor ('no one reads that way anymore'). When any of these things happens, there is a corresponding change in texts, not because they are being read differently, but because they are being written differently.

The only stability, then, inheres in the fact (at least in my model) that interpretive strategies are always being deployed, and this means that communication is a much more chancy affair than we are accustomed to think it. For if there are no fixed texts, but only interpretive strategies making them, and if interpretive strategies are not natural, but learned (and are therefore unavailable to a finite description), what is it that utterers (speakers, authors, critics, me, you) do? In the old model utterers are in the business of handing over ready-made or prefabricated meanings. These meanings are said to be encoded, and the code is assumed to be in the world independently of the individuals who are obliged to attach themselves to it (if they do not they run the danger of being declared deviant). In my model, however, meanings are not extracted but made and made not by encoded forms but by interpretive strategies that call forms into being. It follows then that what utterers do is give hearers and readers the opportunity to make meanings (and texts) by inviting them to put into execution a set of strategies. It is presumed that the invitation will be recognized, and that presumption rests on a projection on the part of a speaker or author of the moves he would make if confronted by the sounds or marks he is uttering or setting down.

It would seem at first that this account of things simply reintroduces the old objection; for isn't this an admission that there is after all a formal encoding, not perhaps of meanings, but of the directions for making them, for executing interpretive strategies? The answer is that they will only *be* directions to those who already have the interpretive strategies in the first place. Rather than producing interpretive acts, they are the product of one. An author hazards his projection, not because of something 'in' the marks, but because of something he assumes to be in his reader. The very existence of the 'marks' is a function of an interpretive community, for they will be recognized (that is, made) only by its members. Those outside that community will be deploying a different set of interpretive strategies (interpretation cannot be withheld) and will therefore be making different marks.

So once again I have made the text disappear, but unfortunately the problems do not disappear with it. If everyone is continually executing interpretive strategies and in that act constituting texts, intentions, speakers, and authors, how can any one of us know whether or not he is a member of the same interpretive community as any other of us? The answer is that he can't, since any evidence brought forward to support the claim would itself be an interpretation (especially if the 'other' were an author long dead). The only 'proof' of membership is fellowship, the nod of recognition from someone in the same community, someone who says to you what neither of us could ever prove to a third party: 'we know'. I say it to you now, knowing full well that you will agree with me (that is, understand) only if you already agree with me.

## Notes

1    See my *Surprised by Sin: The Reader in Paradise Lost* (London and New York: Macmillan, 1967); *Self-Consuming Artifacts: The Experience of Seventeenth-Century Literature* (Berkeley: University of California Press, 1972); *Is There a Text in This Class?* (Cambridge: Harvard University Press, 1980): 'What Is Stylistics and Why Are They Saying Such Terrible Things About It'? (chap. 2); 'How Ordinary Is Ordinary Language'? (chap. 3); 'Facts and Fictions: A Reply to Ralph Rader' (chap. 5).

# Chapter 28

# Janice Radway

## A FEELING FOR BOOKS

## The Book-of-the-Month Club, literary taste and middle-class desire

### Books are for readers

When Harry Scherman laid out his original plan for the Book-of-the-Month Club in 1926, he made it clear that he understood implicitly how the literary field was configured. He also demonstrated a canny sense of how his projected operation would likely challenge the traditional understanding of that configuration. Scherman suggested that he planned to create his committee of selection as a way of acknowledging the dominant view of the literary field as a special domain dealing with a category of printed objects distinctly different from all things commercial.[1] As he himself later put it, 'Obviously, there would be suspicion that the books which would be presented to subscribers would be presented for *commercial* reasons.' To counter that assumption, 'there had to be some real assurance that the books that were going to be sent to them . . . were chosen for their *quality* as really desirable books. That necessitated a committee', he added. 'The members of it had to be known to the public as completely disinterested people.'[2] The original selection committee was established, therefore, to foreground the status of his books as literary objects rather than their role as commodities bound for circulation through the market.

After he hired Henry Canby, Dorothy Canfield Fisher, Heywood Broun, Christopher Morley, and William Allen White, however, Harry Scherman empowered them to do more than function as a concession to the dominant view of publishing. He asked them to provide something other than a mere testimonial to the quality of the merchandise offered by the club. In fact, he asked the committee members to make determinations about the quality of the merchandise itself, and more importantly, he asked them to determine their own criteria for making such determinations in the first place. Neither he nor his partners interfered in their deliberations. They left it to the judges to work out procedures and criteria for selecting the best book of the month. As I have already indicated, however, the committee had its own ideas about how to think about the literary field and about the nature of literary production. Consequently, only a few months into the enterprise, Dorothy Canfield Fisher and her colleagues urged Scherman to rethink some of the basic operating assumptions of the club.

As we have already seen, Fisher was instrumental in promoting reconsideration. She objected to the advertised premise of Harry Scherman's new organization, the idea that one book, better than all the rest, could be identified every month. She worried that promotion of a single title would obscure all the other worthy books published at the same time. And those books, she suggested, should not necessarily be compared with one another. Books were different, just as readers were different. Fisher conceived of her role at the club as a kind of scout on behalf of a variety of readers. She was attempting to match prospective readers with titles that would appropriately and effectively address their needs. Thus she urged Scherman to allow the judges to recommend more than the designated book of the month.

Fisher and the rest of the judges seem to have worried less about the commercial orientation of the Book-of-the-Month Club than Harry Scherman did. William Allen White, who expressed skepticism about his suitability for a literary undertaking when first approached by Scherman, wrote later in a letter to him that 'now if I am worth anything to you it is [as] a mentor on that side of the merchandising operation'.[3] Joan Rubin has shown that he often pronounced books 'salable' and expressed concern about how the committee's more literary selections would affect the club's 'business proposition'.[4] Similarly, Christopher Morley's talents as a book promoter, which he displayed with great panache in his column 'The Bowling Green', accorded well with the fundamental purposes of the Book-of-the-Month Club, which despite Harry Scherman's queasiness and organizational caveats, was commercial to its very core. Antiquarian and bibliophile though he was, Morley did not envision books as static, shelved, or cherished objects alone. For him they achieved their true vitality and dynamic promise only in the hands of active readers.

One of Morley's first literary successes was the novel *Parnassus on Wheels*, which chronicled the activities of a peripatetic bookseller devoted to making books accessible to ordinary people.[5] And at the end of *Ex Libris Carissimis*, a 1932 collection of his essays, he appended a list of his favorite books, which he troped as 'Golden Florins'. For him classics were not eternal treasures in some literary museum but value-bearing, circulating currency.[6] Morley also sought to familiarize the readers of his columns with something other than 'the best books'. He discussed all sorts of writers, major and minor; the latter category he justified by saying that 'some of the most exquisite pleasures of print are to be found in pursuit of the smaller names'.[7]

The Book-of-the-Month Club judges, like the organization they were hired to assist (and like Melvil Dewey, the cheap libraries, and the creators of the Harvard Classics), were devoted to the cause of the circulating book. In their minds the value of a book was not fixed once and for all at the moment of its creation but was established and reestablished anew in the process of exchange every time it made its way into the hands of readers who found particular uses for it in keeping with their own peculiar aims. Even Henry Canby, by all accounts the most literary of the judges, once observed that 'the primary object of all writing about books is to give them currency'.[8] This was especially necessary, he believed, in the bewildering and confusing modern age because people relied on books and literature to tell them how to make sense of the new forms of life that swirled so meaninglessly about them.

In fact, as I have indicated before, Canby left the professoriate to take up the activity of book reviewing because he felt that the conservatism of the literary academy prevented him from devoting his attention to the all-important task of searching out a literature appropriate to the modern age. 'We are not concerned to know only whether Joyce's "Ulysses" is inferior to Homer's or O'Neill's plays to the tragedies of Euripides,' he once wrote. 'Our chief interest is in interpretations not comparisons. We would know what these modern works . . . are good for, what are their defects, and how they might have been bettered.'[9] Canby's turn to reviewing was motivated by his fervent belief that the general American public needed to discover a literature that might counter modern skepticism and materialism without turning its back on every aspect of modernity. 'We shall listen to no philosopher or critic,' he wrote, 'who out of ignorance is afraid of the results of science, saying pooh! pooh! to the machines, and resorting to the seventeenth century or the fourth A.D. or B.C.' He continued, 'That life is out of control now is notorious, but it will never be brought back by cursing from a hill top. It is better to try to ride the machines than to pretend that they can be disinvented; wiser to guide a civilization than to oppose it utterly.'[10]

In a sense Henry Canby continued to believe in the power and efficacy of words to address modern dilemmas. It was that faith, in fact, that caused him to worry so insistently about the difficulties of finding a literature adequate to the challenges of modernity in a world where so many more books were being churned out by faster presses and sped-up editorial processes at increasingly profit-minded publishing houses. As he put it, 'Books are being published daily, and some one must tell the busy and none too discriminating public what they are worth – not to mention the librarians who are so engaged in making out triple cards and bibliographies and fitting titles to vague recollections that they have no time left to read.'[11] Canby took up newspaper reviewing out of the conviction that '[the newspapers] alone . . . have kept pace with the growing swarm of published books'. Without the reviews first placed on book pages and then collected in book supplements, he argued, 'the public would have . . . only the advertisements and the publishers' announcements to classify, analyze, and in some measure describe the regiment of books that marches in advance of our civilization'.[12] Henry Canby's commitment to regular reviewing and to the distribution goals of the Book-of-the-Month Club was a function of his belief that books could effectively provide the guidance modern people needed to make sense of the unprecedented rate and extent of social change they were forced to confront on a daily basis.

Adumbrated here, it should be clear, is an attitude toward books and, by extrapolation, culture at large that privileges the activities and objectives of circulation and use. Henry Canby was never driven simply by an overwhelming desire to identify the best that had been thought and said in the past. He was motivated by a mission to ensure the utility of books (and other cultural products) by getting them into the hands of people who might best understand them and apply the insights they contained. As he put it, 'The best book is worth nothing at all if it never finds a reader.' He noted as well that 'good reading is a highly personal experience, whose quality depends upon the taste, the intellect, the imagination, and the sensitivity of the individual reader. Still he has to get the books. I find too little in histories of literature and criticism of how books get to readers.'[13]

My point here is that just as Harry Scherman's desire to market new books in an endless stream prompted him to foreground the pleasures and uses of reading as an activity rather than to focus on the particularities of books as singular objects, so the judges' interest in book promotion and their matter-of-fact acquiescence to the market-driven nature of publishing pushed them to focus on the processes of book buying and book reading as well. In effect they installed readers and their differentiated reading activities at the center of their evaluative operation. Not all readers bought books, they knew, and not all book buyers bought books to read. Some books were bought as gifts; some were bought to be displayed. Others were purchased as reference tools or as volumes intended to comprise a personal library. And still others were bought to be read through to the end. In their writings Henry Canby, Dorothy Canfield Fisher, and the others suggested that readers often sought different affective experiences in the act of reading, different relationships to the book they had picked up, and different ends as the goal of the reading process. Ironically, then, despite the larger advertising emphasis on the club's search for the single best book of the month, the judges began to elaborate a practical logic of selection that foregrounded not only the variability of readers and reading but also the variability of the evaluative standards used to find books for them.

Even Henry Canby's more narrow view of specifically 'literary' books accorded with this larger perspective. Although he would continue to believe that the literary had a special role to play in what he called modern civilization, he considered its distinctiveness less a matter of quality and more a difference of kind, function, or purpose. The literary, for Canby, was not necessarily better than other sorts of books, nor was it universally useful. Nor did he believe that all instances of the category 'literature' should be ranked along a single scale of value. Rather, Canby argued that, like works of sociology, psychology, general science, history, and biography, literary books appealed to particular audiences and performed distinct functions. They did so because all books concretized the experience of their authors and because different authors turned their experience to different purposes and goals. Books, like all forms of cultural production, according to Canby, attempted different things for different purposes and with different audiences in mind. Canby felt, therefore, that every book ought to be approached on its own terms if readers would do justice to it and get the most from it that they could. The reviewer's proper task, then, in order to facilitate appropriate connections between books and readers, was to clarify precisely what those terms were. The reviewer's job was to provide an adequate and informative definition of the book as a categorical object of a particular kind.

Canby's earliest collection of 'essays in contemporary criticism' had been issued in 1922 under the title *Definitions* as a way of emphasizing the fact that he offered not a 'sequence of chapters developing a single theme and arriving at categorical conclusions' but, rather, a series of essays, quite literally 'attempts' to illuminate the multiple purposes, means, and achievements of contemporary writers in a confused age.[14] Then, as later, Canby did not consider his criticism an Olympian pronouncement issued from on high, measuring all works against a single, universal standard. Rather, he viewed his essays as a series of attempts to open doors through which both writer and reader may enter into a better comprehension of what novelists, poets, and critics have done or are trying to accomplish'.[15] Such a mediating role was necessary, he believed, because the literary world had grown muddied as a consequence of augmented production and because the general business of evaluation and judgment had been thrown into disarray.

Henry Canby differed crucially from cultural critics such as Waldo Frank and Ernest Boyd in that he did not blame the much-remarked-on evaluative confusion of his era on the abandonment of standards altogether. He argued instead that standards had proliferated drastically. Observing that 'one of the common complaints against this slipshod generation is that it has no standards', he countered, 'not a lack of standards but a confusion of standards is our undoing'.[16] And he well understood that such confusion profoundly unsettled the profession of literary criticism as it had previously been conceived. 'Literary criticism', he wrote, 'has become polytheistic and we worship at so many altars that we cannot ourselves name our literary religion'.[17] For Canby the kind of religion of literature promoted by the modernists and the little magazines was a decided anachronism simply because the assumption of a universal standard on which omniscient judgment could be predicated was no longer possible.

The second most powerful judge, Dorothy Canfield Fisher, held views remarkably similar to Henry Canby's. In fact she insisted even more strongly than he did that literary judgments, evaluations, and descriptions needed to vary with their audiences and their objects. Nonetheless, because she believed that there was a fundamental continuity between literature and life, she treated all books as instrumental guides for living and argued that even fiction could enable readers to broaden their experience and to lead richer, more intense, and honorable lives. Similarly, she championed nonfiction titles when they strove to make their technical knowledge both accessible and useful to the general reader. She was known at the club for her interest in continuing education. Fisher was as aware as Henry Canby that readers differed not only in their interests and tastes but in their education and literary preparation as well. Accordingly, she conceptualized her role at the club as a promoter of many different kinds of interactions between books and readers, and she conceptualized her duty as a reviewer in a manner distinctly different from the way she thought of the activities of the traditional literary critic.

In a report on a book of poems by Marion Canby, for instance, she once expatiated at length on her understanding of the difference between book reviewing and literary criticism.[18] It is worth quoting several passages of her analysis, for they lay out clearly the thinking that was shared by all of the Book-of-the-Month Club judges, and they suggest that the judges were quite aware they were not functioning as traditional critics. 'People of experience agree that one trouble with book reviews could be eliminated by firmly specifying at the head of each one . . . the kind of person for whom it is intended. One sort of review is written for actual readers of books, people of intelligence and taste not professionally literary in any way who, seeing a new volume would like to find a statement about it that gives them a fairly clear idea what is inside it and whether it is the kind of book they would be apt to find worth reading.' Actual readers, Fisher suggested, were quite different from professional readers. Thus they needed something different from what was generally provided in literary criticism. Since the worth of a book was apparently a function of the content it offered to inquiring readers, a review ought to inform them about what they would find between its covers, and it ought to advise them if they would be likely to derive satisfaction or pleasure from reading it.

Literary criticism, on the other hand, because it was aimed at the professional reader, stressed judgment and evaluation rather than information and advice. Fisher suggested, in fact, that 'the [literary] sort of review is intended, consciously or unconsciously, not at all for mere readers of books, but for other critics, and for professionally literary folk whose self-appointed business it is correctly to appraise and accurately to calculate the position of each new piece of creative writing, in relation with what has gone before and is likely to come after it in the history of literature'. Evaluation and judgment, from her point of view, belonged to the province of the literary professional, whose job it was to provide a critical account of literary history and tradition. Fisher clearly believed that professional reading was organized differently from that practiced by the nonprofessional, and she obviously thought both entirely legitimate. She suggested, in fact, that 'both kinds of reviews are interesting, worth-while and of value – but only when read by those for whom they are intended. Each kind is exasperating and disappointing when read by people who are looking for the other kind'.

Significantly, Fisher concluded her report on Marion Canby's poems with the observation 'that the reviews written for the Book of the Month Club News are of the first kind'.[19] Like Henry Canby, then, who had abandoned literary criticism, he once reported, because he 'had shaken off some pedantic ideas and no longer yearned to publish articles that only scholars could understand, which no one, not even scholars did', Fisher seems to have understood that criticism and the books critics tended to find valuable were closely bound up with the interests and concerns of a highly specialized, often heavily trained, and quite small professional audience.[20] Since ordinary readers could derive benefit from many different kinds of books, she suggested, the judges ought to concern themselves with more than the literary, and they ought to report accurately on the nature of those books for the club's subscribers. Although she was willing to include high literary titles on the club's list, she was as careful as Henry Canby was to ask herself whether a large, general audience might find a given title pleasing, compelling, or useful. If the judgment was no, she would argue vigorously for a report in the News that would characterize the book honestly and that would discourage readers who might not be up to its challenge or likely to find it interesting.

Of the April 1928 main selection, for instance, Elizabeth Bowen's The Hotel, the Book-of-the-Month Club News noted that 'it is a book . . . that calls for a more than usually careful characterization to subscribers'. The report continued, 'It must be described, first, as a subtle book.' Obviously hoping to avoid baffled or irate customers and a mountain of returns, the *News* cautioned its readers further:

> Those who enjoy writers like Joseph Conrad, Anatole France, Henry James – and to come closer to today – writers somewhat like H. M. Tomlinson, Willa Cather, Edith Wharton, will exult in it. It will yield its full delight, like an old and rare wine, only to those who take it in with an appreciative and unhurried attention. Those readers, on the other hand, who prefer the straightforward narrative – as exemplified by such novelists as Galsworthy, Tarkington, Bennett and innumerable others – while they cannot fail to appreciate the color and sparkle of this gem, may not be enthusiastic about it. If one is not in a proper mood, indeed, one may even find *The Hotel* annoying by reason of its subtlety, although this would be unfair to a deft piece of work.[21]

Similarly, the next issue of the *News* warned potential readers straightaway that Henry Canby had reported that *Mr Weston's Good Wine*, by T. F. Powys, should be avoided 'if you cannot endure symbolism' or 'if the earthly humors of the all-too-human race, especially in the pursuit of love, shock you easily'. In that case, the *News* concluded bluntly, 'you are advised not to read it'.[22] Apparently neither Canby nor Fisher had any compunctions about warning the club's subscribers away from books they thought distinct literary achievements yet esoteric.

The commentary of Henry Canby and Dorothy Canfield Fisher suggests that the judges believed the principal aim of the Book-of-the-Month Club was not to place books in the long sweep of literary history but to match readers with the books appropriate to them. Following from this premise, the logic of the evaluative system they established at the club in its early years developed three pointed concerns. The judges tried first to determine what sort of book they had before them. Then they attempted to understand why a reader might select this book rather than another. Finally they explored how best to describe that book to make its relevant features known to readers, who would approach it with previously formed expectations, desires, and needs. In the final analysis, despite their presentation to the public as authorities who could magisterially issue pronouncements on the basis of special literary expertise, the Book-of-the-Month Club judges developed an evaluative process that was thoroughly contingent and fundamentally reader driven. They tended to subordinate the critical act of literary judgment to the activity of recommendation. And recommendation, as they practiced it, was a self-consciously social activity constituted by their effort to understand and to adopt the point of view of their subscribers. Once they managed to understand readers' desires, needs, and tastes, they subsequently strove to match those aims to goods and authors already available in the public marketplace. In a sense the judges constituted themselves as social facilitators or mediators trying to foster connections between readers, books, and their authors. Thus they resisted taking up the usual critical distance and pose of superiority found in traditional criticism. More frequently in their daily practice they tried not to dictate on the basis of their own taste but sought to imagine themselves as the readers they aimed to address. Only after they had managed that act of imagination and identification did they turn to the monthly output of the publishing industry and seek particular books for particular readers'.[23]

## The planar logic of middlebrow evaluation

Harry Scherman's judges conceived of their business less as a process of evaluation and judgment than as one of definition and sorting. Their job was to read all the books submitted by the trade, to imagine who might find such books interesting or useful, and then to evaluate how well particular books might satisfy those readers most likely to select them. Since the publishers had been instructed by Scherman to send many different kinds of books to the club, the judges quickly recognized that they could not compare apples to oranges or oranges to grapefruits. Not all books were literary books, and even literary books, the judges believed, varied considerably in form, function, and intent. As Canby himself observed, 'There is – to take the novel – the story well calculated to pass a pleasant hour but able to pass nothing else; there is the story with a good idea in it and worth reading for the idea only; there is the story worthless as art but usefully catching some current phase of experience; and there is the fine novel which will stand any test for insight, skill, and truth.' He continued, 'Now it is folly to apply a single standard to all these types of story. It can be done, naturally, but it accomplishes nothing except to eliminate all but the shining best.'[24] The project at the club, as a consequence, was to proliferate gauges and to multiply evaluative standards. The judges asked what every book was useful for. Even lesser books, with modest aims and intentions, they believed, deserved their readers, and those books could sometimes satisfy and serve their readers better than more ambitious titles.

In effect, then, Henry Canby and his colleagues treated all books that came to them as instances of multiple and multifarious types, that is, as examples of different classes or genera, each with its own peculiar functions and uses. 'Is this serious fiction', they asked themselves, 'or hammock literature?' 'Is this a sea saga or a small woman's novel?' 'Is it popular history or too specialized for the general reader?' 'Is it literary criticism or literary biography?' Only after determining the category did they ask themselves whether a book was any good or not. Having determined that a particular title was a literary biography, for instance, they then asked themselves, 'Is it a *good* literary biography?' 'Does it fail as an entertaining yarn?' they similarly wondered. 'Will it please readers who are partial to nature books?' To answer this latter question about quality, they additionally had to ask themselves what, exactly, characterized an excellent example of a particular kind of book. 'What makes a good nature book good?' they wondered. 'Is it the same quality or set of features that establishes the excellence of a biography or a work of serious fiction?'

The Book-of-the-Month Club judges focused on the diversity and variety of the literary field and on its ability to generate many different kinds of books with different features and different aims. In spite of Harry Scherman's ritual repetition of the claim that the club sent out the best book of the month, in practice the judges deemed this kind of absolute hierarchical grading an impossible and undesirable task. Their work, consequently, contested a hierarchical and pyramidal view of the literary field. Although they continued to recognize the existence of a special aesthetic category called Literature, which they rendered with a capital *L*, they also thought of the literary field itself as a universe encompassing all kinds of print productions. Accordingly, they differentiated books from one another on the basis of their differential functions and variable appeals to readers. In their view books were only comparable if they were of the same genus or type. It made no sense to judge a popular history lacking because its verbal style was undistinguished. Nor was it justifiable to eliminate a rollicking good story because its characters were superficially delineated. This is not to say that at the club the larger field was conceived as an open, free space, lacking in organization and structure. It was quite structured, in fact, but according to a different logic and in respect of different principles.

As a way of getting at that logic and its supporting principles, it might be useful to quote Henry Canby again on the variability of the literary as a special category unto itself. For although Canby continued to group most fictional texts under the sign of the literary, he also subdivided that body of texts on the basis of the functions they could perform for their readers. His comments here come from an essay about the difference between literary criticism and reviewing, a subject that concerned him throughout his career, as it did Dorothy Canfield Fisher. Criticism, Canby also felt, rightly concerned itself with literary values. Reviewing, on the other hand, which he believed properly functioned to inform readers about new books, needed to approach the question of value more flexibly. 'It is sometimes necessary to remind the austerer critic', he wrote, 'that there are a hundred books of poetry, of essays, of biography, of fiction, which are by no means of the first rank and yet are highly important, if only as news of what the world, in our present, is thinking and feeling. They cannot be judged, all of them on the top plane of perfect excellence; and if we judge them on any other plane, good, better, best, get inextricably mixed.'[25] Canby, at least, was willing to judge books on other planes and thus to contest the very idea of good, better, and best judged on one set of aesthetic criteria. Fiction, for instance, could be evaluated for the news it provided of the contemporary world rather than for its linguistic craftsmanship. Canby continued significantly, 'There is no help except to set books upon their planes and assort them into their categories – which is merely to define them before beginning to criticize'. The crucial move in the evaluative practice of the Book-of-the-Month Club judges was not judgment at all but the activity of categorization, of sorting onto different planes.

The concept of different planes, it should be noted, constructs a vision of a print universe conceived of not as an organic, uniform, hierarchically ordered space. Rather, the print universe appears as a series of discontinuous, discrete, noncongruent worlds. Those worlds bring together readers with particular needs and demands and writers with special forms of expertise capable of addressing both. The role prescribed for the critic in a uniform literary world is that of Solomonic, omniscient judge. The disposition best suited to this more differentiated world of particular and locally specific purposes, desires, and goals is closer to that of a manager who has been charged with the smooth functioning of a complex system. The skills required of this literary manager – with the literary defined very broadly to include virtually all kinds of books and print – are more like those of the modern, professional librarian than the critic. Trained to bring together inquiring readers with the appropriate forms of technical expertise capable of answering their questions, the modern librarian is primarily oriented to the needs and tastes of readers. Relying on the card catalog and the innovations of the Dewey system of classification, this individual approaches the world of print not as a single universe but rather as a world of differentiated knowledge-production where language is put to multiple and different uses, where it is deployed differentially to describe and manipulate the world in highly specific, technically distinct ways.

Given this view of the world of print as a series of contiguous and equivalent domains, it should not be surprising to note that the category of Literature was treated by the Book-of-the-Month Club judges with a certain amount of ambiguity. On one hand the club's rhetoric about best books and future classics tended to evoke a sense of the literary as both sacred and transcendent, as the apex of all cultural achievement. On the other hand their day-to-day selection procedures and habits of description tended to construe the literary as only one more category among many. In practice, literary books were treated as books of a certain sort, as a special taste dependent on a high degree of education and familiarity with the complexities of literary history. The insight and enlightenment associated with the literary was offered at the club not as a superior form of knowledge but as a particular and peculiar sort with its own uses and applications, equivalent to yet different from other sorts of knowledge, such as knowledge to be found in works of science, political affairs, or history. Thus the judges' pragmatic approach to the larger literary field challenged the sacred status of Literature and contested its claim as the best that had been thought and said in the world. This does not seem particularly surprising when we consider that they lived in an ever-more-secular world impressed every day by the achievements of modern science and its supporting discourses, which foregrounded the material, the utilitarian, the technological, and the technical.

What I think we see at the Book-of-the-Month Club, then, is a disposition to structure the larger literary field according to a logic congenial to the emergent social group discussed in the previous chapter in connection with the debate over the Book-of-the-Month Club – the professional-managerial class. Increasingly educated to think of the world, whether mechanical, social, or natural, as an infinitely complex universe beyond the comprehension of single persons or even single points of view, individuals aspiring to membership in this group of workers were taught by specialized high school and college curricula to divide the universe into discrete domains and particular provinces, such as sociology, political science, the humanities, science, and history. They were asked to think of each of these areas as capable of being rendered comprehensible by highly specific and technical ways of knowing. Aiming to labor not with their hands but with their minds, these potential knowledge workers were asked to learn particular forms of technical competence and professional expertise and to use both to facilitate better description and manipulation of all that was encompassed by their own special domain. They were to convey the technical knowledge they commanded as specialists and professionals to people who were nonspecialists, to clients, consumers, or students in need of usable versions of such knowledge for pragmatic decision making and the conduct of everyday life.

The multiple planes of the literary field as conceived by the Book-of-the-Month Club judges, it seems to me were structured according to this kind of logic, a planar logic that foregrounded the discreteness and particularity of domains and forms of expertise. This view also emphasized the pragmatic disposition of expertise and its fundamentally instrumental orientation in the service of a putatively general population. In effect expertise was constructed as a positivity in relation to a generality, the generality and lack exhibited by Harry Scherman's general reader, that individual who could not reproduce technical competence but who could, out of need and desire, recognize its claims, revere it, and make use of it for practical ends.

This parallel construction is evident in the way Harry Scherman presented his judges to the public. In fact, he did not simply present Canby, Fisher, Morley, Broun, and White as experts. He simultaneously stressed their orientation to the needs of the general reader. In the first prospectus issued for the club in 1926, for instance, he observed that the selecting committee consisted of 'well-known critics and writers, whose complicity of taste and whose judgment as to books have been demonstrated for many years before the public'.[26] Then, beneath full-page portraits of each expert, he listed their professional credentials, stressing equally their special training and competence as well as their devotion to a broad, general taste. Of Broun, Scherman wrote, 'His reporting revealed a rare critical and descriptive faculty which was fully developed when he became a columnist for *The New York Tribune* and afterward *The New York World*. Since then his comment upon things in general as well as upon the special fields of literature and the theater in which he has become an authority, has been followed by the intelligent with constant delight.'[27] Furthermore, Scherman characterized William Allen White as 'one of the most distinguished editors in America' and noted significantly that 'in addition to service on many delegations and foundations, he is a writer of distinction in pure literature as well as journalism'. He continued, 'His admirable sanity, combined with a courageous and progressive attitude in all affairs involving the American mind, has won general recognition.'[28]

The specialist and the generalist were locked together at the club and, more generally, within American culture at this historical moment, in a relation of mutuality, each serving the other. The specialist labored on behalf of the generalist, who in turn obligingly accorded the specialist respect, legitimacy, and ultimately authority itself. What the Book-of-the-Month Club sold, then, along with its subscriptions and endless stream of new books, was a social framework and cognitive map for understanding and organizing the world. In a social formation and economy increasingly driven by the need to generate, to distribute, and to control myriad forms of information and knowledge, the Book-of-the-Month Club performed the important role of acclimating the professional-managerial class and all who aspired to its status to the assumption that books and the experts who wrote them addressed the particular purposes of general readers. Less an innovative force in achieving national distribution of books than an exercise in social training and pedagogy, the Book-of-the-Month Club functioned more significantly, it seems to me, as a key cultural agency constructing the idea of the general reader, yet ironically modeling and thereby promoting belief in the worth of technical expertise and specialized knowledge.

The club promised such a membership the chance to keep up with the ever-advancing production of new knowledge as well as the opportunity to confirm its identity as educated and au courant. In a sense it assuaged an anxiety instilled by the increasingly specialized and technical curricula of the colleges and universities; it calmed the fear that once one had cut formal ties to institutions of higher education, one ran the risk of being left behind by relentlessly changing, highly specialized fields of knowledge. Although one's ongoing participation in a profession and its key associations would enable one to keep up with one's own field, all those other important fields of knowledge might grow increasingly opaque and incomprehensible to the flagging reader. Thus the Book-of-the-Month Club's many handbooks, outlines, guides, omnibuses, and popularizations helped to alleviate this anxiety and, at the same time, to produce a belief in the naturalness of technical knowledge and special competence as well as a sense that these could be translated for general readers who might thereby benefit practically from their advances and insights.

In dispensing its middlebrow cultural products, then, the club also recommended a particular orientation to those products and the culture they represented, a habitus suitable to a world organized and understood in this way. The club suggested that though knowledge and culture were the province of experts, they were valuable to the extent that they produced practical results and utilitarian effects for general readers. This was true even of fiction, they thought, which aimed sometimes to promote relaxation and escape and at other times to produce aesthetic pleasure. Both knowledge and culture were conceived, therefore, in utilitarian and pragmatic fashion. They were not valuable in and for themselves, according to the Book-of-the-Month Club, but for what they could do.

The middlebrow habitus or orientation toward the world that Canby and company taught was an instrumental one, finally, even when they were speaking about Literature with a capital *L*. Though the club began by appropriating an older, genteel view of culture and knowledge as higher forms of learning capable of ennobling all who came in contact with them, it did so in order to market those forms for its own profit, thereby refuting the notion that culture and intellectual inquiry ought to be thought of as finalities without purposes, as instances of the transcendent. The Book-of-the-Month Club extended its own pragmatic, utilitarian disposition to culture to those it addressed as subscribers by attempting to persuade them that a certain facility with the material contained in books could assure them of social success. Thus, while the club selected and sold serious cultural material and thereby continued to underwrite the notion of a higher, sacred culture of learning and art, it also invited its members to take up a relationship to that culture that was troublesome to those who saw themselves as its authoritative guardians.

For Henry Canby, Dorothy Canfield Fisher, and the rest of the Book-of-the-Month Club judges, all books, including fiction, achieved success and even greatness to the degree that they took up issues of everyday life. Value was also a function of a book's capacity to be used in pragmatic fashion to accomplish a particular end or purpose. The judges were wary of the dispassionate, highly intellectualized aesthetic distance associated with experimental forms of literary modernism and the highly academic criticism that had appeared to legitimate it. As a consequence, their guiding philosophy of book selection was less an aesthetic, in the sense of a philosophy or theory of art, than an ethos, a practical disposition or orientation to books that evaluated them according to how well they harmonized with a reader's moral norms, ethical standards, and expectations about pleasure. The Book-of-the-Month Club judges aimed to distribute more books to more readers not by seeking to elevate literary or aesthetic taste but by pursuing the possibilities of functional alignment, by attempting to match books and readers through a correlation of their most basic perceptual schemes for structuring 'the everyday perception of everyday existence.'[29]

This attention to the variability of readers and reading aims produced an evaluative practice at the Book-of-the-Month Club that was as attentive to minor works of crime fiction as it was to works aspiring to the status of great literature. Although Henry Canby and even Dorothy Canfield Fisher sometimes continued to insist on the value of the literary above all else in their nonclub writings, in their work at the club they treated books as a collection of categorically different objects, each category a subset with its own defining features, operative functions, and potential audience. Together the judges attempted to see the merit in a popular biography just as they tried to describe accurately the potential value in a work of free verse, a volume on foreign affairs, or a book on modern science. Although they continued to try to root out what Henry Canby called cheap vulgarity, none of them were very confident that they knew what that was in an age marked by extreme confusion. Thus they tried to follow the exhortation he had published before in *American Estimates*. Canby wrote, 'Let us fight, then, in despite of time, tide, tendency, against cheap vulgarity in literature. But let us disclaim the reformer's easy distinctions as to what is to be saved and what damned.' He continued significantly, 'If the great first cause has foreordained a vital pictorial art to come from the comic strip, or a new literature from "The Saturday Evening Post," why let them come.' [30] In an age of diversifying audiences, proliferating publications, and the destruction of sure and singular standards, Canby and company felt that it was essential for them as book experts to mill about in the crowd, to take for granted the muddle and confusion, and yet to keep their eyes open to all possibilities.

Not surprisingly, Canby and his colleagues produced an ecumenical practice at the Book-of-the-Month Club that enabled Harry Scherman's distribution machine to send out in 1928 alone Bernard Shaw's *The Intelligent Woman's Guide to Socialism and Capitalism*, Felix Salten's *Bambi*, Stephen Vincent Benét's *John Brown's Body*, Paul de Kruif's *Hunger Fighters*, and a book called *Whither Mankind?* edited by Charles Beard, which the *News* praised both because it represented 'the ripest thought, upon a subject of interest, of some of the leading figures of our day' and because it exhibited 'great readability'.[31] In 1929 they sent out and retracted a book titled *Cradle of the Deep*, which had proved to be a hoax; *The Omnibus of Crime*, edited by Dorothy Sayers; *Kristin Lavransdatter*, by Sigrid Unset, who later won the Nobel Prize; and Walter Lippmann's *A Preface to Morals?*[32] In subsequent years the selection grew even more diverse as the club's judges moved away from their early predilection for serious fiction and toward a more self-conscious attempt to serve the full range of subscriber taste and to represent the varied output of the publishing industry. They increased the number of popular histories they offered and added more biographies, accounts of scientific developments and public affairs, and even medical manuals aimed at middle-class parents eager to implement the newest theories of child development in their own families.

## Notes

1   Harry Scherman, 'Original Outline of Plan for the Book-of-the-Month Club', 4–7.
2   'Reminiscences of Harry Scherman', 41: emphasis added.
3   Quoted in Rubin, *Making of Middlebrow Culture*, 142.
4   *Ibid.*
5   Morley, *Parnassus on Wheels*.

6    Morley, *Ex Libris Carissimis*.

7    Morley, *Streamlines*, 130, quoted in Wallach and Bracker, *Christopher Morley*, 21.

8    Canby, 'Exacting Art'.

9    Canby, 'Post Mortem'.

10   Canby, 'New Humanists'.

11   Canby, *Definitions*, 199–200.

12   *Ibid.*, 188.

13   Canby, *American Memoir*, 357.

14   Canby, *Definitions*, vii.

15   *Ibid.*

16   Canby, *American Estimates*, 199.

17   *Ibid.*, 201.

18   Dorothy Canfield Fisher, review of *High Mowing*, by Marion Canby, box 26, folder 1, 'Activities', Fisher Collection.

19   *Ibid.*

20   Canby, *American Memoir*, 278.

21   *Book-of-the-Month Club News*, March 1928, 1–2 (unpaginated).

22   *Ibid.*, April 1928, 4.

23   Joan Rubin has been the pioneer in taking middlebrow culture seriously. My account, as a result, is heavily indebted to her work. I should point out, however, that our attributes and approaches to the topic of literary criticism diverge significantly. In her account of the activities of the judges, Rubin acknowledges that she herself believes it important to maintain standards in the face of the judges' abnegation of them. She therefore holds them responsible for failing to teach such standards to their subscribers. In keeping with her assumption, Rubin evaluates the judges' activities by measuring the distance they had moved from the more responsible evaluation and pedagogy of the 'true critic'. Indeed, she accuses them of the 'withholding, or underexercise, of critical authority' in their reports for the *Book-of-the-Month Club News* because those reports 'tended to substitute narrative for evaluation, information for aesthetics' (*Making of Middlebrow Culture*, 102). I feel that her assertions are based on the familiar acceptance of the aesthetic as a higher form of human cultural production, of criticism as a higher moral calling, and on a view of standards themselves as in some way obvious, eternal, and universal. I would prefer to see all of these as contingent historical forms serving particular and indentifiable social purposes. I want to suggest that the narrative and information supplied in those reports appeared there because the judges were searching for something other than the aesthetically excellent. Thus they *were* exercising critical authority, but in a form unrecognizable to those who insisted that authority be exercised only as criticism and in the exclusive service of literary and aesthetic values.

24   Canby, *Definitions*, 297.

25   *Ibid.*, 298.

26   Harry Scherman, 'Book-of-the-Month Club', 7.

27   *Ibid.*, 6.

28   *Ibid.*, 12.

29   Bourdieu, *Distinction*, 44. I am drawing here on Bourdieu's arguments about the characteristic petit bourgeois approach to art and culture, an approach distinctly related to that of middlebrow culture.

30   Canby, *American Estimates*, 125.

31   *Book-of-the-Month Club News*, October 1928, 1.

32   For the full list of yearly selections to 1957, see Charles Lee, *Hidden Public*, 161–94.

## References

Bourdieu, Pierre, *Distinction: A Social Critique of the Judgement of Taste*, trans. Richard Nice, Cambridge: Harvard University Press, 1984.

Canby, Henry Seidel, *American Estimates*, London: Jonathan Cape, 1929.

—— *American Memoir*, Boston: Houghton Mifflin, 1947.

—— 'An Exacting Art', *Saturday Review of Literature*, March 1, 1930, 32.

—— *Definitions: Essays in Contemporary Criticism*, New York: Harcourt, Brace, 1922.

—— 'The New Humanists', *Saturday Review of Literature*, February 22, 1930, 751.

—— 'Post Mortem', *Saturday Review of Literature*, June 14, 1930, 1122.

Lee, Charles, *The Hidden Public: The Story of the Book-of-the-Month Club*, Garden City, NY: Doubleday, 1958.

Morley, Christopher, *Parnassus on Wheels*, Philadelphia: Lippincott, 1917.

—— *Ex Libris Carissimis*, Philadelphia: University of Pennsylvania Press, 1951.

Oral History Research Office, Butler Library, Columbia University. The Book of the Month Club. Director, Allan Nevins. Interviews by Louis M. Starr, 1955. 'The Reminiscences of Harry Scherman'.

Rubin, Joan Shelley, *The Making of Middlebrow Culture*, Chapel Hill: University of North Carolina Press, 1992.

Wallach, Mark I., and Jon Bracker, *Christopher Morley*, Boston: Twayne, 1976.

# BIBLIOGRAPHY

## Introduction

Adams, Thomas and Barker, Nicolas (1993) 'A New Model for the Study of the Book', in Nicolas Barker, ed., *A Potencie of Life: Books in Society*, London: British Library.

Bowers, Fredson (1949) *Principles of Bibliographical Description*, Princeton: Princeton University Press.

Bradbury, Ray (1953) *Fahrenheit 451*, New York: Ballantine Press.

Darnton, Robert (1990) 'What is the History of Books', in *The Kiss of Lamourette: Reflections in Cultural History*, New York: Norton, pp. 107–36.

Duguid, Paul (1996) 'Material Matters: The Past and Futurology of the Book', in Geoffrey Nunberg, ed., *The Future of the Book*, Berkeley: University of California Press, pp. 63–101.

Eco, Umberto (1983) *The Name of the Rose*, trans. William Weaver, London: Secker and Warburg.

Eisenstein, Elizabeth (1968) 'Some Conjectures about the Impact of Printing on Western Society and Thought: A Preliminary Report', *Journal of Modern History*, 40, 1–56.

Eisenstein, Elizabeth (1979) *The Printing Press as an Agent of Change*, 2 vols, Cambridge: Cambridge University Press.

Eisenstein, Elizabeth (1983) *The Printing Press as an Agent of Change*, 1 vol. edn, Cambridge: Cambridge University Press.

Escarpit, Robert (1958, 1965) *Sociologie de la Littérature / The Sociology of Literature*, trans. Ernest Pick, Painesville, Ohio: Lake Erie College Press.

Febvre, Lucien and Martin, Henri-Jean (1958) *L'Apparition du Livre*, Paris: Albin Michel.

Febvre, Lucien and Martin, Henri-Jean (1976) *The Coming of the Book: The Impact of Printing, 1450–1800*, English trans., London: Verso.

Greg, W. W. (1966) *Collected Papers*, ed. J. C. Maxwell, Oxford: Clarendon Press.

Johns, Adrian (1998) *The Nature of the Book: Print and Knowledge in the Making*, Chicago: University of Chicago Press.

Jordan, John O. and Patten, Robert L., eds (1995) *Literature in the Marketplace: Nineteenth-Century British Publishing and Reading Practices*, Cambridge: Cambridge University Press.

Landow, George P. (1997) *Hypertext 2.0: The Convergence of Contemporary Critical Theory and Technology*, Baltimore and London: Johns Hopkins University Press.

McGann, J. J. (1991) *The Textual Condition*, Princeton: Princeton University Press.

McKerrow, Ronald B. (1927) *An Introduction to Bibliography for Literary Students*, Oxford: Clarendon Press.

Nunberg, Geoffrey (1993) 'The Place of Books in the Age of Electronic Reproduction', *Representations* 42 (1993): 13–37.

Tanselle, G. T. (1979) *Selected Studies in Bibliography*, Charlottesville: University Press of Virginia, pp. 308–53.

## Part I: What is book history?

Adams, Thomas and Barker, Nicolas (1993) 'A New Model for the Study of the Book', in Nicolas Barker, ed., *A Potencie of Life: Books in Society*, London: British Library.

Balsamo, Luigi (1990) *Bibliography: History of a Tradition*, Berkeley, Ca.: B. M. Rosenthal.

Barker, Nicolas (1993a) 'Intentionality and Reception Theory', in Nicolas Barker, ed., *A Potencie of Life: Books in Society*, London: British Library.

Barker, Nicolas, ed., (1993b) *A Potencie of Life: Books in Society: The Clark Lectures 1986–1987*, London: British Library.

Barthes, Roland (1977) *Image Music Text*, London: Fontana Press.

Barzun, Jacques (1986) *On Writing, Editing and Publishing*, Chicago: University of Chicago Press.

Benjamin, Walter (1969) 'The Work of Art in the Age of Mechanical Reproduction', in *Illuminations*, trans. Harry Zohn, New York: Schocken Books.

Bourdieu, Pierre (1993) *The Field of Cultural Production*, ed., Randal Johnson, Cambridge: Polity Press.

Bowers, Fredson (1949) *Principles of Bibliographical Description*, Princeton: Princeton University Press.

Bowers, Fredson (1964) *Bibliography and Textual Criticism*, Oxford: Clarendon Press.

Chartier, Roger (1988) *Cultural History: between Practices and Representations*, Cambridge: Polity Press.

Chartier, Roger ed., (1989) *The Cultures of Print: Power and Uses of Print in Modern Europe*, Cambridge: Polity Press.

Darnton, Robert (1984) *The Great Cat Massacre and Other Episodes in French Cultural History*, New York: Basic Books.

Darnton, Robert (1990) 'What is the History of Books', in *The Kiss of Lamourette: Reflections in Cultural History*, New York: Norton, pp. 107–36.

Davison, Peter, ed. (1992) *The Book Encompassed: Studies in Twentieth Century Bibliography*, Cambridge: Cambridge University Press.

Escarpit, Robert (1958, 1965) *The Sociology of Literature*, trans. Ernest Pick, Painesville, Ohio: Lake Erie College Press.

Escarpit, Robert (1966) *The Book Revolution*, London: George C. Harrap & Co.

Estivals, Robert (1994) 'Histoire du livre et bibliologie', *Canadian Review of Comparative Literature / Revue Canadienne de Littérature Comparée* 21.3: 457–68.

Feather, John (1980) 'Cross-Channel Currents: Historical Bibliography and l'Histoire du livre', *Library Series 6* 2.1: 1–15.

Feather, John (1986a) 'The Book in History and the History of the Book', *Journal of Library History* 21: 12–26.

Feather, John (1986b) *A Dictionary of Book History*, New York and Oxford: Oxford University Press.

Feather, John P. and McKitterick, David (1986) *The History of Books and Libraries: Two Views*, Washington, DC: Library of Congress.

Gaskell, Philip (1972) *A New Introduction to Bibliography*, New York and Oxford: Oxford University Press.

Gaskell, Philip (1978) *From Writer to Reader: Studies in Editorial Method*, Oxford: Clarendon Press.

Génette, Gerard (1997) *Paratexts: Thresholds of Interpretation*, trans. Jane E. Lewin, Cambridge: Cambridge University Press.

Greetham, D. C. (1994) *Textual Scholarship: An Introduction*, New York: Garland Press.

Greg, W. W. (1966) *Collected Papers*, ed. J. C. Maxwell, Oxford: Clarendon Press.

Hall, David D. (1983) 'On Native Ground: From the History of Printing to the History of the Book', *Proceedings of the American Antiquarian Society* 93: 313–36.

Hall, David D. and Hench, J. B., eds (1987) *Needs and Opportunities in the History of the Book: America, 1639–1876*, Worcester: American Antiquarian Society.

Hall, David D. (1996) *Cultures of Print: Essays in the History of the Book*, Amherst: University of Massachusetts Press.

Hoggart, Richard (1958) *The Uses of Literacy: Changing Patterns in English Mass Culture*, New York: Oxford University Press.

Howard-Hill, T. H. (1993–1995) 'The Institutionalization of Bibliography', *Analytical and Enumerative Bibliography* 7.4: 181–91.

Jordan, John O. and Patten, Robert L., eds (1995) *Literature in the Marketplace: Nineteenth-Century British Publishing and Reading Practices*, Cambridge: Cambridge University Press.

Macherey, Pierre (1978) *A Theory of Literary Production*, London.

McGann, Jerome (1983) *A Critique of Modern Textual Criticism*, Chicago: University of Chicago Press.

McGann, Jerome (1985) *The Beauty of Inflections: Literary Investigations in Historical Method and Theory*, Oxford: Clarendon Press.

McGann, J. J. (1991) *The Textual Condition*, Princeton: Princeton University Press.

McKenzie, D. F.(1969) 'Printers of the Mind: Some Notes on Bibliographical Theories and Printing House Practices', *Studies in Bibliography* 22: 1–75.

McKenzie, D. F. (1986) *The Panizzi Lectures, 1985: Bibliography and the Sociology of Texts*, London: British Library.

McKenzie, D. F. (1992) 'History of the Book', in Peter Davidson, ed., *The Bibliographical Society, 1892–1992*, Cambridge: Cambridge University Press.

McKerrow, Ronald B. (1927) *An Introduction to Bibliography for Literary Students*, Oxford: Clarendon Press.

McLuhan, Marshall (1962) *The Gutenburg Galaxy: The Making of Typographic Man*, Toronto: University of Toronto Press.

Nunberg, Geoffrey (1993) 'The Place of Books in the Age of Electronic Reproduction', *Representations* 42 (1993): 13–37.

Nunberg, Geoffrey, ed. (1996) *The Future of the Book*, Berkeley: University of California Press.

Oliphant, D. and Carver, Larry (1990) *New Directions in Textual Studies*, Austin: University of Texas, H. Ransom Center.

Patten, Robert L. (1996) 'When is a Book not a Book', *Biblion*, Spring: 35–63.

Phelps, Deirdre (1994) 'Theory and the Book: Socio-Cultural Theory of the Novel I', *New England Book and Text Studies* 1: 91–101.

Rawson, David A. (1991) 'Review Essay: New Questions and New Approaches in the Study of the "History of the Book"', *Eighteenth-century Studies* 15: 103–12.

Rose, Jonathan (1994) 'How to Do Things with Book History', *Victorian Studies* 37: 461–71.

Rose, Jonathan (1996) 'How Historians Teach the History of the Book', *Canadian Review of Comparative Literature / Revue Canadienne de Littérature Comparée* 23.1: 217–24.

Shillingsburg, Peter L. (1986) *Scholarly Editing in the Computer Age*, Athens: University of Georgia Press.

Shillingsburg, Peter L. (1991) 'Text as Matter, Concept, and Action', *Studies in Bibliography* 44: 31–82.

Sutherland, John (1988) 'Publishing History: A Hole at the Centre of Literary Sociology', *Critical Enquiry* 14.3: 574–89.

Tanselle, G. T. (1981) *The History of Books as a Field of Study*, Chapel Hill: Rare Book Collection, University of North Carolina.

Tanselle, G. T. (1987) *Textual Criticism Since Greg: A Chronicle, 1950–1985*, Charlottesville: University Press of Virginia for the Bibliographical Society of the University of Virginia.

Tanselle, G. T. (1989) *A Rationale of Textual Criticism*, Philadelphia: University of Pennsylvania Press.

Tanselle, G. T. (1990) *Textual Criticism and Scholarly Editing*, Charlottesville: University Press of Virginia for the Bibliographical Society of the University of Virginia.

Willison, I. R. (1991) 'Remarks on the History of the Book in Britain as a Field of Study within the Humanities', *Library Chronicle of the University of Texas* 21: 95–147.

Willison, I. R. (1993) 'The History of the Book in Twentieth-Century Britain and America: Perspective and Evidence', *Proceedings of the American Antiquarian Society* 102: 353–77.

## Part 2: From orality to literacy

Achebe, Chinua (1961) *No Longer at Ease*, New York: Ivan Obolensky.

Allison, A. F. and Rogers, D. M. (1989) *The Contemporary Printed Literature of the English Counter-Reformation between 1558 and 1640*, Aldershot: Scolar Press.

Armbruster, Carol (1993) *Publishing and Readership in Revolutionary France and America*, Westport, Conn.: Greenwood.

Armstrong, Elizabeth (1986) *Robert Estienne: Royal Printer: An Historical Study of the Elder Stephanus*, rev. edn, Abingdon: Sutton Courtenany Press.

Bailyn, Bernard and Hench, John B., eds (1980) *The Press & the American Revolution*, Worcester, Mass.: American Antiquarian Society.

Barber, Giles (1994) *Studies in the Booktrade of the European Enlightenment*, London: Pindar.

Bekker-Nielsen, Hans, ed. (1986) *From Script to Book*, Odense: Odense University Press.

Bell, David N., ed. (1992) *The Libraries of the Cistercians, Gilbertines and Premonstratensians*, London: British Library.

Bell, David N. (1995) *What Nuns Read: Books and Libraries in Medieval English Nunneries*, Cistercian Studies Series, 158, Kalamazoo: Cistercian Publications.

Bell, H. E. (1936–1937) 'The Price of Books in Medieval England', *The Library*, 4th series, 312–32.

Bell, Susan Groag (1982) 'Medieval Women Book Owners: Arbiters of Lay Piety and Ambassadors of Culture', *Signs* 7.4: 742–68.

Bennett, H. S. (1947) 'The Production and Dissemination of Vernacular Manuscripts in the Fifteenth Century', *The Library*, 5th series, 167–78.

Bennett, H. S. (1952) *English Books and Readers 1475–1557*, Cambridge: Cambridge University Press.

Berkvens-Stevelinck, C., Bots, H., Hoffijzer, P. G. and Lankhorst, O. S., eds (1992) *Le Magasin de l'Univers: The Dutch Republic as the Centre of the European Book Trade: Papers Presented at the International Colloquium Held at Wassenaar, 5–7 July 1990*, Leiden: E. J. Brill.

Bernstein, Basil (1974) *Class, Codes and Control. Theoretical Studies towards a Sociology of Language*, vol. 1, 2nd rev. edn, London: Routledge and Kegan Paul.

Bietenholz, Peter G. (1971) *Basle and France in the Sixteenth Century: The Basle Humanists and Printers in their Contacts with Francophone Culture*, Toronto: University of Toronto Press.

Biller, Peter and Hudson, Anne, eds (1994) *Heresy and Literacy, 100–1530*, Cambridge: Cambridge University Press.

Blake, N. F. (1991) *William Caxton and English Literary Culture*, London: Hambledon Press.

Bloch, Eileen (1965) 'Erasmus and the Froben Press: The Making of an Editor', *Library Quarterly* 35: 109–20.

Boerner, Peter (1969) *Tagebuch*, Stuttgart: J. B. Metzler.

Bologna, Guila (1988) *Illuminated Manuscripts: The Book Before Gutenberg*, New York: Weidenfeld and Nicolson.

Boyle, Leonard (1984) *Medieval Latin Palaeography: A Bibliographical Introduction*, Toronto: University of Toronto Press.

Brant, S. (1968) *Das Narrenschiff*, ed. M. Lemmer, Tübingen.

Brown, Cynthia J. (1995) *Poets, Patrons and Printers: Crisis of Authority in Late Medieval France*, Ithaca: Cornell University Press.

Brownrigg, Linda L. (1990) *Seminar in the History of the Book to 1500: Assessing the Evidence*, Los Altos Hills: Red Gull Press.

Brownrigg, Linda L., ed. (1994) *Making the Medieval Book: Techniques of Production*, Oxford: Oxford University Press.

Buhler, Curt Ferdinand (1960) *The Fifteenth Century Book: The Scribes, The Printers, The Decorators*, Philadelphia: University of Pennsylvania Press.

Bury, R. de (1960 [1345]) *Philobiblon*, trans. E. C. Thomas, ed. M. Maclagan, Oxford: Oxford University Press.

Calkins, Robert G. (1983) *Illuminated Books of the Middle Ages*, Ithaca, NY: Cornell University Press.

Carlson, David R. (1993) *English Humanist Books: Writers and Patrons, Manuscripts and Print, 1475–1525*, Toronto: University of Toronto Press.

Carpenter, Kenneth, ed. (1983) *Books and Society in History*, New York: Bowker.

Carter, Thomas Francis (1955) *The Invention of Printing in China and Its Spread Westward*, 2nd ed., rev. by L. Carrington Goodrich, New York: Ronald Press.

Chappell, Warren (1970) *A Short History of the Printed Word*, New York: Knopf.

Chartier, Roger (1987) *The Cultural Uses of Print in Early Modern France*, trans. Lydia G. Cochrane, Princeton: Princeton University Press.

Chartier, Roger, ed. (1989) *The Culture of Print: Power and the Uses of Print in Early Modern Europe*, trans. Lydia G. Cochrane, Princeton: Princeton University Press

Chafe, Wallace L. (1982) 'Integration and involvement in speaking, writing and oral literature', in Deborah Tannen, ed., *Spoken and Written Language: Exploring Orality and Literacy*, Norwood, NJ: Ablex.

Chrisman, Miriam Usher (1982) *Lay Culture, Learned Culture: Books and Social Change in Strasbourg, 1480–1599*, New Haven: Yale University Press.

Clair, Colin (1976) *A History of European Printing*, London: Academic Press.

Clanchy, Michael T. (1979) *From Memory to Written Record: England 1066–1307*, Cambridge, Mass. and Oxford: B. H. Blackwell.

Coleman, Janet (1981) *Medieval Readers and Writers 1350–1400*, New York: Columbia University Press.

Davies, Martin (1995) *Aldus Manutius: Printer and Publisher of Renaissance Venice*, London: British Library.

Davis, Natalie Zemon (1957) 'The Protestant Printing Workers of Lyons in 1551', *Aspects de la propagande religiouse*, Geneva: Droz, 247–57.

De Hamel, Christopher (1986) *A History of Illuminated Manuscripts*, Oxford: Phaidon.

De Hamel, Christopher (1992) *Scribes and Illuminators*, Toronto.

De Roover, Florence Edler [as Florence Edler] (1937) 'Cost Accounting in the Sixteenth Century: The Books of Accounts of Christopher Plantin, Antwerp, Printer and Publisher', *Accounting Review* 12: 226–37.

De Roover, Florence Edler [as Florence Edler] (1953) 'New Facets on the Financing and Marketing of Early Printed Books', *Bulletin of the Business Historical Society* 27: 222–30.

Diringer, David (1953) *The Alphabet: A Key to the History of Mankind*, 2nd edn rev., New York: Philosphical Library.

Eisenstein, Elizabeth (1968) 'Some Conjectures about the Impact of Printing on Western Society and Thought: A Preliminary Report', *Journal of Modern History* 40: 1–56.

Eisenstein, Elizabeth (1979) *The Printing Press as an Agent of Change: Communications and Cultural Transformations in Early-Modern Europe*, 2 vols, Cambridge: Cambridge University Press.

Eisenstein, Elizabeth (1986) *Print Culture and Enlightenment Thought*, Chapel Hill, NC: Hanes Foundation, Rare Book Collection/University Library, The University of North Carolina.

Fabian, Bernhard (1992) *The English Book in 18th-Century Germany*, London: British Library.

Febvre, Lucien, and Martin, Henri-Jean (1958) *L'Apparition du Livre*, Paris: Albin Michel.

Febvre, Lucien and Martin, Henri-Jean (1976) *The Coming of the Book: The Impact of Printing, 1450–1800*, trans. David Gerard, London: NLB.

Finnegan, Ruth (1988) *Literacy and Orality*, Oxford: Blackwell.

Flood, John L. and Kelly, William A., eds (1995) *The German Book, 1450–1750*, London: British Library.

Gameson, Richard, ed. (1994) *The Early Medieval Bible: Its Production, Decoration and Use*, Cambridge: Cambridge University Press.

Ganz, Peter, ed. (1986) *The Role of the Book in Medieval Culture*, Tournhout: Brepols.

Gelb, I. J. (1963) *A Study of Writing*, rev. edn, Chicago: University of Chicago Press.

Geldner, F. (1961) 'Zum altesten Missaldruck', in *Gutenberg-Jahrbuch*, pp. 101–6.

Gellrich, Jesse (1986) *The Idea of the Book in the Middle Ages: Language Theory, Mythology, and Fiction*, Ithaca: Cornell University Press.

Gerson, J. (1973) [1423] 'De Laude scriptorum', in J. Gerson, *Oeuvres completes*, Paris, 9: 423–34.

Gesner, C. (1966) [1545] *Bibliotheca Universalis and Appendix*, Zurich.

Goody, Jack, ed. (1968a) *Literacy in Traditional Societies*, Cambridge: Cambridge University Press.

Goody, Jack (1968b), 'Restricted Literacy in Northern Ghana', in Jack Goody, ed., *Literacy in Traditional Societies*, Cambridge: Cambridge University Press, pp. 198–264.

Goody, Jack (1977) *The Domestication of the Savage Mind*, Cambridge: Cambridge University Press.

Goody, Jack (1987) *The Interface between the Oral and the Written*, Cambridge: Cambridge University Press.

Goody, Jack and Watt, Ian (1968) 'The Consequences of Literacy', in Jack Goody, ed., *Literacy in Traditional Societies*, Cambridge: Cambridge University Press, pp. 27–84.

Grafton, Anthony T. (1980) 'The importance of being printed', *Journal of Interdisciplinary History* 11: 256–86.

Grafton, Anthony (1997) *Commerce with the Classics: Ancient Books and Renaissance Readers*, Ann Arbor: University of Michigan Press.

Greg. W. W. (1956) *Some Aspects and Problems of London Publishing between 1550–1650*, Oxford: Clarendon Press.

Griffiths, Jeremy and Pearsall, Derek, eds (1995) *Book Production and Publishing in Britain, 1375–1475*, Cambridge: Cambridge University Press.

Guxman, M. M. (1970) 'Some general regularities in the formation and development of national languages', in Joshua A. Fishman, ed., *Readings in the Sociology of Language*, The Hague: Mouton, pp. 773–6.

Harris, Victor (1989) *Ancient Literacy*, Cambridge: Cambridge University Press.

Harvey R., Kirsop, W. and McMullin, B. J., eds (1993) *An Index of Civilization: Studies in Publishing and Printing History in Honour of Keith Maslen*, Clayton, Vic.: Centre for Bibliographical and Textual Studies, Monash University.

Haugen, Einar (1966) 'Linguistics and language planning', in William Bright, ed., *Sociolinguistics: Proceedings of the UCLA Sociolinguistics Conference 1964*, The Hague: Mouton, pp. 50–71.

Havelock, Eric A. (1963) *Preface to Plato*, Cambridge, Mass.: Belknap Press of Harvard University Press.

Havelock, Eric A. (1978) *The Greek Concept of Justice: From its Shadow in Homer to its Substance in Plato*, Cambridge, Mass. and London: Harvard University Press.

Havelock, Eric A. (1982) *The Literate Revolution in Greece and Its Cultural Consequences*, Princeton: Princeton University Press.

Havelock, Eric A. and Herschell, Jackson P., eds (1978) *Communication Arts in the Ancient World*, Humanistic Studies in the Communication Arts, New York: Hastings House.

Heidenheimer, H. (1925) 'Das Beglietgedicht zum Justiniani Institutiones-Drucke von 1468, in A. Ruppel, ed., *Gutenberg-Festschrift: Feier des 25 jährigen Bestenhens des Gutenberg-Museums in Mainz*, Mainz, pp. 108–17.

Hellinga, Lotte (1983) *Caxton in Focus: The Beginning of Printing in England*, London: British Library.

Hellinga, Lotte and Goldfinch, John, eds (1987) *Bibliography and the Study of 15th-century Civilization*, London: British Library.

Hindman, Sandra, ed. (1991) *Printing the Written Word: The Social History of Books, Circa 1450–1520*, Ithaca and London: Cornell University Press.

Hindman, Sandra, and Farquhar, James Douglas (1977) *Pen to Press: Illustrated Manuscripts and Printed Books in the First Century of Printing*, College Park, Maryland: University of Maryland Press.

Hirsch, E. D. Jr. (1977) *The Philosophy of Composition*, Chicago and London: University of Chicago Press.

Hirsch, Rudolph (1974) *Printing, Selling, and Reading, 1450–1550*, Wiesbaden: Otto Harrassowitz.

Hussein, Mohamed A. (1972) *Origins of the Book: Egypt's Contribution to the Development of the Book from Papyrus to Codex*, Greenwich, Conn.: New York Graphic Society.

Ing, Janet (1988) *Johann Gutenberg and His Bible: A Historical Study*, New York: Typophiles.

Jardine, Lisa (1993) *Erasmus, Man of Letters: The Construction of Charisma in Print*, Princeton: Princeton University Press.

Johns, Adrian (1991) 'History, Science and the History of the Book: The Making of Natural Philosophy in Early Modern England', *Publishing History* 30: 5–31.

Johns, Adrian (1998) *The Nature of the Book: Print and knowledge in the making*, Chicago: University of Chicago Press.

Kenney, E. J. (1974) *The Classical Text: Aspects of Editing in the Age of the Printed Book*, Berkeley: University of California Press.

Kerckhore, Derrick de (1981) 'A Theory of Greek Tragedy', *Sub-stance* (Summer), University of Wisconsin, Madison.

Kingdom, Robert M. (1956) 'The Flood Tide: Books from Geneva', in *Geneva and the Coming of the Wars of Religion in France, 1553–1563*, Geneva: Droz, pp. 93–105.

Leakey, Richard and Lewin, Roger (1979) *People of the Lake: Mankind and its beginnings*, Garden City, NY: Anchor Press/Doubleday.

Levy-Strauss, Claude (1966) *The Savage Mind*, Chicago: University of Chicago Press. Originally published as *La Pensée Sauvage* (1962).

Leyser, Karl (1994) *Communications and Power in Medieval Europe*, Rio Grande, Ohio: Hambledon.

Lowry, Martin (1979) *The World of Aldus Manutius*, Oxford: Blackwell.

Lowry, Martin (1991) *Nicholas Jenson and the Rise of Venetian Publishing*, Oxford: Blackwell.

Lycosthenes, C. (1551) *Elenchus scriptorum omnium*, Basel.

Martin, Henri-Jean (1993) *Print, Power and People in 17th Century France*, trans. David Gerard, Metuchen, NJ: Scarecrow Press.

Martin, Henri-Jean (1994) *The History and Power of Writing*, trans. Lydia G. Cochrane. Chicago: University of Chicago Press.

Machlup, Fritz (1978–80) *Information through the Printed Word: The Dissemination of Scholarly, Scientific and Intellectual Knowledge*, 4 vols, New York: Praeger.

McKenzie, D. F. (1981) 'Typography and Meaning: The Case of William Congreve', in *Wolfenbutteler Schriften zur Geschichte des Buchwesens* 4, Hamburg: Dr. Ernst Hauswedell & Co., pp. 81–125.

McKenzie, D. F. (1984) 'The Sociology of a Text: Orality, Literacy and Print in Early New Zealand', *The Library*: 333–65.

McKitterick, Rosamund (1989) *The Carolingians and the Written Word*, Cambridge: Cambridge University Press.

McKitterick, Rosamund, ed. (1990) *The Uses of Literacy in Early Medieval Europe*, Cambridge: Cambridge University Press.

McMurtrie, Douglas C. (1943) *The Book: The Story of Printing and Bookmaking*, 3rd rev. edn, New York and Oxford: Oxford University Press.

McNally, Peter F., ed. (1987) *The Advent of Printing: Historians of Science Respond to Elizabeth Eisensteins's The Printing Press as an Agent of Change*, Montreal: McGill University Graduate School of Library and Information Studies.

Meggitt, Mervyn (1968) 'Uses of literacy in New Guinea and Melanesia', in Jack Goody, ed., *Literacy in Traditional Societies*, Cambridge: Cambridge University Press, pp. 300–9.

Mertens, D. (1983) 'Früher Buchdruck und Historiographie', in B. Moeller *et al.*, eds, *Studien zum städtischen Bildungswesen des späten Mittelalters und der frühen, Neuzeit*, Göttingen, pp. 83–111.

Minnis, A. J. (1984) *The Medieval Theory of Authorship*, Toronto.

Moss, Ann (1996) *Printed Commonplace-Books and the Structure of Renaissance Thought*, Oxford: Clarendon Press.

Myers, Robin and Harris, Michael, eds (1990) *Spreading the Word: The Distribution Networks of Print, 1550–1850*, Winchester: St. Paul's Bibliographies.

Needham, Paul (1982) 'Johann Gutenberg and the Catholicon Press', *Papers of the Bibliographical Society of America* 76: 395–456.

Needham, Paul (1992) 'Mainz and Eltville: The True Tale of Three Compositors', *Bulletin du Bibliophile*: 257–304.

Olson, David R. (1977) 'From utterance to text: the bias of language in speech and writing', *Harvard Educational Review* 47: 257–81.

Olson, David R. (1980) 'On the Language and Authority of Textbooks', *Journal of Communication* 30.4 (Winter): 186–96.

Ong, Walter J. (1958) *Ramus, Method and Decay of Dialogue*, Cambridge, Mass.: Harvard University Press.

Ong, Walter J. (1967) *The Presence of the Word*, New Haven and London: Yale University Press.

Ong, Walter J. (1971) *Rhetoric, Romance and Technology*, Ithaca: Cornell University Press.

Ong, Walter J. (1977) *Interfaces of the Word*, Ithaca and London: Cornell University Press.

Ong, Walter J. (1981) *Fighting for Life: Contest, Sexuality, and Consciousness*, Ithaca and London: Cornell University Press.

Ong, Walter J. (1982) *Orality and Literacy: The Technologizing of the Word*, New York: Methuen.

Parkes, Malcolm (1991) *Scribes, Scripts, and Readers: Studies in the Communication, Presentation and Dissemination of Medieval Texts*, London: Hambledon Press.

Parkes, Malcolm (1992) *Pause and Effect: An Introduction to the History of Punctuation in the West*, Aldershot: Scolar Press.

Parkes, Malcolm and Watson, Andrew G. eds (1978) *Medieval Scribes, Manuscripts, and Libraries*, London.

Pearsall, Derek, ed. (1983) *Manuscripts and Readers in Fifteenth-Century England: The Literary Implications of Manuscript Study: Essays from the 1981 Conference at the University of York*, Cambridge: D. S. Brewer.

Pedersen, Johannes (1984) *The Arabic Book*, Princeton, NJ: Princeton University Press.

Petrucci, Armando (1995) *Writers and Readers in Medieval Italy: Studies in the History of Written Culture*, New Haven: Yale University Press.

Plato (1973) *Phaedrus and Letters VII and VIII*, trans. and intro. Walter Hamilton, Harmondsworth: Penguin Books.

Polidori Vergilii Urbinatis (1502) *De inventorifus rerum opus*, Paris.

Popkin, Jeremy D. (1992) 'Print Culture in the Netherlands on the Eve of the Revolution', in *The Dutch Republic in the Eighteenth Century: Decline, Enlightenment and Revolution*, ed., Margareth C. Jacob and Wijnand W. Mijnhardt, Ithaca: Cornell University Press, pp. 273–91.

Richardson, Brian (1994) *Print Culture in Renaissance Italy: The Editor and the Vernacular Text, 1470–1600*, Cambridge: Cambridge University Press.

Richardson, Malcolm (1980) 'Henry V, the English Chancery, and Chancery English', *Speculum* 55.4 (October): 726–50.

Roberts, Colin H. and Skeat, T. C. (1987) *The Birth of the Codex*, London: Oxford University Press for the British Academy.

Robinson, Pamela R. and Zim, Rivkah, eds (1997) *Of the Making of Books: Medieval Manuscripts, their Scribes and Readers: Essays Presented to M. B. Parkes*, Brookfield: Ashgate.

Rouse, Mary and Rouse, Richard (1991) *Authentic Witnesses: Approaches to Medieval Texts and Manuscripts*, Notre Dame.

Saenger, Paul (1982) 'Silent Reading: Its Impact on Late Medieval Script and Society', *Viator* 13: 367–414.

Scholderer, Victor (1970) *Johann Gutenberg: The Inventor of Printing*, 2nd edn, London: British Museum.

Schottenloher, Karl (1931) 'Handeschriftenforschung und Buchdruck im 15. and 16. Jahrhundert', *Zutenberg-Jahrbuch*, 73–106.

Schottenloher, Karl (1989) *Books and the Western World: A Cultural History*, trans. William D. Boyd and Irmgard H. Wolfe, Jefferson, NC: McFarland.

Schreiner, K. (1984) 'Laienbildung als Herausforderung für Kirche und Gesellschaft', *Zeitschrift für historische Forschung* 11: 257–345.

Scribner, Sylvia and Cole, Michael (1978) 'Literacy without schooling: Testing for intellectual effects', *Harvard Educational Review* 48: 448–61.

Shernan, William H. and Dee, John (1995) *The Politics of Reading and Writing in the English Renaissance*, Amherst: University of Massachusetts Press.

Shuger, Deborah Kuller (1994) *The Renaissance Bible: Scholarship, Sacrifice and Subjectivity*, Berkeley: University of California Press.

Steinberg, S. H. (1974) *Five Hundred Years of Printing*, 1955. 3rd rev. edn, Harmondsworth: Penguin.

Stock, Brian (1990) *Listening for the Text*, Baltimore: Johns Hopkins University Press.

Swierk, A. (1972) 'Johannes Gutenburg als Erfinder in Zeugnissen seiner Zeit', in H. Widmann, ed., *Der gegenwartige Stand der Gutenberg-Forschung 1*, Stuttgart, pp. 79–90.

Tambiah, S. J. (1968) 'Literacy in a Buddhist village in north-east Thailand', in Jack Goody, ed., *Literacy in Traditional Societies*, Cambridge: Cambridge University Press, pp. 85–131.

Trapp, J. B., ed. (1983) *Manuscripts in the Fifty Years after the Invention of Printing*, London: Warburg Institute, University of London.

Trithemius, J. (1973) [1494] *De laude scriptorum: Zum Lobe der Schreiber*, ed. and trans. K. Arnold, Wurzburg.

Tyson, Gerald P. and Wagonheim, Sylvia S., eds (1986) *Print and Culture in the Renaissance: Essays on the Advent of Printing in Europe*, Newark: University of Delaware Press.

Widman, H. (1972) 'Gutenburgh im Urteil der Nachwelt', in H. Widmann, ed., *Der gegenwärtige Stand der Gutenburg-Forschung 1*, Stuttgart, pp. 251–72.

Wilks, Ivor (1968) 'The transmission of Islamic learning in the western Sudan', in Jack Goody, ed., *Literacy in Traditional Societies*, Cambridge: Cambridge University Press, pp. 162–97.

Wilson, Edward O. (1975) *Sociobiology: The New Synthesis*, Cambridge, Mass.: Belknap Press of Harvard University Press.

Winterich, John T. (1935) *Early American Books and Printing*, Boston: Houghton Mifflin.

Witten, Laurence (1959) 'The Earliest Books Printed in Spain', *Papers of the Bibliographical Society of America* 53: 91–113.

Wolfram, Walt (1972) 'Sociolinguistic premises and the nature of nonstandard dialects', in Arthur L. Smith, ed., *Language, Communication, and Rhetoric in Black America*, New York: Harper and Row, pp. 28–40.

Zumthor, P. (1983) *Introduction a la poesie orale*, Paris.

Zumthor, P. (1987) *La lettre et la voix*, Paris.

## Part 3: Commodifying print: Books and authors

Albertine, Susan, ed. (1996) *A Living of Words: American Women in Print Culture*, Knoxville: University of Tennessee Press.

Alston, R. C. and H. Fellner (1992) *Publishing, the Book Trade, and the Diffusion of Knowledge*, Chadwyck-Healey.

Altick, Richard (1962) 'The Sociology of Authorship: The Social Origins, Education and Occupations of 1,100 British Writers, 1800–1935', *Bulletin of the New York Public Library* 66: 389–404.

Anderson, Patricia, and Rose, Jonathan, eds (1991) *Dictionary of Literary Biography*, vols 106 and 112: *British Literary Publishing Houses*, Detroit: Gale Research.

Barbert, Biles and Fabian, Bernhard, eds (1981) *Buch und Buchhandel in Europa im achtzehnten Jahrhundert: The Book and the Book Trade in Eighteenth-Century Europe: Wolfenbutteler Symposium, November 1–3, 1977*, Hamburg: Hauswedell.

Barnes, James J. (1964) *Free Trade in Books: A Study of the London Book Trade since 1800*, Oxford: Clarendon Press.

Barnes, James J. (1974) *Authors, Publishers, and Politicians: The Quest for an Anglo-American Copyright Agreement, 1815–1854*, Columbus: Ohio State University Press.

Blagden, Cyprian (1960) *The Stationers' Company: A History, 1403–1959*, London: Allen & Unwin.

Bonham-Carter, Victor (1978) *Authors by Profession*, 2 vols, London: Society of Authors.

Botein, Stephen (1975) '"Mere Mechanics" and an Open Press: The Business and Political Strategies of Colonial American Printers', *Perspectives in American History* 5: 127–225.

Briggs, Asa, ed. (1974) *Essays in the History of Publishing in Celebration of the 250th Anniversary of the House of Longman, 1724–1974*, London: Longman.

Brown, Richard D. (1989) *Knowledge is Power: The Diffusion of Information in Early America, 1700–1865*, Oxford: Oxford University Press.

Charvat, William (1968) *The Profession of Authorship in America, 1800–1870: The Papers of William Charvat*, ed. Matthew J. Bruccoli, Columbus, Ohio: Ohio State University Press.

Charvat, William (1992) [1959] *Literary Publishing in America, 1790–1850*, Amherst: University of Massachusetts Press.

Coser, Lewis A., Kadushin, Charles and Powell, Walter W. (1982) *Books: the Culture and Commerce of Publishing*, New York: Basic Books.

Coultrap-McQuin, Susan (1990) *Doing Literary Business: American Women Writers in the Nineteenth Century*, Chapel Hill: University of North Carolina Press.

Cross, Nigel (1985) *The Common Writer: Life in Nineteenth-Century Grub Street*, Cambridge: Cambridge University Press.

Darnton, Robert (1979) *The Business of Enlightenment: A Publishing History of the Encyclopedie, 1775–1800*, Cambridge, Mass.: Harvard University Press.

Darnton, Robert (1982) *The Literary Underground of the Old Regime*, Cambridge, Mass.: Harvard University Press.

Darnton, Robert (1995) *The Forbidden Best-Sellers of Pre-Revolutionary France*, New York: Norton.

Dooley, Allan C. (1992) *Author and Printer in Victorian England*, Charlottesville: University Press of Virginia.

Dudek, Louis (1960) *Literature and the Press: A History of Printing, Printed Media, and their Relation to Literature*, Toronto: Contact Press.

Dzwonkoski, Peter, ed. (1986) *Dictionary of Literary Biography*, vols 46 and 49: *American Literary Publishing Houses*, Detroit: Gale Research.

Eliot, Simon (1994) *Some Patterns and Trends in British Publishing, 1800–1919*, London: Bibliographical Society.

Feather, John (1988) *A History of British Publishing*, London: Croom Helm.

Feltes, N. N. (1978) *Modes of Production of Victorian Novels*, Chicago: University of Chicago Press.

Feltes, N. N. (1993) *Literary Capital and the Late Victorian Novel*, Madison, WI: University of Wisconsin Press.

Fritschner, Linda Marie (1980) 'Publishers' Readers, Publishers and their Authors', *Publishing History* 7: 45–100.

Goldsmith, Elizabeth C. and Goodman, Dena, eds (1995) *Going public: Women and Publishing in Early Modern France*, Ithaca: Cornell University Press.

Griest, Guinevere L. (1970) *Mudie's Circulating Library and the Victorian Novel*, Bloomington: Indiana University Press.

Gross, John (1969, 1991) *The Rise and Fall of the Man of Letters*, Hardmondsworth: Penguin.

Hepburn, James (1968) *The Author's Empty Purse and the Rise of the Literary Agent*, London: Oxford University Press.

Hesse, Carla (1992) *Publishing and Cultural Politics in Revolutionary Paris, 1789–1810*, Berkeley: University of California Press.

Keating, Peter (1989) *The Haunted Study: A Social History of the English Novel: 1875–1914*, London: Secker and Warburg.

Kiernan, Alvin (1993) *Samuel Johnson and the Impact of Print*, Princeton: Princeton University Press.

Landon, Richard, ed. (1978) *Book Selling and Book Buying: Aspects of the Nineteenth-Century British and North American Book Trade*, Chicago: American Library Association.

Lehmann-Haupt, Hellmut, Wroth, Lawrence C. and Silver, Rollo G. (1951) *The Book in America: A History of the Making and Selling of Books in the United States*, New York: R. R. Bowker.

Lough, J. (1978) *Writer and Public in France from the Middle Ages to the Present Day*, Oxford: Clarendon Press.

McAleer, Joseph (1992) *Popular Reading and Publishing in Britain, 1914–1950*, Oxford: Oxford University Press.

McDonald, Peter (1997) *British Literary Culture and Publishing Practice 1880–1914*, Cambridge: Cambridge University Press.

Martin, Henri-Jean and Roger Chartier, eds (1983) *Histoire de l'Edition Française, Tome 1–4*, Paris: Promodis.

Mumby, Frank Arthur and Norris, Ian (1982) *Publishing and Bookselling: A History from the Earliest Times to the Present Day*, rev. edn, London: Bell & Hyman.

Myers, Robin (1973) *The British Book Trade, from Caxton to the Present Day*, London: Andre Deutsch.

Nowell-Smith, Simon (1968) *International Copyright Law and the Publisher in the Reign of Queen Victoria*, Oxford: Clarendon Press.

Parker, George L. (1985) *The Beginnings of the Book Trade in Canada*, Toronto: University of Toronto Press.

Patten, Robert L. (1978) *Charles Dickens and His Publishers*, Oxford: Clarendon Press.

Plant, Marjorie (1974) [1939] *The English Book Trade: An Economic History of the Making and Sale of Books*, 3rd rev. edn, London: George Allen and Unwin Ltd.

Raven, James (1992) *Judging New Wealth: Popular Publishing and Responses to Commerce in England, 1750–1800*, Oxford: Clarendon Press.

Rose, Mark (1993) *Authors and Owners: The Invention of Copyright*, Cambridge, Mass.: Harvard University Press.

Ross, Trevor (1992) 'Copyright and the Invention of Tradition', *Eighteenth-Century Studies* 26: 1–27.

Schick, Frank L. (1958) *The Paperbound Book in America: The History of Paperbacks and Their European Background*, New York: R. R. Bowker.

Shevelow, K. (1989) *Women and Print Culture*, London: Routledge.

Shillingsburg, Peter L. (1992) *Pegasus in Harness: Victorian Publishing and W. M. Thackeray*, Charlottesville: University Press of Virginia.

Sutherland, John (1978) *Victorian Novelists and Publishers*, Chicago: Chicago University Press.

Sutherland, John (1995) *Victorian Fiction: Writers, Publishers, Readers*, Basingstoke: Macmillan Press.

Tebbel, John (1972–1981) *A History of Book Publishing in the United States*, 4 vols, New York: R. R. Bowker.

Thomas, Gillian (1992) *A Position to Command Respect: Women and the Eleventh Britannica*, Metuchen, NJ: Scarecrow Press.

Tompkins, Jane P. (1985) *Sensational Designs: The Cultural Works of American Fiction, 1790–1860*, New York: Harvard University Press.

Tuchman, Gaye and Nina E. Fortin (1989) *Edging Women Out: Victorian Novelists, Publishers and Social Change*, New Haven and London: Yale University Press.

Unseld, Siegfried (1980) *The Author and His Publisher*, trans. Hunter Hannum and Hildegarde Hannum, Chicago: University of Chicago Press.

Vincent, David (1989) *Literacy and Popular Culture: England, 1750–1914*, Cambridge: Cambridge University Press.

Viscomi, Joseph (1993) *Blake and the Idea of the Book*, Princeton: Princeton University Press.

Wall, Wendy (1993) *The Imprint of Gender: Authorship and Publication in the English Renaissance*, Ithaca: Cornell University Press.

Warner, Michael (1990) *Letters of the Republic: Publication and the Public Sphere in Eighteenth-Century America*, Cambridge, Mass.: Harvard University Press.

West III, James L. W. (1988) *American Authors and the Literary Marketplace since 1900*, Philadelphia: University of Pennsylvania Press.

Williams, Raymond (1962) *The Long Revolution*, London: Penguin Books.

Winship, Michael (1995) *American Literary Publishing in the Mid-Nineteenth Century: The Business of Ticknor and Fields*, Cambridge: Cambridge University Press.

Woodmansee, Martha (1994) *The Author, Art, and the Market*, New York: Columbia University Press.

Woodmansee, Martha and Jaszi, Peter, eds (1994) *The Construction of Authorship: Textual Appropriation in Law and Literature*, Durham, NC: Duke University Press.

Zionkowski, Linda (1992) 'Aesthetics, Copyright and "The Goods of the Mind"', *British Journal for Eighteenth-Century Studies* 15: 163–74.

## Part 4: Books and readers

Allen, James Smith (1991) *In the Public Eye: A History of Reading in Modern France, 1800–1940*, Princeton, NJ: Princeton University Press

Altick, Richard (1957) *The English Common Reader: A Social History of the Mass Reading Public, 1800–1900*, Chicago: University of Chicago Press.

Boyarin, Jonathan, ed. (1993) *The Ethnography of Reading*, Berkeley: University of California Press.

Brooks, Jeffrey (1985) *When Russia Learned to Read*, Princeton: Princeton University Press.

Cavallo, Guglielmo and Chartier, Roger, eds (1999) *A History of Reading in the West*, Cambridge: Polity Press.

Chartier, Roger, ed. (1989) *A History of Private Life: Passions of the Renaissance*, Cambridge, Mass.: Harvard University Press.

Chartier, Roger (1989) 'Texts, Printing, Readings', in Lynn Hunt, ed., *The New Cultural History*, Berkeley: University of California Press, pp. 154–75.

Chartier, Roger (1993) *The Order of Books: Readers, Authors and Libraries in Europe between the 14th and 18th Centuries*, trans. Lydia Cochrane, Cambridge: Polity Press.

Chartier, Roger (1995) *Forms and Meanings: Texts, Performances, and Audiences from Codex to Computer*, Philadelphia: University of Pennsylvania Press.

Cipolla, Carlo M. (1969) *Literacy and Development in the West*, Harmondsworth: Penguin Books.

Cressy, David (1980) *Literacy and the Social Order: Reading and Writing in Tudor and Stuart England*, Cambridge: Cambridge University Press.

Danky, James P. and Wiegand, Wayne, eds (1998) *Print Culture in a Diverse America*, Champaign: University of Illinois Press.

Darnton, Robert (1990) 'First Steps Towards a History of Reading', in *The Kiss of Lamourette*, London: Faber and Faber, pp. 154–90.

Eco, Umberto (1979) *The Role of the Reader: Explorations in the Semiotics of Texts*, Bloomington: Indiana University Press.

Fish, Stanley (1980) *Is There a Text in This Class? The Authority of Interpretive Communities*, Cambridge, Mass.: Harvard University Press.

Flint, Kate (1993) *The Female Reader*, Oxford: Oxford University Press.

Flynn, Elizabeth A. and Schweichart, Patrocinio P., eds (1986) *Gender and Reading: Essays on Readers, Texts, and Contexts*, Baltimore: Johns Hopkins University Press.

Furet, Francois and Ozouf, Jacques (1982) *Reading and Writing: Literacy in France from Calvin to Jules Ferry*, Cambridge: Cambridge University Press.

Gamble, Harry Y. (1995) *Books and Readers in the Early Church: A History of Early Christian Texts*, New Haven: Yale University Press.

Ginzberg, Carlo (1982) *The Cheese and the Worms: The Cosmos of a Sixteenth-Century Miller*, New York: Penguin Books.

Gross, Robert A. (1996) 'Reading Culture, Reading Books', *Proceedings of the American Antiquarian Society* 106: 59–78.

Iser, Wolfgang (1978a) *The Act of Reading: A Theory of Aesthetic Response*, Baltimore: Johns Hopkins University Press.

Iser, Wolfgang (1978b) *The Implied Reader*, Baltimore: Johns Hopkins.

Jaus, Hans Robert (1982) *Towards an Aesthetic of Reception*, University of Minnesota Press.

Kaestle, Carl, Damon-Moore, Helen and Stedman, Lawrence C., eds (1991) *Literacy in the United States: Readers and Reading since 1880*, New Haven: Yale University Press.

Kintgen, Eugene R. (1996) *Reading in Tudor England*, Pittsburgh: University of Pittsburgh Press.

Leavis, Q. D. (1932) *Fiction and the Reading Public*, London: Chatto & Windus.

Machor, James L. (1993) *Readers in History: Nineteenth-Century American Literature and the Contexts of Response*, Baltimore: Johns Hopkins University Press.

Manguel, Alberto (1996) *A History of Reading*, New York: Viking.

Moylan, Michele and Stiles, Lane, eds (1996) *Reading Books: Essays on the Material Text and Literature in America*, Amherst: University of Massachusetts Press.

Radway, Janice (1984a) 'Interpretive Communities and Variable Literacies: The Functions of Romance Reading', *Daedalus* 113 (Summer): 49–73.

Radway, Janice (1984b) *Reading the Romance: Women, Patriarchy, and Popular Literature*, Chapel Hill: University of North Carolina Press.

Radway, Janice (1997) *A Feeling for Books: The Book-of-the-Month Club, Literary Taste, and Middle-Class Desire*, Chapel Hill: University of North Carolina Press.

Raven, James, Small, Helen and Tadmor, Naomi, eds (1996) *The Practice and Representation of Reading in England*, Cambridge: Cambridge University Press.

Rivers, Isabel, ed. (1982) *Books and Their Readers in Eighteenth-century England*, New York: St. Martin's Press.

Suleiman, Susan, and Crosman, Inge, eds (1980) *The Reader in the Text: Essays on Audiences and Interpretation*, Princeton: Princeton University Press.

Tompkins, Jane P., ed. (1980) *Reader-Response Cricitism*, Baltimore: Johns Hopkins University Press.

Travis, Molly Abel (1998) *Reading Cultures: The Construction of Readers in the Twentieth Century*, Carbondale: Southern Illinois University Press.

Ward, Albert (1974) *Book Production, Fiction, and the German Reading Public, 1740–1800*, Oxford: Clarendon Press.

# INDEX